PLAYFAIR
CRICKET

EDITED B

All statistics by

PREFACE

England's success in the Ashes this winter brought great delight to us all. However, victory did not come by chance, but through excellent preparation. One key to England's success was that the three games before the first Test weren't viewed as warm-up matches but as a mini-series that England went all-out to win. Four years ago, these games were used as little more than training exercises. Andy Flower decided to pick the best team for each fixture, and, with this attitude, England did well. So they went in to the first Test in good heart, having played some hard cricket.

Flower's role in all of this is vital. As a person and as a cricketer, he is calm and committed. Having been a world-class performer himself, he understands the moods of players, and can express his ideas and vision with great clarity. Every base is covered, and he ensures the players always go in search of victory, something they have to keep working on. He has brought self-belief to the squad: his methods have been seen to work. But he also has the priceless virtue of not getting stuck in his ways; he is happy to change things and promote new ideas.

Ahead of the first Test, the two sides seemed pretty evenly matched, but that game in Brisbane tipped the balance. As with Cardiff in 2009, Australia found themselves in a very strong position, but could not press home their advantage. Indeed, by the end, with England having made 517 for one in their second innings, Australia were demoralised. I don't take many pictures on my travels, but I did take one of that scoreboard. After that, the momentum largely remained with England. Even in Perth there were positives, with Chris Tremlett immediately looking at home on his return to the side. The team understood that they had not handled the conditions well, but they did not dwell on it. They drew on their record of bouncing back.

As a fellow Essex man, I was delighted that Alastair Cook emerged as the Man of the Series. Some had foolishly written him off after a disappointing summer. But he worked hard on his game and he is very driven to achieve what he can in the game. Ponting's comments questioning his place in the side served only to motivate him, rather than undermine him. Cook understood that you do not lose your ability, but merely lose your confidence in your ability.

Going forward under Flower and captain Andrew Strauss, England are clear that the aim is to be the best side in the world. Meeting the current top-ranked nation, India, this summer is a perfect opportunity to find out how far along that road they have gone. Top-class players want to challenge themselves against the best, and few in the game have ever been better than Sachin Tendulkar. He has set himself standards and he is not prepared to let them drop. His wonderful comment after he made his fiftieth Test century gives you a measure of the man: 'Let others count; I just want to play.'

How much we will see of England's stars in county cricket this summer remains a topic that will continue to cause debate. Their success in Australia has boosted the profile of the game, and if the players can be seen away from the England set-up this will only help. I always enjoyed coming back to Essex after playing for England; on each occasion I went out to play, I knew I was putting my record on the line. I believe that is how it should be. I hope that the England players will want to turn out for their counties when they have the opportunity, and I am pleased that the current regime generally seems happy for them to do so. Rising to the different challenges faced in county cricket is well worth it.

GRAHAM GOOCH

FOREWORD

Welcome to the 64th *Playfair Cricket Annual*. This edition covers a remarkable year that started with England crowned world Twenty20 champions in the Caribbean. It continued with series wins over Bangladesh and Pakistan over the summer. Finally, England retained the Ashes in Australia for the first time since 1986-87. All these events are charted within these pages.

The 50-over ICC World Cup will have to wait for next year's volume (it should just about be concluded in time to meet our deadlines), but has already thrown up one major shock, when Ireland beat England. However, even that story does not compare with the romance of Afghanistan reaching the 20-over World Cup last year. Their path to the tournament was an unbelievably difficult one, but the fact that they got there should give hope not only to other sides wanting to compete at the highest level but also to all those seeking for good news from that troubled country.

As last year, *Playfair* is divided into five sections as follows: Test match cricket, county cricket, international limited-overs cricket (including Twenty20), other cricket (IPL, Champions League, women's Test and limited-overs cricket, universities), and fixtures for the coming season. Each section, where appropriate, begins with a preview of forthcoming events, followed by a review of events during the previous season, then come the player records, and finally the records section.

I have restored the Minor Counties, Second XI and other fixtures to the annual this year, as several people got in touch to demand their return – in one case, someone even organised a petition. It is often said that interest in county cricket is waning; *Playfair*'s readers show that this is not the case, even at the levels below the first-class game.

There are very few other modifications this time round. Within the players' register, I have standardised the references to international Under-19 appearances, so these are given only for those who have appeared in Under-19 'Tests' and remain under the age of 25. In the register, 'Second XI debut' refers to the year in which a player made his first appearance in the Second XI Championship. Also in the register, I have now listed players' IT20 best performances in the same style as their Test and LOI ones. In the county records for limited-overs cricket, the three categories are '50 ov', for limited-overs games of 50 (or more) overs per side, '40 ov' and 'T20' are self-explanatory. I have been asked if I intend to provide career averages for either IT20s or T20s, but I do not believe this is the best use of the limited space available in *Playfair*. If you feel you would like these added, or if there are any other features you would like included, do get in touch.

In order to improve communication, we set up a *Playfair* website last year. Do please visit www.playfaircricket.co.uk. I provide regular updates on there throughout the summer, and during the off-season when England are in action, to cover the latest statistical landmarks and other events of interest. *Playfair* is also moving on to Facebook – a development that may surprise those who know me well! In both cases, I would welcome any suggestions for improvements to the service.

This year's cover justifiably places Graeme Swann on the front. The Nottinghamshire and England spinner has been in remarkable form, taking more than 50 Test wickets in each of the last two calendar years, a feat achieved by no other player. However, in the world game there is no cricketer who currently shines as brightly as Sachin Tendulkar. Over the winter he passed 50 Test centuries, while his 120 against England in the World Cup on 27 February was his 98th three-figure innings in international cricket to date. This summer we have what will surely be the last opportunity to see him in action in this country; few will want to miss the opportunity to see the greatest batsman of the modern era in action. It would not be a surprise if he reached his 100th hundred in the Test at Lord's. In seven innings to date at the home of cricket, he has a best of just 37 and an average of 21.28 – something he will surely want to put right.

Ian Marshall,
Eastbourne, March 2011.

ACKNOWLEDGEMENTS AND THANKS

This book could not be written without the help of many people giving freely of their time and expertise, so I would like to thank the following for all they have done to help ensure this edition of *Playfair Cricket Annual* could be written:

At the counties, I would like to thank the following for their help over the last year: Derbyshire – Nathan Fearn, Tom Holdcroft and John Brown; Durham – Brian Hunt; Essex – Ashley Neave and Tony Choat; Glamorgan – Andrew Hignell; Gloucestershire – Lizzie Allen and Keith Gerrish (soon to be succeeded by Adrian Bull); Hampshire – Tim Tremlett and Tony Weld; Kent – Carolyn Prosser and Jack Foley; Lancashire – Diana Lloyd, Alan West and Darrin White; Leicestershire – Elaine Pickering and Graham York; Middlesex – Rebecca Hart and Don Shelley; Northamptonshire – Tony Kingston; Nottinghamshire – Louise Marshall and Brian Hewes; Somerset – Guy Wolfenden and Gerald Stickley; Surrey – Steve Howes and Keith Booth; Sussex – Simon Dyke and Mike Charman; Warwickshire – Keith Cook and David Wainwright; Worcestershire – Joan Grundy and Neil Smith; Yorkshire – Janet Bairstow and John Potter.

At the universities, Cambridge – Tony Gibbs and Anthony Hyde; Durham – Graeme Fowler; Loughborough – Margaret Folwell; Oxford – Neil Harris. For the international umpires, thank you to Brent Silva; and Chris Kelly for the domestic umpires. To Alan Fordham, thank you for the Principal Fixtures, and Philip August for the Minor Counties. Philip Bailey, as ever, provided the first-class and List A career records, and he continues to be an essential help in compiling the book.

At Headline, my thanks go to Marion Donaldson – she and I were colleagues more than 20 years ago, and I doubt either of us expected we would end up working together on *Playfair*; Rhea Halford moved on to an exciting new role during the writing of the Annual and will be much missed; Louise Rothwell was again a huge help in ensuring that the book was produced as swiftly as possible; Sam Eades, for looking after the publicity; and Sam Habib, for all his help on running the *Playfair* website. John Skermer was diligent and assiduous in checking the proofs. At Letterpart, the *Playfair* typesetter since 1994, Chris Leggett, Caroline Leggett, Lorraine Byfield and the rest of the team did a superb job on the setting. Next year I promise to try not to be so close to our deadlines.

Finally, on a personal level, I would like to thank my young daughters, Kiri and Sophia, who have seen very little of me of late as I have hidden behind a closed study door to finish off the book; and of course to my wife, Sugra, for her support, understanding and patience.

ENGLAND v SRI LANKA

SERIES RECORDS

1981-82 to 2007-08

HIGHEST INNINGS TOTALS

England	in England	551-6d		Lord's	2006
	in Sri Lanka	387		Kandy	2000-01
Sri Lanka	in England	591		The Oval	1998
	in Sri Lanka	628-8d		Colombo (SSC)	2003-04

LOWEST INNINGS TOTALS

England	in England	181		The Oval	1998
	in Sri Lanka	81		Galle	2007-08
Sri Lanka	in England	141		Birmingham	2006
	in Sri Lanka	81		Colombo (SSC)	2000-01

HIGHEST MATCH AGGREGATE 1401 for 24 wickets Lord's 2002
LOWEST MATCH AGGREGATE 645 for 36 wickets Colombo (SSC) 2000-01

HIGHEST INDIVIDUAL INNINGS

England	in England	174	G.A.Gooch	Lord's	1991
	in Sri Lanka	128	R.A.Smith	Colombo (SSC)	1992-93
Sri Lanka	in England	213	S.T.Jayasuriya	The Oval	1998
	in Sri Lanka	213*	D.P.M.D.Jayawardena	Galle	2007-08

HIGHEST AGGREGATE OF RUNS IN A SERIES

England	in England	360	(av 72.00)	K.P.Pietersen	2006
	in Sri Lanka	278	(av 46.33)	A.N.Cook	2007-08
Sri Lanka	in England	277	(av 55.40)	M.S.Atapattu	2002
	in Sri Lanka	474	(av 158.00)	D.P.M.D.Jayawardena	2007-08

RECORD WICKET PARTNERSHIPS – ENGLAND

1st	168	M.E.Trescothick (76)/M.P.Vaughan (115)	Lord's	2002
2nd	202	M.E.Trescothick (161)/M.A.Butcher (94)	Birmingham	2002
3rd	167	N.Hussain (109)/G.P.Thorpe (59)	Kandy	2000-01
4th	128	G.A.Hick (107)/M.R.Ramprakash (53)	The Oval	1998
5th	173	K.P.Pietersen (158)/P.D.Collingwood (57)	Lord's	2006
6th	87	A.J.Lamb (107)/R.M.Ellison (41)	Lord's	1984
	87	A.J.Stewart (54)/C.White (39)	Kandy	2000-01
	87	A.Flintoff (77)/G.J.Batty (14)	Colombo (SSC)	2003-04
7th	109	I.R.Bell (74)/M.J.Prior (63)	Kandy	2007-08
8th	102	A.J.Stewart (123)/A.F.Giles (45)	Manchester	2002
9th	53	M.R.Ramprakash (42)/D.Gough (15)	The Oval	1998
10th	91	G.P.Thorpe (123)/M.J.Hoggard (17*)	Birmingham	2002

RECORD WICKET PARTNERSHIPS – SRI LANKA

1st	113	M.G.Vandort (49)/S.T.Jayasuriya (78)	Kandy	2007-08
2nd	109	W.U.Tharanga (52)/K.C.Sangakkara (65)	Lord's	2006
3rd	262	T.T.Samaraweera (142)/ D.P.M.D.Jayawardena (134)	Colombo (SSC)	2003-04
4th	153	D.P.M.D.Jayawardena (52)/T.M.Dilshan (100)	Kandy	2003-04
5th	150	S.Wettimuny (190)/L.R.D.Mendis (111)	Lord's	1984
6th	138	S.A.R.Silva (102*)/L.R.D.Mendis (94)	Lord's	1984
7th	183	D.P.M.D.Jayawardena (213*)/W.P.J.U.C.Vaas (90)	Galle	2007-08
8th	53	H.D.P.K.Dharmasena (54)/W.P.J.U.C.Vaas (36)	Kandy	2000-01
9th	105	W.P.J.U.C.Vaas (50*)/M.D.N.Kulasekara (64)	Lord's	2006
10th	64	J.R.Ratnayeke (59*)/G.F.Labrooy (42)	Lord's	1988

BEST INNINGS BOWLING ANALYSIS

England	in England	7-70	P.A.J.DeFreitas	Lord's	1991
	in Sri Lanka	6-33	J.E.Emburey	Colombo (PSS)	1981-82
Sri Lanka	in England	9-65	M.Muralitharan	The Oval	1998
	in Sri Lanka	7-46	M.Muralitharan	Galle	2003-04

BEST MATCH BOWLING ANALYSIS

England	in England	8-115	P.A.J.DeFreitas	Lord's	1991
	in Sri Lanka	8- 95	D.L.Underwood	Colombo (PSS)	1981-82
Sri Lanka	in England	16-220	M.Muralitharan	The Oval	1998
	in Sri Lanka	11- 93	M.Muralitharan	Galle	2003-04

HIGHEST WICKET AGGREGATE IN A SERIES

England	in England	15	(av 24.60)	M.J.Hoggard	2006
	in Sri Lanka	18	(av 29.94)	A.F.Giles	2003-04
Sri Lanka	in England	24	(av 16.87)	M.Muralitharan	2006
	in Sri Lanka	26	(av 12.30)	M.Muralitharan	2003-04

RESULTS SUMMARY

ENGLAND v SRI LANKA – IN ENGLAND

	Tests	Series			Lord's			Oval			Birmingham			Manchester			Nottingham		
		E	SL	D	E	SL	D	E	SL	D	E	SL	D	E	SL	D	E	SL	D
1984	1	–	–	1	–	–	1	–	–	–	–	–	–	–	–	–	–	–	–
1988	1	1	–	–	1	–	–	–	–	–	–	–	–	–	–	–	–	–	–
1991	1	1	–	–	1	–	–	–	–	–	–	–	–	–	–	–	–	–	–
1998	1	–	1	–	–	–	–	–	1	–	–	–	–	–	–	–	–	–	–
2002	3	2	–	1	–	1	–	–	–	–	1	–	–	1	–	–	–	–	–
2006	3	1	1	1	–	1	–	–	–	–	1	–	–	–	–	–	–	1	–
	10	5	2	3	2	–	3	–	1	–	2	–	–	1	–	–	–	1	–

ENGLAND v SRI LANKA – IN SRI LANKA

	Tests	Series			Colombo (PSS)			Colombo (SSC)			Galle			Kandy		
		E	SL	D	E	SL	D	E	SL	D	E	SL	D	E	SL	D
1981-82	1	1	–	–	1	–	–	–	–	–	–	–	–	–	–	–
1992-93	1	–	1	–	–	–	–	–	1	–	–	–	–	–	–	–
2000-01	3	2	1	–	–	–	–	1	–	–	–	1	–	1	–	–
2003-04	3	–	1	2	–	–	–	–	1	–	–	–	1	–	–	1
2007-08	3	–	1	2	–	–	–	–	–	1	–	–	1	–	1	–
	11	3	4	4	1	–	–	1	2	1	–	1	2	1	1	1
Totals	21	8	6	7												

ENGLAND v INDIA

SERIES RECORDS

1932 to 2008-09

HIGHEST INNINGS TOTALS

England	in England	653-4d	Lord's	1990
	in India	652-7d	Madras	1984-85
India	in England	664	The Oval	2007
	in India	591	Bombay	1992-93

LOWEST INNINGS TOTALS

England	in England	101	The Oval	1971
	in India	102	Bombay	1981-82
India	in England	42	Lord's	1974
	in India	83	Madras	1976-77

HIGHEST MATCH AGGREGATE 1614 for 30 wickets Manchester 1990
LOWEST MATCH AGGREGATE 482 for 31 wickets Lord's 1936

HIGHEST INDIVIDUAL INNINGS

England	in England	333	G.A.Gooch	Lord's	1990
	in India	207	M.W.Gatting	Madras	1984-85
India	in England	221	S.M.Gavaskar	The Oval	1979
	in India	224	V.G.Kambli	Bombay	1992-93

HIGHEST AGGREGATE OF RUNS IN A SERIES

England	in England	752	(av 125.33)	G.A.Gooch	1990
	in India	594	(av 99.00)	K.F.Barrington	1961-62
India	in England	602	(av 100.33)	R.S.Dravid	2002
	in India	586	(av 83.71)	V.G.Kambli	1992-93

RECORD WICKET PARTNERSHIPS – ENGLAND

1st	225	G.A.Gooch (116)/M.A.Atherton (131)	Manchester	1990
2nd	241	G.Fowler (201)/M.W.Gatting (207)	Madras	1984-85
3rd	308	G.A.Gooch (333)/A.J.Lamb (139)	Lord's	1990
4th	266	W.R.Hammond (217)/T.S.Worthington (128)	The Oval	1936
5th	254	K.W.R.Fletcher (113)/A.W.Greig (148)	Bombay	1972-73
6th	171	I.T.Botham (114)/R.W.Taylor (43)	Bombay	1979-80
7th	125	D.W.Randall (126)/P.H.Edmonds (64)	Lord's	1982
8th	168	R.Illingworth (107)/P.Lever (88*)	Manchester	1971
9th	103	C.White (94*)/M.J.Hoggard (32)	Nottingham	2002
10th	70	P.J.W.Allott (41*)/R.G.D.Willis (28)	Lord's	1982

RECORD WICKET PARTNERSHIPS – INDIA

1st	213	S.M.Gavaskar (221)/C.P.S.Chauhan (80)	The Oval	1979
2nd	314	G.Gambhir (179)/R.S.Dravid (136)	Chandigarh	2008-09
3rd	316	G.R.Viswanath (222)/Yashpal Sharma (140)	Madras	1981-82
4th	249	S.R.Tendulkar (193)/S.C.Ganguly (128)	Leeds	2002
5th	214	M.Azharuddin (110)/R.J.Shastri (111)	Calcutta	1984-85
6th	130	S.M.H.Kirmani (43)/Kapil Dev (97)	The Oval	1982
7th	235	R.J.Shastri (142)/S.M.H.Kirmani (102)	Bombay	1984-85
8th	128	R.J.Shastri (93)/S.M.H.Kirmani (67)	Delhi	1981-82
9th	104	R.J.Shastri (93)/Madan Lal (44)	Delhi	1981-82
10th	73	A.Kumble (110*)/S.Sreesanth (35)	The Oval	2007

BEST INNINGS BOWLING ANALYSIS

England	in England	8-31	F.S.Trueman	Manchester	1952
	in India	7-46	J.K.Lever	Delhi	1976-77
India	in England	6-35	L.Amar Singh	Lord's	1936
	in India	8-55	M.H.Mankad	Madras	1951-52

BEST MATCH BOWLING ANALYSIS

England	in England	11- 93	A.V.Bedser	Manchester	1946
	in India	13-106	I.T.Botham	Bombay	1979-80
India	in England	10-188	C.Sharma	Birmingham	1986
	in India	12-108	M.H.Mankad	Madras	1951-52

HIGHEST AGGREGATE OF WICKETS IN A SERIES

England	in England	29	(av 13.31)	F.S.Trueman	1952
	in India	29	(av 17.55)	D.L.Underwood	1976-77
India	in England	18	(av 20.33)	Z.Khan	2007
	in India	35	(av 18.91)	B.S.Chandrasekhar	1972-73

RESULTS SUMMARY

ENGLAND v INDIA – IN ENGLAND

	Tests	Series E	I	D	Lord's E	I	D	Manchester E	I	D	The Oval E	I	D	Leeds E	I	D	Nottingham E	I	D	Birmingham E	I	D
1932	1	1	–	–	1	–	–	–	–	–	–	–	–	–	–	–	–	–	–	–	–	–
1936	3	2	–	1	1	–	–	–	–	1	1	–	–	–	–	–	–	–	–	–	–	–
1946	3	1	–	2	1	–	–	–	–	1	–	–	1	–	–	–	–	–	–	–	–	–
1952	4	3	–	1	1	–	–	1	–	–	–	–	1	1	–	–	–	–	–	–	–	–
1959	5	5	–	–	1	–	–	1	–	–	1	–	–	1	–	–	1	–	–	–	–	–
1967	3	3	–	–	1	–	–	–	–	–	1	–	–	–	–	–	1	–	–	–	–	–
1971	3	–	1	2	–	–	1	–	–	1	–	1	–	–	–	–	–	–	–	–	–	–
1974	3	3	–	–	1	–	–	1	–	–	1	–	–	–	–	–	–	–	1	–	–
1979	4	1	–	3	–	–	1	–	1	–	–	–	1	–	1	–	–	1	–	–	–
1982	3	1	–	2	1	–	–	–	–	1	–	–	1	–	–	–	–	–	–	–	–	–
1986	3	–	2	1	–	1	–	–	–	–	–	–	–	–	1	–	–	–	–	1
1990	3	1	–	2	1	–	–	–	–	1	–	–	1	–	–	–	–	–	–	–	–
1996	3	1	–	2	–	–	1	–	1	–	–	–	1	–	–	–	1	1	–	–
2002	4	1	1	2	1	–	–	–	–	1	–	1	–	1	–	–	1	–	–	–
2007	3	–	1	2	–	–	1	–	1	–	–	1	–	–	1	–	–	–	–	–
	48	23	5	20	10	1	4	3	–	5	2	1	7	3	2	1	1	1	2	4	–	1

ENGLAND v INDIA – IN INDIA

	Tests	Series E	I	D	Bombay E	I	D	Calcutta E	I	D	Madras E	I	D	Delhi E	I	D	Kanpur E	I	D	Bangalore E	I	D	Chandigarh E	I	D	Ahmedabad E	I	D
1933-34	3	2	–	1	1	–	–	–	–	1	1	–	–	–	–	–	–	–	–	–	–	–	–	–	–	–	–	–
1951-52	5	1	1	3	1	–	–	–	–	1	1	–	–	–	1	–	–	–	–	–	–	–	–	–	–	–
1961-62	5	–	2	3	–	–	1	–	1	–	–	1	–	–	1	–	1	–	–	–	–	–	–	–	–
1963-64	5	–	–	5	–	–	1	–	–	1	–	–	1	–	–	1	–	–	1	–	–	–	–	–	–
1972-73	5	1	2	2	–	–	1	–	1	–	1	–	–	–	1	–	–	1	–	–	–	–	–	–	–
1976-77	5	3	1	1	1	–	–	1	–	–	1	–	–	1	–	–	–	1	–	–	–	–	–	–	–
1979-80	1	1	–	–	1	–	–	–	–	–	–	–	–	–	–	–	–	–	–	–	–	–	–	–	–
1981-82	6	1	–	5	–	–	1	–	–	1	–	–	1	–	–	1	–	–	1	–	–	–	–	–	–
1984-85	5	2	1	2	–	1	–	1	–	–	1	–	–	–	1	–	–	–	–	–	–	–	–	–	–
1992-93	3	–	3	–	–	1	–	–	1	–	1	–	–	–	–	–	–	–	–	–	–	–	–	–	–
2001-02	3	–	1	2	–	–	1	–	–	1	–	–	1	–	–	–	–	–	–	–	1	–	–	1
2008-09	2	–	1	1	–	–	–	–	–	1	–	1	–	–	–	–	–	–	–	–	–	–	–	1	–	–
	48	10	13	25	2	3	5	1	3	5	3	5	2	3	–	4	1	–	5	–	1	2	–	1	1	–	–	1

Totals	96	33	18	45

TOURING TEAMS REGISTER 2011

Neither Sri Lanka nor India had selected their 2011 touring teams at the time of going to press. The following players who had represented those teams in Test matches since 16 November 2009 were still available for selection:

SRI LANKA

Full Names	Birthdate	Birthplace	Team	Type	F-C Debut
DILSHAN, Tillekeratne M.	14.10.76	Kalutara	Bloomfield	RHB/OB	1993-94
FERNANDO, C.R.Dilhara	19.07.79	Colombo	Sinhalese	RHB/RFM	1997-98
HERATH, H.M.Rangana K.B.	19.03.78	Kurunegala	Wayamba	LHB/SLA	1996-97
JAYAWARDENA, D.P.Mahela D.	27.05.77	Colombo	Sinhalese	RHB/RM	1995-96
JAYAWARDENA, H.A.Prasanna W.	09.10.79	Colombo	Bloomfield	RHB/WK	1997-98
KALUHALAMULLA, H.K.Suraj Randiv	30.01.85	Matara	Bloomfield	RHB/OB	2002-03
KULASEKARA, K.M.D.Nuwan	22.07.82	Nittambuwa	Colts	RHB/RFM	2002-03
LAKMAL, R.A.Suranga	10.03.87	Matara	Tamil Union	RHB/RMF	2007-08
MALINGA, Separamadu Lasith	28.08.83	Galle	Nondescripts	RHB/RF	2001-02
MATHEWS, Angelo Davis	02.06.87	Colombo	Colts	RHB/RFM	2006-07
MENDIS, B.Ajantha W.	11.03.85	Moratuwa	Sri Lanka Army	RHB/LBG	2006-07
MIRANDO, M.Thilan Thushara	01.03.81	Balapitiya	Sinhalese	LHB/LFM	1998-99
PARANAVITANA, N.Tharanga	15.04.82	Kegalle	Sinhalese	LHB/OB	2001-02
PRASAD, K.T.G.Dammika	30.05.83	Ragama	Sinhalese	RHB/RFM	2001-02
SAMARAWEERA, Thilan T.	22.09.76	Colombo	Sinhalese	RHB/OB	1995-96
SANGAKKARA, Kumar C.	27.10.77	Matale	Kandurata	LHB/WK	1997-98
WELAGEDARA, U.W.M.B.Chanaka A.	20.03.81	Matale	Tamil Union	RHB/LFM	2002-03

NB: H.K.S.R.Kaluhalamulla is also known as S.Randiv; M.T.T.Mirando is also known as T.Thushara.

INDIA

Full Names	Birthdate	Birthplace	Team	Type	F-C Debut
BADRINATH, Subramaniam	30.08.80	Madras	Tamil Nadu	RHB/OB	2000-01
DHONI, Mahendra Singh	07.07.81	Ranchi	Chennai SK	RHB/WK	1999-00
DRAVID, Rahul Sharad	11.01.73	Indore	Karnataka	RHB/OB	1990-91
GAMBHIR, Gautam	14.10.81	Delhi	Delhi	LHB/LB	1999-00
HARBHAJAN SINGH	03.07.80	Jullundur	Mumbai Indians	RHB/OB	1997-98
KARTHIK, Krishnakumar Dinesh	01.06.85	Madras	Tamil Nadu	RHB/WK	2002-03
KHAN, Zaheer	07.10.78	Shrirampur	Mumbai	RHB/LFM	1999-00
LAXMAN, Vangipurappu Venkata Sai	01.11.74	Hyderabad	Hyderabad	RHB/OB	1992-93
MISHRA, Amit	24.11.82	Delhi	Haryana	RHB/LB	2000-01
MITHUN, Abhimanyu	25.10.89	Dasarahalli	Karnataka	RHB/RM	2009-10
OJHA, Pragyan Prayish	05.09.86	Khurda	Hyderabad	LHB/SLA	2004-05
PUJARA, Cheteshwar Arvind	25.01.88	Rajkot	Saurashtra	RHB/LB	2005-06
RAINA, Suresh Kumar	27.11.86	Ghaziabad	Uttar Pradesh	LHB/OB	2002-03
SAHA, Wriddhaman Prasanta	24.10.84	Shaktigarh	Bengal	RHB/WK	2007-08
SEHWAG, Virender	20.10.78	Delhi	Delhi	RHB/OB	1997-98
SHARMA, Ishant	02.09.88	Delhi	Delhi	RHB/RFM	2006-07
SREESANTH, Shanthakumaran	06.02.83	Kothamangalam	Kerala	RHB/RFM	2002-03
TENDULKAR, Sachin Ramesh	24.04.73	Bombay	Mumbai	RHB/OB	1988-89
UNADKAT, Jaidev Dipakbhai	18.10.91	Porbandar	Saurashtra	RHB/LMF	2010
VIJAY, Murali	01.04.84	Madras	Tamil Nadu	RHB/OB	2006-07
YUVRAJ SINGH	12.12.81	Chandigarh	Punjab	LHB/SLA	1996-97

When the final squads are announced, a complete version of the touring party will be posted on www.playfaircricket.co.uk

STATISTICAL HIGHLIGHTS IN 2010 TESTS

Including Tests from No. 1943 (South Africa v England, 3rd Test) and No. 1946 (Australia v Pakistan, 2nd Test) to No. 1984 (Australia v England, 4th Test) and No. 1987 (South Africa v India, 2nd Test). († *National record*).

TEAM HIGHLIGHTS
HIGHEST INNINGS TOTALS

707	India v Sri Lanka	Colombo (SSC)
643-6d	India v South Africa	Kolkata
642-4d	Sri Lanka v India	Colombo (SSC)
620-4d	South Africa v India	Centurion
620-5d	England v Australia	Adelaide

LOWEST INNINGS TOTALS

72	Pakistan v England	Birmingham
74	Pakistan v England	Lord's
80	Pakistan v England	Nottingham
88	Australia v Pakistan	Leeds
98	Australia v England	Melbourne

MATCH AGGREGATES OF 1500 RUNS

1501-32	New Zealand (553-7d & 258-5d) v Bangladesh (408 & 282)	Hamilton

BATSMEN'S MATCH (Qualification: 1200 runs, average 70 per wicket)

86.94 (1478-17)	Sri Lanka v India	Colombo (SSC)

LARGE MARGINS OF VICTORY

Inns & 225 runs	England (446) beat Pakistan (74 & 147)	Lord's
354 runs	England (354 & 262-9d) beat Pakistan (182 & 80)	Nottingham

NARROW MARGINS OF VICTORY

36 runs	Australia (127 & 381) beat Pakistan (333 & 139)	Sydney
One wicket	India (405 & 216-9) beat Australia (428 & 192)	Mohali

FOUR HUNDREDS IN AN INNINGS

India (643-6d) v South Africa		Kolkata

BATTING HIGHLIGHTS
TRIPLE HUNDREDS

C.H.Gayle	333	West Indies v Sri Lanka	Galle

DOUBLE HUNDREDS

H.M.Amla	253*	South Africa v India	Nagpur
A.N.Cook	235*	England v Australia	Brisbane
A.B.de Villiers	278*†	South Africa v Pakistan	Abu Dhabi
J.H.Kallis	201*	South Africa v India	Centurion
B.B.McCullum	225	New Zealand v India	Hyderabad (RGI)
K.P.Pietersen	227	England v Australia	Adelaide
R.T.Ponting	209	Australia v Pakistan	Hobart
K.C.Sangakkara	219	Sri Lanka v India	Colombo (SSC)
S.R.Tendulkar (2)	214	India v Australia	Bangalore
	203	India v Sri Lanka	Colombo (SSC)
I.J.L.Trott	226	England v Bangladesh	Lord's

10

FASTEST HUNDRED

A.B.de Villiers (129)	75 balls†	South Africa v India	Centurion

HUNDRED BEFORE LUNCH

A.B.de Villiers (0-119*)		South Africa v India	Centurion

200 RUNS IN A DAY

C.H.Gayle	333	(0-219*)	West Indies v Sri Lanka	Galle

NINE SIXES IN AN INNINGS

C.H.Gayle	(333)	9	West Indies v Sri Lanka	Galle

HUNDRED ON TEST DEBUT

A.N.Petersen	100	South Africa v India	Kolkata
S.K.Raina	120	India v Sri Lanka	Colombo (SSC)
K.S.Williamson	131	New Zealand v India	Ahmedabad

LONG INNINGS (Qualification: 600 mins and/or 400 balls)

Min	Balls			
675	473	H.M.Amla (253*)	South Africa v India	Nagpur
653	437	C.H.Gayle (333)	West Indies v Sri Lanka	Galle
630	428	A.N.Cook (235*)	England v Australia	Brisbane
601	418	A.B.de Villiers (278*)	South Africa v Pakistan	Abu Dhabi

NOTABLE PARTNERSHIPS

Qualifications: 1st-4th wkts: 250 runs; 5th-6th: 225; 7th: 200; 8th: 175; 9th: 150; 10th: 100.

Second Wicket

329*	A.N.Cook/I.J.L.Trott	England v Australia	Brisbane

Third Wicket

340	H.M.Amla/J.H.Kallis	South Africa v India	Nagpur
308	M.Vijay/S.R.Tendulkar	India v Australia	Bangalore

Fourth Wicket

352	R.T.Ponting/M.J.Clarke	Australia v Pakistan	Hobart

Fifth Wicket

256	S.R.Tendulkar/S.K.Raina	India v Sri Lanka	Colombo (SSC)
253	M.J.Clarke/M.J.North	Australia v New Zealand	Wellington

Sixth Wicket

339†	M.J.Guptill/B.B.McCullum	New Zealand v Bangladesh	Hamilton
307	M.E.K.Hussey/B.J.Haddin	Australia v England	Brisbane

Seventh Wicket

259*†	V.V.S.Laxman/M.S.Dhoni	India v South Africa	Kolkata

Eighth Wicket

332†	I.J.L.Trott/S.C.J.Broad	England v Pakistan	Lord's

Tenth Wicket

107*†	A.B.de Villiers/M.Morkel	South Africa v Pakistan	Abu Dhabi
105	Harbhajan Singh/S.Sreesanth	India v New Zealand	Hyderabad (RGI)

275 runs were added for the third wicket for India v Bangladesh (Mirpur): S.R.Tendulkar and R.S.Dravid added 222 runs, and then after Dravid's injury Tendulkar and M.Vijay added a further 53 runs.

BOWLING HIGHLIGHTS

SEVEN WICKETS IN AN INNINGS

| Z.Khan | 7- 87 India v Bangladesh | Mirpur |
| D.W.Steyn | 7- 51 South Africa v India | Nagpur |

TEN WICKETS IN A MATCH

J.M.Anderson	11- 71 England v Pakistan	Nottingham
M.G.Johnson	10-132 Australia v New Zealand	Hamilton
Z.Khan	10-149 India v Bangladesh	Mirpur
D.W.Steyn	10-108 South Africa v India	Nagpur
G.P.Swann	10-217 England v Bangladesh	Chittagong

FIVE WICKETS IN AN INNINGS ON DEBUT

| Tanvir Ahmed | 6-120 Pakistan v South Africa | Abu Dhabi |
| Wahab Riaz | 5- 63 Pakistan v England | The Oval |

HAT-TRICKS

| P.M.Siddle | Australia v England | Brisbane |

200 RUNS CONCEDED IN AN INNINGS

| H.K.S.R.Kaluhalamulla 73-16-222-2 | Sri Lanka v India | Colombo (SSC) |

60 OVERS IN AN INNINGS

P.L.Harris	62-9-165-2	South Africa v West Indies	Basseterre
B.A.W.Mendis	63-10-172-4	Sri Lanka v India	Colombo (SSC)
H.K.S.R.Kaluhalamulla	73-16-222-2	Sri Lanka v India	Colombo (SSC)
Shakib Al Hasan	66-27-124-4	Bangladesh v England	Mirpur

WICKET-KEEPING HIGHLIGHTS

SIX WICKET-KEEPING DISMISSALS IN AN INNINGS

| M.J.Prior | 6ct | England v Australia | Melbourne |

NINE WICKET-KEEPING DISMISSALS IN A MATCH

| B.J.Haddin | 9ct | Australia v Pakistan | Sydney |
| M.V.Boucher | 9ct | South Africa v India | Durban |

FIELDING HIGHLIGHTS

FIVE CATCHES IN A MATCH IN THE FIELD

| D.P.M.D.Jayawardena | 5ct | Sri Lanka v India | Galle |

LEADING TEST AGGREGATES IN 2010
1000 RUNS IN 2010

	M	I	NO	HS	Runs	Avge	100	50
S.R.Tendulkar (I)	14	23	3	214	1562	78.10	7	5
V.Sehwag (I)	14	25	2	173	1422	61.82	5	8
I.J.L.Trott (E)	14	24	4	226	1325	66.25	4	4
A.N.Cook (E)	14	24	2	235*	1287	58.50	5	4
H.M.Amla (SA)	11	19	3	253*	1249	78.06	5	4
J.H.Kallis (SA)	11	19	4	201*	1198	79.86	6	2

RECORD CALENDAR YEAR RUNS AGGREGATE

	M	I	NO	HS	Runs	Avge	100	50
M.Yousuf Youhana (P) (2006)	11	19	1	202	1788	99.33	9	3

RECORD CALENDAR YEAR RUNS AVERAGE

	M	I	NO	HS	Runs	Avge	100	50
G.St A.Sobers (WI) (1958)	7	12	3	365*	1193	132.55	5	3

1000 RUNS IN DEBUT CALENDAR YEAR

	M	I	NO	HS	Runs	Avge	100	50
M.A.Taylor (A) (1989)	11	20	1	219	1219	64.15	4	5
A.N.Cook (E) (2006)	13	24	2	127	1013	46.04	4	3

50 WICKETS IN 2010

	M	O	R	W	Avge	Best	5wI	10wM
G.P.Swann (E)	14	576.0	1662	64	25.96	6-65	6	1
D.W.Steyn (SA)	11	390.1	1285	60	21.41	7-51	4	1
J.M.Anderson (E)	11	463.0	1309	57	22.96	6-17	3	1

RECORD CALENDAR YEAR WICKETS AGGREGATE

	M	O	R	W	Avge	Best	5wI	10wM
M.Muralitharan (SL) (2006)	11	588.4	1521	90	16.90	8-70	9	5
S.K.Warne (A) (2005)	14	691.4	2043	90	22.70	6-46	6	2

50 WICKET-KEEPING DISMISSALS IN 2010

	M	Dis	Ct	St
M.J.Prior (E)	14	56	54	2

RECORD CALENDAR YEAR DISMISSALS AGGREGATE

	M	Dis	Ct	St
I.A.Healy (A) (1993)	16	67	58	9
M.V.Boucher (SA) (1998)	13	67	65	2

20 CATCHES BY FIELDERS IN 2010

	M	Ct
P.D.Collingwood (E)	12	22

RECORD CALENDAR YEAR FIELDER'S AGGREGATE

	M	Ct
G.C.Smith (SA) (2008)	15	30

TEST MATCH SCORES
BANGLADESH v INDIA (1st Test)

At Chittagong Divisional Stadium, on 17, 18, 19, 20, 21 January 2010.
Toss: Bangladesh. Result: **INDIA** won by 113 runs.
Debut: Bangladesh – Shafiul Islam.

INDIA

G.Gambhir	c Rahim b Shahadat	23	c Nafis b Islam		116
*V.Sehwag	c Iqbal b Shakib	52	c Raqibul b Shakib		45
R.S.Dravid	b Shahadat	4	(4) run out		24
S.R.Tendulkar	not out	105	(5) lbw b Rubel		16
V.V.S.Laxman	st Rahim b Shakib	7	(6) not out		69
Yuvraj Singh	c Rubel b Shakib	12	(7) c Ashraful b Shahadat		25
†K.D.Karthik	c Raqibul b Shahadat	0	(8) c Rubel b Mahmudullah		27
A.Mishra	lbw b Shahadat	14	(3) c Iqbal b Mahmudullah		50
Z.Khan	c Raqibul b Shakib	11	b Shakib		0
I.Sharma	c Rahim b Shahadat	1	not out		7
S.Sreesanth	c Kayes b Shakib	1			
Extras	(B 1, LB 6, W 1, NB 5)	13	(B 1, LB 5, W 3, NB 5)		14
Total	**(70.5 overs)**	**243**	**(8 wkts dec; 87 overs)**		**413**

BANGLADESH

Tamim Iqbal	b Khan	31	c Dravid b Sehwag		52
Imrul Kayes	lbw b Khan	23	c Karthik b Khan		1
Shahriar Nafis	c Laxman b Sharma	4	c Sehwag b Sharma		21
Mohammad Ashraful	c Dravid b Sharma	2	c Dravid b Sharma		27
Raqibul Hasan	c Karthik b Sreesanth	17	lbw b Sharma		13
*Shakib Al Hasan	c Sehwag b Khan	17	c Sehwag b Mishra		17
†Mushfiqur Rahim	c Sehwag b Mishra	44	sub (P.P.Ojha) b Mishra		101
Mahmudullah	c Karthik b Sreesanth	69	c Karthik b Khan		20
Shahadat Hossain	c Yuvraj b Mishra	11	b Mishra		24
Shafiul Islam	c Yuvraj b Mishra	6	c and b Mishra		8
Rubel Hossain	not out	0	not out		4
Extras	(B 4, LB 1, W 1, NB 12)	18	(B 4, LB 3, NB 6)		13
Total	**(65.2 overs)**	**242**	**(75.2 overs)**		**301**

BANGLADESH	O	M	R	W	O	M	R	W
Shafiul Islam	9	1	41	0	15	0	87	1
Shahadat Hossain	18	2	71	5	16	1	53	1
Rubel Hossain	10	0	40	0	15	0	94	1
Shakib Al Hasan	29.5	10	62	5	27	2	112	2
Mahmudullah	3	0	17	0	13	0	52	2
Mohammad Ashraful	1	0	5	0	1	0	9	0

INDIA	O	M	R	W	O	M	R	W
Khan	20	4	54	3	20	5	90	2
Sreesanth	11	1	55	2	12.2	0	53	0
Sharma	13	3	47	2	15	4	48	3
Mishra	16.2	2	66	3	22.2	3	92	4
Yuvraj Singh	5	1	15	0	(6) 1.4	1	4	0
Sehwag					(5) 4	1	7	1

FALL OF WICKETS

	I	B	I	B
Wkt	1st	1st	2nd	2nd
1st	79	53	90	8
2nd	79	58	188	47
3rd	85	58	233	79
4th	107	68	245	97
5th	149	89	272	135
6th	150	98	313	145
7th	182	206	362	170
8th	209	228	394	230
9th	230	235	–	258
10th	243	242	–	301

Umpires: B.F.Bowden (*New Zealand*) (58) and M.Erasmus (*South Africa*) (1).
Referee: A.J.Pycroft (*Zimbabwe*) (7). **Test No. 1948/6 (B62/1434)**

BANGLADESH v INDIA (2nd Test)

At Shere Bangla National Stadium, Mirpur, on 24, 25, 26, 27 January 2010.
Toss: Bangladesh. Result: **INDIA** won by ten wickets.
Debuts: None.

BANGLADESH

Tamim Iqbal	b Khan	0		c Dhoni b Khan	151
Imrul Kayes	c Dhoni b Sharma	0		c sub (K.D.Karthik) b Khan	5
Junaid Siddique	c Dhoni b Khan	7		c Dhoni b Khan	55
Mohammad Ashraful	st Dhoni b Ojha	39	(5)	c Dhoni b Ojha	25
Raqibul Hasan	c Dravid b Sharma	4	(6)	b Khan	5
*Shakib Al Hasan	c Dhoni b Khan	34	(7)	c Gambhir b Ojha	7
†Mushfiqur Rahim	lbw b Sharma	30	(8)	not out	10
Mahmudullah	not out	96	(9)	c Vijay b Khan	0
Shahadat Hossain	st Dhoni b Ojha	8	(4)	c sub (A.Mishra) b Harbhajan	40
Shafiul Islam	c Dravid b Sharma	9		b Khan	0
Rubel Hossain	b Harbhajan	4		b Khan	0
Extras	(LB 2)	2		(B 7, LB 5, W 2)	14
Total	**(73.5 overs)**	**233**		**(90.3 overs)**	**312**

INDIA

G.Gambhir	c Rahim b Islam	68	(2)	not out	0
V.Sehwag	c Rahim b Shahadat	56	(1)	not out	0
R.S.Dravid	retired hurt	111			
S.R.Tendulkar	c Kayes b Shakib	143			
M.Vijay	c Mahmudullah b Shakib	30			
†*M.S.Dhoni	st Rahim b Raqibul	89			
Harbhajan Singh	c Rahim b Islam	13			
Z.Khan	c Shahadat b Islam	0			
I.Sharma	c Rahim b Ashraful	13			
P.P.Ojha	not out	1			
Yuvraj Singh					
Extras	(B 3, LB 6, W 1, NB 10)	20		(B 2)	2
Total	**(8 wkts dec; 133 overs)**	**544**		**(0 wkts; 0.2 overs)**	**2**

INDIA	O	M	R	W		O	M	R	W	FALL OF WICKETS			
Khan	19	3	62	3		20.3	2	87	7		B	I	B	I
Sharma	18	3	66	4		15	2	50	0	Wkt	1st	1st	2nd	2nd
Ojha	16	1	49	2	(4)	22	4	77	2	1st	0	103	19	–
Harbhajan Singh	18.5	3	48	1	(3)	26	7	75	1	2nd	4	146	219	–
Yuvraj Singh	2	0	6	0						3rd	13	421	222	–
Sehwag					(5)	7	2	11	0	4th	44	436	290	–
										5th	51	459	291	–
BANGLADESH										6th	106	467	301	–
Shafiul Islam	23	1	86	3						7th	127	518	304	–
Shahadat Hossain	22	2	91	1						8th	155	544	304	–
Rubel Hossain	28	1	115	0						9th	213	–	304	–
Shakib Al Hasan	34	3	118	2	(1)	0.2	0	0	0	10th	233	–	312	–
Mohammad Ashraful	9	0	38	1										
Mahmudullah	15	0	78	0										
Junaid Siddique	1	0	9	0										
Raqibul Hasan	1	0	1	1										

Umpires: B.F.Bowden (*New Zealand*) (59) and M.Erasmus (*South Africa*) (2).
Referee: A.J.Pycroft (*Zimbabwe*) (8).
R.S.Dravid retired hurt at 368-2.

Test No. 1949/7 (B63/I435)

INDIA v SOUTH AFRICA (1st Test)

At Vidarbha C.A.Stadium, Nagpur, on 6, 7, 8, 9 February 2010.
Toss: South Africa. Result: **SOUTH AFRICA** won by an innings and 6 runs.
Debuts: India – S.Badrinath, W.P.Saha.

SOUTH AFRICA

*G.C.Smith	b Khan	6
A.G.Prince	c Dhoni b Khan	0
H.M.Amla	not out	253
J.H.Kallis	c Vijay b Harbhajan	173
A.B.de Villiers	c Badrinath b Sehwag	53
J.P.Duminy	lbw b Harbhajan	9
†M.V.Boucher	c Mishra b Khan	39
D.W.Steyn	not out	0
W.D.Parnell		
M.Morkel		
P.L.Harris		
Extras	(B 8, LB 8, NB 9)	25
Total	**(6 wkts dec; 176 overs; 696 mins)**	**558**

INDIA

G.Gambhir	c Boucher b Morkel	12	b Morkel		1
V.Sehwag	c Duminy b Parnell	109	c Smith b Steyn		16
M.Vijay	b Steyn	4	c Morkel b Harris		32
S.R.Tendulkar	c Boucher b Steyn	7	b Harris		100
S.Badrinath	c Prince b Steyn	56	c Boucher b Parnell		6
†*M.S.Dhoni	c Kallis b Harris	6	c De Villiers b Harris		25
W.P.Saha	b Steyn	0	lbw b Steyn		36
Harbhajan Singh	lbw b Steyn	8	lbw b Parnell		39
Z.Khan	b Steyn	2	c Harris b Kallis		33
A.Mishra	b Steyn	0	b Steyn		0
I.Sharma	not out	0	not out		0
Extras	(B 14, LB 6, W 5, NB 4)	29	(B 15, LB 8, W 6, NB 2)		31
Total	**(64.4 overs; 294 mins)**	**233**	**(107.1 overs; 463 mins)**		**319**

INDIA	O	M	R	W		O	M	R	W		FALL OF WICKETS			
Khan	31	7	96	3								SA	I	I
Sharma	28	4	85	0							Wkt	1st	1st	2nd
Harbhajan Singh	46	1	166	2							1st	5	31	1
Mishra	53	5	140	0							2nd	6	40	24
Sehwag	18	1	55	1							3rd	346	56	96
											4th	454	192	122
SOUTH AFRICA											5th	476	221	192
Steyn	16.4	6	51	7		18.1	1	57	3		6th	554	221	209
Morkel	15	4	58	1		21	6	65	1		7th	–	222	259
Harris	17	2	39	1	(4)	38	17	76	3		8th	–	226	318
Parnell	7	1	31	1	(3)	13	2	58	2		9th	–	228	318
Kallis	6	0	14	0		12	3	19	1		10th	–	233	319
Duminy	3	0	20	0		5	0	21	0					

Umpires: S.J.Davies (*Australia*) (22) and I.J.Gould (*England*) (10).
Referee: A.J.Pycroft (*Zimbabwe*) (9).   **Test No. 1950/23 (I436/SA349)**

INDIA v SOUTH AFRICA (2nd Test)

At Eden Gardens, Kolkata, on 14, 15, 16, 17, 18 February 2010.
Toss: South Africa. Result: **INDIA** won by an innings and 57 runs.
Debut: South Africa – A.N.Petersen.

SOUTH AFRICA

*G.C.Smith	b Khan	4	lbw b Mishra		20
A.N.Petersen	c Dhoni b Khan	100	c Badrinath b Harbhajan		21
H.M.Amla	c Dhoni b Khan	114	not out		123
J.H.Kallis	c Laxman b Harbhajan	10	c Dhoni b Mishra		20
†A.B.de Villiers	run out	12	(6) lbw b Mishra		3
A.G.Prince	lbw b Harbhajan	1	(5) c Sharma b Harbhajan		23
J.P.Duminy	lbw b Harbhajan	0	lbw b Harbhajan		6
D.W.Steyn	lbw b Mishra	5	lbw b Harbhajan		1
P.L.Harris	c Dhoni b Sharma	1	(10) c sub (K.D.Karthik) b Sharma		4
W.D.Parnell	lbw b Khan	12	(9) c Harbhajan b Sharma		22
M.Morkel	not out	11	lbw b Harbhajan		12
Extras	(B 1, LB 4, W 10, NB 11)	26	(B 6, LB 5, W 1, NB 18, Pen 5)		35
Total	**(85 overs; 375 mins)**	**296**	**(131.3 overs; 559 mins)**		**290**

INDIA

G.Gambhir	run out	25
V.Sehwag	c Prince b Duminy	165
M.Vijay	c De Villiers b Morkel	7
S.R.Tendulkar	c Kallis b Harris	106
V.V.S.Laxman	not out	143
S.Badrinath	b Steyn	1
A.Mishra	c Kallis b Morkel	28
†*M.S.Dhoni	not out	132
Harbhajan Singh		
Z.Khan		
I.Sharma		
Extras	(B 6, LB 9, W 13, NB 8)	36
Total	**(6 wkts dec; 153 overs; 678 mins)**	**643**

INDIA	O	M	R	W	O	M	R	W	FALL OF WICKETS
Khan	22	5	90	4	6	0	32	0	SA I SA
Sharma	18	3	67	1	(3) 25	5	84	2	Wkt 1st 1st 2nd
Mishra	21	3	70	1	(4) 40	12	78	3	1st 9 73 36
Harbhajan Singh	24	2	64	3	(2) 48.3	23	59	5	2nd 218 82 54
Sehwag					10	2	20	0	3rd 229 331 111
Tendulkar					2	1	1	0	4th 251 335 158
									5th 253 336 164
SOUTH AFRICA									6th 253 384 172
Steyn	30	5	115	1					7th 254 – 180
Morkel	26	3	115	2					8th 255 – 250
Parnell	20	1	103	0					9th 261 – 264
Kallis	12	1	40	0					10th 296 – 290
Harris	50	5	182	1					
Duminy	15	0	73	1					

Umpires: S.J.Davies (*Australia*) (23) and I.J.Gould (*England*) (11).
Referee: A.J.Pycroft (*Zimbabwe*) (10). Test No. 1951/24 (I437/SA350)

NEW ZEALAND v BANGLADESH (Only Test)

At Seddon Park, Hamilton, on 15, 16, 17, 18, 19 February 2010.
Toss: Bangladesh. Result: **NEW ZEALAND** won by 121 runs.
Debut: New Zealand – P.J.Ingram.

NEW ZEALAND

T.G.McIntosh	c Kayes b Islam	7	(2) run out		89
B.J.Watling	c Siddique b Rubel	13	(1) run out		1
P.J.Ingram	c Shahadat b Rubel	42	run out		13
L.R.P.L.Taylor	c Rahim b Rubel	40	c Kayes b Mahmudullah		51
M.J.Guptill	c Rahim b Rubel	189	not out		56
*D.L.Vettori	b Shakib	10	c Ashraful b Mahmudullah		13
†B.B.McCullum	b Rubel	185	not out		19
D.R.Tuffey	not out	31			
J.S.Patel	not out	12			
T.G.Southee					
C.S.Martin					
Extras	(B 1, LB 10, W 5, NB 8)	24	(B 5, LB 2, W 6, NB 3)		16
Total	(7 wkts dec; 135 overs; 549 mins)	553	(5 wkts dec; 71 overs; 314 mins)		258

BANGLADESH

Tamim Iqbal	c McCullum b Southee	68	c Tuffey b Vettori		30
Imrul Kayes	c Taylor b Vettori	28	b Patel		29
Junaid Siddique	c Taylor b Martin	21	b Martin		8
Aftab Ahmed	c Taylor b Tuffey	33	run out		8
Mohammad Ashraful	c Watling b Tuffey	12	lbw b Vettori		2
*Shakib Al Hasan	c McCullum b Martin	87	b Southee		100
†Mushfiqur Rahim	c Guptill b Vettori	7	c McIntosh b Tuffey		22
Mahmudullah	lbw b Vettori	115	c Tuffey b Patel		42
Shahadat Hossain	c McCullum b Martin	13	not out		17
Shafiul Islam	not out	12	c McCullum b Southee		13
Rubel Hossain	run out	0	c McIntosh b Southee		0
Extras	(B 4, LB 1, W 7)	12	(B 4, LB 1, W 6)		11
Total	(97.3 overs; 396 mins)	408	(76 overs; 300 mins)		282

BANGLADESH	O	M	R	W		O	M	R	W
Shahadat Hossain	24	1	136	0		11	2	32	0
Shafiul Islam	31	2	111	1		14	3	47	0
Rubel Hossain	29	1	166	5	(4)	12	0	44	0
Shakib Al Hasan	37	6	89	1	(3)	15	1	44	0
Aftab Ahmed	4	0	10	0					
Mahmudullah	7	0	21	0	(5)	19	1	84	2
Mohammad Ashraful	3	0	9	0					

NEW ZEALAND	O	M	R	W		O	M	R	W
Martin	25	2	116	3		12	1	48	1
Southee	16	2	62	1		11	4	41	3
Patel	10	3	53	0	(5)	17	2	75	2
Tuffey	18	2	84	2		12	5	33	1
Vettori	28.3	7	88	3	(3)	24	6	80	2

FALL OF WICKETS				
	NZ	B	NZ	B
Wkt	1st	1st	2nd	2nd
1st	17	79	2	35
2nd	57	118	52	51
3rd	66	132	124	72
4th	126	162	196	78
5th	158	179	227	78
6th	497	196	–	157
7th	525	341	–	225
8th	–	362	–	252
9th	–	402	–	282
10th	–	408	–	282

Umpires: R.E.Koertzen (*South Africa*) (106) and R.J.Tucker (*Australia*) (1).
Referee: A.G.Hurst (*Australia*) (37).   Test No. 1952/9 (NZ357/B64)

BANGLADESH v ENGLAND (1st Test)

At Chittagong Divisional Stadium, on 12, 13, 14, 15, 16 March 2010.
Toss: Bangladesh. Result: **ENGLAND** won by 181 runs.
Debuts: England – M.A.Carberry, S.T.Finn.

ENGLAND

*A.N.Cook	c and b Mahmudullah	173	c Ahmed b Mahmudullah	39
M.A.Carberry	lbw b Mahmudullah	30	lbw b Razzak	34
I.J.L.Trott	c Rahim b Rubel	39	c Siddique b Shakib	14
K.P.Pietersen	b Razzak	99	lbw b Shakib	32
P.D.Collingwood	c Iqbal b Razzak	145	c Mahmudullah b Razzak	3
I.R.Bell	c Rubel b Shakib	84	not out	39
†M.J.Prior	not out	0	c Shahadat b Shakib	7
G.P.Swann			c Siddique b Shakib	32
S.C.J.Broad				
T.T.Bresnan				
S.T.Finn				
Extras	(B 6, LB 9, W 3, NB 11)	29	(B 5, LB 2, NB 2)	9
Total	(6 wkts dec; 138.3 overs; 560 mins)	599	(7 wkts dec; 49.3 overs; 206 mins)	209

BANGLADESH

Tamim Iqbal	b Bresnan	86	b Swann	14
Imrul Kayes	c Prior b Broad	4	c Prior b Finn	23
Junaid Siddique	c and b Broad	7	c Collingwood b Swann	106
Aftab Ahmed	c Bell b Swann	1	c Prior b Bresnan	26
Mahmudullah	c Collingwood b Swann	51	b Bresnan	5
*Shakib Al Hasan	b Swann	1	lbw b Swann	4
Shahadat Hossain	c Collingwood b Finn	14	(10) c Prior b Bresnan	12
†Mushfiqur Rahim	c sub (J.C.Tredwell) b Swann	79	(7) b Swann	95
Naeem Islam	run out	38	(8) c Carberry b Swann	36
Abdur Razzak	not out	0	(9) lbw b Broad	1
Rubel Hossain	b Swann	0	not out	0
Extras	(B 1, LB 12, W 1, NB 1)	15	(B 2, LB 7)	9
Total	(90.3 overs; 380 mins)	296	(124 overs; 495 mins)	331

BANGLADESH	O	M	R	W		O	M	R	W
Shahadat Hossain	17	2	73	0		6	0	19	0
Rubel Hossain	19	0	97	1		6	1	28	0
Shakib Al Hasan	34.3	4	133	1	(5)	16.3	1	62	4
Naeem Islam	12	1	42	0		3	0	14	0
Mahmudullah	23	1	78	2	(3)	8	0	26	1
Abdur Razzak	31	1	157	2		10	2	53	2
Aftab Ahmed	1	0	2	0					
Tamim Iqbal	1	0	2	0					

ENGLAND	O	M	R	W		O	M	R	W
Broad	21	4	70	2		24	7	65	1
Bresnan	25	10	72	1		24	7	63	3
Swann	29.3	8	90	5	(4)	49	11	127	5
Finn	14	5	48	1	(3)	18	7	47	1
Pietersen	1	0	3	0		7	1	15	0
Trott						2	0	5	0

FALL OF WICKETS

Wkt	E 1st	B 1st	E 2nd	B 2nd
1st	72	13	65	33
2nd	149	27	87	45
3rd	319	51	126	99
4th	412	145	130	105
5th	596	149	131	110
6th	599	159	144	277
7th	–	183	209	294
8th	–	296	–	301
9th	–	296	–	327
10th	–	296	–	331

Umpires: A.L.Hill (*New Zealand*) (16) and R.J.Tucker (*Australia*) (2).
Referee: J.J.Crowe (*New Zealand*) (39).   **Test No. 1953/5 (E896/B65)**

BANGLADESH v ENGLAND (2nd Test)

At Shere Bangla National Stadium, Mirpur, on 20, 21, 22, 23, 24 March 2010.
Toss: Bangladesh. Result: **ENGLAND** won by nine wickets.
Debuts: Bangladesh – Jahurul Islam; England – J.C.Tredwell.

BANGLADESH

Tamim Iqbal	c Prior b Tredwell	85		c Broad b Swann	52
Imrul Kayes	c Finn b Broad	12		b Broad	4
Junaid Siddique	lbw b Swann	39		c and b Tredwell	34
Jahurul Islam	lbw b Swann	0		b Swann	43
Mahmudullah	c Collingwood b Finn	59		c Prior b Bresnan	6
*Shakib Al Hasan	lbw b Tredwell	49		st Prior b Tredwell	96
†Mushfiqur Rahim	c Prior b Bresnan	30		b Broad	3
Naeem Islam	not out	59	(9)	c Pietersen b Tredwell	3
Abdur Razzak	lbw b Swann	3	(10)	lbw b Finn	8
Shafiul Islam	c Prior b Bresnan	53	(8)	c Trott b Tredwell	28
Rubel Hossain	c Prior b Swann	17		not out	0
Extras	(B 1, LB 10, NB 2)	13		(LB 3, W 5)	8
Total	**(117.1 overs; 455 mins)**	**419**		**(102 overs; 379 mins)**	**285**

ENGLAND

*A.N.Cook	c Kayes b Razzak	21		not out	109
I.J.L.Trott	b Shakib	64		run out	19
K.P.Pietersen	c Kayes b Shakib	45		not out	74
P.D.Collingwood	lbw b Rubel	0			
I.R.Bell	c Jahurul b Shakib	138			
†M.J.Prior	b Shakib	62			
T.T.Bresnan	st Rahim b Razzak	91			
G.P.Swann	run out	6			
S.C.J.Broad	lbw b Mahmudullah	3			
J.C.Tredwell	st Rahim b Razzak	37			
S.T.Finn	not out	0			
Extras	(B 9, LB 12, W 1, NB 7)	29		(B 2, LB 4, NB 1)	7
Total	**(173.3 overs; 701 mins)**	**496**		**(1 wkt; 44 overs; 182 mins)**	**209**

ENGLAND	O	M	R	W	O	M	R	W
Broad	18	5	69	1	16	2	72	0
Bresnan	21	7	57	2	13	2	34	1
Swann	36.1	5	114	4 (5)	30	7	73	2
Finn	10	2	61	1	9	3	21	1
Tredwell	31	5	99	2 (3)	34	8	82	4
Collingwood	1	0	8	0				

BANGLADESH	O	M	R	W	O	M	R	W
Shafiul Islam	14	3	45	0	6	0	22	0
Abdur Razzak	39.3	8	132	3	15	0	67	0
Shakib Al Hasan	66	27	124	4	8	0	31	0
Mahmudullah	20	4	53	1	7	1	38	0
Rubel Hossain	26	4	88	1	4	0	26	0
Naeem Islam	10	0	29	0	4	0	19	0
Tamim Iqbal	1	0	4	0				

FALL OF WICKETS				
	B	E	B	E
Wkt	1st	1st	2nd	2nd
1st	53	29	23	42
2nd	119	105	86	
3rd	122	107	110	
4th	167	174	130	
5th	226	272	156	
6th	254	415	169	
7th	301	426	232	
8th	314	434	258	
9th	388	481	275	
10th	419	496	285	

Umpires: A.L.Hill (*New Zealand*) (17) and R.J.Tucker (*Australia*) (3).
Referee: J.J.Crowe (*New Zealand*) (40).   **Test No. 1954/6 (E897/B66)**

NEW ZEALAND v AUSTRALIA (1st Test)

At Basin Reserve, Wellington, on 19, 20, 21, 22, 23 March 2010.
Toss: Australia. Result: **AUSTRALIA** won by ten wickets.
Debuts: New Zealand – B.J.Arnel; Australia – R.J.Harris.

AUSTRALIA

P.J.Hughes	c Taylor b Arnel	20	not out		86
S.M.Katich	lbw b Arnel	79	not out		18
*R.T.Ponting	run out	41			
M.E.K.Hussey	c Watling b Martin	4			
M.J.Clarke	st McCullum b Vettori	168			
M.J.North	not out	112			
†B.J.Haddin	not out	11			
M.G.Johnson					
N.M.Hauritz					
R.J.Harris					
D.E.Bollinger					
Extras	(B 2, LB 15, W 2, NB 5)	24	(NB 2)		2
Total	**(5 wkts dec; 131 overs; 562 mins)**	**459**	**(0 wkts; 23 overs; 91 mins)**		**106**

NEW ZEALAND

T.G.McIntosh	c Hussey b Harris	9	(2) c Katich b Hauritz		83
B.J.Watling	lbw b Bollinger	0	(1) lbw b Bollinger		33
P.J.Ingram	run out	5	c Haddin b Bollinger		1
L.R.P.L.Taylor	c North b Bollinger	21	lbw b Hauritz		25
M.J.Guptill	c Haddin b Bollinger	30	c North b Harris		6
*D.L.Vettori	c Ponting b Harris	46	b Hauritz		77
†B.B.McCullum	c Harris b Bollinger	24	c Clarke b Harris		104
D.R.Tuffey	run out	0	not out		47
T.G.Southee	c Haddin b Johnson	5	c Clarke b Harris		0
B.J.Arnel	c Ponting b Bollinger	0	lbw b Harris		3
C.S.Martin	not out	0	b Johnson		0
Extras	(LB 4, W 2, NB 11)	17	(B 1, LB 14, W 1, NB 11)		27
Total	**(59.1 overs; 247 mins)**	**157**	**(134.5 overs; 540 mins)**		**407**

NEW ZEALAND	O	M	R	W		O	M	R	W
Martin	30	3	115	1		6	0	43	0
Southee	19	4	68	0					
Arnel	26	4	89	2	(2)	10	2	31	0
Tuffey	22	7	49	0					
Vettori	33	5	111	1	(3)	7	1	32	0
Guptill	1	0	10	0					

AUSTRALIA	O	M	R	W		O	M	R	W
Bollinger	13	4	28	5		27	3	80	2
Harris	17	4	42	2		24	3	77	4
Johnson	11.1	5	37	1		29.5	7	107	1
Hauritz	14	4	39	0		49	16	119	3
North	4	1	6	0		5	2	9	0

FALL OF WICKETS

	A	NZ	NZ	A
Wkt	1st	1st	2nd	2nd
1st	25	3	70	–
2nd	104	14	78	–
3rd	115	31	115	–
4th	176	43	136	–
5th	429	112	183	–
6th	–	148	309	–
7th	–	148	388	–
8th	–	154	392	–
9th	–	156	396	–
10th	–	157	407	–

Umpires: Asad Rauf (*Pakistan*) (28) and I.J.Gould (*England*) (12).
Referee: J.Srinath (*India*) (14).   **Test No. 1955/49 (NZ358/A719)**

NEW ZEALAND v AUSTRALIA (2nd Test)

At Seddon Park, Hamilton, on 27, 28, 29, 30, 31 March 2010.
Toss: Australia. Result: **AUSTRALIA** won by 176 runs.
Debuts: None.

AUSTRALIA

S.R.Watson	c Arnel b Southee	12	c Watling b Southee	65
S.M.Katich	c Watling b Vettori	88	c McCullum b Arnel	106
*R.T.Ponting	run out	22	c Watling b Southee	6
M.E.K.Hussey	c McCullum b Southee	22	c McCullum b Arnel	67
M.J.Clarke	c Southee b Patel	28	lbw b Arnel	63
M.J.North	lbw b Southee	9	c McCullum b Vettori	90
†B.J.Haddin	c and b Southee	12	b Patel	48
M.G.Johnson	c McIntosh b Vettori	0	c Patel b Vettori	41
N.M.Hauritz	not out	12	not out	41
R.J.Harris	lbw b Vettori	10	not out	18
D.E.Bollinger	b Vettori	4		
Extras	(B 4, LB 6, NB 2)	12	(B 2, LB 1, NB 4)	7
Total	**(74.3 overs; 306 mins)**	**231**	**(8 wkts dec; 153 overs; 596 mins)**	**511**

NEW ZEALAND

T.G.McIntosh	b Bollinger	4	(2) b Johnson	19
B.J.Watling	b Bollinger	46	(1) c Haddin b Johnson	24
M.S.Sinclair	b Johnson	11	lbw b Clarke	29
L.R.P.L.Taylor	c Haddin b Bollinger	138	c Haddin b Johnson	22
M.J.Guptill	c Ponting b Harris	4	c Ponting b Johnson	58
*D.L.Vettori	c Haddin b Harris	15	lbw b Hauritz	22
†B.B.McCullum	c Ponting b Johnson	5	c Hussey b Bollinger	51
J.S.Patel	c Ponting b Johnson	7	c North b Bollinger	3
T.G.Southee	not out	22	c Clarke b Johnson	45
B.J.Arnel	c Haddin b Johnson	7	c Haddin b Johnson	0
C.S.Martin	b Harris	0	not out	5
Extras	(W 1, NB 4)	5	(B 12, LB 10, NB 2)	24
Total	**(63.3 overs; 278 mins)**	**264**	**(91.1 overs; 362 mins)**	**302**

NEW ZEALAND	O	M	R	W	O	M	R	W		FALL OF WICKETS			
Martin	12	3	42	0	14	1	60	0			A	NZ	A	NZ
Southee	19	3	61	4	23	4	89	2		*Wkt*	*1st*	*1st*	*2nd*	*2nd*
Arnel	12	2	53	0	26	6	77	3		1st	25	4	85	40
Vettori	19.3	5	36	4	48	10	140	2		2nd	63	30	91	53
Patel	12	2	29	1	39	8	141	1		3rd	129	114	246	107
Sinclair					3	2	1	0		4th	172	143	247	119
										5th	180	167	389	152
AUSTRALIA										6th	199	193	443	239
Bollinger	14	3	57	3	16	2	87	2		7th	200	234	443	249
Harris	15.3	3	50	3	14	3	38	0		8th	200	236	453	273
Johnson	16	2	59	4	(4) 20.1	6	73	6		9th	217	263	–	295
Hauritz	13	1	68	0	(6) 17	5	37	1		10th	231	264	–	302
Watson	5	1	30	0	(3) 6	2	18	0						
Clarke					(5) 16	4	27	1						
North					2	2	0	0						

Umpires: Alim Dar (*Pakistan*) (60) and Asad Rauf (*Pakistan*) (29).
Referee: J.Srinath (*India*) (15).   **Test No. 1956/50 (NZ359/A720)**

ENGLAND v BANGLADESH (1st Test)

At Lord's, London, on 27, 28, 29, 30, 31 May 2010.
Toss: Bangladesh. Result: **ENGLAND** won by eight wickets.
Debuts: England – E.J.G.Morgan; Bangladesh – Robiul Islam.

ENGLAND

*A.J.Strauss	b Mahmudullah	83	c Rahim b Shakib		82
A.N.Cook	lbw b Shahadat	7	lbw b Mahmudullah		23
I.J.L.Trott	c Kayes b Shahadat	226	not out		36
K.P.Pietersen	b Shakib	18	not out		10
I.R.Bell	b Rubel	17			
E.J.G.Morgan	c Rahim b Shahadat	44			
†M.J.Prior	run out	16			
T.T.Bresnan	c Siddique b Shahadat	25			
G.P.Swann	c Rubel b Shakib	22			
J.M.Anderson	b Shahadat	13			
S.T.Finn	not out	3			
Extras	(LB 10, W 8, NB 13)	31	(LB 5, W 1, NB 6)		12
Total	**(125 overs; 534 mins)**	**505**	**(2 wkts; 35.1 overs; 123 mins)**		**163**

BANGLADESH

Tamim Iqbal	run out	55	c Trott b Finn		103
Imrul Kayes	c Strauss b Finn	43	c Bell b Finn		75
Junaid Siddique	c Prior b Finn	58	c Bresnan b Finn		74
Jahurul Islam	c Prior b Anderson	20	c and b Trott		46
Mohammad Ashraful	lbw b Finn	4	c Prior b Anderson		21
*Shakib Al Hasan	c Strauss b Anderson	25	(7) c Morgan b Finn		16
†Mushfiqur Rahim	b Finn	16	(8) c Prior b Finn		0
Mahmudullah	b Anderson	17	(9) c Prior b Bresnan		19
Shahadat Hossain	b Anderson	20	(6) b Bresnan		0
Rubel Hossain	c Cook b Bresnan	9	c Strauss b Bresnan		4
Robiul Islam	not out	9	not out		0
Extras	(LB 2, W 3, NB 1)	6	(B 7, LB 14, W 2, NB 1)		24
Total	**(93 overs; 385 mins)**	**282**	**(110.2 overs; 467 mins)**		**382**

BANGLADESH	O	M	R	W	O	M	R	W	FALL OF WICKETS				
										E	B	B	E
Shahadat Hossain	28	3	98	5	2	0	19	0	*Wkt*	*1st*	*1st*	*2nd*	*2nd*
Robiul Islam	22	2	107	0	1	0	12	0	1st	7	88	185	67
Shakib Al Hasan	27	3	109	2	16	1	48	1	2nd	188	134	189	147
Rubel Hossain	23	0	109	1	1	0	8	0	3rd	227	179	289	–
Mahmudullah	23	3	59	2	15.1	1	71	1	4th	258	185	321	–
Mohammad Ashraful	2	0	13	0					5th	370	191	322	–
									6th	400	221	347	–
ENGLAND									7th	463	234	354	–
Anderson	31	6	78	4	29	8	84	1	8th	478	255	361	–
Bresnan	24	5	76	1	26.2	9	93	3	9th	498	266	381	–
Finn	25	5	100	4	24	6	87	5	10th	505	282	382	–
Swann	11	6	19	0	27	5	81	0					
Trott	2	0	7	0	4	0	16	1					

Umpires: B.F.Bowden (*New Zealand*) (60) and E.A.R.de Silva (*Sri Lanka*) (44).
Referee: A.G.Hurst (*Australia*) (38).   **Test No. 1957/7 (E898/B67)**

ENGLAND v BANGLADESH (2nd Test)

At Old Trafford, Manchester, on 4, 5, 6 June 2010.
Toss: England. Result: **ENGLAND** won by an innings and 80 runs.
Debut: England – A.Shahzad.

ENGLAND

*A.J.Strauss	c Kayes b Shafiul	21
A.N.Cook	c Siddique b Razzak	29
I.J.L.Trott	b Shafiul	3
K.P.Pietersen	st Rahim b Shakib	64
I.R.Bell	b Shakib	128
E.J.G.Morgan	c Jahurul b Shahadat	37
†M.J.Prior	c Jahurul b Shakib	93
G.P.Swann	lbw b Razzak	20
A.Shahzad	c Razzak b Shakib	5
J.M.Anderson	not out	2
S.T.Finn	lbw b Shakib	0
Extras	(B 6, LB 5, W 4, NB 2)	17
Total	**(121.3 overs; 485 mins)**	**419**

BANGLADESH

Tamim Iqbal	c Prior b Anderson	108		c Prior b Anderson	2
Imrul Kayes	c Shahzad b Finn	36		c Shahzad b Finn	9
Junaid Siddique	c Prior b Swann	1		c Pietersen b Anderson	6
Jahurul Islam	b Swann	5	(5)	c Prior b Finn	0
Mohammad Ashraful	c Morgan b Shahzad	11	(4)	c Trott b Anderson	14
*Shakib Al Hasan	c Anderson b Swann	10		b Shahzad	1
†Mushfiqur Rahim	c Anderson b Swann	11		c sub (K.R.Brown) b Finn	13
Mahmudullah	b Shahzad	8		c Prior b Finn	38
Shafiul Islam	b Shahzad	4	(10)	c Strauss b Finn	4
Abdur Razzak	not out	0	(9)	c Morgan b Swann	19
Shahadat Hossain	lbw b Swann	0		not out	4
Extras	(B 4, LB 7, W 8, NB 3)	22		(B 13)	13
Total	**(54.1 overs; 240 mins)**	**216**		**(34.1 overs; 163 mins)**	**123**

BANGLADESH	O	M	R	W		O	M	R	W
Shahadat Hossain	21	3	84	1					
Shafiul Islam	21	2	63	2					
Mahmudullah	12	1	31	0					
Shakib Al Hasan	37.3	4	121	5					
Abdur Razzak	30	3	109	2					

ENGLAND	O	M	R	W		O	M	R	W
Anderson	14	4	45	1		10	3	16	3
Finn	8	1	39	1		10	2	42	5
Swann	22.1	4	76	5	(4)	7.1	0	34	1
Shahzad	10	2	45	3	(3)	7	2	18	1

FALL OF WICKETS			
	E	B	B
Wkt	1st	1st	2nd
1st	44	126	2
2nd	48	153	14
3rd	83	169	18
4th	153	169	21
5th	223	185	37
6th	376	206	39
7th	399	210	76
8th	414	214	97
9th	419	216	119
10th	419	216	123

Umpires: B.F.Bowden (*New Zealand*) (61) and E.A.R.de Silva (*Sri Lanka*) (45).
Referee: A.G.Hurst (*Australia*) (39).   **Test No. 1958/8 (E899/B68)**

WEST INDIES v SOUTH AFRICA (1st Test)

At Queen's Park Oval, Port-of-Spain, Trinidad, on 10, 11, 12, 13 June 2010.
Toss: South Africa. Result: **SOUTH AFRICA** won by 163 runs.
Debuts: West Indies – N.T.Pascal; South Africa – L.L.Tsotsobe.

SOUTH AFRICA

*G.C.Smith	c Bravo b Shillingford	23	b Benn		90
A.N.Petersen	lbw b Shillingford	31	lbw b Benn		22
H.M.Amla	c Bravo b Benn	2	c Deonarine b Shillingford		5
J.H.Kallis	lbw b Shillingford	28	lbw b Benn		40
P.L.Harris	c Shillingford b Benn	10			
A.B.de Villiers	c Ramdin b Benn	68	(5) not out		19
A.G.Prince	c Dowlin b Gayle	57	(6) not out		16
†M.V.Boucher	c Pascal b Bravo	69			
D.W.Steyn	st Ramdin b Benn	39			
M.Morkel	b Benn	2			
L.L.Tsotsobe	not out	3			
Extras	(B 9, LB 4, W 1, NB 6)	20	(B 6, LB 3, NB 5)		14
Total	**(129.4 overs)**	**352**	**(4 wkts dec; 62 overs)**		**206**

WEST INDIES

*C.H.Gayle	b Morkel	6	lbw b Morkel		73
T.M.Dowlin	c Smith b Morkel	4	lbw b Morkel		1
B.P.Nash	c Boucher b Morkel	1	c Boucher b Steyn		13
S.Chanderpaul	c Boucher b Steyn	26	c De Villiers b Kallis		15
N.Deonarine	b Steyn	29	lbw b Steyn		23
D.J.Bravo	c Boucher b Morkel	1	c Prince b Harris		49
†D.Ramdin	not out	25	c De Villiers b Tsotsobe		9
S.Shillingford	lbw b Steyn	0	c Petersen b Harris		27
S.J.Benn	b Steyn	0	lbw b Petersen		42
R.Rampaul	b Steyn	0	not out		18
N.T.Pascal	c Petersen b Kallis	0	b Steyn		10
Extras	(B 2, LB 3, W 2, NB 1)	8	(B 11, LB 2)		13
Total	**(47.1 overs)**	**102**	**(80.3 overs)**		**293**

WEST INDIES	O	M	R	W		O'	M	R	W
Rampaul	19	3	56	0		6	2	21	0
Pascal	11	1	32	0		6	1	27	0
Bravo	16.4	6	33	1	(5)	4	1	9	0
Benn	47	9	120	5	(3)	25	3	74	3
Shillingford	35	4	96	3	(4)	21	2	66	1
Gayle	1	0	2	1					

SOUTH AFRICA	O	M	R	W		O'	M	R	W
Steyn	14	5	29	5		15.3	1	65	3
Morkel	13	7	19	4		12	3	49	2
Tsotsobe	8	0	18	0		13	5	20	1
Harris	6	1	25	0		26.3	3	91	2
Kallis	6.1	2	6	1		11	3	49	1
Smith						0.3	0	4	0
Petersen						2	1	2	1

FALL OF WICKETS

Wkt	SA 1st	WI 1st	SA 2nd	WI 2nd
1st	55	7	56	2
2nd	60	9	79	39
3rd	68	12	157	94
4th	91	71	178	114
5th	107	72	–	152
6th	229	72	–	192
7th	238	72	–	194
8th	324	75	–	260
9th	330	75	–	264
10th	352	102	–	293

Umpires: Asad Rauf (*Pakistan*) (30) and S.J.Davis (*Australia*) (24).
Referee: R.S.Mahanama (*Sri Lanka*) (29). **Test No. 1959/23 (WI463/SA351)**

WEST INDIES v SOUTH AFRICA (2nd Test)

At Warner Park, Basseterre, St Kitts, on 18, 19, 20, 21, 22 June 2010.
Toss: South Africa. Result: **MATCH DRAWN**.
Debuts: None.

SOUTH AFRICA

*G.C.Smith	b Roach	132	c Ramdin b Shillingford	46
A.N.Petersen	c Roach b Shillingford	52	b Bravo	39
H.M.Amla	c Bravo b Shillingford	44	c sub (D.J.G.Sammy) b Shillingford	41
J.H.Kallis	c Rampaul b Shillingford	110	not out	62
A.B.de Villiers	not out	135	not out	31
A.G.Prince	c Gayle b Benn	9		
†M.V.Boucher	run out	17		
D.W.Steyn	not out	20		
P.L.Harris				
M.Morkel				
L.L.Tsotsobe				
Extras	(LB 5, W 2, NB 17)	24	(B 1, LB 1, W 13, NB 1)	16
Total	**(6 wkts dec; 147 overs)**	**543**	**(3 wkts dec; 94 overs)**	**235**

WEST INDIES

*C.H.Gayle	b Morkel	50
T.M.Dowlin	c De Villiers b Morkel	10
N.Deonarine	b Steyn	65
S.Chanderpaul	c and b Harris	166
B.P.Nash	run out	114
D.J.Bravo	c Boucher b Harris	53
†D.Ramdin	c Petersen b Tsotsobe	1
S.Shillingford	c De Villiers b Kallis	7
S.J.Benn	c Kallis b Morkel	26
R.Rampaul	c Boucher b Morkel	31
K.A.J.Roach	not out	1
Extras	(B 1, LB 7, W 7, NB 7)	22
Total	**(181.1 overs)**	**546**

WEST INDIES	O	M	R	W		O	M	R	W
Roach	22	4	72	1		13	3	33	0
Rampaul	18	4	65	0		2	0	7	0
Benn	30	3	124	1		28	4	61	0
Bravo	18	2	58	0	(5)	11	4	37	1
Shillingford	52	4	193	3	(4)	30	5	80	2
Deonarine	3	0	20	0					
Nash	4	0	6	0	(6)	9	4	12	0
Dowlin					(7)	1	0	3	0

SOUTH AFRICA	O	M	R	W
Steyn	29	4	105	1
Morkel	34.1	9	116	4
Tsotsobe	28	10	68	1
Harris	62	9	165	2
Kallis	23	7	65	1
Petersen	5	0	39	0

FALL OF WICKETS

	SA	WI	SA
Wkt	1st	1st	2nd
1st	99	13	74
2nd	211	106	131
3rd	283	151	131
4th	421	371	–
5th	442	471	–
6th	490	476	–
7th	–	486	–
8th	–	486	–
9th	–	545	–
10th	–	546	–

Umpires: Asad Rauf (*Pakistan*) (31) and S.J.A.Taufel (*Australia*) (62).
Referee: J.J.Crowe (*New Zealand*) (41).   **Test No. 1960/24 (WI464/SA352)**

WEST INDIES v SOUTH AFRICA (3rd Test)

At Kensington Oval, Bridgetown, Barbados, on 26, 27, 28, 29 June 2010.
Toss: West Indies. Result: **SOUTH AFRICA** won by seven wickets.
Debut: West Indies – B.J.Bess.

WEST INDIES

*C.H.Gayle	b Steyn	20	c Boucher b Steyn		10
D.M.Richards	lbw b Morkel	0	c Petersen b Steyn		17
N.Deonarine	b Botha	46	c Prince b Steyn		0
S.Chanderpaul	c Kallis b Botha	22	not out		71
B.P.Nash	lbw b Botha	2	c Kallis b Botha		12
D.J.Bravo	c Smith b Steyn	61	b Harris		2
†D.Ramdin	c Steyn b Kallis	27	c Boucher b Botha		1
S.Shillingford	c Botha b Kallis	0	lbw b Botha		25
S.J.Benn	c Amla b Botha	24	b Morkel		9
K.A.J.Roach	c Boucher b Steyn	2	c Boucher b Morkel		8
B.J.Bess	not out	11	c Kallis b Morkel		0
Extras	(B 4, LB 7, W 5)	16	(B 1, LB 1, W 1, NB 3)		6
Total	**(73.5 overs)**	**231**	**(65.1 overs)**		**161**

SOUTH AFRICA

*G.C.Smith	c Richards b Benn	70	c Chanderpaul b Roach		10
A.N.Petersen	c Chanderpaul b Roach	1	b Roach		6
H.M.Amla	c Nash b Benn	5	c Benn b Roach		25
P.L.Harris	c Gayle b Bess	11			
J.H.Kallis	b Benn	43	(4) not out		0
A.B.de Villiers	c Ramdin b Benn	73	(5) not out		4
A.G.Prince	not out	78			
†M.V.Boucher	run out	17			
J.Botha	lbw b Benn	9			
D.W.Steyn	b Roach	4			
M.Morkel	c Bravo b Benn	9			
Extras	(B 5, LB 6, W 7, NB 8)	26	(W 2, NB 2)		4
Total	**(134.4 overs)**	**346**	**(3 wkts; 8.4 overs)**		**49**

SOUTH AFRICA	O	M	R	W		O	M	R	W		FALL OF WICKETS				
Steyn	13	3	37	3		11	4	36	3			WI	SA	WI	SA
Morkel	10	2	48	1		14.1	5	33	3		Wkt	1st	1st	2nd	2nd
Kallis	12	1	36	2	(5)	4	0	10	0		1st	12	17	27	14
Botha	19.5	2	56	4		20	5	46	3		2nd	21	41	27	29
Harris	19	3	43	0	(3)	16	3	34	1		3rd	76	60	36	45
											4th	90	122	70	–
WEST INDIES											5th	105	145	74	–
Roach	25	6	59	2		4.4	1	22	3		6th	181	279	75	–
Bess	9	0	65	1		4	0	27	0		7th	187	312	128	–
Shillingford	25	2	85	0							8th	204	326	151	–
Benn	46.4	13	81	6							9th	207	333	161	–
Bravo	27	12	43	0							10th	231	346	161	–
Gayle	2	1	2	0											

Umpires: S.J.Davis (*Australia*) (25) and S.J.A.Taufel (*Australia*) (63).
Referee: J.J.Crowe (*New Zealand*) (42).   **Test No. 1961/25 (WI465/SA353)**

PAKISTAN v AUSTRALIA (1st Test)

At Lord's, London, on 13, 14, 15, 16 July 2010.
Toss: Pakistan. Result: **AUSTRALIA** won by 150 runs.
Debuts: Pakistan – Azhar Ali, Umar Amin; Australia – T.D.Paine, S.P.D.Smith.

AUSTRALIA

S.R.Watson	b Aamer	4	c Farhat b Asif		31
S.M.Katich	c Kamran Akmal b Asif	80	c Kamran Akmal b Gul		83
*R.T.Ponting	c Amin b Aamer	26	lbw b Asif		0
M.J.Clarke	lbw b Asif	47	b Gul		12
M.E.K.Hussey	not out	56	c Farhat b Gul		0
M.J.North	b Asif	0	(7) c Kamran Akmal b Asif		20
†T.D.Paine	c Kamran Akmal b Gul	7	(8) b Afridi		47
S.P.D.Smith	lbw b Kaneria	1	(9) lbw b Kaneria		12
M.G.Johnson	b Kaneria	8	(6) b Gul		30
B.W.Hilfenhaus	b Aamer	1	not out		56
D.E.Bollinger	b Aamer	4	b Kaneria		21
Extras	(B 10, LB 2, W 2, NB 10)	24	(B 6, LB 5, W 2, NB 9)		22
Total	**(76.5 overs; 340 mins)**	**253**	**(91 overs; 415 mins)**		**334**

PAKISTAN

Imran Farhat	c Paine b Hilfenhaus	4	c Watson b Smith		24
Salman Butt	b Watson	63	st Paine b North		92
Azhar Ali	c Paine b Hilfenhaus	16	c Paine b Hilfenhaus		42
Umar Amin	c Paine b Johnson	1	c Katich b North		33
Umar Akmal	lbw b Watson	5	c Clarke b North		22
†Kamran Akmal	lbw b Watson	0	b Smith		46
*Shahid Afridi	c Johnson b Watson	31	c Hussey b North		2
Mohammad Aamer	c Paine b Bollinger	0	c Hussey b North		19
Umar Gul	c Watson b Bollinger	7	c Ponting b Smith		1
Danish Kaneria	c Smith b Watson	14	c Ponting b North		2
Mohammad Asif	not out	4	not out		1
Extras	(LB 2, NB 1)	3	(B 2, LB 1, NB 2)		5
Total	**(40.5 overs; 186 mins)**	**148**	**(91.1 overs; 363 mins)**		**289**

PAKISTAN	O	M	R	W	O	M	R	W		FALL OF WICKETS			
Mohammad Aamer	19.5	2	72	4	18	3	67	0			A	P	A	P
Mohammad Asif	19	5	63	3	21	3	77	3		Wkt	1st	1st	2nd	2nd
Umar Gul	17	3	32	1	21	5	61	4		1st	8	11	61	50
Shahid Afridi	3	0	25	0	(5) 14	0	44	1		2nd	51	45	73	152
Danish Kaneria	18	7	49	2	(4) 17	2	74	2		3rd	171	54	97	186
										4th	174	75	97	216
AUSTRALIA										5th	174	83	149	227
Bollinger	11	2	38	2	12	4	43	0		6th	206	117	188	229
Hilfenhaus	12	2	37	2	16	8	37	1		7th	208	117	188	283
Johnson	10	2	31	1	18	5	74	0		8th	213	129	208	285
Watson	7.5	1	40	5	(5) 6	0	26	0		9th	222	133	282	287
Smith					(4) 21	5	51	3		10th	253	148	334	289
North					18.1	1	55	6						

Umpires: I.J.Gould (*England*) (13) and R.E.Koertzen (*South Africa*) (107).
Referee: B.C.Broad (*England*) (39).   **Test No. 1962/56 (P347/A721)**

PAKISTAN v AUSTRALIA (2nd Test)

At Headingley, Leeds, on 21, 22, 23, 24 July 2010.
Toss: Australia. Result: **PAKISTAN** won by three wickets.
Debuts: None.

AUSTRALIA

Batsman	First innings		Second innings	
S.R.Watson	lbw b Asif	5	b Amin	24
S.M.Katich	lbw b Aamer	13	b Aamer	11
*R.T.Ponting	lbw b Asif	6	c Kamran Akmal b Aamer	66
M.J.Clarke	b Gul	3	c Kamran Akmal b Asif	77
M.E.K.Hussey	lbw b Gul	5	c Umar Akmal b Aamer	8
M.J.North	c Kamran Akmal b Amin	16	b Aamer	0
†T.D.Paine	c Kamran Akmal b Asif	17	c Ali b Kaneria	33
S.P.D.Smith	b Aamer	10	b Gul	77
M.G.Johnson	b Aamer	0	lbw b Asif	12
B.W.Hilfenhaus	run out	3	c Umar Akmal b Kaneria	17
D.E.Bollinger	not out	2	not out	0
Extras	(LB 6, NB 2)	8	(B 4, LB 10, W 2, NB 8)	24
Total	(33.1 overs; 170 mins)	**88**	(95.3 overs; 446 mins)	**349**

PAKISTAN

Batsman	First innings		Second innings	
Imran Farhat	lbw b Watson	43	b Bollinger	67
*Salman Butt	b Hilfenhaus	45	c Clarke b Hilfenhaus	13
Azhar Ali	c Paine b Watson	30	c Paine b Bollinger	51
Umar Amin	c North b Hilfenhaus	25	c Paine b Bollinger	0
Umar Akmal	c Paine b Johnson	21	c Paine b Hilfenhaus	8
Shoaib Malik	c Paine b Watson	26	c North b Hilfenhaus	10
†Kamran Akmal	c North b Watson	15	c Hussey b Johnson	13
Mohammad Aamer	lbw b Watson	0	not out	5
Umar Gul	b Watson	0	not out	1
Danish Kaneria	run out	15		
Mohammad Asif	not out	9		
Extras	(B 11, LB 9, NB 9)	29	(LB 7, NB 5)	12
Total	(64.5 overs; 290 mins)	**258**	(7 wkts; 50.4 overs; 228 mins)	**180**

PAKISTAN	O	M	R	W		O	M	R	W
Mohammad Aamer	11	4	20	3		27	6	86	4
Mohammad Asif	10.1	1	30	3		26	4	83	2
Umar Gul	9	3	16	2		15.3	1	80	1
Umar Amin	2	0	7	1		6	1	12	1
Danish Kaneria	1	0	9	0		21	2	74	2

AUSTRALIA	O	M	R	W		O	M	R	W
Bollinger	17	4	50	4		13	2	51	3
Hilfenhaus	20.5	3	77	2		13	2	39	3
Watson	11	3	33	6	(4)	5	1	18	0
Johnson	15	0	71	1	(3)	10.4	1	41	1
Smith	1	0	7	0		2	2	24	0

FALL OF WICKETS

Wkt	A 1st	P 1st	A 2nd	P 2nd
1st	20	80	15	27
2nd	20	133	55	137
3rd	27	140	144	137
4th	29	171	158	146
5th	41	195	164	150
6th	60	222	217	161
7th	73	222	246	179
8th	73	224	283	–
9th	86	234	320	–
10th	88	258	349	–

Umpires: I.J.Gould (*England*) (14) and R.E.Koertzen (*South Africa*) (108).
Referee: B.C.Broad (*England*) (40).   **Test No. 1963/57 (P348/A722)**

SRI LANKA v INDIA (1st Test)

At Galle International Stadium, on 18, 19 (*no play*), 20, 21, 22 July 2010.
Toss: Sri Lanka. Result: **SRI LANKA** won by ten wickets.
Debut: India – A.Mithun.

SRI LANKA

N.T.Paranavitana	c Dhoni b Sharma	111	not out		23
T.M.Dilshan	c Dhoni b Mithun	25	not out		68
*K.C.Sangakkara	c Tendulkar b Sehwag	103			
D.P.M.D.Jayawardena	lbw b Sharma	48			
T.T.Samaraweera	lbw b Mithun	0			
A.D.Mathews	c Laxman b Sharma	41			
†H.A.P.W.Jayawardena	lbw b Mithun	27			
H.M.R.K.B.Herath	not out	80			
S.L.Malinga	c Harbhajan b Mithun	64			
M.Muralitharan	not out	5			
U.W.M.B.C.A.Welagedara					
Extras	(B 2, LB 9, NB 5)	16	(W 1, NB 4)		5
Total	**(8 wkts dec; 124 overs; 537 mins)**	**520**	**(0 wkts; 14.1 overs; 70 mins)**		**96**

INDIA

G.Gambhir	lbw b Malinga	2	c H.A.P.W.Jayawardena b Malinga		0
V.Sehwag	c Paranavitana b Welagedara	109	c D.P.M.D.Jayawardena b Welagedara		31
R.S.Dravid	run out	18	c Sangakkara b Malinga		44
S.R.Tendulkar	lbw b Muralitharan	8	lbw b Malinga		84
V.V.S.Laxman	c Dilshan b Malinga	22	run out		69
Yuvraj Singh	c D.P.M.D.Jayawardena b Muralitharan	52	c D.P.M.D.Jayawardena b Muralitharan		4
†*M.S.Dhoni	b Muralitharan	33	b Malinga		4
Harbhajan Singh	st H.A.P.W.Jayawardena b Herath	4	lbw b Muralitharan		8
I.Sharma	not out	5	(10) not out		31
P.P.Ojha	c D.P.M.D.Jayawardena b Muralitharan	13	(11) c D.P.M.D.Jayawardena b Muralitharan		13
A.Mithun	b Muralitharan	8	(9) lbw b Malinga		25
Extras	(B 1, LB 1, W 2, NB 10)	14	(B 5, LB 9, W 2, NB 8)		24
Total	**(65 overs; 296 mins)**	**276**	**(115.4 overs; 457 mins)**		**338**

INDIA	O	M	R	W	O	M	R	W	FALL OF WICKETS			
Sharma	28	5	145	3	(2) 4	0	28	0		SL	I	I	SL
Mithun	28	3	105	4	(1) 5	0	33	0	Wkt	1st	1st	2nd	2nd
Harbhajan Singh	30	4	98	0	(4) 2.1	0	24	0	1st	55	2	0	–
Ojha	28	1	115	0	(3) 3	0	11	0	2nd	236	68	42	–
Sehwag	10	0	46	1					3rd	259	101	161	–
									4th	260	169	172	–
SRI LANKA									5th	322	178	181	–
Malinga	13	0	55	2	17	2	50	5	6th	344	252	186	–
Welagedara	11	1	69	1	10	2	43	1	7th	393	259	197	–
Herath	18	1	62	1	27	3	60	0	8th	508	259	246	–
Mathews	5	0	19	0	7	3	13	0	9th	–	266	314	–
Muralitharan	17	1	63	5	44.4	7	128	3	10th	–	276	338	–
Dilshan	1	0	6	0	10	1	30	0					

Umpires: D.J.Harper (*Australia*) (89) and R.J.Tucker (*Australia*) (4).
Referee: A.J.Pycroft (*Zimbabwe*) (11).　　　　**Test No. 1964/33 (SL193/I1438)**

SRI LANKA v INDIA (2nd Test)

At Sinhalese Sports Club, Colombo, on 26, 27, 28, 29, 30 July 2010.
Toss: Sri Lanka. Result: **MATCH DRAWN**.
Debuts: Sri Lanka – H.K.S.R.Kaluhalamulla (*also known as S.Randiv*); India – S.K.Raina.

SRI LANKA

N.T.Paranavitana	b Sharma	100	c Laxman b Harbhajan		34
T.M.Dilshan	c Laxman b Ojha	54	c Sharma b Mithun		14
*K.C.Sangakkara	c Dravid b Sehwag	219	not out		42
D.P.M.D.Jayawardena	c Raina b Harbhajan	174	lbw b Sehwag		5
T.T.Samaraweera	not out	76	not out		10
A.D.Mathews					
†H.A.P.W.Jayawardena					
K.T.G.D.Prasad					
C.R.D.Fernando					
H.K.S.R.Kaluhalamulla					
B.A.W.Mendis					
Extras	(B 4, LB 8, W 2, NB 5)	19	(B 8, LB 8, NB 8)		24
Total	**(4 wkts dec; 159.4 overs; 635 mins)**	**642**	**(3 wkts; 45 overs; 177 mins)**		**129**

INDIA

M.Vijay	lbw b Mendis	58
V.Sehwag	st H.A.P.W.Jayawardena b Kaluhalamulla	99
R.S.Dravid	lbw b Kaluhalamulla	3
S.R.Tendulkar	c H.A.P.W.Jayawardena b Dilshan	203
V.V.S.Laxman	lbw b Mendis	29
S.K.Raina	c Sangakkara b Mendis	120
†*M.S.Dhoni	c and b Dilshan	76
Harbhajan Singh	c Sangakkara b Dilshan	0
A.Mithun	b Mendis	41
I.Sharma	c Sangakkara b Fernando	27
P.P.Ojha	not out	18
Extras	(B 9, LB 7, W 4, NB 13)	33
Total	**(225.2 overs; 930 mins)**	**707**

INDIA	O	M	R	W		O	M	R	W
Mithun	23	5	117	0		6	1	17	1
Sharma	23	5	102	1		4	0	31	0
Ojha	46	9	172	1	(5)	13	6	13	0
Harbhajan Singh	42.4	4	147	1		13	0	35	1
Sehwag	20	0	71	1	(3)	9	1	17	1
Raina	5	0	21	0					

SRI LANKA	O	M	R	W
Prasad	22	2	101	0
Fernando	31.2	1	116	1
Mathews	9	1	24	0
Kaluhalamulla	73	16	222	2
Mendis	63	10	172	4
Dilshan	27	6	56	3

FALL OF WICKETS

	SL	I	SL
Wkt	1st	1st	2nd
1st	99	165	50
2nd	273	169	73
3rd	466	173	97
4th	642	241	–
5th	–	497	–
6th	–	592	–
7th	–	592	–
8th	–	643	–
9th	–	668	–
10th	–	707	–

Umpires: D.J.Harper (*Australia*) (90) and R.J.Tucker (*Australia*) (5).
Referee: A.J.Pycroft (*Zimbabwe*) (12).   **Test No. 1965/34 (SL194/I439)**

SRI LANKA v INDIA (3rd Test)

At P.Saravanamuttu Stadium, Colombo, on 3, 4, 5, 6, 7 August 2010.
Toss: Sri Lanka. Result: **INDIA** won by five wickets.
Debuts: None.

SRI LANKA

N.T.Paranavitana	c Dhoni b Sharma	8		c Dhoni b Sehwag	16
T.M.Dilshan	run out	41		c Vijay b Sehwag	13
*K.C.Sangakkara	c Sehwag b Ojha	75		c Raina b Ojha	28
D.P.M.D.Jayawardena	lbw b Ojha	56	(5)	c Dravid b Ojha	5
T.T.Samaraweera	not out	137	(6)	c Dhoni b Mithun	83
A.D.Mathews	lbw b Ojha	45	(7)	c Tendulkar b Mishra	5
†H.A.P.W.Jayawardena	lbw b Ojha	9	(8)	lbw b Mishra	0
H.K.S.R.Kaluhalamulla	c Dravid b Sehwag	8	(4)	lbw b Ojha	6
S.L.Malinga	c and b Mishra	4		lbw b Sehwag	15
B.A.W.Mendis	c Raina b Sharma	3		c Raina b Mishra	78
U.W.M.B.C.A.Welagedara	c Dhoni b Sharma	1		not out	4
Extras	(B 8, LB 4, W 7, NB 16)	35		(B 4, W 4, NB 6)	14
Total	**(138 overs; 562 mins)**	**425**		**(85.2 overs; 359 mins)**	**267**

INDIA

M.Vijay	c Mendis b Malinga	14		c D.P.M.D.Jayawardena b Kaluhalamulla	27
V.Sehwag	c Welagedara b Kaluhalamulla	109		c D.P.M.D.Jayawardena b Kaluhalamulla	0
R.S.Dravid	lbw b Mathews	23		b Kaluhalamulla	7
S.R.Tendulkar	c H.A.P.W.Jayawardena b Malinga	41		c H.A.P.W.Jayawardena b Kaluhalamulla	54
V.V.S.Laxman	c D.P.M.D.Jayawardena b Mendis	56	(6)	not out	103
S.K.Raina	c Sangakkara b Mendis	62	(7)	not out	41
†*M.S.Dhoni	c H.A.P.W.Jayawardena b Malinga	15			
A.Mithun	c D.P.M.D.Jayawardena b Kaluhalamulla	46			
A.Mishra	c Dilshan b Kaluhalamulla	40			
I.Sharma	c Paranavitana b Kaluhalamulla	8	(5)	c Sangakkara b Kaluhalamulla	4
P.P.Ojha	not out	1			
Extras	(B 6, LB 6, W 1, NB 8)	21		(B 5, LB 6, W 2, NB 9)	22
Total	**(106.1 overs; 457 mins)**	**436**		**(5 wkts; 68.3 overs; 302 mins)**	**258**

INDIA	O	M	R	W		O	M	R	W
Mithun	22	2	78	0		8	1	22	1
Sharma	23	6	72	3		17	3	54	0
Mishra	42	3	140	1	(5) 17.2	1	47	3
Ojha	46	10	115	4	(3) 28	5	89	3
Sehwag	5	0	8	1	(4) 15	0	51	3

SRI LANKA	O	M	R	W		O	M	R	W
Malinga	30	3	119	3		12	1	49	0
Welagedara	15	0	88	0	(4) 8.3	2	34	0
Mendis	30	4	109	2	(5) 14	0	65	0
Mathews	4	0	13	1	(3) 2	0	5	0
Kaluhalamulla	25.1	6	80	4	(2) 29	3	82	5
Dilshan	2	0	15	0		3	0	12	0

FALL OF WICKETS

Wkt	SL 1st	I 1st	SL 2nd	I 2nd
1st	15	49	32	10
2nd	102	92	39	27
3rd	157	183	63	49
4th	241	199	77	62
5th	330	304	78	171
6th	359	321	87	—
7th	381	350	87	—
8th	386	414	125	—
9th	421	433	243	—
10th	425	436	267	—

Umpires: S.J.A.Taufel (*Australia*) (64) and R.J.Tucker (*Australia*) (6).
Referee: A.J.Pycroft (*Zimbabwe*) (13).   Test No. 1966/35 (SL195/I440)

ENGLAND v PAKISTAN (1st Test)

At Trent Bridge, Nottingham, on 29, 30, 31 July, 1 August 2010.
Toss: England. Result: **ENGLAND** won by 354 runs.
Debuts: None.

ENGLAND

*A.J.Strauss	c Kamran Akmal b Aamer	45	c Kamran Akmal b Aamer		0
A.N.Cook	c Farhat b Aamer	8	c Kamran Akmal b Asif		12
I.J.L.Trott	lbw b Aamer	38	b Gul		26
K.P.Pietersen	b Asif	9	c Kamran Akmal b Gul		22
P.D.Collingwood	lbw b Asif	82	lbw b Gul		1
E.J.G.Morgan	lbw b Asif	130	run out		17
†M.J.Prior	run out	6	not out		102
G.P.Swann	lbw b Asif	2	lbw b Kaneria		28
S.C.J.Broad	b Gul	3	c Farhat b Malik		24
J.M.Anderson	lbw b Asif	0	c Kamran Akmal b Malik		2
S.T.Finn	not out	0	not out		9
Extras	(B 5, LB 14, W 5, NB 7)	31	(B 4, LB 11, W 1, NB 3)		19
Total	**(104.1 overs; 470 mins)**	**354**	**(9 wkts dec; 75.3 overs; 350 mins)**		**262**

PAKISTAN

Imran Farhat	b Anderson	19	c Strauss b Anderson		15
*Salman Butt	c Prior b Anderson	1	c Collingwood b Broad		8
Azhar Ali	c Prior b Anderson	14	lbw b Broad		0
Umar Amin	c Swann b Finn	2	lbw b Anderson		1
Umar Akmal	c Swann b Finn	4	(6) lbw b Anderson		4
Shoaib Malik	c Strauss b Anderson	38	(7) c Collingwood b Anderson		9
†Kamran Akmal	c Collingwood b Finn	0	(8) lbw b Finn		0
Mohammad Aamer	c Swann b Anderson	25	(5) c Pietersen b Finn		4
Umar Gul	not out	65	c Collingwood b Anderson		9
Danish Kaneria	b Broad	7	not out		16
Mohammad Asif	run out	0	c Swann b Anderson		0
Extras	(B 5, LB 2)	7	(B 4, LB 8, W 1, NB 1)		14
Total	**(54 overs; 242 mins)**	**182**	**(29 overs; 141 mins)**		**80**

PAKISTAN	O	M	R	W		O	M	R	W
Mohammad Aamer	24	7	41	3		16	3	35	1
Mohammad Asif	27	9	77	5		17	1	56	1
Umar Gul	18.1	5	61	1		15	2	41	3
Danish Kaneria	21	0	100	0	(5)	12	0	71	1
Shoaib Malik	11	2	39	0	(6)	10.3	0	31	2
Azhar Ali	1	0	9	0					
Umar Amin	1	0	3	0	(4)	5	1	13	0
Imran Farhat	1	0	5	0					
ENGLAND									
Anderson	22	7	54	5		15	8	17	6
Broad	17	4	59	1		8	2	23	2
Finn	13	5	50	3		6	3	28	2
Swann	2	1	12	0					

FALL OF WICKETS

	E	P	E	P
Wkt	1st	1st	2nd	2nd
1st	42	5	2	10
2nd	93	32	18	10
3rd	116	35	65	11
4th	118	41	66	31
5th	337	45	72	37
6th	344	47	98	41
7th	351	105	147	41
8th	354	108	203	50
9th	354	147	213	65
10th	354	182	–	80

Umpires: E.A.R.de Silva (*Sri Lanka*) (46) and A.L.Hill (*New Zealand*) (18).
Referee: R.S.Madugalle (*Sri Lanka*) (116).   **Test No. 1967/68 (E900/P349)**

ENGLAND v PAKISTAN (2nd Test)

At Edgbaston, Birmingham, on 6, 7, 8, 9 August 2010.
Toss: Pakistan. Result: **ENGLAND** won by nine wickets.
Debut: Pakistan – Zulqarnain Haider.

PAKISTAN

Imran Farhat	c Prior b Broad	0	b Swann		29
*Salman Butt	c Swann b Finn	7	c Strauss b Anderson		0
Azhar Ali	lbw b Broad	0	b Swann		19
Shoaib Malik	c Prior b Anderson	3	c Prior b Finn		3
Umar Akmal	lbw b Finn	17	lbw b Swann		20
Umar Amin	c Collingwood b Broad	23	st Prior b Swann		14
†Zulqarnain Haider	c Prior b Broad	0	c Strauss b Swann		88
Mohammad Aamer	c Cook b Anderson	12	c Strauss b Broad		16
Umar Gul	c Pietersen b Anderson	0	(10) not out		13
Saeed Ajmal	not out	5	(9) c Collingwood b Swann		50
Mohammad Asif	c Pietersen b Anderson	0	c Pietersen b Broad		14
Extras	(LB 4, NB 1)	5	(B 16, LB 14)		30
Total	**(39.3 overs; 179 mins)**	**72**	**(117.5 overs; 479 mins)**		**296**

ENGLAND

*A.J.Strauss	c Haider b Aamer	25	not out	53
A.N.Cook	c Akmal b Asif	17	b Aamer	4
I.J.L.Trott	c sub (Yasir Hameed) b Amin	55	not out	53
K.P.Pietersen	c and b Ajmal	80		
P.D.Collingwood	c Farhat b Ajmal	28		
E.J.G.Morgan	c Haider b Asif	6		
†M.J.Prior	lbw b Ajmal	15		
G.P.Swann	c and b Ajmal	4		
S.C.J.Broad	c sub (Yasir Hameed) b Ajmal	0		
J.M.Anderson	lbw b Aamer	0		
S.T.Finn	not out	0		
Extras	(B 10, LB 9, W 1, NB 1)	21	(B 5, NB 3)	8
Total	**(83.1 overs; 394 mins)**	**251**	**(1 wkt; 36.3 overs; 152 mins)**	**118**

ENGLAND	O	M	R	W	O	M	R	W	FALL OF WICKETS				
Anderson	14.3	6	20	4	28	13	62	1		P	E	P	E
Broad	17	7	38	4	28.5	8	66	2	Wkt	1st	1st	2nd	2nd
Finn	8	3	10	2	16	5	57	1	1st	8	44	1	7
Swann					37	20	65	6	2nd	9	44	53	–
Collingwood					7	2	14	0	3rd	12	177	54	–
Pietersen					1	0	2	0	4th	29	205	76	–
									5th	33	220	82	–
PAKISTAN									6th	36	243	101	–
Mohammad Aamer	20	4	57	2	11	1	31	1	7th	63	248	153	–
Mohammad Asif	20	5	41	2	6	0	20	0	8th	64	248	268	–
Umar Gul	9	1	24	0					9th	67	251	269	–
Saeed Ajmal	26.1	5	82	5	(3) 14.3	1	42	0	10th	72	251	296	–
Umar Amin	8	2	28	1									
Shoaib Malik					(4) 5	0	20	0					

Umpires: S.J.Davis (*Australia*) (26) and M.Erasmus (*South Africa*) (3).
Referee: R.S.Madugalle (*Sri Lanka*) (117).   **Test No. 1968/69 (E901/P350)**

ENGLAND v PAKISTAN (3rd Test)

At The Oval, London, on 18, 19, 20, 21 August 2010.
Toss: England. Result: **PAKISTAN** won by four wickets.
Debut: Pakistan – Wahab Riaz.

ENGLAND

Batsman	First innings		Second innings	
*A.J.Strauss	c Kamran Akmal b Riaz	15	c Hameed b Aamer	4
A.N.Cook	c Kamran Akmal b Asif	6	c Kamran Akmal b Riaz	110
I.J.L.Trott	c Hameed b Riaz	12	(4) c Ali b Aamer	36
K.P.Pietersen	c Kamran Akmal b Riaz	6	(5) b Ajmal	23
P.D.Collingwood	b Aamer	5	(6) c Kamran Akmal b Aamer	3
E.J.G.Morgan	c Kamran Akmal b Riaz	17	(7) b Ajmal	5
†M.J.Prior	not out	84	(8) c Kamran Akmal b Aamer	5
G.P.Swann	c Umar Akmal b Asif	8	(9) b Ajmal	6
S.C.J.Broad	lbw b Riaz	48	(10) c Asif b Aamer	6
J.M.Anderson	lbw b Asif	0	(3) c Kamran Akmal b Ajmal	11
S.T.Finn	lbw b Ajmal	0	not out	1
Extras	(B 10, LB 11, W 6, NB 5)	32	(LB 5, W 2, NB 5)	12
Total	**(62.3 overs; 309 mins)**	**233**	**(77 overs; 332 mins)**	**222**

PAKISTAN

Batsman	First innings		Second innings	
Imran Farhat	b Anderson	11	lbw b Swann	33
Yasir Hameed	c Prior b Finn	36	c Swann b Anderson	0
Wahab Riaz	lbw b Swann	27		
*Salman Butt	c Prior b Swann	17	(3) c Collingwood b Swann	48
Mohammad Yousuf	c and b Swann	56	(4) b Anderson	33
Azhar Ali	not out	92	(5) run out	5
Umar Akmal	run out	38	(6) not out	16
†Kamran Akmal	c Morgan b Broad	10	(7) lbw b Swann	0
Mohammad Aamer	c Prior b Broad	6	(8) not out	4
Saeed Ajmal	b Anderson	0		
Mohammad Asif	c Anderson b Swann	8		
Extras	(LB 4, W 1, NB 2)	7	(B 4, LB 2, W 2, NB 1)	9
Total	**(100.2 overs; 441 mins)**	**308**	**(6 wkts; 41.4 overs; 185 mins)**	**148**

PAKISTAN	O	M	R	W		O	M	R	W
Mohammad Aamer	15	4	49	1		19	5	52	5
Mohammad Asif	20	5	68	3		16	7	45	0
Wahab Riaz	18	6	63	5		8	1	40	1
Saeed Ajmal	9.3	1	32	1		31	7	71	4
Imran Farhat						3	0	9	0
ENGLAND									
Anderson	24	6	79	2		14	5	39	2
Broad	25	4	72	2		6	0	35	0
Finn	20	4	74	1	(4)	3	0	18	0
Swann	27.2	9	68	4	(3)	18.4	4	50	3
Collingwood	4	0	11	0					

FALL OF WICKETS

	E	P	E	P
Wkt	1st	1st	2nd	2nd
1st	9	48	4	5
2nd	35	48	40	57
3rd	40	76	156	103
4th	47	110	194	124
5th	67	179	195	131
6th	74	236	202	132
7th	94	251	206	–
8th	213	269	210	–
9th	214	270	220	–
10th	233	308	222	–

Umpires: S.J.Davis (*Australia*) (27) and A.L.Hill (*New Zealand*) (19).
Referee: R.S.Madugalle (*Sri Lanka*) (118).　　　　**Test No. 1969/70 (E902/P351)**

ENGLAND v PAKISTAN (4th Test)

At Lord's, London, on 26, 27, 28, 29 August 2010.
Toss: Pakistan. Result: **ENGLAND** won by an innings and 225 runs.
Debuts: None.

ENGLAND

*A.J.Strauss	b Asif	13
A.N.Cook	c Kamran Akmal b Aamer	10
I.J.L.Trott	c Kamran Akmal b Riaz	184
K.P.Pietersen	c Kamran Akmal b Aamer	0
P.D.Collingwood	lbw b Aamer	0
E.J.G.Morgan	c Hameed b Aamer	0
†M.J.Prior	c Kamran Akmal b Aamer	22
G.P.Swann	c Ali b Aamer	0
S.C.J.Broad	lbw b Ajmal	169
J.M.Anderson	c Hameed b Ajmal	6
S.T.Finn	not out	0
Extras	(B 4, LB 17, W 7, NB 14)	42
Total	**(139.2 overs; 610 mins)**	**446**

PAKISTAN

Imran Farhat	c Prior b Anderson	6	c Cook b Broad	5
Yasir Hameed	c Swann b Broad	2	lbw b Anderson	3
*Salman Butt	b Swann	26	lbw b Broad	21
Mohammad Yousuf	b Broad	0	c Trott b Finn	10
Azhar Ali	c Cook b Swann	10	b Swann	12
Umar Akmal	b Finn	6	not out	79
†Kamran Akmal	c Prior b Finn	13	c Prior b Anderson	1
Mohammad Aamer	lbw b Finn	0	b Swann	0
Wahab Riaz	lbw b Swann	2	c Pietersen b Swann	0
Saeed Ajmal	not out	4	run out	8
Mohammad Asif	c and b Swann	0	c Collingwood b Swann	1
Extras	(LB 4, NB 1)	5	(B 1, LB 2, W 3, NB 1)	7
Total	**(33 overs; 158 mins)**	**74**	**(36.5 overs; 174 mins)**	**147**

PAKISTAN	O	M	R	W	O	M	R	W		FALL OF WICKETS		
										E	P	P
Mohammad Aamer	28	6	84	6					Wkt	1st	1st	2nd
Mohammad Asif	29	6	97	1					1st	31	9	7
Wahab Riaz	27.2	4	92	1					2nd	39	9	9
Saeed Ajmal	44	5	126	2					3rd	39	10	41
Yasir Hameed	1	1	0	0					4th	39	46	41
Imran Farhat	10	1	26	0					5th	47	53	63
									6th	102	57	64
ENGLAND									7th	102	57	65
Anderson	10	6	10	1	13	4	35	2	8th	434	70	73
Broad	6	4	10	2	6	1	24	1	9th	446	74	97
Finn	9	4	38	3	4	0	23	1	10th	446	74	147
Swann	8	3	12	4	13.5	1	62	5				

Umpires: B.F.Bowden (*New Zealand*) (62) and A.L.Hill (*New Zealand*) (20).
Referee: R.S.Madugalle (*Sri Lanka*) (119).   **Test No. 1970/71 (E903/P352)**

INDIA v AUSTRALIA (1st Test)

At Punjab C.A.Stadium, Mohali, Chandigarh, on 1, 2, 3, 4, 5 October 2010.
Toss: Australia. Result: **INDIA** won by one wicket.
Debuts: None.

AUSTRALIA

Batsman		1st		2nd
S.R.Watson	c Gambhir b Harbhajan	126	b Sharma	56
S.M.Katich	lbw b Khan	6	c Dhoni b Ojha	37
*R.T.Ponting	run out	71	c Raina b Sharma	4
M.J.Clarke	c Dravid b Harbhajan	14	c Dhoni b Sharma	4
M.E.K.Hussey	lbw b Khan	17	lbw b Harbhajan	28
M.J.North	b Khan	0	c sub (C.A.Pujara) b Harbhajan	10
†T.D.Paine	c Laxman b Khan	92	c sub (C.A.Pujara) b Ojha	9
M.G.Johnson	c Dhoni b Khan	47	c Dhoni b Khan	3
N.M.Hauritz	c Gambhir b Harbhajan	9	b Khan	6
B.W.Hilfenhaus	not out	20	b Khan	6
D.E.Bollinger	c Sharma b Ojha	0	not out	1
Extras	(B 4, LB 9, NB 13)	26	(B 12, LB 4, NB 5)	21
Total	**(151.4 overs; 646 mins)**	**428**	**(60.5 overs; 292 mins)**	**192**

INDIA

Batsman		1st		2nd
G.Gambhir	lbw b Johnson	25	lbw b Hilfenhaus	0
V.Sehwag	c Clarke b Johnson	59	c Hussey b Hilfenhaus	17
R.S.Dravid	c Paine b Bollinger	77	c Paine b Bollinger	13
I.Sharma	b Bollinger	18	(10) lbw b Hilfenhaus	31
S.R.Tendulkar	lbw b North	98	(4) c Hussey b Bollinger	38
S.K.Raina	lbw b Johnson	86	(5) c North b Hilfenhaus	0
†*M.S.Dhoni	c Watson b Johnson	14	(8) run out	2
Harbhajan Singh	c Paine b Johnson	0	(9) c Ponting b Bollinger	2
Z.Khan	b Hauritz	6	(6) c Clarke b Hauritz	10
V.V.S.Laxman	c Clarke b Hauritz	2	(7) not out	73
P.P.Ojha	not out	0	not out	5
Extras	(B 5, LB 13, W 1, NB 1)		(B 10, LB 8, W 6, NB 1)	25
Total	**(108.1 overs; 487 mins)**	**405**	**(9 wkts; 58.4 overs; 300 mins)**	**216**

INDIA	O	M	R	W		O	M	R	W
Khan	30	7	94	5		11.5	1	43	3
Sharma	11.4	1	71	0		9	2	34	2
Ojha	51.4	16	113	1	(4)	17	1	59	2
Harbhajan Singh	49	12	114	3	(3)	23	7	40	2
Sehwag	9.2	1	23	0					

AUSTRALIA	O	M	R	W		O	M	R	W
Hilfenhaus	25	2	100	2		19	3	57	4
Bollinger	16	2	49	2		8	0	32	3
Johnson	20	5	64	5		16.4	2	50	0
Hauritz	29.1	4	116	2			1	45	1
Watson	6	0	19	0	(6)	4	0	8	0
North	12	3	39	1	(5)	4	0	8	0

FALL OF WICKETS

	A	I	A	I
Wkt	1st	1st	2nd	2nd
1st	13	81	87	0
2nd	154	106	91	31
3rd	218	230	96	48
4th	218	230	138	48
5th	222	354	154	76
6th	275	382	165	119
7th	357	382	165	122
8th	373	399	170	124
9th	427	401	183	205
10th	428	405	192	–

Umpires: B.F.Bowden (*New Zealand*) (63) and I.J.Gould (*England*) (15).
Referee: B.C.Broad (*England*) (41).   Test No. 1971/77 (I441/A723)

INDIA v AUSTRALIA (2nd Test)

At M.Chinnaswamy Stadium, Bangalore, on 9, 10, 11, 12, 13 October 2010.
Toss: Australia. Result: **INDIA** won by seven wickets.
Debuts: India – C.A.Pujara; Australia – P.R.George.

AUSTRALIA

S.R.Watson	c Dhoni b Ojha	57	lbw b Ojha		32
S.M.Katich	c Dravid b Harbhajan	43	c Dhoni b Harbhajan		24
*R.T.Ponting	lbw b Raina	77	lbw b Khan		72
M.J.Clarke	c Raina b Harbhajan	14	st Dhoni b Ojha		3
M.E.K.Hussey	c Sehwag b Khan	34	lbw b Ojha		20
M.J.North	c Sreesanth b Harbhajan	128	b Harbhajan		3
†T.D.Paine	st Dhoni b Ojha	59	c Dhoni b Sreesanth		23
M.G.Johnson	lbw b Ojha	0	b Khan		11
N.M.Hauritz	run out	17	not out		21
B.W.Hilfenhaus	not out	16	b Sreesanth		0
P.R.George	st Dhoni b Harbhajan	2	c Dhoni b Khan		0
Extras	(B 9, LB 12, W 1, NB 9)	31	(B 1, LB 5, W 3, NB 5)		14
Total	**(141 overs; 604 mins)**	**478**	**(75.2 overs; 326 mins)**		**223**

INDIA

M.Vijay	c Paine b Johnson	139	lbw b Watson		37
V.Sehwag	c Johnson b Hilfenhaus	30	c Paine b Hilfenhaus		7
R.S.Dravid	c North b Johnson	1	(5) not out		21
S.R.Tendulkar	b George	214	not out		53
C.A.Pujara	lbw b Johnson	4	(3) b Hauritz		72
S.K.Raina	c Hilfenhaus b Clarke	32			
†*M.S.Dhoni	c Clarke b Hauritz	30			
Harbhajan Singh	c Ponting b Watson	4			
Z.Khan	c Clarke b George	0			
P.P.Ojha	not out	0			
S.Sreesanth	lbw b Hauritz	0			
Extras	(B 6, LB 26, W 8)	40	(B 8, LB 5, W 4)		17
Total	**(144.5 overs; 636 mins)**	**495**	**(3 wkts; 45 overs; 199 mins)**		**207**

INDIA	O	M	R	W		O	M	R	W
Khan	23	5	84	1		11.2	1	41	3
Sreesanth	21	1	79	0		14	2	48	2
Ojha	42	7	120	3		25	5	57	3
Harbhajan Singh	43	3	148	4		21	2	63	2
Sehwag	4	1	7	0		4	0	8	0
Raina	8	1	19	1					

AUSTRALIA	O	M	R	W		O	M	R	W
Hilfenhaus	31	6	77	1		7	0	27	1
Johnson	28	2	105	4		14	4	42	0
George	21	3	48	2	(4)	7	0	29	0
Hauritz	39.5	4	153	2	(3)	12	0	76	1
Clarke	8	0	27	1					
Watson	12	2	35	1	(5)	5	0	20	1
Katich	5	0	18	0					

FALL OF WICKETS

	A	I	A	I
Wkt	1st	1st	2nd	2nd
1st	99	37	58	17
2nd	113	38	58	89
3rd	132	346	65	146
4th	198	350	126	–
5th	256	411	131	–
6th	405	486	181	–
7th	415	491	185	–
8th	458	494	217	–
9th	459	495	218	–
10th	478	495	223	–

Umpires: B.F.Bowden (*New Zealand*) (64) and I.J.Gould (*England*) (16).
Referee: B.C.Broad (*England*) (42).

Test No. 1972/78 (I442/A724)

INDIA v NEW ZEALAND (1st Test)

At Sardar Patel Stadium, Motera, Ahmedabad, on 4, 5, 6, 7, 8 November 2010.
Toss: India. Result: **MATCH DRAWN**.
Debuts: New Zealand – H.K.Bennett, K.S.Williamson.

INDIA

G.Gambhir	b Ryder	21	c Hopkins b Martin		0
V.Sehwag	b Vettori	173	run out		1
R.S.Dravid	b Martin	104	c Hopkins b Martin		1
S.R.Tendulkar	c and b Patel	40	b Martin		12
V.V.S.Laxman	lbw b Patel	40	lbw b Vettori		91
S.K.Raina	c McCullum b Williamson	3	c Taylor b Martin		0
†*M.S.Dhoni	c Watling b Vettori	10	b Martin		22
Harbhajan Singh	c Hopkins b Vettori	69	c Watling b Taylor		115
Z.Khan	b Vettori	1	lbw b Vettori		9
P.P.Ojha	lbw b Patel	11	not out		9
S.Sreesanth	not out	2	c Hopkins b Taylor		4
Extras	(B 5, LB 2, W 1, NB 5)	13	(B 10, NB 1)		11
Total	**(151.5 overs; 600 mins)**	**487**	**(102.4 overs; 427 mins)**		**266**

NEW ZEALAND

T.G.McIntosh	c Dhoni b Khan	0	lbw b Khan		0
B.B.McCullum	st Dhoni b Ojha	65	not out		11
B.J.Watling	b Ojha	6	not out		2
L.R.P.L.Taylor	c Laxman b Harbhajan	56			
J.D.Ryder	lbw b Sreesanth	103			
K.S.Williamson	c Laxman b Ojha	131			
*D.L.Vettori	c Dhoni b Raina	41			
†G.J.Hopkins	lbw b Ojha	14			
J.S.Patel	b Sreesanth	14			
H.K.Bennett	b Khan	4			
C.S.Martin	not out	3			
Extras	(B 5, LB 12, NB 5)	22	(B 4, W 5)		9
Total	**(165.4 overs; 694 mins)**	**459**	**(1 wkt; 10 overs; 39 mins)**		**22**

NEW ZEALAND	O	M	R	W		O	M	R	W
Martin	24	5	75	1		27	8	63	5
Bennett	15	2	47	0					
Vettori	54.5	12	118	4	(2)	38	8	81	2
Ryder	17	4	56	1					
Patel	29	6	135	3	(3)	23	1	72	0
Williamson	12	0	49	1	(4)	4	0	18	0
Taylor					(5)	4.4	2	4	2
McCullum					(6)	6	1	18	0

INDIA	O	M	R	W		O	M	R	W
Khan	28.4	6	70	2		4	2	7	1
Sreesanth	26	2	88	2		1	0	4	0
Ojha	53	14	107	4		3	2	1	0
Harbhajan Singh	43	7	112	1					
Sehwag	1	0	7	0					
Raina	12	1	42	1	(4)	1	0	1	0
Tendulkar	2	0	16	0					
Dhoni					(5)	1	0	5	0

FALL OF WICKETS

	I	NZ	I	NZ
Wkt	1st	1st	2nd	2nd
1st	60	8	0	4
2nd	297	27	1	—
3rd	317	131	2	—
4th	317	137	15	—
5th	392	331	15	—
6th	392	417	65	—
7th	410	417	228	—
8th	412	445	228	—
9th	478	445	260	—
10th	487	459	266	—

Umpires: S.J.Davis (*Australia*) (28) and H.D.P.K.Dharmasena (*Sri Lanka*) (1).
Referee: R.S.Madugalle (*Sri Lanka*) (120). **Test No. 1973/48 (I443/NZ360)**

INDIA v NEW ZEALAND (2nd Test)

At Rajiv Gandhi International Stadium, Hyderabad, on 12, 13, 14, 15, 16 November 2010.
Toss: New Zealand. Result: **MATCH DRAWN**.
Debuts: None.

NEW ZEALAND

T.G.McIntosh	b Khan	102	c sub (C.A.Pujara) b Ojha		49
B.B.McCullum	c Dhoni b Sreesanth	4	c Raina b Sreesanth		225
M.J.Guptill	lbw b Ojha	85	c Dhoni b Ojha		18
L.R.P.L.Taylor	c Dhoni b Khan	24	b Sreesanth		7
J.D.Ryder	c Laxman b Harbhajan	70	c Dhoni b Raina		20
†G.J.Hopkins	lbw b Khan	4	(8) not out		11
K.S.Williamson	lbw b Khan	4	(6) lbw b Harbhajan		69
*D.L.Vettori	lbw b Harbhajan	11	(7) c Dravid b Raina		23
T.G.Southee	st Dhoni b Harbhajan	10	b Sreesanth		11
B.J.Arnel	not out	6	not out		1
C.S.Martin	c Sehwag b Harbhajan	3			
Extras	(B 2, LB 20, W 1, NB 4)	27	(B 4, LB 3, W 2, NB 5)		14
Total	**(117.3 overs; 521 mins)**	**350**	**(8 wkts dec; 135 overs; 575 mins)**		**448**

INDIA

G.Gambhir	c Hopkins b Southee	54	not out		14
V.Sehwag	b Vettori	96	not out		54
R.S.Dravid	lbw b Southee	45			
S.R.Tendulkar	c Taylor b Vettori	13			
V.V.S.Laxman	lbw b Martin	74			
S.K.Raina	c Guptill b Vettori	20			
†*M.S.Dhoni	c McCullum b Vettori	14			
Harbhajan Singh	not out	111			
Z.Khan	c Arnel b Southee	7			
P.P.Ojha	run out	0			
S.Sreesanth	lbw b Vettori	24			
Extras	(B 4, LB 8, W 1, NB 1)	14			
Total	**(143.4 overs; 662 mins)**	**472**	**(0 wkts; 17 overs; 57 mins)**		**68**

INDIA	O	M	R	W		O	M	R	W
Khan	27	8	69	4		7.3	1	21	0
Sreesanth	21	1	88	1		27	5	121	3
Harbhajan Singh	35.3	10	76	4	(4)	38	3	117	1
Ojha	27	4	80	1	(3)	47.3	14	137	2
Raina	7	2	15	0	(6)	13	2	38	2
Tendulkar					(5)	2	0	7	0

NEW ZEALAND	O	M	R	W		O	M	R	W
Martin	29	6	87	1					
Southee	33	6	119	3	(1)	4	0	11	0
Arnel	24	5	79	0	(2)	5	1	11	0
Vettori	49.4	7	135	5					
Williamson	7	0	31	0					
Taylor	1	0	9	0	(4)	3	0	13	0
Guptill					(3)	5	0	33	0

FALL OF WICKETS

	NZ	I	NZ	I
Wkt	1st	1st	2nd	2nd
1st	4	160	125	–
2nd	151	160	174	–
3rd	206	184	187	–
4th	253	259	221	–
5th	269	311	345	–
6th	287	326	396	–
7th	312	336	431	–
8th	331	355	447	–
9th	338	367	–	–
10th	350	472	–	–

Umpires: H.D.P.K.Dharmasena (*Sri Lanka*) (2) and S.J.A.Taufel (*Australia*) (65).
Referee: R.S.Madugalle (*Sri Lanka*) (121).   **Test No. 1974/49 (I444/NZ361)**

INDIA v NEW ZEALAND (3rd Test)

At Vidarbha C.A.Stadium, Nagpur, on 20, 21, 22, 23 November 2010.
Toss: New Zealand. Result: **INDIA** won by an innings and 198 runs.
Debut: New Zealand – A.J.McKay.

NEW ZEALAND

T.G.McIntosh	b Sreesanth	4		lbw b Harbhajan	8
M.J.Guptill	c Dhoni b Sreesanth	6	(4)	lbw b Ojha	0
L.R.P.L.Taylor	lbw b Sharma	20	(5)	c sub (C.A.Pujara) b Harbhajan	29
J.D.Ryder	c Raina b Harbhajan	59	(6)	c Sharma b Raina	22
K.S.Williamson	c Sehwag b Ojha	0	(7)	b Sharma	8
*D.L.Vettori	b Sharma	3	(8)	lbw b Raina	13
†G.J.Hopkins	c Raina b Ojha	7	(3)	c Gambhir b Harbhajan	8
B.B.McCullum	c Dhoni b Sharma	40	(2)	lbw b Ojha	25
T.G.Southee	c Sehwag b Ojha	38		b Sharma	31
A.J.McKay	b Sharma	5		not out	20
C.S.Martin	not out	2		b Sharma	0
Extras	(B 1, LB 5, NB 3)	9		(B 10, LB 1)	11
Total	**(66.3 overs; 312 mins)**	**193**		**(51.2 overs; 215 mins)**	**175**

INDIA

G.Gambhir	c Taylor b Southee	78
V.Sehwag	c and b Vettori	74
R.S.Dravid	c Guptill b Williamson	191
S.R.Tendulkar	c Hopkins b McKay	61
V.V.S.Laxman	b Martin	12
S.K.Raina	c sub (B.J.Watling) b Vettori	3
†*M.S.Dhoni	c and b Vettori	98
Harbhajan Singh	c McCullum b Martin	20
I.Sharma	not out	7
S.Sreesanth	not out	0
P.P.Ojha		
Extras	(B 12, LB 5, W 4, NB 1)	22
Total	**(8 wkts dec; 165 overs; 711 mins)**	**566**

INDIA	O	M	R	W	O	M	R	W
Sreesanth	12	4	28	2	7	3	25	0
Sharma	18	4	43	4	6.2	2	15	3
Ojha	19.3	2	57	3	17	2	67	2
Harbhajan Singh	17	2	59	1	19	4	56	3
Raina					2	1	1	2

NEW ZEALAND	O	M	R	W
Martin	28	4	82	2
Southee	29	5	94	1
McKay	31	5	120	1
Vettori	58	7	178	3
Williamson	11	0	45	1
Guptill	7	0	27	0
Taylor	1	0	3	0

FALL OF WICKETS			
	NZ	I	NZ
Wkt	1st	1st	2nd
1st	11	113	18
2nd	16	192	38
3rd	42	296	38
4th	43	309	62
5th	51	328	93
6th	82	521	110
7th	124	549	123
8th	159	562	124
9th	165	–	175
10th	193	–	175

Umpires: N.J.Llong (*England*) (9) and S.J.A.Taufel (*Australia*) (66).
Referee: R.S.Madugalle (*Sri Lanka*) (122). **Test No. 1975/50 (1445/NZ362)**

PAKISTAN v SOUTH AFRICA (1st Test)

At Dubai Sports City Stadium, on 12, 13, 14, 15, 16 November 2010.
Toss: South Africa. Result: **MATCH DRAWN**.
Debut: Pakistan – Adnan Akmal.

SOUTH AFRICA

*G.C.Smith	c Umar b Riaz	100	(2) lbw b Ajmal		34
A.N.Petersen	c Khan b Rehman	67	(1) lbw b Rehman		26
H.M.Amla	c Adnan Akmal b Riaz	80	not out		118
J.H.Kallis	c Adnan Akmal b Ajmal	73	not out		135
P.L.Harris	c Khan b Gul	0			
A.B.de Villiers	b Gul	5			
A.G.Prince	lbw b Gul	1			
†M.V.Boucher	lbw b Rehman	9			
J.Botha	b Rehman	10			
D.W.Steyn	not out	10			
M.Morkel	lbw b Ajmal	10			
Extras	(B 9, LB 2, W 1, NB 3)	15	(B 1, LB 2, W 1, NB 1)		5
Total	**(123 overs)**	**380**	**(2 wkts dec; 95 overs)**		**318**

PAKISTAN

Mohammad Hafeez	c Smith b Harris	60	c Botha b Steyn		34
Taufiq Umar	lbw b Morkel	42	c Kallis b Botha		22
Azhar Ali	c Amla b Morkel	56	b Harris		63
Younus Khan	c De Villiers b Botha	35	not out		131
*Misbah-ul-Haq	c Amla b Botha	9	not out		76
Umar Akmal	c Steyn b Botha	4			
†Adnan Akmal	c Boucher b Steyn	10			
Abdur Rehman	c De Villiers b Morkel	1			
Umar Gul	not out	12			
Wahab Riaz	c Boucher b Morkel	5			
Saeed Ajmal	c Boucher b Morkel	2			
Extras	(LB 12)	12	(B 6, LB 4, W 5, NB 2)		17
Total	**(95 overs)**	**248**	**(3 wkts; 117 overs)**		**343**

PAKISTAN	O	M	R	W		O	M	R	W
Umar Gul	30	4	100	3		18	0	73	0
Wahab Riaz	18	3	61	2					
Abdur Rehman	32	2	101	3		36	5	105	1
Saeed Ajmal	35	6	95	2	(5)	27	2	102	1
Mohammad Hafeez	1	0	1	0	(4)	11	3	20	0
Younus Khan	7	2	11	0	(2)	3	0	15	0

SOUTH AFRICA	O	M	R	W		O	M	R	W
Steyn	18	3	58	1		22	6	82	1
Morkel	21	7	54	5		22	4	46	0
Harris	25	7	47	1		31	10	57	1
Kallis	8	3	16	0	(5)	4	2	10	0
Botha	23	6	61	3	(4)	38	7	138	1

FALL OF WICKETS

	SA	P	SA	P
Wkt	1st	1st	2nd	2nd
1st	153	105	47	41
2nd	190	111	76	75
3rd	307	176	–	157
4th	318	196	–	–
5th	327	202	–	–
6th	329	220	–	–
7th	345	225	–	–
8th	347	228	–	–
9th	363	246	–	–
10th	380	248	–	–

Umpires: E.A.R.de Silva (*Sri Lanka*) (47) and D.J.Harper (*Australia*) (91).
Referee: A.J.Pycroft (*Zimbabwe*) (14). **Test No. 1976/17 (P353/SA354)**

PAKISTAN v SOUTH AFRICA (2nd Test)

At Sheikh Zayed Stadium, Abu Dhabi, on 20, 21, 22, 23, 24 November 2010.
Toss: Pakistan. Result: **MATCH DRAWN**.
Debuts: Pakistan – Asad Shafiq, Tanvir Ahmed.

SOUTH AFRICA

*G.C.Smith	c Akmal b Ahmed	10	(1) c Khan b Rehman		35
A.N.Petersen	c Misbah b Ahmed	2	(2) b Rehman		62
H.M.Amla	c Akmal b Ahmed	4	c Umar b Hafeez		10
J.H.Kallis	b Ahmed	105	(3) lbw b Rehman		25
A.B.de Villiers	not out	278	(5) not out		47
A.G.Prince	c Shafiq b Hafeez	32	(6) b Gul		15
†M.V.Boucher	b Ahmed	45	(7) not out		7
J.Botha	b Rehman	12			
D.W.Steyn	c Hafeez b Rehman	27			
P.L.Harris	c Akmal b Ahmed	19			
M.Morkel	not out	35			
Extras	(B 6, LB 1, W 2, NB 6)	15	(LB 1, NB 1)		2
Total	**(9 wkts dec; 153 overs)**	**584**	**(5 wkts dec; 55 overs)**		**203**

PAKISTAN

Mohammad Hafeez	lbw b Steyn	2	lbw b Harris	34
Taufiq Umar	c Amla b Kallis	43	lbw b Botha	30
Azhar Ali	c Smith b Steyn	90	not out	28
Younus Khan	c Amla b Steyn	14	lbw b Harris	0
*Misbah-ul-Haq	lbw b Steyn	77	not out	58
Asad Shafiq	c Kallis b Harris	61		
†Adnan Akmal	c Amla b Harris	17		
Abdur Rehman	lbw b Botha	60		
Umar Gul	lbw b Harris	21		
Tanvir Ahmed	c Prince b Morkel	30		
Mohammad Sami	not out	2		
Extras	(B 5, LB 8, W 2, NB 2)	17	(LB 2, W 1)	3
Total	**(144.1 overs)**	**434**	**(3 wkts; 67 overs)**	**153**

PAKISTAN	O	M	R	W		O	M	R	W
Umar Gul	36	6	137	0		7	0	32	1
Tanvir Ahmed	28	6	120	6		5	1	29	0
Mohammad Sami	24	1	101	0	(4)	5	0	28	0
Younus Khan	3	1	11	0					
Abdur Rehman	50	9	150	2	(3)	22	1	81	3
Mohammad Hafeez	12	0	58	1	(5)	16	4	32	1

SOUTH AFRICA	O	M	R	W		O	M	R	W
Steyn	30	8	98	4		13	2	40	0
Morkel	33	13	94	1		11	3	29	0
Kallis	21	6	77	1	(4)	2	0	13	0
Botha	14.1	3	54	1	(5)	17	4	40	1
Harris	46	17	98	3	(3)	23	14	28	2
Petersen						1	0	1	0

FALL OF WICKETS

	SA	P	SA	P
Wkt	1st	1st	2nd	2nd
1st	2	2	81	66
2nd	6	119	113	66
3rd	33	153	130	66
4th	212	156	148	–
5th	268	263	182	–
6th	341	309	–	–
7th	383	317	–	–
8th	442	353	–	–
9th	477	412	–	–
10th	–	434	–	–

Umpires: E.A.R.de Silva (*Sri Lanka*) (48) and D.J.Harper (*Australia*) (92).
Referee: A.J.Pycroft (*Zimbabwe*) (15).   **Test No. 1977/18 (P354/SA355)**

SRI LANKA v WEST INDIES (1st Test)

At Galle International Stadium, on 15, 16, 17, 18, 19 November 2010.
Toss: West Indies. Result: **MATCH DRAWN**.
Debuts: West Indies – D.M.Bravo, A.D.Russell.

WEST INDIES

C.H.Gayle	b Mendis	333
A.B.Barath	c D.P.M.D.Jayawardena b Kaluhalamulla	50
D.M.Bravo	c Samaraweera b Mendis	58
S.Chanderpaul	c D.P.M.D.Jayawardena b Kaluhalamulla	32
B.P.Nash	lbw b Mendis	64
D.J.Bravo	lbw b Mendis	5
†C.S.Baugh	not out	8
*D.J.G.Sammy	b Mendis	0
A.D.Russell	b Mendis	2
S.Shillingford	st H.A.P.W.Jayawardena b Kaluhalamulla	1
K.A.J.Roach		
Extras	(B 2, LB 6, W 7, NB 12)	27
Total	**(9 wkts dec; 163.2 overs; 656 mins)**	**580**

SRI LANKA

N.T.Paranavitana	b Roach	10	c Sammy b Shillingford		95
T.M.Dilshan	c Shillingford b Russell	0	b Roach		54
*K.C.Sangakkara	b D.J.Bravo	73	c Sammy b Roach		4
D.P.M.D.Jayawardena	c Baugh b Roach	59	c and b Nash		58
T.T.Samaraweera	run out	52	not out		19
A.D.Mathews	c Sammy b Shillingford	27	not out		5
†H.A.P.W.Jayawardena	c Roach b Shillingford	58			
H.K.S.R.Kaluhalamulla	b Shillingford	12			
K.T.G.D.Prasad	c Russell b Shillingford	47			
B.A.W.Mendis	c D.M.Bravo b Roach	4			
M.T.T.Mirando	not out	4			
Extras	(B 8, LB 8, W 3, NB 13)	32	(LB 1, W 4, NB 1)		6
Total	**(95.2 overs; 387 mins)**	**378**	**(4 wkts; 81.2 overs; 356 mins)**		**241**

SRI LANKA	O	M	R	W	O	M	R	W		FALL OF WICKETS		
										WI	SL	SL
Mirando	21	4	79	0					Wkt	1st	1st	2nd
Prasad	30	3	116	0					1st	110	6	102
Mendis	59	6	169	6					2nd	306	61	110
Kaluhalamulla	48.2	3	183	3					3rd	392	132	197
Dilshan	3	0	15	0					4th	559	193	233
Mathews	2	0	10	0					5th	565	227	–
WEST INDIES									6th	566	264	–
Roach	19	2	75	3	17	3	55	2	7th	566	295	–
Russell	15	1	73	1	8	1	31	0	8th	579	367	–
Shillingford	33.2	3	123	4	(4) 30	4	79	1	9th	580	374	–
Sammy	11	2	41	0	(5) 9	2	14	0	10th	–	378	–
D.J.Bravo	16	4	47	1	(3) 12.2	1	40	0				
Gayle	1	0	3	0								
Nash					(6) 5	0	21	1				

Umpires: S.J.Davis (*Australia*) (29) and R.A.Kettleborough (*England*) (1).
Referee: A.G.Hurst (*Australia*) (40).   **Test No. 1978/13 (SL196/WI466)**
M.T.T.Mirando is also known as T.Thushara.

SRI LANKA v WEST INDIES (2nd Test)

At R.Premadasa Stadium, Colombo, on 23, 24, 25, 26 (*no play*), 27 November 2010.
Toss: Sri Lanka. Result: **MATCH DRAWN**.
Debut: Sri Lanka – R.A.S.Lakmal.

SRI LANKA

N.T.Paranavitana	c D.J.Bravo b Roach	16	not out		20
T.M.Dilshan	b Roach	4	c Baugh b D.J.Bravo		26
*K.C.Sangakkara	c Gayle b Sammy	150	not out		1
D.P.M.D.Jayawardena	b Sammy	2			
T.T.Samaraweera	c Shillingford b D.J.Bravo	80			
A.D.Mathews	c Baugh b Roach	25			
†H.A.P.W.Jayawardena	b Benn	34			
K.M.D.N.Kulasekara	c D.J.Bravo b Roach	17			
H.M.R.K.B.Herath	not out	24			
B.A.W.Mendis	b Roach	2			
R.A.S.Lakmal					
Extras	(B 4, LB 12, W 14, NB 3)	33	(B 5, LB 4, W 1)		10
Total	(9 wkts dec; 115.2 overs; 507 mins)	387	(1 wkt dec; 15 overs; 66 mins)		57

WEST INDIES

C.H.Gayle	c Mathews b Lakmal	31	c D.P.M.D.Jayawardena b Dilshan		3
A.B.Barath	lbw b Kulasekara	3	lbw b Mendis		8
D.M.Bravo	c Herath b Dilshan	80	not out		0
S.Chanderpaul	lbw b Mendis	8	not out		0
B.P.Nash	lbw b Dilshan	29			
D.J.Bravo	st H.A.P.W.Jayawardena b Herath	20			
†C.S.Baugh	b Herath	50			
*D.J.G.Sammy	c Mathews b Lakmal	2			
S.J.Benn	c Paranavitana b Herath	0			
S.Shillingford	not out	5			
K.A.J.Roach	b Mendis	3			
Extras	(LB 4, NB 8)	12	(NB 1)		1
Total	(71.3 overs; 311 mins)	243	(2 wkts; 11 overs; 43 mins)		12

WEST INDIES

	O	M	R	W	O	M	R	W
Roach	28.2	5	100	5	5	0	15	0
Sammy	35	8	80	2	4	1	16	0
D.J.Bravo	18	5	61	1	4	1	8	1
Benn	19	4	57	1	2	0	9	0
Shillingford	15	0	73	0				

SRI LANKA

	O	M	R	W		O	M	R	W
Mendis	16.3	1	56	2	(3)	3	2	1	1
Lakmal	16	1	85	2	(1)	2	0	7	0
Kulasekara	11	5	17	1					
Herath	23	3	76	3		1	1	0	0
Mathews	3	2	1	0					
Dilshan	3	0	4	2	(2)	5	2	4	1

FALL OF WICKETS

	SL	WI	SL	WI
Wkt	1st	1st	2nd	2nd
1st	10	7	55	9
2nd	31	51	–	11
3rd	34	77	–	
4th	204	160	–	
5th	273	161	–	
6th	305	205	–	
7th	349	208	–	
8th	383	209	–	
9th	387	240	–	
10th	–	243	–	

Umpires: Asad Rauf (*Pakistan*) (32) and R.A.Kettleborough (*England*) (2).
Referee: A.G.Hurst (*Australia*) (41). **Test No. 1979/14 (SL197/WI467)**

SRI LANKA v WEST INDIES (3rd Test)

At Pallekele International Cricket Stadium, on 1, 2, 3 (*no play*), 4, 5 (*no play*) December 2010.
Toss: Sri Lanka. Result: **MATCH DRAWN**.
Debuts: None.

WEST INDIES

C.H.Gayle	lbw b Lakmal	0
D.S.Smith	lbw b Mendis	55
D.M.Bravo	lbw b Fernando	68
S.Chanderpaul	c D.P.M.D.Jayawardena b Mendis	54
B.P.Nash	c H.A.P.W.Jayawardena b Herath	67
D.J.Bravo	st H.A.P.W.Jayawardena b Herath	0
†C.S.Baugh	lbw b Herath	2
*D.J.G.Sammy	lbw b Herath	8
S.J.Benn	not out	29
K.A.J.Roach	not out	12
N.T.Pascal		
Extras	(LB 4, W 1, NB 3)	8
Total	**(8 wkts; 103.3 overs; 425 mins)**	**303**

SRI LANKA

N.T.Paranavitana
T.M.Dilshan
*K.C.Sangakkara
D.P.M.D.Jayawardena
T.T.Samaraweera
A.D.Mathews
†H.A.P.W.Jayawardena
H.M.R.K.B.Herath
C.R.D.Fernando
B.A.W.Mendis
R.A.S.Lakmal
Extras
Total

SRI LANKA	O	M	R	W
Lakmal	17.3	5	41	1
Mathews	10	4	34	0
Dilshan	10	1	20	0
Fernando	15	2	72	1
Mendis	28	6	78	2
Herath	23	5	54	4

FALL OF WICKETS

	WI
Wkt	*1st*
1st	0
2nd	115
3rd	142
4th	241
5th	242
6th	252
7th	253
8th	274
9th	–
10th	–

Umpires: Asad Rauf (*Pakistan*) (33) and B.N.J.Oxenford (*Australia*) (1).
Referee: A.G.Hurst (*Australia*) (42).   **Test No. 1980/15 (SL198/WI468)**

AUSTRALIA v ENGLAND (1st Test)

At Woolloongabba, Brisbane, on 25, 26, 27, 28, 29 November 2010.
Toss: England. Result: **MATCH DRAWN**.
Debut: Australia – X.J.Doherty.

ENGLAND

*A.J.Strauss	c Hussey b Hilfenhaus	0	st Haddin b North		110
A.N.Cook	c Watson b Siddle	67	not out		235
I.J.L.Trott	b Watson	29	not out		135
K.P.Pietersen	c Ponting b Siddle	43			
P.D.Collingwood	c North b Siddle	4			
I.R.Bell	c Watson b Doherty	76			
†M.J.Prior	b Siddle	0			
S.C.J.Broad	lbw b Siddle	0			
G.P.Swann	lbw b Siddle	10			
J.M.Anderson	b Doherty	11			
S.T.Finn	not out	0			
Extras	(LB 8, W 7, NB 5)	20	(B 17, LB 4, W 10, NB 6)		37
Total	**(76.5 overs; 360 mins)**	**260**	**(1 wkt dec; 152 overs; 630 mins)**		**517**

AUSTRALIA

S.R.Watson	c Strauss b Anderson	36	not out		41
S.M.Katich	c and b Finn	50	c Strauss b Broad		4
*R.T.Ponting	c Prior b Anderson	10	not out		51
M.J.Clarke	c Prior b Finn	9			
M.E.K.Hussey	c Cook b Finn	195			
M.J.North	c Collingwood b Swann	1			
†B.J.Haddin	c Collingwood b Swann	136			
M.G.Johnson	b Finn	0			
X.J.Doherty	c Cook b Finn	16			
P.M.Siddle	c Swann b Finn	6			
B.W.Hilfenhaus	not out	1			
Extras	(B 4, LB 12, W 4, NB 1)	21	(B 4, LB 1, W 1, Pen 5)		11
Total	**(158.4 overs; 662 mins)**	**481**	**(1 wkt; 26 overs; 119 mins)**		**107**

AUSTRALIA	O	M	R	W		O	M	R	W
Hilfenhaus	19	4	60	1		32	8	82	0
Siddle	16	3	54	6		24	4	90	0
Johnson	15	2	66	0	(4)	27	5	104	0
Watson	12	2	30	1	(6)	21	5	66	0
Doherty	13.5	3	41	2		35	5	107	0
North	1	0	1	0	(3)	19	3	47	1

ENGLAND	O	M	R	W		O	M	R	W
Anderson	37	13	99	2		5	2	15	0
Broad	33	7	72	0		7	1	18	1
Swann	43	5	128	2		8	0	33	0
Finn	33.4	1	125	6		4	0	25	0
Collingwood	12	1	41	0					
Pietersen					(5)	2	0	6	0

FALL OF WICKETS

	E	A	E	A
Wkt	1st	1st	2nd	2nd
1st	0	78	188	5
2nd	41	96	–	–
3rd	117	100	–	–
4th	125	140	–	–
5th	197	143	–	–
6th	197	450	–	–
7th	197	458	–	–
8th	228	462	–	–
9th	254	472	–	–
10th	260	481	–	–

Umpires: Alim Dar (*Pakistan*) (61) and B.R.Doctrove (*West Indies*) (30).
Referee: J.J.Crowe (*New Zealand*) (43).   **Test No. 1981/322 (A725/E904)**

47

AUSTRALIA v ENGLAND (2nd Test)

At Adelaide Oval, on 3, 4, 5, 6, 7 December 2010.
Toss: Australia. Result: **ENGLAND** won by an innings and 71 runs.
Debuts: None.

AUSTRALIA

S.R.Watson	c Pietersen b Anderson	51	c Strauss b Finn		57
S.M.Katich	run out	0	c Prior b Swann		43
*R.T.Ponting	c Swann b Anderson	0	c Collingwood b Swann		9
M.J.Clarke	c Swann b Anderson	2	c Cook b Pietersen		80
M.E.K.Hussey	c Collingwood b Swann	93	c Anderson b Finn		52
M.J.North	c Prior b Finn	26	lbw b Swann		22
†B.J.Haddin	c Finn b Broad	56	c Prior b Anderson		12
R.J.Harris	lbw b Swann	0	lbw b Anderson		0
X.J.Doherty	run out	6	b Swann		5
P.M.Siddle	c Cook b Anderson	3	b Swann		6
D.E.Bollinger	not out	0	not out		7
Extras	(LB 6, W 1, NB 1)	8	(B 5, LB 1, W 5)		11
Total	(85.5 overs; 377 mins)	245	(99.1 overs; 392 mins)		304

ENGLAND

*A.J.Strauss	b Bollinger	1
A.N.Cook	c Haddin b Harris	148
I.J.L.Trott	c Clarke b Harris	78
K.P.Pietersen	c Katich b Doherty	227
P.D.Collingwood	lbw b Watson	42
I.R.Bell	not out	68
†M.J.Prior	not out	27
S.C.J.Broad		
G.P.Swann		
J.M.Anderson		
S.T.Finn		
Extras	(B 8, LB 13, W 8)	29
Total	(5 wkts dec; 152 overs; 673 mins)	620

ENGLAND	O	M	R	W		O	M	R	W
Anderson	19	4	51	4		22	4	92	2
Broad	18.5	6	39	1		11	3	32	0
Finn	16	1	71	1	(4)	18	2	60	2
Swann	29	2	70	2	(3)	41.1	12	91	5
Collingwood	3	0	8	0		4	0	13	0
Pietersen						3	0	10	1

AUSTRALIA	O	M	R	W
Harris	29	5	84	2
Bollinger	29	1	130	1
Siddle	30	3	121	0
Watson	19	7	44	1
Doherty	27	3	158	1
North	18	0	62	0

FALL OF WICKETS

	A	E	A	A
Wkt	1st	1st	1st	2nd
1st	0	3		84
2nd	0	176		98
3rd	2	351		134
4th	96	452		238
5th	156	568		261
6th	207	—		286
7th	207	—		286
8th	226	—		286
9th	243	—		295
10th	245	—		304

Umpires: M.Erasmus (*South Africa*) (4) and A.L.Hill (*New Zealand*) (21).
Referee: J.J.Crowe (*New Zealand*) (44).   **Test No. 1982/323 (A726/E905)**

AUSTRALIA v ENGLAND (3rd Test)

At WACA Ground, Perth, on 16, 17, 18, 19 December 2010.
Toss: England. Result: **AUSTRALIA** won by 267 runs.
Debuts: None.

AUSTRALIA

S.R.Watson	lbw b Finn	13	lbw b Tremlett		95
P.J.Hughes	b Tremlett	2	c Collingwood b Finn		12
*R.T.Ponting	c Collingwood b Anderson	12	c Prior b Finn		1
M.J.Clarke	c Prior b Tremlett	4	b Tremlett		20
M.E.K.Hussey	c Prior b Swann	61	c Swann b Tremlett		116
S.P.D.Smith	c Strauss b Tremlett	7	c Prior b Tremlett		36
†B.J.Haddin	c Swann b Anderson	53	b Tremlett		7
M.G.Johnson	c Anderson b Finn	62	c Bell b Collingwood		1
R.J.Harris	b Anderson	3	c Bell b Finn		3
P.M.Siddle	not out	35	c Collingwood b Anderson		8
B.W.Hilfenhaus	c Cook b Swann	13	not out		0
Extras	(LB 3)	3	(LB 6, W 4, NB 2)		12
Total	**(76 overs; 322 mins)**	**268**	**(86 overs; 390 mins)**		**309**

ENGLAND

*A.J.Strauss	c Haddin b Harris	52		c Ponting b Johnson	15
A.N.Cook	c Hussey b Johnson	32		lbw b Harris	13
I.J.L.Trott	lbw b Johnson	4		c Haddin b Johnson	31
K.P.Pietersen	lbw b Johnson	0		c Watson b Hilfenhaus	3
P.D.Collingwood	lbw b Johnson	5		c Smith b Harris	11
I.R.Bell	c Ponting b Harris	53	(7)	lbw b Harris	16
†M.J.Prior	b Siddle	12	(8)	c Hussey b Harris	10
G.P.Swann	c Haddin b Harris	11	(9)	b Johnson	9
C.T.Tremlett	b Johnson	2	(10)	not out	1
J.M.Anderson	c Watson b Johnson	0	(6)	b Harris	3
S.T.Finn	not out	1		c Smith b Harris	2
Extras	(B 8, LB 4, W 1, NB 2)	15		(LB 8, NB 1)	9
Total	**(62.3 overs; 267 mins)**	**187**		**(37 overs; 167 mins)**	**123**

ENGLAND	O	M	R	W		O	M	R	W		FALL OF WICKETS			
												A	E	A	E
Anderson	20	3	61	3		26	7	65	1			A	E	A	E
Tremlett	23	3	63	3		24	4	87	5		Wkt	1st	1st	2nd	2nd
Finn	15	1	86	2		21	4	97	3		1st	2	78	31	23
Collingwood	2	0	3	0	(5)	6	3	3	1		2nd	17	82	34	37
Swann	16	0	52	2	(4)	9	0	51	0		3rd	28	82	64	55
											4th	36	94	177	81
AUSTRALIA											5th	69	98	252	81
Hilfenhaus	21	6	53	0		10	4	16	1		6th	137	145	271	94
Harris	15	4	59	3		11	1	47	6		7th	189	181	276	111
Siddle	9	2	25	1	(4)	4	1	8	0		8th	201	186	284	114
Johnson	17.3	5	38	6	(3)	12	3	44	3		9th	233	186	308	120
											10th	268	187	309	123

Umpires: B.R.Doctrove (*West Indies*) (31) and M.Erasmus (*South Africa*) (5).
Referee: J.J.Crowe (*New Zealand*) (45).   **Test No. 1983/324 (A727/E906)**

AUSTRALIA v ENGLAND (4th Test)

At Melbourne Cricket Ground, on 26, 27, 28, 29 December 2010.
Toss: England. Result: **ENGLAND** won by an innings and 157 runs.
Debuts: None.

AUSTRALIA

S.R.Watson	c Pietersen b Tremlett	5	lbw b Bresnan		54
P.J.Hughes	c Pietersen b Bresnan	16	run out		23
*R.T.Ponting	c Swann b Tremlett	10	b Bresnan		20
M.J.Clarke	c Prior b Anderson	20	c Strauss b Swann		13
M.E.K.Hussey	c Prior b Anderson	8	c Bell b Bresnan		0
S.P.D.Smith	c Prior b Anderson	6	b Anderson		38
†B.J.Haddin	c Strauss b Bresnan	5	not out		55
M.G.Johnson	c Prior b Anderson	0	b Tremlett		6
R.J.Harris	not out	10	absent hurt		–
P.M.Siddle	c Prior b Tremlett	11	(9) c Pietersen b Swann		40
B.W.Hilfenhaus	c Prior b Tremlett	0	(10) c Prior b Bresnan		0
Extras	(LB 2, NB 5)	7	(B 1, LB 6, W 2)		9
Total	**(42.5 overs; 227 mins)**	**98**	**(85.4 overs; 342 mins)**		**258**

ENGLAND

*A.J.Strauss	c Hussey b Siddle	69
A.N.Cook	c Watson b Siddle	82
I.J.L.Trott	not out	168
K.P.Pietersen	lbw b Siddle	51
P.D.Collingwood	c Siddle b Johnson	8
I.R.Bell	c Siddle b Johnson	1
†M.J.Prior	c Ponting b Siddle	85
T.T.Bresnan	c Haddin b Siddle	4
G.P.Swann	c Haddin b Hilfenhaus	22
C.T.Tremlett	b Hilfenhaus	4
J.M.Anderson	b Siddle	1
Extras	(B 10, LB 2, W 3, NB 3)	18
Total	**(159.1 overs; 713 mins)**	**513**

ENGLAND	O	M	R	W		O	M	R	W
Anderson	16	4	44	0		20	1	71	1
Tremlett	11.5	5	26	4		17	3	71	1
Bresnan	13	6	25	2	(4)	21.4	8	50	4
Swann	2	1	1	0	(3)	27	11	59	2

AUSTRALIA	O	M	R	W
Hilfenhaus	37	13	83	2
Harris	28.4	9	91	0
Johnson	29	2	134	2
Siddle	33.1	10	75	6
Watson	10	1	34	0
Smith	18	3	71	0
Clarke	3.2	0	13	0

FALL OF WICKETS

	A	E	A
Wkt	1st	1st	2nd
1st	15	159	53
2nd	37	170	99
3rd	37	262	102
4th	58	281	104
5th	66	286	134
6th	77	459	158
7th	77	465	172
8th	77	508	258
9th	92	512	258
10th	98	513	–

Umpires: Alim Dar (*Pakistan*) (62) and A.L.Hill (*New Zealand*) (22).
Referee: R.S.Madugalle (*Sri Lanka*) (123).   Test No. 1984/325 (A728/E907)

AUSTRALIA v ENGLAND (5th Test)

At Sydney Cricket Ground, on 3, 4, 5, 6, 7 January 2011.
Toss: Australia. Result: **ENGLAND** won by an innings and 83 runs.
Debuts: Australia – M.A.Beer, U.T.Khawaja.

AUSTRALIA

S.R.Watson	c Strauss b Bresnan	45	run out		38
P.J.Hughes	c Collingwood b Tremlett	31	c Prior b Bresnan		13
U.T.Khawaja	c Trott b Swann	37	c Prior b Anderson		21
*M.J.Clarke	c Anderson b Bresnan	4	c Prior b Anderson		41
M.E.K.Hussey	b Collingwood	33	c Pietersen b Bresnan		12
†B.J.Haddin	c Prior b Anderson	6	c Prior b Tremlett		30
S.P.D.Smith	c Collingwood b Anderson	18	not out		54
M.G.Johnson	b Bresnan	53	b Tremlett		0
P.M.Siddle	c Strauss b Anderson	2	c Anderson b Swann		43
B.W.Hilfenhaus	c Prior b Anderson	34	c Prior b Anderson		7
M.A.Beer	not out	2	b Tremlett		2
Extras	(B 5, LB 7, W 1, NB 2)	15	(B 11, LB 4, W 3, NB 2)		20
Total	(106.1 overs; 423 mins)	280	(84.4 overs; 369 mins)		281

ENGLAND

*A.J.Strauss	b Hilfenhaus	60
A.N.Cook	c Hussey b Watson	189
I.J.L.Trott	b Johnson	0
K.P.Pietersen	c Beer b Johnson	36
J.M.Anderson	b Siddle	7
P.D.Collingwood	c Hilfenhaus b Beer	13
I.R.Bell	c Clarke b Johnson	115
†M.J.Prior	c Haddin b Hilfenhaus	118
T.T.Bresnan	c Clarke b Johnson	35
G.P.Swann	not out	36
C.T.Tremlett	c Haddin b Hilfenhaus	12
Extras	(B 3, LB 11, W 5, NB 4)	23
Total	(177.5 overs; 730 mins)	644

ENGLAND	O	M	R	W		O	M	R	W
Anderson	30.1	7	66	4		18	5	61	3
Tremlett	26	9	71	1		20.4	4	79	3
Bresnan	30	5	89	3	(4)	18	6	51	2
Swann	16	4	37	1	(3)	28	8	75	1
Collingwood	4	2	5	1					

AUSTRALIA	O	M	R	W
Hilfenhaus	38.5	7	121	3
Johnson	36	5	168	4
Siddle	31	5	111	1
Watson	20	7	49	1
Beer	38	3	112	1
Smith	13	0	67	0
Hussey	1	0	2	0

FALL OF WICKETS			
	A	E	A
Wkt	1st	1st	2nd
1st	55	98	46
2nd	105	99	52
3rd	113	165	117
4th	134	181	124
5th	143	226	161
6th	171	380	171
7th	187	487	171
8th	189	589	257
9th	265	609	267
10th	280	644	281

Umpires: Alim Dar (*Pakistan*) (63) and B.F.Bowden (*New Zealand*) (65).
Referee: R.S.Madugalle (*Sri Lanka*) (124). **Test No. 1985/326 (A729/E908)**

AUSTRALIA v ENGLAND 2010-11

AUSTRALIA – BATTING AND FIELDING

	M	I	NO	HS	Runs	Avge	100	50	Ct/St
M.E.K.Hussey	5	9	–	195	570	63.33	2	3	5
S.R.Watson	5	10	1	95	435	48.33	–	4	5
B.J.Haddin	5	9	1	136	360	45.00	1	3	8/1
S.P.D.Smith	3	6	1	54*	159	31.80	–	1	2
S.M.Katich	2	4	–	50	97	24.25	–	1	1
M.J.Clarke	5	9	–	80	193	21.44	–	1	3
P.M.Siddle	5	9	1	43	154	19.25	–	–	2
M.G.Johnson	4	7	–	62	122	17.42	–	1	–
M.J.North	2	3	–	26	49	16.33	–	–	1
P.J.Hughes	3	6	–	31	97	16.16	–	–	–
R.T.Ponting	4	8	1	51*	113	16.14	–	1	4
B.W.Hilfenhaus	4	7	2	34	55	11.00	–	–	1
X.J.Doherty	2	3	–	16	27	9.00	–	–	–
R.J.Harris	3	4	–	10*	14	3.50	–	–	–

Also played (one Test): M.A.Beer 2*, 2 (1 ct); D.E.Bollinger 0*, 7*; U.T.Khawaja 37, 21.

AUSTRALIA – BOWLING

	O	M	R	W	Avge	Best	5wI	10wM
R.J.Harris	83.4	19	281	11	25.54	6- 47	1	–
P.M.Siddle	147.1	28	484	14	34.57	6- 54	2	–
M.G.Johnson	136.3	22	554	15	36.93	6- 38	1	–
B.W.Hilfenhaus	157.5	42	415	7	59.28	3-121	–	–

Also bowled: M.A.Beer 38-3-112-1; D.E.Bollinger 29-1-130-1; M.J.Clarke 3.2-0-13-0; X.J.Doherty 75.5-11-306-3; M.E.K.Hussey 1-0-2-0; M.J.North 38-3-110-1; S.P.D.Smith 31-3-138-0; S.R.Watson 76-19-223-3.

ENGLAND – BATTING AND FIELDING

	M	I	NO	HS	Runs	Avge	100	50	Ct/St
A.N.Cook	5	7	1	235*	766	127.66	3	2	5
I.J.L.Trott	5	7	2	168*	445	89.00	2	1	1
I.R.Bell	5	6	1	115	329	65.80	1	3	3
K.P.Pietersen	5	6	–	227	360	60.00	1	1	5
M.J.Prior	5	6	1	118	252	50.40	1	1	23
A.J.Strauss	5	7	–	110	307	43.85	1	3	8
G.P.Swann	5	5	1	36*	88	22.00	–	–	6
T.T.Bresnan	2	2	–	35	39	19.50	–	–	–
P.D.Collingwood	5	6	–	42	83	13.83	–	–	9
C.T.Tremlett	3	4	1	12	19	6.33	–	–	–
J.M.Anderson	5	5	–	11	22	4.40	–	–	4
S.T.Finn	3	3	2	2	3	3.00	–	–	2

Also played (two Tests): S.C.J.Broad 0.

ENGLAND – BOWLING

	O	M	R	W	Avge	Best	5wI	10wM
T.T.Bresnan	82.4	25	215	11	19.54	4- 50	–	–
C.T.Tremlett	122.3	28	397	17	23.35	5- 87	1	–
J.M.Anderson	213.1	50	625	24	26.04	4- 44	–	–
S.T.Finn	107.4	9	464	14	33.14	6-125	1	–
G.P.Swann	219.1	43	597	15	39.80	5- 91	1	–

Also bowled: S.C.J.Broad 69.5-17-161-2; P.D.Collingwood 31-6-73-2; K.P.Pietersen 5-0-16-1.

SOUTH AFRICA v INDIA (1st Test)

At Centurion Park (Verwoerdburg), Pretoria, on 16, 17, 18, 19, 20 December 2010.
Toss: South Africa. Result: **SOUTH AFRICA** won by an innings and 25 runs.
Debut: India – J.D.Unadkat.

INDIA

Batsman	1st innings	R	2nd innings	R
G.Gambhir	c Harris b Morkel	5	lbw b Steyn	80
V.Sehwag	c Amla b Steyn	0	c Smith b Harris	63
R.S.Dravid	lbw b Morkel	14	c Boucher b Morkel	43
S.R.Tendulkar	lbw b Steyn	36	(5) not out	111
V.V.S.Laxman	b Steyn	7	(6) c De Villiers b Tsotsobe	8
S.K.Raina	c Prince b Kallis	33	(7) c Harris b Kallis	5
†*M.S.Dhoni	lbw b Morkel	27	(8) c Boucher b Steyn	90
Harbhajan Singh	run out	2	(9) c Kallis b Harris	1
I.Sharma	c Kallis b Morkel	0	(4) c Amla b Steyn	23
S.Sreesanth	c Steyn b Morkel	0	c De Villiers b Morkel	3
J.D.Unadkat	not out	0	c Prince b Steyn	1
Extras	(LB 6, W 3, NB 3)	12	(B 13, LB 5, W 8, NB 5)	31
Total	**(38.4 overs; 202 mins)**	**136**	**(128.1 overs; 585 mins)**	**459**

SOUTH AFRICA

Batsman	Dismissal	R
*G.C.Smith	c Dhoni b Harbhajan	62
A.N.Petersen	c Gambhir b Harbhajan	77
H.M.Amla	c Dhoni b Sharma	140
J.H.Kallis	not out	201
A.B.de Villiers	c Dhoni b Sharma	129
A.G.Prince		
†M.V.Boucher		
D.W.Steyn		
P.L.Harris		
M.Morkel		
L.L.Tsotsobe		
Extras	(B 2, LB 3, W 2, NB 4)	11
Total	**(4 wkts dec; 130.1 overs; 580 mins)**	**620**

SOUTH AFRICA	O	M	R	W	O	M	R	W
Steyn	10	1	34	3	30.1	6	105	4
Morkel	12.4	5	20	5	31	6	94	2
Tsotsobe	9	2	50	0	24	3	98	1
Kallis	6	1	20	1	(5) 13	3	56	1
Harris	1	0	6	0	(4) 30	5	88	2

INDIA	O	M	R	W
Sreesanth	24	1	97	0
Sharma	27.1	2	120	2
Unadkat	26	4	101	0
Harbhajan Singh	36	2	169	2
Raina	7	0	77	0
Tendulkar	10	1	51	0

FALL OF WICKETS

Wkt	1st I	1st SA	2nd I
1st	1	111	137
2nd	24	166	170
3rd	27	396	214
4th	66	620	242
5th	67	–	256
6th	71	–	277
7th	110	–	449
8th	110	–	450
9th	116	–	456
10th	136	–	459

Umpires: S.J.Davis (*Australia*) (30) and I.J.Gould (*England*) (17).
Referee: A.J.Pycroft (*Zimbabwe*) (16). **Test No. 1986/25 (SA356/I446)**

SOUTH AFRICA v INDIA (2nd Test)

At Kingsmead, Durban, on 26, 27, 28, 29 December 2010.
Toss: South Africa. Result: **INDIA** won by 87 runs.
Debuts: None.

INDIA

V.Sehwag	c Kallis b Steyn	25	c Boucher b Tsotsobe		32
M.Vijay	c Boucher b Steyn	19	c Amla b Morkel		9
R.S.Dravid	c Boucher b Steyn	25	c Boucher b Tsotsobe		2
S.R.Tendulkar	c Kallis b Tsotsobe	13	c De Villiers b Steyn		6
V.V.S.Laxman	c Tsotsobe b Steyn	38	c Boucher b Steyn		96
C.A.Pujara	c Boucher b Tsotsobe	19	b Morkel		10
†*M.S.Dhoni	c Petersen b Steyn	35	c Boucher b Tsotsobe		21
Harbhajan Singh	c De Villiers b Steyn	21	c Kallis b Morkel		4
Z.Khan	c Boucher b Morkel	0	c De Villiers b Harris		27
I.Sharma	not out	1	c Amla b Kallis		0
S.Sreesanth	c Boucher b Morkel	0	not out		0
Extras	(B 1, LB 2, W 4, NB 2)	9	(B 8, LB 4, W 9)		21
Total	**(65.1 overs)**	**205**	**(70.5 overs; 342 mins)**		**228**

SOUTH AFRICA

A.N.Petersen	b Khan	24	(2)	c Pujara b Harbhajan	26
*G.C.Smith	c Dhoni b Khan	9	(1)	c Dhoni b Sreesanth	37
H.M.Amla	lbw b Harbhajan	33		c Dhoni b Sreesanth	16
J.H.Kallis	run out	10		c Sehwag b Sreesanth	17
A.B.de Villiers	c Dhoni b Sreesanth	10		lbw b Harbhajan	33
A.G.Prince	b Khan	13		not out	39
†M.V.Boucher	not out	16		lbw b Khan	1
D.W.Steyn	c Dravid b Harbhajan	1		c Pujara b Khan	10
P.L.Harris	c Pujara b Harbhajan	0		b Khan	7
M.Morkel	c Harbhajan b Sharma	0		c Dhoni b Sharma	20
L.L.Tsotsobe	c Vijay b Harbhajan	0		run out	0
Extras	(B 2, W 1, NB 12)	15		(LB 1, NB 8)	9
Total	**(37.2 overs; 192 mins)**	**131**		**(72.3 overs; 338 mins)**	**215**

SOUTH AFRICA	O	M	R	W	O	M	R	W
Steyn	19	6	50	6	15.5	1	60	2
Morkel	19.1	3	68	2	15	1	47	3
Tsotsobe	11	3	40	2	13	3	43	2
Kallis	8	2	18	0	13	2	30	1
Harris	8	1	26	0	14	2	36	1
INDIA								
Khan	13	2	36	3	17	3	57	3
Sreesanth	8	0	41	1	(3) 14	2	45	3
Sharma	9	2	42	1	(2) 11.3	0	36	1
Harbhajan Singh	7.2	2	10	4	29	5	70	2
Tendulkar					1	0	6	0

FALL OF WICKETS

	I	SA	I	SA
Wkt	1st	1st	2nd	2nd
1st	43	23	42	63
2nd	48	46	44	82
3rd	79	67	48	82
4th	117	74	56	123
5th	130	96	93	136
6th	156	100	141	143
7th	190	103	148	155
8th	193	103	218	182
9th	205	127	223	215
10th	205	131	228	215

Umpires: Asad Rauf (*Pakistan*) (34) and S.J.Davis (*Australia*) (31).
Referee: A.J.Pycroft (*Zimbabwe*) (17).

Test No. 1987/26 (SA357/I447)

SOUTH AFRICA v INDIA (3rd Test)

At Newlands, Cape Town, on 2, 3, 4, 5, 6 January 2011.
Toss: India. Result: **MATCH DRAWN**.
Debuts: None.

SOUTH AFRICA

A.N.Petersen	c Dhoni b Sharma	21	(2) lbw b Harbhajan	22
*G.C.Smith	lbw b Khan	6	(1) lbw b Harbhajan	29
H.M.Amla	c Pujara b Sreesanth	59	(4) b Harbhajan	2
J.H.Kallis	c Dhoni b Khan	161	(5) not out	109
A.B.de Villiers	c Dhoni b Sreesanth	26	(6) b Khan	13
A.G.Prince	b Sreesanth	47	(7) c Sreesanth b Sharma	22
†M.V.Boucher	c Dhoni b Sreesanth	0	(8) lbw b Tendulkar	55
D.W.Steyn	c Pujara b Khan	0	(9) c sub (M.Vijay) b Harbhajan	28
M.Morkel	c Dhoni b Sreesanth	8	(10) c Sreesanth b Harbhajan	28
P.L.Harris	c Pujara b Sharma	7	(3) lbw b Harbhajan	0
L.L.Tsotsobe	not out	8	c Sehwag b Harbhajan	8
Extras	(B 1, LB 6, W 1, NB 11)	19	(LB 7, W 2, NB 12)	21
Total	**(112.5 overs; 522 mins)**	**362**	**(102 overs; 478 mins)**	**341**

INDIA

G.Gambhir	c Boucher b Harris	93	c Boucher b Steyn	64
V.Sehwag	c Smith b Steyn	13	c Smith b Morkel	11
R.S.Dravid	run out	5	c Prince b Tsotsobe	31
S.R.Tendulkar	b Morkel	146	not out	14
V.V.S.Laxman	run out	15	not out	32
C.A.Pujara	lbw b Steyn	2		
†*M.S.Dhoni	c Prince b Steyn	0		
Harbhajan Singh	c sub (J.P.Duminy) b Steyn	40		
Z.Khan	c Prince b Morkel	23		
I.Sharma	c Boucher b Steyn	1		
S.Sreesanth	not out	4		
Extras	(LB 20, W 1, NB 1)	22	(B 7, W 5, NB 2)	14
Total	**(117.1 overs; 536 mins)**	**364**	**(3wkts; 82 overs; 352 mins)**	**166**

INDIA	O	M	R	W		O	M	R	W
Khan	29.5	6	89	3		20	2	64	1
Sreesanth	29	6	114	5		24	3	79	0
Sharma	27	6	77	2		18	1	62	1
Harbhajan Singh	27	3	75	0		38	1	120	7
Tendulkar						2	0	9	1

SOUTH AFRICA	O	M	R	W		O	M	R	W
Steyn	31	11	75	5		18	6	43	1
Morkel	29.1	7	106	2		15	6	26	1
Tsotsobe	26	5	82	0		13	4	29	1
Harris	29	8	72	1		30	19	29	0
Petersen	2	0	9	0	(6)	5	2	0	0
Smith					(5)	4	0	27	0

FALL OF WICKETS

	SA	I	SA	I
Wkt	1st	1st	2nd	2nd
1st	17	19	50	27
2nd	34	28	52	106
3rd	106	204	53	120
4th	164	235	64	–
5th	262	237	98	–
6th	262	247	130	–
7th	272	323	233	–
8th	283	341	287	–
9th	310	350	333	–
10th	362	364	341	–

Umpires: I.J.Gould (*England*) (18) and S.J.A.Taufel (*Australia*) (67).
Referee: A.J.Pycroft (*Zimbabwe*) (18).　　　　**Test No. 1988/27 (SA358/I1448)**

NEW ZEALAND v PAKISTAN (1st Test)

At Seddon Park, Hamilton, on 7, 8, 9 January 2011.
Toss: Pakistan. Result: **PAKISTAN** won by ten wickets.
Debut: New Zealand – R.A.Young.

NEW ZEALAND

T.G.McIntosh	c Khan b Ahmed	5	st Akmal b Rehman		3
B.B.McCullum	c Ali b Gul	56	c Akmal b Riaz		35
M.J.Guptill	c Misbah b Rehman	50	c Umar b Rehman		11
L.R.P.L.Taylor	c Akmal b Rehman	6	run out		8
J.D.Ryder	run out	22	lbw b Riaz		0
K.S.Williamson	c Akmal b Ahmed	50	c Ali b Riaz		1
†R.A.Young	lbw b Rehman	14	c Ali b Gul		12
*D.L.Vettori	lbw b Ahmed	0	lbw b Rehman		3
T.G.Southee	c Khan b Gul	56	c sub (Umar Akmal) b Gul		17
B.J.Arnel	c Riaz b Ahmed	8	not out		0
C.S.Martin	not out	0	c Khan b Gul		7
Extras	(LB 6, W 1, NB 1)	8	(NB 5)		5
Total	**(97.5 overs; 423 mins)**	**275**	**(38.3 overs; 184 mins)**		**110**

PAKISTAN

Mohammad Hafeez	c McIntosh b Martin	0
Taufiq Umar	c Williamson b Arnel	54
Azhar Ali	c Young b Martin	24
Younus Khan	c and b Arnel	23
*Misbah-ul-Haq	lbw b Arnel	62
Asad Shafiq	lbw b Southee	83
†Adnan Akmal	c Ryder b Southee	44
Abdur Rehman	b Arnel	28
Umar Gul	lbw b Vettori	17
Tanvir Ahmed	c Southee b Martin	18
Wahab Riaz	not out	0
Extras	(B 4, LB 6, W 1, NB 3)	14
Total	**(122.1 overs; 512 mins)**	**367**

(2) not out 9
(1) not out 12

(0 wkts; 3.4 overs; 15 mins) 21

PAKISTAN	O	M	R	W	O	M	R	W
Umar Gul	24	3	84	2	8.3	3	28	3
Tanvir Ahmed	18.5	2	63	4	4	1	20	0
Wahab Riaz	17	4	47	0 (4)	11	1	38	3
Younus Khan	6	1	20	0				
Abdur Rehman	30	13	51	3 (3)	15	6	24	3
Mohammad Hafeez	2	1	4	0				

NEW ZEALAND	O	M	R	W	O	M	R	W
Martin	25.1	7	86	3	2	0	11	0
Southee	32	10	82	4	1.4	0	10	0
Arnel	28	6	95	4				
Vettori	29	12	48	1				
Williamson	6	0	33	0				
Guptill	2	0	13	0				

FALL OF WICKETS				
	NZ	P	NZ	P
Wkt	1st	1st	2nd	2nd
1st	9	0	36	–
2nd	92	72	44	–
3rd	99	104	60	–
4th	135	107	60	–
5th	158	256	61	–
6th	176	256	61	–
7th	177	332	71	–
8th	261	332	90	–
9th	274	365	96	–
10th	275	367	110	–

Umpires: D.J.Harper (*Australia*) (93) and R.J.Tucker (*Australia*) (7).
Referee: R.S.Mahanama (*Sri Lanka*) (30).   **Test No. 1989/49 (NZ363/P355)**

NEW ZEALAND v PAKISTAN (2nd Test)

At Basin Reserve, Wellington, on 15, 16, 17, 18, 19 January 2011.
Toss: New Zealand. Result: **MATCH DRAWN**.
Debuts: None.

NEW ZEALAND

M.J.Guptill	c Akmal b Ahmed	29	lbw b Rehman		73
B.B.McCullum	lbw b Gul	2	c Ahmed b Rehman		64
K.S.Williamson	c Akmal b Gul	21	c Akmal b Ahmed		15
L.R.P.L.Taylor	c Akmal b Riaz	78	lbw b Gul		52
J.D.Ryder	c Akmal b Ahmed	0	b Hafeez		17
J.E.C.Franklin	c Akmal b Rehman	33	c Khan b Hafeez		6
†R.A.Young	c Akmal b Ahmed	57	c Ali b Rehman		20
*D.L.Vettori	c Misbah b Rehman	110	b Gul		1
T.G.Southee	c Misbah b Gul	1	not out		22
B.J.Arnel	lbw b Gul	1	lbw b Gul		0
C.S.Martin	not out	4	c Akmal b Gul		1
Extras	(B 7, LB 1, W 10, NB 2)	20	(B 2, LB 6, W 1, NB 13)		22
Total	**(127.1 overs; 559 mins)**	**356**	**(90.5 overs; 403 mins)**		**293**

PAKISTAN

Taufiq Umar	c Guptill b Vettori	70	(2) lbw b Southee		0
Mohammad Hafeez	c Young b Southee	1	(1) c Taylor b Martin		32
Azhar Ali	c Taylor b Martin	67	lbw b Martin		10
Younus Khan	c Ryder b Vettori	73	c Young b Southee		81
*Misbah-ul-Haq	lbw b Martin	99	not out		70
Asad Shafiq	c Taylor b Vettori	0	lbw b Vettori		24
†Adnan Akmal	c Martin b Vettori	22	not out		2
Abdur Rehman	c McCullum b Martin	5			
Umar Gul	c McCullum b Martin	19			
Tanvir Ahmed	c Taylor b Southee	7			
Wahab Riaz	not out	7			
Extras	(B 1, LB 2, W 2, NB 1)	6	(LB 6, NB 1)		7
Total	**(133 overs; 556 mins)**	**376**	**(5 wkts; 92 overs; 374 mins)**		**226**

PAKISTAN	O	M	R	W	O	M	R	W
Umar Gul	32	3	87	4	20.5	4	61	4
Tanvir Ahmed	25	5	93	3	10	0	36	1
Younus Khan	1	0	9	0				
Wahab Riaz	16	3	46	1	8	1	38	0
Abdur Rehman	45.1	11	96	2	(3) 39	6	119	3
Mohammad Hafeez	8	0	17	0	(5) 13	3	31	2

NEW ZEALAND								
Martin	32	7	91	4	24	6	63	2
Southee	28	7	102	2	15	2	49	2
Arnel	16	4	50	0	(4) 9	5	17	0
Franklin	9	1	30	0	(5) 1	1	6	0
Vettori	47	11	100	4	(3) 34	13	57	1
Guptill	1	1	0	0	3	0	16	0
Ryder					4	0	2	0

FALL OF WICKETS

	NZ	P	NZ	P
Wkt	1st	1st	2nd	2nd
1st	3	2	120	4
2nd	46	134	166	35
3rd	98	144	166	42
4th	98	286	192	215
5th	166	294	208	215
6th	180	324	268	–
7th	318	333	268	–
8th	322	360	275	–
9th	338	363	275	–
10th	356	376	293	–

Umpires: D.J.Harper (*Australia*) (94) and R.J.Tucker (*Australia*) (8).
Referee: R.S.Mahanama (*Sri Lanka*) (31).   **Test No. 1990/50 (NZ364/P356)**

ENGLAND TEST MATCH AVERAGES 2010

These averages cover the 13 Tests played by England included in this book, against Bangladesh away then at home, Pakistan at home and Australia away.

BATTING AND FIELDING

	M	I	NO	HS	Runs	Avge	100	50	Ct/St
I.R.Bell	9	11	2	138	735	81.66	3	4	5
I.J.L.Trott	13	21	4	226	1250	73.52	4	4	6
A.N.Cook	13	21	2	235*	1334	70.21	6	2	9
M.J.Prior	13	17	4	118	664	51.07	2	4	54/2
K.P.Pietersen	13	19	2	227	842	49.52	1	5	12
A.J.Strauss	11	17	1	110	648	40.50	1	6	17
T.T.Bresnan	5	4	–	91	155	38.75	–	1	1
E.J.G.Morgan	6	8	–	130	256	32.00	1	–	4
S.C.J.Broad	8	8	–	169	253	31.62	1	–	2
P.D.Collingwood	11	15	–	145	340	22.66	1	1	21
G.P.Swann	13	15	1	36*	218	15.57	–	–	15
C.T.Tremlett	3	4	1	12	19	6.33	–	–	–
S.T.Finn	11	12	9	9*	16	5.33	–	–	3
J.M.Anderson	11	13	1	13	56	4.66	–	–	7

Also played (one Test): M.A.Carberry 30, 34 (1 ct); A.Shahzad 5 (2 ct); J.C.Tredwell 37 (1 ct).

BOWLING

	O	M	R	W	Avge	Best	5wI	10wM
J.M.Anderson	437.4	126	1164	56	20.78	6- 17	2	1
C.T.Tremlett	122.3	28	397	17	23.35	5- 87	1	–
G.P.Swann	538	127	1480	59	25.08	6- 65	6	1
S.T.Finn	304.4	64	1207	46	26.23	6-125	3	–
T.T.Bresnan	216	65	610	22	27.72	4- 50	–	–
J.C.Tredwell	65	13	181	6	30.16	4- 82	–	–
S.C.J.Broad	262.4	65	764	22	34.72	4- 38	–	–

Also bowled: P.D.Collingwood 43-8-106-2; K.P.Pietersen 14-1-36-1; A.Shahzad 17-4-63-4; I.J.L.Trott 8-0-28-1.

INTERNATIONAL UMPIRES AND REFEREES 2011

ELITE PANEL OF UMPIRES 2011

The Elite Panel of ICC Umpires and Referees was introduced in April 2002 to raise standards and guarantee impartial adjudication. Two umpires from this panel stand in Test matches while one officiates with a home umpire from the Supplementary International Panel in limited-overs internationals. A new panel will be appointed for 12 months from 1 July.

Full Names	Birthdate	Birthplace	Tests	Debut	LOI	Debut
ALIM Sarwar DAR	06.06.68	Jhang, Pakistan	63	2003-04	138	1999-00
ASAD RAUF	12.05.56	Lahore, Pakistan	34	2004-05	83	1999-00
BOWDEN, Brent Fraser	11.04.63	Auckland, New Zealand	65	1999-00	150	1994-95
DAVIS, Stephen James	09.04.52	London, England	31	1997-98	97	1992-93
DE SILVA, E.Asoka Ranjit	28.03.56	Kalutara, Sri Lanka	48	2000	110	1999-00
DOCTROVE, Billy Raymond	03.07.55	Marigot, Dominica	31	2000	101	1997-98
ERASMUS, Marais	27.02.64	George, South Africa	5	2009-10	26	2007-08
GOULD, Ian James	19.08.57	Taplow, England	18	2008-09	48	2006
HARPER, Daryl John	23.10.51	Adelaide, Australia	94	1998-99	169	1993-94
HILL, Anthony Lloyd	26.06.51	Auckland, New Zealand	22	2001-02	79	1997-98
TAUFEL, Simon James Arthur	21.01.71	Sydney, Australia	67	2000-01	159	1998-99
TUCKER, Rodney James	28.08.64	Sydney, Australia	8	2009-10	18	2008-09

ELITE PANEL OF REFEREES 2011

Full Names	Birthdate	Birthplace	Tests	Debut	LOI	Debut
BROAD, Brian Christopher	29.09.57	Bristol, England	42	2003-04	177	2003-04
CROWE, Jeffrey John	14.09.58	Auckland, New Zealand	45	2004-05	131	2003-04
HURST, Alan George	15.07.50	Melbourne, Australia	42	2004-05	97	2004-05
MADUGALLE, Ranjan Senerath	22.04.59	Kandy, Sri Lanka	124	1993-94	252	1993-94
MAHANAMA, Roshan Siriwardena	31.05.66	Colombo, Sri Lanka	31	2004	151	2004
PYCROFT, Andrew John	06.06.56	Harare, Zimbabwe	18	2009	30	2009
SRINATH, Javagal	31.08.69	Mysore, India	15	2006	100	2006-07

INTERNATIONAL UMPIRES PANEL 2011

Nominated by their respective cricket boards, members from this panel officiate in home LOI and supplement the Elite panel for Test matches. Specialist third umpires have been selected to undertake adjudication involving television replays. The number of Test matches/LOI in which they have stood is shown in brackets.

			Third Umpire
Australia	B.N.J.Oxenford (1/21)	P.R.Reiffel (-/8)	S.D.Fry (-/1)
Bangladesh	Nadir Shah (-/37)	Enamul Haque (-/31)	Sharfuddoula (-/4)
England	R.A.Kettleborough (2/12)	N.J.Llong (9/39)	R.K.Illingworth (-/2)
			R.J.Bailey (-/-)
India	A.M.Saheba (3/47)	S.K.Tarapore (-/16)	S.S.Hazare (-/5)
			S.Asnani (-/2)
New Zealand	G.A.V.Baxter (-/33)	C.B.Gaffaney (-/4)	B.G.Frost (-/-)
Pakistan	Zamir Haider (-/11)	Nadeem Ghauri (5/43)	Ahsan Raza (-/2)
South Africa	J.D.Cloete (-/6)	B.G.Jerling (4/94)	S.George (-/-)
Sri Lanka	H.D.P.K.Dharmasena (2/20)	R.E.L.Martinesz (-/2)	T.H.Wijewardene (4/49)
West Indies	N.A.Malcolm (-/22)	P.J.Nero (-/-)	G.O.Brathwaite (-/-)
			J.S.Wilson (-/-)
Zimbabwe	O.Chirombe (-/3)	R.B.Tiffin (44/118)	T.J.Matibiri (-/-)

Test Match statistics to 1 April 2011; LOI statistics to 18 February 2011.

TEST MATCH CAREER RECORDS

These records, complete to 1 April 2011, contain all players registered for county cricket in 2011 at the time of going to press, plus those who have played Test cricket since 16 November 2009 (Test No. 1932). Records are for performances for the country shown, and do not include figures for multi-national teams.

ENGLAND – BATTING AND FIELDING

	M	I	NO	HS	Runs	Avge	100	50	Ct/St
K.Ali	1	2	–	9	10	5.00	–	–	–
T.R.Ambrose	11	16	1	102	447	29.80	1	3	31
J.M.Anderson	57	76	31	34	524	11.64	–	–	25
G.J.Batty	7	8	1	38	144	20.57	–	–	3
I.R.Bell	62	106	11	199	4192	44.12	12	26	53
I.D.Blackwell	1	1	–	4	4	4.00	–	–	–
R.S.Bopara	10	15	–	143	502	33.46	3	–	5
T.T.Bresnan	7	5	–	91	164	32.80	–	1	3
S.C.J.Broad	34	46	6	169	1096	27.40	1	5	9
M.A.Carberry	1	2	–	34	64	32.00	–	–	1
R.Clarke	2	3	–	55	96	32.00	–	1	1
P.D.Collingwood	68	115	10	206	4259	40.56	10	20	96
A.N.Cook	65	115	7	235*	5130	47.50	16	24	57
D.G.Cork	37	56	8	59	864	18.00	–	3	18
R.D.B.Croft	21	34	8	37*	421	16.19	–	–	10
R.K.J.Dawson	7	13	3	19*	114	11.40	–	–	3
S.T.Finn	11	12	9	9*	16	5.33	–	–	3
J.S.Foster	7	12	3	48	226	25.11	–	–	17/1
S.J.Harmison	62	84	23	49*	742	12.16	–	–	7
M.J.Hoggard	67	92	27	38	473	7.27	–	–	24
G.O.Jones	34	53	4	100	1172	23.91	1	6	128/5
S.P.Jones	18	18	5	44	205	15.76	–	–	4
R.W.T.Key	15	26	1	221	775	31.00	1	3	11
A.Khan	1	–	–	–	–	–	–	–	–
J.Lewis	1	2	–	20	27	13.50	–	–	–
A.McGrath	4	5	–	81	201	40.20	–	2	3
D.L.Maddy	3	4	–	24	46	11.50	–	–	4
S.I.Mahmood	8	11	1	34	81	8.10	–	–	–
E.J.G.Morgan	6	8	–	130	256	32.00	1	–	4
G.Onions	8	10	7	17*	30	10.00	–	–	3
M.S.Panesar	39	51	17	26	187	5.50	–	–	9
D.J.Pattinson	1	2	–	13	21	10.50	–	–	–
K.P.Pietersen	71	123	6	227	5666	48.42	17	21	44
L.E.Plunkett	9	13	2	44*	126	11.45	–	–	3
M.J.Prior	40	61	11	131*	2148	42.96	4	16	117/4
M.R.Ramprakash	52	92	6	154	2350	27.32	2	12	39
C.M.W.Read	15	23	4	55	360	18.94	–	1	48/6
C.P.Schofield	2	3	–	57	67	22.33	–	1	–
O.A.Shah	6	10	–	88	269	26.90	–	2	2
A.Shahzad	1	1	–	5	5	5.00	–	–	2
R.J.Sidebottom	22	31	11	31	313	15.65	–	–	5
A.J.Strauss	82	147	6	177	6084	43.14	19	24	94
G.P.Swann	29	36	6	85	741	24.70	–	4	25
J.C.Tredwell	1	1	–	37	37	37.00	–	–	1
C.T.Tremlett	9	12	3	25*	69	9.85	–	–	1
M.E.Trescothick	76	143	10	219	5825	43.79	14	29	95
I.J.L.Trott	18	30	4	226	1600	61.53	5	5	9

ENGLAND – BOWLING

	O	M	R	W	Avge	Best	5wI	10wM
K.Ali	36	5	136	5	27.20	3- 80	–	–
J.M.Anderson	2009.2	448	6595	212	31.10	7- 43	10	1
G.J.Batty	232.2	34	733	11	66.63	3- 55	–	–
I.R.Bell	18	3	76	1	76.00	1- 33	–	–
I.D.Blackwell	19	2	71	0	–	–	–	–
R.S.Bopara	49.2	7	199	1	199.00	1- 39	–	–
T.T.Bresnan	247	72	707	25	28.28	4- 50	–	–
S.C.J.Broad	1115.3	235	3489	99	35.24	6- 91	3	–
R.Clarke	29	11	60	4	15.00	2- 7	–	–
P.D.Collingwood	317.3	51	1018	17	59.88	3- 23	–	–
A.N.Cook	1	0	1	0	–	–	–	–
D.G.Cork	1279.4	264	3906	131	29.81	7- 43	5	–
R.D.B.Croft	769.5	195	1825	49	37.24	5- 95	1	–
R.K.J.Dawson	186	20	677	11	61.54	4-134	–	–
S.T.Finn	304.4	64	1207	46	26.23	6-125	3	–
S.J.Harmison	2198.4	426	7091	222	31.94	7- 12	8	1
M.J.Hoggard	2318.1	493	7564	248	30.50	7- 61	7	1
S.P.Jones	470.1	78	1666	59	28.23	6- 53	3	–
A.Khan	29	1	122	1	122.00	1-111	–	–
J.Lewis	41	9	122	3	40.66	3- 68	–	–
A.McGrath	17	1	56	4	14.00	3- 16	–	–
D.L.Maddy	14	1	40	0	–	–	–	–
S.I.Mahmood	188.2	25	762	20	38.10	4- 22	–	–
G.Onions	238.1	43	869	28	31.03	5- 38	1	–
M.S.Panesar	1507	308	4331	126	34.37	6- 37	8	1
D.J.Pattinson	30.1	2	96	2	48.00	2- 95	–	–
K.P.Pietersen	145.3	10	584	5	116.80	1- 0	–	–
L.E.Plunkett	256.2	40	916	23	39.82	3- 17	–	–
M.R.Ramprakash	149.1	16	477	4	119.25	1- 2	–	–
C.P.Schofield	18	2	73	0	–	–	–	–
O.A.Shah	5	0	31	0	–	–	–	–
A.Shahzad	17	4	63	4	15.75	3- 45	–	–
R.J.Sidebottom	802	188	2231	79	28.24	7- 47	5	1
G.P.Swann	1238.3	260	3598	128	28.10	6- 65	10	1
J.C.Tredwell	65	13	181	6	30.16	4- 82	–	–
C.T.Tremlett	265.4	64	783	30	26.10	5- 87	1	–
M.E.Trescothick	50	6	155	1	155.00	1- 34	–	–
I.J.L.Trott	19	0	86	1	86.00	1- 16	–	–

TEST

AUSTRALIA – BATTING AND FIELDING

	M	I	NO	HS	Runs	Avge	100	50	Ct/St
M.A.Beer	1	2	1	2*	4	4.00	–	–	1
D.E.Bollinger	12	14	7	21	54	7.71	–	–	2
M.J.Clarke	69	114	12	168	4742	46.49	14	20	69
X.J.Doherty	2	3	–	16	27	9.00	–	–	–
P.R.George	1	2	–	2	2	1.00	–	–	–
B.J.Haddin	32	54	6	169	1904	39.66	3	8	118/3
R.J.Harris	5	7	2	18*	42	8.40	–	–	1
N.M.Hauritz	17	24	7	75	426	25.05	–	2	3
B.W.Hilfenhaus	17	26	10	56*	242	15.12	–	1	5
P.J.Hughes	10	19	1	160	712	39.55	2	2	3
M.E.K.Hussey	59	103	12	195	4650	51.09	13	24	57
M.G.Johnson	42	60	8	123*	1152	22.15	1	6	10
S.M.Katich	56	99	6	157	4188	45.03	10	25	39
U.T.Khawaja	1	2	–	37	58	29.00	–	–	–
A.B.McDonald	4	6	1	68	107	21.40	–	1	2
C.J.McKay	1	1	–	10	10	10.00	–	–	1
M.J.North	21	35	2	128	1171	35.48	5	4	17
T.D.Paine	4	8	–	92	287	35.87	–	2	16/1
R.T.Ponting	152	259	28	257	12363	53.51	39	56	178
C.J.L.Rogers	1	2	–	15	19	9.50	–	–	1
P.M.Siddle	22	31	7	43	410	17.08	–	–	12
S.P.D.Smith	5	10	1	77	259	28.77	–	2	3
S.W.Tait	3	5	2	8	20	6.66	–	–	1
S.R.Watson	27	49	2	126	1953	41.55	2	15	21

AUSTRALIA – BOWLING

	O	M	R	W	Avge	Best	5wI	10wM
M.A.Beer	38	3	112	1	112.00	1-112	–	–
D.E.Bollinger	400.1	78	1296	50	25.92	5- 28	2	–
M.J.Clarke	284	46	822	21	39.14	6- 9	1	–
X.J.Doherty	75.5	11	306	3	102.00	2- 41	–	–
P.R.George	28	3	77	2	38.50	2- 48	–	–
R.J.Harris	154.1	32	488	20	24.40	6- 47	1	–
N.M.Hauritz	700	143	2204	63	34.98	5- 53	2	–
B.W.Hilfenhaus	630.3	143	1906	55	34.65	4- 57	–	–
M.E.K.Hussey	31	4	105	2	52.50	1- 3	–	–
M.G.Johnson	1614.5	294	5378	181	29.71	8- 61	7	2
S.M.Katich	173.1	21	635	21	30.23	6- 65	1	–
A.B.McDonald	122	40	300	9	33.33	3- 25	–	–
C.J.McKay	28	5	101	1	101.00	1- 56	–	–
M.J.North	209.4	37	591	14	42.21	6- 55	1	–
R.T.Ponting	89.5	23	242	5	48.40	1- 0	–	–
P.M.Siddle	774.2	191	2376	74	32.10	6- 54	4	–
S.P.D.Smith	62	10	220	3	73.33	3- 51	–	–
S.W.Tait	69	6	302	5	60.40	3- 97	–	–
S.R.Watson	433.3	85	1351	43	31.41	6- 33	2	–

TEST **SOUTH AFRICA – BATTING AND FIELDING**

	M	I	NO	HS	Runs	Avge	100	50	Ct/St
H.M.Amla	51	90	7	253*	3897	46.95	12	19	46
J.Botha	5	6	2	25	83	20.75	–	–	3
M.V.Boucher	138	194	23	125	5295	30.96	5	34	497/22
A.B.de Villiers	66	113	13	278*	4741	47.41	12	23	93/1
F.de Wet	2	2	–	20	20	10.00	–	–	1
J.P.Duminy	12	20	2	166	518	28.77	1	3	12
A.J.Hall	21	33	4	163	760	26.20	1	3	16
P.L.Harris	37	48	5	46	460	10.69	–	–	16
C.W.Henderson	7	7	–	30	65	9.28	–	–	2
J.H.Kallis	144	244	37	201*	11864	57.31	40	54	162
N.D.McKenzie	58	94	7	226	3253	37.39	5	16	54
R.McLaren	1	1	1	33*	33	–	–	–	–
M.Morkel	31	37	4	40	481	14.57	–	–	7
M.Ntini	101	116	45	32*	699	9.84	–	–	25
W.D.Parnell	3	2	–	22	34	17.00	–	–	1
A.N.Petersen	9	17	–	100	572	33.64	1	3	5
A.G.Prince	62	98	16	162*	3556	43.36	11	10	42
G.C.Smith	90	157	9	277	7445	50.30	22	29	116
D.W.Steyn	46	58	13	76	620	13.77	–	1	13
L.L.Tsotsobe	5	5	2	8*	19	6.33	–	–	1
M.van Jaarsveld	9	15	2	73	397	30.53	–	3	11
C.M.Willoughby	2	–	–	–	–	–	–	–	–

SOUTH AFRICA – BOWLING

	O	M	R	W	Avge	Best	5wI	10wM
H.M.Amla	7	0	28	0	–	–	–	–
J.Botha	169.3	29	573	17	33.70	4- 56	–	–
M.V.Boucher	1.2	0	6	1	6.00	1- 6	–	–
A.B.de Villiers	33	6	99	2	49.50	2- 49	–	–
F.de Wet	71	19	186	6	31.00	4- 55	–	–
J.P.Duminy	111.5	11	408	11	37.09	3- 89	–	–
A.J.Hall	500.1	95	1617	45	35.93	3- 1	–	–
P.L.Harris	1468.1	336	3901	103	37.87	6-127	3	–
C.W.Henderson	327	79	928	22	42.18	4-116	–	–
J.H.Kallis	3046.1	769	8605	269	31.98	6- 54	5	–
N.D.McKenzie	15	0	68	0	–	–	–	–
R.McLaren	13	4	43	1	43.00	1- 30	–	–
M.Morkel	1018.1	187	3415	113	30.22	5- 20	4	–
M.Ntini	3472.2	759	11242	390	28.82	7- 37	18	4
W.D.Parnell	51	5	227	5	45.40	2- 17	–	–
A.N.Petersen	12	1	36	1	36.00	1- 2	–	–
A.G.Prince	16	1	47	1	47.00	1- 2	–	–
G.C.Smith	224.2	28	832	8	104.00	2-145	–	–
D.W.Steyn	1585.5	303	5526	238	23.21	7- 51	16	4
L.L.Tsotsobe	145	35	448	9	49.77	3- 43	–	–
M.van Jaarsveld	7	0	28	0	–	–	–	–
C.M.Willoughby	50	18	125	1	125.00	1- 47	–	–

TEST   **WEST INDIES – BATTING AND FIELDING**

	M	I	NO	HS	Runs	Avge	100	50	Ct/St
A.B.Barath	4	7	–	104	200	28.57	1	1	2
C.S.Baugh	8	13	1	68	256	21.33	–	2	7/1
S.J.Benn	17	27	3	42	381	15.87	–	–	7
B.J.Bess	1	2	1	11*	11	11.00	–	–	–
D.J.Bravo	40	71	1	113	2200	31.42	3	13	41
D.M.Bravo	3	4	1	80	206	68.66	–	3	1
S.Chanderpaul	129	219	34	203*	9063	48.98	22	55	52
C.D.Collymore	30	52	27	16*	197	7.88	–	–	6
N.Deonarine	8	13	1	82	370	30.83	–	2	5
T.M.Dowlin	6	11	–	95	343	31.18	–	3	5
C.H.Gayle	91	159	6	333	6373	41.65	13	33	85
B.P.Nash	18	27	–	114	1049	38.85	2	8	6
N.T.Pascal	2	2	–	10	12	6.00	–	–	1
D.Ramdin	42	73	8	166	1482	22.80	1	8	119/3
R.Rampaul	5	9	3	40*	114	19.00	–	–	1
D.M.Richards	3	6	–	69	125	20.83	–	1	4
K.A.J.Roach	10	15	5	17	72	7.20	–	–	5
A.D.Russell	1	1	–	2	2	2.00	–	–	1
D.J.G.Sammy	11	18	–	48	301	16.72	–	1	11
R.R.Sarwan	83	146	8	291	5759	41.73	15	31	50
S.Shillingford	5	7	1	27	65	10.83	–	–	3
D.S.Smith	32	56	2	108	1370	25.37	1	5	27
J.E.Taylor	29	46	6	106	629	15.72	1	1	5
G.C.Tonge	1	2	1	23*	25	25.00	–	–	–

WEST INDIES – BOWLING

	O	M	R	W	Avge	Best	5wI	10wM
A.B.Barath	1	0	3	0	–	–	–	–
S.J.Benn	730.1	126	2112	51	41.41	6- 81	3	–
B.J.Bess	13	0	92	1	92.00	1- 65	–	–
D.J.Bravo	1077.4	213	3426	86	39.83	6- 55	2	–
S.Chanderpaul	280	50	845	8	105.62	1- 2	–	–
C.D.Collymore	1056.1	245	3004	93	32.30	7- 57	4	1
N.Deonarine	83.5	21	246	4	61.50	2- 74	–	–
T.M.Dowlin	1	0	3	0	–	–	–	–
C.H.Gayle	1142.5	224	2995	72	41.59	5- 34	2	–
B.P.Nash	73	13	217	2	108.50	1- 21	–	–
N.T.Pascal	17	2	59	0	–	–	–	–
R.Rampaul	122	23	439	4	109.75	1- 21	–	–
K.A.J.Roach	314.4	63	1017	36	28.25	6- 48	2	–
A.D.Russell	23	2	104	1	104.00	1- 73	–	–
D.J.G.Sammy	302.4	57	900	29	31.03	7- 66	3	–
R.R.Sarwan	337	33	1163	23	50.56	4- 37	–	–
S.Shillingford	241.2	24	795	14	56.78	4-123	–	–
D.S.Smith	1	0	3	0	–	–	–	–
J.E.Taylor	822.3	150	2923	82	35.64	5- 11	3	–
G.C.Tonge	28	3	113	1	113.00	1- 28	–	–

TEST

NEW ZEALAND – BATTING AND FIELDING

	M	I	NO	HS	Runs	Avge	100	50	Ct/St
A.R.Adams	1	2	–	11	18	9.00	–	–	1
B.J.Arnel	5	10	3	8*	34	4.85	–	–	3
H.K.Bennett	1	1	–	4	4	4.00	–	–	–
S.E.Bond	18	20	7	41*	168	12.92	–	–	8
G.D.Elliott	5	9	1	25	86	10.75	–	–	2
D.R.Flynn	16	29	5	95	689	28.70	–	4	7
J.E.C.Franklin	27	38	6	122*	683	21.34	1	2	11
P.G.Fulton	10	16	1	75	314	20.93	–	1	12
M.J.Guptill	15	28	1	189	944	34.96	1	6	11
G.J.Hopkins	4	7	1	15	71	11.83	–	–	9
P.J.Ingram	2	4	–	42	61	15.25	–	–	–
B.B.McCullum	57	97	6	225	3389	37.24	6	19	167/11
T.G.McIntosh	17	33	2	136	854	27.54	2	4	10
A.J.McKay	1	2	1	20*	25	25.00	–	–	–
H.J.H.Marshall	13	19	2	160	652	38.35	2	2	1
C.S.Martin	61	89	46	12*	109	2.53	–	–	13
I.E.O'Brien	22	34	5	31	219	7.55	–	–	7
J.S.Patel	12	16	3	27*	167	12.84	–	–	7
J.D.Ryder	16	29	2	201	1211	44.85	3	6	10
M.S.Sinclair	33	56	5	214	1635	32.05	3	4	31
T.G.Southee	13	22	4	77*	385	21.38	–	2	4
S.B.Styris	29	48	4	170	1586	36.04	5	6	23
L.R.P.L.Taylor	30	55	1	154*	2221	41.12	5	12	52
D.R.Tuffey	26	36	10	80*	427	16.42	–	1	15
D.L.Vettori	104	159	22	140	4159	30.35	6	22	57
L.Vincent	23	40	1	224	1332	34.15	3	9	19
B.J.Watling	5	10	2	60*	203	25.37	–	1	7
K.S.Williamson	5	9	–	131	299	33.22	1	2	1
R.A.Young	2	4	–	57	103	25.75	–	1	3

NEW ZEALAND – BOWLING

	O	M	R	W	Avge	Best	5wI	10wM
A.R.Adams	31.4	5	105	6	17.50	3- 44	–	–
B.J.Arnel	156	35	502	9	55.77	4- 95	–	–
H.K.Bennett	15	2	47	0	–	–	–	–
S.E.Bond	562	113	1922	87	22.09	6- 51	5	1
G.D.Elliott	47	9	140	4	35.00	2- 8	–	–
J.E.C.Franklin	747.1	136	2648	80	33.10	6-119	3	–
M.J.Guptill	32.2	3	136	3	45.33	3- 37	–	–
B.B.McCullum	6	1	18	0	–	–	–	–
A.J.McKay	31	5	120	1	120.00	1-120	–	–
H.J.H.Marshall	1	0	4	0	–	–	–	–
C.S.Martin	2036	426	6899	199	34.66	6- 54	9	1
I.E.O'Brien	732.2	158	2429	73	33.27	6- 75	1	–
J.S.Patel	556	121	1794	40	44.85	5-110	1	–
J.D.Ryder	82	23	280	5	56.00	2- 7	–	–
M.S.Sinclair	7	2	14	0	–	–	–	–
T.G.Southee	433.1	86	1489	35	42.54	5- 55	1	–
S.B.Styris	326.4	77	1015	20	50.75	3- 28	–	–
L.R.P.L.Taylor	15	3	43	2	21.50	2- 4	–	–
D.R.Tuffey	812.5	209	2445	77	31.75	6- 54	2	–
D.L.Vettori	4449.4	1105	11613	344	33.75	7- 87	19	3
L.Vincent	1	0	2	0	–	–	–	–
K.S.Williamson	40	0	176	2	88.00	1- 45	–	–

TEST **INDIA – BATTING AND FIELDING**

	M	I	NO	HS	Runs	Avge	100	50	Ct/St
S.Badrinath	2	3	–	56	63	21.00	–	1	2
M.S.Dhoni	54	82	9	148	2925	40.06	4	20	148/25
R.S.Dravid	149	257	29	270	12040	52.80	31	59	199
G.Gambhir	38	68	5	206	3234	51.33	9	16	29
Harbhajan Singh	93	129	21	115	2008	18.59	2	8	42
K.D.Karthik	23	37	1	129	1000	27.77	1	7	51/5
M.Kartik	8	10	1	43	88	9.77	–	–	2
Z.Khan	78	103	22	75	1045	12.90	–	3	18
V.V.S.Laxman	120	198	31	281	7903	47.32	16	49	122
A.Mishra	10	13	2	50	205	18.63	–	1	6
A.Mithun	3	4	–	46	120	30.00	–	–	–
P.P.Ojha	11	13	9	18*	67	16.75	–	–	3
C.A.Pujara	3	5	–	72	107	21.40	–	1	6
S.K.Raina	8	12	1	120	373	33.90	1	2	9
W.P.Saha	1	2	–	36	36	18.00	–	–	–
V.Sehwag	86	148	6	319	7611	53.59	22	26	66
I.Sharma	31	43	19	31*	319	13.29	–	–	10
S.Sreesanth	24	34	11	35	263	11.43	–	–	5
S.R.Tendulkar	177	290	32	248*	14692	56.94	51	59	106
J.D.Unadkat	1	2	1	1*	2	2.00	–	–	–
M.Vijay	9	14	–	139	537	38.35	1	2	7
Yuvraj Singh	34	52	6	169	1639	35.63	3	9	30

INDIA – BOWLING

	O	M	R	W	Avge	Best	5wI	10wM
M.S.Dhoni	3	0	19	0	–	–	–	–
R.S.Dravid	20	4	39	1	39.00	1- 18	–	–
Harbhajan Singh	4413.5	809	12518	393	31.85	8- 84	25	5
M.Kartik	322	74	820	24	34.16	4- 44	–	–
Z.Khan	2626	528	8658	271	31.94	7- 87	10	1
V.V.S.Laxman	54	12	126	2	63.00	1- 2	–	–
A.Mishra	475	72	1429	36	39.69	5- 71	1	–
A.Mithun	92	12	372	6	62.00	4-105	–	–
P.P.Ojha	589.5	124	1697	42	40.40	4-107	–	–
S.K.Raina	55	7	214	6	35.66	2- 1	–	–
V.Sehwag	541.3	70	1643	39	42.12	5-104	1	–
I.Sharma	940.4	166	3238	90	35.97	5-118	1	–
S.Sreesanth	792.1	150	2778	79	35.16	5- 40	3	–
S.R.Tendulkar	682.4	82	2388	45	53.06	3- 10	–	–
J.D.Unadkat	26	4	101	0	–	–	–	–
Yuvraj Singh	125.1	13	431	8	53.87	2- 9	–	–

TEST   PAKISTAN – BATTING AND FIELDING

	M	I	NO	HS	Runs	Avge	100	50	Ct/St
Abdur Rauf	3	6	–	31	52	8.66	–	–	–
Abdur Rehman	6	7	1	60	128	21.33	–	1	1
Adnan Akmal	4	5	1	44	95	23.75	–	–	16/1
Asad Shafiq	3	4	–	83	168	42.00	–	2	1
Azhar Ali	10	19	2	92*	629	37.00	–	6	7
Azhar Mahmood	21	34	4	136	900	30.00	3	1	14
Danish Kaneria	61	84	33	29	360	7.05	–	–	18
Faisal Iqbal	26	44	2	139	1124	26.76	1	8	22
Fawad Alam	3	6	–	168	250	41.66	1	–	3
Imran Farhat	39	75	2	128	2327	31.87	3	14	40
Kamran Akmal	53	92	6	158*	2648	30.79	6	12	184/22
Khurram Manzoor	7	12	1	93	326	29.63	–	3	3
Misbah-ul-Haq	23	40	6	161*	1459	42.91	2	10	28
Mohammad Aamer	14	28	6	30*	278	12.63	–	–	3
Mohammad Asif	23	38	13	29	141	5.64	–	–	3
Mohammad Hafeez	15	29	2	104	849	31.44	2	4	5
Mohammad Sami	35	54	14	49	475	11.87	–	–	7
Mohammad Yousuf	90	156	12	223	7530	52.29	24	33	65
Naved-ul-Hasan	9	15	3	42*	239	19.91	–	–	3
Saeed Ajmal	9	16	7	50	98	10.88	–	1	2
Salman Butt	33	62	–	122	1889	30.46	3	10	12
Sarfraz Ahmed	1	2	–	5	6	3.00	–	–	4
Shahid Afridi	27	48	1	156	1716	36.51	5	8	10
Shoaib Malik	32	54	6	148*	1606	33.45	2	8	16
Tanvir Ahmed	3	3	–	30	55	18.33	–	–	1
Taufiq Umar	29	54	3	135	2002	39.25	4	11	36
Umar Akmal	13	25	2	129	822	35.73	1	5	7
Umar Amin	4	8	–	33	99	12.37	–	–	1
Umar Gul	34	48	7	65*	490	11.95	–	1	7
Wahab Riaz	5	6	2	27	41	10.25	–	–	1
Yasir Arafat	3	3	1	50*	94	47.00	–	1	–
Yasir Hameed	25	49	3	170	1491	32.41	2	8	20
Younus Khan	67	119	8	313	5617	50.60	17	23	74
Zulqarnain Haider	1	2	–	88	88	44.00	–	1	2

PAKISTAN – BOWLING

	O	M	R	W	Avge	Best	5wI	10wM
Abdur Rauf	75	11	278	6	46.33	2- 59	–	–
Abdur Rehman	394.1	74	1079	31	34.80	4-105	–	–
Azhar Ali	1	0	9	0	–	–	–	–
Azhar Mahmood	502.3	111	1402	39	35.94	4- 50	–	–
Danish Kaneria	2949.3	517	9082	261	34.79	7- 77	15	2
Faisal Iqbal	1	0	7	0	–	–	–	–
Imran Farhat	71.1	4	284	3	94.66	2- 69	–	–
Mohammad Aamer	477.5	103	1484	51	29.09	6- 84	3	–
Mohammad Asif	861.5	200	2583	106	24.36	6- 41	7	1
Mohammad Hafeez	188	34	482	8	60.25	2- 48	–	–
Mohammad Sami	1224.5	192	4391	84	52.27	5- 36	2	–
Mohammad Yousuf	1	0	3	0	–	–	–	–
Naved-ul-Hasan	260.5	36	1044	18	58.00	3- 30	–	–
Saeed Ajmal	457.5	70	1311	33	39.72	5- 82	1	–
Salman Butt	22.5	1	106	1	106.00	1- 36	–	–
Shahid Afridi	532.2	69	1709	48	35.60	5- 52	1	–
Shoaib Malik	374.1	47	1291	21	61.47	4- 42	–	–
Tanvir Ahmed	90.5	15	361	14	25.78	6-120	1	–
Taufiq Umar	13	2	44	0	–	–	–	–
Umar Amin	22	4	63	3	21.00	1- 7	–	–
Umar Gul	1200.2	184	4241	125	33.92	6-135	4	–
Wahab Riaz	123.2	23	425	13	32.69	5- 63	1	–
Yasir Arafat	104.3	12	438	9	48.66	5-161	1	–
Yasir Hameed	13	1	72	0	–	–	–	–
Younus Khan	110	16	407	7	58.14	2- 23	–	–

TEST　　　　**SRI LANKA – BATTING AND FIELDING**

	M	I	NO	HS	Runs	Avge	100	50	Ct/St
T.M.Dilshan	66	105	11	168	3990	42.44	11	16	73
C.R.D.Fernando	35	40	13	36*	198	7.33	–	–	10
H.M.R.K.B.Herath	24	29	6	80*	311	13.52	–	1	5
D.P.M.D.Jayawardena	116	190	13	374	9527	53.82	28	38	165
H.A.P.W.Jayawardena	36	45	6	154*	1172	30.05	2	3	67/25
H.K.S.R.Kaluhalamulla	3	3	–	12	26	8.66	–	–	–
K.M.D.N.Kulasekara	12	17	1	64	262	16.37	–	1	4
R.A.S.Lakmal	2	–	–	–	–	–	–	–	–
S.L.Malinga	30	37	13	64	275	11.45	–	1	7
A.D.Mathews	13	17	2	99	527	35.13	–	2	4
B.A.W.Mendis	15	15	4	78	151	13.72	–	1	2
M.T.T.Mirando	10	14	3	15*	94	8.54	–	–	3
M.Muralitharan	132	162	56	67	1259	11.87	–	1	70
N.T.Paranavitana	16	28	2	111	963	37.03	2	5	7
K.T.G.D.Prasad	6	5	–	47	113	22.60	–	–	1
T.T.Samaraweera	63	98	17	231	4395	54.25	12	25	37
K.C.Sangakkara	94	156	12	287	8244	57.25	24	34	163/20
W.P.J.U.C.Vaas	111	162	35	100*	3089	24.32	1	13	31
U.W.M.B.C.A.Welagedara	6	6	2	8	27	6.75	–	–	2

SRI LANKA – BOWLING

	O	M	R	W	Avge	Best	5wI	10wM
T.M.Dilshan	217.2	41	633	19	33.31	4- 10	–	–
C.R.D.Fernando	900.4	132	3260	90	36.22	5- 42	3	–
H.M.R.K.B.Herath	944.1	168	2820	78	36.15	5- 99	4	–
D.P.M.D.Jayawardena	91.1	18	292	6	48.66	2- 32	–	–
H.K.S.R.Kaluhalamulla	175.3	28	567	14	40.50	5- 82	1	–
K.M.D.N.Kulasekara	279.4	56	879	26	33.80	4- 21	–	–
R.A.S.Lakmal	35.3	6	132	3	44.00	2- 84	–	–
S.L.Malinga	868.1	112	3349	101	33.15	5- 50	3	–
A.D.Mathews	131	24	421	6	70.16	1- 13	–	–
B.A.W.Mendis	644.3	98	1948	61	31.93	6-117	3	1
M.T.T.Mirando	278	35	1040	28	37.14	5- 83	1	–
M.Muralitharan	7285.5	1786	18023	795	22.67	9- 51	67	22
N.T.Paranavitana	15	0	76	1	76.00	1- 26	–	–
K.T.G.D.Prasad	174.2	12	784	13	60.30	3- 82	–	–
T.T.Samaraweera	215.1	36	679	14	48.50	4- 49	–	–
K.C.Sangakkara	11	0	38	0	–	–	–	–
W.P.U.C.J.Vaas	3906.2	895	10501	355	29.58	7- 71	12	2
U.W.M.B.C.A.Welagedara	165.3	19	707	12	58.91	4- 87	–	–

TEST

ZIMBABWE – BATTING AND FIELDING

	M	I	NO	HS	Runs	Avge	100	50	Ct/St
S.M.Ervine	5	8	–	86	261	32.62	–	3	7
M.W.Goodwin	19	37	4	166*	1414	42.84	3	8	10

ZIMBABWE – BOWLING

	O	M	R	W	Avge	Best	5wI	10wM
S.M.Ervine	95	18	388	9	43.11	4-116	–	–
M.W.Goodwin	19.5	3	69	0	–	–	–	–

BANGLADESH – BATTING AND FIELDING

	M	I	NO	HS	Runs	Avge	100	50	Ct/St
Abdur Razzak	8	15	5	33	160	16.00	–	–	3
Aftab Ahmed	16	31	3	82*	582	20.78	–	1	7
Imrul Kayes	13	26	–	75	453	17.42	–	1	12
Jahurul Islam	3	6	–	46	114	19.00	–	–	3
Junaid Siddique	18	35	–	106	942	26.91	1	7	11
Mahmudullah	9	18	2	115	590	36.87	1	4	7
Mohammad Ashraful	55	107	4	158*	2306	22.38	5	7	24
Mushfiqur Rahim	23	45	3	101	1140	27.14	1	6	32/7
Naeem Islam	4	8	1	59*	180	25.71	–	1	1
Raqibul Hasan	7	14	–	65	268	19.14	–	1	7
Robiul Islam	1	2	2	9*	9	–	–	–	–
Rubel Hossain	8	15	6	17	43	4.77	–	–	4
Shafiul Islam	5	10	1	53	137	15.22	–	1	–
Shahadat Hossain	29	55	15	40	394	9.85	–	–	7
Shahriar Nafees	16	32	–	138	835	26.09	1	4	12
Shakib Al Hasan	21	40	2	100	1179	31.02	1	5	8
Tamim Iqbal	19	36	–	151	1445	40.13	4	8	8

BANGLADESH – BOWLING

	O	M	R	W	Avge	Best	5wI	10wM
Abdur Razzak	313.3	41	1079	16	67.43	3- 93	–	–
Aftab Ahmed	57.2	8	237	5	47.40	2- 31	–	–
Imrul Kayes	1	0	7	0	–	–	–	–
Junaid Siddique	3	0	11	0	–	–	–	–
Mahmudullah	227.5	21	799	22	36.31	5- 51	1	–
Mohammad Ashraful	265.1	11	1188	20	59.40	2- 42	–	–
Naeem Islam	46	3	150	1	150.00	1- 11	–	–
Raqibul Hasan	3	1	5	1	5.00	1- 0	–	–
Robiul Islam	23	2	119	0	–	–	–	–
Rubel Hossain	213	10	997	12	83.08	5-166	–	–
Shafiul Islam	133	12	502	7	71.71	3- 86	–	–
Shahadat Hossain	722.2	74	2992	66	45.33	6- 27	4	–
Shakib Al Hasan	847.1	172	2410	75	32.13	7- 36	7	–
Tamim Iqbal	4	0	10	0	–	–	–	–

INTERNATIONAL TEST MATCH RESULTS

Matches completed by 1 April 2011.

	Opponents	Tests	E	A	SA	WI	NZ	I	P	SL	Z	B	Tied	Drawn
England	Australia	326	102	133	–	–	–	–	–	–	–	–	–	91
	South Africa	138	56	–	29	–	–	–	–	–	–	–	–	53
	West Indies	145	43	–	–	53	–	–	–	–	–	–	–	49
	New Zealand	94	45	–	–	–	8	–	–	–	–	–	–	41
	India	99	34	–	–	–	–	19	–	–	–	–	–	46
	Pakistan	71	22	–	–	–	–	–	13	–	–	–	–	36
	Sri Lanka	21	8	–	–	–	–	–	–	6	–	–	–	7
	Zimbabwe	6	3	–	–	–	–	–	–	–	0	–	–	3
	Bangladesh	8	8	–	–	–	–	–	–	–	–	0	–	–
Australia	South Africa	83	–	47	18	–	–	–	–	–	–	–	–	18
	West Indies	108	–	52	–	32	–	–	–	–	–	–	1	23
	New Zealand	50	–	26	–	–	7	–	–	–	–	–	–	17
	India	78	–	34	–	–	–	20	–	–	–	–	1	23
	Pakistan	57	–	28	–	–	–	–	12	–	–	–	–	17
	Sri Lanka	20	–	13	–	–	–	–	–	1	–	–	–	6
	Zimbabwe	3	–	3	–	–	–	–	–	–	0	–	–	–
	Bangladesh	4	–	4	–	–	–	–	–	–	–	0	–	–
South Africa	West Indies	25	–	–	16	3	–	–	–	–	–	–	–	6
	New Zealand	35	–	–	20	–	4	–	–	–	–	–	–	11
	India	27	–	–	12	–	–	7	–	–	–	–	–	8
	Pakistan	18	–	–	8	–	–	–	3	–	–	–	–	7
	Sri Lanka	17	–	–	8	–	–	–	–	4	–	–	–	5
	Zimbabwe	7	–	–	6	–	–	–	–	–	0	–	–	1
	Bangladesh	8	–	–	8	–	–	–	–	–	–	0	–	–
West Indies	New Zealand	37	–	–	–	10	9	–	–	–	–	–	–	18
	India	82	–	–	–	30	–	11	–	–	–	–	–	41
	Pakistan	44	–	–	–	14	–	–	15	–	–	–	–	15
	Sri Lanka	15	–	–	–	3	–	–	–	6	–	–	–	6
	Zimbabwe	6	–	–	–	4	–	–	–	–	–	–	–	2
	Bangladesh	6	–	–	–	3	–	–	–	–	–	2	–	1
New Zealand	India	50	–	–	–	–	9	16	–	–	–	–	–	25
	Pakistan	50	–	–	–	–	7	–	23	–	–	–	–	20
	Sri Lanka	26	–	–	–	–	9	–	–	7	–	–	–	10
	Zimbabwe	13	–	–	–	–	7	–	–	–	0	–	–	6
	Bangladesh	9	–	–	–	–	8	–	–	–	–	0	–	1
India	Pakistan	59	–	–	–	–	–	9	12	–	–	–	–	38
	Sri Lanka	35	–	–	–	–	–	14	–	6	–	–	–	15
	Zimbabwe	11	–	–	–	–	–	7	–	–	2	–	–	2
	Bangladesh	7	–	–	–	–	–	6	–	–	–	0	–	1
Pakistan	Sri Lanka	37	–	–	–	–	–	–	15	9	–	–	–	13
	Zimbabwe	14	–	–	–	–	–	–	8	–	2	–	–	4
	Bangladesh	6	–	–	–	–	–	–	6	–	–	0	–	–
Sri Lanka	Zimbabwe	15	–	–	–	–	–	–	–	10	0	–	–	5
	Bangladesh	12	–	–	–	–	–	–	–	12	–	0	–	–
Zimbabwe	Bangladesh	8	–	–	–	–	–	–	–	–	4	1	–	3
		1990	321	340	125	152	68	109	107	61	8	3	2	694

	Tests	Won	Lost	Drawn	Tied	Toss Won
England	908	321	261	326	–	439
Australia	729	340	192	195	2	368
South Africa	358	125	124	109	–	172
West Indies	468	152	154	161	1	244
New Zealand	364	68	147	149	–	184
India	448	109	139	199	1	226
Pakistan	356	107	99	150	–	168
Sri Lanka	198	61	70	67	–	104
Zimbabwe	83	8	49	26	–	49
Bangladesh	68	3	59	6	–	36

INTERNATIONAL TEST CRICKET RECORDS

(To 1 April 2011)

TEAM RECORDS

HIGHEST INNINGS TOTALS

952-6d	Sri Lanka v India	Colombo (RPS)	1997-98
903-7d	England v Australia	The Oval	1938
849	England v West Indies	Kingston	1929-30
790-3d	West Indies v Pakistan	Kingston	1957-58
765-6d	Pakistan v Sri Lanka	Karachi	2008-09
760-7d	Sri Lanka v India	Ahmedabad	2009-10
758-8d	Australia v West Indies	Kingston	1954-55
756-5d	Sri Lanka v South Africa	Colombo (SSC)	2006
751-5d	West Indies v England	St John's	2003-04
749-9d	West Indies v England	Bridgetown	2008-09
747	West Indies v South Africa	St John's	2004-05
735-6d	Australia v Zimbabwe	Perth	2003-04
729-6d	Australia v England	Lord's	1930
726-9d	India v Sri Lanka	Mumbai	2009-10
713-3d	Sri Lanka v Zimbabwe	Bulawayo	2003-04
708	Pakistan v England	The Oval	1987
707	India v Sri Lanka	Colombo (SSC)	2010
705-7d	India v Australia	Sydney	2003-04
701	Australia v England	The Oval	1934
699-5	Pakistan v India	Lahore	1989-90
695	Australia v England	The Oval	1930
692-8d	West Indies v England	The Oval	1995
687-8d	West Indies v England	The Oval	1976
682-6d	South Africa v England	Lord's	2003
681-8d	West Indies v England	Port-of-Spain	1953-54
679-7d	Pakistan v India	Lahore	2005-06
676-7	India v Sri Lanka	Kanpur	1986-87
675-5d	India v Pakistan	Multan	2003-04
674-6	Pakistan v India	Faisalabad	1984-85
674-6d	Australia v England	Cardiff	2009
674	Australia v India	Adelaide	1947-48
671-4	New Zealand v Sri Lanka	Wellington	1990-91
668	Australia v West Indies	Bridgetown	1954-55
664	India v England	The Oval	2007
660-5d	West Indies v New Zealand	Wellington	1994-95

659-8d	Australia v England	Sydney	1946-47
658-8d	England v Australia	Nottingham	1938
658-9d	South Africa v West Indies	Durban	2003-04
657-7d	India v Australia	Calcutta	2000-01
657-8d	Pakistan v West Indies	Bridgetown	1957-58
656-8d	Australia v England	Manchester	1964
654-5	England v South Africa	Durban	1938-39
653-4d	England v India	Lord's	1990
653-4d	Australia v England	Leeds	1993
652-7d	England v India	Madras	1984-85
652-7d	Australia v South Africa	Johannesburg	2001-02
652-8d	West Indies v England	Lord's	1973
652	Pakistan v India	Faisalabad	1982-83
651	South Africa v Australia	Cape Town	2008-09
650-6d	Australia v West Indies	Bridgetown	1964-65

The highest for Zimbabwe is 563-9d (v WI, Harare, 2001), and for Bangladesh 488 (v Z, Chittagong, 2004-05).

LOWEST INNINGS TOTALS

1p;&-2q† One batsman absent

26	New Zealand v England	Auckland	1954-55
30	South Africa v England	Port Elizabeth	1895-96
30	South Africa v England	Birmingham	1924
35	South Africa v England	Cape Town	1898-99
36	Australia v England	Birmingham	1902
36	South Africa v Australia	Melbourne	1931-32
42	Australia v England	Sydney	1887-88
42	New Zealand v Australia	Wellington	1945-46
42†	India v England	Lord's	1974
43	South Africa v England	Cape Town	1888-89
44	Australia v England	The Oval	1896
45	England v Australia	Sydney	1886-87
45	South Africa v Australia	Melbourne	1931-32
46	England v West Indies	Port-of-Spain	1993-94
47	South Africa v England	Cape Town	1888-89
47	New Zealand v England	Lord's	1958
47	West Indies v England	Kingston	2003-04

The lowest for Pakistan is 53† (v A, Sharjah, 2002-03), for Sri Lanka 71 (v P, Kandy, 1994-95), for Zimbabwe 54 (v SA, Cape Town, 2004-05), and for Bangladesh 62 (v SL, Colombo PPS, 2006-07).

BATTING RECORDS
5000 RUNS IN TESTS

Runs			M	I	NO	HS	Avge	100	50
14692	S.R.Tendulkar	I	177	290	32	248*	56.94	51	59
12363	R.T.Ponting	A	152	259	28	257	53.51	39	56
12063	R.S.Dravid	I/ICC	150	259	29	270	52.44	31	59
11953	B.C.Lara	WI/ICC	131	232	6	400*	52.88	34	48
11947	J.H.Kallis	SA/ICC	145	246	38	201*	57.43	40	54
11174	A.R.Border	A	156	265	44	205	50.56	27	63
10927	S.R.Waugh	A	168	260	46	200	51.06	32	50
10122	S.M.Gavaskar	I	125	214	16	236*	51.12	34	45
9527	D.P.M.D.Jayawardena	SL	116	190	13	374	53.82	28	38
9063	S.Chanderpaul	WI	129	219	34	203*	48.98	22	55
8900	G.A.Gooch	E	118	215	6	333	42.58	20	46
8832	Javed Miandad	P	124	189	21	280*	52.57	23	43
8830	Inzamam-ul-Haq	P/ICC	120	200	22	329	49.60	25	46

Runs			M	I	NO	HS	Avge	100	50
8625	M.L.Hayden	A	103	184	14	380	50.73	30	29
8540	I.V.A.Richards	WI	121	182	12	291	50.23	24	45
8463	A.J.Stewart	E	133	235	21	190	39.54	15	45
8244	K.C.Sangakkara	SL	94	156	12	287	57.25	24	34
8231	D.I.Gower	E	117	204	18	215	44.25	18	39
8114	G.Boycott	E	108	193	23	246*	47.72	22	42
8032	G.St A.Sobers	WI	93	160	21	365*	57.78	26	30
8029	M.E.Waugh	A	128	209	17	153*	41.81	20	47
7903	V.V.S.Laxman	I	120	198	31	281	47.32	16	49
7728	M.A.Atherton	E	115	212	7	185*	37.70	16	46
7696	J.L.Langer	A	105	182	12	250	45.27	23	30
7694	V.Sehwag	I/ICC	87	150	6	319	53.43	22	27
7624	M.C.Cowdrey	E	114	188	15	182	44.06	22	38
7558	C.G.Greenidge	WI	108	185	16	226	44.72	19	34
7530	Mohammad Yousuf	P	90	156	12	223	52.29	24	33
7525	M.A.Taylor	A	104	186	13	334*	43.49	19	40
7515	C.H.Lloyd	WI	110	175	14	242*	46.67	19	39
7487	D.L.Haynes	WI	116	202	25	184	42.29	18	39
7457	G.C.Smith	SA/ICC	91	159	9	277	49.71	22	29
7422	D.C.Boon	A	107	190	20	200	43.65	21	32
7289	G.Kirsten	SA	101	176	15	275	45.27	21	34
7249	W.R.Hammond	E	85	140	16	336*	58.45	22	24
7212	S.C.Ganguly	I	113	188	17	239	42.17	16	35
7172	S.P.Fleming	NZ	111	189	10	274*	40.06	9	46
7110	G.S.Chappell	A	87	151	19	247*	53.86	24	31
6996	D.G.Bradman	A	52	80	10	334	99.94	29	13
6973	S.T.Jayasuriya	SL	110	188	14	340	40.07	14	31
6971	L.Hutton	E	79	138	15	364	56.67	19	33
6868	D.B.Vengsarkar	I	116	185	22	166	42.13	17	35
6806	K.F.Barrington	E	82	131	15	256	58.67	20	35
6744	G.P.Thorpe	E	100	179	28	200*	44.66	16	39
6373	C.H.Gayle	WI	91	159	6	333	41.65	13	33
6361	P.A.de Silva	SL	93	159	11	267	42.97	20	22
6227	R.B.Kanhai	WI	79	137	6	256	47.53	15	28
6215	M.Azharuddin	I	99	147	9	199	45.03	22	21
6167	H.H.Gibbs	SA	90	154	7	228	41.95	14	26
6149	R.N.Harvey	A	79	137	10	205	48.41	21	24
6084	A.J.Strauss	E	82	147	6	177	43.14	19	24
6080	G.R.Viswanath	I	91	155	10	222	41.93	14	35
5949	R.B.Richardson	WI	86	146	12	194	44.39	16	27
5825	M.E.Trescothick	E	76	143	10	219	43.79	14	29
5807	D.C.S.Compton	E	78	131	15	278	50.06	17	28
5768	Salim Malik	P	103	154	22	237	43.69	15	29
5764	N.Hussain	E	96	171	16	207	37.19	14	33
5762	C.L.Hooper	WI	102	173	15	233	36.46	13	27
5759	R.R.Sarwan	WI	83	146	8	291	41.73	15	31
5719	M.P.Vaughan	E	82	147	9	197	41.44	18	18
5666	K.P.Pietersen	E	71	123	6	227	48.42	17	21
5617	Younus Khan	P	67	119	8	313	50.60	17	23
5570	A.C.Gilchrist	A	96	137	20	204*	47.60	17	26
5502	M.S.Atapattu	SL	90	156	15	249	39.02	16	17
5444	M.D.Crowe	NZ	77	131	11	299	45.36	17	18
5410	J.B.Hobbs	E	61	102	7	211	56.94	15	28
5357	K.D.Walters	A	74	125	14	250	48.26	15	33
5345	I.M.Chappell	A	75	136	10	196	42.42	14	26
5334	J.G.Wright	NZ	82	148	7	185	37.82	12	23

Runs			M	I	NO	HS	Avge	100	50
5312	M.J.Slater	A	74	131	7	219	42.84	14	21
5312	M.V.Boucher	SA/ICC	139	196	23	125	30.70	5	34
5248	Kapil Dev	I	131	184	15	163	31.05	8	27
5234	W.M.Lawry	A	67	123	12	210	47.15	13	27
5200	I.T.Botham	E	102	161	6	208	33.54	14	22
5138	J.H.Edrich	E	77	127	9	310*	43.54	12	24
5130	A.N.Cook	E	65	115	7	235*	47.50	16	24
5105	A.Ranatunga	SL	93	155	12	135*	35.69	4	38
5062	Zaheer Abbas	P	78	124	11	274	44.79	12	20

The most for Zimbabwe is 4794 (112 innings) by A.Flower, and for Bangladesh 3026 by Habibul Bashar (99 innings).

750 RUNS IN A SERIES

Runs			Series	M	I	NO	HS	Avge	100	50
974	D.G.Bradman	A v E	1930	5	7	–	334	139.14	4	–
905	W.R.Hammond	E v A	1928-29	5	9	1	251	113.12	4	–
839	M.A.Taylor	A v E	1989	6	11	1	219	83.90	2	5
834	R.N.Harvey	A v SA	1952-53	5	9	–	205	92.66	4	3
829	I.V.A.Richards	WI v E	1976	4	7	–	291	118.42	3	2
827	C.L.Walcott	WI v A	1954-55	5	10	–	155	82.70	5	2
824	G.St A.Sobers	WI v P	1957-58	5	8	2	365*	137.33	3	3
810	D.G.Bradman	A v E	1936-37	5	9	–	270	90.00	3	1
806	D.G.Bradman	A v SA	1931-32	5	5	1	299*	201.50	4	–
798	B.C.Lara	WI v E	1993-94	5	8	–	375	99.75	2	2
779	E.de C.Weekes	WI v I	1948-49	5	7	–	194	111.28	4	2
774	S.M.Gavaskar	I v WI	1970-71	4	8	3	220	154.80	4	3
766	A.N.Cook	E v A	2010-11	5	7	1	235*	127.66	3	2
765	B.C.Lara	WI v E	1995	6	10	1	179	85.00	3	3
761	Mudassar Nazar	P v I	1982-83	6	8	2	231	126.83	4	1
758	D.G.Bradman	A v E	1934	5	8	–	304	94.75	2	1
753	D.C.S.Compton	E v SA	1947	5	8	–	208	94.12	4	2
752	G.A.Gooch	E v I	1990	3	6	–	333	125.33	3	2

HIGHEST INDIVIDUAL INNINGS

400*	B.C.Lara	WI v E	St John's	2003-04
380	M.L.Hayden	A v Z	Perth	2003-04
375	B.C.Lara	WI v E	St John's	1993-94
374	D.P.M.D.Jayawardena	SL v SA	Colombo (SSC)	2006
365*	G.St A.Sobers	WI v P	Kingston	1957-58
364	L.Hutton	E v A	The Oval	1938
340	S.T.Jayasuriya	SL v I	Colombo (RPS)	1997-98
337	Hanif Mohammed	P v WI	Bridgetown	1957-58
336*	W.R.Hammond	E v NZ	Auckland	1932-33
334*	M.A.Taylor	A v P	Peshawar	1998-99
334	D.G.Bradman	A v E	Leeds	1930
333	G.A.Gooch	E v I	Lord's	1990
333	C.H.Gayle	WI v SL	Galle	2010-11
329	Inzamam-ul-Haq	P v NZ	Lahore	2001-02
325	A.Sandham	E v WI	Kingston	1929-30
319	V.Sehwag	I v SA	Chennai	2007-08
317	C.H.Gayle	WI v SA	St John's	2004-05
313	Younus Khan	P v SL	Karachi	2008-09
311	R.B.Simpson	A v E	Manchester	1964
310*	J.H.Edrich	E v NZ	Leeds	1965
309	V.Sehwag	I v P	Multan	2003-04
307	R.M.Cowper	A v E	Melbourne	1965-66

304	D.G.Bradman	A v E	Leeds	1934
302	L.G.Rowe	WI v E	Bridgetown	1973-74
299*	D.G.Bradman	A v SA	Adelaide	1931-32
299	M.D.Crowe	NZ v SL	Wellington	1990-91
293	V.Sehwag	I v SL	Mumbai	2009-10
291	I.V.A.Richards	WI v E	The Oval	1976
291	R.R.Sarwan	WI v E	Bridgetown	2008-09
287	R.E.Foster	E v A	Sydney	1903-04
287	K.C.Sangakkara	SL v SA	Colombo (SSC)	2006
285*	P.B.H.May	E v WI	Birmingham	1957
281	V.V.S.Laxman	I v A	Calcutta	2000-01
280*	Javed Miandad	P v I	Hyderabad	1982-83
278*	A.B.de Villiers	SA v P	Abu Dhabi	2010-11
278	D.C.S.Compton	E v P	Nottingham	1954
277	B.C.Lara	WI v A	Sydney	1992-93
277	G.C.Smith	SA v E	Birmingham	2003
275*	D.J.Cullinan	SA v NZ	Auckland	1998-99
275	G.Kirsten	SA v E	Durban	1999-00
275	D.P.M.D.Jayawardena	SL v I	Ahmedabad	2009-10
274*	S.P.Fleming	NZ v SL	Colombo (SSC)	2002-03
274	R.G.Pollock	SA v A	Durban	1969-70
274	Zaheer Abbas	P v E	Birmingham	1971
271	Javed Miandad	P v NZ	Auckland	1988-89
270*	G.A.Headley	WI v E	Kingston	1934-35
270	D.G.Bradman	A v E	Melbourne	1936-37
270	R.S.Dravid	I v P	Rawalpindi	2003-04
270	K.C.Sangakkara	SL v Z	Bulawayo	2003-04
268	G.N.Yallop	A v P	Melbourne	1983-84
267*	B.A.Young	NZ v SL	Dunedin	1996-97
267	P.A.de Silva	SL v NZ	Wellington	1990-91
267	Younus Khan	P v I	Bangalore	2004-05
266	W.H.Ponsford	A v E	The Oval	1934
266	D.L.Houghton	Z v SL	Bulawayo	1994-95
262*	D.L.Amiss	E v WI	Kingston	1973-74
262	S.P.Fleming	NZ v SA	Cape Town	2005-06
261*	R.R.Sarwan	WI v B	Kingston	2004
261	F.M.M.Worrell	WI v E	Nottingham	1950
260	C.C.Hunte	WI v P	Kingston	1957-58
260	Javed Miandad	P v E	The Oval	1987
259	G.M.Turner	NZ v WI	Georgetown	1971-72
259	G.C.Smith	SA v E	Lord's	2003
258	T.W.Graveney	E v WI	Nottingham	1957
258	S.M.Nurse	WI v NZ	Christchurch	1968-69
257*	Wasim Akram	P v Z	Sheikhupura	1996-97
257	R.T.Ponting	A v I	Melbourne	2003-04
256	R.B.Kanhai	WI v I	Calcutta	1958-59
256	K.F.Barrington	E v A	Manchester	1964
255*	D.J.McGlew	SA v NZ	Wellington	1952-53
254	D.G.Bradman	A v E	Lord's	1930
254	V.Sehwag	I v P	Lahore	2005-06
253*	H.M.Amla	SA v I	Nagpur	2009-10
253	S.T.Jayasuriya	SL v P	Faisalabad	2004-05
251	W.R.Hammond	E v A	Sydney	1928-29
250	K.D.Walters	A v NZ	Christchurch	1976-77
250	S.F.A.F.Bacchus	WI v I	Kanpur	1978-79
250	J.L.Langer	A v E	Melbourne	2002-03

The highest for Bangladesh is 158* by Mohammad Ashraful (v I, Chittagong, 2004-05).

20 HUNDREDS

				Opponents									
			200	Inn	E	A	SA	WI	NZ	I	P	SL	Z	B
51	S.R.Tendulkar	I	6	290	7	11	7	3	4	–	2	9	3	5
40	J.H.Kallis	SA	1	246	7	4	–	8	5	6	6	–	3	1
39	R.T.Ponting	A	5	259	8	–	8	7	2	6	5	1	1	1
34	S.M.Gavaskar	A	4	214	4	8	–	13	2	–	5	2	–	–
34	B.C.Lara	WI	9	232	7	9	4	–	1	2	4	5	1	1
32	S.R.Waugh	A	1	260	10	–	2	7	2	2	3	3	1	2
31	R.S.Dravid	I	5	259	4	2	2	3	6	–	5	3	3	3
30	M.L.Hayden †	A	2	184	5	–	6	5	1	6	1	3	2	–
29	D.G.Bradman	A	12	80	19	–	4	2	–	4	–	–	–	–
28	D.P.M.D.Jayawardena	SL	6	190	6	1	5	1	3	6	1	–	1	4
27	A.R.Border	A	2	265	8	–	–	3	5	4	6	1	–	–
26	G.St A.Sobers	WI	2	160	10	4	–	–	1	8	3	–	–	–
25	Inzamam-ul-Haq	P	2	200	5	1	–	4	3	3	–	5	2	2
24	G.S.Chappell	A	4	151	9	–	5	3	1	6	–	–	–	–
24	I.V.A.Richards	WI	3	182	8	5	–	–	1	8	2	–	–	–
24	Mohammad Yousuf	P	4	156	6	1	–	7	1	4	–	1	2	2
24	K.C.Sangakkara	SL	7	156	1	1	2	3	3	5	5	–	2	2
23	J.L.Langer	A	3	182	5	–	2	3	4	3	4	2	–	–
23	Javed Miandad	P	6	189	2	6	–	2	7	5	–	1	–	–
22	W.R.Hammond	E	7	140	–	9	6	1	4	2	–	–	–	–
22	M.Azharuddin	I	–	147	6	2	4	–	2	–	3	5	–	–
22	M.C.Cowdrey	E	–	188	–	5	3	6	2	3	3	–	1	–
22	G.Boycott	E	1	193	–	7	1	5	2	4	3	–	–	–
22	V.Sehwag	I	6	150	1	3	5	2	2	–	4	5	–	–
22	G.C.Smith	SA	4	159	6	1	–	7	1	–	3	1	1	3
22	S.Chanderpaul	WI	1	219	5	4	5	–	1	5	1	–	–	1
21	R.N.Harvey	A	2	137	6	–	8	3	–	4	–	–	–	–
21	G.Kirsten	SA	3	176	5	2	–	3	2	3	2	1	1	2
21	D.C.Boon	A	1	190	7	–	3	3	6	1	1	–	–	–
20	K.F.Barrington	E	1	131	–	5	2	3	3	6	1	–	–	–
20	P.A.de Silva	SL	2	159	2	1	–	2	5	8	–	1	1
20	M.E.Waugh	A	–	209	6	–	4	4	1	5	1	3	1	–
20	G.A.Gooch	E	2	215	–	4	–	5	4	5	1	1	–	–

† Includes century scored for Australia v ICC in 2005-06.

The most for New Zealand is 17 by M.D.Crowe (131 innings), for Zimbabwe 12 by A.Flower (112), and for Bangladesh 5 by Mohammad Ashraful (107 innings).

The most double hundreds by batsmen not included above are 6 by M.S.Atapattu (16 hundreds for Sri Lanka), 4 by L.Hutton (19 for England), 4 by C.G.Greenidge (19 for West Indies), and 4 by Zaheer Abbas (12 for Pakistan).

HIGHEST PARTNERSHIP FOR EACH WICKET

1st	415	N.D.McKenzie/G.C.Smith	SA v B	Chittagong	2007-08
2nd	576	S.T.Jayasuriya/R.S.Mahanama	SL v I	Colombo (RPS)	1997-98
3rd	624	K.C.Sangakkara/D.P.M.D.Jayawardena	SL v SA	Colombo (SSC)	2006
4th	437	D.P.M.D.Jayawardena/T.T.Samaraweera	SL v P	Karachi	2008-09
5th	405	S.G.Barnes/D.G.Bradman	A v E	Sydney	1946-47
6th	351	D.P.M.D.Jayawardena/H.A.P.W.Jayawardena	SL v I	Ahmedabad	2009-10
7th	347	D.St E.Atkinson/C.C.Depeiza	WI v A	Bridgetown	1954-55
8th	332	I.J.L.Trott/S.C.J.Broad	E v P	Lord's	2010
9th	195	M.V.Boucher/P.L.Symcox	SA v P	Johannesburg	1997-98
10th	151	B.F.Hastings/R.O.Collinge	NZ v P	Auckland	1972-73
	151	Azhar Mahmood/Mushtaq Ahmed	P v SA	Rawalpindi	1997-98

76

BOWLING RECORDS
200 WICKETS IN TESTS

Wkts			M	Balls	Runs	Avge	5 wI	10 wM
800	M.Muralitharan	SL/ICC	133	44039	18180	22.72	67	22
708	S.K.Warne	A	145	40705	17995	25.41	37	10
619	A.Kumble	I	132	40850	18355	29.65	35	8
563	G.D.McGrath	A	124	29248	12186	21.64	29	3
519	C.A.Walsh	WI	132	30019	12688	24.44	22	3
434	Kapil Dev	I	131	27740	12867	29.64	23	2
431	R.J.Hadlee	NZ	86	21918	9612	22.30	36	9
421	S.M.Pollock	SA	108	24453	9733	23.11	16	1
414	Wasim Akram	P	104	22627	9779	23.62	25	5
405	C.E.L.Ambrose	WI	98	22104	8500	20.98	22	3
393	Harbhajan Singh	I	93	26483	12518	31.85	25	5
390	M.Ntini	SA	101	20834	11242	28.82	18	4
383	I.T.Botham	E	102	21815	10878	28.40	27	4
376	M.D.Marshall	WI	81	17584	7876	20.94	22	4
373	Waqar Younis	P	87	16224	8788	23.56	22	5
362	Imran Khan	P	88	19458	8258	22.81	23	6
355	D.K.Lillee	A	70	18467	8493	23.92	23	7
355	W.P.J.U.C.Vaas	SL	111	23438	10501	29.58	12	2
345	D.L.Vettori	NZ/ICC	105	26860	11724	33.98	19	3
330	A.A.Donald	SA	72	15519	7344	22.25	20	3
325	R.G.D.Willis	E	90	17357	8190	25.20	16	–
310	B.Lee	A	76	16531	9554	30.81	10	–
309	L.R.Gibbs	WI	79	27115	8989	29.09	18	2
307	F.S.Trueman	E	67	15178	6625	21.57	17	3
297	D.L.Underwood	E	86	21862	7674	25.83	17	6
291	C.J.McDermott	A	71	16586	8332	28.63	14	2
271	Z.Khan	I	78	15756	8658	31.94	10	1
270	J.H.Kallis	SA/ICC	145	18337	8643	32.01	5	–
266	B.S.Bedi	I	67	21364	7637	28.71	14	1
261	Danish Kaneria	P	61	17697	9082	34.79	15	2
259	J.Garner	WI	58	13169	5433	20.97	7	–
259	J.N.Gillespie	A	71	14234	6770	26.13	8	–
252	J.B.Statham	E	70	16056	6261	24.84	9	1
249	M.A.Holding	WI	60	12680	5898	23.68	13	2
248	R.Benaud	A	63	19108	6704	27.03	16	1
248	M.J.Hoggard	E	67	13909	7564	30.50	7	1
246	G.D.McKenzie	A	60	17681	7328	29.78	16	3
242	B.S.Chandrasekhar	I	58	15963	7199	29.74	16	2
238	D.W.Steyn	SA	46	9515	5526	23.21	16	4
236	A.V.Bedser	E	51	15918	5876	24.89	15	5
236	Abdul Qadir	P	67	17126	7742	32.80	15	5
236	J.Srinath	I	67	15104	7196	30.49	10	1
235	G.St A.Sobers	WI	93	21599	7999	34.03	6	–
234	A.R.Caddick	E	62	13558	6999	29.91	13	1
229	D.Gough	E	58	11821	6503	28.39	9	–
228	R.R.Lindwall	A	61	13650	5251	23.03	12	–
226	S.J.Harmison	E/ICC	63	13375	7192	31.82	8	1
226	A.Flintoff	E/ICC	79	14951	7410	32.78	3	–
218	C.L.Cairns	NZ	62	11698	6410	29.40	13	1
216	C.V.Grimmett	A	37	14513	5231	24.21	21	7
216	H.H.Streak	Z	65	13559	6079	28.14	7	–
212	M.G.Hughes	A	53	12285	6017	28.38	7	1
212	J.M.Anderson	E	57	12056	6595	31.10	10	1
208	S.C.G.MacGill	A	44	11237	6038	29.02	12	2
208	Saqlain Mushtaq	P	49	14070	6206	29.83	13	3
202	A.M.E.Roberts	WI	47	11136	5174	25.61	11	2
202	J.A.Snow	E	49	12021	5387	26.66	8	1
200	J.R.Thomson	A	51	10535	5601	28.00	8	–

The most for Bangladesh is 100 in 33 Tests by Mohammad Rafique.

35 WICKETS IN A SERIES

Wkts			Series	M	Balls	Runs	Avge	5 wI	10 wM
49	S.F.Barnes	E v SA	1913-14	4	1356	536	10.93	7	3
46	J.C.Laker	E v A	1956	5	1703	442	9.60	4	2
44	C.V.Grimmett	A v SA	1935-36	5	2077	642	14.59	5	3
42	T.M.Alderman	A v E	1981	6	1950	893	21.26	4	–
41	R.M.Hogg	A v E	1978-79	6	1740	527	12.85	5	2
41	T.M.Alderman	A v E	1989	6	1616	712	17.36	6	1
40	Imran Khan	P v I	1982-83	6	1339	558	13.95	4	2
40	S.K.Warne	A v E	2005	5	1517	797	19.92	3	2
39	A.V.Bedser	E v A	1953	5	1591	682	17.48	5	1
39	D.K.Lillee	A v E	1981	6	1870	870	22.30	2	1
38	M.W.Tate	E v A	1924-25	5	2528	881	23.18	5	1
37	W.J.Whitty	A v SA	1910-11	5	1395	632	17.08	2	–
37	H.J.Tayfield	SA v E	1956-57	5	2280	636	17.18	4	1
36	A.E.E.Vogler	SA v E	1909-10	5	1349	783	21.75	4	1
36	A.A.Mailey	A v E	1920-21	5	1465	946	26.27	4	2
36	G.D.McGrath	A v E	1997	6	1499	701	19.47	2	–
35	G.A.Lohmann	E v SA	1895-96	3	520	203	5.80	4	2
35	B.S.Chandrasekhar	I v E	1972-73	5	1747	662	18.91	4	–
35	M.D.Marshall	WI v E	1988	5	1219	443	12.65	3	1

The most for New Zealand is 33 by R.J.Hadlee (3 Tests v A, 1985-86), for Sri Lanka 30 by M.Muralitharan (3 Tests v Z, 2001-02), for Zimbabwe 22 by H.H.Streak (3 Tests v P, 1994-95), and for Bangladesh 18 by Enamul Haque[2] (2 Tests v Z, 2004-05).

15 WICKETS IN A TEST († On debut)

19- 90	J.C.Laker	E v A	Manchester	1956
17-159	S.F.Barnes	E v SA	Johannesburg	1913-14
16-136†	N.D.Hirwani	I v WI	Madras	1987-88
16-137†	R.A.L.Massie	A v E	Lord's	1972
16-220	M.Muralitharan	SL v E	The Oval	1998
15- 28	J.Briggs	E v SA	Cape Town	1888-89
15- 45	G.A.Lohmann	E v SA	Port Elizabeth	1895-96
15- 99	C.Blythe	E v SA	Leeds	1907
15-104	H.Verity	E v A	Lord's	1934
15-123	R.J.Hadlee	NZ v A	Brisbane	1985-86
15-124	W.Rhodes	E v A	Melbourne	1903-04
15-217	Harbhajan Singh	I v A	Madras	2000-01

The best analysis for South Africa is 13-132 by M.Ntini (v WI, Port-of-Spain, 2004-05), for West Indies 14-149 by M.A.Holding (v E, The Oval, 1976), for Pakistan 14-116 by Imran Khan (v SL, Lahore, 1981-82), for Zimbabwe 11-257 by A.G.Huckle (v NZ, Bulawayo, 1997-98), and for Bangladesh 12-200 by Enamul Haque[2] (v Z, Dhaka, 2004-05).

NINE WICKETS IN AN INNINGS

10-53	J.C.Laker	E v A	Manchester	1956
10-74	A.Kumble	I v P	Delhi	1998-99
9-28	G.A.Lohmann	E v SA	Johannesburg	1895-96
9-37	J.C.Laker	E v A	Manchester	1956
9-51	M.Muralitharan	SL v Z	Kandy	2001-02
9-52	R.J.Hadlee	NZ v A	Brisbane	1985-86
9-56	Abdul Qadir	P v E	Lahore	1987-88
9-57	D.E.Malcolm	E v SA	The Oval	1994
9-65	M.Muralitharan	SL v E	The Oval	1998
9-69	J.M.Patel	I v A	Kanpur	1959-60
9-83	Kapil Dev	I v WI	Ahmedabad	1983-84

9- 86	Sarfraz Nawaz	P v A	Melbourne	1978-79
9- 95	J.M.Noreiga	WI v I	Port-of-Spain	1970-71
9-102	S.P.Gupte	I v WI	Kanpur	1958-59
9-103	S.F.Barnes	E v SA	Johannesburg	1913-14
9-113	H.J.Tayfield	SA v E	Johannesburg	1956-57
9-121	A.A.Mailey	A v E	Melbourne	1920-21

The best analysis for Zimbabwe is 8-109 by P.A.Strang (v NZ, Bulawayo, 2000-01), and for Bangladesh 7-95 by Enamul Haque[2] (v Z, Dhaka, 2004-05).

HAT-TRICKS

F.R.Spofforth	Australia v England	Melbourne	1878-79
W.Bates	England v Australia	Melbourne	1882-83
J.Briggs[7]	England v Australia	Sydney	1891-92
G.A.Lohmann	England v South Africa	Port Elizabeth	1895-96
J.T.Hearne	England v Australia	Leeds	1899
H.Trumble	Australia v England	Melbourne	1901-02
H.Trumble	Australia v England	Melbourne	1903-04
T.J.Matthews (2)[2]	Australia v South Africa	Manchester	1912
M.J.C.Allom[1]	England v New Zealand	Christchurch	1929-30
T.W.J.Goddard	England v South Africa	Johannesburg	1938-39
P.J.Loader	England v West Indies	Leeds	1957
L.F.Kline	Australia v South Africa	Cape Town	1957-58
W.W.Hall	West Indies v Pakistan	Lahore	1958-59
G.M.Griffin[7]	South Africa v England	Lord's	1960
L.R.Gibbs	West Indies v Australia	Adelaide	1960-61
P.J.Petherick[1/7]	New Zealand v Pakistan	Lahore	1976-77
C.A.Walsh[3]	West Indies v Australia	Brisbane	1988-89
M.G.Hughes[3/7]	Australia v West Indies	Perth	1988-89
D.W.Fleming[1]	Australia v Pakistan	Rawalpindi	1994-95
S.K.Warne	Australia v England	Melbourne	1994-95
D.G.Cork[7]	England v West Indies	Manchester	1995
D.Gough[7]	England v Australia	Sydney	1998-99
Wasim Akram[4]	Pakistan v Sri Lanka	Lahore	1998-99
Wasim Akram[4]	Pakistan v Sri Lanka	Dhaka	1998-99
D.N.T.Zoysa[5]	Sri Lanka v Zimbabwe	Harare	1999-00
Abdul Razzaq	Pakistan v Sri Lanka	Galle	2000-01
G.D.McGrath	Australia v West Indies	Perth	2000-01
Harbhajan Singh	India v Australia	Calcutta	2000-01
Mohammad Sami[7]	Pakistan v Sri Lanka	Lahore	2001-02
J.J.C.Lawson[7]	West Indies v Australia	Bridgetown	2002-03
Alok Kapali[7]	Bangladesh v Pakistan	Peshawar	2003
A.M.Blignaut	Zimbabwe v Bangladesh	Harare	2003-04
M.J.Hoggard	England v West Indies	Bridgetown	2003-04
J.E.C.Franklin	New Zealand v Bangladesh	Dhaka	2004-05
I.K.Pathan[6/7]	India v Pakistan	Karachi	2005-06
R.J.Sidebottom[7]	England v New Zealand	Hamilton	2007-08
P.M.Siddle	Australia v England	Brisbane	2010-11

[1] On debut. [2] Hat-trick in each innings. [3] Involving both innings. [4] In successive Tests. [5] His first 3 balls (second over of the match). [6] The fourth, fifth and sixth balls of the match. [7] On losing side.

WICKET-KEEPING RECORDS
100 DISMISSALS IN TESTS†

Total			Tests	Ct	St
521	M.V.Boucher	South Africa/ICC	139	499	22
416	A.C.Gilchrist	Australia	96	379	37
395	I.A.Healy	Australia	119	366	29
355	R.W.Marsh	Australia	96	343	12
270†	P.J.L.Dujon	West Indies	79	265	5
269	A.P.E.Knott	England	95	250	19
241†	A.J.Stewart	England	82	227	14
228	Wasim Bari	Pakistan	81	201	27
219	R.D.Jacobs	West Indies	65	207	12
219	T.G.Evans	England	91	173	46
206	Kamran Akmal	Pakistan	53	184	22
201†	A.C.Parore	New Zealand	67	194	7
198	S.M.H.Kirmani	India	88	160	38
189	D.L.Murray	West Indies	62	181	8
187	A.T.W.Grout	Australia	51	163	24
176	I.D.S.Smith	New Zealand	63	168	8
174	R.W.Taylor	England	57	167	7
173	M.S.Dhoni	India	54	148	25
172†	B.B.McCullum	New Zealand	51	161	11
165	R.C.Russell	England	54	153	12
152	D.J.Richardson	South Africa	42	150	2
151†	A.Flower	Zimbabwe	55	142	9
151†	K.C.Sangakkara	Sri Lanka	48	131	20
147†	Moin Khan	Pakistan	66	127	20
141	J.H.B.Waite	South Africa	49	124	17
133	G.O.Jones	England	34	128	5
130	Rashid Latif	Pakistan	37	119	11
130	K.S.More	India	49	110	20
130	W.A.S.Oldfield	Australia	54	78	52
122	D.Ramdin	West Indies	42	119	3
121	B.J.Haddin	Australia	32	118	3
121	M.J.Prior	England	40	117	4
119	R.S.Kaluwitharana	Sri Lanka	49	93	26
112†	J.M.Parks	England	43	101	11
107	N.R.Mongia	India	44	99	8
104	Salim Yousuf	Pakistan	32	91	13
101†	J.R.Murray	West Indies	31	98	3

The most for Bangladesh is 87 (78 ct, 9 st) by Khaled Masud in 44 Tests.
† *Excluding catches taken in the field*

25 DISMISSALS IN A SERIES

28	R.W.Marsh	Australia v England	1982-83
27 (inc 2st)	R.C.Russell	England v South Africa	1995-96
27 (inc 2st)	I.A.Healy	Australia v England (6 Tests)	1997
26 (inc 3st)	J.H.B.Waite	South Africa v New Zealand	1961-62
26	R.W.Marsh	Australia v West Indies (6 Tests)	1975-76
26 (inc 5st)	I.A.Healy	Australia v England (6 Tests)	1993
26 (inc 1st)	M.V.Boucher	South Africa v England	1998
26 (inc 2st)	A.C.Gilchrist	Australia v England	2001
26 (inc 2st)	A.C.Gilchrist	Australia v England	2006-07
25 (inc 2st)	I.A.Healy	Australia v England	1994-95
25 (inc 2st)	A.C.Gilchrist	Australia v England	2002-03
25	A.C.Gilchrist	Australia v India	2007-08

TEN DISMISSALS IN A TEST

11	R.C.Russell	England v South Africa	Johannesburg	1995-96
10	R.W.Taylor	England v India	Bombay	1979-80
10	A.C.Gilchrist	Australia v New Zealand	Hamilton	1999-00

SEVEN DISMISSALS IN AN INNINGS

7	Wasim Bari	Pakistan v New Zealand	Auckland	1978-79
7	R.W.Taylor	England v India	Bombay	1979-80
7	I.D.S.Smith	New Zealand v Sri Lanka	Hamilton	1990-91
7	R.D.Jacobs	West Indies v Australia	Melbourne	2000-01

FIVE STUMPINGS IN AN INNINGS

5	K.S.More	India v West Indies	Madras	1987-88

FIELDING RECORDS
100 CATCHES IN TESTS

Total			Tests	Total			Tests
200	R.S.Dravid	India/ICC	150	120	I.T.Botham	England	102
181	M.E.Waugh	Australia	128	120	M.C.Cowdrey	England	114
178	R.T.Ponting	Australia	152	119	G.C.Smith	South Africa/ICC	91
171	S.P.Fleming	New Zealand	111	115	C.L.Hooper	West Indies	102
166	J.H.Kallis	South Africa/ICC	145	112	S.R.Waugh	Australia	168
165	D.P.M.D.Jayawardena	Sri Lanka	116	110	R.B.Simpson	Australia	62
164	B.C.Lara	West Indies/ICC	131	110	W.R.Hammond	England	85
157	M.A.Taylor	Australia	104	109	G.St A.Sobers	West Indies	93
156	A.R.Border	Australia	156	108	S.M.Gavaskar	India	125
128	M.L.Hayden	Australia	103	106	S.R.Tendulkar	India	177
125	S.K.Warne	Australia	145	105	I.M.Chappell	Australia	75
122	G.S.Chappell	Australia	87	105	M.Azharuddin	India	99
122	I.V.A.Richards	West Indies	121	105	G.P.Thorpe	England	100
122	V.V.S.Laxman	India	120	103	G.A.Gooch	England	118

The most for Pakistan is 93 by Javed Miandad (124), for Zimbabwe 60 by A.D.R.Campbell (60) and for Bangladesh 24 by Mohammad Ashraful (53).

15 CATCHES IN A SERIES

15	J.M.Gregory	Australia v England	1920-21

SEVEN CATCHES IN A TEST

7	G.S.Chappell	Australia v England	Perth	1974-75
7	Yajurvindra Singh	India v England	Bangalore	1976-77
7	H.P.Tillekeratne	Sri Lanka v New Zealand	Colombo (SSC)	1992-93
7	S.P.Fleming	New Zealand v Zimbabwe	Harare	1997-98
7	M.L.Hayden	Australia v Sri Lanka	Galle	2003-04

FIVE CATCHES IN AN INNINGS

5	V.Y.Richardson	Australia v South Africa	Durban	1935-36
5	Yajurvindra Singh	India v England	Bangalore	1976-77
5	M.Azharuddin	India v Pakistan	Karachi	1989-90
5	K.Srikkanth	India v Australia	Perth	1991-92
5	S.P.Fleming	New Zealand v Zimbabwe	Harare	1997-98

APPEARANCE RECORDS
100 TEST MATCH APPEARANCES

			Opponents									
			E	A	SA	WI	NZ	I	P	SL	Z	B
177	S.R.Tendulkar	India	24	31	25	16	22	–	18	25	9	7
168	S.R.Waugh	Australia	46	–	16	32	23	18	20	8	3	2
156	A.R.Border	Australia	47	–	6	31	23	20	22	7	–	–
152†	R.T.Ponting	Australia	35	–	21	21	15	25	15	12	3	4
150†	R.S.Dravid	India/ICC	17	28	20	17	15	–	15	20	9	7
145†	S.K.Warne	Australia	36	–	24	19	20	14	15	13	1	2
145†	J.H.Kallis	South Africa/ICC	28	23	–	24	14	16	15	12	6	6
139†	M.V.Boucher	South Africa/ICC	25	18	–	24	14	14	15	14	6	8
133	A.J.Stewart	England	–	33	23	24	16	9	13	9	6	–
133†	M.Muralitharan	Sri Lanka/ICC	16	12	15	12	14	22	16	–	14	11
132	A.Kumble	India	19	20	21	17	11	–	15	18	7	4
132	C.A.Walsh	West Indies	36	38	10	–	10	15	18	3	2	–
131	Kapil Dev	India	27	20	4	25	10	–	29	14	2	–
131†	B.C.Lara	West Indies/ICC	30	30	18	–	11	17	12	8	2	2
129	S.Chanderpaul	West Indies	30	17	21	–	13	18	13	7	6	4
128	M.E.Waugh	Australia	29	–	18	28	14	14	15	9	1	–
125	S.M.Gavaskar	India	38	20	–	27	9	–	24	7	–	–
124†	G.D.McGrath	Australia	30	–	17	23	14	11	17	8	1	2
124	Javed Miandad	Pakistan	22	24	–	17	18	28	–	12	3	–
121	I.V.A.Richards	West Indies	36	34	–	–	7	28	16	–	–	–
120†	Inzamam-ul-Haq	Pakistan/ICC	19	13	13	15	12	10	–	20	11	6
120	V.V.S.Laxman	India	13	25	19	16	10	–	15	13	6	3
119	I.A.Healy	Australia	33	–	12	28	11	9	14	11	1	–
118	G.A.Gooch	England	–	42	3	26	15	19	10	3	–	–
117	D.I.Gower	England	–	42	–	19	13	24	17	2	–	–
116	D.L.Haynes	West Indies	36	33	1	–	10	19	16	1	–	–
116	D.B.Vengsarkar	India	26	24	–	25	11	–	22	8	–	–
116	D.P.M.D.Jayawardena	Sri Lanka	16	10	13	11	11	18	18	–	8	11
115	M.A.Atherton	England	–	33	18	27	11	7	11	4	4	–
114	M.C.Cowdrey	England	–	43	14	21	18	8	10	–	–	–
113	S.C.Ganguly	India	12	24	17	12	8	–	12	14	9	5
111	S.P.Fleming	New Zealand	19	14	15	11	–	13	9	13	11	6
111	W.P.J.U.C.Vaas	Sri Lanka	15	12	11	9	10	14	18	–	15	7
110	S.T.Jayasuriya	Sri Lanka	14	13	15	10	13	10	17	–	13	5
110	C.H.Lloyd	West Indies	34	29	–	–	8	28	11	–	–	–
108	G.Boycott	England	–	38	7	29	15	13	6	–	–	–
108	C.G.Greenidge	West Indies	29	32	–	–	10	23	14	–	–	–
108	S.M.Pollock	South Africa	23	13	–	16	11	12	12	13	5	3
107	D.C.Boon	Australia	31	–	6	22	17	11	11	9	–	–
105†	J.L.Langer	Australia	21	–	11	18	14	14	13	8	3	2
105†	D.L.Vettori	New Zealand/ICC	17	17	11	9	–	15	8	11	7	9
104	M.A.Taylor	Australia	33	–	11	20	11	9	12	8	–	–
104	Wasim Akram	Pakistan	18	13	4	17	9	12	–	19	10	2
103†	M.L.Hayden	Australia	–	19	15	11	18	6	7	2	4	–
103	Salim Malik	Pakistan	19	15	1	7	18	22	–	15	6	–
102	I.T.Botham	England	–	36	–	20	15	14	14	3	–	–
102	C.L.Hooper	West Indies	24	25	10	–	2	19	14	6	2	–
101	G.Kirsten	South Africa	22	18	–	13	13	10	11	9	3	4
101	M.Ntini	South Africa	18	15	–	15	11	10	9	12	3	8
100	G.P.Thorpe	England	–	16	27	23	11	6	13	4	–	–

† Includes appearance in the Australia v ICC 'Test' in 2005-06. The most for Zimbabwe is 67 by G.W.Flower, and for Bangladesh 55 by Mohammad Ashraful.

100 CONSECUTIVE TEST APPEARANCES

153	A.R.Border	Australia	March 1979 to March 1994
107	M.E.Waugh	Australia	June 1993 to October 2002
106	S.M.Gavaskar	India	January 1975 to February 1987

50 TESTS AS CAPTAIN

			Won	Lost	Drawn	Tied
93	A.R.Border	Australia	32	22	38	1
83	G.C.Smith	South Africa	38	24	21	–
80	S.P.Fleming	New Zealand	28	27	25	–
77	R.T.Ponting	Australia	48	16	13	–
74	C.H.Lloyd	West Indies	36	12	26	–
57	S.R.Waugh	Australia	41	9	7	–
56	A.Ranatunga	Sri Lanka	12	19	25	–
54	M.A.Atherton	England	13	21	20	–
53	W.J.Cronje	South Africa	27	11	15	–
51	M.P.Vaughan	England	26	11	14	–
50	I.V.A.Richards	West Indies	27	8	15	–
50	M.A.Taylor	Australia	26	13	11	–

The most for India is 49 by S.C.Ganguly, for Pakistan 48 by Imran Khan, for Zimbabwe 21 by A.D.R.Campbell and H.H.Streak, and for Bangladesh 18 by Habibul Bashar.

50 TEST UMPIRING APPEARANCES

128	S.A.Bucknor	(West Indies)	28.04.1989 to 22.03.2009
106	R.E.Koertzen	(South Africa)	26.12.1992 to 19.02.2010
94	D.J.Harper	(Australia)	28.11.1998 to 19.01.2011
92	D.R.Shepherd	(England)	01.08.1985 to 07.06.2005
78	D.B.Hair	(Australia)	25.01.1992 to 08.06.2008
73	S.Venkataraghavan	(India)	29.01.1993 to 20.01.2004
67	S.J.A.Taufel	(Australia)	26.12.2000 to 06.01.2011
66	H.D.Bird	(England)	05.07.1973 to 24.06.1996
65	B.F.Bowden	(New Zealand)	11.03.2000 to 07.01.2011
63	Alim Dar	(Pakistan)	21.10.2003 to 07.01.2011

THE FIRST-CLASS COUNTIES REGISTER, RECORDS AND 2010 AVERAGES

Career best statistics are to 1 March 2011. Test Match career bests have been updated to 1 April 2011 and LOI career bests to 18 February 2011.

ABBREVIATIONS – General

*	not out/unbroken partnership	IT20	International Twenty20
b	born	l-o	limited-overs
BB	Best innings bowling analysis	LOI	Limited-Overs Internationals
Cap	Awarded 1st XI County Cap	Tests	International Test Matches
f-c	first-class	F-c	Overseas tours involving first-class
HS	Highest Score	Tours	appearances

Awards

PCA 2010	Professional Cricketers' Association Player of 2010
Wisden 2009	One of *Wisden Cricketers' Almanack*'s Five Cricketers of 2009
YC 2010	Cricket Writers' Club Young Cricketer of 2010

ECB Competitions

BHC	Benson & Hedges Cup (1972-2002)
CB40	Clydesdale Bank 40 (2010)
CC	LV= County Championship
CGT	Cheltenham & Gloucester Trophy (2001-06)
FPT	Friends Provident Trophy (2007-09)
NL	National League (1999-2005)
NWT	NatWest Trophy (1981-2000)
P40	NatWest PRO 40 League (2006-09)
SL	Sunday League (1969-98)
T20	Twenty20 Competition

Education

ARU	Anglia Ruskin University
BHS	Boys' High School
C	College
CFE	College of Further Education
CHE	College of Higher Education
CS	Comprehensive School
GS	Grammar School
HS	High School
I	Institute
IHE	Institute of Higher Education
RGS	Royal Grammar School
S	School
SFC	Sixth Form College
SM	Secondary Modern School
SS	Secondary School
TC	Technical College
T(H)S	Technical (High) School
U	University
UWIC	University of Wales Institute, Cardiff

Playing Categories

LBG	Bowls right-arm leg-breaks and googlies
LF	Bowls left-arm fast
LFM	Bowls left-arm fast-medium
LHB	Bats left-handed
LM	Bowls left-arm medium pace
LMF	Bowls left-arm medium fast
OB	Bowls right-arm off-breaks
RF	Bowls right-arm fast
RFM	Bowls right-arm fast-medium
RHB	Bats right-handed
RM	Bowls right-arm medium pace

RMF	Bowls right-arm medium-fast
RSM	Bowls right-arm slow-medium
SLA	Bowls left-arm leg-breaks
SLC	Bowls left-arm 'Chinamen'
WK	Wicket-keeper

Teams (see also p 220)

ACT	Australian Capital Territory
ADBP	Agricultural Development Bank of Pakistan
B	Bangladesh
BS	Basnahira South
CC&C	Combined Campuses & Colleges
CD	Central Districts
EL	England Lions
EP	Eastern Province
FS	Free State
GW	Griqualand West
KRL	Khan Research Laboratories
ME	Mashonaland Eagles
MT	Matabeleland Tuskers
MWR	Mid West Rhinos
NBP	National Bank of Pakistan
ND	Northern Districts
NSW	New South Wales
NT	Northern Transvaal
NW	North West
(O)FS	(Orange) Free State
PIA	Pakistan International Airlines
PNSC	Pakistan National Shipping Corporation
PTC	Pakistan Telecommunication Co
Q	Queensland
REDCO	Really Efficient Development Co
SAU	South African Universities
SNGPL	Sui Northern Gas Pipelines Limited
SR	Southern Rocks
SSGC	Sui Southern Gas Corporation
Tas	Tasmania
T&T	Trinidad & Tobago
Uni	Unicorns
UP	Uttar Pradesh
Vic	Victoria
WA	Western Australia
WAPDA	Water & Power Development Authority
WP	Western Province

DERBYSHIRE

Formation of Present Club: 4 November 1870
Inaugural First-Class Match: 1871
Colours: Chocolate, Amber and Pale Blue
Badge: Rose and Crown
County Champions: (1) 1936
Gillette/NatWest/C&G/FP Trophy Winners: (1) 1981
Benson and Hedges Cup Winners: (1) 1993
Pro 40/National League (Div 1) Winners: (0); best – 4th (Div 2) 2002
Sunday League Winners: (1) 1990
Clydesdale Bank 40 Winners: (0); best – 4th (Group B) 2010
Twenty20 Cup Winners: (0) best – Quarter-Finalist 2005

Chief Executive: Keith Loring, Derbyshire County Cricket Club, Grandstand Road, Derby DE21 6AF • Tel: 01332 388101 • Fax: 0844 500 8322 • Email: info@derbyshireccc.com • Web: www.derbyshireccc.com

Head of Cricket: J.E.Morris. **Assistant Coach:** Andy Brown. **Captain:** L.D.Sutton. **Vice-Captain:** None. **Overseas Players:** M.J.Guptill and U.T.Khawaja. **2011 Beneficiary:** None. **Head Groundsman:** Neil Godrich. **Scorer:** John M.Brown. ‡ New registration. NQ Not qualified for England.

ADSHEAD, Stephen John (Bridley Moor HS, Redditch), b Redditch, Worcs 29 Jan 1980. 5'9". RHB, WK. Herefordshire 1999. Leicestershire 2000 (1 non-CC match). Worcestershire 2003 (2 matches). Gloucestershire 2004-09; cap 2004. Derbyshire debut 2010. HS 156* Gs v Essex (Southend) 2009. De HS 49 v Sussex (Horsham) 2010. LO HS 87 Gs v Durham (Chester-le-St) 2009 (FPT). T20 HS 81.

BORRINGTON, Paul Michael (Repton S; Chellarton S; Loughborough U), b Nottingham 24 May 1988. Son of A.J.Borrington (Derbyshire 1971-80). 5'10". RHB, OB. Debut (Derbyshire) 2005. Loughborough UCCE 2008-09. HS 105 LU v Hants (Southampton) 2009. De HS 85 v Worcs (Worcester) 2008. BB – . LO HS 25 v Glamorgan (Derby) 2009 (P40).

CLARE, Jonathan Luke (St Theodore's HS), b Burnley, Lancs 14 Jun 1986. 6'4". RHB, RMF. Debut (Derbyshire) 2007, taking 5-90 v Notts (Chesterfield). Lancashire 2nd XI. Derbyshire 2nd XI debut 2006. HS 129* and BB 7-74 v Northants (Northampton) 2008. LO HS 34 v Kent (Chesterfield) 2009 (P40). LO HS 3-39 v Scotland (Derby) 2008 (FPT). T20 HS 18. T20 BB 2-20.

DURSTON, Wesley John (Millfield S; University C, Worcester), b Taunton, Somerset 6 Oct 1980. 5'10". RHB, OB. Somerset 2002-09. Derbyshire debut 2010. Unicorns 2010 (l-o only). HS 146* Sm v Derbys (Derby) 2005. De HS 69 v Sussex (Horsham) 2009. BB 3-23 Sm v Sri Lanka A (Taunton) 2004. CC BB 2-31 Sm v Surrey (Bath) 2006. De BB 1-9 v Middx (Derby) 2010. LO HS 117 Unicorns v Sussex (Arundel) 2010 (CB40). LO BB 3-44 Sm v Surrey (Taunton) 2006 (P40). T20 HS 111 v Notts (Nottingham) 2010 – De record. T20 BB 3-25.

FOOTITT, Mark Harold Alan (Carlton le Willows S; West Notts C), b Nottingham 25 Nov 1985. 6'2". RHB, LFM. Nottinghamshire 2005-09. MCC 2006. No f-c appearances in 2008. Derbyshire debut 2010. HS 30 v Surrey (Oval) 2010. BB 5-45 Nt v West Indies A (Nottingham) 2006. CC BB 5-59 Nt v Essex (Nottingham) 2007. De BB 4-78 v Northants (Northampton) 2010. LO HS 1 v Northants (Derby) 2010 (CB40). LO BB 3-20 v Middx (Derby) 2010 (CB40). T20 HS – . T20 BB – .

GROENEWALD, Timothy Duncan (Maritzburg C; South Africa U), b Pietermaritzburg, South Africa 10 Jan 1984. 6'0". RHB, RFM. Debut Cambridge UCCE 2006. Warwickshire 2006-08. Derbyshire debut 2009. HS 78 Wa v Bangladesh A (Birmingham) 2008. CC HS 76 Wa v Durham (Chester-le-St) 2006. De HS 50 v Northants (Chesterfield) 2009. BB 6-50 v Surrey (Croydon) 2009. LO HS 36 Wa v Lancs (Manchester) 2007 (FPT). LO BB 3-25 Wa v Worcs (Birmingham) 2007 (P40). T20 HS 41. T20 BB 3-18.

‡^{NQ}**GUPTILL, Martin** James, b Auckland, New Zealand 30 Sep 1986. RHB, OB. Auckland 2005-06 to date. **Tests** (NZ): 15 (2008-09 to 2010-11); HS 189 v B (Hamilton) 2009-10; BB 3-37 v P (Napier) 2009-10. **LOI** (NZ): 44 (2008-09 to 2010-11); HS 122* v WI (Auckland) 2008-09 – on debut; BB 2-7 v B (Napier) 2009-10. **IT20** (NZ): 23 (2008-09 to 2010-11); HS 54 v P (Auckland) 2010-11. – F-c Tours (NZ): I 2008-09 (NZ A), 2010-11; SL 2009; Z 2010-11 (NZ A). HS 189 (*see Tests*). BB 3-37 (*see Tests*). LO HS 156 Auck v Canterbury (Christchurch) 2009-10. LO BB 2-7 (*see LOI*). T20 HS 97*. T20 BB – .

HIGGINBOTTOM, Matthew (New Mills SS; Leeds Met U), b Stockport, Cheshire 20 Oct 1990. 6'2". LHB, RM. Derbyshire 2nd XI debut 2009. Bradford/Leeds MCCU 2009-10. Awaiting 1st XI debut.

^{NQ}**HUGHES, Chesney** Francis, b Anguilla 20 January 1991. 6'2". LHB, SLA. British passport. Debut (Derbyshire) 2010. Derbyshire 2nd XI debut 2009. Leeward Is 2009-10 to date (l-o only). HS 156 v Northants (Chesterfield) 2010. BB 1-9 v Worcs (Derby) 2010. LO HS 81 Leeward Is v Windward Is (Kingston) 2010-11. LO BB 1-17 WI U19s v Leeward Is (Enmore) 2007-08. T20 HS 65. T20 BB 1-17.

JONES, Philip Steffan (Stradey CS, Llanelli; Neath TC; Loughborough U; Homerton C, Cambridge), b Llanelli, Carms, Wales 9 Feb 1974. 6'2". RHB, RMF. Cambridge U 1997; blue 1997. Somerset 1997-2003, 2007-08; cap 2001. Northamptonshire 2004-05. Derbyshire 2006, 2009 to date; cap 2010. Kent 2009. Wales MC 1994-97. HS 114 Sm v Leics (Leicester) 2007. De HS 86 v Worcs (Worcester) 2010. 50 wkts (2); most – 59 (2001, 2006). BB 6-25 v Glamorgan (Cardiff) 2006. LO HS 42 Sm v Glamorgan (Taunton) 2008 (FPT). LO BB 6-56 Nh v Ire (Clontarf) 2004 (CGT). T20 HS 40. T20 BB 3-20.

‡^{NQ}**KHAWAJA, Usman** Tariq, b Islamabad, Pakistan 18 Dec 1986. 5'9". LHB, RM. NSW 2007-08 to date. **Tests** (A): 1 (2010-11); HS 37 v E (Sydney) 2010-11. HS 214 and BB 1-21 NSW v S Australia (Adelaide) 2010-11. LO HS 121 NSW v S Australia (Sydney) 2010-11. T20 HS 65.

LINEKER, Matthew Steven (Swanwick Hall S), b Derby 22 Jan 1985. 6'5". LHB, SLA. Derbyshire 2nd XI debut 2006. Nottinghamshire 2nd XI 2008. Awaiting 1st XI debut.

^{NQ}**MADSEN, Wayne** Lee (Kearsney C, Durban; U of South Africa), b Durban, South Africa 2 Jan 1984. Nephew of M.B.Madsen (Natal 1967-68 to 1978-79), T.R.Madsen (Natal 1976-77 to 1989-90) and H.R.Fotheringham (Natal, Transvaal 1971-72 to 1989-90) and cousin of G.S.Fotheringham (KwaZulu-Natal 2008-09 to date). 5'11". RHB, OB. KwaZulu-Natal 2003-04 to 2007-08. Dolphins 2006-07 to 2007-08. Derbyshire debut 2009, scoring 170 v Glos (Cheltenham). HS 179 v Northants (Northampton) 2010. BB 3-45 KZ-Natal v EP (Pt Elizabeth) 2007-08. De BB 1-68 v Glam (Cardiff) 2010. LO HS 71 v Middx (Derby) 2010 (CB40). LO BB 2-18 v Glamorgan (Derby) 2010 (P40). T20 HS 29.

NEEDHAM, Jake (Nottingham Bluecoat S, Aspley), b Portsmouth, Hants 30 Sep 1986. 6'1". RHB, OB. Debut (Derbyshire) 2005. No f-c appearances in 2010. HS 48 v Notts (Chesterfield) 2007. BB 6-49 v Leics (Leicester) 2008. LO HS 42 v Somerset (Taunton) 2007 (P40). LO BB 3-36 v Essex (Colchester) 2010 (CB40). T20 HS 7*. T20 BB 4-21.

‡**PALLADINO, Antonio** Paul (Cardinal Pole SS; Anglia Polytechnic U), b Tower Hamlets, London 29 Jun 1983. 6'0". RHB, RMF. Cambridge UCCE 2003-05. Essex 2003-10. Namibia 2009-10. HS 66 Ex v Durham (Chelmsford) 2010. BB 6-41 Ex v Kent (Canterbury) 2003. LO HS 31 Namibia v Boland (Windhoek) 2009-10. LO BB 3-32 Ex v Glamorgan (Chelmsford) 2003 (NL). T20 HS 8*. T20 BB 4-21.

PARK, Garry Terence (Eshowe HS, Natal; Anglia Ruskin U), b Empangeni, Zululand, South Africa 19 Apr 1983. Elder brother of C.M.Park (Cambridge MCCU 2010) and younger brother of S.M.Park (Unicorns 2010). 5'7". RHB, RM, occ WK. Cambridge UCCE 2003-05. Durham 2006-08. Derbyshire debut 2009. Cambridgeshire 2005. 1000 runs (1): 1059 (2009). HS 178* v Kent (Derby) 2009. BB 3-25 v Surrey (Derby) 2009. LO HS 64 v Surrey (Croydon) 2009 (P40). LO BB 2-40 v Middx (Uxbridge) 2009 (P40). T20 HS 66. T20 BB 3-11.

POYNTON, Thomas (John Taylor HS, Barton-under-Needwood; Repton S), b Burton upon Trent, Staffs 25 Nov 1989. 5'10". RHB, WK. Debut (Derbyshire) 2007. No f-c appearances in 2009. HS 25 and BB 2-96 v Glamorgan (Cardiff) 2010. LO HS 24 v Warwks (Birmingham) 2009 (P40). T20 HS 3.

REDFERN, Daniel James (Adam's GS, Newport, Shropshire), b Shrewsbury, Shropshire 18 Apr 1990. 5'9". LHB, OB. Debut (Derbyshire) 2007. HS 95 v Northants (Northampton) 2009. BB 1-7 (twice). LO HS 57* v Yorks (Derby) 2007 (P40). LO BB 2-10 v Kent (Chesterfield) 2009 (P40). T20 HS 9.

SHEIKH, Atif, b Nottingham 18 Feb 1991. RHB, LMF. Debut (Derbyshire) 2010. England U19s 2010. Derbyshire 2nd XI debut 2008. HS 6 and BB 3-78 v Glos (Derby) 2010 – only f-c game.

SLATER, Benjamin Thomas (Netherthorpe S; Leeds Met U), b Chesterfield 26 Aug 1991. 5'10". LHB, LBG. Derbyshire 2nd XI debut 2009. Bradford/Leeds MCCU 2009-10. Awaiting 1st XI debut.

ᴺᴼ**SMITH, Gregory** Marc (St Stithins C), b Johannesburg, South Africa 20 Apr 1983. 5'9". RHB, RM/OB. Debut (SA Academy) 2003-04. Griqualand West 2003-04. Derbyshire debut 2006 (Kolpak registration); cap 2009; captain 2010 (*part*). Mountaineers 2010-11. HS 165* v Glamorgan (Derby) 2010. BB 5-54 v Northants (Chesterfield) 2010. LO HS 88 v Kent (Derby) 2007 (P40). LO BB 4-53 v Lancs (Derby) 2009 (P40). T20 HS 100*. T20 BB 5-27.

‡**SUTTON, Luke** David (Millfield S; Durham U), b Keynsham, Somerset 4 Oct 1976. 5'11". RHB, WK. Somerset 1997-98. Derbyshire 2000-05; cap 2002; captain 2004-05. Lancashire 2006-10; cap 2007. Rejoins Derbyshire in 2011 as captain. HS 151* La v Yorks (Manchester) 2006. De HS 140* v Sussex (Derby) 2001. LO HS 83 v Lancs (Derby) 2003 (NL). T20 HS 61*.

‡**TURNER, Mark** Leif (Thornhill CS), b Sunderland, Co Durham 23 Oct 1984. 5'11". RHB, RMF. Durham 2005-06. Somerset 2007-09, no f-c appearances in 2010. HS 57 Sm v Derbys (Taunton) 2007. BB 4-30 Sm v LU (Taunton) 2007. CC BB 3-53 Sm v Lancs (Manchester) 2008. LO HS 15* Sm v Essex (Taunton) 2009 (P40). LO BB 4-36 Sm v Worcs (Bath) 2010 (CB40). T20 HS 11*. T20 BB 3-25.

WHITELEY, Ross Andrew (Repton S), b Sheffield, Yorks 13 Sep 1988. RHB, WK. Debut (Derbyshire) 2008. No f-c appearances in 2009-10. Derbyshire 2nd XI debut 2006. HS 27 v Leics (Leicester) 2008 – on debut. LO HS 24 v Glamorgan (Cardiff) 2008.

GODDARD, Lee James (Batley GS; Huddersfield TC; Loughborough U), b Dewsbury, Yorks 22 Oct 1982. 5'10". RHB, WK. Loughborough UCCE 2003. Derbyshire 2004, 2006, 2010. Durham 2007. No f-c appearances for Du in 2008-09. HS 91 v Surrey (Derby) 2006. LO HS 36 v Kent (Canterbury) 2006 (P40). T20 HS 22*.

HUNTER, Ian David (Fyndoune Community C, Sacriston; New C, Durham), b Durham City 11 Sep 1979. 6'2". RHB, RMF. Durham 2000-03. Derbyshire 2004-09. No f-c appearances in 2010. HS 65 Du v Northants (Northampton) 2002. De HS 48 v Somerset (Taunton) 2006. BB 5-46 v Essex (Chelmsford) 2009. LO HS 39 Du v Leics (Leicester) 2002 (BHC). LO BB 4-29 Du v Essex (Ilford) 2000 (NL). T20 HS 25*. T20 BB 3-26.

LUNGLEY, Tom (St John Houghton SS; SE Derbyshire C), b Derby 25 Jul 1979. 6'1". LHB, RM. Derbyshire 2000-10; cap 2007. HS 50 v Warwks (Derby) 2008. 50 wkts (1): 59 (2007). BB 5-20 v Leics (Derby) 2007. LO HS 45 v Essex (Chelmsford) 2001 (NL). LO BB 4-28 v Essex (Derby) 2001 (NL). T20 HS 25. T20 BB 5-27 v Leics (Leicester) 2009 – De record.

NO**PETERSON, Robin** John, b Pt Elizabeth, South Africa 4 Aug 1979. LHB, SLA. EP 1998-99 to 2003-04. Warriors 2004-05 to 2008-09. Cape Cobras 2009-10 to date. Derbyshire 2010 (Kolpak registration). **Tests** (SA): 6 (2003 to 2007-08); HS 61 v B (Dhaka) 2003 – on debut; BB 5-33 v B (Chittagong) 2007-08. **LOI** (SA): 40 (2002-03 to 2010-11); HS 36 v WI (Centurion) 2003-04; BB 3-42 v P (Dubai) 2010-11. **IT20** (SA): 7 (2005-06 to 2010-11); HS 34 v A (Centurion) 2008-09; BB 3-30 v A (Johannesburg) 2008-09. F-c Tours (SA): E 2003; WI 2000-01 (SA A); P 2003-04; B 2003, 2007-08. HS 130 EP v Gauteng (Johannesburg) 2002-03. De HS 58 v Northants (Chesterfield) 2010. 50 wkts (1): 51 (2010). BB 6-67 EP v Border (East London) 1999-00. De BB 4-10 v Sussex (Derby) 2010. LO HS 101 EP v Border (Pt Elizabeth) 2001-02. LO BB 7-24 Warriors v Eagles (East London) 2007-08. T20 HS 72*. T20 BB 3-24.

ROGERS, C.J.L. – *see MIDDLESEX.*

SADLER, John Leonard (St Thomas A'Becket S, Sandal), b Dewsbury, Yorks 19 Nov 1981. 5'11". LHB, LBG. Leicestershire 2003-07. Derbyshire 2008-10. 1000 runs (1): 1024 (2006). HS 145 Le v Surrey (Leicester) 2003 and 145 Le v Sussex (Hove) 2003. De HS 50 v Bangladesh A (Derby) 2008. BB 1-5 Le v Middx (Southgate) 2007. De BB 1-57 v Essex (Derby) 2008. LO HS 113* Le v Derbys (Leicester) 2007 (FPT). LO BB 1-33 Le v Yorks (Leeds) 2007 (FPT). T20 HS 73. T20 BB – .

WAGG, G.G. – *see GLAMORGAN.*

L.E.Bosman, E.P.Jones and C.K.Langeveldt left the staff without making a County First-Class or List A appearance for Derbyshire in 2010.

DERBYSHIRE 2010

RESULTS SUMMARY

	Place	Won	Lost	Tied	Drew	NR
LV= County Championship (2nd Division)	9th	3	7		6	
All First-Class Matches		3	7		6	1
Clydesdale Bank 40 (Group B)	4th	4	8			
Friends Provident t20 (North Group)	5th	6	8			2

LV= COUNTY CHAMPIONSHIP AVERAGES

BATTING AND FIELDING

Cap		M	I	NO	HS	Runs	Avge	100	50	Ct/St
2008	C.J.L.Rogers	15	27	3	200	1285	53.54	4	5	19
	C.F.Hughes	12	21	2	156	784	41.26	2	4	12
	W.L.Madsen	16	29	1	179	940	33.57	4	2	11
2010	P.S.Jones	12	18	4	86	427	30.50	–	1	4
2009	G.M.Smith	16	27	1	165*	721	27.73	1	4	4
	G.T.Park	11	19	2	124*	431	25.35	1	2	6
	S.J.Adshead	4	7	2	49	125	25.00	–	–	13
	D.J.Redfern	9	15	1	85	331	23.64	–	1	3
	R.J.Peterson	15	24	3	58	484	23.04	–	2	9
	W.J.Durston	6	11	–	69	240	21.81	–	1	9
	T.D.Groenewald	13	19	9	35*	216	21.60	–	–	3
	P.M.Borrington	7	13	1	79*	246	20.50	–	1	4
	L.J.Goddard	8	11	1	67	165	16.50	–	1	24
	T.Poynton	4	6	–	25	88	14.66	–	–	5
2007	G.G.Wagg	4	7	–	37	82	11.71	–	–	1
	J.L.Sadler	3	4	–	16	45	11.25	–	–	3
2007	T.Lungley	7	10	1	21	85	9.44	–	–	6
	M.H.A.Footitt	9	12	3	30	69	7.66	–	–	3
	J.L.Clare	4	6	–	24	45	7.50	–	–	4

Also batted: A.Sheikh (1 match) 6, 0 (1 ct).

BOWLING

	O	M	R	W	Avge	Best	5wI	10wM
G.G.Wagg	77	13	246	10	24.60	3-31	–	–
J.L.Clare	69.3	8	324	11	29.45	4-42	–	–
R.J.Peterson	553.3	129	1566	51	30.70	4-10	–	–
P.S.Jones	313.5	68	959	31	30.93	4-26	–	–
G.M.Smith	414.3	77	1368	42	32.57	5-54	1	–
T.Lungley	165.0	25	630	19	33.15	3-39	–	–
T.D.Groenewald	413.5	105	1295	38	34.07	5-86	1	–
M.H.A.Footitt	239.2	48	786	23	34.17	4-78	–	–
Also bowled:								
A.Sheikh	25.0	1	152	5	30.40	3-78	–	–
G.T.Park	83.3	9	327	9	36.33	2-20	–	–

W.J.Durston 16-0-76-1; C.F.Hughes 11-0-81-1; W.L.Madsen 8.2-0-68-1; T.Poynton
8-0-96-2; D.J.Redfern 3-0-14-0; C.J.L.Rogers 1-0-5-0.

Derbyshire played no first-class fixtures outside the County Championship in 2010, their
fixture against Loughborough MCCU was abandoned without a ball bowled. The First-Class
Averages (pp 220–237) give the records of their players in all first-class county matches.

DERBYSHIRE RECORDS

FIRST-CLASS CRICKET

Highest Total	For 801-8d		v	Somerset	Taunton	2007
	V 662		by	Yorkshire	Chesterfield	1898
Lowest Total	For 16		v	Notts	Nottingham	1879
	V 23		by	Hampshire	Burton upon T	1958
Highest Innings	For 274	G.A.Davidson	v	Lancashire	Manchester	1896
	V 343*	P.A.Perrin	for	Essex	Chesterfield	1904

Highest Partnership for each Wicket

1st	322	H.Storer/J.Bowden	v	Essex	Derby	1929
2nd	417	K.J.Barnett/T.A.Tweats	v	Yorkshire	Derby	1997
3rd	316*	A.S.Rollins/K.J.Barnett	v	Leics	Leicester	1997
4th	328	P.Vaulkhard/D.Smith	v	Notts	Nottingham	1946
5th	302*†	J.E.Morris/D.G.Cork	v	Glos	Cheltenham	1993
6th	212	G.M.Lee/T.S.Worthington	v	Essex	Chesterfield	1932
7th	258	M.P.Dowman/D.G.Cork	v	Durham	Derby	2000
8th	198	K.M.Krikken/D.G.Cork	v	Lancashire	Manchester	1996
9th	283	A.Warren/J.Chapman	v	Warwicks	Blackwell	1910
10th	132	A.Hill/M.Jean-Jacques	v	Yorkshire	Sheffield	1986

† 346 runs were added for this wicket in two separate partnerships

Best Bowling	For 10- 40	W.Bestwick	v	Glamorgan	Cardiff	1921
(Innings)	V 10- 45	R.L.Johnson	for	Middlesex	Derby	1994
Best Bowling	For 17-103	W.Mycroft	v	Hampshire	Southampton	1876
(Match)	V 16-101	G.Giffen	for	Australians	Derby	1886

Most Runs – Season	2165	D.B.Carr	(av 48.11)	1959
Most Runs – Career	23854	K.J.Barnett	(av 41.12)	1979-98
Most 100s – Season	8	P.N.Kirsten		1982
Most 100s – Career	53	K.J.Barnett		1979-98
Most Wkts – Season	168	T.B.Mitchell	(av 19.55)	1935
Most Wkts – Career	1670	H.L.Jackson	(av 17.11)	1947-63
Most Career W-K Dismissals	1304	R.W.Taylor	(1157 ct; 147 st)	1961-84
Most Career Catches in the Field	563	D.C.Morgan		1950-69

LIMITED-OVERS CRICKET

Highest Total	50ov	365-3		v	Cornwall	Derby	1986
	40ov	304-3		v	Kent	Maidstone	2005
	T20	222-5		v	Yorkshire	Leeds	2010
Lowest Total	50ov	79		v	Surrey	The Oval	1967
	40ov	60		v	Kent	Canterbury	2008
	T20	98		v	Lancashire	Manchester	2005
Highest Innings	50ov	173*	M.J.Di Venuto	v	Derbys CB	Derby	2000
	40ov	141*	C.J.Adams	v	Kent	Chesterfield	1992
	T20	111	W.J.Durston	v	Notts	Nottingham	2010
Best Bowling	50ov	8-21	M.A.Holding	v	Sussex	Hove	1988
	40ov	6- 7	M.Hendrick	v	Notts	Nottingham	1972
	T20	5-27	T.Lungley	v	Leics	Leicester	2009

DURHAM

Formation of Present Club: 23 May 1882
Inaugural First-Class Match: 1992
Colours: Navy Blue, Yellow and Maroon
Badge: Coat of Arms of the County of Durham
County Champions: (2) 2008, 2009
Gillette/NatWest/C&G/FP Trophy Winners: (1) 2007
Benson and Hedges Cup Winners: (0); best –
Quarter-Finalist 1998, 2000, 2001
Pro 40/National League (Div 1) Winners: (0); best – 6th
2009
Sunday League Winners: (0); best – 7th 1993
Clydesdale Bank 40 Winners: (0); best – 5th (Group C)
2010
Twenty20 Cup Winners: (0); best – Semi-Finalist 2008

Chief Executive: David Harker, Emirates Durham International Cricket Ground, Chester-le-Street, Co Durham DH3 3QR • Tel: 0191 387 1717 • Fax: 0191 387 1616 • Email: marketing@durhamccc.co.uk • Web: www.durhamccc.co.uk

Director of Cricket: G.Cook. **Assistant Coaches:** J.J.B.Lewis and A.Walker. **Captain:** P.Mustard (f-c) and D.M.Benkenstein (l-o). **Vice-Captain:** none. **Overseas Player:** none. **2011 Beneficiary:** none. **Head Groundsman:** David Measor. **Scorer:** Brian Hunt. ‡ New registration.^{NQ} Not qualified for England.

Durham initially awarded caps immediately after their players joined the staff but revised this policy in 1998, again capping players on merit, past 'awards' having been nullified. Durham abolished both their capping and 'awards' systems after the 2005 season.

BENKENSTEIN, Dale Martin (Durban HS; Michaelhouse HS), b Salisbury, Rhodesia 9 Jun 1974. Son of M.M.Benkenstein (Rhodesia, Natal B 1970-71 to 1980-81); brother of twins B.R. (Natal B 1993-94) and B.N. Benkenstein (Natal B, GW 1994-95 to 1996-97). 5'9". RHB, RM/OB. Natal/KwaZulu-Natal 1993-94 to 2003-04. Dolphins 2004-05 to 2007-08. MCC 2004. British passport. Durham debut/cap 2005; captain 2006-08, l-o captain 2011. *Wisden* 2008. **LOI** (SA): 23 (1998-99 to 2002-03); HS 69 v WI (Cape Town) 1998-99; BB 3-5 v Kenya (Colombo) 2002-03. F-c Tours (SA A): WI 2000; NZ 1998-99 (SA); SL 1995 (SA U-24), 1998. 1000 runs (4); most – 1500 (2006). HS 259 KZ-Natal v Northerns (Durban) 2001-02. Du HS 181 v Somerset (Taunton) 2009. BB 4-16 Dolphins v Warriors (Durban) 2005-06. Du BB 4-29 v Northants (Northampton) 2005. LO HS 107* Natal v North West (Fochville) 1997-98. LO BB 4-16 v Surrey (Chester-le-St) 2005. T20 HS 57*. T20 BB 3-10.

BLACKWELL, Ian David (Brookfield Community S), b Chesterfield, Derbys 10 Jun 1978. 6'2". LHB, SLA. Derbyshire 1997-99. Somerset 2000-08; cap 2001; captain 2006 (*part*). Durham debut 2009. **Tests:** 1 (2005-06); HS 4 and BB- v I (Nagpur) 2005-06. **LOI:** 34 (2002-03 to 2005-06); HS 82 v I (Colombo) 2002-03; BB 3-26 v A (Adelaide) 2002-03. F-c Tour: I 2005-06. 1000 runs (3); most – 1256 (2005). HS 247* Sm v Derbys (Taunton) 2003 – off 156 balls and including 204 off 98 balls in reduced post-lunch session. Won Walter Lawrence Trophy 2005 for 67-ball hundred v Derbys (Taunton). Du HS 158 v Warwks (Birmingham) 2009. BB 7-85 v Lancs (Manchester) 2009. LO HS 134* Sm v Sussex (Taunton) 2005 (NL). LO BB 5-26 Sm v Derbys (Taunton) 2005 (NL). T20 HS 82. T20 BB 4-26.

BORTHWICK, Scott George (Farringdon Community Sports C, Sunderland), b Sunderland 19 Apr 1990. 5'9". LHB, LBG. Debut (Durham) 2009. Durham 2nd XI debut 2006. England U19 2008-09 to 2009. HS 68 v Notts (Chester-le-St) 2010. BB 4-27 v MCC (Abu Dhabi) 2010. CC BB 3-95 v Hants (Southampton) 2009 – on debut. LO HS 10* v Notts (Nottingham) 2010 (CB40). LO BB 2-11 v Worcs (Chester-le-St) 2009 (P40). T20 HS – . T20 BB 3-23.

BRATHWAITE, Ruel Marlon Ricardo (Queen's C, Barbados; Dulwich C; Loughborough U; Queen's C, Cambridge), b Bridgetown, Barbados 6 Sep 1985. 6'2". RHB, RFM. British passport. Loughborough UCCE 2006-08. British U 2006. MCC 2007. Cambridge U 2009. Durham debut 2010 (1 match). HS 76* LU v Worcs (Worcester) 2007. Du HS 2 and Du BB 3-93 v Somerset (Chester-le-St) 2010. BB 5-54 CU v Oxford U (Cambridge) 2009. LO HS – . LO BB 1-19 WI v EL (Worcester) 2007. T20 HS 0. T20 BB 1-33.

BREESE, Gareth Rohan (Wolmer's BHS, Kingston; Kingston U of Technology, Jamaica), b Montego Bay, Jamaica 9 Jan 1976. 5'7". RHB, OB. Jamaica 1995-96 to 2005-06; captain/overseas player 2003-04 to 2005-06. British passport (Welsh father). Durham debut 2004; cap 2005. **Tests** (WI): 1 (2002-03); HS 5 and BB 2-108 v I (Madras) 2002-03. F-c Tours (WI): E 2002 (WI A); I 2002-03. HS 165* v Somerset (Taunton) 2004. BB 7-60 Jamaica v Barbados (Bridgetown) 2000-01. Du BB 5-41 (10-151 match) v Yorks (Scarborough) 2004 – scored 35 and 68 to complete match double. LO HS 68* v Notts (Chester-le-St) 2007 (FPT). LO BB 5-41 v Derbys (Chester-le-St) 2008 (FPT). T20 HS 37. T20 BB 4-14.

CLAYDON, Mitchell Eric (Westfield Sports HS, Sydney), b Fairfield, NSW, Australia 25 Nov 1982. 6'4". LHB, RMF. Yorkshire 2005-06. Durham debut 2007. Canterbury 2010-11. HS 40 v Lancs (Manchester) 2008. BB 4-90 v Sussex (Hove) 2009. LO HS 19 v Glos (Bristol) 2009 (FPT). LO BB 4-39 Cant v Otago (Timaru) 2010-11. T20 HS 12*. T20 BB 5-26.

COETZER, Kyle James (Aberdeen GS), b Aberdeen, Scotland 14 Apr 1984. 5'11". RHB, RM. Debut (Durham) 2004. Scotland 2004 to date. **LOI** (Scot): 5 (2008 to 2010); HS 51 v E (Edinburgh) 2010. BB – . **IT20** (Scot): 9 (2008 to 2009-10); HS 48* v Kenya (Belfast) 2008; BB 3-25 v Afghanistan (Abu Dhabi) 2009-10. F-c Tour (Scot): Kenya 2009-10. HS 172 v MCC (Abu Dhabi) 2010. CC HS 142 v Warwks (Chester-le-St) 2007. BB 2-16 Scot v Kenya (Nairobi) 2009-10. Du BB – . LO HS 127 Scot v Oman (Johannesburg) 2008-09. LO BB – . T20 HS 64. T20 BB 3-25.

COLLINGWOOD, Paul David (Blackfyne CS; Derwentside C), b Shotley Bridge 26 May 1976. 5'11". RHB, RM. Debut (Durham) 1996 v Northants (Chester-le-St) taking wicket of D.J.Capel with his first ball before scoring 91 and 16; cap 1998; benefit 2007. MBE 2005. *Wisden* 2007. **ECB central contract 2010-11. Tests**: 68 (2003-04 to 2010-11); HS 206 v A (Adelaide) 2006-07; BB 3-23 v NZ (Wellington) 2007-08. **LOI**: 193 (2001 to 2010-11, 25 as captain); HS 120* v A (Melbourne) 2006-07; BB 6-31 v B (Nottingham) 2005 – record analysis for E, and first to score a hundred (112*) and take six wickets in same LOI. **IT20**: 35 (2005 to 2010-11, 30 as captain); HS 79 v WI (Oval) 2007; BB 4-22 v SL (Southampton) 2006. F-c Tours: A 2006-07, 2010-11; SA 2004-05; WI 2003-04, 2008-09; NZ 2007-08; I 2005-06, 2008-09; P 2005-06; SL 2003-04, 2007-08; B 2009-10. 1000 runs (2); most – 1120 (2005), inc six hundreds (Du record). HS 206 (see Tests). Du HS 190 v SL (Chester-le-St) 2002 and 190 v Derbys (Derby) 2005, sharing Du record 4th wkt partnership of 250 with D.M.Benkenstein. BB 5-52 v Somerset (Stockton) 2005. LO HS 120* (see LOI). LO BB 6-31 (see LOI). T20 HS 79 (see IT20). T20 BB 5-14 v Derbys (Chester-le-St) 2008 – Du record.

DAVIES, Anthony **Mark** (Northfield CS, Billingham; Stockton SFC), b Stockton-on-Tees 4 Oct 1980. 6'3". RHB, RMF. Debut (Durham) 2002; cap 2005. Nottinghamshire 2007 (on loan). F-c Tour (Eng A): NZ 2008-09. HS 62 v Somerset (Stockton) 2005. 50 wkts (1): 50 (2004). BB 8-24 (11-75 match) v Hants (Basingstoke) 2008. LO HS 31* v Warwks (Chester-le-St) 2002 (NL). LO BB 4-13 v Sussex (Chester-le-St) 2001 (NL). T20 HS 6. T20 BB 2-14.

NQDi VENUTO, Michael James (St Virgil's C; Hobart), b Hobart, Australia 12 Dec 1973. 6'0". LHB, RM/LBG. Tasmania 1991-92 to 2007-08. Sussex 1999; cap 1999. Derbyshire 2000-06; cap 2000; appointed captain for 2004 but missed entire season – back surgery. Durham debut 2007, carrying his bat for 155* v Worcs (Worcester) on debut. Italian passport 2008. **LOI** (A): 9 (1996-97 to 1997-98); HS 89 v SA (Johannesburg) 1996-97. F-c Tours: Z 1995-96 (Tas); Scotland/Ireland 1998 (Aus A). 1000 runs (10); most – 1654 (2009), inc six hundreds (Du record). HS 254* v Sussex (Chester-le-St) 2009. BB 1-0 Tas v Q (Brisbane) 1999-00. UK BB 1-3 Sx v Somerset (Taunton) 1999. LO HS 173* v Derbys CB (Derby) 2000 (NWT). LO BB 1-10 Tas v Q (Hobart) 1995-96. T20 HS 95*. T20 BB 3-19.

HARMISON, Ben William (Ashington HS), b Ashington, Northumb 9 Jan 1986. Younger brother of S.J.Harmison. 6'5". LHB, RMF. Debut (Durham) 2006, scoring 110 v Oxford UCCE (Oxford). Scored 105 in his second match (v West Indies A) to emulate A.Fairbairn (Middlesex 1947) in scoring hundreds in first two f-c matches, those matches being in England. HS 110 (see above). CC HS 101 v Warwks (Chester-le-St) 2007. BB 4-27 v Surrey (Guildford) 2008. LO HS 67 v Notts (Chester-le-St) 2009 (P40). LO BB 3-43 v Scotland (Chester-le-St) 2008 (FPT). T20 HS 24. T20 BB 3-20.

HARMISON, Stephen James (Ashington HS), b Ashington, Northumb 23 Oct 1978. Elder brother of B.W.Harmison. 6'4". RHB, RF. Debut (Durham) 1996; cap 1999. ICC World XI 2005-06. Lions 2007-08. MCC 2007. *Wisden* 2004. MBE 2005. **Tests**: 63 (2002 to 2009); HS 49* v SA (Oval) 2008; BB 7-12 (9-73 match) v WI (Kingston) 2003-04. **LOI**: 58 (2002-03 to 2008-09); HS 18* v WI (Providence) 2008-09; BB 5-33 v A (Bristol) 2005; hat-trick v I (Nottingham) 2004. **IT20**: 2 (2005 to 2006); HS – ; BB 1-13 v A (Southampton) 2005. F-c Tours: A 2002-03, 2005-06 (RW), 2006-07; SA 1998-99 (Eng A), 2004-05; WI 2003-04, 2009; NZ 2007-08; I 2005-06, 2008-09; P 2005-06; SL 2007-08; Z 1998-99 (Eng A); B 2003-04. HS 49* (see Tests). Du HS 36* v Hants (Chester-le-St) 2008. 50 wkts (6); most – 65 (2008). BB 7-12 (see Tests). Du BB 7-29 (9-74 match) v Warwks (Chester-le-St) 2010. Hat-tricks (2): v Worcs (Chester-le-St) 2005 and v Sussex (Hove) 2008. LO HS 25* v Somerset (Chester-le-St) 2008 (P40). LO BB 5-33 (see LOI). T20 HS 6. T20 BB 5-41.

MUCHALL, Gordon James (Durham S), b Newcastle upon Tyne, Northumb 2 Nov 1982. 6'0". RHB, RM. Northumberland 1999. Older brother of P.B.Muchall (Northumberland). Debut (Durham) 2002; cap 2005. F-c Tours: SL 2002-03 (ECB Acad). HS 219 v Kent (Canterbury) 2006, sharing Du record 6th wkt partnership of 249 with P.Mustard (see below). BB 3-26 v Yorks (Leeds) 2003. LO HS 101* v Yorks (Leeds) 2005 (NL). LO BB 1-15 v Sussex (Hove) 2003 (NL). T20 HS 64*. T20 BB 1-8.

MUSTARD, Philip (Usworth CS), b Sunderland 8 Oct 1982. Cousin of C.Rushworth (see below). 5'11". LHB, WK. Debut (Durham) 2002; captain 2010 (part) to date. **LOI**: 10 (2007-08); HS 83 v NZ (Napier) 2007-08. **IT20**: 2 (2007-08); HS 40 v NZ (Christchurch) 2007-08. HS 130 v Kent (Canterbury) 2006. LO HS 108 v Northants (Northampton) 2007 (FPT). T20 HS 70*.

ONIONS, Graham (St Thomas More RC S, Blaydon), b Gateshead 9 Sep 1982. 6'1". RHB, RFM. Debut (Durham) 2004. MCC 2007-08. *Wisden* 2009. Missed entire 2010 season through back injury. **Tests**: 8 (2009 to 2009-10); HS 17* v A (Lord's) 2009; BB 5-38 v WI (Lord's) 2009 – on debut. **LOI**: 4 (2009 to 2009-10); HS 1 v A (Centurion) 2009-10; BB 2-58 v SL (Johannesburg) 2009-10. F-c Tours: SA 2009-10; I 2007-08 (EL); B 2006-07 (Eng A). HS 41 v Yorks (Leeds) 2007. 50 wkts (2); most – 69 (2009). BB 8-101 v Warwks (Birmingham) 2007. LO HS 19 v Derbys (Derby) 2008 (FPT). LO BB 3-39 v Derbys (Derby) 2005 (NL). T20 HS 31. T20 BB 3-25.

PLUNKETT, Liam Edward (Nunthorpe SS; Teesside Tertiary C), b Middlesbrough, Yorks 6 Apr 1985. 6'3". RHB, RFM. Debut (Durham) 2003. Dolphins 2007-08. **Tests**: 9 (2005-06 to 2007); HS 44* v WI (Leeds) 2007; BB 3-17 v SL (Birmingham) 2006. **LOI**: 29 (2005-06 to 2010-11); HS 56 v P (Lahore) 2005-06; BB 3-24 v A (Sydney) 2006-07. **IT20**: 1 (2006); HS – ; BB 1-37 v SL (Southampton) 2006. F-c Tours: WI 2010-11 (EL); NZ 2008-09 (EL); I 2005-06, 2007-08 (EL); P 2005-06. HS 94* v Sussex (Hove) 2009. 50 wkts (3); most – 60 (2009). BB 6-63 (11-119) v Worcs (Chester-le-St) 2009. LO HS 72 v Somerset (Chester-le-St) 2008 (P40). LO BB 4-15 v Essex (Chester-le-St) 2007 (FPT). T20 HS 31. T20 BB 3-16.

RICHARDSON, Michael John (Rondebosch HS; Stonyhurst C, Nottingham U), b Pt Elizabeth, South Africa 4 Oct 1986. Son of D.J.Richardson (South Africa, EP and NT 1977-78 to 1997-98), grandson of J.H.Richardson (NE Transvaal and Transvaal B 1952-53 to 1960-61), nephew of R.P.Richardson (WP 1984-85 to 1988-89). 5'10". RHB, WK. MCC YC 2008-09. Debut (Durham) 2010. HS 2 v Durham MCCU (Durham) 2010 – only 1st XI appearance to date.

RUSHWORTH, Christopher (Castle View CS, Sunderland), b Sunderland 11 Jul 1986. Cousin of P.Mustard (*see above*). 6'2". RHB, RMF. Debut (Durham) 2010. Durham 2nd XI debut 2004. Northumberland 2004-05. HS 28 v Yorks (Chester-le-St) 2010. BB 4-90 v Essex (Chelmsford) 2010. LO HS 7* v Notts (Nottingham) 2010 (CB40). LO BB 3-6 v Scotland (Chester-le-St) 2010.

SMITH, William Rew (Bedford S; Collingwood C, Durham), b Luton, Beds 28 Sep 1982. 5'9". RHB, OB. Nottinghamshire 2002-06. Durham UCCE 2003-05; captain 2004-05. British U 2004-05. Durham debut 2007; captain 2009-10 (part). Bedfordshire 1999-2002. HS 201* v Surrey (Guildford) 2008. BB 3-34 DU v Leics (Leicester) 2005. CC BB 1-5 v Lancs (Chester-le-St) 2007. LO HS 103 v Worcs (Chester-le-St) 2007 (FPT). LO BB 1-6 v Derbys (Chester-le-St) 2008 (FPT). T20 HS 55. T20 BB 1-31.

STOKES, Benjamin Andrew (Cockermouth S), b Christchurch, Canterbury, New Zealand 4 Jun 1991. 6'0". LHB, RM. Debut (Durham) 2010. Durham 2nd XI debut 2007 when aged 16y 99d. England U19s 2009 to 2009-10. F-c Tour (EL): WI 2010-11. HS 161* v Kent (Canterbury) 2010. BB 2-32 v Hants (Chester-le-St) 2010. LO HS 39 v Scotland (Glasgow) and v Notts (Nottingham) 2010 (CB40). BB 2-22 v Surrey (Oval) 2009 (FPT) and v Warwks (Chester-le-St) 2010 (CB40). T20 HS 44. T20 BB 1-23.

STONEMAN, Mark Daniel (Whickham CS), b Newcastle upon Tyne, Northumb 26 Jun 1987. 5'11". LHB, RM. Debut (Durham) 2007. HS 118 v Durham MCCU (Durham) 2010. CC HS 101 v Sussex (Chester-le-St) 2007. LO HS 25 v Notts (Nottingham) 2010 (CB40). T20 HS 46.

THORP, Callum David (Servite C, Tuart Hill, Perth), b Mount Lawley, Perth, Australia 11 Feb 1975. 6'3". RHB, RMF. W Australia 2002-03 to 2003-04. Durham debut 2005. HS 79* v MCC (Abu Dhabi) 2010. CC HS 75 v Hants (Southampton) 2006. 50 wkts (1): 50 (2008). BB 7-88 v Kent (Canterbury) 2008. LO HS 52 v Bangladeshis (Chester-le-St) 2005. LO BB 6-17 v Scotland (Edinburgh) 2006 (CGT). T20 HS 13. T20 BB 2-32.

EVANS, L. – *see NORTHAMPTONSHIRE.*

GIDMAN, W.P.R. – *see GLOUCESTERSHIRE.*

KILLEEN, Neil (Greencroft CS; Derwentside C; Teesside U), b Shotley Bridge 17 Oct 1975. 6'2". RHB, RMF. Durham 1995-2008; cap 1999; benefit 2006. MCC 1999-2000. No f-c appearances in 2009-10. Tour (MCC): B 1999-00. HS 48 v Somerset (Chester-le-St) 1995. 50 wkts (1): 58 (1999). BB 7-70 v Hants (Chester-le-St) 2003. LO HS 32 v Middx (Lord's) 1996 (SL). LO BB 6-31 v Derbys (Derby) 2000 (NL) – Du l-o record. T20 HS 17*. T20 BB 4-7.

P.R.Hindmarch, J.A.Morkel, L.R.P.L.Taylor and K.Turner left the staff without making a County First-Class or List A appearance in 2010.

COUNTY CAPS AWARDED IN 2010

Derbyshire	P.S.Jones
Durham	–
Essex	M.J.Walker
Glamorgan	J.Allenby, J.A.R.Harris
Gloucestershire	J.N.Batty, C.D.J.Dent, J.M.R.Taylor, E.G.C.Young
Hampshire	N.D.McKenzie
Kent	–
Lancashire	S.Chanderpaul, S.J.Croft, K.W.Hogg, T.C.Smith
Leicestershire	M.J.Hoggard
Middlesex	G.K.Berg, N.R.Dexter, A.C.Gilchrist, D.J.Malan
Northamptonshire	–
Nottinghamshire	H.M.Amla
Somerset	–
Surrey	–
Sussex	M.S.Panesar
Warwickshire	Imran Tahir
Worcestershire (colours)	J.G.Cameron, S.H.Choudhry, A.Richardson, B.J.M.Scott, Shakib Al Hasan
Yorkshire	A.Lyth, R.M.Pyrah, A.Shahzad, D.J.Wainwright

Durham abolished their capping system after 2005. Gloucestershire award caps on first-class debut. Worcestershire award club colours on Championship debut. Glamorgan's capping system is now based on a player's number of appearances and not on his performances.

DURHAM 2010

RESULTS SUMMARY

	Place	Won	Lost	Tied	Drew	NR
LV= County Championship (1st Division)	5th	5	3		8	
All First-Class Matches		6			9	
Clydesdale Bank 40 (Group C)	5th	5	6			1
Friends Provident t20 (North Group)	8th	4	8			4

LV= COUNTY CHAMPIONSHIP AVERAGES

BATTING AND FIELDING

Cap		M	I	NO	HS	Runs	Avge	100	50	Ct/St
	B.A.Stokes	13	19	3	161*	740	46.25	2	2	8
	M.J.Di Venuto	16	27	3	129	1092	45.50	3	7	29
2005	G.J.Muchall	9	14	1	140*	508	39.07	2	1	3
	P.Mustard	16	24	5	120	742	39.05	2	4	40/2
	I.D.Blackwell	15	24	2	86	794	36.09	–	8	2
2005	D.M.Benkenstein	16	26	1	114	799	31.96	1	5	13
	B.W.Harmison	5	9	–	96	265	29.44	–	2	2
	M.D.Stoneman	10	16	1	78	407	27.13	–	4	5
	K.J.Coetzer	6	12	1	72	280	25.45	–	2	2
	S.G.Borthwick	10	14	3	68	269	24.45	–	2	8
	M.E.Claydon	12	15	4	38*	185	16.81	–	–	2
	W.R.Smith	4	7	–	44	114	16.28	–	–	2
2005	A.M.Davies	5	4	2	27	32	16.00	–	–	–
	L.E.Plunkett	14	17	–	51	238	14.00	–	1	8
	C.D.Thorp	5	6	1	29	64	12.80	–	–	2
	C.Rushworth	9	14	2	28	127	10.58	–	–	1
1999	S.J.Harmison	8	11	6	11*	29	5.80	–	–	2

Also batted (one match each): R.M.R.Brathwaite 2, 0*; G.R.Breese (cap 2005) 8, 5 (1 ct); P.D.Collingwood (cap 1998) 12.

BOWLING

	O	M	R	W	Avge	Best	5wI	10wM
S.J.Harmison	240.4	50	801	30	26.70	7- 29	1	–
I.D.Blackwell	455.3	129	1205	43	28.02	5- 78	2	–
B.W.Harmison	86.4	10	402	14	28.71	4- 70	–	–
M.E.Claydon	287.1	49	1087	35	31.05	3- 17	–	–
C.D.Thorp	148.3	39	427	13	32.84	4- 54	–	–
C.Rushworth	214.4	43	821	21	39.09	4- 90	–	–
L.E.Plunkett	384.4	57	1386	35	39.60	4-107	–	–
S.G.Borthwick	153.5	18	615	15	41.00	2- 22	–	–

Also bowled:
B.A.Stokes 66.3 6 328 5 65.60 2- 32
D.M.Benkenstein 81-43-143-4; R.M.R.Brathwaite 30.1-2-118-4; K.J.Coetzer 7-0-33-0; P.D.Collingwood 7-2-11-1; A.M.Davies 128-45-273-2; G.J.Muchall 1-02-0; W.R.Smith 4-0-27-0.

The First-Class Averages (pp 220–237) give the records of Durham players in all first-class county matches (Durham's other opponents being Durham MCCU), with the exception of P.D.Collingwood and L.E.Plunkett, whose first-class figures for Durham are as above.

DURHAM RECORDS

FIRST-CLASS CRICKET

Highest Total	For 648-5d		v	Notts	Chester-le-St[2] 2009
	V 810-4d		by	Warwicks	Birmingham 1994
Lowest Total	For 67		v	Middlesex	Lord's 1996
	V 56		by	Somerset	Chester-le-St[2] 2003
Highest Innings	For 273	M.L.Love	v	Hampshire	Chester-le-St[2] 2003
	V 501*	B.C.Lara	for	Warwicks	Birmingham 1994

Highest Partnership for each Wicket

1st	334*	S.Hutton/M.A.Roseberry	v	Oxford U	Oxford 1996
2nd	258	J.J.B.Lewis/M.L.Love	v	Notts	Chester-le-St[2] 2001
3rd	205	G.Fowler/S.Hutton	v	Yorkshire	Leeds 1993
4th	250	P.D.Collingwood/D.M.Benkenstein	v	Derbyshire	Derby 2005
5th	222	D.M.Benkenstein/G.R.Breese	v	Middlesex	Lord's 2006
6th	249	G.J.Muchall/P.Mustard	v	Kent	Canterbury 2006
7th	315	D.M.Benkenstein/O.D.Gibson	v	Yorkshire	Leeds 2006
8th	147	P.Mustard/L.E.Plunkett	v	Yorkshire	Leeds 2009
9th	127	D.G.C.Ligertwood/S.J.E.Brown	v	Surrey	Stockton 1996
10th	103	M.M.Betts/D.M.Cox	v	Sussex	Hove 1996

Best Bowling	For 10- 47	O.D.Gibson	v	Hampshire	Chester-le-St[2] 2007
(Innings)	V 9- 36	M.S.Kasprowicz	for	Glamorgan	Cardiff 2003
Best Bowling	For 14-177	A.Walker	v	Essex	Chelmsford 1995
(Match)	V 13-110	M.S.Kasprowicz	for	Glamorgan	Chester-le-St[2] 2003

Most Runs – Season	1654	M.J.Di Venuto	(av 78.76)	2009
Most Runs – Career	7854	J.J.B.Lewis	(av 31.41)	1997-2006
Most 100s – Season	6	P.D.Collingwood		2005
	6	M.J.Di Venuto		2009
Most 100s – Career	17	D.M.Benkenstein		2005-10
Most Wkts – Season	80	O.D.Gibson	(av 20.75)	2007
Most Wkts – Career	518	S.J.E.Brown	(av 28.30)	1992-2002
Most Career W-K Dismissals	404	P.Mustard	(389 ct; 15 st)	2002-10
Most Career Catches in the Field	123	P.D.Collingwood		1996-2010

LIMITED-OVERS CRICKET

Highest Total	50ov	332-4	v	Worcs	Chester-le-St[2] 2007
	40ov	319-3	v	Worcs	Worcester 2004
	T20	225-2	v	Leics	Chester-le-St[2] 2010

Lowest Total	50ov	82	v	Worcs	Chester-le-St[1] 1968
	40ov	72	v	Warwicks	Birmingham 2002
	T20	93	v	Kent	Canterbury 2009

Highest Innings	50ov	138	M.J.Di Venuto	v	Derbyshire	Chester-le-St[2] 2008
	40ov	131*	W.Larkins	v	Hampshire	Portsmouth 1994
	T20	80*	L.R.P.L.Taylor	v	Leics	Chester-le-St[2] 2010

Best Bowling	50ov	7-32	S.P.Davis	v	Lancashire	Chester-le-St[1] 1983
	40ov	6-31	N.Killeen	v	Derbyshire	Derby 2000
	T20	5-14	P.D.Collingwood	v	Derbyshire	Chester-le-St[2] 2008

[1] Chester-le-Street CC (Ropery Lane) [2] Emirates Durham International Cricket Ground

97

ESSEX

Formation of Present Club: 14 January 1876
Inaugural First-Class Match: 1894
Colours: Blue, Gold and Red
Badge: Three Seaxes above Scroll bearing 'Essex'
County Champions: (6) 1979, 1983, 1984, 1986, 1991, 1992
Gillette/NatWest/C&G/FP Trophy Winners: (3) 1985, 1997, 2008
Benson and Hedges Cup Winners: (2) 1979, 1998
Pro 40/National League (Div 1) Winners: (2) 2005, 2006
Sunday League Winners: (3) 1981, 1984, 1985
Clydesdale Bank 40 Winners: (0); best – Semi-Finalist 2010
Twenty20 Cup Winners: (0); best – Semi-Finalist 2006, 2008, 2010

Chief Executive: David E.East, The Ford County Ground, New Writtle Street, Chelmsford CM2 0PG • Tel: 01245 252420 • Fax: 01245 254030 • Email: administration.essex@ecb.co.uk • Web: www.essexcricket.org.uk

First Team Coach: A.P.Grayson. **Batting Coach:** G.A.Gooch. **Bowling Coach:** C.E.W.Silverwood. **Captain:** J.S.Foster. **Vice-Captain:** none. **Overseas Player:** S.B.Styris. **2011 Beneficiary:** J.S.Foster. **Head Groundsman:** Stuart Kerrison. **Scorer:** A.E. (Tony) Choat. ‡ New registration.^{NQ} Not qualified for England.

BOPARA, Ravinder Singh (Brampton Manor HS; Barking Abbey Sports C), b Newham, London 4 May 1985. 5'8". RHB, RM. Debut (Essex) 2002; cap 2005. Auckland 2009-10. Dolphins 2010-11. MCC 2006, 2008. YC 2008. **Tests:** 10 (2007-08 to 2009); HS 143 v WI (Lord's) 2009; BB 1-39 v SL (Galle) 2007-08. **LOI:** 54 (2006-07 to 2010); HS 60 v I (Kanpur) 2008-09; BB 4-38 v B (Birmingham) 2010. **IT20:** 11 (2008 to 2010); HS 55 v WI (Oval) 2009. F-c Tours: WI 2008-09, 2010-11 (EL); SL 2007-08. 1000 runs (1): 1256 (2008). HS 229 v Northants (Chelmsford) 2007. BB 5-75 v Surrey (Chelmsford) 2006. LO HS 201* v Leics (Leicester) 2008 (FPT) – Ex record. LO BB 5-63 Dolphins v Warriors (Pietermaritzburg) 2010-11. T20 HS 105*. T20 BB 3-13.

CHAMBERS, Maurice Anthony (Homerton TC; Sir George Monoux C), b Port Antonio, Portland, Jamaica 14 Sep 1987. 6'3". RHB, RFM. Debut (Essex) 2005. No f-c appearances 2006-07 – stress fracture of the back. MCC YC 2004. F-c Tours (EL): WI 2010-11. HS 14 and BB 6-68 (10-123 match) v Notts (Chelmsford) 2010. LO HS 1* v Leics (Leicester) 2008 (P40). LO BB 1-26 v Yorks (Chelmsford) 2008. T20 HS 10*. T20 BB 3-31.

COMBER, Michael Andrew (Clacton County HS), b Colchester 26 Oct 1989. 6'3". RHB, RMF. Debut (Essex) 2010. Essex 2nd XI debut 2007. HS 19 and BB 2-34 v Bangladeshis (Chelmsford) 2010. CC HS 0. CC BB 1-4 v Durham (Chelmsford) 2010. LO HS 52* v Northants (Southend) 2010 (CB40). T20 HS 5.

COOK, Alastair Nathan (Bedford S), b Gloucester 25 Dec 1984. 6'3". LHB, OB. Debut (Essex) 2003; cap 2005. MCC 2004-07. YC 2005. **ECB central contract 2010-11. Tests:** 65 (2005-06 to 2010-11); HS 235* v A (Brisbane) 2010-11. Scored 60 and 104* v I (Nagpur) 2005-06 on debut. Third, after D.G.Bradman and S.R.Tendulkar, to score seven Test hundreds before his 23rd birthday. Second, after M.A.Taylor, to score 1000 runs in the calendar year of his debut. BB – . **LOI:** 26 (2006 to 2009-10); HS 102 v I (Southampton) 2007. **IT20:** 4 (2007 to 2009-10); HS 26 v SA (Centurion) 2009-10. F-c Tours (C=captain): A 2006-07, 2010-11; SA 2009-10; WI 2005-06 (Eng A), 2008-09; NZ 2007-08; I 2005-06, 2008-09; SL 2004-05 (Eng A), 2007-08; B 2009-10C. 1000 runs (4+1); most – 1466 (2005). HS (see Tests). CC HS 195 v Northants (Northampton) 2005. BB 3-13 v Northants (Chelmsford) 2005. LO HS 125 v Surrey (Croydon) 2007 (FPT). BB – . T20 HS 100*.

FOSTER, James Savin (Forest S, Snaresbrook; Collingwood C, Durham U), b Whipps Cross 15 Apr 1980. 6'0". RHB, WK. British U 2000-01. Essex debut 2000; cap 2001; captain 2010 (*part*) to date; benefit 2011. Durham UCCE 2001. MCC 2004, 2008-10. **Tests**: 7 (2001-02 to 2002-03); HS 48 v I (Bangalore) 2001-02. **LOI**: 11 (2001-02); HS 13 v I (Bombay) 2001-02. **IT20**: 5 (2009); HS 14* v P (Oval) 2009. F-c Tours: A 2002-03; WI 2000-01 (Eng A); NZ 2001-02; I 2001-02, 2007-08 (Eng A). 1000 runs (1): 1037 (2004). HS 212 v Leics (Chelmsford) 2004. BB 1-122 v Northants (Northampton) 2008 – in contrived circumstances. LO HS 83* v Durham, inc 5 sixes in 5 balls off S.G.Borthwick (Chester-le-St) 2009 (P40). T20 HS 62*.

GODLEMAN, Billy Ashley (Islington Green S), b Islington, London 11 Feb 1989. 6'3". LHB, LB. Middlesex 2005-09. Essex debut 2010. England U19s 2006 to 2007-08. HS 113* M v Somerset (Taunton) 2007 – on CC debut. Ex HS 106 v Somerset (Taunton) 2010. BB – . LO HS 32 M v Scotland (Jury's) 2009 (FPT). T20 HS 69.

MASTERS, David Daniel (Fort Luton HS; Mid Kent CHE), b Chatham, Kent 22 Apr 1978. Son of K.D.Masters (Kent 1983-84), elder brother of D.Masters (*see LEICESTERSHIRE*). 6'4". RHB, RMF. Kent 2000-02. Leicestershire 2003-07; cap 2007. Essex debut/cap 2008. HS 119 Le v Sussex (Hove) 2003. Ex HS 67 v Leics (Chelmsford) 2009. 50 wkts (1): 53 (2010). BB 6-24 v Leics (Chelmsford) 2008. LO HS 39 Le v Glos (Cheltenham) 2006 (P40). LO BB 5-17 v Surrey (Oval) 2008 (FPT). T20 HS 14. T20 BB 3-7.

MICKLEBURGH, Jaik Charles (Bungay HS), b Norwich, Norfolk 30 Mar 1990. RHB, RM. Debut (Essex) 2008. Essex 2nd XI debut aged 16 years 160 days. Norfolk 2007. England U19s 2009. HS 174 v Durʰam (Chester-le-St) 2010. BB – . LO HS 46 v Netherlands (Amstelveen) 2010 (CB40). T20 HS 32.

NAPIER, Graham Richard (The Gilberd S, Colchester), b Colchester 6 Jan 1980. 5'9½". RHB, RM. Debut (Essex) 1997; cap 2003. Wellington 2008-09. MCC 2004. F-c Tour (Eng A): I 2003-04. HS 125 v Notts (Chelmsford) 2007. BB 6-103 v Glamorgan (Southend) 2008. LO HS 79 Essex CB v Lancs CB (Chelmsford) 2000 (NWT). LO BB 6-29 v Worcs (Chelmsford) 2001 (NL). T20 HS 152* v Sussex (Chelmsford) 2008 – record T20 Cup score (58b, 10 fours, 16 sixes); 2nd highest score in all T20. T20 BB 4-10 v Northants (Chelmsford) 2008 – Ex record.

OSBORNE, Max (Sawyers Hall C), b Orsett 21 Nov 1990. 6'3". RHB, RMF. Debut (Essex) 2010. Essex 2nd XI debut 2009. HS 5 and CC BB 1-25 v Durham (Chelmsford) 2010. BB 3-35 v Bangladeshis (Chelmsford) 2010.

PETTINI, Mark Lewis (Comberton Village C; Hills Road SFC, Cambridge; Cardiff U), b Brighton, Sussex 7 Aug 1983. RHB, RM. 5'10". Debut (Essex) 2001; cap 2006; captain 2007 (*part*) to 2010 (*part*). MCC 2005. 1000 runs (1): 1218 (2006). HS 208* v Derbys (Chelmsford) 2006. BB – . LO 144 v Surrey (Oval) 2007 (FPT). T20 HS 87.

PHILLIPS, Timothy James (Felsted S; St Hild & St Bede C, Durham U), b Cambridge 13 Mar 1981. 6'1". LHB, SLA. Essex 1999, 2001-02; cap 2006. Durham UCCE 2001-02. HS 89 v Worcs (Worcester) 2005. BB 5-41 v Derbys (Chelmsford) 2006. LO HS 41 v Somerset (Taunton) 2009 (P40). LO BB 5-34 v Lancs (Chelmsford) 2006 (P40). T20 HS 57*. T20 BB 2-11.

‡**SHAH, Owais** Alam (Isleworth & Syon S), b Karachi, Pakistan 22 Oct 1978. 6'0". RHB, OB. Middlesex 1996-2010; cap 2000; captain 2004 (*part*); benefit 2008. Cape Cobras 2010-11. MCC 2002-08. YC 2001. **Tests**: 6 (2005-06 to 2008-09); HS 88 v I (Bombay) 2005-06. **LOI**: 71 (2001 to 2009-10); HS 107* v I (Oval) 2007; BB 3-15 v Ire (Belfast) 2009. **IT20**: 17 (2007 to 2009); HS 55* v WI (Oval) 2007. F-c Tours (Eng A): A 1996-97; WI 2005-06 (*part*), 2008-09 (E); I 2005-06 (E – *part*); SL 1997-98, 2004-05, 2007-08 (E). 1000 runs (8); most – 1728 (2005). HS 203 M v Derbys (Southgate) 2001. BB 3-33 M v Glos (Bristol) 1999. LO HS 134 M v Sussex (Arundel) 1999 (NL). LO BB 4-11 M v Leics (Lord's) 2009 (P40). T20 HS 80. T20 BB 2-26.

STYRIS, Scott Bernard (Hamilton HBS), b Brisbane, Australia 10 Jul 1975. 5'10". RHB, RMF. ND 1994-95 to date. Middlesex 2005-06; cap 2006. Auckland 2005-06 to 2009-10. Durham 2007. Essex 2010 T20 only. **Tests** (NZ): 29 (2002-2007-08); HS 170 v SA (Auckland) 2003-04; BB 3-28 v I (Wellington) 2002-03. **LOI** (NZ): 180 (1999-00 to 2010-11); HS 141 v SL (Bloemfontein) 2002-03; BB 6-25 v WI (Port-of-Spain) 2002. **IT20** (NZ): 31 (2004-05 to 2010-11); HS 66 v A (Auckland) 2004-05; BB 3-5 v Z (Providence) 2009-10. F-c Tours (NZ): E 2000 (NZ A), 2004; A 2004-05; SA 2000-01, 2005-06, 2007-08; WI 2002; I 2003-04; SL 2002-03; Z 2005; B 2004-05. HS 212* ND v Otago (Hamilton) 2001-02. UK HS 133 and UK BB 6-71 M v Lancs (Lord's) 2006. LO HS 141 (*see LOI*). LO BB 6-25 (*see LOI*). T20 HS 106*. T20 BB 3-5.

Ten DOESCHATE, Ryan Neil (Fairbairn C; Cape Town U), b Port Elizabeth, South Africa 30 Jun 1980. 5'10½". RHB, RMF. Debut (Essex) 2003; cap 2006. EU passport – Dutch ancestry. Netherlands 2005 to date. **LOI** (Ne): 27 (2006 to 2010); HS 109* v Bermuda (Nairobi) 2006-07; BB 4-31 v Canada (Nairobi) 2006-07. **IT20** (Ne): 9 (2008 to 2009-10); HS 56 v Kenya (Belfast) 2008; BB 3-23 v Scotland (Belfast) 2008. F-c Tours (Ne): SA 2006-07, 2007-08; K 2005-06, 2009-10; Ireland 2005. HS 259* and BB 6-20 (9-112 match) Netherlands v Canada (Pretoria) 2006. Ex HS 159* v Surrey (Guildford) 2009. Ex BB 6-57 v New Zealanders (Chelmsford) 2008. CC BB 5-13 v Hants (Chelmsford) 2010. LO HS 134* Ne v Namibia (Benoni) 2008-09. LO BB 5-50 v Glos (Bristol) 2007 (FPT). T20 HS 102. T20 BB 4-24.

WALKER, Matthew Jonathan (King's S, Rochester), b Gravesend, Kent 2 Jan 1974. Grandson of Jack Walker (Kent 1949). 5'8". LHB, RM. Kent 1992-93 to 2008; UK debut 1994; cap 2000; benefit 2008. Essex debut 2009; cap 2010. F-c Tour: Z 1992-93 (K). 1000 runs (4); most – 1419 (2006). HS 275* K v Somerset (Canterbury) 1996. Ex HS 150 v Middx (Lord's) 2009. BB 3-35 v Kent (Canterbury) 2010. LO HS 117 K v Warwks (Canterbury) 1997 (BHC). LO BB 4-24 K v Yorks (Leeds) 2001 (NL). T20 HS 74*.

WESTLEY, Thomas (Linton Village C; Hills Road SFC), b Cambridge 13 March 1989. 6'2". RHB, OB. Debut (Essex) 2007. MCC 2007, 2009. Durham MCCU 2010. Essex 2nd XI debut 2004 when aged 15 years 88 days. Cambridgeshire 2005. HS 132 v Derbys (Derby) 2009 and v Kent (Chelmsford) 2010. BB 4-55 DU v Durham (Durham) 2010. CC BB 2-33 v Glamorgan (Cardiff) 2009. LO HS 36 v Worcs (Chelmsford) 2007 (P40). LO BB 1-34 v Northants (Northampton) 2010 (CB40).

WHEATER, Adam Jack (Millfield S), b Whipps Cross 13 Feb 1990. RHB, WK. Debut (Essex) 2008. Cambridge MCCU 2010. MT 2010-11. Essex 2nd XI debut when aged 16 years 190 days. HS 126 MT v SR (Bulawayo) 2010-11. Ex HS 36 v Cambridge UCCE (Cambridge) 2009. CC HS 22 v Derbys (Derby) 2008 – on debut. LO HS 69 MT v SR (Bulawayo) 2010-11. T20 HS 14.

WRIGHT, Christopher Julian Clement (Eggars S, Alton; Anglia Ruskin U), b Chipping Norton, Oxon 14 Jul 1985. 6'3". RHB, RFM. Cambridge UCCE 2004-05. Middlesex 2004-07. Tamil Union 2005-06. Essex debut 2008. HS 76 CU v Essex (Cambridge) 2005. CC HS 71* v Middx (Chelmsford) 2008. BB 6-22 v Leics (Leicester) 2008. LO HS 23 v Kent (Chelmsford) 2008 (FPT). LO BB 3-3 v Northants (Southend) 2008. T20 HS 6*. T20 BB 4-24.

NQDANISH Parabha Shanker **KANERIA** (St Patrick's HS; Government Islamia C), b Karachi, Pakistan 16 Dec 1980. 6'1". Cousin of Anil Dalpat (Pakistan); 2nd Hindu to represent Pakistan. RHB, LBG. Debut (PNSC) 1998-99. Karachi 1998-99 to 2006-07. Habib Bank 2000-01 to date. Essex 2004-10; cap 2004. Sind 2007-08 to date. **Tests** (P): 61 (2000-01 to 2010); HS 29 v E (Leeds) 2006; BB 7-77 v B (Dhaka) 2001-02. **LOI** (P): 18 (2001-02 to 2006-07); HS 6* v Z (Kingston) 2006-07; BB 3-31 v NZ (Dambulla) 2003. F-c Tours (P): E 2006, 2010; A 2004-05, 2009-10; SA 2006-07; WI 2004-05; NZ 2003-04, 2009-10; I 2004-05, 2007-08; SL 2001 (Pak A), 2005-06, 2009; B 2001-02; K 2000 (Pak A). HS 65 v Notts (Nottingham) 2007. 50 wkts (3+1); most – 75 (2009). BB 8-59 (13-81 match) Habib Bank v SSGC (Karachi) 2008-09. UK BB 8-116 (12-203 match) v Leics (Chelmsford) 2009. Hat-trick v Derbys (Derby) 2009. LO HS 64 Habib Bank v KRL (Rawalpindi) 2009-10. LO BB 6-33 Sind v Punjab (Karachi) 2009-10. T20 HS 12. T20 BB 4-22.

NQFLOWER, Grant William (St George's C), b Salisbury, Rhodesia 20 Dec 1970. 5'10". Younger brother of A.Flower (Mashonaland, Essex, S Australia and Zimbabwe 1986-87 to 2006). RHB, SLA. Debut (Zimbabwe) 1989-90. Mashonaland 1993-94 to 2003-04. MCC 1996-97. Leicestershire 2002 (one match); cap 2002. Essex 2005-10; cap 2005. **Tests** (Z): 67 (1992-93 to 2003-04); HS 201* v P (Harare) 1994-95 sharing with A.Flower in 4th wicket partnership of 269, the highest stand between brothers in Test cricket; BB 4-41 (8-104 match) v B (Chittagong) 2001-02. **LOI** (Z): 221 (1992-93 to 2010-11, 1 as captain); HS 142* v B (Bulawayo) 2000-01; BB 4-32 v Kenya (Dhaka) 1998-99. F-c Tours (Z): E 1990, 2000; A 1994-95; SA 1999-00; WI 1999-00; NZ 1995-96, 1997-98, 2000-01; I 1992-93, 2000-01, 2001-02; P 1993-94, 1996-97, 1998-99; SL 1996-97, 1997-98, 2001-02; B 2001-02. HS 243* Mashonaland v Matabeleland (Harare) 1996-97. UK HS 203 v Northants (Chelmsford) 2007. BB 7-31 Z v Lahore (Lahore) 1998-99. UK BB 4-66 Le v Warwks (Birmingham) 2002. Ex BB 3-28 v Glos (Bristol) 2006. LO HS 148* Mashonaland v Midlands (Kwekwe) 2002-03. LO BB 4-32 (see LOI). T20 HS 61. T20 BB 3-20.

NQMcGAIN, Bryce Edward, b Mornington, Victoria, Australia 25 Mar 1972. 6'0". RHB, LBG. Victoria 2001-02 to date. Essex 2010. **Tests** (A): 1 (2008-09); HS 2 and BB- (Cape Town) 2008-09. F-c Tours (A): SA 2008-09, I 2008-09 (Aus A). HS 25 Vic v NSW (Sydney) 2007-08. Ex HS 24 v Warwks (Southend) 2010. BB 6-112 Vic v NSW (Sydney) 2006-07. Ex BB 5-151 v Kent (Canterbury) 2010. LO HS 51 Denmark v Leics CB (Cossington) 2002 (CGT). LO BB 3-11 Vic v Tas (Hobart) 2007-08. T20 HS 6*. T20 BB 2-10.

NQMARTIN, Christopher Stewart b Christchurch, Canterbury, New Zealand 10 Dec 1974. RHB, RFM. Canterbury 1997-98 to 2004-05, 2009-10. South Island 1999-00. Auckland 2005-06 to 2008-09, 2010-11. Warwickshire 2008. Essex 2010 (one f-c match). **Tests** (NZ): 61 (2000-01 to 2010-11); HS 12* v B (Dunedin) (2007-08); BB 6-54 v SL (Wellington) 2004-05. **LOI** (NZ): 20 (2000-01 to 2007-08); HS 3 v Z (Taupo) 2000-01; BB 3-62 v SL (Napier) 2005-06. **IT20** (NZ): 6 (2007-08); HS 5* v E (Auckland) 2007-08; BB 2-14 v Kenya (Durban) 2007-08. F-c Tours (NZ): E 2000 (NZ A), 2004, 2008; A 2001-02, 2004-05, 2008-09; SA 2000-01, 2004-05 (NZ A), 2005-06, 2007-08; I 2010-11; P 2001-02; SL 2005-06 (NZ A), 2009; Z 2005, 2010-11 (NZ A). HS 25 Canterbury v ND (Gisborne) 2001-02. Ex HS 11 and Ex BB 1-84 v Yorks (Scarborough) 2010. BB 6-54 (see Tests). CC BB 5-84 Wa v Glos (Birmingham) 2008. LO HS 13 Auckland v CD (Auckland) 2005-06. LO BB 6-24 NZ A v SL A (Moratuwa) 2008-09. T20 HS 5*. T20 BB 3-33.

MAUNDERS, John Kenneth (Ashford HS; Spelthorne C), b Ashford, Middlesex 4 Apr 1981. 5'10". LHB, RM. Middlesex 1999. Leicestershire 2003-07. Essex 2008-10. HS 180 Le v Glos (Cheltenham) 2006. Ex HS 150 v Leics (Chelmsford) 2009. BB 4-15 Le v Worcs (Worcester) 2006. LO HS 109* Le v Derbys (Leicester) 2007 (FPT). LO BB 2-16 Le v Warwks (Birmingham) 2005 (CGT). T20 HS 25*. T20 BB 2-14.

PALLADINO, A.P. – see DERBYSHIRE.

M.S.Westfield left the staff without making a County First-Class or List A appearance for Essex in 2010.

ESSEX 2010

RESULTS SUMMARY

	Place	Won	Lost	Tied	Drew	NR
LV= County Championship (1st Division)	9th	2	6		8	
All First-Class Matches		3	6		8	
Clydesdale Bank 40 (Group B)	SF	9	3			1
Friends Provident t20 (South Group)	SF	11	7			

LV= COUNTY CHAMPIONSHIP AVERAGES

BATTING AND FIELDING

Cap		M	I	NO	HS	Runs	Avge	100	50	Ct/St
2005	R.S.Bopara	8	15	2	142	550	42.30	2	3	4
2005	A.N.Cook	7	12	–	102	474	39.50	1	3	6
2010	M.J.Walker	11	22	2	105	782	39.10	1	4	8
2006	R.N.ten Doeschate	11	19	2	85	577	33.94	–	5	9
2001	J.S.Foster	16	27	1	169	839	32.26	1	4	48/5
	J.C.Mickleburgh	15	28	–	174	839	29.96	1	3	10
	B.A.Godleman	11	20	–	106	532	26.60	1	2	9
	T.Westley	9	18	1	132	440	25.88	1	2	1
2006	M.L.Pettini	15	27	3	96	599	24.95	–	2	7
	B.E.McGain	2	4	2	24	46	23.00	–	–	1
2006	T.J.Phillips	9	14	3	46*	208	18.90	–	–	7
	A.P.Palladino	4	8	1	66	130	18.57	–	1	1
	J.K.Maunders	6	10	–	70	179	17.90	–	1	6
2008	D.D.Masters	14	22	1	50	356	16.95	–	1	8
	C.J.C.Wright	11	17	5	28*	161	13.41	–	–	2
2003	G.R.Napier	4	6	1	35	67	13.40	–	–	1
	A.Carter	3	5	1	16*	45	11.25	–	–	2
	M.A.Chambers	10	15	5	14	53	5.30	–	–	5
2004	Danish Kaneria	6	9	1	9	28	3.50	–	–	1

Also batted: M.A.Comber (1 match) 0, 0; G.W.Flower (2 – cap 2005) 36*, 5, 2 (2 ct); C.S.Martin (1) 0*, 11; M.Osborne (1) 5, 0*.

BOWLING

	O	M	R	W	Avge	Best	5wI	10wM
D.D.Masters	487	138	1223	53	23.07	5- 43	1	–
A.Carter	100.5	15	311	13	23.92	5- 40	1	–
M.A.Chambers	236.5	43	826	32	25.81	6- 68	2	1
B.E.McGain	64.3	4	260	10	26.00	5-151	1	–
R.N.ten Doeschate	191.3	16	716	27	26.51	5- 13	1	–
A.P.Palladino	104	25	333	12	27.75	4- 57	–	–
Danish Kaneria	226.4	45	753	23	32.73	4- 51	–	–
C.J.C.Wright	301.5	55	1156	31	37.29	5- 70	1	–
T.J.Phillips	245.2	44	752	20	37.60	4- 94	–	–

Also bowled:

T.Westley	68	10	174	6	29.00	2- 68	

R.S.Bopara 25-2-99-4; M.A.Comber 8-1-16-1; A.N.Cook 8-1-36-1; G.W.Flower 9-0-32-1; C.S.Martin 25-10-84-1; J.C.Mickleburgh 1.1-0-11-0; G.R.Napier 95-18-280-3; M.Osborne 16-2-56-1; M.J.Walker 18-2-71-3.

The First-Class Averages (pp 220–237) give the records of Essex players in all first-class county matches (Essex's other opponents being the Bangladeshis), with the exception of R.S.Bopara, A.N.Cook, Danish Kaneria, J.S.Foster and T.Westley, whose first-class figures for Essex are as above.

ESSEX RECORDS

FIRST-CLASS CRICKET

Highest Total	For 761-6d		v	Leics	Chelmsford	1990
	V 803-4d		by	Kent	Brentwood	1934
Lowest Total	For 30		v	Yorkshire	Leyton	1901
	V 14		by	Surrey	Chelmsford	1983
Highest Innings	For 343*	P.A.Perrin	v	Derbyshire	Chesterfield	1904
	V 332	W.H.Ashdown	for	Kent	Brentwood	1934

Highest Partnership for each Wicket

1st	316	G.A.Gooch/P.J.Prichard	v	Kent	Chelmsford	1994
2nd	403	G.A.Gooch/P.J.Prichard	v	Leics	Chelmsford	1990
3rd	347*	M.E.Waugh/N.Hussain	v	Lancashire	Ilford	1992
4th	314	Salim Malik/N.Hussain	v	Surrey	The Oval	1991
5th	339	J.C.Mickleburgh/J.S.Foster	v	Durham	Chester-le-St[2]	2010
6th	206	J.W.H.T.Douglas/J.O'Connor	v	Glos	Cheltenham	1923
	206	B.R.Knight/R.A.G.Luckin	v	Middlesex	Brentwood	1962
7th	261	J.W.H.T.Douglas/J.Freeman	v	Lancashire	Leyton	1914
8th	263	D.R.Wilcox/R.M.Taylor	v	Warwicks	Southend	1946
9th	251	J.W.H.T.Douglas/S.N.Hare	v	Derbyshire	Leyton	1921
10th	218	F.H.Vigar/T.P.B.Smith	v	Derbyshire	Chesterfield	1947

Best Bowling	For 10- 32	H.Pickett	v	Leics	Leyton	1895
(Innings)	V 10- 40	E.G.Dennett	for	Glos	Bristol	1906
Best Bowling	For 17-119	W.Mead	v	Hampshire	Southampton	1895
(Match)	V 17- 56	C.W.L.Parker	for	Glos	Gloucester	1925

Most Runs – Season	2559	G.A.Gooch	(av 67.34)	1984
Most Runs – Career	30701	G.A.Gooch	(av 51.77)	1973-97
Most 100s – Season	9	J.O'Connor		1929, 1934
	9	D.J.Insole		1955
Most 100s – Career	94	G.A.Gooch		1973-97
Most Wkts – Season	172	T.P.B Smith	(av 27.13)	1947
Most Wkts – Career	1610	T.P.B.Smith	(av 26.68)	1929-51
Most Career W-K Dismissals	1231	B.Taylor	(1040 ct; 191 st)	1949-73
Most Career Catches in the Field	519	K.W.R.Fletcher		1962-88

LIMITED-OVERS CRICKET

Highest Total	50ov	391-5		v	Surrey	The Oval	2008
	40ov	316-4		v	Glamorgan	Chelmsford	2004
	T20	242-3		v	Sussex	Chelmsford	2008
Lowest Total	50ov	57		v	Lancashire	Lord's	1996
	40ov	69		v	Derbyshire	Chesterfield	1974
	T20	99		v	Kent	Chelmsford	2007
Highest Innings	50ov	201*	R.S.Bopara	v	Leics	Leicester	2008
	40ov	176	G.A.Gooch	v	Glamorgan	Southend	1983
	T20	152*	G.R.Napier	v	Sussex	Chelmsford	2008
Best Bowling	50ov	5- 8	J.K.Lever	v	Middlesex	Westcliff	1972
		5- 8	G.A.Gooch	v	Cheshire	Chester	1995
	40ov	8-26	K.D.Boyce	v	Lancashire	Manchester	1971
	T20	4-10	G.R.Napier	v	Northants	Chelmsford	2008

GLAMORGAN

GlamorganCricket
CricedMorgannwg

Formation of Present Club: 6 July 1888
Inaugural First-Class Match: 1921
Colours: Blue and Gold
Badge: Gold Daffodil
County Champions: (3) 1948, 1969, 1997
Gillette/NatWest/C&G/FP Trophy Winners: (0); best – Finalist 1977
Benson and Hedges Cup Winners: (0); best – Finalist 2000
Pro 40/National League (Div 1) Winners: (2) 2002, 2004
Sunday League Winners: (1) 1993
Clydesdale Bank 40 Winners: (0); best – 7th (Group A) 2010
Twenty20 Cup Winners: (0); best – Semi-Finalist 2004

Chief Executive: A.D.Hamer, SWALEC Stadium, Cardiff, CF11 9XR • Tel: 0871 282 3401 • Fax: 0871 282 3405 • email: info@glamorgancricket.co.uk • Web: www.glamorgancricket.com

Managing Director of Cricket: C.P.Metson. **Head Coach:** M.P.Mott. **Assistant Coaches:** R.V.Almond and S.L.Watkin. **Captain:** A.N.Petersen. **Vice-Captain:** tbc. **Overseas Players:** M.J.Cosgrove and A.N.Petersen. **2011 Beneficiary:** M.J.Powell. **Head Groundsman:** Keith Exton. **Scorer:** Andrew K.Hignell. ‡ New registration. [NQ] Not qualified for England.

ALLENBY, James (Christ Church GS, Perth), b Perth, W Australia 12 Sep 1982. 6'0". RHB, RM. Leicestershire 2006-09. Glamorgan debut 2009; cap 2010. HS 138* Le v Bangladesh A (Leicester) 2008. CC HS 137 v Surrey (Oval) 2009. BB 5-59 v Glos (Cheltenham) 2010. LO HS 91* Le v Middx (Lord's) 2007 (P40). LO BB 5-43 Le v Derbys (Leicester) 2007 (FPT). T20 HS 110. T20 BB 5-21 Le v Lancs (Manchester) 2008, inc 4 wkts in 4 balls.

ASHLING, Christopher Paul (Millfield S, UWIC), b Manchester 26 Nov 1988. 5'7". RHB, RFM. Debut (Glamorgan) 2009. Cardiff UCCE 2008. Wales MC 2008-09. Lancashire 2nd XI debut 2005. HS 20 v Derbys (Derby) 2010. BB 3-18 v West Indies A (Cardiff) 2010. CC BB 2-66 v Leics (Leicester) 2009. LO HS 6* v Leics (Leicester) 2009 (P40). LO BB 2-33 v Lancs (Cardiff) 2009 (P40). T20 HS 6. T20 BB 2-39.

BRAGG, William David (Rougemont S, Newport; UWIC), b Newport, Monmouthshire 24 Oct 1986. 5'9". LHB, WK. Debut (Glamorgan) 2007. No f-c appearances in 2008. Wales MC 2004-09. HS 92 v Glos (Bristol) 2009. BB – . LO HS 78 v Leics (Leicester) 2009 (P40). BB – . T20 HS 15.

BROWN, David Owen (Queen Elizabeth GS, Blackburn; Collingwood C, Durham U), b Burnley, Lancs 8 Dec 1982. Younger brother of M.J.Brown (*see SURREY*). RHB, RM. 6'0". Durham UCCE 2003-05. British U 2005. Gloucestershire 2006-08; cap 2006. Glamorgan debut 2010. HS 99 v West Indies A (Cardiff) 2010 (only f-c appearance for Gm). CC HS 83 Gs v Worcs (Cheltenham) 2008. BB 5-38 Gs v Derbys (Derby) 2008. LO HS 63* Gs v Surrey (Bristol) 2006 (CGT) – on debut. LO BB 3-29 Gs v Glam (Colwyn Bay) 2007 (FPT). T20 HS 56. T20 BB 2-30.

COOKE, Christopher Barry, b Johannesburg, South Africa 30 May 1986. RHB, WK. WP 2009-10. Glamorgan 2nd XI debut 2010. Awaiting 1st XI debut.

^{NO}COSGROVE, Mark James, b Elizabeth, Adelaide, S Australia 14 Jun 1984. 5'10". LHB, RM. S Australia 2002-03 to 2009-10. Glamorgan debut 2006 – scoring 114 v Derbys (Cardiff); cap 2006. Tasmania 2010-11. **LOI** (A): 3 (2005-06 to 2006-07); HS 74 v B (Fatullah) 2005-06 – on debut; BB 1-1 v WI (Kuala Lumpur) 2006-07. 1000 runs (1): 1187 (2010). HS 233 v Derbys (Derby) 2006. BB 3-3 S Aus v Tas (Adelaide) 2006-07. Gm BB 3-30 v Derbys (Derby) 2009. LO HS 121 S Aus v WA (Perth) 2005-06. LO BB 2-21 S Aus v Q (Brisbane) 2005-06 and v Worcs (Cardiff) 2010 (CB40). T20 HS 89. T20 BB 2-11.

COSKER, Dean Andrew (Millfield S), b Weymouth, Dorset 7 Jan 1978. 5'11". RHB, SLA. Debut (Glamorgan) 1996; cap 2000; benefit 2010. MCC 2010. F-c Tours (Eng A): SA 1998-99; SL 1997-98; Z 1998-99; K 1997-98. HS 52 v Glos (Bristol) 2005. 50 wkts (1): 51 (2010). BB 6-91 (11-126 match) v Essex (Cardiff) 2009. LO HS 50* v Northants (Northampton) 2009 (FPT). LO BB 5-54 v Essex (Chelmsford) 2003 (NL). T20 HS 16*. T20 BB 3-18.

CROFT, Robert Damien Bale (St John Lloyd Catholic CS, Llanelli; Neath Tertiary C; W Glamorgan IHE), b Morriston, Swansea 25 May 1970. 5'10½". RHB, OB. Debut (Glamorgan) 1989; cap 1992; benefit 2000; captain 2003 (*part*) to 2006 (*part*). **Tests**: 21 (1996 to 2001); HS 37* v SA (Manchester) 1998; BB 5-95 v NZ (Christchurch) 1996-97. **LOI**: 50 (1996 to 2001); HS 32 v SL (Perth) 1998-99; BB 3-51 v SA (Oval) 1998. F-c Tours: A 1998-99; SA 1993-94 (Eng A), 1995-96 (Gm); WI 1991-92 (Eng A), 1997-98; NZ 1996-97; SL 2000-01, 2003-04; Z 1990-91 (Gm), 1994-95 (Gm), 1996-97. HS 143 v Somerset (Taunton) 1995. 50 wkts (10); most – 76 (1996). Took 1,000th f-c wicket 2007. BB 8-66 (14-169 match) v Warwks (Swansea) 1992. LO HS 143 v Lincs (Lincoln) 2004 (CGT). LO BB 6-20 v Worcs (Cardiff) 1994 (SL). T20 HS 62*. T20 BB 3-12.

GLOVER, John Charles (Llantarnam CS; St Aidan's C, Durham), b Cardiff 29 Aug 1989. 6'4", RHB, RMF. Durham MCCU 2008-10. Glamorgan 2nd XI debut 2009. Wales MC 2008-09. Awaiting 1st XI debut. Development contract. HS 14 and BB 5-38 DU v Durham (Durham) 2009.

HARRIS, James Alexander Russell (Pontardulais CS; Gorseinon C), b Morriston, Swansea 16 May 1990. 6'0". RHB, RFM. Debut (Glamorgan) 2007 – aged 16 years 351 days – youngest Glamorgan player to take a first-class wicket; cap 2010. Glamorgan 2nd XI debut 2005 when aged 14 years 353 days. Wales MC 2005-08. England U19s 2007. F-c Tour (Eng A): WI 2010-11. HS 87* v Notts (Swansea) 2007. 50 wkts (1): 63 (2010). BB 7-66 (12-118 match) v Glos (Bristol) 2007 – youngest (17 years 3 days) to take 10 wickets in any CC match. LO HS 21 v Derbys (Derby) 2009 (FPT). LO BB 4-48 v Kent (Canterbury) 2008 (P40). T20 HS 18. T20 BB 4-23.

HARRISON, David Stuart (W Monmouth CS; Usk C, Pontypool), b Newport, Monmouthshire 30 Jul 1981. Elder brother of A.J.Harrison (Glamorgan 2005-06); son of S.C.Harrison (Glamorgan 1971-77). 6'4". RHB, RMF. Debut (Glamorgan) 1999; cap 2006. No appearances 2007. MCC 2005. HS 88 v Essex (Chelmsford) 2004. 50 wkts (1): 57 (2004). BB 7-45 v Worcs (Worcester) 2010. LO HS 37* and LO BB 5-26 v Yorks (Leeds) 2002 (NL). T20 HS 8. T20 BB 2-17.

JAMES, Nicholas Alexander (King Edward VI S, Aston), b Sandwell, Birmingham 17 Sep 1986. 5'9". LHB, SLA. Warwickshire 2008. Glamorgan debut 2010. Staffordshire 2005-07. England U19 2005 to 2005-06. HS 60* v West Indies A (Cardiff) 2010. BB 1-6 Wa v Cambridge UCCE (Cambridge) 2008. Awaiting CC debut. LO HS 30 Wa v Worcs (Birmingham) 2006 (CGT). LO BB 2-19 v Worcs (Worcester) 2010 (CB40). T20 HS 12*.

JONES, Alexander John (Cowbridge CS), b Bridgend 10 Nov 1988. RHB, LMF. Glamorgan 2nd XI debut 2008. Wales MC 2007-10. Cardiff MCCU 2009-10. Awaiting f-c debut. LO HS 5 and LO BB- v Somerset (Taunton) 2010 (CB40).

NORMAN, Aneurin John (Millfield S), b Cardiff 22 Mar 1991. RHB, RM. Glamorgan 2nd XI debut 2008. Wales MC 2008-10. Awaiting 1st XI debut. Development contract.

‡**O'SHEA, Michael** Peter (Barry CS; Millfield S), b Cardiff 4 Sep 1987. 5'11". RHB, OB. Glamorgan 2005-09; no f-c appearances 2006, 2008. Rejoins in 2011. Wales MC 2005-08. England U19s 2004-05 to 2006. HS 50 v Kent (Canterbury) 2009. LO HS 90 Unicorns v Worcs (Kidderminster) 2010 (CB40). LO BB 2-37 v Hants (Swansea) 2007 (FPT). T20 HS 5.

OWEN, William Thomas (Prestatyn HS; UWIC), b St Asaph, Flintshire 2 Sep 1988. 6'0". RHB, RMF. Debut (Glamorgan) 2007. Wales MC 2007-10. HS 38 v Northants (Northampton) 2010. BB 3-65 v West Indies A (Cardiff) 2010. LO HS 12 and LO BB 5-49 v Unicorns (Bournemouth) 2010 (CB40). T20 HS 8. T20 BB – .

‡NQ**PETERSEN, Alviro** Nathan, Port Elizabeth, South Africa 25 November 1980. RHB, RM. Northerns 2000-01 to 2005-06. Titans 2004-05 to 2005-06. Lions 2005-06 to date. North West 2008-09. Joins Glamorgan as captain in 2011. **Tests** (SA): 9 (2009-10 to 2010-11); HS 100 v I (Kolkata) 2009-10 – on debut; BB 1-2 v WI (Port-of-Spain) 2010. **LOI** (SA): 14 (2006-07 to 2010); HS 80 v Z (Potchefstroom) 2006-07; BB – . **IT20** (SA): 2 (2010); HS 8 v WI (North Sound) 2010. F-c Tours (SA): WI 2010; I 2007-08 (SA A), 2009-10; Z 2007 (SA A); B 2010 (SA A); UAE (v P) 2010-11. HS 152 NW v Northerns (Potchefstroom) 2008-09; BB 2-7 Northerns v Easterns (Benoni) 2001-02. LO HS 124 Lions v Eagles (Bloemfontein) 2006-07. LO BB 1-13 Lions v Dolphins (Durban) 2006-07. T20 HS 84*. T20 BB – .

POWELL, Michael John (Crickhowell SS; Pontypool CFE), b Abergavenny, Monmouthshire 3 Feb 1977. 6'1". RHB, OB, occ WK. Debut (Glamorgan) 1997 scoring 200* v Oxford U (Oxford); cap 2000; benefit 2010. MCC 2005. 1000 runs (5); most – 1327 (2006). HS 299 v Glos (Cheltenham) 2006 – record score for Glamorgan in England. BB 2-39 v Oxford U (Oxford) 1999. CC BB – . LO HS 114* v Hants (Cardiff) 2008 (FPT). LO BB 1-26 v Lincs (Lincoln) 2004 (CGT). T20 HS 68*.

REED, Michael Thomas (Cardiff U), b Leicester 10 Sep 1988. RHB, RFM. Glamorgan 2nd XI debut 2009. Wales MC 2009-10. Cardiff MCCU 2010. Awaiting 1st XI debut. Development contract.

REES, Gareth Peter (Coedcae CS; Bath U), b Swansea 8 Apr 1985. 6'1". LHB, LM. Wales MC 2003-05. Debut (Glamorgan) 2006; cap 2008. 1000 runs (2); most – 1088 (2008). HS 154 v Surrey (Oval) 2008. LO HS 123* v Essex (Chelmsford) 2009 (FPT). T20 HS 35.

SHANTRY, Adam John (Priory S; Shrewsbury SFC), b Bristol 13 Nov 1982. 6'2½". Son of B.K.Shantry (Gloucestershire 1978-79), brother of J.D.Shantry (see *WORCESTERSHIRE*). LHB, LFM. Northamptonshire 2003-04. Warwickshire 2006-07. Glamorgan debut 2008. Shropshire 2001. HS 100 v Leics (Colwyn Bay) 2009. BB 5-49 Wa v West Indies A (Birmingham) 2006. Gm BB 5-52 (10-129 match) v Warwks (Birmingham) 2008. LO HS 19* v Northants (Northampton) 2009 (FPT). LO BB 5-37 Nh v New Zealanders (Northampton) 2004. T20 HS – . T20 BB – .

‡**WAGG, Graham** Grant (Ashlawn S, Rugby), b Rugby, Warwks 28 Apr 1983. 6'0". RHB, LM. Warwickshire 2002-04; contract terminated after ECB imposed a 15-month ban, expiring 1 Jan 2006, for taking cocaine. Derbyshire 2006-10; cap 2007. F-c Tour (Eng A): I 2003-04. HS 108 De v Northants (Northampton) 2008. 50 wkts (2); most – 59 (2008). BB 6-35 De v Surrey (Derby) 2009. LO HS 48* De v Middx (Lord's) 2010 (CB40). LO BB 4-35 De v Durham (Derby) 2008 (FPT). T20 HS 62. T20 BB 3-23.

WALLACE, Mark Alexander (Crickhowell HS), b Abergavenny, Monmouthshire 19 Nov 1981. 5'9". LHB, WK. Debut (Glamorgan) 1999; cap 2003. F-c Tour (ECB Acad): SL 2002-03. HS 139 v Surrey (Oval) 2009. LO HS 85 v Surrey (Cardiff) 2008 (P40). T20 HS 42*.

‡NQWALTERS, Stewart Jonathan (Guildford GS, Perth, WA), b Mornington, Victoria, Australia 25 Jun 1983. 6'1". RHB, RM. Surrey 2006-10. HS 188 Sy v Leics (Oval) 2009. BB 1-4 Sy v Durham (Chester-le-St) 2007. LO HS 91 Sy v Northants (Oval) 2008 (P40). LO BB 1-12 Sy v Yorks (Scarborough) 2007 (P40). T20 HS 53*. T20 BB 1-9.

WATERS, Huw Thomas (Llantaram CS; Monmouth S), b Cardiff 26 Sep 1986. 6'2". RHB, RMF. Debut (Glamorgan) 2005. No f-c appearances in 2009. Wales MC 2004-07. HS 34 v Kent (Canterbury) 2005. BB 5-86 v Somerset (Taunton) 2006. LO HS 8 v Hants (Swansea) 2007 (FPT). LO BB 3-47 v Durham (Chester-le-St) 2007 (P40). T20 HS 11*. T20 BB 3-30.

WRIGHT, Ben James (Cowbridge CS), b Preston, Lancs 5 Dec 1987. 5'9". RHB, RM. Debut (Glamorgan) 2006. No f-c appearances in 2008. HS 172 v Glos (Cardiff) 2010. BB 1-14 v Essex (Chelmsford) 2007. LO HS 79 v Lancs (Colwyn Bay) 2010 (CB40). LO BB 1-19 v Derbys (Derby) 2009 (FPT). T20 HS 55*. T20 BB 1-16.

RELEASED/RETIRED
(Having made a County First-Class or List A appearance in 2010)

DALRYMPLE, James William Murray (Radley C; St Peter's C, Oxford), b Nairobi, Kenya 21 Jan 1981. Brother of S.H.Dalrymple (Oxford U 2002-04). 5'11". RHB, OB. Oxford UCCE/U 2001-03; captain 2002; blue 2001-02-03. British U 2001-02. Middlesex 2001-07; cap 2004. Glamorgan 2008-10; cap 2008; captain 2009-10. **LOI**: 27 (2006 to 2006-07); HS 67 v SL (Lord's) 2006; BB 2-5 v I (Jaipur) 2006-07. **IT20**: 3 (2006 to 2006-07); HS 32 v A (Sydney) 2006-07; BB 1-10 v P (Bristol) 2006. F-c Tour (Eng A): WI 2005-06. 1000 runs (1): 1009 (2009). HS 244 M v Surrey (Oval) 2004. Gm HS 128 v Derbys (Derby) 2009. BB 5-49 OU v Cambridge U (Cambridge) 2003. CC BB 4-53 M v Hants (Southgate) 2005. Gm BB 3-11 v Leics (Colwyn Bay) 2009. LO HS 107 M v Glamorgan (Lord's) 2004 (CGT). LO BB 4-14 M v Essex (Southgate) 2001 (NL). T20 HS 63. T20 BB 3-25.

MAYNARD, T.L. – *see SURREY.*

TAIT, S.W. – *see SURREY.*

GLAMORGAN 2010

RESULTS SUMMARY

	Place	Won	Lost	Tied	Drew	NR
LV= County Championship (2nd Division)	3rd	7	4		5	
All First-Class Matches		7	4		6	
Clydesdale Bank 40 (Group A)	7th	2	8			2
Friends Provident t20 (South Group)	8th	6	10			

LV= COUNTY CHAMPIONSHIP AVERAGES

BATTING AND FIELDING

Cap		M	I	NO	HS	Runs	Avge	100	50	Ct/St
2006	M.J.Cosgrove	15	26	2	142	1187	49.45	5	4	10
2010	J.Allenby	16	25	4	105	933	44.42	1	10	16
2009	G.P.Rees	16	28	4	106*	863	35.95	2	4	6
	B.J.Wright	16	25	1	172	821	34.20	2	4	7
	T.L.Maynard	10	16	–	98	474	29.62	–	4	9
2000	M.J.Powell	6	10	1	55	250	27.77	–	1	–
2003	M.A.Wallace	16	24	1	113	626	27.21	1	4	43/4
2008	J.W.M.Dalrymple	15	22	–	105	554	25.18	1	2	19
2000	D.A.Cosker	16	24	10	49*	268	19.14	–	–	7
1992	R.D.B.Croft	8	12	2	63	184	18.40	–	1	–
2010	J.A.R.Harris	13	19	2	49	257	15.11	–	–	2
2006	D.S.Harrison	12	18	–	35	253	14.05	–	–	2
	W.D.Bragg	2	4	–	44	56	14.00	–	–	1
	C.P.Ashling	2	4	1	20	29	9.66	–	–	–
	H.T.Waters	11	13	4	16	67	7.44	–	–	1

Also batted: W.T.Owen (2 matches) 0*, 38, 0.

BOWLING

	O	M	R	W	Avge	Best	5wI	10wM
J.A.R.Harris	443.4	115	1293	63	20.52	5-56	2	–
J.Allenby	330.1	82	885	41	21.58	5-59	1	–
D.A.Cosker	432	101	1128	51	22.11	5-93	1	–
D.S.Harrison	323.3	44	1156	37	31.24	7-45	2	–
H.T.Waters	297.4	79	898	26	34.53	4-39	–	–
R.D.B.Croft	312	64	766	22	34.81	4-20	–	–
J.W.M.Dalrymple	127	13	391	11	35.54	4-71	–	–

Also bowled: C.P.Ashling 44-3-178-3; M.J.Cosgrove 35-5-140-3; T.L.Maynard 3-0-20-0; W.T.Owen 36-6-139-0; G.P.Rees 1-0-3-0; M.A.Wallace 1-0-3-0; B.J.Wright 2-0-7-0.

The First-Class Averages (pp 220–237) give the records of Glamorgan players in all first-class county matches (Glamorgan's other opponents being West Indies A), with the exception of D.A.Cosker and J.A.R.Harris, whose first-class figures for Glamorgan are as above.

GLAMORGAN RECORDS

FIRST-CLASS CRICKET

Highest Total	For 718-3d			v	Sussex	Colwyn Bay	2000
	V 712			by	Northants	Northampton	1998
Lowest Total	For 22			v	Lancashire	Liverpool	1924
	V 33			by	Leics	Ebbw Vale	1965
Highest Innings	For 309*	S.P.James		v	Sussex	Colwyn Bay	2000
	V 322*	M.B.Loye		for	Northants	Northampton	1998

Highest Partnership for each Wicket

1st	374	M.T.G.Elliott/S.P.James	v	Sussex	Colwyn Bay	2000
2nd	252	M.P.Maynard/D.L.Hemp	v	Northants	Cardiff	2002
3rd	313	D.E.Davies/W.E.Jones	v	Essex	Brentwood	1948
4th	425*	A.Dale/I.V.A.Richards	v	Middlesex	Cardiff	1993
5th	264	M.Robinson/S.W.Montgomery	v	Hampshire	Bournemouth	1949
6th	240	J.Allenby/M.A.Wallace	v	Surrey	The Oval	2009
7th	211	P.A.Cottey/O.D.Gibson	v	Leics	Swansea	1996
8th	202	D.Davies/J.J.Hills	v	Sussex	Eastbourne	1928
9th	203*	J.J.Hills/J.C.Clay	v	Worcs	Swansea	1929
10th	143	T.Davies/S.A.B.Daniels	v	Glos	Swansea	1982

Best Bowling	For 10- 51	J.Mercer	v	Worcs	Worcester	1936
(Innings)	V 10- 18	G.Geary	for	Leics	Pontypridd	1929
Best Bowling	For 17-212	J.C.Clay	v	Worcs	Swansea	1937
(Match)	V 16- 96	G.Geary	for	Leics	Pontypridd	1929

Most Runs – Season	2276	H.Morris	(av 55.51)		1990
Most Runs – Career	34056	A.Jones	(av 33.03)		1957-83
Most 100s – Season	10	H.Morris			1990
Most 100s – Career	54	M.P.Maynard			1985-2005
Most Wkts – Season	176	J.C.Clay	(av 17.34)		1937
Most Wkts – Career	2174	D.J.Shepherd	(av 20.95)		1950-72
Most Career W-K Dismissals	933	E.W.Jones	(840 ct; 93 st)		1961-83
Most Career Catches in the Field	656	P.M.Walker			1956-72

LIMITED-OVERS CRICKET

Highest Total	50ov	429		v	Surrey	The Oval	2002
	40ov	305-6		v	Worcs	Cardiff	2001
	T20	206-6		v	Somerset	Taunton	2006
Lowest Total	50ov	76		v	Northants	Northampton	1968
	40ov	42		v	Derbyshire	Swansea	1979
	T20	94-9		v	Essex	Cardiff	2010
Highest Innings	50ov	162*	I.V.A.Richards	v	Oxfordshire	Swansea	1993
	40ov	155*	J.H.Kallis	v	Surrey	Pontypridd	1999
	T20	116*	I.J.Thomas	v	Somerset	Taunton	2004
Best Bowling	50ov	5-13	R.J.Shastri	v	Scotland	Edinburgh	1988
	40ov	7-16	S.D.Thomas	v	Surrey	Swansea	1998
	T20	5-16	R.E.Watkins	v	Glos	Cardiff	2009

GLOUCESTERSHIRE

Formation of Present Club: 1871
Inaugural First-Class Match: 1870
Colours: Blue, Gold, Brown, Silver, Green and Red
Badge: Coat of Arms of the City and County of Bristol
County Champions (since 1890): (0); best – 2nd 1930, 1931, 1947, 1959, 1969, 1986
Gillette/NatWest/C&G/FP Trophy Winners: (5) 1973, 1999, 2000, 2003, 2004
Benson and Hedges Cup Winners: (3) 1977, 1999, 2000
Pro 40/National League (Div 1) Winners: (1) 2000
Sunday League Winners: (0); best – 2nd 1988
Clydesdale Bank 40 Winners: (0); best – 3rd Group B 2010
Twenty20 Cup Winners: (0); best – Finalist 2007

Chief Executive: Tom E.M.Richardson, County Ground, Nevil Road, Bristol BS7 9EJ • Tel: 0117 910 8000 • Fax: 0117 924 1193 • Email: info@glosccc.co.uk • Web: www.glosccc.co.uk

Director of Cricket: J.G.Bracewell. **Assistant Coach:** S.N.Barnes. **Captain:** A.P.R.Gidman. **Vice-Captain:** tbc. **Overseas Player:** M.Muralitharan (T20 only). **2011 Beneficiary:** none. **Head Groundsman:** Sean Williams. **Scorer:** Adrian Bull. ‡ New registration. NQ Not qualified for England.

Gloucestershire revised their capping policy in 2004 and now award players with their County Caps when they make their first-class debut.

BANERJEE, Vikram (King Edward's S, Birmingham; Downing C, Cambridge; b Bradford, Yorks 20 Mar 1984. 6'0". LHB, SLA. Cambridge UCCE 2004-06; blue 2004-05-06. Gloucestershire debut/cap 2006. HS 35 and BB 5-74 v Surrey (Oval) 2010. LO HS 6 v Surrey (Bristol) 2009 (FPT). LO BB 3-47 v Sussex (Bristol) 2009 (FPT). T20 HS 5*. T20 BB 2-30.

BATTY, Jonathan Neil (Wheatley Park S, Oxon; Repton S; Durham U; Keble C, Oxford), b Chesterfield, Derbys 18 Apr 1974. 5'10". RHB, WK. Comb U 1994-95. Oxford U 1996; blue 1996. Surrey 1997-2009; cap 2001; captain 2004; benefit 2009. Gloucestershire debut/cap 2010. Oxfordshire 1993-96. Minor C 1996. 1000 runs (1): 1025 (2006). HS 168* Sy v Essex (Chelmsford) 2003. Gs HS 61 v Derbys (Derby) 2010. BB 1-21 Sy v Lancs (Manchester) 2000. LO HS 158* Sy v Hants (Oval) 2005 (CGT). T20 HS 59.

BEARD, Michael Adam (Lord Williams's S, Thame), b Oxford 24 Oct 1992. 6'5". LHB, LMF. Gloucestershire 2nd XI debut 2009. Awaiting 1st XI debut.

COCKBAIN, Ian Andrew (Maghull HS), Liverpool, Lancs 17 Feb 1987. Son of I.Cockbain (Lancs and Minor Cos 1979-94). RHB, RM. Lancashire 2nd XI 2006-08. MCC YC 2008-10. Gloucestershire 2nd XI debut 2010. Awaiting 1st XI debut.

COUGHTRIE, Richard George (Oxford Brookes U), b North Shields, Co Durham 1 Sep 1988. RHB, WK. Oxford MCCU 2009-10. Gloucestershire 2nd XI debut 2010. Awaiting 1st XI debut. HS 43 OU v Middx (Oxford) 2010.

110

DAWSON, Richard Kevin James (Batley GS; Exeter U), b Doncaster, Yorks 4 Aug 1980. 6'3". RHB, OB. British U 2000. Yorkshire 2001-06; cap 2004. MCC 2002. Northamptonshire 2007. Gloucestershire debut/cap 2008. Devon 1999-2000. **Tests**: 7 (2001-02 to 2002-03); HS 19* v A (Perth) 2002-03; BB 4-134 v I (Chandigarh) 2001-02 – on debut. F-c Tours: A 2002-03; NZ 2001-02; I 2001-02; SL 2002-03 (ECB Acad), 2004-05 (Eng A). HS 87 Y v Kent (Canterbury) 2002. Gs HS 50 and Gs BB 4-76 v Glamorgan (Cardiff) 2009. BB 6-82 Y v Glamorgan (Scarborough) 2001. LO HS 41 Y v Leics (Scarborough) 2002 (NL). LO BB 4-13 Y v Derbys (Derby) 2002 (BHC). T20 HS 27*. T20 BB 3-24.

DENT, Christopher David James (Backwell CS; Alton C), b Bristol 20 Jan 1991. 5'9". LHB, WK, occ SLA. Debut (Gloucestershire) 2010; cap 2010. Gloucestershire 2nd XI debut 2007, aged 16y 80d. England U19s 2009-10. HS 98 v Derbys (Derby) 2010. BB – . LO HS 8 v Yorks (Cheltenham) 2010 (CB40). LO BB 1-17 v Neth (Rotterdam) 2010 (CB40). T20 HS 63.

‡[NQ]**FULLER, James** Kerr, b Cape Town, South Africa 24 Jan 1990. British passport. RHB, RFM. Otago 2009-10. HS 24 Otago v Wellington (Wellington) 2009-10. BB 1-33 Otago v ND (Whangarei) 2009-10.

GIDMAN, Alex Peter Richard (Wycliffe C), b High Wycombe, Bucks 22 Jun 1981. Elder brother of W.R.S.Gidman (*see below*). 6'3". RHB, RM. Debut (Gloucestershire); cap 2004; captain 2009 to date. MCC YC 2001. MCC 2004, 2007, 2010. Otago 2007-08. F-c Tour (Eng A): SL 2004-05. Appointed captain of Eng A tour to India 2003-04 but withdrew because of hand injury. 1000 runs (4); most – 1244 (2006). HS 176 v Surrey (Bristol) 2009. BB 4-47 v Glamorgan (Cardiff) 2005. LO HS 116 v Sussex (Hove) 2009 (FPT). LO BB 5-42 Eng A v Bangladesh A (Mirpur) 2006-07. T20 HS 64. T20 BB 2-24.

‡**GIDMAN, William** Robert Simon (Wycliffe C; Berkshire C of Agriculture), b High Wycombe, Bucks 14 Feb 1985. Younger brother of A.P.R.Gidman (*see above*). 6'2". LHB, RM. Durham 2007. No f-c appearances in 2008-10, awaiting CC debut. MCC YC 2004-06. HS 8 and BB 3-37 Du v Sri Lanka A (Chester-le-St) 2007. LO HS 21 MCC v Bangladesh A (Durham) 2008. LO BB 4-36 Du v Hants (Chester-le-St) 2010 (CB40).

LEWIS, Jonathan (Churchfields S, Swindon; Swindon C), b Aylesbury, Bucks 26 Aug 1975. 6'2". RHB, RMF. Debut (Gloucestershire) 1995; cap 1998; captain 2006-08; benefit 2007. MCC 2005, 2010. Wiltshire 1993, 1995. Northamptonshire staff 1994. **Tests**: 1 (2006); HS 20 and BB 3-68 v SL (Nottingham) 2006. **LOI**: 13 (2005 to 2007); HS 17 v I (Leeds) 2007; BB 4-24 v A (Brisbane) 2006-07. **IT20**: 2 (2005 to 2006-07); HS 1 v A (Sydney) 2006-07; BB 4-24 v A (Southampton) 2005. F-c Tours (Eng A): WI 2000-01; SL 2004-05. HS 62 v Worcs (Cheltenham) 1999. 50 wkts (8); most – 74 (2003). BB 8-95 v Zimbabweans (Gloucester) 2000. CC BB 7-38 (10-75 match) v Somerset (Bristol) 2006. Hat-trick v Notts (Nottingham) 2000. LO HS 54 v Durham (Cheltenham) 2009 (P40). LO BB 5-19 v Hants (Southampton) 2005 (NL). T20 HS 43. T20 BB 4-24.

McCARTER, Graeme John, b Londonderry, N.Ireland 10 Oct 1992. RHB, RFM. Gloucestershire 2nd XI debut 2008, aged 15y 292d. Awaiting 1st XI debut.

[NQ]**MARSHALL, Hamish** John Hamilton (Mahurangi C, Warkworth; King C, Auckland), b Warkworth, New Zealand 15 Feb 1979. Twin brother of J.A.H.Marshall (ND and NZ 1997-98 to date). Irish passport, qualified to play in April 2011. 5'9". RHB, RM. ND 1998-99 to date. Gloucestershire debut 2006 (scoring 102 v Worcs on UK debut); cap 2006; Kolpak registration 2008-11. Buckinghamshire 2003. **Tests** (NZ): 13 (2000-01 to 2005-06); HS 160 v SL (Napier) 2004-05. **LOI** (NZ): 66 (2003-04 to 2006-07); HS 101* v P (Faisalabad) 2003-04. **IT20** (NZ): 3 (2004-05 to 2005-06); HS 8 v A (Auckland) 2004-05. F-c Tours (NZ): A 2004-05; SA 2000-01, 2005-06; Z 2005; B 2004-05. 1000 runs (1): 1218 (2006). HS170 ND v Canterbury (Rangiora) 2009-10. Gs HS 168 v Leics (Cheltenham) 2006. BB 4-24 v Leics (Leicester) 2009. LO HS 122 v Sussex (Hove) 2007 (P40). LO BB 2-21 v Hants (Southampton) 2009 (P40). T20 HS 100.

MILES, Craig Neil (Bradon Forest S, Swindon; Filton C, Bristol), b Swindon, Wilts 20 July 1994. 6'4". RHB, RMF. Gloucestershire 2nd XI debut 2009. Awaiting 1st XI debut.

[‡NQ]**MURALITHARAN, Muttiah** (St Anthony's C, Kandy), Kandy, Sri Lanka 17 Apr 1972. RHB, OB. Central Province 1989-90 to 2003-04. Tamil Union 1991-92 to 2003-04. Lancashire 1999 (taking 7-44 and 7-73 v Warwks at Southport on debut), 2001, 2005, 2007; cap 1999. Kent 2003; cap 2003. Signs for Gloucestershire in 2011 for T20 only. *Wisden* 1998. **Tests** (SL): 133 (1992-93 to 2010); HS 67 v I (Kandy) 2001-02; BB 9-51 (13-115 match) v Z (Kandy) 2001-02. **LOI** (SL): 341 (1993 to 2010-11); HS 33* v B (Dhaka) 2008-09; BB 7-30 v I (Sharjah) 2000-01. **IT20** (SL): 12 (2006-07 to 2010-11); HS 1 v P (Colombo, RPS) 2009; BB 3-29 v WI (Oval) 2009. F-c Tours (SL): E 1991, 1998, 2002, 2006; A 1995-96, 2005-06, 2007-08; SA 1992-93 (SL U24), 1994-95, 1997-98, 2000-01, 2002-03; WI 1996-97, 2003, 2007-08; NZ 1994-95, 1996-97; I 1993-94, 1997-98, 2006-07, 2009-10; P 1995-96, 1999-00, 2001-02, 2008-09; Z 1994-95, 2005-06; 2008-09. HS 67 (*see Tests*). CC HS 28 La v Sussex (Liverpool) 2007. 50 wkts (3+3); most – 96 (2003-04). BB 9-51 (*see Tests*). CC BB 7-39 (11-61 match) La v Derbys (Derby) 1999. LO HS 33* (*see LOI*). LO BB 7-30 (*see LOI*). T20 HS 11. T20 BB 4-16.

NORWELL, Liam Connor, b Bournemouth, Dorset 27 Dec 1991. RHB, RMF. Gloucestershire 2nd XI debut 2009. Awaiting 1st XI debut.

PAYNE, David Alan (Lytchett Minster S), b Poole, Dorset, 15 Feb 1991. 6'2". RHB, LMF. Gloucestershire 2nd XI debut 2008. Dorset 2009. England U19s 2010. Awaiting f-c debut. LO HS 13 and LO BB 7-29 v Essex (Chelmsford) 2010 (CB40), inc 4 wkts in 4 balls and 6 wkts in 9 balls – Gs 1-o record. T20 HS 1*. T20 BB 3-25.

SAXELBY, Ian David (Oakham S), b Nottingham 22 May 1989. 6'2". RHB, RMF. Nephew of K.Saxelby (Nottinghamshire 1978-90) and M.Saxelby. (Notts, Durham and Derbys 1989-2000). Debut (Gloucestershire) 2008; cap 2008. No 1st XI appearances in 2010. Nottinghamshire 2nd XI debut 2006. England U19s 2008. HS 60* v Northants (Northampton) 2009. BB 3-31 v Essex (Southend) 2009 and v Leics (Leicester) 2009. LO HS 7* and BB 4-31 v Surrey (Bristol) 2009 (FPT). T20 HS 2. T20 BB 2-32.

TAYLOR, Christopher Glyn (Colston's Collegiate S), b Southmead, Bristol 27 Sep 1976. 5'7". RHB, OB. Debut (Gloucestershire) 2000, scoring 104 v Middx – first to score a hundred at Lord's in a Championship match on his first-class debut; cap 2001; captain 2004-05. 1000 runs (2); most – 1101 (2008). HS 196 v Notts (Nottingham) 2001. BB 4-52 v Northants (Northampton) 2007. LO HS 105 v Northants (Northampton) 2010 (CB40). LO BB 2-5 v Northants (Northampton) 2004 (NL). T20 HS 83. T20 BB 1-22.

TAYLOR, Jack Martin Robert (Chipping Norton S), b Banbury, Oxfordshire 12 Nov 1991. 5'11". RHB, OB. Debut (Gloucestershire) 2010; cap 2010. Gloucestershire 2nd XI debut 2007, aged 15y 191d. Oxfordshire 2009-10. HS 6 v Derbys (Bristol) 2010. BB 1-8 v Surrey (Bristol) 2010.

WADE, David Neil (Bishop Luffa C of E S, Chichester; Havant C), b Chichester, W Sussex 27 Sep 1983. RHB, RFM. Gloucestershire 2nd XI debut 2010. Awaiting 1st XI debut.

YOUNG, Edward George Christopher (Wellington C; Oxford Brookes U), b Chertsey, Surrey 21 May 1989. 6'1". RHB, SLA. Brother of P.J.W.Young (Oxford UCCE 2006-08). Oxford MCCU 2009-10. Gloucestershire debut/cap 2010. HS 79 OU v Northants (Oxford) 2010. Gs HS 38 and Gs BB 1-75 v Leics (Leicester) 2010. BB 2-74 OU v Notts (Oxford) 2009. LO HS 25 v Yorks (Leeds) 2010 (CB40). LO BB 2-42 v Netherlands (Bristol) 2010 (CB40).

RELEASED/RETIRED
(Having made a County First-Class or List A appearance in 2010)

ALI, Abdul-Kadeer (Handsworth GS), b Moseley, Birmingham 7 Mar 1983. 6'1". Brother of M.M.Ali (*see WORCESTERSHIRE*), cousin of Kabir Ali (*see HAMPSHIRE*). RHB, RM/LB. Worcestershire 2000-04. Gloucestershire 2005-10; cap 2005. F-c Tour (Eng A): I 2003-04. HS 161 v Northants (Bristol) 2008. BB 1-4 v Glamorgan (Bristol) 2005. LO HS 114 v Hants (Southampton) 2007 (P40). LO BB 1-4 Wo v Worcs CB (Worcester) 2003 (CGT). T20 HS 53. T20 BB 2-28.

NO**FRANKLIN, James** Edward Charles (Wellington C; Victoria U), Wellington, New Zealand 7 Nov 1980. 6'4½". LHB, LFM. Wellington 1998-99 to date. Gloucestershire 2004-10; cap 2004. Glamorgan 2006. **Tests** (NZ): 27 (2000-01 to 2010-11); HS 122* v SA (Cape Town) 2006-07; BB 6-119 v A (Auckland) 2004-05. Hat-trick v B (Dhaka) 2004-05. **LOI** (NZ): 83 (2000-01 to 2010-11); HS 98* v I (Bangalore) 2010-11; BB 5-42 v E (Chester-le-St) 2004. **IT20** (NZ): 16 (2005-06 to 2010-11); HS 43 v A (Wellington) 2009-10; BB 3-23 v SL (Auckland) 2006-07. F-c Tours (NZ): E 2004; A 2004-05; SA 2004-05 (NZ A), 2005-06; Z 2005, 2010-11 (NZ A); B 2004-05. HS 219 Wellington v Auckland (Auckland) 2008-09. UK/Gs HS 109 v Derbys (Cheltenham) 2009; became only the second man for Gs to score a hundred and take a hat-trick in the same match. BB 7-14 v Derbys (Bristol) 2010. Hat-trick (*see above*). LO HS 133* v Derbys (Bristol) 2010. LO BB 5-42 (*see LOI*). T20 HS 90. T20 BB 3-23.

HUSSAIN, G.M. – *see SOMERSET*.

IRELAND, A.J. – *see MIDDLESEX*.

KIRBY, S.P. – *see SOMERSET*.

PORTERFIELD, W.T.S. – *see WARWICKSHIRE*.

SNELL, Stephen David (Sandown HS), b Winchester, Hampshire 27 Feb 1983. 6'0". RHB, WK. Gloucestershire 2005-10; cap 2005. MCC YC 2002-04. HS 127 v Worcs (Worcester) 2008. LO HS 95 v Middx (Cheltenham) 2010 (CB40). T20 HS 50.

R.J.Woodman left the staff without making a County First-Class or List A appearance in 2010.

GLOUCESTERSHIRE 2010

RESULTS SUMMARY

	Place	Won	Lost	Tied	Drew	NR
LV= County Championship (2nd Division)	5th	6	9		1	
All First-Class Matches		6	9		1	
Clydesdale Bank 40 (Group B)	3rd	9	3			
Friends Provident t20 (South Group)	9th	5	11			

LV= COUNTY CHAMPIONSHIP AVERAGES

BATTING AND FIELDING

Cap†		M	I	NO	HS	Runs	Avge	100	50	Ct/St
2008	W.T.S.Porterfield	7	14	–	175	531	37.92	2	1	6
2006	H.J.H.Marshall	15	27	2	89*	884	35.36	–	7	15
2004	J.E.C.Franklin	16	29	3	108	862	33.15	1	4	7
2001	C.G.Taylor	15	27	2	89	803	32.12	–	6	11
2010	C.D.J.Dent	16	31	3	98	725	25.89	–	4	24
2004	A.P.R.Gidman	16	29	–	99	679	23.41	–	3	16
2005	Kadeer Ali	6	12	1	74	240	21.81	–	2	5
2005	S.D.Snell	10	19	1	71	322	17.88	–	2	18
1998	J.Lewis	16	28	2	50	419	16.11	–	1	7
2010	J.N.Batty	15	30	2	61	450	16.07	–	1	53/3
2006	V.Banerjee	7	14	3	35	108	9.81	–	–	1
2009	G.M.Hussain	15	26	10	28*	153	9.56	–	–	1
2005	S.P.Kirby	10	17	5	22*	100	8.33	–	–	2
2010	J.M.R.Taylor	2	4	–	6	11	2.75	–	–	2
2007	A.J.Ireland	8	12	2	11	21	2.10	–	–	1

Also batted (2 matches): E.G.C.Young (cap 2010) 1, 19, 38 (3 ct).

BOWLING

	O	M	R	W	Avge	Best	5wI	10wM
A.J.Ireland	222.5	33	784	36	21.77	5-25	2	–
G.M.Hussain	417.4	86	1497	67	22.34	5-36	2	–
J.Lewis	419.3	103	1222	54	22.62	4-25	–	–
J.E.C.Franklin	334.2	69	1083	46	23.54	7-14	1	–
S.P.Kirby	261.4	59	835	29	28.79	4-50	–	–
V.Banerjee	222	28	793	23	34.47	5-74	2	–

Also bowled:
A.P.R.Gidman 53 7 203 9 22.55 2-10

C.D.J.Dent 11-0-43-0; H.J.H.Marshall 61-19-153-0; W.T.S.Porterfield 5-0-49-0; C.G.Taylor 52.2-5-172-3; J.M.R.Taylor 5-2-13-1; E.G.C.Young 38-1-154-1.

Gloucestershire played no first-class fixtures outside the County Championship in 2010. The First-Class Averages (pp 220–237) give the records of their players in all first-class county matches, with the exception of S.P.Kirby and E.G.C.Young, whose first-class figures for Gloucestershire are as above.

† Gloucestershire revised their capping policy in 2004 and now award players with their County Caps when they make their first-class debut.

GLOUCESTERSHIRE RECORDS

FIRST-CLASS CRICKET

Highest Total	For	695-9d		v	Middlesex	Gloucester	2004
	V	774-7d		by	Australians	Bristol	1948
Lowest Total	For	17		v	Australians	Cheltenham	1896
	V	12		by	Northants	Gloucester	1907
Highest Innings	For	341	C.M.Spearman	v	Middlesex	Gloucester	2004
	V	319	C.J.L.Rogers	for	Northants	Northampton	2006

Highest Partnership for each Wicket

1st	395	D.M.Young/R.B.Nicholls		v	Oxford U	Oxford	1962
2nd	256	C.T.M.Pugh/T.W.Graveney		v	Derbyshire	Chesterfield	1960
3rd	336	W.R.Hammond/B.H.Lyon		v	Leics	Leicester	1933
4th	321	W.R.Hammond/W.L.Neale		v	Leics	Gloucester	1937
5th	261	W.G.Grace/W.O.Moberley		v	Yorkshire	Cheltenham	1876
6th	320	G.L.Jessop/J.H.Board		v	Sussex	Hove	1903
7th	248	W.G.Grace/E.L.Thomas		v	Sussex	Hove	1896
8th	239	W.R.Hammond/A.E.Wilson		v	Lancashire	Bristol	1938
9th	193	W.G.Grace/S.A.P.Kitcat		v	Sussex	Bristol	1896
10th	131	W.R.Gouldsworthy/J.G.Bessant		v	Somerset	Bristol	1923

Best Bowling	For	10-40	E.G.Dennett		v	Essex	Bristol	1906
(Innings)	V	10-66	A.A.Mailey		for	Australians	Cheltenham	1921
		10-66	K.Smales		for	Notts	Stroud	1956
Best Bowling	For	17-56	C.W.L.Parker		v	Essex	Gloucester	1925
(Match)	V	15-87	A.J.Conway		for	Worcs	Moreton-in-M	1914

Most Runs – Season		2860	W.R.Hammond	(av 69.75)	1933
Most Runs – Career		33664	W.R.Hammond	(av 57.05)	1920-51
Most 100s – Season		13	W.R.Hammond		1938
Most 100s – Career		113	W.R.Hammond		1920-51
Most Wkts – Season		222	T.W.J.Goddard	(av 16.80)	1937
		222	T.W.J.Goddard	(av 16.37)	1947
Most Wkts – Career		3170	C.W.L.Parker	(av 19.43)	1903-35
Most Career W-K Dismissals		1054	R.C.Russell	(950 ct; 104 st)	1981-2004
Most Career Catches in the Field		719	C.A.Milton		1948-74

LIMITED-OVERS CRICKET

Highest Total	50ov	401-7		v	Bucks	Wing	2003
	40ov	344-6		v	Northants	Cheltenham	2001
	T20	227-4		v	Somerset	Bristol	2006
Lowest Total	50ov	82		v	Notts	Bristol	1987
	40ov	49		v	Middlesex	Bristol	1978
	T20	68		v	Hampshire	Bristol	2010
Highest Innings	50ov	177	A.J.Wright	v	Scotland	Bristol	1997
	40ov	153	C.M.Spearman	v	Warwicks	Gloucester	2003
	T20	100*	I.J.Harvey	v	Warwicks	Birmingham	2003
Best Bowling	50ov	6-21	C.A.Walsh	v	Kent	Bristol	1990
		6-21	C.A.Walsh	v	Cheshire	Bristol	1992
	40ov	7-29	D.A.Payne	v	Essex	Chelmsford	2010
	T20	4-22	I.D.Fisher	v	Somerset	Bristol	2004

HAMPSHIRE

Formation of Present Club: 12 August 1863
Inaugural First-Class Match: 1864
Colours: Blue, Gold and White
Badge: Tudor Rose and Crown
County Champions: (2) 1961, 1973
Gillette/NatWest/C&G/FP Trophy Winners: (3) 1991, 2005, 2009
Benson and Hedges Cup Winners: (2) 1988, 1992
Pro 40/National League (Div 1) Winners: (0); best – 2nd 2008
Sunday League Winners: (3) 1975, 1978, 1986
Clydesdale Bank 40 Winners: (0); best – 4th Group C 2010
Twenty20 Cup Winners: (1) 2010

Chairman and CEO: Rod Bransgrove, The Rose Bowl, Botley Road, West End, Southampton SO30 3XH • Tel: 023 8047 2002 • Fax: 023 8047 2122 • Email: enquiries@rosebowlplc.com • Web: www.rosebowlplc.com

Cricket Secretary and Director of Rose Bowl Plc: T.M.Tremlett. **First XI Manager:** G.W.White. **Captain:** D.G.Cork. **Vice-Captain:** N.Pothas. **Overseas Players:** Imran Tahir and Shahid Afridi (T20). **2011 Beneficiary:** N.Pothas. **Head Groundsman:** Nigel Gray. **Scorer:** A.E. (Tony) Weld. ‡ New registration. ^NQ Not qualified for England.

ADAMS, James Henry Kenneth (Sherborne S; University C, London; Loughborough U), b Winchester 23 Sep 1980. 6'2". LHB, LM. British U 2002-04. Hampshire debut 2002; cap 2006. Loughborough UCCE 2003-04 – scoring 107 v Somerset (Taunton) on debut. Dorset 1998. F-c Tour (EL): WI 2010-11. 1000 runs (2); most – 1351 (2009). HS 262* v Notts (Nottingham) 2006. BB 2-16 v Durham (Chester-le-St) 2004. LO HS 131 v Warwks (Birmingham) 2010 (CB40). LO BB 1-34 v Essex (Chelmsford) 2007 (FPT). T20 HS 101*. T20 BB –.

ALI, Kabir (Moseley CS and SFC), b Moseley, Birmingham 24 Nov 1980. 6'0". Cousin of A.K.Ali (*see GLOUCESTERSHIRE*) and K.M.Ali (*see WORCESTERSHIRE*). RHB, RMF. Worcestershire 1999-2009. Rajasthan 2006-07. Hampshire debut 2010. **Tests:** 1 (2003); HS 9 and BB 3-80 v SA (Leeds) 2003. **LOI:** 14 (2003 to 2006); HS 39* v P (Rawalpindi) 2005-06; BB 4-45 v I (Delhi) 2005-06. F-c Tours: WI 2005-06 (Eng A); SL 2002-03 (ECB Acad). HS 84* Wo v Durham (Stockton) 2003. H HS 18 v Durham (Chester-le-St) 2010. 50 wkts (5); most – 71 (2002). BB 8-50 Wo v Lancs (Manchester) 2007. Took 8-53 before lunch first day Wo v Yorks (Scarborough) 2003. H BB 5-33 v Essex (Chelmsford) 2010 – on H debut. LO HS 92 Wo v Essex (Worcester) 2003 (NL). LO BB Wo 5-36 v Yorks (Leeds) 2002 (NL). T20 HS 49. T20 BB 4-44.

BALCOMBE, David John (St John's S, Leatherhead; St Hild & St Bede C, Durham), b City of London 24 Dec 1984. 6'4". RHB, RFM. Durham UCCE 2005-07. British U 2006. Hampshire debut 2007. HS 73 DU v Leics (Leicester) 2005. H HS 30 v Yorks (Southampton) 2010. BB 5-112 DU v Durham (Durham) 2005. H BB 3-58 v Yorks (Leeds) 2007. LO HS 2 (twice). LO BB 2-39 v Somerset (Taunton) 2008. T20 HS 3. T20 BB – .

BATES, Alexander **Michael** (Lord Wandsworth C, Hook), b Portsmouth 10 Oct 1990. 5'10". RHB, WK. Debut (Hampshire) 2010. Hampshire 2nd XI debut 2007. Berkshire 2009. England U19s 2009-10. HS 31 v Lancs (Liverpool) 2010. LO HS 2* v Leics (Leicester) 2010 (CB40). T20 HS 10.

BRIGGS, Danny Richard (Isle of Wight C), b Newport, IoW, 30 Apr 1991. 6'2". RHB, SLA. Debut (Hampshire) 2009. Hampshire 2nd XI debut 2007, aged 16y 120d. F-c Tour (EL): WI 2010-11. HS 38* EL v Barbados (Bridgetown) 2010-11. CC HS 36 v Somerset (Southampton) 2009 – on debut. BB 4-74 EL v CC&C (Bridgetown) 2010-11. CC BB 4-93 v Kent (Canterbury) 2010. LO HS 10* v Leics (Leicester) 2010 (CB40). LO BB 2-36 v Notts (Southampton) 2009 (P40). T20 HS 9. T20 BB 3-5.

CARBERRY, Michael Alexander (St John Rigby Catholic C), b Croydon, Surrey 29 Sep 1980. 6'0". LHB, OB. Surrey 2001-02. Kent 2003-05. Hampshire debut/cap 2006. MCC 2008. **Tests**: 1 (2009-10); HS 34 v B (Chittagong) 2009-10. F-c Tours: B 2006-07 (Eng A), 2009-10. 1000 runs (2); most – 1251 (2009). HS 204 v Warwks (Southampton) 2009. BB 2-85 v Durham (Chester-le-St) 2006. LO HS 121* v Ireland (Southampton) 2009 (FPT). LO BB 2-11 v Notts (Nottingham) 2009 (FPT). T20 HS 90. T20 BB 1-16.

CORK, Dominic Gerald (St Joseph's C, Stoke-on-Trent; Newcastle CFE), b Newcastle-under-Lyme, Staffs 7 Aug 1971. 6'2". RHB, RFM. Derbyshire 1990-2003; cap 1993; captain 1998-2003; benefit 2001. Lancashire 2004-08; cap 2004. Hampshire debut/cap 2009; captain 2010 (part) to date. Wisden 1995. PCA 1995. Staffordshire 1989-90. **Tests**: 37 (1995 to 2002); HS 59 v NZ (Auckland) 1996-97; BB 7-43 v WI (Lord's) 1995 – on debut (record England analysis by Test match debutant); hat-trick v WI (Manchester) 1995 – the first in Test history to occur in the opening over of a day's play. **LOI**: 32 (1992 to 2002-03); HS 31* v NZ (Napier) 1996-97; BB 3-27 v WI (Lord's) 1995. F-c Tours: A 1992-93 (Eng A), 1998-99; SA 1993-94 (Eng A), 1995-96; WI 1991-92 (Eng A); NZ 1996-97; I 1994-95 (Eng A); P 2000-01 (part). HS 200* De v Durham (Derby) 2000. H HS 55 v Essex (Southampton) 2010. 50 wkts (7); most – 90 (1995). BB 9-43 (13-93 match) De v Northants (Derby) 1995. H BB 5-14 v Worcs (Worcester) 2009. Took 8-53 before lunch on his 20th birthday for De v Essex (Derby) 1991. 2 hat-tricks: 1994 and 1995 (see Tests). LO HS 93 De v Derbys CB (Derby) 2000 (NWT). LO BB 6-21 De v Glamorgan (Chesterfield) 1997 (SL). T20 HS 28. T20 BB 4-16.

DAWSON, Liam Andrew (John Bentley S, Calne), b Swindon, Wilts 1 Mar 1990. 5'8". RHB, SLA. Debut (Hampshire) 2007. England U19s 2007 to 2008. Wiltshire 2006-07. HS 100* v Notts (Nottingham) 2008. BB 2-3 v Sussex (Southampton) 2009. LO HS 69* v Essex (Chelmsford) 2009 (P40). LO BB 4-45 v Middx (Lord's) 2008 (P40). T20 HS 23. T20 BB 3-25.

‡^{NQ}**De WET, Friedel** (Grenswag Hoerskool; Pretoria TC), b Durban, South Africa 26 Jun 1980. RHB, RFM. Northerns 2001-02 to 2002-03. North West 2004-05 to date. Lions 2005-06 to date. Joins Hampshire in 2011 (Kolpak registration). **Tests** (SA): 2 (2009-10); HS 20 and BB 4-55 v E (Pretoria) 2009-10. F-c Tour (SA A): 1 2007-08. HS 56 Lions v Titans (Pretoria) 2007-08. 50 wkts (0+1): 61 (2006-07). BB 7-61 Lions v Cape Cobras (Cape Town) 2005-06. LO HS 56* NW v FS (Potchefstroom) 2005-06. LO BB 5-59 Lions v Eagles (Johannesburg) 2006-07. T20 HS 17. T20 BB 2-18.

^{NQ}**ERVINE, Sean** Michael (Lomagundi C, Chinhoyi), b Harare, Zimbabwe 6 Dec 1982. Elder brother of C.R.Ervine (Midlands, SR 2003-04 to date); son of R.M.Ervine (Rhodesia 1977-78); grandson of M.A.Den (Rhodesia 1935-36); nephew of N.B.Ervine (Rhodesia 1977-78) and G.M.Den (Rhodesia and EP 1963-64 to 1969-70). Irish passport. 6'2". LHB, RM. CFX Academy 2000-01 to 2001. Midlands 2001-02 to 2003-04. Hampshire debut/cap 2005 (Kolpak registration). WA 2006-07 to 2007-08. SR 2009-10. **Tests** (Z): 5 (2003 to 2003-04); HS 86 v (Harare) 2003-04; BB 4-146 v A (Perth) 2003-04. **LOI** (Z): 42 (2001-02 to 2003-04); HS 100 v I (Adelaide) 2003-04; BB 3-29 v P (Sharjah) 2001-02. F-c Tours (Z): E 2003; A 2003-04. HS 237* v Somerset (Southampton) 2010. BB 6-82 Midlands v Mashonaland (Kwekwe) 2002-03. H BB 5-60 v Glamorgan (Cardiff) 2005. LO HS 167* v Ireland (Southampton) 2009 (FPT). LO BB 5-50 v Glamorgan (Cardiff) 2005 (CGT). T20 HS 74*. T20 BB 4-12.

GRIFFITHS, David Andrew (Sandown HS, IoW), b Newport, IoW 10 Sep 1985. 6'1". LHB, RFM. Debut (Hampshire) 2006. HS 31* v Surrey (Southampton) 2007. BB 5-85 v Essex (Chelmsford) 2010. LO HS 3* v Worcs (Worcester) 2008 (FPT). LO BB 4-29 v Glos (Southampton) 2009 (P40). T20 HS 4*. T20 BB 3-13.

HOWELL, Benny Alexander Cameron (The Oratory S), b Bordeaux, France 5 Oct 1988. Son of J.B.Howell (Warwickshire 2nd XI 1978). 5'11". RHB, RM. Hampshire 2nd XI debut 2005. Berkshire 2007. Awaiting f-c debut. LO HS 12 and LO BB 1-23 v Leics (Southampton) 2010 (CB40). T20 HS 29*. T20 BB 2-14.

‡NQ**IMRAN TAHIR,** Mohammad (Government Pakistan Angels HS and MAO College, Lahore), b Lahore, Pakistan 4 Jun 1979. 5'11". RHB, LB. Lahore City 1996-97 to 1997-98. WAPDA 1998-99. REDCO 1999-00. Lahore Whites 2000-01. SNGPL 2001-02 to 2003-04. Sialkot 2002-03. Middlesex 2003. Lahore Blues 2004-05. PIA 2004-05 to 2006-07. Lahore Ravi 2005-06. Yorkshire (1 match) 2007. Titans 2007-08 to 2009-10. Hampshire 2008-09; cap 2009. Easterns 2008-09 to 2009-10. Warwickshire 2010; cap 2010. Dolphins 2010-11. Staffordshire 2004-05. Qualified for SA on 1 Apr 2009. F-c Tour (Pak A): SL 2004-05. HS 77* v Somerset (Southampton) 2009. 50 wkts (1+1); most – 74 (2004-05). BB 8-76 REDCO v Karachi Blues (Lahore) 1999-00. UK BB 7-66 (12-189 match) v Lancs (Manchester) 2008 – on H debut. LO HS 41* Staffs v Lancs (Stone) 2004 (CGT). LO BB 5-27 v Sussex (Southampton) 2008 (P40). T20 HS 13. T20 BB 3-13.

JONES, Simon Philip (Coedcae CS; Millfield S), b Morriston, Swansea 25 Dec 1978. Son of I.J.Jones (Glamorgan and England 1960-68). 6'3½". LHB, RFM. Glamorgan 1998-2007; cap 2002. Worcestershire 2008 (no 1st XI appearances in 2009). Hampshire debut 2010. MCC 2002-04. MBE 2005. *Wisden* 2005. **Tests**: 18 (2002 to 2005); HS 44 v I (Lord's) 2002 – on debut; BB 6-53 v A (Manchester) 2005. **LOI**: 8 (2004-05 to 2005); HS 1; BB 2-43 v Z (Bulawayo) 2004-05 – on debut. F-c Tours: A 2002-03 (*part*); SA 2004-05; WI 2003-04; I 2003-04 (Eng A – *part*). HS 46 Gm v Yorks (Scarborough) 2001. BB 6-45 Gm v Derbys (Cardiff) 2002. H HS 0* and H BB 4-60 v Warwks (Southampton) 2010. LO HS 26 Gm v Hants (Swansea) 2007 (FPT). LO BB 5-32 Wo v Hants (Worcester) 2008 (FPT). T20 HS 11*. T20 BB 4-10.

LUMB, Michael John (St Stithians C, Johannesburg), b Johannesburg, South Africa 12 Feb 1980. Son of R.G.Lumb (Yorkshire 1970-84); nephew of A.J.S.Smith (SAU and Natal 1972-73 to 1983-84). 6'0". LHB, RM. Yorkshire 2000-06; ECB qualified and CC debut 2001; cap 2003. Hampshire debut 2007; cap 2008. F-c Tour (Eng A): I 2003-04. 1000 runs (2); most – 1038 (2003). HS 219 v Notts (Nottingham) 2009. BB 2-10 Y v Kent (Canterbury) 2001. H BB – . LO HS 110 EL v Pakistan A (Dubai) 2009-10. T20 HS 124* v Essex (Southampton) 2009 – H record. T20 BB 3-32.

NQ**McKENZIE, Neil** Douglas (King Edward VII HS; Rand Afrikaans U), b Johannesburg, South Africa 24 Nov 1975. 5'9½". RHB, RM. Transvaal/Gauteng 1994-95 to 1998-99. Northerns 1999-00 to 2003-04. Lions 2004-05 to date; captain 2004-05 to 2009-10 (*part*). Somerset 2007. Durham 2008. Hampshire debut/cap 2010 (Kolpak registration). *Wisden* 2008. **Tests** (SA): 58 (2000 to 2008-09); HS 226 v B (Chittagong) 2007-08, sharing Test record 1st wkt partnership of 415 with G.C.Smith; BB – . **LOI** (SA): 64 (1999-00 to 2008-09); HS 131* v Kenya (Cape Town) 2001-02; BB – . **IT20** (SA): 2 (2005-06 to 2008-09); HS 7* v A (Brisbane) 2008-09. F-c Tours (SA): E 2003, 2008; A 2001-02, 2008-09; WI 2000-01; NZ 2003-04; I 2007-08; P 2003-04; SL 2000; Z 2001-02, 2004 (SA A); B 2003, 2007-08. HS 226 (*see Tests*). UK HS 141 v Oxford MCCU (Oxford) 2010. CC HS 115* v Notts (Nottingham) 2010. BB 2-13 Lions v Eagles (Kimberley) 2007-08. H BB 2-30 v Lancs (Liverpool) 2010. LO HS 131* (*see LOI*). LO BB 2-19 Gauteng v GW (Kimberley) 1997-98. T20 HS 85*. T20 BB 1-4.

MASCARENHAS, Adrian Dimitri (Trinity C, Perth, Australia), b Hammersmith, London 30 Oct 1977. 6'2". Resident in Australia 1979-96. RHB, RMF. Debut (Hampshire) 1996, taking 6-88 v Glamorgan (Southampton); took 16 wickets in first two CC matches; cap 1998; benefit 2007; captain 2008-10. No f-c or l-o appearances in 2010 after Achilles injury. Dorset 1996. **LOI**: 20 (2007 to 2009); HS 52 v I (Bristol) 2007; hit sixes off five successive balls from Yuvraj Singh v I (Oval) 2007; BB 3-23 v I (Lord's) 2007. **IT20**: 14 (2007 to 2009); HS 31 v NZ (Auckland) 2007-08; BB 3-13 v Z (Cape Town) 2007-08. HS 131 v Kent (Canterbury) 2006. 50 wkts (1): 56 (2004). BB 6-25 v Derbys (Southampton) 2004. LO HS 79 v Worcs (Southampton) 1999 (NL) and 79 v Kent (Canterbury) 2004 (NL). LO BB 5-27 v Glos (Southampton) 2002 (NL). T20 HS 57*. T20 BB 5-14 v Sussex (Hove) 2004 – H record.

MILLER, Jamie Robin M., b Zimbabwe 6 Sep 1991. RHB, LBG. Hampshire 2nd XI debut 2010. Awaiting 1st XI debut.

‡^{NO}**MYBURGH, Johannes** Gerhardus (Pretoria BHS; U of SA), b Pretoria, South Africa 22 Oct 1980. 5'7". Elder brother of S.J.Myburgh (Northerns 2005-06 to 2009-10) and brother-in-law of F.de Wet (*see above*). RHB, OB. Northerns 1997-98 to 2006-07. Titans 2004-05. Canterbury 2007-08 to 2009-10. EU qualified through wife's visa. HS 203 Northerns B v Easterns (Pretoria) 1997-98. BB 4-56 Canterbury v ND (Hamilton) 2008-09. LO HS 112 Canterbury v Auckland (Christchurch) 2009-10. LO BB 2-22 Canterbury v CD (Christchurch) 2009-10. T20 HS 88. T20 BB 3-16.

POTHAS, Nic (King Edward VII S; Rand Afrikaans U), b Johannesburg, South Africa 18 Nov 1973. ECB qualified – EU (Greek) passport. 6'3". RHB, WK, occ RM. Transvaal 1993-94 to 1996-97. Gauteng 1997-98 to 2000-01. Hampshire debut 2002; cap 2003; benefit 2011. **LOI** (SA): 3 (2000-01); HS 24 v P (Singapore) 2000 – on debut. F-c Tours (SA): E 1996 (SA A); WI 2000 (SA A); SL 1998. HS 165 Gauteng v KZ-Natal (Johannesburg) 1998-99. H HS 146* v Worcs (Worcester) 2003. BB 1-16 v Middx (Lord's) 2006. Held 7 catches in an innings v Lancs (Manchester) 2006. LO HS 114* v Glamorgan (Cardiff) 2005 (C&G). T20 HS 59.

‡**RAVENSCROFT, Timothy** John (Elizabeth C, Guernsey), b Guernsey 21 Jan 1992. 5'10". RHB, OB. Awaiting 1st XI debut.

RIAZUDDIN, Hamza (Bradfield C), b Chelsea, London 19 Dec 1989. 5'11". RHB, RMF. Debut (Hampshire) 2008. England U19s 2009. Berkshire 2008. HS 4 and CC BB 1-21 v Somerset (Taunton) 2008. BB 1-0 v OU (Oxford) 2010. LO HS 23* v Durham (Chester-le-St) 2010 (CB40). LO BB 2-47 v Somerset (Southampton) 2009 (P40). T20 HS 13*. T20 BB 4-15.

ROUSE, Adam Paul, b Harare, Zimbabwe 30 Jun 1992. RHB, WK. Hampshire 2nd XI debut 2008, aged 15y 331d. England U19s 2010. Awaiting 1st XI debut.

‡^{NO}**SHAHID KHAN AFRIDI**, Sahibzada Mohammad (Ibrahim Alibhai S; Islamia Science C, Karachi) b Kohat, Pakistan, 1 Mar 1980. Brother of Tariq Afridi (Karachi 1999-00) and Ashfaq Afridi (Karachi Blues 2008-09). RHB, LBG. Debut Combined XI v Eng A 1995-96. Karachi 1995-96 to 2003-04. Habib Bank 1997-98 to 2008-09. Leicestershire 2001; cap 2001. Derbyshire 2003. GW 2003-04. Sind 2007-08 to 2008-09. T20 contract for 2011. **Tests** (P): 27 (1998-99 to 2010, 1 as captain); HS 156 v I (Faisalabad) 2005-06; BB 5-52 v A (Karachi) 1998-99 – on debut. **LOI** (P): 312 (1996-97 to 2010-11, 21 as captain); HS 124 v B (Dambulla) 2010; BB 6-38 v A (Dubai) 2010. Scored a 37-ball hundred (*LOI record*) which included then joint record 11 sixes v SL (Nairobi) 1996-97 in his first LOI innings. **IT20** (P): 42 (2006-07 to 2010-11,18 as captain); HS 54* v SL (Lord's) 2009; BB 4-11 v Netherlands (Lord's) 2009. F-c Tours (P): E 2006, 2010; A 1996-97, 2004-05; WI 1999-00, 2005; I 1998-99, 2004-05; SL 2005-06; Z 2002-03; B 1998-99. HS 164 Le v Northants (Northampton) 2001. BB 6-101 Habib Bank v KRL (Rawalpindi) 1997-98. UK BB 5-84 Le v Essex (Chelmsford) 2001. LO HS 124 (*see LOI*). LO BB 6-38 (*see LOI*). T20 HS 54*. T20 BB 4-11.

TOMLINSON, James Andrew (Harrow Way S, Andover; Cardiff U), b Winchester 12 Jun 1982. 6'1". LHB, LMF. British U 2002-03. Hampshire debut 2002; cap 2008. Wiltshire 2001. HS 42 v Somerset (Southampton) 2010. 50 wkts (1): 67 (2008). BB 8-46 (10-194 match) v Somerset (Taunton) 2008. LO HS 14 v Durham (Chester-le-St) 2010 (CB40). LO BB 4-47 v Glamorgan (Southampton) 2006 (CGT). T20 HS 5. T20 BB 1-20.

VINCE, James Michael (Warminster S), b Cuckfield, Sussex 14 Mar 1991. 6'2". RHB, RM. Debut (Hampshire) 2009. Hampshire 2nd XI debut 2006. Wiltshire 2007-08. HS 180 v Yorks (Scarborough) 2010. BB – . LO HS 93 v Essex (Chelmsford) 2009 (P40). T20 HS 77.

WOOD, Christopher Philip (Alton C), b Basingstoke 27 June 1990. 6'2". RHB, LMF. Debut (Hampshire) 2010. Hampshire 2nd XI debut 2007. England U19s 2009. HS 35 and CC BB 3-32 v Lancs (Liverpool) 2010. BB 5-54 v Oxford MCCU (Oxford) 2010. LO HS 3 v Warwks (Southampton) 2010 (CB40). LO BB 4-33 v Scotland (Aberdeen) 2010 (CB40). T20 HS 18. T20 BB 3-27.

RELEASED/RETIRED
(Having made a County First-Class or List A appearance in 2010)

BENHAM, Christopher (Yately CS; Loughborough U), b Frimley, Surrey 24 Mar 1983. 6'1". RHB, RM/OB. Loughborough UCCE 2004. Hampshire 2004-10. HS 111 v Loughborough UCCE (Southampton) 2009. CC HS 95 v Warwks (Southampton) 2006. BB – . LO HS 158 v Glamorgan (Southampton) 2006. T20 HS 59.

[NO]**CHRISTIAN, Daniel** Trevor, b Camperdown, NSW, Australia 4 May 1983. RHB, RFM. S Australia 2007-08 to date. Hampshire 2010. **IT20** (A): 3 (2009-10); HS 4* and BB 2-29 v WI (Sydney) 2009-10. HS 106 S Aus v NSW (Sydney) 2010-11. H HS 36 and H BB 2-115 v Somerset (Taunton) 2010. BB 5-24 (9-87 match) S Aus v WA (Perth) (2009-10). LO HS 100 S Aus v Q (Townsville) 2010-11. LO BB 4-32 S Aus v Vic (Geelong) 2010-11. T20 HS 54. T20 BB 4-23.

[NO]**HERATH**, Herath Mudiyanselage **Rangana** Keerthi Bandara, b Kurunegala, Sri Lanka 19 Mar 1978. LHB, SLA. Kurunegala Youth 1996-97 to 1997-98. Moors Sports Club 1998-99 to 2009-10. Colombo District 2000-01 to 2001-02. North Central Province 2003-04 to 2004-05. Wayamba 2008-09 to date. Surrey 2009. Hampshire 2010. **Tests** (SL): 24 (1999-00 to 2010-11); HS 80* v I (Galle) 2010; BB 5-99 v P (Colombo, PSS) 2009. **LOI** (SL): 11 (2003-04 to 2010-11); HS 2 v NZ (Dambulla) 2010 and v WI (Colombo, SSC) 2010-11; BB 3-28 v SA (Dambulla) 2004. F-c Tours (SL): E 1999 (SL A), 2007 (SL A); SA 2003-04 (SL A), 2008-09 (SL A); WI 2007-08; NZ 2004-05; I 2003-04 (SL A), 2009-10; P 1999-00, 2004-05; Z 1999-00, 2004, 2007-08 (SL A); B 2005-06 (SL A), 2008-09. HS 80* (see Tests). H HS 17* v Yorks (Southampton) 2010. 50 wkts (0+2); most – 72 (2000-01). BB 8-43 (11-72 match) Moors SC v Police SC (Colombo) 2003-04. H BB 4-98 v Somerset (Southampton) 2010. LO HS 88* SL A v SA A (Benoni) 2008-09. LO BB 4-19 SL A v Z Select (Bulawayo) 2007-08. T20 HS 9. T20 BB 3-14.

[NO]**HUGHES, Phillip** Joel, b Macksville, NSW, Australia 30 Nov 1988. LHB, OB. NSW 2007-08 to date. Middlesex 2009, scoring 118 and 65* on debut. Hampshire 2010. **Tests** (A): 10 (2008-09 to 2010-11); HS 160 (and 115) v SA (Durban) 2008-09. F-c Tours (A): E 2009; SA 2008-09; NZ 2009-10; I 2008-09 (Aus A). HS 198 NSW v S Australia (Adelaide) 2008-09. UK HS 195 M v Surrey (Oval) 2009. H HS 38 v Kent (Canterbury) 2010. LO HS 119 M v Somerset (Lord's) 2009 (FPT). T20 HS 83.

PIETERSEN, K.P. – see *SURREY*.

Abdul Razzaq left the staff, without making a County First-Class or List A appearance in 2010.

HAMPSHIRE 2010

RESULTS SUMMARY

	Place	Won	Lost	Tied	Drew	NR
LV= County Championship (1st Division)	7th	3	6		7	
All First-Class Matches		3	6		8	
Clydesdale Bank 40 (Group C)	4th	6	6			
Friends Provident t20 (South Group)	**Winners**	11	8			

LV= COUNTY CHAMPIONSHIP AVERAGES

BATTING AND FIELDING

Cap		M	I	NO	HS	Runs	Avge	100	50	Ct/St
2008	M.J.Lumb	5	7	–	158	381	54.42	1	1	4
2006	J.H.K.Adams	16	29	1	196	1351	48.25	3	8	16
2006	M.A.Carberry	15	27	1	162	1221	46.96	5	4	9
2005	S.M.Ervine	16	26	4	237*	944	42.90	1	5	7
2010	N.D.McKenzie	14	24	4	115*	801	40.05	2	4	21
2003	N.Pothas	9	15	–	87	531	35.40	–	4	33
	J.M.Vince	15	25	2	180	795	34.56	1	3	11
2009	D.G.Cork	13	17	3	55	380	27.14	–	2	8
	C.C.Benham	6	11	–	45	268	24.36	–	–	8
	L.A.Dawson	7	11	1	74	230	23.00	–	2	3
	H.M.R.K.B.Herath	4	6	3	17*	59	19.66	–	–	1
	C.P.Wood	2	4	–	35	68	17.00	–	–	
	P.J.Hughes	3	6	–	38	85	14.16	–	–	
2008	J.A.Tomlinson	15	21	5	42	198	12.37	–	–	3
	A.M.Bates	7	10	2	31	92	11.50	–	–	23
	D.A.Griffiths	5	9	6	9*	34	11.33	–	–	1
	D.J.Balcombe	7	6	1	30	56	11.20	–	–	2
	D.R.Briggs	12	14	3	28	116	10.54	–	–	2
	Kabir Ali	4	8	–	18	64	8.00	–	–	2

Also played (1 match): D.T.Christian 28, 36; S.P.Jones 0*, 0*.

BOWLING

	O	M	R	W	Avge	Best	5wI	10wM
D.G.Cork	407.2	102	1042	45	23.15	5-50	2	–
Kabir Ali	137.2	27	488	19	25.68	5-33	2	–
D.J.Balcombe	214.1	42	721	24	30.04	3-69	–	–
D.A.Griffiths	152	18	646	19	34.00	5-85	1	–
J.A.Tomlinson	559.1	149	1624	46	35.30	7-85	2	–
D.R.Briggs	358.2	53	1262	32	39.43	4-93	–	–
H.M.R.K.B.Herath	175.3	42	463	10	46.30	4-98	–	–
S.M.Ervine	345.5	74	1023	18	56.83	4-31	–	–

Also bowled:

	O	M	R	W	Avge	Best	5wI	10wM
C.P.Wood	41	9	156	6	26.00	3-32	–	–

J.H.K.Adams 2-1-5-0; M.A.Carberry 37-9-100-4; D.T.Christian 22.1-1-115-2; L.A.Dawson 18-1-61-1; S.P.Jones 22.5-60-4; N.D.McKenzie 32-3-95-2; J.M.Vince 4.2-0-24-0.

The First-Class Averages (pp 220–237) give the records of Hampshire players in all first-class county matches (Hampshire's other opponents being Oxford MCCU).

HAMPSHIRE RECORDS

FIRST-CLASS CRICKET

Highest Total	For 714-5d		v	Notts	Southampton	2005
	V 742		by	Surrey	The Oval	1909
Lowest Total	For 15		v	Warwicks	Birmingham	1922
	V 23		by	Yorkshire	Middlesbrough	1965
Highest Innings	For 316	R.H.Moore	v	Warwicks	Bournemouth	1937
	V 303*	G.A.Hick	for	Worcs	Southampton	1997

Highest Partnership for each Wicket

1st	347	V.P.Terry/C.L.Smith	v	Warwicks	Birmingham	1987
2nd	321	G.Brown/E.I.M.Barrett	v	Glos	Southampton	1920
3rd	344	G.Brown/C.P.Mead	v	Yorkshire	Portsmouth	1927
4th	278	J.H.K.Adams/J.M.Vince	v	Yorkshire	Scarborough	2010
5th	235	G.Hill/D.F.Walker	v	Sussex	Portsmouth	1937
6th	411	R.M.Poore/E.G.Wynyard	v	Somerset	Taunton	1899
7th	325	G.Brown/C.H.Abercrombie	v	Essex	Leyton	1913
8th	257	N.Pothas/A.J.Bichel	v	Glos	Cheltenham	2005
9th	230	D.A.Livingstone/A.T.Castell	v	Surrey	Southampton	1962
10th	192	H.A.W.Bowell/W.H.Livsey	v	Worcs	Bournemouth	1921

Best Bowling	For 9- 25	R.M.H.Cottam	v	Lancashire	Manchester	1965
(Innings)	V 10- 46	W.Hickton	for	Lancashire	Manchester	1870
Best Bowling	For 16- 88	J.A.Newman	v	Somerset	Weston-s-Mare	1927
(Match)	V 17-103	W.Mycroft	for	Derbyshire	Southampton	1876

Most Runs – Season	2854	C.P.Mead	(av 79.27)		1928
Most Runs – Career	48892	C.P.Mead	(av 48.84)		1905-36
Most 100s – Season	12	C.P.Mead			1928
Most 100s – Career	138	C.P.Mead			1905-36
Most Wkts – Season	190	A.S.Kennedy	(av 15.61)		1922
Most Wkts – Career	2669	D.Shackleton	(av 18.23)		1948-69
Most Career W-K Dismissals	700	R.J.Parks	(630 ct; 70 st)		1980-92
Most Career Catches in the Field	629	C.P.Mead			1905-36

LIMITED-OVERS CRICKET

Highest Total	50ov	371-4		v	Glamorgan	Southampton	1975
	40ov	353-8		v	Middlesex	Lord's	2005
	T20	225-2		v	Middlesex	Southampton	2006
Lowest Total	50ov	75		v	Essex	Chelmsford	2007
	40ov	43		v	Essex	Basingstoke	1972
	T20	85		v	Sussex	Southampton	2008
Highest Innings	50ov	177	C.G.Greenidge	v	Glamorgan	Southampton	1975
	40ov	172	C.G.Greenidge	v	Surrey	Southampton	1987
	T20	124*	M.J.Lumb	v	Essex	Southampton	2009
Best Bowling	50ov	7-30	P.J.Sainsbury	v	Norfolk	Southampton	1965
	40ov	6-20	T.E.Jesty	v	Glamorgan	Cardiff	1975
	T20	5-14	A.D.Mascarenhas	v	Sussex	Hove	2004

KENT

Formation of Present Club: 1 March 1859
Substantial Reorganisation: 6 December 1870
Inaugural First-Class Match: 1864
Colours: Maroon and White
Badge: White Horse on a Red Ground
County Champions: (6) 1906, 1909, 1910, 1913, 1970, 1978
Joint Champions: (1) 1977
Gillette/NatWest/C&G/FP Trophy Winners: (2) 1967, 1974
Benson and Hedges Cup Winners: (3) 1973, 1976, 1978
Pro 40/National League (Div 1) Winners: (1) 2001
Sunday League Winners: (4) 1972, 1973, 1976, 1995
Clydesdale Bank 40 Winners: (0); best – 2nd Group C 2010
Twenty20 Cup Winners: (1) 2007

Acting Chief Executive: Jamie Clifford, St Lawrence Ground, Canterbury, CT1 3NZ • Tel: 01227 456886 • Fax: 01227 762168 • Email: kent@ecb.co.uk • Web: www.kentccc.co.uk

Head Coach: P.Farbrace. **1st Team Assistant Coach/Cricket Performance Manager:** P.Relf. **Captain:** R.W.T.Key. **Vice-Captain:** M.van Jaarsveld. **Overseas Player:** J.D.Nel. **2011 Beneficiary:** R.W.T.Key. **Head Groundsman:** Andrew Peirson. **Scorer:** Jack C.Foley. ‡ New registration. NQ Not qualified for England.

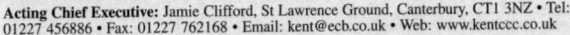

NQAZHAR MAHMOOD Sagar (F.G. No. 1 HS, Islamabad), b Rawalpindi, Pakistan 28 Feb 1975. 5'11". RHB, RFM. Islamabad 1993-94 to 1997-98, 2001-02 to 2006-07. United Bank 1995-96 to 1996-97. Rawalpindi 1998-99 to 2004-05. MCC 2001. PIA 2001-02. Surrey 2002-07; cap 2004. Habib Bank 2006-07, 2010-11. Kent debut 2008 (British passport holder) scoring 116 v Notts (Canterbury); cap 2008. **Tests** (P): 21 (1997-98 to 2001); HS 136 v SA (Johannesburg) 1997-98; BB 4-50 v E (Lord's) 2001. Scored 128* and 50* v SA (Rawalpindi) 1997-98 on debut. **LOI** (P): 143 (1996-97 to 2006-07); HS 67 v I (Adelaide) 1999-00; BB 6-18 v WI (Sharjah) 1999-00. F-c Tours (P): E 1997 (Pak A), 2001; A 1999-00; SA 1997-98; I 1998-99; SL 2000; Z 1997-98. HS 204* Sy v Middx (Oval) 2005. K HS 116 (*see above*). 50 wkts (0+1): 59 (1996-97). BB 8-61 Sy v Lancs (Oval) 2002. K BB 6-55 v Yorks (Canterbury) 2008. LO HS 101* Sy v Glamorgan (Oval) 2006 (C&G). LO BB 6-18 (*see LOI*). T20 HS 65*. T20 BB 4-20.

BALL, Adam James (Beths GS, Bexley) b Greenwich, London 1 March 1993. 6'0". RHB, LFM. Kent 2nd XI debut 2009, aged 16 years 117 days. England U19s 2010 to 2010-11. Awaiting f-c debut. LO HS 5 and LO BB 1-16 v Durham (Chester-le-St) 2010 (CB40) – only 1st XI appearance.

BELL-DRUMMOND, Daniel James (Millfield S), b Lewisham, London 4 Aug 1993. 6'0". RHB, RMF. Kent 2nd XI debut 2009, aged 16 years 21 days. England U19s 2010 to 2010-11. Awaiting 1st XI debut.

BILLINGS, Samuel William (Haileybury), b Pembury 15 Jun 1991. 5'11". RHB, WK. Kent 2nd XI debut 2007, aged 15 years 349 days. Awaiting 1st XI debut.

BLAKE, Alexander James (Hayes SS; Leeds Met U), b Farnborough 25 Jan 1989. 6'1". LHB, RMF. Debut (Kent) 2008. Kent 2nd XI debut 2005. Leeds/Bradford UCCE 2009. HS 105* v Yorks (Leeds) 2010. BB 2-9 v Pakistanis (Canterbury) 2010. CC BB 1-60 v Hants (Southampton) 2010. LO HS 81* v Scotland (Canterbury) 2010 (CB40). LO BB 1-25 v Glamorgan (Cardiff) 2007 (P40). T20 HS 33.

COLES, Matthew Thomas (Maplesden Noakes S; Mid-Kent C), b Maidstone 26 May 1990. 6'3". LHB, RMF. Debut (Kent) 2009. Kent 2nd XI debut 2007. HS 51 v Lancs (Canterbury) 2010. BB 4-55 v Warwks (Canterbury) 2010. LO HS 5 (*twice*) 2009 (P40). LO BB 4-47 v Hants (Southampton) 2010 (CB40). T20 HS 16*. T20 BB 3-30.

COOK, Simon James (Matthew Arnold S), b Oxford 15 Jan 1977. 6'4". RHB, RMF. Middlesex 1999-2004; cap 2003. Kent debut 2005; cap 2007. HS 93* M v Notts (Lord's) 2001. K HS 71 v Yorks (Leeds) 2006. BB 8-63 M v Northants (Northampton) 2002. K BB 6-35 v Sussex (Canterbury) 2007. LO HS 67* M v Durham (Lord's) 2003 (NL). LO BB 6-37 M v Leics (Leicester) 2004 (NL). T20 HS 25*. T20 BB 3-13.

DENLY, Joseph Liam (Chaucer TC), b Canterbury 16 Mar 1986. 6'0". RHB, LB. Debut (Kent) 2004; cap 2008. **LOI:** 9 (2009 to 2009-10); HS 67 v Ireland (Belfast) 2009 – on debut. **IT20:** 5 (2009 to 2009-10); HS 14 and BB 1-9 v SA (Centurion) 2009-10. F-c Tours (EL): NZ 2008-09; I 2007-08. 1000 runs (1): 1003 (2007). HS 149 v Somerset (Tunbridge W) 2008. BB 2-13 v Surrey (Canterbury) 2007. LO HS 115 v Warwks (Birmingham) 2009 (FPT). LO BB 1-20 E XI v SA A (Potchefstroom) 2009-10. T20 HS 91. T20 BB 1-9.

GOODMAN, James Elliot (St Olave's GS), b Farnborough 19 Nov 1990. 5'10". RHB, RM. Debut (Kent) 2010. Kent 2nd XI debut 2006, aged 15 years 194 days. England U19s 2009-10. HS 59 and BB 1-16 v Pakistanis (Canterbury) 2010 – only f-c appearance. LO HS 26* v Surrey (Canterbury) 2009 (P40).

JONES, Geraint Owen (Harristown State HS, Toowoomba and MacGregor State HS, Brisbane, Australia), b Kundiawa, Papua New Guinea 14 Jul 1976. Welsh parents. 5'10". RHB, WK. Debut (Kent) 2001; cap 2003. MBE 2005. **Tests:** 34 (2003-04 to 2006-07); HS 100 v NZ (Leeds) 2004. **LOI:** 49 (2004 to 2006); HS 80 v Z (Bulawayo) 2004-05. **IT20:** 2 (2005 to 2006); HS 19 v A (Southampton) 2005. F-c Tours: A 2006-07; SA 2004-05; WI 2003-04; I 2005-06; P 2005-06; SL 2003-04. 1000 runs (2); most – 1345 (2009). HS 178 v Somerset (Canterbury) 2010. LO HS 86 v Surrey (Oval) 2008 (FPT). T20 HS 56.

JOSEPH, Robert ('Robbie') Hartman (Sutton Valence S; St Mary's C, Twickenham), b Antigua 20 Jan 1982. Resided in England since 1997. 6'1". RHB, RFM. Debut (First-Class Counties XI v NZ) 2000. Kent debut 2004. Leeward Is 2008-09. F-c Tour (EL): NZ 2008-09. HS 36* v Sussex (Hove) 2007. 50 wkts (1): 55 (2008). BB 6-32 (9-62 match) v Durham (Chester-le-St) 2008. LO HS 15 v (Canterbury) 2005 (NL). LO BB 5-13 v Derbys (Canterbury) 2008 (P40). T20 HS 1*. T20 BB 2-14.

KEY, Robert William Trevor (Colfe's S), b East Dulwich, London 12 May 1979. 6'1". RHB, RM/OB. Debut (Kent) 1998; cap 2001; captain 2006 to date; benefit 2011. MCC 2002-04, 2009. *Wisden* 2004. **Tests:** 15 (2002 to 2004-05); HS 221 v WI (Lord's) 2004. **LOI:** 5 (2003 to 2004); HS 19 v WI (Lord's) 2004. **IT20:** 1 (2009); HS 10* v Netherlands (Lord's) 2009. F-c Tours: A 2002-03; SA 1998-99 (Eng A), 2004-05; NZ 2008-09 (EL – captain); SL 2002-03 (ECB Acad); Z 1998-99 (Eng A). 1000 runs (6); most – 1896 (2004). HS 270* v Glamorgan (Cardiff) 2009. BB 2-31 v Somerset (Canterbury) 2010. LO HS 120* v Essex (Canterbury) 2008 (P40). T20 HS 98*.

NQ NEL, Johann Dewald (George Watson's C, Edinburgh), b Klerksdorp, Transvaal, South Africa 6 Jun 1980. 6'0". RHB, RMF. Scotland 2004-10. Worcestershire 2007. Kent debut 2010. **LOI** (Scot): 19 (2006 to 2010); HS 11* v Afghanistan (Ayr) 2010; BB 4-25 v Ireland (Aberdeen) 2008. **IT20** (Scot): 10 (2007-08 to 2009-10); HS 13* v P (Durban) 2007-08; BB 3-10 v Kenya (Belfast) 2008. HS 36 Scotland v Afghanistan (Ayr) 2010. CC HS 8 Wo v Yorks (Leeds) 2007. K HS 4 v Pakistanis (Canterbury) 2010. BB 6-62 (9-119 match) v Yorks (Leeds) 2010. LO HS 36* Scotland v Durham (Edinburgh) 2006 (CGT). LO BB 4-25 Scotland v Ireland (Aberdeen) 2008. T20 HS 13*. T20 BB 3-10.

NORTHEAST, Sam Alexander (Harrow S), b Ashford 16 Oct 1989. 5'11". RHB, OB. Debut (Kent) 2007. No 1st XI appearances in 2008. England U19s 2009. HS 128* v Glos (Bristol) 2009. BB – . LO HS 69 v Surrey (Canterbury) 2009 (P40). T20 HS 21.

PIESLEY, Christopher Damien (Fulston Manor S, Sittingbourne), b Chatham 12 Mar 1992. LHB, OB. Debut (Kent) 2010. Kent 2nd XI debut 2008. HS 43 v Pakistanis (Canterbury) 2010 – only f-c appearance.

RILEY, Adam Edward N. (Beths GS, Bexley), b Sidcup 23 Mar 1992. 6'2". RHB, OB. Kent 2nd XI debut 2010. Awaiting 1st XI debut.

SHAW, Stuart Ashley (Shavington HS, Crewe), b Crewe, Cheshire 14 Apr 1991. 5'11". RHB, LFM. Kent 2nd XI debut 2010. Awaiting f-c and l-o debut. T20 HS 3*. T20 BB 1-10.

STEVENS, Darren Ian (Hinckley C), b Leicester 30 Apr 1976. 5'11". RHB, RM. Leicestershire 1997-2004; cap 2002. MCC 2002. Kent debut/cap 2005. F-c Tour (ECB Acad): SL 2002-03. 1000 runs (2); most – 1277 (2005). HS 208 v Glamorgan (Canterbury) 2005 and v Middx (Uxbridge) 2009. BB 4-36 v Yorks (Canterbury) 2006. LO HS 133 Le v Northumb (Jesmond) 2000 (NWT). LO BB 5-32 v Scotland (Edinburgh) 2005 (NL). T20 HS 77. T20 BB 4-14 v Essex (Chelmsford) 2007 – K record.

TREDWELL, James Cullum (Southlands Community CS, New Romney), b Ashford 27 Feb 1982. 6'0". LHB, OB. Debut (Kent) 2001; cap 2007. MCC 2004, 2008. **Tests**: 1 (2009-10); HS 37 and BB 4-82 v B (Dhaka) 2009-10. **LOI**: 3 (2009-10 to 2010-11); HS 16 v A (Hobart) 2010-11; BB – . F-c Tours: I 2003-04 (Eng A, captain); B 2009-10. HS 123* v New Zealanders (Canterbury) 2008. CC HS 116* v Yorks (Tunbridge W) 2007. 50 wkts (1): 69 (2009). BB 8-66 (11-120 match) v Glamorgan (Canterbury) 2009. LO HS 88 v Surrey (Oval) 2007 (FPT). LO BB 6-27 v Middx (Southgate) 2009 (FPT). T20 HS 34. T20 BB 4-21.

VAN JAARSVELD, Martin (Warmbaths S; Pretoria U), b Klerksdorp, South Africa 18 Jun 1974. 6'2". RHB, OB. N Transvaal/Northerns 1994-95 to 2003-04. Northamptonshire 2004. Titans 2004-05 to 2008-09. Kent debut/cap 2005 scoring 118 and 111 v Warwks (Canterbury) – second player after C.W.G.Bassano (Derbyshire) to score two hundreds on a county debut. PCA 2008. Qualified for England in 2010. **Tests** (SA): 9 (2002-03 to 2004-05); HS 73 v WI (Johannesburg) 2003-04. **LOI** (SA): 11 (2002-03 to 2004); HS 45 v E (Birmingham) 2003; BB 1-0 v B (Kimberley) 2002-03. Took wickets with his first and third balls in LOI. F-c Tours (SA): A 2002-03 (SA A); NZ 2003-04; I 2004-05; SL 1998-99 (SA A), 2004; Z 1998-99 (SA Acad). 1000 runs (6+1); most – 1509 (2005). HS 262* v Glamorgan (Cardiff) 2005. BB 5-33 v Surrey (Oval) 2008. LO HS 132* Titans v Eagles (Bloemfontein) 2008-09 and v Somerset (Canterbury) 2009 (FPT). LO BB 3-13 Titans v Cape Cobras (Centurion) 2008-09. T20 HS 82. T20 BB 3-25.

^{NQ}**BANDARA**, Herath Mudiyanselage Charitha **Malinga**, b Nagoda, Sri Lanka, 31 Dec 1979. 5'8". RHB, LBG. Kalutara Town 1996-97. Nondescripts 1998-99 to 2002-03. Tamil Union 2003-04. Southern Province 2003-04. Galle 2004-05. Gloucestershire 2005; cap 2005. Ragama 2006-07 to date. Basnahira South 2008-09 to 2009-10. **Tests** (SL): 8 (1998 to 2005-06); HS 43 v P (Kandy) 2005-06; BB 3-84 v I (Ahmedabad) 2005-06. **LOI** (SL): 31 (2005-06 to 2009-10); HS 31 v P (Colombo, RPS) 2009; BB 4-31 v SA (Hobart) 2005-06. **IT20** (SL): 4 (2006-07 to 2009); HS 7 v NZ (Colombo, RPS) 2009; BB 3-32 v I (Colombo, RPS) 2008-09. F-c Tours (SL): E 1999 (SL A), 2006; A 2007-08; SA 2008-09 (SL A): WI 2006-07 (SL A); I 2005-06; B 2005-06. HS 108 BS v Ruhuna (Colombo, CCC) 2009-10. CC HS 70 and CC BB 5-71 Gs v Middx (Bristol) 2005. K HS 29 v Notts (Tunbridge W) 2010. BB 8-49 SL A v England A (Colombo, NCC) 2004-05. UK BB 5-45 Gs v Bangladesh A (Bristol) 2005. K BB 4-42 v Hants (Canterbury) 2010. LO HS 64 Ragama v Tamil Union (Colombo, PSS) 2008-09. LO BB 5-22 Nondescripts v Sebastianites (Colombo, NCC) 1999-00. T20 HS 31*. T20 BB 3-14.

DIXEY, Paul Garrod (King's S, Canterbury; Hatfield C, Durham U), b Canterbury 2 Nov 1987. 5'8". RHB, WK. Kent 2005-10; no f-c appearances for K 2007-09. MCC 2007. Durham UCCE 2007-09. HS 103 DU v Lancs (Durham) 2009. K HS 24 v Bangladesh A (Canterbury) 2005 – on debut. LO HS 16 v Northants (Canterbury) 2009 (P40).

EDWARDS, Philip Duncan (Borden GS; Anglia Ruskin U, Cambridge), b Minster, Isle of Sheppey, 16 Apr 1984. 6'4". RHB, RMF. Cambridge UCCE 2004-05. Kent 2009-10. Suffolk 2007-08. HS 43 CU v Middx (Cambridge) 2004. K HS 13 v Notts (Nottingham) 2009. BB 3-72 v Surrey (Canterbury) 2009. LO HS 2* v Lancs (Manchester) 2009 (P40). LO BB 3-57 v Derbys (Chesterfield) 2009 (P40).

FERLEY, Robert Steven (King Edward VII HS; Sutton Valence S; Grey C, Durham U), b Norwich, Norfolk 4 Feb 1982. 5'8". RHB, SLA. Durham UCCE 2001-03. British U 2001-03. Kent 2003-10. Nottinghamshire 2007-08. Norfolk 1998. 78* DU v Durham (Chester-le-St) 2003. CC HS 43* Nt v Essex (Chelmsford) 2007. K HS 29 v Surrey (Canterbury) 2004. BB 6-136 v Middx (Canterbury) 2006. LO HS 52 v Warwks (Birmingham) 2010 (CB40). LO BB 4-33 v Yorks (Scarborough) 2006 (P40). T20 HS 16*. T20 BB 3-17.

HOCKLEY, James Bernard (Kelsey Park S, Beckenham), b Beckenham 16 Apr 1979. 6'2". RHB, OB. Kent 1998-2002, 2009-10. HS 82 v Yorks (Canterbury) 2010. HS 11 v Essex (Chelmsford) 2010. LO HS 121 v Warwks (Canterbury) 2002 (CGT). LO BB 2-32 v Northants (Canterbury) 2009 (P40). T20 HS 18. T20 BB 1-9.

KHAN, A. – *see* SUSSEX.

LAWSON, Mark Anthony Kenneth (Castle Hall Language C, Mirfield), b Leeds, Yorks 24 Oct 1985. 5'8". RHB, LB. Yorkshire 2004-07. Middlesex (1 match) 2008. Derbyshire 2008-09. Kent 2010. HS 44 Y v Hants (Southampton) 2006. K HS 31 and K BB 4-93 v Pakistanis (Canterbury) 2010 – on K debut. BB 6-88 Y v Middx (Scarborough) 2006. LO HS 20 Y v Warwks (Birmingham) 2005 (NL). LO BB 2-36 v Glamorgan (Derby) 2009 (FPT). T20 HS 4*. T20 BB 2-20.

NTINI, Makhaya (Dale C: East London TC), b Mdingi, nr King William's Town, South Africa 6 Jul 1977. 6'0". RHB, RFM. Border 1995-96 to 2003-04. Warriors 2004-05 to date. Warwickshire 2005. Kent 2010. **Tests** (SA): 101 (1997-98 to 2009-10); HS 32* v E (Leeds) 2003; BB 7-37 (13-132 match – SA record) v WI (Port-of-Spain) 2004-05. **LOI** (SA): 173 (1997-98 to 2008-09); HS 42* v NZ (Napier) 2003-04; BB 6-22 v A (Cape Town) 2005-06 – SA record analysis. **IT20** (SA): 10 (2005-06 to 2010-11); HS 5 v NZ (Johannesburg) 2005-06; BB 2-22 v WI (Johannesburg) 2007-08. F-c Tours (SA): E 1998, 2003, 2008; A 2001-02, 2005-06, 2008-09; WI 2000-01, 2004-05; NZ 2003-04; I 2004-05, 2007-08; P 2003-04, 2007-08; SL 2000-01, 2004, 2006; Z 2001-02; B 2002-03, 2007-08. HS 34* Border v Gauteng (Johannesburg) 1999-00. CC HS 27 Wa v Hants (Southampton) 2005. K HS 13 v Durham (Canterbury) 2010. BB 7-37 (*see Tests*). UK BB 6-51 (10-104 match) v Durham (Chester-le-St) 2010. LO HS 42* (*see LOI*). LO BB 6-22 (*see LOI*). T20 HS 11. T20 BB 4-21.

W.W.Lee left the staff, without making a County First-Class or List A appearance in 2010.

BENEFITS AWARDED IN 2011

Derbyshire	–
Durham	–
Essex	J.S.Foster
Glamorgan	M.J.Powell
Gloucestershire	–
Hampshire	N.Pothas
Kent	R.W.T.Key
Lancashire	M.J.Chilton
Leicestershire	C.W.Henderson (testimonial)
Middlesex	–
Northamptonshire	–
Nottinghamshire	–
Somerset	–
Surrey	–
Sussex	M.J.G.Davis (testimonial)
Warwickshire	I.R.Bell
Worcestershire	–
Yorkshire	G.L.Brophy

KENT 2010

RESULTS SUMMARY

	Place	Won	Lost	Tied	Drew	NR
LV= County Championship (1st Division)	8th	3	7		6	
All First-Class Matches		3	7		8	
Clydesdale Bank 40 (Group C)	2nd	7	3			2
Friends Provident t20 (South Group)	7th	7	9			

LV= COUNTY CHAMPIONSHIP AVERAGES

BATTING AND FIELDING

Cap		M	I	NO	HS	Runs	Avge	100	50	Ct/St
2005	D.I.Stevens	14	24	3	197	935	44.52	4	2	6
2005	M.van Jaarsveld	16	28	2	110*	1082	41.61	2	6	35
2003	G.O.Jones	16	29	–	178	865	29.82	2	2	48/5
2001	R.W.T.Key	15	27	2	261	674	26.96	1	1	1
2007	J.C.Tredwell	11	18	2	115	472	29.50	1	1	20
	S.A.Northeast	16	28	–	71	468	24.57	–	4	6
	A.J.Blake	8	15	1	105*	331	23.64	1	–	4
2008	Azhar Mahmood	7	13	–	64	289	22.23	–	2	–
2008	J.L.Denly	16	29	–	95	610	21.03	–	3	9
	M.T.Coles	12	20	4	51	322	20.12	–	1	3
	J.B.Hockley	5	9	–	82	139	15.44	–	1	6
	H.M.C.M.Bandara	6	10	3	29	105	15.00	–	–	5
2007	S.J.Cook	14	22	6	26*	161	10.06	–	–	1
	A.Khan	12	18	5	24	115	8.84	–	–	5
	M.Ntini	5	8	3	13	25	5.00	–	–	–

Also batted (1 match each): P.D.Edwards 6*, 13; R.S.Ferley 19, 1; R.H.Joseph 7*, 5; J.D.Nel 2 (1 ct).

BOWLING

	O	M	R	W	Avge	Best	5wI	10wM
M.Ntini	164	44	474	24	19.75	6-51	2	1
D.I.Stevens	267.1	71	725	27	26.85	4-38	–	–
Azhar Mahmood	257.3	51	774	28	27.64	5-62	2	–
J.C.Tredwell	348.1	61	1098	37	29.67	7-22	2	–
S.J.Cook	310.3	58	1108	34	32.58	4-62	–	–
A.Khan	372.2	82	1258	38	33.10	5-43	1	–
M.T.Coles	234	32	881	24	36.70	4-55	–	–
H.M.C.M.Bandara	210.4	32	745	18	41.38	4-42	–	–
Also bowled:								
J.D.Nel	36	10	119	9	13.22	6-62	1	–

A.J.Blake 14-1-60-1; J.L.Denly 47-2-205-2; P.D.Edwards 14-3-77-1; R.S.Ferley 26-2-142-2; J.B.Hockley 24-3-88-2; G.O.Jones 1-0-8-0; R.H.Joseph 27-4-112-2; R.W.T.Key 11.2-3-31-2; S.A.Northeast 3-1-2-0; M.van Jaarsveld 110-14-299-3.

The First-Class Averages (pp 220–237) give the records of Kent players in all first-class county matches (Kent's other opponents being Loughborough MCCU and the Pakistanis).

KENT RECORDS

FIRST-CLASS CRICKET

Highest Total	For 803-4d		v	Essex	Brentwood	1934
	V 676		by	Australians	Canterbury	1921
Lowest Total	For 18		v	Sussex	Gravesend	1867
	V 16		by	Warwicks	Tonbridge	1913
Highest Innings	For 332	W.H.Ashdown	v	Essex	Brentwood	1934
	V 344	W.G.Grace	for	MCC	Canterbury	1876

Highest Partnership for each Wicket

1st	300	N.R.Taylor/M.R.Benson	v	Derbyshire	Canterbury	1991
2nd	366	S.G.Hinks/N.R.Taylor	v	Middlesex	Canterbury	1990
3rd	323	R.W.T.Key/M.van Jaarsveld	v	Surrey	Tunbridge W	2005
4th	368	P.A.de Silva/G.R.Cowdrey	v	Derbyshire	Maidstone	1995
5th	277	F.E.Woolley/L.E.G.Ames	v	N Zealanders	Canterbury	1931
6th	315	P.A.de Silva/M.A.Ealham	v	Notts	Nottingham	1995
7th	248	A.P.Day/E.Humphreys	v	Somerset	Taunton	1908
8th	177	G.O.Jones/Yasir Arafat	v	Warwicks	Canterbury	2007
9th	171	M.A.Ealham/P.A.Strang	v	Notts	Nottingham	1997
10th	235	F.E.Woolley/A.Fielder	v	Worcs	Stourbridge	1909

Best Bowling	For	10- 30	C.Blythe	v	Northants	Northampton	1907
(Innings)	V	10- 48	C.H.G.Bland	for	Sussex	Tonbridge	1899
Best Bowling	For	17- 48	C.Blythe	v	Northants	Northampton	1907
(Match)	V	17-106	T.W.J.Goddard	for	Glos	Bristol	1939

Most Runs – Season	2894	F.E.Woolley	(av 59.06)		1928
Most Runs – Career	47868	F.E.Woolley	(av 41.77)		1906-38
Most 100s – Season	10	F.E.Woolley		1928, 1934	
Most 100s – Career	122	F.E.Woolley			1906-38
Most Wkts – Season	262	A.P.Freeman	(av 14.74)		1933
Most Wkts – Career	3340	A.P.Freeman	(av 17.64)		1914-36
Most Career W-K Dismissals	1253	F.H.Huish	(901 ct; 352 st)		1895-1914
Most Career Catches in the Field	773	F.E.Woolley			1906-38

LIMITED-OVERS CRICKET

Highest Total	50ov	384-6		v	Berkshire	Finchampstead	1994
	40ov	327-6		v	Leics	Canterbury	1993
	T20	217		v	Glos	Gloucester	2010
Lowest Total	50ov	60		v	Somerset	Taunton	1979
	40ov	83		v	Middlesex	Lord's	1984
	T20	91		v	Surrey	The Oval	2006
Highest Innings	50ov	136*	C.L.Hooper	v	Berkshire	Finchampstead	1994
	40ov	146	A.Symonds	v	Lancashire	Tunbridge Wells	2004
	T20	112	A.Symonds	v	Middlesex	Maidstone	2004
Best Bowling	50ov	8-31	D.L.Underwood	v	Scotland	Edinburgh	1987
	40ov	6- 9	R.A.Woolmer	v	Derbyshire	Chesterfield	1979
	T20	4-14	D.I.Stevens	v	Essex	Chelmsford	2007

LANCASHIRE

Formation of Present Club: 12 January 1864
Inaugural First-Class Match: 1865
Colours: Red, Green and Blue
Badge: Red Rose
County Champions (since 1890): (7) 1897, 1904, 1926,
1927, 1928, 1930, 1934
Joint Champions: (1) 1950
Gillette/NatWest/C&G/FP Trophy Winners: (7) 1970, 1971,
1972, 1975, 1990, 1996, 1998
Benson and Hedges Cup Winners: (4) 1984, 1990, 1995,
1996
Pro 40/National League (Div 1) Winners: (1) 1999.
Sunday League Winners: (4) 1969, 1970, 1989, 1998
Clydesdale Bank 40 Winners: (0); best – 4th Group A 2010
Twenty20 Cup Winners: (0); best – Finalist 2005

Chief Executive: Jim Cumbes, Old Trafford, Manchester M16 0PX • Tel: 0161 282 4000 •
Fax: 0161 282 4100 • Email: enquiries@lccc.co.uk • Web: www.lccc.co.uk

Director of Cricket: M.Watkinson. **Head Coach:** Peter Moores. **Captain:** G.Chapple.
Vice-Captain: none. **Overseas Players:** none. **2011 Beneficiary:** M.J.Chilton. **Head Groundsman:** Matthew Merchant. **Scorer:** Alan West. ‡ New registration. NQ Not qualified for England.

ANDERSON, James Michael (St Theodore RC HS and SFC, Burnley), b Burnley 30 Jul 1982. 6'2". LHB, RFM. Debut (Lancashire) 2002; cap 2003. YC 2003. *Wisden* 2008. **ECB central contract 2010-11. Tests**: 57 (2003 to 2010-11); HS 34 v SA (Leeds) 2008; BB 7-43 v NZ (Nottingham) 2008. **LOI**: 137 (2002-03 to 2010-11); HS 20* v A (Brisbane) 2010-11; BB 5-23 v SA (Port Elizabeth) 2009-10. Hat-trick v P (Oval) 2003 – 1st for Eng in 373 LOI. **IT20**: 19 (2006-07 to 2009-10); HS 1* v A (Sydney) 2006-07; BB 3-23 v Netherlands (Lord's) 2009. F-c Tours: A 2006-07, 2010-11; SA 2004-05, 2009-10; WI 2003-04, 2005-06 (Eng A) (*part*), 2008-09; NZ 2007-08; I 2005-06 (*part*), 2008-09; SL 2003-04, 2007-08. HS 37* v Durham (Manchester) 2005. 50 wkts (2); most – 60 (2005). BB 7-43 (*see Tests*). La BB 6-23 v Hants (Southampton) 2002. Hat-trick v Essex (Manchester) 2003. LO HS 20* (*see LOI*). LO BB 5-23 (*see LOI*). T20 HS 16. T20 BB 3-23.

BROWN, Karl Robert (Hesketh Fletcher HS, Atherton), b Bolton 17 May 1988. 5'10". RHB, RMF. Debut (Lancashire) 2006. HS 40 v Kent (Liverpool) 2008. BB 2-30 v Notts (Nottingham) 2009. LO HS 65* v Unicorns (Manchester) 2010 (CB40).

CHAPPLE, Glen (West Craven HS; Nelson & Colne C), b Skipton, Yorks 23 Jan 1974. 6'1". RHB, RMF. Debut (Lancashire) 1992; cap 1994. **LOI**: 1 (2006); HS 14 and BB – v Ireland (Belfast) 2006. F-c Tours (Eng A): A 1996-97; WI 1995-96 (La); I 1994-95. HS 155 v Somerset (Manchester) 2001. Scored 100 off 27 balls in contrived circumstances v Glamorgan (Manchester) 1993. 50 wkts (5); most – 55 (1994). BB 7-53 v Durham (Blackpool) 2007. LO HS 81* v Derbys (Manchester) 2002 (CGT). LO BB 6-18 v Essex (Lord's) 1996 (NWT) – La record. T20 HS 55*. T20 BB 3-36.

130

CHEETHAM, Steven Philip (Bury GS; Holy Cross SFC), b Oldham 5 Sep 1987. 6'5". RHB, RFM. Debut (Lancashire) 2007. Surrey 2010 (on loan). No f-c appearances in 2008 and 2009. HS 0* and BB 2-71 Sy v Leics (Leicester) 2010. La BB 1-44 v Durham UCCE (Durham) 2007. LO HS 13* Sy v Worcs (Oval) 2010 (CB40). LO BB 4-32 Sy v Unicorns (Wormsley) 2010 (CB40).

CHILTON, Mark James (Manchester GS; Durham U), b Sheffield, Yorks 2 Oct 1976. 6'3". RHB, RM. Debut (Lancashire) 1997; cap 2002; captain 2005-07; benefit 2011. British U 1998. 1000 runs (1): 1154 (2003). HS 131 v Kent (Manchester) 2006. BB 2-3 v Durham UCCE (Durham) 2009. CC BB 1-1 (twice). LO HS 115 v Surrey (Croydon) 2004 (NL). LO BB 5-26 Brit U v Sussex (Cambridge) 1997 (BHC). T20 HS 38.

CROFT, Steven John (Highfield HS, Blackpool; Myerscough C), b Blackpool 11 Oct 1984. 5'10". RHB, RMF. Debut (Lancashire) 2005; cap 2010. Auckland 2008-09. HS 122 v Notts (Manchester) 2008. BB 4-51 v Notts (Nottingham) 2008. LO HS 93* v Glamorgan (Colwyn Bay) 2010 (CB40). LO BB 4-24 v Scotland (Manchester) 2008 (FPT). T20 HS 88. T20 BB 3-6.

CROSS, Gareth David (Moorside S; Eccles C), b Bury 20 Jun 1984. 5'9". RHB, RMF, WK. Debut (Lancashire) 2005. No f-c appearances in 2009. HS 100* v Hants (Southampton) 2006. LO HS 76 v Warwks (Birmingham) 2007 (P40). LO BB 2-26 v Durham (Chester-le-St) 2008 (FPT). T20 HS 65*.

HOGG, Kyle William (Saddleworth HS), b Birmingham, Warwks 2 Jul 1983. Son of W.Hogg (Lancashire and Warwickshire 1976-83); grandson of S.Ramadhin (Trinidad, Lancashire and West Indies 1949-50 to 1965). 6'4". LHB, RFM. Debut (Lancashire) 2001; cap 2010. Otago 2006-07. Worcestershire 2007 (on loan). Nottinghamshire 2007 (on loan). F-c Tour (ECB Acad): SL 2002-03. HS 88 v Yorks (Manchester) 2010. BB 5-48 v Leics (Manchester) 2002 - on CC debut. LO HS 66* v Scotland (Manchester) 2008 (FPT). LO BB 4-20 v Hants (Southampton) 2002 (NL). T20 HS 44. T20 BB 2-10.

HORTON, Paul James (St Margaret's HS, Liverpool), b Sydney, Australia 20 Sep 1982. 5'10". RHB, RM. UK resident since 1997. Debut (Lancashire) 2003; cap 2007. MT 2010-11. 1000 runs (2); most – 1116 (2007). HS 209 MT v SR (Masvingo) 2010-11. La HS 173 v Somerset (Taunton) 2009. LO HS 111* v Derbys (Manchester) 2009 (FPT). T20 HS 71.

KEEDY, Gary (Garforth CS), b Wakefield, Yorks 27 Nov 1974. 6'0". LHB, SLA. Yorkshire 1994 (one match). Lancashire debut 1995; cap 2000; benefit 2009. F-c Tour: WI 1995-96 (La). HS 64 v Sussex (Hove) 2008. 50 wkts (3); most – 72 (2004). BB 7-68 (10-128 match) v Durham (Manchester) 2010. LO HS 33 v Derbys (Derby) 2008. LO BB 5-30 v Sussex (Manchester) 2000 (NL). T20 HS 9*. T20 BB 4-15.

KERRIGAN, Simon Christopher (Corpus Christi RC HS, Preston), b Preston 10 May 1989. RHB, SLA. Debut (Lancashire) 2010. Lancashire 2nd XI debut 2007. HS 16* v Somerset (Taunton) 2010. BB 6-74 v Essex (Manchester) 2010. T20 HS 4*. T20 BB 3-17.

MAHMOOD, Sajid Iqbal (North C, Bolton), b Bolton 21 Dec 1981. 6'4". RHB, RF. Debut (Lancashire) 2002; cap 2007. MCC 2005, 2009. **Tests**: 8 (2006 to 2009-10); HS 34 and BB 4-22 v P (Leeds) 2006. **LOI**: 26 (2004 to 2009-10); HS 22* v P (Birmingham) 2006; BB 4-50 v SL (North Shore, Antigua) 2006-07. **IT20**: 4 (2006 to 2009-10); HS 1* v SA (Centurion) 2009-10; BB 1-31 v SA (Johannesburg) 2009-10. F-c Tours (Eng A): A 2006-07 (Eng); WI 2005-06; NZ 2008-09; I 2003-04; SL 2004-05. HS 94 v Sussex (Manchester) 2004. BB 6-30 v Durham (Chester-le-St) 2009. LO HS 29 v Staffs (Stone) 2004 (CGT). LO BB 5-16 v SL A (Liverpool) 2007. T20 HS 34. T20 BB 4-21.

MOORE, Stephen Colin (St Stithian's C, Johannesburg; Exeter U), b Johannesburg, South Africa 4 Nov 1980. 6'1". RHB, RM. Worcestershire 2003-09. Lancashire debut 2010. MCC 2009. F-c Tour (EL): NZ 2008-09. 1000 runs (3); most – 1451 (2008). HS 246 Wo v Derbys (Worcester) 2005. La HS 61 v Essex (Chelmsford) and v Warwks (Birmingham) 2010. BB 1-13 Wo v Lancs (Worcester) 2004. LO HS 118 v Surrey (Croydon) 2010 (CB40). LO BB 1-1 Wo v Scotland (Worcester) 2004 (NL). T20 HS 83*.

NEWBY, Oliver James (Ribblesdale HS; Myerscough C), b Blackburn 26 Aug 1984. 6'5". RHB, RMF. Debut (Lancashire) 2003. Nottinghamshire 2005 (on loan). Gloucestershire (on loan) 2008; cap 2008. No f-c appearances in 2010. HS 38* Nt v Kent (Nottingham) 2005 – on Notts debut. La HS 26 v Warwks (Manchester) 2007. BB 5-69 Gs v Northants (Bristol) 2008. La BB 4-21 v Durham MCCU (Durham) 2009. LO HS 12* v Derbys (Derby) 2009 (FPT). LO BB 4-41 v Glamorgan (Cardiff) 2009 (FPT). T20 HS 6*. T20 BB 2-34.

PARRY, Stephen David (Audenshaw HS), b Manchester 12 Jan 1986. 5'11". RHB, SLA. Debut (Lancashire) 2007 taking 5-23 v Durham UCCE (Durham). No 1st XI appearances in 2008. Cumberland 2005-06. HS 2 and CC BB 2-51 v Durham (Manchester) 2009. BB 5-23 (*see above*). LO HS 31 v Essex (Chelmsford) 2009 (FPT). LO BB 3-48 EL v India A (Worcester) 2010. T20 HS 7. T20 BB 4-28.

PROCTER, Luke Anthony (Counthill S, Oldham), b Oldham 24 June 1988. 5'11". LHB, RM. Debut (Lancashire) 2010. Lancashire 2nd XI debut 2006. Cumberland 2007. HS 32 and BB 1-26 v Somerset (Taunton) 2010. LO HS 97 v WI A (Manchester) 2010. LO BB 3-29 v Unicorns (Colwyn Bay) 2010 (CB40).

SMITH, Thomas Christopher (Parkland HS, Chorley; Runshaw C, Leyland), b Liverpool 26 Dec 1985. 6'3". LHB, RMF. Debut (Lancashire) 2005; cap 2010. Leicestershire (on loan) 2008. F-c Tour (Eng A): B 2006-07. HS 128 v Hants (Southampton) 2009. BB 6-46 v Yorks (Manchester) 2009. LO HS 87* v Glamorgan (Cardiff) 2009 (FPT). LO BB 3-8 v Leics (Manchester) 2006 (CGT). T20 HS 92*. T20 BB 3-12.

RELEASED/RETIRED
(Having made a County First-Class or List A appearance in 2010)

[NQ]**CHANDERPAUL, Shivnarine** (Cove and John SS, Unity Village), b Unity Village, Demerara, Guyana 16 Aug 1974. 5'6". LHB, LB. Guyana 1991-92 to date. Durham 2007-09. Lancashire 2010; cap 2010. **Tests** (WI): 129 (1993-94 to 2010-11, 14 as captain); HS 203* v SA (Georgetown) 2004-05; BB 1-2 v A (Adelaide) 1996-97. **LOI** (WI): 263 (1994-95 to 2010-11, 16 as captain); HS 150 v SA (E London) 1998-99; BB 3-18 v I (Sharjah) 1997-98. **IT20** (WI): 22 (2005-06 to 2010); HS 41 v E (Oval) 2007. F-c Tours (WI) (C=Captain): E 1995, 2000, 2004, 2007, 2009; A 1995-96, 1996-97, 2000-01, 2005-06C, 2009-10; SA 1998-99, 2003-04, 2007-08; NZ 1994-95, 1999-00, 2005-06C, 2008-09; I 1994-95, 2002-03; P 1997-98, 2001-02 (Sharjah), 2006-07; SL 2005C, 2010-11; Z 2001, 2003-04; B 1999-00, 2002-03; K 2001. 1000 runs (1+1); most – 1107 (2004-05). HS 303* Guyana v Jamaica (Kingston) 1995-96. CC HS 201* Du v Worcs (Worcester) 2009. La HS 120 v Kent (Canterbury) 2010. BB 4-48 Guyana v Leeward Is (Basseterre) 1992-93. LO HS 150 (*see LOI*). LO BB 4-22 Guyana v Trinidad (Hampton Court) 1995-96. T20 HS 64.

^{NQ}**KATICH, Simon** Mathew (Trinity C, WA: U of WA), b Middle Swan, Midland, W Australia 21 Aug 1975. 6'0". LHB, SLC. WA 1996-97 to 2001-02. Durham 2000; cap 2000. Yorkshire (one match) 2002. NSW 2002-03 to date. Hampshire 2003-05, cap 2003. Derbyshire 2007; cap/captain 2007. Lancashire (one match) 2010. **Tests** (A): 56 (2001 to 2010-11); HS 157 v WI (Bridgetown) 2008; BB 6-65 v Z (Sydney) 2003-04. **LOI** (A): 45 (2000-01 to 2006-07); HS 107* v SL (Brisbane) 2005-06. **IT20** (A): 3 (2004-05 to 2005-06); HS 39 v SA (Johannesburg) 2005-06. F-c Tours (A): E 2001, 2005, 2009, 2010 (v P); SA 2008-09; WI 2008; NZ 2004-05, 2009-10; I 2004-05, 2008-09 (Aus A), 2008-09, 2010-11; SL 1999-00, 2003-04. 1000 runs (3+4); most – 1506 (2007-08). HS 306 NSW v Q (Sydney) 2007-08. UK HS 221 De v Somerset (Taunton) 2007. La HS 32 v Yorks (Manchester) 2010. BB 7-130 NSW v Vic (Melbourne) 2002-03. UK BB 4-21 H v Northants (Southampton) 2003. LO HS 136* NSW v Vic (Bowral) 2003-04. LO BB 3-21 Aus A v SA (Adelaide) 2001-02. T20 HS 75.

MONTGOMERY, Gary Stephen (Warwick S; Henley C, Coventry), b Leamington Spa, Warwks, 8 Oct 1982. 6'2". RHB, LMF. Lancashire 2nd XI debut 2009. Has played goalkeeper in Football League for Kidderminster Harriers, Coventry City, Rotherham United and Grimsby Town. Awaiting f-c debut. LO HS 0*. LO BB 1-61 v Unicorns (Colwyn Bay) 2010 (CB40).

^{NQ}**POWELL, Daren** Brent-Lyle (St Alban's S; St Elizabeth Technical HS), b Malvenn, St Elizabeth, Jamaica 15 Apr 1978. 6'0". RHB, RFM. Jamaica 2000-01 to 2009-10. Gauteng 2003-04. Derbyshire 2004. Hampshire 2007. Lancashire 2010. **Tests** (WI): 37 (2002 to 2008-09); HS 36* v E (Lord's) 2007; BB 5-25 v SL (Kandy) 2005. **LOI** (WI): 55 (2002-03 to 2008-09); HS 48* v SA (St George's) 2006-07; BB 4-27 v I (Cuttack) 2006-07. **IT20** (WI): 5 (2007 to 2007-08); HS 1* v B (Johannesburg) 2007-08; BB 1-6 v SA (Pt Elizabeth) 2007-08. F-c Tours (WI): E 2002 (WI A), 2006 (WI A), 2007; A 2005-06; SA 2007-08; NZ 2005-06, 2008-09; I 2002-03; P 2006-07; SL 2005; B 2002-03. HS 69 Jamaica v Barbados (Bridgetown) 2008-09. UK HS 62 WI A v Durham (Chester-le-St) 2006. CC HS 25 H v Surrey (Southampton) 2007. La HS 16* v Essex (Manchester) 2010. BB 6-49 De v Durham UCCE (Derby) 2004. CC BB 4-8 H v Worcs (Southampton) 2007. La BB 2-45 v Yorks (Manchester) 2010. LO HS 48* (*see LOI*). LO BB 5-23 Jamaica v T&T (Discovery Bay) 2002-03. T20 HS 1*. T20 BB 2-15.

^{NQ}**PRINCE, Ashwell** Gavin (St Thomas Senior SS, UPE), b Port Elizabeth, South Africa, 28 May 1977. LHB, OB. EP 1995-96 to 1997-98. WP 1997-98 to 2003-04. WP Boland 2004-05. Cape Cobras 2005-06 to 2007-08. Nottinghamshire 2008. Warriors 2008-09 to date. Lancashire 2009-10. **Tests** (SA): 62 (2001-02 to 2010-11, 2 as captain); HS 162* v B (Centurion) 2008-09; BB 1-2 v NZ (Cape Town) 2006. **LOI** (SA): 52 (2002-03 to 2007); HS 89* v WI (Port of Spain) 2005; BB – . **IT20** (SA): 1 (2005-06); HS 5 v NZ (Johannesburg) 2005-06. F-c Tours (SA): E 2008; A 2005-06; WI 2000 (SA A), 2005, 2010; I 2007-08, 2009-10; P 2007-08; SL 2006; Z 2007 (SA A); B 2007-08; UAE 2010-11 (v P). 1000 runs (0+1): 1180 (2008-09). HS 254 Warriors v Titans (Centurion) 2008-09; CC HS 135* v Notts (Manchester) 2009. BB 2-11 SA v Middx (Uxbridge) 2008. CC BB – . LO HS 128 Warriors v Dolphins (East London) 2009-10. LO BB – . T20 HS 69. T20 BB – .

SUTTON, L.D. – *see DERBYSHIRE.*

A.Flintoff, N.L.McCullum and A.Shankar left the staff, without making a County First-Class or List A appearance in 2010.

LANCASHIRE 2010

RESULTS SUMMARY

	Place	Won	Lost	Tied	Drew	NR
LV= County Championship (1st Division)	4th	5	3	8		
All First-Class Matches		5	3	8		1
Clydesdale Bank 40 (Group A)	4th	6	6			
Friends Provident t20 (North Group)	QF	9	6			1

LV= COUNTY CHAMPIONSHIP AVERAGES
BATTING AND FIELDING

Cap		M	I	NO	HS	Runs	Avge	100	50	Ct/St
2010	S.Chanderpaul	8	14	1	120	698	53.69	2	5	2
	A.G.Prince	7	13	2	115	450	40.90	1	4	7
2010	S.J.Croft	16	26	3	93	883	38.39	–	8	13
2010	K.W.Hogg	9	13	4	88	301	33.44	–	2	3
2007	S.I.Mahmood	15	20	2	72	564	31.33	–	5	2
2002	M.J.Chilton	16	29	4	69	750	30.00	–	4	6
	G.D.Cross	7	11	1	100*	290	29.00	1	1	12
2007	L.D.Sutton	13	21	2	118	530	27.89	2	–	37/5
2010	T.C.Smith	14	25	3	128	576	26.18	2	2	14
1994	G.Chapple	14	22	6	54*	403	25.18	–	2	4
	S.C.Moore	9	17	–	61	426	25.05	–	2	6
2007	P.J.Horton	16	30	2	123	634	22.64	1	3	19
2000	G.Keedy	7	9	2	34	89	12.71	–	–	–
	D.B.L.Powell	4	4	1	16*	29	9.66	–	–	–
2003	J.M.Anderson	4	5	1	25*	35	8.75	–	–	–
	S.C.Kerrigan	13	15	5	16*	45	4.50	–	–	3

Also batted: K.R.Brown (2 matches) 21, 0, 4; S.M.Katich (1) 32, 8 (1 ct); L.A.Procter (2) 13, 19, 32.

BOWLING

	O	M	R	W	Avge	Best	5wI	10wM
G.Chapple	372.4	89	1027	52	19.75	5-27	2	–
J.M.Anderson	130.5	39	345	16	21.56	6-44	1	–
G.Keedy	246.5	43	688	31	22.19	7-68	2	1
T.C.Smith	279.5	58	913	32	28.53	6-94	1	–
S.C.Kerrigan	319	66	967	30	32.23	6-74	3	–
K.W.Hogg	202.2	48	650	20	32.50	4-53	–	–
S.I.Mahmood	348	54	1263	33	38.27	5-55	1	–
Also bowled:								
D.B.L.Powell	99	16	343	7	49.00	2-45		

S.J.Croft 14-2-51-1; L.A.Procter 7.3-0-47-1.

Lancashire played no other first-class fixtures outside the County Championship in 2010. The First-Class Averages (pp 220–237) give the records of Lancashire players in all first-class matches, with the exception of J.M.Anderson and S.M.Katich, whose first-class figures for Lancashire are as above.

LANCASHIRE RECORDS

FIRST-CLASS CRICKET

Highest Total	For 863		v	Surrey	The Oval	1990
	V 707-9d		by	Surrey	The Oval	1990
Lowest Total	For 25		v	Derbyshire	Manchester	1871
	V 22		by	Glamorgan	Liverpool	1924
Highest Innings	For 424	A.C.MacLaren	v	Somerset	Taunton	1895
	V 315*	T.W.Hayward	for	Surrey	The Oval	1898

Highest Partnership for each Wicket

1st	368	A.C.MacLaren/R.H.Spooner	v	Glos	Liverpool	1903
2nd	371	F.B.Watson/G.E.Tyldesley	v	Surrey	Manchester	1928
3rd	364	M.A.Atherton/N.H.Fairbrother	v	Surrey	The Oval	1990
4th	358	S.P.Titchard/G.D.Lloyd	v	Essex	Chelmsford	1996
5th	360	S.G.Law/C.L.Hooper	v	Warwicks	Birmingham	2003
6th	278	J.Iddon/H.R.W.Butterworth	v	Sussex	Manchester	1932
7th	248	G.D.Lloyd/I.D.Austin	v	Yorkshire	Leeds	1997
8th	158	J.Lyon/R.M.Ratcliffe	v	Warwicks	Manchester	1979
9th	142	L.O.S.Poidevin/A.Kermode	v	Sussex	Eastbourne	1907
10th	173	J.Briggs/R.Pilling	v	Surrey	Liverpool	1885

Best Bowling	For 10-46	W.Hickton	v	Hampshire	Manchester	1870
(Innings)	V 10-40	G.O.B.Allen	for	Middlesex	Lord's	1929
Best Bowling	For 17-91	H.Dean	v	Yorkshire	Liverpool	1913
(Match)	V 16-65	G.Giffen	for	Australians	Manchester	1886

Most Runs – Season	2633	J.T.Tyldesley	(av 56.02)	1901
Most Runs – Career	34222	G.E.Tyldesley	(av 45.20)	1909-36
Most 100s – Season	11	C.Hallows		1928
Most 100s – Career	90	G.E.Tyldesley		1909-36
Most Wkts – Season	198	E.A.McDonald	(av 18.55)	1925
Most Wkts – Career	1816	J.B.Statham	(av 15.12)	1950-68
Most Career W-K Dismissals	925	G.Duckworth	(635 ct; 290 st)	1923-38
Most Career Catches in the Field	556	K.J.Grieves		1949-64

LIMITED-OVERS CRICKET

Highest Total	50ov	381-3		v	Herts	Radlett	1999
	40ov	310-7		v	Somerset	Taunton	2003
	T20	220-5		v	Derbyshire	Derby	2009
Lowest Total	50ov	59		v	Worcs	Worcester	1963
	40ov	68		v	Yorkshire	Leeds	2000
		68		v	Surrey	The Oval	2002
	T20	91		v	Derbyshire	Manchester	2003
Highest Innings	50ov	162*	A.R.Crook	v	Bucks	Wormsley	2005
	40ov	143	A.Flintoff	v	Essex	Chelmsford	1999
	T20	102*	L.Vincent	v	Derbyshire	Manchester	2008
Best Bowling	50ov	6-18	G.Chapple	v	Essex	Lord's	1996
	40ov	6-25	G.Chapple	v	Yorkshire	Leeds	1998
	T20	4-12	A.Flintoff	v	Durham	Chester-le-St	2008

LEICESTERSHIRE

Formation of Present Club: 25 March 1879
Inaugural First-Class Match: 1894
Colours: Dark Green and Scarlet
Badge: Gold Running Fox on Green Ground
County Champions: (3) 1975, 1996, 1998
Gillette/NatWest/C&G/FP Trophy Winners: (0); best –
Finalist 1992, 2001
Benson and Hedges Cup Winners: (3) 1972, 1975, 1985
Pro 40/National League (Div 1) Winners: (0); best – 2nd
2001
Sunday League Champions: (2) 1974, 1977
Clydesdale Bank 40 Winners: (0); best – 6th Group C
2010
Twenty20 Cup Winners: (2) 2004, 2006

Chief Executive: Mike Siddall, County Ground, Grace Road, Leicester LE2 8AD • Tel:
0871 282 1879 • Fax: 0871 282 1873 • Email: enquiries@leicestershireccc.co.uk • Web:
www.leicestershireccc.co.uk

Head Coach/Academy Director: Phil Whitticase. **Captain:** M.J.Hoggard. **Vice-Captain:**
tba. **Overseas Player:** A.B.McDonald. **2011 Beneficiary:** C.W.Henderson. **Head Groundsman:** Andrew Ward. **Scorer:** Graham A.York. ‡ New registration. NQ Not qualified for
England.

BOYCE, Matthew Andrew Golding (Oakham S; Nottingham U), b Cheltenham, Glos
13 Aug 1985. 5'9". LHB, RM. Debut (Leicestershire) 2006. HS 106 v Warwks (Birmingham) 2008. BB – . LO HS 80 v Hants (Leicester) 2009 (FPT). T20 HS 34.

BUCK, Nathan Liam (Newbridge HS; Ashby S), b Leicester 26 Apr 1991. 6'2" RHB, RMF.
Debut (Leicestershire) 2009. Leicestershire 2nd XI debut 2008. England U19s 2009 to
2009-10. F-c Tour (EL): WI 2010-11. HS 26 v Glos (Leicester) 2010. BB 4-44 v Derbys
(Derby) 2010. LO HS 21 v Glamorgan (Leicester) 2009 (P40). LO BB 2-16 v Hants
(Southampton) 2010 (CB40). T20 HS 3*. T20 BB 3-20.

COBB, Joshua James (Oakham S), b Leicester 17 Aug 1990. 5'11½". Son of R.A.Cobb
(Leics and N Transvaal 1980-89). RHB, LB. Debut (Leicestershire) 2007. Leicestershire
2nd XI debut 2006, aged 16y 5d. England U19s 2009. HS 148* v Middx (Lord's) 2008. BB
2-11 v Glos (Leicester) 2008. LO HS 43* v Hants (Leicester) 2010 (CB40). LO BB 1-12 v
Middx (Lord's) 2009 (P40). T20 HS 15. T20 BB 2-16.

Du TOIT, Jacques (Elspark S; Oosterlig C; Pretoria U), b Port Elizabeth, South Africa
2 Jan 1980. RHB, RMF. British passport. Easterns 1998-99 to 2004-05. Leicestershire debut
2008. Colombo CC 2010-11. HS 154 v Cambridge MCCU (Cambridge) 2010. HS 122 v
Surrey (Leicester) 2010. BB 3-31 v Glos (Leicester) 2008. LO HS 144 v Glamorgan
(Colwyn Bay) 2008 (P40). LO BB 2-30 Easterns v KZ-Natal (Benoni) 2004-05. T20 HS 69.
T20 BB 2-15.

GURNEY, Harry Frederick (Garendon HS; Loughborough GS; Leeds U), b Nottingham
25 Oct 1986. 6'2". RHB, LFM. Debut (Leicestershire) 2007. Bradford/Leeds UCCE
2006-07 (not f-c). HS 24* v Middx (Leicester) 2009. BB 5-82 v Surrey (Leicester) 2009.
LO HS 7 v Kent (Canterbury) 2010 (CB40). LO BB 5-24 v Hants (Leicester) 2010 (CB40).
T20 HS 5*. T20 BB 3-21.

HENDERSON, Claude William (Worcester HS), b Worcester, Cape Province, South Africa 14 Jun 1972. Elder brother of J.M.Henderson (Boland, Transvaal, North West, Free State and Eagles 1994-95 to 2005-06). Applying for UK citizenship. 6'1½". RHB, SLA. Boland 1990-91 to 1997-98. WP 1998-99 to 2003-04. Leicestershire debut/cap 2004 (the first Kolpak registration). Lions 2006-07 to 2007-08. Cape Cobras 2008-09 to date. **Tests** (SA): 7 (2001-02 to 2002-03); HS 30 and BB 4-116 v A (Adelaide) 2001-02. **LOI** (SA): 4 (2001-02); HS – ; BB 4-17 v Z (Harare) 2001-02. F-c Tours (SA): A 2001-02; SL 1998 (SA A); Z 2001-02. HS 81 v Glos (Leicester) 2007. 50 wkts (1): 56 (2010). BB 7-57 Boland v EP (Paarl) 1994-95. Le BB 7-74 v Durham (Leicester) 2004. LO HS 45 Lions v Eagles (Johannesburg) 2006-07. LO BB 6-29 Boland v Easterns (Paarl) 1997-98. T20 HS 32. T20 BB 3-23.

HOGGARD, Matthew James (Grangefield S, Pudsey), b Leeds, Yorks 31 Dec 1976. 6'2". RHB, RMF. Yorkshire 1996-2009; cap 2000; benefit 2008. Free State 1998-99 to 1999-00. Leicestershire debut/cap 2010; captain 2010 to date. MCC 2004-07. MBE 2005. *Wisden* 2005. **Tests**: 67 (2000 to 2007-08); HS 38 v WI (Oval) 2004; BB 7-61 (12-205 match) v SA (Johannesburg) 2004-05; hat-trick v WI (Bridgetown) 2003-04. **LOI**: 26 (2001-02 to 2005-06); HS 7 v I (Cochin) 2005-06; BB 5-49 v Z (Harare) 2001-02. F-c Tours: A 2002-03, 2006-07; SA 2004-05; WI 2003-04; NZ 2001-02, 2007-08; I 2001-02, 2005-06; P 2000-01, 2005-06; SL 2000-01, 2003-04, 2007-08; B 2003-04. HS 89* v Glamorgan (Leeds) 2004. Le HS 6 (*twice*). 50 wkts (3); most – 50 (2005, 2010). BB 7-49 Y v Somerset (Leeds) 2003. Le BB 6-63 v Middx (Lord's) 2010. Hat-tricks (2): (*see Tests*) and Y v Sussex (Hove) 2009. LO HS 17* v Kent (Canterbury) 2010 (CB40). LO BB 5-28 Y v Leics (Leicester) 2000 (NL). T20 HS 18. T20 BB 3-19.

JEFFERSON, William Ingleby (Beeston Hall S, Norfolk; Oundle S; St Hild & St Bede C, Durham U), b Derby 25 Oct 1979. Son of R.I.Jefferson (Cambridge U and Surrey 1961-66); grandson of J.Jefferson (Army 1919, Comb Services 1922). 6'10". RHB, RMF. British U 2000-02. Essex 2000-06; cap 2002. Durham UCCE 2001-02. Nottinghamshire 2007-09. Leicestershire debut 2010. F-c Tour (Eng A): B 2006-07. 1000 runs (1): 1555 (2004). HS 222 Ex v Hants (Southampton) 2004. Le HS 135 v Surrey (Oval) 2010. BB 1-16 Ex v Yorks (Leeds) 2005. LO HS 132 Ex v Essex CB (Chelmsford) 2003 (CGT). LO BB 2-9 Ex v Worcs (Worcester) 2005 (NL). T20 HS 83.

JONES, William Stephen (Harrow S; Cardiff U), b Perth, Australia 29 Mar 1990. RHB, LB. Leicestershire 2nd XI debut 2010. Hertfordshire 2009. Awaiting 1st XI debut. Summer contract.

[NO]**McDONALD, Andrew** Barry (Murray HS, Lavington, NSW), b Wodonga, Victoria, Australia, 15 Jun 1981. 6'4". RHB, RFM. Victoria 2001-02 to date. Leicestershire debut 2010. **Tests** (A): 4 (2008-09); HS 68 v SA (Cape Town) 2008-09; BB 3-25 v SA (Durban) 2008-09. F-c Tours (A): E 2009; SA 2008-09. HS 176* v Middx (Leicester) 2010. BB 6-34 Vic v Q (Brisbane) 2006-07. Le BB 5-40 v Worcs (Leicester) 2010. LO HS 67 Vic v WA (Melbourne) 2008-09. LO BB 4-50 Vic v Q (Brisbane) 2009-10. T20 HS 67. T20 BB 5-13 v Notts (Nottingham) 2010 – Le record.

MALIK, Muhammad Nadeem (Wilford Meadows CS; Bilborough C), b Nottingham 6 Oct 1982. 6'5". RHB, RFM. Nottinghamshire 2001-03, 2007 – on loan. Worcestershire 2004-07. Leicestershire debut 2008, taking 5-51 (8-119 match) v Middx (Leicester). Notts 2nd XI debut 1999, aged 16y 337d. HS 41 v Essex (Leicester) 2008. Le BB 6-46 v Essex (Chelmsford) 2008. LO HS 11 Nt v Worcs (Nottingham) 2002 (NL). LO BB 4-40 v Hants (Southampton) 2010 (CB40). T20 HS 3*. T20 BB 4-16.

NAIK, Jigar Kumar Hakumatrai (Rushey Mead SS; Gateway SFC; Nottingham Trent U; Loughborough U), b Leicester 10 Aug 1984. 6'2". RHB, OB. Debut (Leicestershire) 2006. Loughborough UCCE 2007. Colombo CC 2010-11. HS 109* v Derbys (Leicester) 2009. BB 7-96 v Surrey (Oval) 2010. LO HS 18 v Derbys (Derby) 2009 (P40). LO BB 3-21 v Lancs (Leicester) 2009 (P40). T20 HS 7*. T20 BB 2-22.

NEW, Thomas James (Quarrydale S), b Sutton in Ashfield, Notts 18 Jan 1985. 5'10". LHB, RM, WK. Debut (Leicestershire) 2004; cap 2009. Derbyshire 2008 – on loan. HS 125 v Oxford UCCE (Oxford) 2007. CC HS 109 v Middx (Leicester) 2008. BB 2-18 v Glos (Leicester) 2007. LO HS 68 v Northants (Oakham) 2006 (CGT). T20 HS 18.

NIXON, Paul Andrew (Ullswater HS, Penrith), b Carlisle, Cumberland 21 Oct 1970. 6'0". LHB, WK, occ RM. Leicestershire 1989-99, 2003 to date; cap 1994; benefit 2007; captain 2007 (*part*) to 2009 (*part*). MCC 1999-00. Kent 2000-02; cap 2000. Cumberland 1987. **LOI:** 19 (2006-07); HS 49 v NZ (Perth) 2006-07. **IT20:** 1 (2006-07); HS 31* v A (Sydney) 2006-07. F-c Tours: SA 1996-97 (Le); I 1994-95 (Eng A); P 2000-01; B 1999-00 (MCC). 1000 runs (1): 1046 (1994). HS 173* v Kent (Canterbury) 2009. BB 1-7 v Glos (Bristol) 2010. LO HS 101 v Sri Lanka A (Galle) 1998-99. T20 HS 65.

SMITH, Gregory Philip (Oundle S; St Hild & St Bede C, Durham U), b Leicester 16 Nov 1988. 6'0". RHB, LBG. Debut (Leicestershire) 2008. Durham MCCU 2009-10. England U19s 2008. HS 158* v Glos (Leicester) 2010. BB 1-64 v Glos (Leicester) 2008. LO HS 58 v Surrey (Oval) 2008 (P40).

TAYLOR, James William Arthur (Shrewsbury S), b Nottingham 6 Jan 1990. RHB, LB. Debut (Leicestershire) 2008; cap 2009. MCC 2010. Shropshire 2007. England U19s 2008 to 2009. YC 2009. F-c Tour (EL): WI 2010-11. 1000 runs (2); most – 1207 (2009). HS 207* v Surrey (Oval) 2009. BB – . LO HS 103* and LO BB 4-61 v Warwks (Leicester) 2010 (CB40). T20 HS 62*. T20 BB 1-10.

THAKOR, Shivsinh Jaysinh (Loughborough GS), b Leicester 22 Oct 1993. RHB, RM. Leicestershire 2nd XI debut 2008, aged 14y 218d. England U19s 2010-11. Awaiting 1st XI debut.

WHITE, Wayne Andrew (John Port S, Etwall; Nottingham Trent U), b Derby 22 Apr 1985. 6'2". RHB, RMF. Derbyshire 2005-08. Leicestershire debut 2009. HS 101* v Derbys (Derby) 2010. BB 5-87 De v Northants (Northampton) 2007. Le BB 4-58 v Northants (Leicester) 2010. LO HS 46* v Glamorgan (Leicester) 2009 (P40). LO BB 6-29 v Notts (Leics) 2010 (CB40). T20 HS 26. T20 BB 3-27.

WYATT, Alexander Charles Frederick (Oakham S), b Roehampton 23 Jul 1990. 6'7". RHB, RMF. Debut (Leicestershire) 2009. Leicestershire 2nd XI debut 2007. HS 3 and BB 3-42 v West Indians (Leicester) 2009. CC HS 1 and BB 2-44 v Glos (Bristol) 2009. LO HS 1 v Kent (Leicester) 2010 (CB40). LO BB 1-24 v Notts (Nottingham) 2010 (CB40). T20 HS – . T20 BB 3-14.

RELEASED/RETIRED
(Having made a County First-Class or List A appearance in 2010)

BENNING, James Graham Edward (Beacon S; Chesham S; Caterham S), b Mill Hill, N London 4 May 1983. 6'0". RHB, RM. Surrey 2003-09. Leicestershire 2009-10. Buckinghamshire 2000-01. HS 128 Sy v Oxford UCCE (Oxford) 2004. CC HS 112 Sy v Glos (Oval) 2006. Le HS 72 v Northants (Northampton) 2009. BB 3-43 v Glamorgan (Leicester) 2009. LO HS 189* Sy v Glos (Bristol) 2006 (CGT). LO BB 4-43 Sy v Leics (Oval) 2003 (NL). T20 HS 88. T20 BB 1-7.

CLIFF, Samuel James (Colonel Frank Seely S, Calverton, Notts), b Nottingham 3 Oct 1987. 6'2". RHB, RMF. Leicestershire 2007-10. HS 26 v Northants (Leicester) 2009. BB 4-42 v Derbys (Leicester) 2008. LO HS 9 v Notts (Nottingham) 2009 (FPT). LO BB 4-26 v Derbys (Leicester) 2008 (P40). T20 HS 4. T20 BB 1-24.

RELEASED/RETIRED continued on p 152

LEICESTERSHIRE 2010

RESULTS SUMMARY

	Place	Won	Lost	Tied	Drew	NR
LV= County Championship (2nd Division)	4th	7	5		4	
All First-Class Matches		7	5		5	
Clydesdale Bank 40 (Group C)	6th	4	8			
Friends Provident t20 (North Group)	7th	6	9			1

LV= COUNTY CHAMPIONSHIP AVERAGES

BATTING AND FIELDING

Cap		M	I	NO	HS	Runs	Avge	100	50	Ct/St
	G.P.Smith	5	10	4	158*	509	84.83	2	3	6
2009	J.W.A.Taylor	16	27	4	206*	1027	44.65	3	3	15
	A.B.McDonald	6	11	1	176*	442	44.20	2	1	2
	J.du Toit	12	18	1	122	745	43.82	1	6	14
1994	P.A.Nixon	16	27	1	106	915	35.19	1	7	4
	W.A.White	8	12	2	101*	346	34.60	1	1	3
	W.I.Jefferson	10	18	–	135	598	33.22	1	4	14
	M.A.G.Boyce	14	26	3	90	750	32.60	–	6	19
2009	T.J.New	16	25	3	91	690	31.36	–	6	42/1
	J.K.H.Naik	7	10	2	36	181	22.62	–	–	4
	J.J.Cobb	4	8	1	27	97	13.85	–	–	2
2004	C.W.Henderson	16	21	1	33	265	13.25	–	–	6
	A.J.Harris	4	7	4	20*	27	9.00	–	–	2
	M.N.Malik	7	8	2	34	53	8.83	–	–	–
	N.L.Buck	15	20	5	26	93	6.20	–	–	4
2010	M.J.Hoggard	15	17	6	6	31	2.81	–	–	5
	H.F.Gurney	4	4	1	4	6	2.00	–	–	–

Also batted: J.G.E.Benning (1 match) 29, 26* (1 ct).

BOWLING

	O	M	R	W	Avge	Best	5wI	10wM
J.K.H.Naik	186	32	586	31	18.90	7-96	1	–
C.W.Henderson	489.3	136	1179	56	21.05	6-21	3	–
M.J.Hoggard	416.4	105	1222	50	24.44	6-63	3	–
A.B.McDonald	103	21	320	12	26.66	5-40	1	–
N.L.Buck	381.5	88	1340	49	27.34	4-44	–	–
M.N.Malik	167	41	521	19	27.42	4-32	–	–
Also bowled:								
H.F.Gurney	76	15	276	8	34.50	3-82	–	–
A.J.Harris	96.4	23	385	9	42.77	3-43	–	–
W.A.White	116.2	18	464	6	77.33	4-58	–	–

J.G.E.Benning 19-2-59-3; M.A.G.Boyce 1-0-2-0; J.J.Cobb 6-1-31-0; J.du Toit 2-0-20-0;
P.A.Nixon 2.1-1-7-1; J.W.A.Taylor 4-0-15-0.

The First-Class Averages (pp 220–237) give the records of Leicestershire players in all first-class county matches (Leicestershire's other opponents being Cambridge MCCU), with the exception of G.P.Smith, whose first-class figures for Leicestershire are as above, and:
J.W.A.Taylor 17-28-4-206*-1083-45.15-3-4-15ct. 4-0-15-0.

LEICESTERSHIRE RECORDS

FIRST-CLASS CRICKET

Highest Total	For 701-4d		v	Worcs	Worcester	1906
	V 761-6d		by	Essex	Chelmsford	1990
Lowest Total	For 25		v	Kent	Leicester	1912
	V 24		by	Glamorgan	Leicester	1971
	24		by	Oxford U	Oxford	1985
Highest Innings	For 309*	H.D.Ackerman	v	Glamorgan	Cardiff	2006
	V 341	G.H.Hirst	for	Yorkshire	Leicester	1905

Highest Partnership for each Wicket

1st	390	B.Dudleston/J.F.Steele	v	Derbyshire	Leicester	1979
2nd	289*	J.C.Balderstone/D.I.Gower	v	Essex	Leicester	1981
3rd	436*	D.L.Maddy/B.J.Hodge	v	L'boro UCCE	Leicester	2003
4th	360*	J.W.A.Taylor/A.B.McDonald	v	Middlesex	Leicester	2010
5th	322	B.F.Smith/P.V.Simmons	v	Notts	Worksop	1998
6th	284	P.V.Simmons/P.A.Nixon	v	Durham	Chester-le-St	1996
7th	219*	J.D.R.Benson/P.Whitticase	v	Hampshire	Bournemouth	1991
8th	195	J.W.A.Taylor/J.K.H.Naik	v	Derbyshire	Leicester	2009
9th	160	R.T.Crawford/ W.W.Odell	v	Worcs	Leicester	1902
10th	228	R.Illingworth/K.Higgs	v	Northants	Leicester	1977

Best Bowling	For 10- 18	G.Geary	v	Glamorgan	Pontypridd	1929
(Innings)	V 10- 32	H.Pickett	for	Essex	Leyton	1895
Best Bowling	For 16- 96	G.Geary	v	Glamorgan	Pontypridd	1929
(Match)	V 16-102	C.Blythe	for	Kent	Leicester	1909

Most Runs – Season		2446	L.G.Berry	(av 52.04)	1937
Most Runs – Career		30143	L.G.Berry	(av 30.32)	1924-51
Most 100s – Season		7	L.G.Berry		1937
		7	W.Watson		1959
		7	B.F.Davison		1982
Most 100s – Career		45	L.G.Berry		1924-51
Most Wkts – Season		170	J.E.Walsh	(av 18.96)	1948
Most Wkts – Career		2131	W.E.Astill	(av 23.18)	1906-39
Most Career W-K Dismissals		905	R.W.Tolchard	(794 ct; 111 st)	1965-83
Most Career Catches in the Field		426	M.R.Hallam		1950-70

LIMITED-OVERS CRICKET

Highest Total	50ov	406-5		v	Berkshire	Leicester	1996
	40ov	344-4		v	Durham	Chester-le-St	1996
	T20	221-3		v	Yorkshire	Leeds	2004
Lowest Total	50ov	56		v	Northants	Leicester	1964
	40ov	36		v	Sussex	Leicester	1973
	T20	97-9		v	Durham	Leicester	2004
Highest Innings	50ov	201	V.J.Wells	v	Berkshire	Leicester	1996
	40ov	154*	B.J.Hodge	v	Sussex	Horsham	2004
	T20	111	D.L.Maddy	v	Yorkshire	Leeds	2004
Best Bowling	50ov	6-16	C.M.Willoughby	v	Somerset	Leicester	2005
	40ov	6-17	K.Higgs	v	Glamorgan	Leicester	1973
	T20	5-13	A.B.McDonald	v	Notts	Nottingham	2010

MIDDLESEX

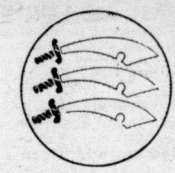

Formation of Present Club: 2 February 1864
Inaugural First-Class Match: 1864
Colours: Blue
Badge: Three Seaxes
County Champions (since 1890): (10) 1903, 1920, 1921, 1947, 1976, 1980, 1982, 1985, 1990, 1993
Joint Champions: (2) 1949, 1977
Gillette/NatWest/C&G/FP Trophy Winners: (4) 1977, 1980, 1984, 1988
Benson and Hedges Cup Winners: (2) 1983, 1986
Pro 40/National League (Div 1) Winners: (0); best – 1st (Div 2) 2004
Sunday League Winners: (1) 1992
Clydesdale Bank 40 Winners: (0); best – 6th Group B 2010
Twenty20 Cup Winners: (1) 2008

Secretary: Vincent J.Codrington, Lord's Cricket Ground, London NW8 8QN • Tel: 020 7289 1300 • Fax: 020 7289 5831 • Email: enquiries@middlesexccc.com • Web: www.middlesexccc.com

Managing Director of Cricket: Angus R.C.Fraser. **Head Coach:** Richard J.Scott. **Assistant Coach:** Richard L.Johnson. **Captain:** N.J.Dexter. **Vice-Captain:** tba. **Overseas Players:** R.McLaren (T20 only) and C.J.L.Rogers. **2011 Beneficiary:** none. **Head Groundsman:** Mick Hunt. **Scorer:** Don K.Shelley. ‡ New registration. ^{NQ} Not qualified for England.

‡^{NQ}**BALBIRNIE, Andrew** (St Andrew's C, Dublin; UWIC), b Dublin, Ireland 28 Dec 1990. 6'2". RHB, OB. Summer contract. MCC YCs 2010. **LOI** (Ire): 4 (2010); HS 17 v Canada (Amstelveen) 2010. LO HS 17 (*see LOI*).

BERG, Gareth Kyle (South African College S), b Cape Town, South Africa 18 Jan 1981. 6'0". RHB, RMF. England qualified through residency. Debut (Middlesex) 2008; cap 2010. WP Academy (1999-00) and WP B (2001-02 to 2002-03). Northants 2nd XI 2004. Middlesex 2nd XI 2007. HS 125 v Derbys (Lord's) 2010. BB 5-55 v Glos (Lord's) 2009. LO HS 65 v Surrey (Lord's) 2008 (FPT). LO BB 4-50 v Surrey (Oval) 2008 (FPT). T20 HS 41. T20 BB 2-31.

‡^{NQ}**COLLYMORE, Corey** Dalanelo (Alexandra SS), b St Peter, Barbados 21 Dec 1977. 6'0". RHB, RFM. Barbados 1998-99 to 2008-09. Warwickshire 2003. Sussex 2008-10; cap 2008. **Tests** (WI): 30 (1998-99 to 2007); HS 16* v Z (Bulawayo) 2003-04 and 16* v E (Chester-le-St) 2007; BB 7-57 v SL (Kingston) 2007. **LOI** (WI): 84 (1999 to 2006-07); HS 13* v I (Toronto) 1999; BB 5-51 v SL (Colombo) 2001-02. F-c tours (WI): E 2000, 2004, 2007; A 2005-06; SA 2003-04; P 2006-07; Z 2002, 2003-04; K 2000-01. HS 23 Sx v Notts (Horsham) 2009. 50 wkts (1): 57 (2010). BB 7-57 (*see Tests*). CC BB 6-48 Sx v Leics (Leicester) 2010. LO HS 13* (*see LOI*). LO BB 5-27 Barbados v Leeward Is (Weymouth) 2005-06. T20 HS 4. T20 BB 1-21.

‡**CROOK, Steven** Paul (Rostrevor C; Magill U), b Modbury, S Australia 28 May 1983. Younger brother of A.R.Crook (S Australia, Aus Academy, Lancashire, Northamptonshire 1998-99 to 2008). 5'11". RHB, RFM. British passport. Lancashire 2003-05. Northamptonshire 2005-09. Aus Academy 2001-02. HS 97 Nh v Yorks (Northampton) 2005. BB 5-71 Nh v Essex (Northampton) 2009. LO HS 72 Nh v Essex (Chelmsford) 2009 (FPT). LO BB 4-20 Nh v Sussex (Northampton) 2006 (P40). T20 HS 27. T20 BB 2-24.

141

DAVEY, Joshua Henry (Culford S), b Aberdeen, Scotland 3 Aug 1990. RHB, RM. Debut (Middlesex) 2010. Middlesex 2nd XI debut 2008. Suffolk 2009. **LOI** (Scot): 4 (2010); HS 24 v Netherlands (Rotterdam) 2010; BB 5-9 v Afghanistan (Ayr) 2010. HS 72 and BB 2-41 v Oxford MCCU (Oxford) 2010 – on debut. CC HS 61 v Glos (Bristol) 2010. CC BB – . LO HS 24 (*see LOI*). LO BB 5-9 (*see LOI*). T20 HS 7*. T20 BB – .

DEXTER, Neil John (Northwood HS, Durban; Varsity C; U of South Africa), b Johannesburg, South Africa 21 Aug 1984. 6'0". RHB, RM. Kent 2005-08. Essex 2008. Middlesex debut 2009; cap 2010; captain 2010 (*part*) to date. HS 146 (and 118) v Kent (Uxbridge) 2009. BB 3-50 v Worcs (Lord's) 2010. LO HS 135* K v Glamorgan (Cardiff) 2006 (CGT). LO BB 3-17 K v Leics (Canterbury) 2006 (P40). T20 HS 73. T20 BB 3-27.

FINN, Steven Thomas (Parmiter's S, Garston), b Watford, Herts 4 Apr 1989. 6'7½". RHB, RFM. Debut (Middlesex) 2005; cap 2009. YC 2010. **ECB central contract 2010-11. Tests:** 11 (2009-10 to 2010-11); HS 9* v P (Nottingham) 2010; BB 6-125 v A (Brisbane) 2010-11. **LOI:** 3 (2010-11); HS 35 v A (Brisbane) 2010-11; BB 2-51 (Sydney) 2010-11. F-c Tours: A 2010-11; B 2009-10. HS 26* v Worcs (Kidderminster) 2008. 50 wkts (2); most – 64 (2010). BB 9-37 (14-106 match) v Worcs (Worcester) 2010. LO HS 35 (*see LOI*). LO BB 3-23 v Somerset (Taunton) 2007 (P40). T20 HS 8. T20 BB 3-22.

HOUSEGO, Daniel Mark (Oratory S, Reading), b Windsor, Berkshire 12 Oct 1988. 5'8". RHB, LB. Debut (Middlesex) 2008. Middlesex 2nd XI debut 2005. Berkshire 2006. HS 102* v Oxford MCCU (Oxford) 2010. CC HS 36 v Derbys (Derby) 2008 – on debut. BB – . T20 HS 18.

‡**NOIRELAND, Anthony** John (Plumtree HS), b Masvingo, Zimbabwe 30 Aug 1984. RHB, RM. Midlands 2002-03 to 2004-05. Gloucestershire 2007-10; cap 2007. Kolpak registration. **LOI** (Z): 26 (2005-06 to 2006-07); HS 8* v K (Bulawayo) 2005-06; BB 3-41 v B (Harare) (twice) – 2006 and 2006-07. **IT20** (Z): 1 (2006-07); HS 2* and BB 1-33 v B (Khulna) 2006-07. HS 16* Gs v Middx (Bristol) 2008. BB 7-36 Zimbabwe A v Bangladesh A (Mirpur) 2006-07. UK BB 6-31 Gs v Leics (Bristol) 2009. LO HS 17 Midlands v Matabeleland (Harare) 2005-06. LO BB 4-16 Zimbabwe A v Kenya (Harare) 2005-06. T20 HS 8*. T20 BB 3-10.

LONDON, Adam Brian (Bishop Wand S, Sunbury), b Ashford 12 Oct 1988. 5'8". LHB, OB. Debut (Middlesex) 2009. Middlesex 2nd XI debut 2006. HS 77 v Northants (Northampton) 2010. BB 1-15 v Oxford MCCU (Oxford) 2010. CC BB – . LO HS and BB – .

‡**NOMcLAREN, Ryan** (Grey C, Bloemfontein; Free State U), b Kimberley, South Africa 9 Feb 1983. 6'4". Son of P.McLaren (GW 1977-78 to 1994-95), nephew of Keith McLaren (GW 1971-72 to 1984-85), cousin of A.P.McLaren (GW 1998-99 to date, Eagles 2007-08 to 2008-09, Knights 2010-11). LHB, RMF. FS 2003-04 to 2004-05. Eagles 2004-05 to 2009-10. Kent 2007-09 (Kolpak registration); cap 2007. Knights 2010-11. Joins Middlesex for T20 only in 2011. **Tests** (SA): 1 (2009-10); HS 33* and BB 1-30 v E (Johannesburg) 2009-10. **LOI** (SA): 10 (2009-10 to 2010); HS 12 v WI (Port-of-Spain) 2010; BB 3-51 v Z (Benoni) 2009-10 – on debut. **IT20** (SA): 5 (2009-10 to 2010-11); HS 6* and BB 5-19 (SA record analysis) v WI (North Sound) 2009-10. HS 140 Eagles v Warriors (Bloemfontein) 2005-06. UK HS 65* v Durham (Canterbury) 2008. 50 wkts (1+1); most – 54 (2006-07). BB 8-38 Eagles v Cape Cobras (Stellenbosch) 2006-07. UK BB 6-75 v Notts (Nottingham) 2008. LO HS 82* Eagles v Dolphins (Durban) 2007-08. LO BB 5-46 K v Surrey (Oval) 2008 (FPT). T20 HS 46*. T20 BB 5-19.

MALAN, Dawid Johannes (Paarl HS), b Roehampton, Surrey 3 Sep 1987. Son of D.J.Malan (WP B and Transvaal B 1978-79 to 1981-82), elder brother of C.C.Malan (Loughborough UCCE 2009). 6'0". LHB, LB. Boland 2005-06. MCC YC 2006-07. Middlesex debut 2008; cap 2010. 1000 runs (1): 1001 runs (2010). HS 132* v Northants (Uxbridge) 2008 – on M debut. BB 2-4 v Leics (Southgate) 2009. LO HS 60 v Surrey (Oval) 2009 (P40). LO BB 2-4 v Scotland (Edinburgh) 2009 (FPT). T20 HS 103 v Lancs (Oval) 2008 – M record. T20 BB 2-10.

MORGAN, Eoin Joseph Gerard (Catholic University S), b Dublin, Ireland 10 Sep 1986. 6'0". LHB, RM. British passport. Ireland 2004 to 2007-08. Middlesex debut 2006; cap 2008. **Tests**: 6 (2010); HS 130 v P (Nottingham) 2010. **LOI** (E/Ire): 61 (23 for Ire 2006 to 2008-09; 38 for E 2009 to 2010-11); HS 115 Ire v Canada (Nairobi) 2006-07. **IT20**: 16 (2009 to 2010-11); HS 85* v SA (Johannesburg) 2009-10 – E record. F-c Tours (Ire): A 2010-11 (E); NZ 2008-09 (Eng A); Namibia 2005-06; UAE 2006-07, 2007-08. 1000 runs (1): 1085 (2008). HS 209* Ire v UAE (Abu Dhabi) 2006-07. CC HS 137* v Glos (Bristol) 2008. BB 2-24 v Notts (Lord's) 2007. LO HS 161 v Kent (Canterbury) 2009 (FPT). LO BB – . T20 HS 85*.

MURTAGH, Timothy James (John Fisher S; St Mary's C), b Lambeth, London 2 Aug 1981. Elder brother of C.P.Murtagh (Loughborough UCCE and Surrey 2005-09); nephew of A.J.Murtagh (Hampshire and EP 1973-77). 6'0". LHB, RFM. British U 2000-03. Surrey 2001-06. Middlesex debut 2007; cap 2008. MCC 2010. HS 74* Sy v Middx (Oval) 2004 and 74* Sy v Warwks (Croydon) 2005. M HS 51* v Leics (Southgate) 2009. 50 wkts (2); most – 64 (2008). BB 7-82 v Derbys (Derby) 2009. LO HS 35* v Surrey (Lord's) 2008 (FPT). LO BB 4-14 Sy v Derbys (Derby) 2005 (NL). T20 HS 40*. T20 BB 6-24 Sy v Middx (Lord's) 2005 – Sy record and 2nd best UK figs.

NEWMAN, Scott Alexander (Trinity S, Croydon; Coulsdon C; Brighton U), b Epsom, Surrey 3 Nov 1979. 6'2". LHB, RM. Surrey 2002-09, scoring 99 v Hants on debut; cap 2005. Nottinghamshire 2009 (on loan). Middlesex debut 2010. MCC 2010. F-c Tour (Eng A): I 2003-04. 1000 runs (4); most – 1404 (2006). HS 219 (and 117) Sy v Glamorgan (Oval) 2005. M HS 126 v Derbys (Derby) 2010. BB – . LO HS 177 Sy v Yorks (Oval) 2009 (FPT). T20 HS 81*.

PATEL, Ravi Hasmukh (Merchant Taylors' S, Northwood), b Harrow 4 Aug 1991. RHB, SLA. Debut (Middlesex) 2010 – only f-c game. Middlesex 2nd XI debut 2008. Summer contract. HS 19* and BB 3-52 v Oxford MCCU (Oxford) 2010. LO HS and BB – .

[NQ]**ROBSON, Sam** David (Marcellin C, Randwick), b Paddington, Sydney, NSW, Australia 1 Jul 1989. 6'0". RHB, LB. Debut (Middlesex) 2009. Middlesex 2nd XI debut 2008. HS 204 v Oxford MCCU (Oxford) 2010. CC HS 110 v Essex (Lord's) 2009. BB – . LO HS 48 v Hants (Southampton) 2009 (FPT).

‡[NQ]**ROGERS, Christopher** John Llewellyn (Wesley C, Perth; Curtin U, Perth), b St George, Sydney, Australia 31 Aug 1977. Son of W.J.Rogers (NSW 1968-69 to 1969-70). 5'10". LHB, LBG. WA 1998-99 to 2007-08. Derbyshire 2004, 2008-10; cap 2008; captain 2008 (part) to 2010 (part). Leicestershire 2005. Northamptonshire 2006. Victoria 2008-09 to date. Shropshire 2003. Wiltshire 2005. **Tests** (A): 1 (2007-08); HS 15 v I (Perth) 2007-08. F-c Tour (Aus A): P 2007-08. 1000 runs (4+2); most – 1461 (2009). HS 319 Nh v Glos (Northampton) 2006. BB 1-16 Nh v Leics (Northampton) 2006. LO HS 140 Vic v S Aus (Melbourne) 2009-10. LO BB 2-22 Nh v Durham (Northampton) 2006. T20 HS 58.

ROLAND-JONES, Tobias Skelton ('Toby'), b Ashford 29 Jan 1988. 6'4". RHB, RMF. Debut (Middlesex) 2010. Middlesex 2nd XI debut 2008. Leeds/Bradford UCCE 2009. HS 26 and BB 5-41 v Surrey (Lord's) 2010. LO HS 23* and LO BB 3-55 v Yorks (Scarborough) 2010 (CB40).

ROSSINGTON, Adam Matthew (Mill Hill S), b Edgware 5 May 1993. 5'11". RHB, WK. Debut (Middlesex) 2010. Middlesex 2nd XI debut 2010. England U19s 2010-11, scoring 113 v SL on debut. Summer contract. HS 1 v Oxford MCCU (Oxford) 2010 – only f-c appearance.

[NQ]**SCOLLAY, Thomas** Edward (St Phillips C), b Alice Springs, Northern Territory, Australia 28 Nov 1987. RHB, OB. Awaiting f-c debut. Middlesex 2nd XI debut 2010. Hampshire 2nd XI 2008. LO HS 32 and LO BB 1-21 v Yorks (Lord's) 2010 (CB40).

SCOTT, Ben James Matthew (Whitton S, Richmond; Richmond C), b Isleworth 4 Aug 1981. Uncle of J.I.Pope (*see LEICESTERSHIRE*). 5'8". RHB, WK. Surrey 2003. Middlesex debut 2004; cap 2007. Worcestershire 2010 (on loan). MCC YC 2000. F-c Tour (Eng A): NZ 2008-09. HS 164* v Northants (Uxbridge) 2008. BB – . LO HS 73* v Surrey (Southgate) 2006 (CGT). T20 HS 43*.

SIMPSON, John Andrew (St Gabriel's RC HS), b Bury, Lancs 13 Jul 1988. 5'10". LHB, WK. Debut (Middlesex) 2009. Lancashire 2nd XI debut 2004. Cumberland 2007. MCC YCs 2008. England U19s 2004-05 to 2005. HS 101* v Northants (Northampton) 2010. LO HS 82 v Glos (Cheltenham) 2010 (CB40). T20 HS 13.

SMITH, Thomas Michael John (Seaford Head Community C; Sussex Downs C), b Eastbourne, Sussex 22 Aug 1987. 5'9". RHB, SLA. Sussex 2007-09. No f-c appearances in 2008. Surrey 2009 (l-o only). Middlesex debut. HS 33 v Derbys (Derby) 2010. BB 1-30 v Sussex (Hove) 2010. LO HS 65 Sy v Leics (Leicester) 2009 (P40). LO BB 3-26 v Derbys (Lord's) 2010 (CB40). T20 HS 9*. T20 BB 5-24.

NQSTIRLING, Paul Robert (Belfast HS), b Belfast, N Ireland 3 Sep 1990. 5'10". RHB, OB. Ireland 2007-08 to date. Awaiting Middlesex f-c and l-o debut. **LOI** (Ire): 23 (2008 to 2010-11); HS 177 v Canada (Toronto) 2010; BB 4-11 v Netherlands (Amstelveen) 2010. **IT20** (Ire): 6 (2009 to 2010); HS 22 v Canada (Colombo, SSC) 2009-10; BB – . F-c Tour (Ire): WI 2009-10. HS 100 Ire v Kenya (Eglinton) 2009. BB – . LO HS 177 (*see LOI*). LO BB 4-11 (*see LOI*). T20 HS 43. T20 BB 1-13.

STRAUSS, Andrew John (Radley C; Durham U), b Johannesburg, South Africa 2 Mar 1977. 5'11". LHB, LM. Debut (Middlesex) 1998; cap 2001; captain 2002 (*part*) to 2004 (*part*); benefit 2009. MCC 2002. ND 2007-08. Oxfordshire 1996. British U (List A) 1997-98. *Wisden* 2004. MBE 2005. **ECB central contract 2010-11. Tests**: 82 (2004 to 2010-11, 32 as captain); HS 177 v NZ (Napier) 2007-08. Scored 112 & 83 (run out) v NZ (Lord's) on debut and 126 & 94* v SA (Pt Elizabeth) 2004-05 on his debut overseas. **LOI**: 120 (2003-04 to 2010-11, 55 as captain); HS 154 v B (Birmingham) 2010; BB – . **IT20**: 4 (2005 to 2008-09); HS 33 v SL (Southampton) 2006. F-c Tours (C=captain): A 2006-07, 2010-11C; SA 2004-05, 2009-10C; WI 2008-09C; NZ 2007-08; I 2005-06, 2008-09; P 2005-06. 1000 runs (4); most – 1529 (2003). HS 177 (*see Tests*). M HS 176 v Durham (Lord's) 2001. BB 1-16 v Notts (Lord's) 2007. LO HS 163 v Surrey (Oval) 2008 (FPT) – M record. LO BB – . T20 HS 60.

WILLIAMS, Robert Edward Morgan (Marlborough C; St Mary's C, Durham U), b Pembury, Kent 19 Jan 1987. 6'0". RHB, RMF. Durham UCCE 2007-09. Middlesex debut 2007; no 1st XI appearances in 2008 after a minor fracture in his back. MCC 2007. HS 31 DU v Lancs (Durham) 2009. M HS 15 and M BB 5-112 v Essex (Chelmsford) 2007 – on M debut. BB 5-70 DU v Lancs (Durham) 2007. LO HS 2* and LO BB 2-60 v Bangladeshis (Lord's) 2010. T20 HS and BB – .

RELEASED/RETIRED
(Having made a County First-Class or List A appearance in 2010)

NQCOLLINS, Pedro Tyrone (St James S), b Boscobelle, Barbados 12 Aug 1976. Half-brother of F.H.Edwards (Barbados & West Indies 2001-02 to date). 6'2". RHB, LFM. Barbados 1996-97 to date. Busta Cup XI 2001-02. Surrey 2008-09 (Kolpak registration). Middlesex 2010. **Tests** (WI): 32 (1998-99 to 2006); HS 24 v I (Kingston) 2001-02; BB 6-53 v B (Kingston) 2004. **LOI** (WI): 30 (1999-00 to 2004-05); HS 10* v NZ (Wellington) 1999-00; BB 5-43 v A (Adelaide) 2004-05. F-c Tours (WI): E 2004; SA 1997-98 (WI A), 2007-08; NZ 1999-00; I 1998-99 (WI A), 2002-03; P (Sharjah) 2001-02; SL 2001-02; Z 2001; B 1998-99 (WI A), 1999-00, 2002-03; Kenya 2001. HS 25 Barbados v T&T (Pointe-a-Pierre) 2003-04. CC HS 23 Sy v Kent (Canterbury) 2009. M HS 13 v Leics (Lord's) 2010. 50 wkts (0+1): 54 (2003-04). BB 6-24 Barbados v Windward Is (Portsmouth, Dominica) 2006-07. CC BB 5-75 Sy v Derbys (Derby) 2009. M BB 4-46 v Derbys (Derby) 2010. LO HS 55* Barbados v Guyana (Georgetown) 2001-02. LO BB 7-11 Barbados v WI U19 (Blairmont, Berbice) 2007-08. T20 HS 1*. T20 BB 3-13.

144

EVANS, Daniel (Brierton CS, Hartlepool), b Hartlepool, Co Durham 24 Jul 1987. 6'5". RHB, RFM. Middlesex 2007-10. Durham 2nd XI 2004-06. England U19s 2006. HS 19* v Northants (Lord's) 2010. BB 6-35 v Essex (Chelmsford) 2008. LO HS 1* v Warwks (Birmingham) 2009 (FPT). LO BB 3-36 v Surrey (Oval) 2008 (FPT). T20 HS 5*. T20 BB – .

NQGILCHRIST, Adam Craig, b Bellingen, NSW, Australia 14 Nov 1971. 6'1". LHB, occ OB, WK. NSW 1992-93 to 1993-94. WA 1994-95 to 2007-08. Middlesex T20 and one l-o match in 2010; cap 2010. **Tests** (A): 96 (1999-00 to 2007-08); HS 204* v SA (Johannesburg) 2001-02. **LOI** (A): 287 (1996-97 to 2007-08); HS 172 v Z (Hobart) 2003-04. **IT20** (A): 13 (2004-05 to 2007-08); HS 48 v E (Sydney) 2006-07. F-c Tours (A): E 1995 (Young A), 1997, 2001, 2005; SA 2001-02, 2005-06; WI 2002-03; NZ 1999-00, 2004-05; I 2000-01, 2004-05; SL/UAE 2002-03; SL 2003-04; B 2005-06. HS 204* (*see Tests*). LO HS 172 (*see LOIs*). LO BB – . T20 HS 109*.

NQO'BRIEN, Iain Edward, b Lower Hutt, Wellington, New Zealand 10 Jul 1976. RHB, RFM. Wellington 2000-01 to 2009-10. Leicestershire 2009. Middlesex 2010. **Tests** (NZ): 22 (2004-05 to 2009-10); HS 31 v P (Wellington) 2009-10; BB 6-75 v WI (Napier) 2008-09. **LOI** (NZ): 10 (2007-08 to 2008-09); HS 3* v I (Napier) 2008-09; BB 3-68 v A (Sydney) 2008-09. **IT20** (NZ): 4 (2008-09 to 2009); HS – ; BB 2-30 v I (Wellington) 2008-09. F-c Tours (NZ): E 2008; A 2008-09; SA 2007-08; SL 2005-06 (NZ A), 2009; B 2008-09. HS 44 Wellington v Canterbury (Wellington) 2006-07. CC HS 31 Le v Glos (Bristol) 2009. M HS 14* v Sussex (Uxbridge) 2010. BB 8-55 (13-117 match) Wellington v Auckland (Wellington) 2006-07. CC BB 7-48 v Glos (Lord's) 2010. LO HS 19* Wellington v Canterbury (Christchurch) 2008-09. LO BB 5-35 Wellington v CD (Wellington) 2004-05. T20 HS 3*. T20 BB 5-23.

SHAH, O.A. – *see ESSEX.*

THOMPSON, Jackson Gladwin (St Benedict's C; Gloucestershire U), b Nasik, Maharashtra, India 7 Feb 1986. 6'3". LHB, OB. Gloucestershire 2007; cap 2007. No f-c appearances for Middlesex. Unicorns 2010 (l-o only). Oxfordshire 2007. HS 21 Gs v Middx (Bristol) 2007 – on debut. LO HS 54 Unicorns v Worcs (Kidderminster) 2010 (CB40). LO BB – . T20 HS 32. T20 BB 1-8.

TOOR, Kabir Singh (John Lyon S, Harrow), b Northwood, Herts 30 Apr 1990. 5'8". RHB, LB. Middlesex 2010. Middlesex 2nd XI debut 2006, when aged 16 years 87 days. HS 15 and BB 1-36 v Oxford MCCU (Oxford) 2010 – only f-c match. LO HS 5 v Northants (Uxbridge) 2009 (P40). LO BB 1-25 v Derbys (Uxbridge) 2009 (P40).

UDAL, Shaun David (Cove CS, Cove, Farnborough, Hants 18 Mar 1969. Grandson of G.F.U.Udal (Middlesex and RAF 1932; Leics 1946); great great grandson of J.S.Udal (MCC 1871-75; Fiji 1894-95). 6'2". RHB, OB. Hampshire 1989-2007; cap 1992; benefit 2002. Middlesex 2008-10; cap 2008; captain 2009-10 (*part*). **Tests**: 4 (2005-06); HS 33* v P (Faisalabad) 2005-06; BB 4-14 v I (Bombay) 2005-06. **LOI**: 11 (1994 to 2005-06); HS 11* v Z (Brisbane) 1994-95; BB 2-37 v A (Sydney) 1994-95. F-c Tours: A 1994-95; I 2005-06; P 1995-96 (Eng A); 2005-06. HS 117* H v Warwks (Southampton) 1997. M HS 91 v Worcs (Lord's) 2008. 50 wkts (2); most – 74 (1993). BB 8-50 H v Sussex (Southampton) 1992. M BB 6-36 (10-95 match) v Glamorgan (Swansea) 2009. LO HS 79* v Scotland (Edinburgh) 2009 (FPT). LO BB 5-43 H v Surrey (Oval) 1998 (SL). T20 HS 40*. T20 BB 3-19.

NQWARNER, David Andrew, b Paddington, Sydney, NSW, Australia 27 Oct 1986. 5'7". LHB, LBG. NSW 2008-09 to date. Durham 2009 – T20 only. Middlesex T20 and one l-o match 2010. **LOI** (A): 7 (2008-09 to 2009); HS 69 v SA (Sydney) 2008-09. **IT20** (A): 25 (2008-09 to 2010-11); HS 89 v SA (Melbourne) 2008-09 – on IT20 debut, becoming the first man to play for Australia before making a f-c debut since 1877. HS 99 NSW v Vic (Melbourne) 2010-11. BB 1-0 NSW v Vic (Newcastle) 2009-10. LO HS 165* NSW v Tas (Sydney) 2008-09. LO BB 1-11 NSW v Q (Brisbane) 2009-10. T20 HS 107*.

T.Henderson left the staff without making a County First-Class or List A appearance in 2010.

MIDDLESEX 2010

RESULTS SUMMARY

	Place	Won	Lost	Tied	Drew	NR
LV= County Championship (2nd Division)	8th	4	7		5	
All First-Class Matches		5	7		5	
Clydesdale Bank 40 (Group B)	6th	3	7			2
Friends Provident t20 (South Group)	6th	8	8			

LV= COUNTY CHAMPIONSHIP AVERAGES

BATTING AND FIELDING

Cap		M	I	NO	HS	Runs	Avge	100	50	Ct/St
2010	N.J.Dexter	12	21	2	118	907	47.73	2	5	10
2010	D.J.Malan	16	29	3	115	1001	38.50	3	5	19
2000	O.A.Shah	13	23	1	156	804	36.54	2	3	10
2010	G.K.Berg	15	26	5	125	761	36.23	1	3	7
	S.A.Newman	15	27	–	126	945	35.00	2	6	8
2001	A.J.Strauss	8	15	–	92	460	30.66	–	3	16
	J.A.Simpson	16	27	2	101*	657	26.28	1	2	42/2
	A.B.London	3	5	–	77	120	24.00	–	1	3
	S.D.Robson	7	13	–	59	291	22.38	–	2	6
	J.H.Davey	3	5	–	61	94	18.80	–	1	2
2008	T.J.Murtagh	15	23	10	50*	241	18.53	–	1	4
	T.M.J.Smith	4	7	1	33	110	18.33	–	–	3
2008	S.D.Udal	13	19	1	55	216	12.00	–	1	6
	D.Evans	3	4	2	19*	23	11.50	–	–	1
	T.S.Roland-Jones	7	11	1	26	109	10.90	–	–	2
	I.E.O'Brien	7	9	1	14*	39	4.87	–	–	1
2009	S.T.Finn	7	11	3	18	34	4.25	–	–	1
	P.T.Collins	10	13	4	13	36	4.00	–	–	1

Also batted (1 match each): D.M.Housego 32, 4 (1 ct); E.J.G.Morgan (cap 2008) 58, 58*.

BOWLING

	O	M	R	W	Avge	Best	5wI	10wM
T.S.Roland-Jones	206.2	27	688	36	19.11	5- 41	2	–
S.T.Finn	261.1	54	844	36	23.44	9- 37	2	1
I.E.O'Brien	205.1	36	628	23	27.30	7- 48	1	–
P.T.Collins	284.4	51	999	36	27.75	4- 46	–	–
N.J.Dexter	120	25	378	13	29.07	3- 50	–	–
S.D.Udal	284.3	38	917	27	33.96	5-128	1	–
G.K.Berg	235	32	877	24	36.54	4- 72	–	–
T.J.Murtagh	459.2	127	1405	38	36.97	5- 52	2	–
Also bowled:								
D.Evans	81.4	16	324	9	36.00	5- 87	1	–
D.J.Malan	74.1	2	339	6	56.50	2- 51	–	–

J.H.Davey 13-2-42-0; S.D.Robson 2-0-17-0; O.A.Shah 43.5-5-133-4; T.M.J.Smith 72-12-262-2.

The First-Class Averages (pp 220–237) give the records of Middlesex players in all first-class county matches (Middlesex's other opponents being Oxford MCCU), with the exception of S.T.Finn, E.J.G.Morgan and A.J.Strauss, whose first-class figures for Middlesex are as above.

MIDDLESEX RECORDS

FIRST-CLASS CRICKET

Highest Total	For	642-3d		v	Hampshire	Southampton	1923
	V	850-7d		by	Somerset	Taunton	2007
Lowest Total	For	20		v	MCC	Lord's	1864
	V	31		by	Glos	Bristol	1924
Highest Innings	For	331*	J.D.B.Robertson	v	Worcs	Worcester	1949
	V	341	C.M.Spearman	for	Glos	Gloucester	2004

Highest Partnership for each Wicket

1st	372	M.W.Gatting/J.L.Langer	v	Essex	Southgate	1998
2nd	380	F.A.Tarrant/J.W.Hearne	v	Lancashire	Lord's	1914
3rd	424*	W.J.Edrich/D.C.S.Compton	v	Somerset	Lord's	1948
4th	325	J.W.Hearne/E.H.Hendren	v	Hampshire	Lord's	1919
5th	338	R.S.Lucas/T.C.O'Brien	v	Sussex	Hove	1895
6th	270	J.D.Carr/P.N.Weekes	v	Glos	Lord's	1994
7th	271*	E.H.Hendren/F.T.Mann	v	Notts	Nottingham	1925
8th	182*	M.H.C.Doll/H.R.Murrell	v	Notts	Lord's	1913
9th	160*	E.H.Hendren/T.J.Durston	v	Essex	Leyton	1927
10th	230	R.W.Nicholls/W.Roche	v	Kent	Lord's	1899

Best Bowling	For	10- 40	G.O.B.Allen	v	Lancashire	Lord's	1929
(Innings)	V	9- 38	R.C.R-Glasgow†	for	Somerset	Lord's	1924
Best Bowling	For	16-114	G.Burton	v	Yorkshire	Sheffield	1888
(Match)		16-114	J.T.Hearne	v	Lancashire	Manchester	1898
	V	16-100	J.E.B.B.P.Q.C.Dwyer	for	Sussex	Hove	1906

Most Runs – Season	2669	E.H.Hendren	(av 83.41)	1923
Most Runs – Career	40302	E.H.Hendren	(av 48.81)	1907-37
Most 100s – Season	13	D.C.S.Compton		1947
Most 100s – Career	119	E.H.Hendren		1907-37
Most Wkts – Season	158	F.J.Titmus	(av 14.63)	1955
Most Wkts – Career	2361	F.J.Titmus	(av 21.27)	1949-82
Most Career W-K Dismissals	1223	J.T.Murray	(1024 ct; 199 st)	1952-75
Most Career Catches in the Field	561	E.H.Hendren		1907-37

LIMITED-OVERS CRICKET

Highest Total	50ov	341-7		v	Somerset	Lord's	2009
	40ov	337-5		v	Somerset	Southgate	2003
	T20	213-4		v	Glamorgan	Richmond	2010
Lowest Total	50ov	41		v	Essex	Westcliff	1972
	40ov	23		v	Yorkshire	Leeds	1974
	T20	104-6		v	Kent	Canterbury	2009
Highest Innings	50ov	163	A.J.Strauss	v	Surrey	The Oval	2008
	40ov	147*	M.R.Ramprakash	v	Worcs	Lord's	1990
	T20	106	A.C.Gilchrist	v	Kent	Canterbury	2010
Best Bowling	50ov	6-15	W.W.Daniel	v	Sussex	Hove	1980
	40ov	6- 6	R.W.Hooker	v	Surrey	Lord's	1969
	T20	5-13	M.Kartik	v	Essex	Lord's	2007

† R.C.Robertson-Glasgow

NORTHAMPTONSHIRE

Formation of Present Club: 31 July 1878
Inaugural First-Class Match: 1905
Colours: Maroon
Badge: Tudor Rose
County Champions: (0); best – 2nd 1912, 1957, 1965, 1976
Gillette/NatWest/C&G/FP Trophy Winners: (2) 1976, 1992
Benson and Hedges Cup Winners: (1) 1980
Pro 40/National League (Div 1) Winners: (0); best – 2nd 2006, 2007
Sunday League Winners: (0); best – 3rd 1991
Clydesdale Bank 40 Winners: (0); best – 5th Group B
Twenty20 Cup Winners: (0); best – Semi-Finalist 2009

Chief Executive: Mark J.Tagg, County Ground, Wantage Road, Northampton, NN1 4TJ
• Tel: 01604 514455 • Fax: 01604 609288 • Email: post@nccc.co.uk • Web: www.nccc.co.uk

First XI Coach: David J.Capel. **Captain:** A.J.Hall. **Vice-Captain:** none. **Overseas Players:** J.Botha (T20 only) and W.P.J.U.C.Vaas. **2011 Beneficiary:** none. **Head Groundsman:** Paul Marshall. **Scorer:** A.C. (Tony) Kingston. ‡ New registration. ᴺᴼ Not qualified for England.

BAKER, Gavin Charles (Haberdashers' Aske's S, Elstree; Loughborough U), b Edgware, Middx 3 Oct 1988. 5'11". RHB, RMF. Loughborough MCCU 2009-10. Northamptonshire debut 2010. Middlesex 2nd XI 2008. Hertfordshire 2009. HS 66 LU v Hants (Southampton) 2009. CC HS 35 v Derbys (Chesterfield) 2010. BB 2-35 LU v Kent (Canterbury) 2010. CC BB – . LO HS 0 and LO BB 1-63 v Glos (Northampton) 2010 (CB40).

‡ᴺᴼ**BOTHA, Johan**, b Johannesburg, South Africa 2 May 1982. RHB, OB. EP 2000-01 to 2003-04. Border 2004-05. Warriors 2004-05 to date. Joins Northamptonshire in 2011 for T20 only. **Tests** (SA): 5 (2005-06 to 2010-11); HS 25 v B (Dhaka) 2007-08; BB 4-56 v WI (Bridgetown) 2010. **LOI** (SA): 69 (2005-06 to 2010-11); HS 46 v A (Melbourne, Dock) 2005-06; BB 4-19 v Kenya (Bloemfontein) 2008-09. **IT20** (SA): 26 (2005-06 to 2010-11); HS 28* v WI (Pt Elizabeth) 2007-08; BB 3-16 v I (Nottingham) 2009. F-c Tours (SA): A 2005-06; WI 2010; SL 2005-06 (SA A); Z 2007-08 (SA A); B 2007-08; UAE 2010-11 (v P). HS 109 Warriors v Dolphins (Pt Elizabeth) 2009-10. BB EP v Northerns (Pt Elizabeth) 2003-04. LO HS 55* Warriors v Cape Cobras (Cape Town) 2006-07. LO BB 4-19 (*see LOI*). T20 HS 44*. T20 BB 4-19.

BRETT, Thomas (Latimer Arts Community C), b Kettering 13 Nov 1989. 6'2". RHB, SLA. Debut (Northamptonshire) 2010. Northamptonshire 2nd XI debut 2007. Bedfordshire 2008-09. HS and BB – v Oxford MCCU (Oxford) 2010 – only f-c match. LO HS 2* v Glos (Northampton) 2010 (CB40). LO BB 1-24 v Netherlands (Rotterdam) 2010 (CB40).

BROOKS, Jack Alexander (Wheatley Park S), b Oxford 4 Jun 1984. 6'2". RHB, RFM. Debut (Northamptonshire) 2009. Oxfordshire 2004-09. HS 53 v Glos (Bristol) 2010. BB 4-76 v Derbys (Chesterfield) 2009. LO HS 10 v Middx (Uxbridge) 2009 (P40). LO BB 3-41 v Yorks (Northampton) 2010 (CB40). T20 HS 5*. T20 BB 3-24.

DAGGETT, Lee Martin (Woodhey HS, and Holy Cross C, Bury; Durham U) b Bury, Lancs 1 Oct 1982. 6'0". RHB, RFM. Durham UCCE 2003-05. British U 2004. Warwickshire 2006-08. Leicestershire 2008. Northamptonshire debut 2009. HS 48 v Leics (Northampton) 2010. BB 8-94 DU v Durham (Chester-le-St) 2004. CC BB 6-30 Wa v Durham (Birmingham) 2006. Nh BB 4-25 v Worcs (Worcester) 2010. LO HS 14* and BB 4-17 v Netherlands (Northampton) 2010 (CB40). T20 HS 3*. T20 BB 2-19.

DAVIS, Christian Arthur Linghorne (Bedford S), b Milton Keynes, Bucks 11 Oct 1992. 6'0". RHB, LFM. Northamptonshire 2nd XI debut 2010. Bedfordshire 2010. England U19s 2010-11. Awaiting f-c debut. LO HS and BB – .

EVANS, Luke (St Aidan's S, Sunderland), b Sunderland 26 Apr 1987. 6'7". RHB, RMF. Durham 2007-10. No 1st XI appearances in 2008. Northamptonshire debut 2010 (on loan). HS 8* and BB 3-53 v Glos (Bristol) 2010. LO HS 1* Du v Warwks (Birmingham) 2010 (CB40). LO BB 2-53 Du v Notts (Chester-le-St) 2009 (P40).

NQHALL, Andrew James (Alberton HS), b Alberton, Johannesburg, South Africa 31 Jul 1975. 6'0". RHB, RFM. Transvaal/Gauteng 1995-96 to 2000-01. Easterns 2001-02 to 2003-04. Worcestershire 2003-04. Lions 2004-05 to 2005-06. Kent 2005-07; cap 2005. Northamptonshire debut 2008 (Kolpak registration); cap 2009; captain 2010 (*part*) to date. Dolphins 2009-10. ME 2010-11. Durham CB 1999. Suffolk 2002. **Tests** (SA): 21 (2001-02 to 2006-07); HS 163 v I (Kanpur) 2004-05; BB 3-1 v SL (Johannesburg) 2002-03. **LOI** (SA): 88 (1998-99 to 2007); HS 81 v SL (Galle) 2000-01; BB 5-18 v E (Bridgetown) 2006-07. **IT20** (SA): 2 (2005-06); HS 11 v A (Brisbane) 2005-06; BB 3-22 v A Johannesburg) 2005-06. F-c Tours (SA): E 2003; WI 2004-05; I 2004-05; SL 2006; Z 1995-96 (Transvaal B), 2007-08 (SA A). 1000 runs (1): 1161 (2009). HS 163 (*see Tests*). UK HS 159 v Leics (Northampton) 2009. UK BB 6-77 (11-99 match) Easterns v WP (Pt Elizabeth) 2002-03. UK BB 5-29 v Essex (Northampton) 2009. LO HS 129* Gauteng v Border (E London) 1999-00. LO BB 5-18 (*see LOI*). T20 HS 66* and T20 BB 6-21 v Worcs (Northampton) 2008 (Nh record analysis, and 1st man in UK to score 50 and take 5 wkts in a game).

HOWGEGO, Benjamin Henry Nicholas (King's S, Ely; Stowe S; Exeter U), b King's Lynn, Norfolk 3 Mar 1988. 5'11". LHB, RM. Debut (Northamptonshire) 2008. Northamptonshire 2nd XI debut 2005. HS 80 v Derbys (Chesterfield) 2010. BB – . LO HS 7 v Middx (Uxbridge) 2009 (P40). T20 HS 1.

KEOGH, Robert Ian (Queensbury S; Dunstable C), b Luton, Beds 21 Oct 1991. 5'11". RHB, OB. Northamptonshire 2nd XI debut 2009. Bedfordshire 2009-10. Awaiting f-c debut. LO HS 11 v Yorks (Northampton) 2010 (CB40).

LOYE, Malachy Bernhard (Moulton S), b Northampton 27 Sep 1972. 6'2". RHB, OB. Northamptonshire 1991-2002 and 2010; cap 1994. PCA 1998. Lancashire 2003-09, scoring 126 v Surrey (Oval) and 113 v Notts (Manchester) in his first two innings; cap 2003; benefit 2008. Auckland 2006-07. **LOI**: 7 (2006-07); HS 45 v A (Sydney) 2006-07. F-c Tours (Eng A): SA 1993-94, 1998-99; Z 1994-95 (Nh), 1998-99. 1000 runs (6); most – 1296 (2006). HS 322* v Glamorgan (Northampton) 1998 – record Nh score until 2001. BB 1-8 La v Kent (Blackpool) 2003. Nh BB – . LO HS 127 La v Durham (Manchester) 2006 (CGT). T20 HS 100.

LUCAS, David Scott (Djanogly CTC, Nottingham), b Nottingham 19 Aug 1978. 6'2". RHB, LMF. Nottinghamshire 1999-2002. Yorkshire 2005. Northamptonshire debut 2007; cap 2009. Lincolnshire 2006. HS 55* v Essex (Chelmsford) 2009. 50 wkts (1): 60 (2009). BB 7-24 (12-73 match) v Glos (Cheltenham) 2009. LO HS 32* v Lancs (Manchester) 2009 (FPT). LO BB 4-27 Nt v Derbys (Derby) 2000 (NL). T20 HS 5*. T20 BB 2-37.

MIDDLEBROOK, James Daniel (Pudsey Crawshaw S), b Leeds, Yorks 13 May 1977. 6'1". RHB, OB. Yorkshire 1998-2001. Essex 2002-09; cap 2003. Northamptonshire debut 2010. MCC 2010. HS 127 Ex v Middx (Lord's) 2007. Nh HS 84 v Derbys (Chesterfield) 2010. 50 wkts (1): 56 (2003). BB 6-82 (10-170 match) Y v Hants (Southampton) 2000 – including 4 wickets in 5 balls. Nh BB 3-23 v Worcs (Worcester) 2010. Hat-trick Ex v Kent (Canterbury) 2003. LO HS 57* v Derbys (Derby) 2010 (CB40). LO BB 4-27 Ex v Somerset (Taunton) 2006 (CGT). T20 HS 43. T20 BB 3-13.

MURPHY, David (Richard Hale S, Hertford; Loughborough U), b Welwyn Garden City, Herts 24 June 1989. 5'11". RHB, WK. Loughborough MCCU 2009-10. Northamptonshire debut 2009. Northamptonshire 2nd XI debut 2007. HS 76 LU v Kent (Canterbury) 2010. Nh HS 55 v Glos (Northampton) 2010. LO HS 31* v Netherlands (Northampton) 2010 (CB40). T20 HS 0.

NEWTON, Robert Irving (Framlingham C), b Taunton, Somerset 18 Jan 1990. 5'8". RHB, OB. Debut (Northamptonshire) 2010. Northamptonshire 2nd XI debut 2006. HS 102 v Leics (Northampton) 2010. BB – . LO HS 66 v Essex (Northampton) 2010 (CB40). T20 HS 7.

O'BRIEN, Niall John (Marian C, Dublin), b Dublin, Ireland 8 Nov 1981. 5'6". Son of B.A.O'Brien (Ireland 1966-81); elder brother of K.J.O'Brien (Nottinghamshire and Ireland 2006-07 to date). LHB, WK. Kent 2004-06. Ireland 2005-06 to date. Northamptonshire debut 2007. **LOI** (Ire): 40 (2006 to 2010-11); HS 72 v Scotland (Belfast) 2007. **IT20** (Ire): 16 (2008 to 2009-10); HS 50 v Canada (Colombo, SSC) 20090-10. Nh HS 176 Ireland v UAE (Windhoek) 2005. Nh HS 168 v Glamorgan (Northampton) 2008. BB 1-4 K v Cambridge UCCE (Cambridge) 2006. LO HS 95 v Leics (Northampton) 2008. T20 HS 84.

PETERS, Stephen David (Coopers Coborn & Co S), b Harold Wood, Essex 10 Dec 1978. 5'11". RHB, occ LB. Essex 1996-2001, scoring 110 and 12* v Cambridge U (Cambridge) on debut. Worcestershire 2002-05. Northamptonshire debut 2006; cap 2007. 1000 runs (4); most – 1320 (2010). HS 199 v Middx (Lord's) 2010. BB 1-19 Ex v Oxford U (Chelmsford) 1999. LO HS 107 v Yorks (Leeds) 2007 (FPT). T20 HS 61*.

SALES, David John Grimwood (Caterham S; Cumnor House S), b Carshalton, Surrey 3 Dec 1977. 6'0". RHB, RM. Debut (Northamptonshire) 1996 v Worcs (Kidderminster) scoring 0 and 210* – record Championship score on f-c debut; youngest (18 years 237 days) to score 200 in a Championship match; cap 1999; captain 2004-07; benefit 2007. Missed entire 2009 season with knee injury. Wellington 2001-02. MCC 2010. F-c Tours (Eng A): NZ 1999-00; SL 1997-98; K 1997-98; B 1999-00. Sustained severe knee injury prior to start of England Plays season of WI 2000-01 – no f-c appearances 2001. 1000 runs (6); most – 1384 (2007). HS 303* v Essex (Northampton) 1999 – youngest Englishman (21 years 240 days) to score a f-c 300. BB 4-25 v SL A (Northampton) 1999. CC BB 2-7 v Yorks (Scarborough) 1999. LO HS 161 v Yorks (Northampton) 2006 (CGT) – Nh record. T20 HS 78*. T20 BB 1-10.

NQVAAS, Warnakulasuriya Patabendige Joseph Ushantha **Chaminda** (St Joseph's C, Maradana), b Mattumagala, Sri Lanka 27 Jan 1974. LHB, LFM. Colts 1990-91 to date. Hampshire 2003. Worcestershire 2005. Middlesex 2007; cap 2007. Northamptonshire debut 2010. **Tests** (SL): 111 (1994-95 to 2009); HS 100* v B (Colombo, SSC) 2007; BB 7-71 (14-191 match) v WI (Colombo, SSC) 2001-02. **LOI** (SL): 322 (1993-94 to 2008, 1 as captain); HS 50* v P (Sharjah) 2000-01; BB 8-19 v Z (Colombo, SSC) 2001-02, world record LOI analysis and inc first of two LOI hat-tricks. **IT20** (6): (2006-07 to 2007-08); HS 21 v A (Cape Town) 2007-08; BB 2-14 v B (Johannesburg) 2007-08. F-c Tours (SL): E 2002, 2006; A 1995-96, 2004, 2007-08; SA 1994-95, 1997-98, 2000-01, 2002-03; WI 2003, 2007-08; NZ 1994-95, 1996-97, 2004-05, 2006-07; I 1993-94, 1997-98, 2005-06; P 1995-96, 1999-00, 2001-02, 2004-05, 2008-09; Z 1994-95, 1999-00, 2004; B 1998-99 (v P), 2008-09. HS 134 Colts v Burgher (Colombo, SSC) 2004-05. UK HS 79 M v Glamorgan (Lord's) 2007. Nh HS 17 v Surrey (Northampton) 2010. 50 wkts (0+2); most – 62 (2001-02). BB 7-54 (11-93 match) W Province v S Province (Colombo, RPS) 2004-05. UK BB 5-126 M v Notts (Lord's) 2007. Nh BB 4-49 v Middx (Lord's) 2010. LO HS 76* Colts v Nondescripts (Colombo, NCC) 2009-10. LO BB (see LOI). T20 HS 73. T20 BB 3-16.

WAKELY, Alexander George (Bedford S), b Hammersmith, London 3 Nov 1988. 6'2". RHB, OB. Debut (Northamptonshire) 2007. Bedfordshire 2004-05. Northamptonshire 2nd XI debut when aged 15 years 295 days. HS 113* v Glamorgan (Cardiff) 2009. BB 2-62 v Somerset (Taunton) 2007 – on debut. LO HS 35 v Netherlands (Rotterdam) 2010 (CB40). BB 2-14 v Lancs (Northampton) 2007 (P40). T20 HS 55.

WHITE, Robert Allan (Stowe S; Durham U; Loughborough U), b Chelmsford, Essex 15 Oct 1979. 5'11". RHB, LB. Debut (Northamptonshire) 2000; cap 2008. Loughborough UCCE 2003. British U 2003. 1000 runs (1): 1037 (2008). HS 277 and BB 2-30 v Glos (Northampton) 2002 – highest maiden f-c hundred in UK; included 107 before lunch on first day. LO HS 111 v Warwks (Northampton) 2008 (FPT). LO BB 2-18 v Sussex (Northampton) 2002 (NL). T20 HS 94*.

WILLEY, David Jonathan (Northampton S), b Northampton 28 Feb 1990. Son of P.Willey (Northants, Leics, England 1966-91). 6'1". LHB, LFM. Debut (Northamptonshire) 2009. Bedfordshire 2008. England U19s 2009. HS 60 v Leics (Leicester) 2009. BB 2-21 v Kent (Canterbury) 2009. LO HS 25 v Essex (Southend) 2010 (CB40). LO BB 2-40 v Middx (Lord's) 2010 (CB40). T20 HS 19. T20 BB 3-9.

RELEASED/RETIRED
(Having made a County First-Class or List A appearance in 2010)

NQBOJE, Nico ('Nicky' (Grey C, Bloemfontein), b Bloemfontein, South Africa 20 Mar 1973. 5'10". Brother of E.H.L.Boje (OFS 1989-1990 to 1990-91). LHB, SLA. (O)FS 1990-91 to 2001-02. Nottinghamshire 2002. Eagles 2004-05 to 2006-07. Northamptonshire 2007-10 (Kolpak registration); cap 2008; captain 2008-10 (part). Warriors 2010-11. **Tests** (SA): 43 (1999-00 to 2006); HS 85 v I (Bangalore) 1999-00; BB 5-62 v SL (Colombo) 2000-01. **LOI** (SA): 115 (1995-96 to 2005); HS 129 v NZ (Pretoria) 2000-01; BB 5-21 v A (Cape Town) 2001-02. **IT20** (SA): 1 (2005-06); HS- and BB 1-27 v NZ (Johannesburg) 2005-06. F-c Tours (SA): E 1996 (SA A); A 2001-02, 2002-03 (SA A), 2005-06; WI 2000-01, 2004-05; NZ 1998-99, 2003-04; I 1996-97, 1999-00; SL 1995 (SA U-24), 1998 (SA A), 2000, 2004, 2006; Z 1994-95. HS 226* v Worcs (Northampton) 2008. BB 8-93 Eagles v Dolphins (Durban) 2005-06. Nh BB 6-110 v Leics (Leicester) 2007. LO HS 129 (see LOI). LO BB 5-21 (see LOI). T20 HS 58*. T20 BB 3-10.

[NO]CHIGUMBURA, Elton, b Kwekwe, Zimbabwe 14 Mar 1986. RHB, RMF. Mashonaland (Eagles) 2001-02 to date. Northerns 2006-07 to 2008-09. Northamptonshire 2010. SR 2010-11. **Tests** (Z): 6 (2004 to 2004-05); HS 71 and BB 5-54 v B (Chittagong) 2004-05. **LOI** (Z): 122 (2004 to 2010-11); HS 79 v Kenya (Mombasa) 2008-09; BB 4-28 v Kenya (Nairobi) 2008-09. **IT20** (Z): 14 (2006-07 to 2010-11); HS 34 v WI (Port of Spain) 2009-10; BB 4-31 v E (Cape Town) 2007-08. F-c Tours (Z): SA 2004-05; P 2007-08; B 2003-04 (Zim A), 2004-05, 2006-07 (Zim A), 2008-09. HS 186 Northerns v Westerns (Harare) 2007-08. Nh HS 44 v Glamorgan (Northampton) 2010. BB 5-33 Z v SA Composite XI (Paarl) 2007-08. Nh BB 5-92 v Derbys (Chesterfield) 2010. LO HS 97* Manicaland v Matabeleland (Harare) 2005-06. LO BB 4-23 Northerns v Westerns (Harare) 2007-08. T20 HS 103*. T20 BB 5-13.

HARRISON, Paul William (Forest S and Collyer's C, Horsham; Loughborough U), b Cuckfield, Sussex 22 May 1984. 6'2". RHB, RM, WK. Loughborough UCCE 2004-06. Warwickshire (one non-CC match) 2005. British U 2006. Leicestershire 2006-07. Northamptonshire 2009-10. HS 54 LU v Notts (Nottingham) 2005. Nh and CC HS 44 v Glos (Bristol) 2010. LO HS 61 Le v Yorks (Scarborough) 2006 (P40). T20 HS 26.

TRIPATHI, Vishal, b Burnley, Lancs 3 Mar 1988. RHB, LB. Northamptonshire 2010. HS 71 v Derbys (Northampton) 2010. BB – . LO HS 0. T20 HS 6.

WIGLEY, David Harry (St Mary's RCS, Menston, Ilkley; Loughborough U), b Bradford, Yorks 26 Oct 1981. 6'4". RHB, RFM. Yorkshire 2002 (one match). Loughborough UCCE 2003-04. British U 2004. Worcestershire 2003, 2005. Northamptonshire 2006-09. Gloucestershire 2008; cap 2008 (1 match). HS 70 v Middx (Northampton) 2007. BB 6-72 v Glos (Northampton) 2009. LO HS 10 v Middx (Southgate) 2007 (P40). LO BB 4-37 Wo v Leics (Worcester) 2004 (NL). T20 HS 1. T20 BB 1-8.

L.Vincent left the staff without making a County First-Class or List A appearance in 2010.

LEICESTERSHIRE RELEASED/RETIRED (continued from p 138)

HARRIS, Andrew James (Hadfield CS; Glossopdale Community C), b Ashton-under-Lyne, Lancs 26 Jun 1973. 6'1". RHB, RM. Derbyshire 1994-99; cap 1996. Nottinghamshire 2000-08; cap 2000; benefit 2008. Gloucestershire (1 match) 2008. Worcestershire (2 matches) 2008. Leicestershire 2009-10. F-c Tour (Eng A): A 1996-97. HS 41* Nt v Northants (Northampton) 2002. Le HS 22* v Kent (Canterbury) 2009. Dismissed 'Timed Out' v Durham UCCE (Nottingham) 2003 – third instance in f-c cricket. 50 wkts (2); most – 67 (2002). BB 7-54 (11-122 match) Nt v Northants (Nottingham) 2002. Le BB 5-26 v Glos (Leicester) 2009. LO HS 34 Nt v Durham (Nottingham) 2006 (CGT). LO BB Nt 5-35 v Hants (Nottingham) 2000 (NL). T20 HS 6*. T20 BB 2-13.

MASTERS, Daniel (Medway Community C), b Chatham, Kent 7 Dec 1986. Son of K.D.Masters (Kent 1983-84), younger brother of D.D.Masters (see ESSEX). 6'0". RHB, RFM. Awaiting f-c debut. LO HS 2 v Kent (Canterbury) 2010 (CB40). LO BB 1-46 v Warwks (Leicester) 2010 (CB40).

POPE, Joel Ian (Whitton S), b Ashford, Middx 23 Oct 1988. Nephew of B.J.M.Scott (see MIDDLESEX). 5'6". RHB, WK. Middlesex 2nd XI 2006. MCC YC 2007. Leicestershire 2nd XI debut 2007. Awaiting f-c debut. LO HS 9 (twice).

NORTHAMPTONSHIRE 2010

RESULTS SUMMARY

	Place	Won	Lost	Tied	Drew	NR
LV= County Championship (2nd Division)	6th	6	7		3	
All First-Class Matches		6	7		4	
Clydesdale Bank 40 (Group B)	5th	4	8			
Friends Provident t20 (North Group)	QF	7	7	3		

LV= COUNTY CHAMPIONSHIP AVERAGES

BATTING AND FIELDING

Cap		M	I	NO	HS	Runs	Avge	100	50	Ct/St
2007	S.D.Peters	15	29	2	199	1296	48.00	3	7	16
	N.J.O'Brien	3	6	–	49	216	36.00	–	–	7/1
2008	N.Boje	9	15	1	98	471	33.64	–	4	3
	R.I.Newton	6	11	–	102	357	32.45	1	2	1
	D.Murphy	9	15	6	55	276	30.66	–	2	26
	A.G.Wakely	12	21	–	98	614	29.23	1	4	5
2009	A.J.Hall	15	27	3	133	696	29.00	1	3	21
	B.H.N.Howgego	7	13	2	80	292	26.54	–	1	3
	J.D.Middlebrook	12	21	3	84	459	25.50	–	3	6
1999	D.J.G.Sales	15	28	–	127	680	24.28	1	2	20
	V.Tripathi	3	6	–	71	141	23.50	–	1	3
1994	M.B.Loye	9	17	–	164	378	22.23	1	1	–
2008	R.A.White	9	18	1	95	361	21.23	–	2	2
2009	D.S.Lucas	10	17	2	40*	316	21.06	–	–	1
	E.Chigumbura	6	10	1	44	189	21.00	–	–	1
	P.W.Harrison	4	7	1	44	126	21.00	–	–	7/2
	D.J.Willey	2	4	2	18*	41	20.50	–	–	1
	L.M.Daggett	11	17	8	48	167	18.55	–	–	3
	J.A.Brooks	13	20	3	53	177	10.41	–	1	2

Also batted: G.C.Baker (1 match) 14, 35; D.A.Burton (1) 0, 2* (1 ct); L.Evans (2) 0*, 8*, 8 (1 ct); W.P.J.U.C.Vaas (2) 0, 17 (1 ct).

BOWLING

	O	M	R	W	Avge	Best	5wI	10wM
E.Chigumbura	114	17	482	20	24.10	5-92	1	–
A.J.Hall	318	57	1047	33	31.72	4-44	–	–
D.S.Lucas	282.4	54	993	31	32.03	5-64	1	–
L.M.Daggett	303.4	64	1009	30	33.63	4-25	–	–
J.A.Brooks	351.3	79	1227	34	36.08	4-88	–	–
J.D.Middlebrook	251.2	40	863	18	47.94	3-23	–	–
N.Boje	230.3	42	796	15	53.06	2-47	–	–
Also bowled:								
D.A.Burton	20	4	75	5	15.00	5-75	1	–
W.P.J.U.C.Vaas	73.2	20	161	6	26.83	4-49	–	–
D.J.Willey	41.5	3	171	5	34.20	2-47	–	–
L.Evans	57	10	201	5	40.20	3-53	–	–

G.C.Baker 13-3-54-0; B.H.N.Howgego 2-0-16-0; R.I.Newton 2.1-0-19-0; D.J.G.Sales 1-0-10-0; V.Tripathi 2-0-11-0; A.G.Wakely 9.1-0-57-1; R.A.White 1-0-7-0.

The First-Class Averages (pp 220–237) give the records of Northamptonshire players in all first-class county matches (Northamptonshire's other opponents being Oxford MCCU), with the exception of G.C.Baker, L.Evans and D.Murphy, whose first-class figures for Northamptonshire are as above.

NORTHAMPTONSHIRE RECORDS

FIRST-CLASS CRICKET

Highest Total	For 781-7d		v	Notts	Northampton	1995
	V 673-8d		by	Yorkshire	Leeds	2003
Lowest Total	For 12		v	Glos	Gloucester	1907
	V 33		by	Lancashire	Northampton	1977
Highest Innings	For 331*	M.E.K.Hussey	v	Somerset	Taunton	2003
	V 333	K.S.Duleepsinhji	for	Sussex	Hove	1930

Highest Partnership for each Wicket

1st	375	R.A.White/M.J.Powell	v	Glos	Northampton	2002
2nd	344	G.Cook/R.J.Boyd-Moss	v	Lancashire	Northampton	1986
3rd	393	A.Fordham/A.J.Lamb	v	Yorkshire	Leeds	1990
4th	370	R.T.Virgin/P.Willey	v	Somerset	Northampton	1976
5th	401	M.B.Loye/D.Ripley	v	Glamorgan	Northampton	1998
6th	376	R.Subba Row/A.Lightfoot	v	Surrey	The Oval	1958
7th	293	D.J.G.Sales/D.Ripley	v	Essex	Northampton	1999
8th	164	D.Ripley/N.G.B.Cook	v	Lancashire	Manchester	1987
9th	156	R.Subba Row/S.Starkie	v	Lancashire	Northampton	1955
10th	148	B.W.Bellamy/J.V.Murdin	v	Glamorgan	Northampton	1925

Best Bowling	For	10-127	V.W.C.Jupp	v	Kent	Tunbridge W	1932
(Innings)	V	10- 30	C.Blythe	for	Kent	Northampton	1907
Best Bowling	For	15- 31	G.E.Tribe	v	Yorkshire	Northampton	1958
(Match)	V	17- 48	C.Blythe	for	Kent	Northampton	1907

Most Runs – Season	2198	D.Brookes	(av 51.11)		1952
Most Runs – Career	28980	D.Brookes	(av 36.13)		1934-59
Most 100s – Season	8	R.A.Haywood			1921
Most 100s – Career	67	D.Brookes			1934-59
Most Wkts – Season	175	G.E.Tribe	(av 18.70)		1955
Most Wkts – Career	1102	E.W.Clark	(av 21.26)		1922-47
Most Career W-K Dismissals	810	K.V.Andrew	(653 ct; 157 st)		1953-66
Most Career Catches in the Field	469	D.S.Steele			1963-84

LIMITED-OVERS CRICKET

Highest Total	50ov	360-2		v	Staffs	Northampton	1990
	40ov	319-7		v	Scotland	Northampton	2003
	T20	224-5		v	Glos	Milton Keynes	2005
Lowest Total	50ov	62		v	Leics	Leicester	1974
	40ov	41		v	Middlesex	Northampton	1972
	T20	88		v	Lancashire	Manchester	2010
Highest Innings	50ov	161	D.J.G.Sales	v	Yorkshire	Northampton	2006
	40ov	172*	W.Larkins	v	Warwicks	Luton	1983
	T20	111*	L.Klusener	v	Worcs	Kidderminster	2007
Best Bowling	50ov	7-10	C.Pietersen	v	Denmark	Brondby	2005
	40ov	7-39	A.Hodgson	v	Somerset	Northampton	1976
	T20	6-21	A.J.Hall	v	Worcs	Northampton	2008

NOTTINGHAMSHIRE

Formation of Present Club: March/April 1841
Substantial Reorganisation: 11 December 1866
Inaugural First-Class Match: 1864
Colours: Green and Gold
Badge: Badge of City of Nottingham
County Champions (since 1890): (6) 1907, 1929, 1981, 1987, 2005, 2010
Gillette/NatWest/C&G/FP Trophy Winners: (1) 1987
Benson and Hedges Cup Winners: (1) 1989
Pro 40/National League (Div 1) Winners: (0); best – 2nd 2007
Sunday League Winners: (1) 1991
Clydesdale Bank 40 Winners: (0); best – 3rd Group C 2010
Twenty20 Cup Winners: (0); best – Finalist 2006

Chief Executive: Derek Brewer, Trent Bridge, Nottingham NG2 6AG • Tel: 0115 982 3000 • Fax: 0115 945 5730 • Email: administration@nottsccc.co.uk • Webs: www.nottsccc.co.uk • www.trentbridge.co.uk

Director of Cricket: Mick Newell. **Club Coach:** Paul Johnson. **Captain:** C.M.W.Read.
Vice-Captain: P.J.Franks. **Overseas Players:** D.J.Hussey and A.C.Voges. **2011 Beneficiary:** none. **Head Groundsman:** Steve Birks. **Scorer:** L. Brian Hewes. ‡ New registration. NQ Not qualified for England.

NQ**ADAMS, Andre** Ryan (Westlake BHS, Auckland), b Mangere, Auckland, New Zealand 17 Jul 1975. 5'9". RHB, RMF. Auckland 1997-98 to date. Essex 2004-06, scoring 124 on debut (*see below*); cap 2004. Nottinghamshire debut/cap 2007 (Kolpak registration). Herefordshire 2001. **Tests** (NZ): 1 (2001-02); HS 11 and BB 3-44 v E (Auckland) 2001-02. **LOI** (NZ): 42 (2000-01 to 2006-07); HS 45 v P (Rawalpindi) 2001-02; BB 5-22 v I (Queenstown) 2002-03. **IT20** (NZ): 4 (2004-05 to 2005-06); HS 7 v A (Auckland) 2004-05; BB 2-20 v SL (Auckland) 2006-07. HS 124 Ex v Leics (Leicester) 2004 (91 balls, 7 sixes, 13 fours; 100 off 80 balls) on UK debut. Nt HS 84 v Yorks (Scarborough) 2009. BB 6-25 Auckland v Wellington. UK BB 6-79 v Lancs (Nottingham) 2010. Hat-trick Ex v Somerset (Taunton) 2005. LO HS 90* North Is Selection XI v Sri Lankans (New Plymouth) 2000-01. LO BB 5-7 Auckland v ND (Auckland) 1999-00. T20 HS 54*. T20 BB 5-20.

BALL, Jacob Timothy ('**Jake**') (Meden CS), b Mansfield 14 Mar 1991. 6'0". RHB, RM. Nephew of B.N.French (Notts and England 1976-95). Nottinghamshire 2nd XI debut 2008. England U19s 2010. Awaiting f-c debut. LO HS 6 and BB 3-32 v Leics (Nottingham) 2010 (CB40).

BROAD, Stuart Christopher John (Oakham S), b Nottingham 24 Jun 1986. 6'5". LHB, RFM. Son of B.C.Broad (Glos, Notts, OFS and England 1979-94). Debut (Leicestershire) 2005; cap 2007. Nottinghamshire debut 2008. YC 2006. *Wisden* 2009. ECB central contract 2010-11. **Tests:** 34 (2007-08 to 2010-11); HS 169 v P (Lord's) 2010, sharing in record Test and UK f-c 8th-wkt partnership of 332 with I.J.L.Trott. BB 6-91 v A (Leeds) 2009. **LOI:** 73 (2006 to 2010); HS 45* v I (Manchester) 2007; BB 5-23 v SA (Nottingham) 2008. **IT20:** 29 (2006 to 2010); HS 10* v WI (Oval) 2009; BB 3-17 v P (Oval) 2009. F-c Tours: A 2010-11; SA 2009-10; WI 2005-06 (Eng A), 2008-09; NZ 2007-08; I 2008-09; SL 2007-08; B 2006-07 (Eng A), 2009-10. HS 169 (*see Tests*). CC HS 91* Le v Derbys (Leicester) 2007. Nt HS 60 v Worcs (Nottingham) 2009. BB 8-52 (11-131 match) v Warwks (Birmingham) 2010. LO HS 45* (*see LOI*). LO BB 5-23 (*see LOI*). T20 HS 10*. T20 BB 3-13.

BROWN, Alistair Duncan (Caterham S), b Beckenham, Kent 11 Feb 1970. 5'10". RHB, OB, occ WK. Surrey 1992-2008; cap 1994; benefit 2002. TCCB XI 1996. Walter Lawrence Trophy for fastest f-c hundred 1998. Nottinghamshire debut/cap 2009. **LOI:** 16 (1996 to 2001); HS 118 v I (Manchester) 1996. 1000 runs (8); most – 1382 (1993). HS 295* Sy v Leics (Oakham) 2000 – record score (all levels) in Rutland. Nt HS 148 v Hants (Southampton) 2009. BB 3-25 Sy v Somerset (Guildford) 2006. Nt BB 1-16 v Yorks (Nottingham) 2009. LO HS 268 Sy v Glamorgan (Oval) 2002 (CGT) – world record 1-o score (160 balls, 12 sixes, 30 fours). LO BB 3-39 Sy v Notts (Nottingham) 2000 (NL). T20 HS 83.

CARTER, Andrew (Lincoln C), b Lincoln 27 Aug 1988. RHB, RMF. Debut (Nottinghamshire) 2009. Essex 2010 (on loan). Nottinghamshire 2nd XI debut 2006. Lincolnshire 2007-10. HS 16* and BB 5-40 Ex v Kent (Canterbury) 2010. Nt HS 14 v Worcs (Worcester) 2009. Nt BB 1-27 v Oxford UCCE (Oxford) 2009. LO HS 12 v Sussex (Hove) 2009 (P40). LO BB 3-32 v Essex (Southend) 2009 (P40). T20 BB – .

EDWARDS, Neil James (Cape Cornwall CS; Richard Huish C), b Treliske, Truro, Cornwall 14 Oct 1983. 6'3". LHB, RM. Somerset 2002-08. Nottinghamshire debut 2010. Cornwall 2000-06. 1000 runs (1): 1251 (2007). HS 212 Sm v Loughborough UCCE (Taunton) 2007. CC HS 160 Sm v Hants (Taunton) 2003. Nt HS 85 v Kent (Nottingham) 2010. BB 1-16 Sm v Derbys (Taunton) 2004. LO HS 65 Sm v Yorks (Taunton) 2006 (P40). T20 HS 1.

ELSTONE, Scott Liam (Friary Grange C), b Burton-on-Trent, Staffs 10 Jun 1990. 5'8". RHB, OB. Awaiting f-c debut. Nottinghamshire 2nd XI debut 2006, aged 16 years and 81 days. LO HS 30 v Durham (Nottingham) 2010 (CB40). LO BB 1-22 v Scotland (Nottingham) 2010 (CB40).

FLETCHER, Luke Jack (Henry Mellish S, Nottingham), b Nottingham 18 Sep 1988. 6'6". RHB, RMF. Debut (Nottinghamshire) 2008. Nottinghamshire 2nd XI debut 2007. HS 92 v Hants (Southampton) 2009. BB 4-38 v Somerset (Nottingham) 2009. LO HS 40* v Durham (Chester-le-St) 2009 (P40). LO BB 2-35 v Worcs (Nottingham) 2009 (FPT). T20 HS 1*. T20 BB 2-23.

FRANKS, Paul John (Southwell Minster CS), b Mansfield 3 Feb 1979. 6'2". LHB, RMF. Debut (Nottinghamshire) 1996; cap 1999; benefit 2007. Canterbury 2002-03. MWR 2010-11. YC 2000. **LOI:** 1 (2000); HS 4 v WI (Nottingham) 2000. F-c Tours (Eng A): SA 1998-99; WI 2000-01; NZ 1999-00; SL 2004-05; B 1999-00. HS 123* v Leics (Leicester) 2003. 50 wkts (2); most – 63 (1999). BB 7-56 v Middx (Lord's) 2000. Hat-trick v Warwks (Nottingham) 1997. LO HS 84* v Lincs (Lincoln) 2003 (CGT). LO BB 6-27 v Durham (Chester-le-St) 2000 (NL). T20 HS 29*. T20 BB 2-12.

HALES, Alexander Daniel (Chesham S), b Hillingdon, Middx 3 Jan 1989. 6'5". RHB, RM, occ WK. Debut (Nottinghamshire) 2008. Nottinghamshire 2nd XI debut 2007. Buckinghamshire 2006-07. MCC YCs 2006-07. England U19s 2008. HS 136 v Hants (Nottingham) 2010. BB 2-63 v Yorks (Nottingham) 2009. LO HS 150* v Worcs (Nottingham) 2009 (P40). T20 HS 83.

NQHUSSEY, David John (Prendiville Catholic C; Edith Cowan U), b Morley, Perth, Australia 15 Jul 1977. Younger brother of M.E.K.Hussey (WA, Northants, Glos, Durham and Australia 1994-95 to date). 5'11". RHB, OB. Victoria 2002-03 to date. Nottinghamshire debut/cap 2004, scoring 107* v Oxford UCCE (Oxford) – UK debut. Sussex CB (List A) 2001. **LOI** (A): 30 (2008 to 2010-11); HS 111 v Scotland (Edinburgh) 2009; BB 4-21 v E (Adelaide) 2010-11. **IT20** (A): (2007-08 to 2010-11); HS 88* v SA (Johannesburg) 2008-09; BB 3-25 v SA (Melbourne) 2008-09. F-c Tour (Aus A): P 2007-08. 1000 runs (4+1); most – 1315 (2004). HS 275 v Essex (Nottingham) 2007. Scored 170, 116 and 140 in successive innings 2004. BB 4-105 v Hants (Nottingham) 2005. LO HS 130 Vic v Q (Brisbane) 2005-06. LO BB 4-21 (*see LOI*). T20 HS 100*. T20 BB 3-25.

MULLANEY, Steven John (St Mary's RC S, Astley), b Warrington, Cheshire 19 Nov 1986. 5'9". RHB, RM. Lancashire 2006-08. No f-c appearances in 2009. Nottinghamshire debut 2010, scoring 100* v Hants (Southampton). HS 165* La v Durham UCCE (Durham) 2007. Nt HS (*see above*). LO HS 41 v Leics (Leicester) 2010 (CB40). LO BB 3-13 La v Derbys (Derby) 2007 (FPT). T20 HS 53. T20 BB 3-12.

PATEL, Akhil (Kimberley CS, Nottingham), b Nottingham 18 Jun 1990. Younger brother of S.R.Patel (*below*). 5'10". LHB, SLC. Derbyshire 2007. Nottinghamshire debut 2009, scoring 69* v Oxford UCCE (Oxford). CC HS 37 v Sussex (Nottingham) 2009. BB 1-34 v Oxford UCCE (Oxford) 2009. LO HS 41 v Glos (Nottingham) 2009 (P40). LO BB 2-34 v Hants (Southampton) 2009 (P40).

PATEL, Samit Rohit (Worksop C), b Leicester 30 Nov 1984. 5'8". Elder brother of A.Patel (*above*). RHB, SLA. Debut (Nottingham) 2002; cap 2008. Nottinghamshire 2nd XI debut 1999, aged 14 years 274 days. **LOI**: 11 (2008 to 2008-09); HS 31 and BB 5-41 v SA (Oval) 2008. F-c Tour (EL): NZ 2008-09. HS 176 v Glos (Nottingham) 2007. BB 6-84 (9-124 match) v Sussex (Nottingham) 2009. LO HS 114 v Durham (Chester-le-St) 2008 (FPT). LO BB 6-13 v Ireland (Dublin) 2009 (FPT). T20 HS 84*. T20 BB 3-11.

PATTINSON, Darren John, b Grimsby, Lincs 2 Aug 1979. Elder brother of J.L.Pattinson (Victoria 2008-09 to date). RHB, RFM. Victoria 2006-07 to date. Nottinghamshire debut 2008 taking 5-22 (8-85 match) v Kent (Canterbury); cap 2008. **Tests**: 1 (2008); HS 13 and BB 2-95 v SA (Leeds) 2008. HS 59 v Durham (Chester-le-St) 2009. BB 8-35 Vic v WA (Perth) 2010-11. Nt BB 6-30 v Lancs (Nottingham) 2008. LO HS 13* v Lancs (Nottingham) 2008. LO BB 4-29 v Warwks (Nottingham) 2008. T20 HS 5. T20 BB 4-19.

‡PHILLIPS, Ben James (Langley Park S and SFC, Beckenham), b Lewisham, London 30 Sep 1974. 6'6". RHB, RFM. Kent 1996-98. Northamptonshire 2002-06; cap 2005. Somerset 2008-10, having joined staff in 2007 but missed entire season through injury. HS 100* K v Lancs (Manchester) 1997. BB 6-29 Nh v Cambridge UCCE (Cambridge) 2006. CC BB 5-47 K v Sussex (Horsham) 1997. LO HS 51* Sm v Worcs (Bath) 2010 (CB40). LO BB 4-25 K v Northants (Canterbury) 2000 (NL). T20 HS 41*. T20 BB 4-18.

READ, Christopher Mark Wells (Torquay GS; Bath U), b Paignton, Devon 10 Aug 1978. 5'8". RHB, WK. Gloucestershire (l-o only) 1997. Debut 1997-98 for England A in Kenya. Nottinghamshire debut 1998; cap 1999; captain 2008 to date; benefit 2009. MCC 2002. Devon 1995-97. **Tests**: 15 (1999 to 2006-07); HS 55 v P (Leeds) 2006. Made six dismissals twice in successive innings 2006-07 to establish an Ashes record. **LOI**: 36 (1999-00 to 2006-07); HS 30* v SA (Manchester) 2003. **IT20**: 1 (2006); HS 13 v P (Bristol) 2006. F-c Tours: A 2006-07; SA 1998-99 (Eng A), 1999-00; WI 2000-01 (Eng A), 2003-04, 2005-06 (Eng A); SL 1997-98 (Eng A), 2002-03 (ECB Acad), 2003-04; Z 1998-99 (Eng A); B 2003-04; K 1997-98 (Eng A). 1000 runs (2); most – 1203 (2009). HS 240 v Essex (Chelmsford) 2007. BB – . LO HS 135 v Durham (Nottingham) 2006 (CGT). T20 HS 58*.

SHRECK, Charles Edward (Truro S), b Truro, Cornwall 6 Jan 1978. 6'7". RHB, RFM. Debut (Nottinghamshire) 2003; cap 2006. Wellington 2005-06 to 2007-08. MCC 2008. Cornwall 1997-2002. HS 19 v Essex (Chelmsford) 2003. 50 wkts (2); most – 61 (2006, 2008). BB 8-31 (12-129 match) v Middx (Nottingham) 2006. Hat-trick v Middx (Lord's) 2006. LO HS 9* Wellington v CD (Palmerston N) 2005-06. LO BB 5-19 Cornwall v Worcs (Truro) 2002 (CGT). Took 5-35 v Worcs (Nottingham) 2002 (NL) – on 1st XI debut. T20 HS 6*. T20 BB 4-22.

SWANN, Graeme Peter (Sponne S, Towcester), b Northampton 24 Mar 1979. Son of R.Swann (Northumberland 1969-72; Bedfordshire 1988-95); younger brother of A.J.Swann (Northamptonshire and Lancashire 1996-2004). 6'0". RHB, OB. Northamptonshire 1998-2004; cap 1999. Nottinghamshire debut/cap 2005. MCC 2005. Bedfordshire 1996. *Wisden* 2009. **ECB central contract 2010-11. Tests:** 29 (2008-09 to 2010-11); HS 85 v SA (Centurion) 2009-10. BB 6-65 v P (Birmingham) 2010. **LOI:** 44 (1999-00 to 2010-11); HS 34 v SL (Dambulla) 2007-08; BB 5-28 v A (Chester-le-St) 2009. **IT20:** 22 (2007-08 to 2010-11); HS 15* v NZ (Auckland) 2007-08; BB 3-14 v P (Dubai) 2009-10. F-c Tours: A 2010-11; SA 1998-99 (Eng A), 1999-00, 2009-10; WI 2000-01 (Eng A *part*), 2008-09; I 2008-09; SL 2004-05 (Eng A); Z 1998-99 (Eng A); B 2009-10. HS 183 Nh v Glos (Bristol) 2002 – including 114 before lunch on third day. Nt HS 97 v Essex (Chelmsford) 2007. 50 wkts (1): 57 (1999). BB 7-33 Nh v Derbys (Northampton) 2003. Nt BB 7-100 v Glamorgan (Swansea) 2007. LO HS 83 Nh v Leics (Northampton) 2001 (NL). LO BB 5-17 v Glos (Nottingham) 2007 (P40). T20 HS 90*. T20 BB 3-14.

[NQ]**VOGES, Adam** Charles (Edith Cowan U, Perth), b Perth, Australia 4 Oct 1979. 6'0". RHB, SLC. WA 2002-03 to date. Hampshire (l-o) 2007. Nottinghamshire debut/cap 2008. **LOI** (A): 15 (2006-07 to 2010-11); HS 80* v E (Perth) 2010-11. BB 1-22 v I (Vadodara) 2009-10. **IT20** (A): 4 (2007-08 to 2009); HS 26 v NZ (Perth) 2007-08 and 26 v NZ (Sydney) 2007-08; BB 2-5 v I (Melbourne) 2007-08. F-c Tours (Aus A): I 2008-09; P 2007-08. HS 180 WA v Tas (Hobart) 2007-08. Nt HS 139 v Sussex (Horsham) 2009. BB 4-92 WA v S Aus (Adelaide) 2006-07. Nt BB 3-21 v Durham (Nottingham) 2008. LO HS 104* WA v S Aus (Adelaide) 2008-09. LO BB 3-25 v Sussex (Hove) 2009 (P40). T20 HS 82*. T20 BB 2-4.

WAGH, Mark Anant (King Edward's S, Birmingham; Keble C, Oxford), b Birmingham, Warwks 20 Oct 1976. 6'2". RHB, OB. Oxford U 1996-98; blue 1996-97-98; captain 1997. Warwickshire 1997-2006; cap 2000. British U 1996-1998. Mashonaland A 1998-99. Nottinghamshire debut/cap 2007. 1000 runs (6); most – 1310 (2007). HS 315 Wa v Middx (Lord's) 2001. Nt HS 152 v Northants (Northampton) 2007. BB 7-222 Wa v Lancs (Birmingham) 2003. Nt BB 2-6 v Somerset (Taunton) 2007. LO HS 102* Wa v Kent (Birmingham) 2004 (NL). LO BB 4-35 Wa v Glamorgan (Birmingham) 2004 (NL). T20 HS 56. T20 BB 2-16.

WHITE, Graeme Geoffrey (Stowe S), b Milton Keynes, Bucks 18 Apr 1987. 5'11". RHB, SLA. Nottinghamshire 2006-09. Nottinghamshire debut 2010. HS 65 and CC BB 1-18 Nh v Glamorgan (Colwyn Bay) 2007. Nt HS 29 and Nt BB 1-104 v Kent (Tunbridge W) 2010. BB 2-35 Nh v Cambridge UCCE (Cambridge) 2007. LO HS 14 Nh v Middx (Southgate) 2007 (P40). LO BB 5-35 v Scotland (Edinburgh) 2010 (CB40). T20 HS 26*. T20 BB 3-22.

NQ**AMLA, Hashim** Mohamed, b Durban, South Africa 31 Mar 1983. Younger brother of A.M.Amla (Natal B, KwaZulu-Natal, Dolphins 1997-98 to date). RHB, RM/OB. KwaZulu-Natal 1999-00 to 2003-04. Dolphins 2004-05 to date. Essex 2009. Nottinghamshire 2010; cap 2010. **Tests** (SA): 51 (2004-05 to 2010-11); HS 253* v I (Nagpur) 2009-10; BB – . **LOI** (SA): 42 (2007-08 to 2010-11); HS 140 v B (Benoni) 2008-09. **IT20** (SA): 3 (2008-09 to 2010-11); HS 26 v A (Brisbane) 2008-09. F-c Tours (SA): E 2008; A 2008-09; WI 2010; I 2004-05, 2007-08 (SA A), 2007-08, 2009-10; P 2007-08; SL 2005-06 (SA A), 2006; Z 2004 (SA A), 2007 (SA A); B 2007-08; UAE 2010-11 (v P). HS 253* (*see Tests*). CC HS 181 Ex v Glamorgan (Chelmsford) 2009 – on debut. Nt HS 129 v Kent (Nottingham) 2010. BB 1-10 SA A v India A (Kimberley) 2001-02. LO HS 140 (*see LOIs*). T20 HS 57.

SHAFAYAT, Bilal Mustapha (Greenwood Dale; Nottingham Bluecoat SFC), b Nottingham 10 Jul 1984. 5'7". RHB, RMF. Nottinghamshire 2001-04, 2007-10. National Bank of Pakistan 2004-05. Northamptonshire 2005-06. Pakistan Customs 2007-08 to 2008-09. Habib Bank 2010-11. Captained Eng U19 tour of Australia 2002-03. F-c Tour (Eng A): I 2003-04. 1000 runs (1): 1058 (2005). HS 161 Nh v Derbys (Derby) 2005. Nt HS 159 v Durham MCCU (Durham) 2010. BB 2-25 Nh v P (Northampton) 2006. Nt BB 1-22 v Durham UCCE (Nottingham) 2003. CC BB 1-24 v Essex (Chelmsford) 2007. LO HS 104 v Northants (Northampton) 2007 (FPT). LO BB 4-33 Nh v Worcs (Worcester) 2005 (NL). T20 HS 40. T20 BB 2-13.

SIDEBOTTOM, R.J. – *see YORKSHIRE.*

WOOD, Matthew James (Exmouth Community C; Exeter U), b Exeter, Devon 30 Sep 1980. 5'11". RHB, OB. Somerset 2001-07; cap 2005. Nottinghamshire 2008-10. MCC 2007. Devon 1998-2004. 1000 (1): 1058 (2005). HS 297 Sm v Yorks (Taunton) 2005. Nt HS 98 v Sussex (Hove) 2008. LO HS 129 Sm v Yorks (Taunton) 2005 (NL). T20 HS 94.

D.P.Nannes left the staff without making a County First-Class or List A appearance in 2010.

NOTTINGHAMSHIRE 2010

RESULTS SUMMARY

	Place	Won	Lost	Tied	Drew	NR
LV= County Championship (1st Division)	1st	7	5		4	
All First-Class Matches		7	5		5	
Clydesdale Bank 40 (Group C)	3rd	7	4			1
Friends Provident t20 (North Group)	SF	11	5	2		

LV= COUNTY CHAMPIONSHIP AVERAGES

BATTING AND FIELDING

Cap		M	I	NO	HS	Runs	Avge	100	50	Ct/St
2010	H.M.Amla	4	6	1	129	377	75.40	1	4	1
2004	D.J.Hussey	5	7	1	251*	399	66.50	1		7
2008	A.C.Voges	3	5	–	126	254	50.80	1	1	1
1999	C.M.W.Read	16	24	4	124*	916	45.80	2	5	59/4
	S.J.Mullaney	11	17	4	100*	512	39.38	1	3	6
2007	M.A.Wagh	15	23	1	139	853	38.77	2	3	8
	A.D.Hales	12	20	1	136	677	35.63	1	4	12
2009	A.D.Brown	16	24	1	134	805	35.00	1	6	11
1999	P.J.Franks	15	21	1	79	651	32.55	–	6	1
2008	S.R.Patel	16	26	2	104	641	26.70	1	3	9
	M.J.Wood	4	6	–	72	148	24.66	–	2	1
	N.J.Edwards	6	9	–	85	189	21.00	–	1	15
	L.J.Fletcher	5	8	3	23*	81	16.20	–	–	2
2007	A.R.Adams	14	20	5	37	240	16.00	–	–	13
	B.M.Shafayat	6	10	–	49	118	11.80	–	–	4
2008	D.J.Pattinson	12	13	4	27	93	10.33	–	–	4
2006	C.E.Shreck	5	7	1	7*	10	1.66	–	–	4
2004	R.J.Sidebottom	6	8	6	18*	44	–	–	–	3

Also batted: S.C.J.Broad (2 matches) 1, 6, 0; G.P.Swann (1 – cap 2005) 1; G.G.White (1) 29 (1 ct).

BOWLING

	O	M	R	W	Avge	Best	5wI	10wM
S.C.J.Broad	66	7	299	19	15.72	8-52	2	1
R.J.Sidebottom	218	58	582	27	21.55	5-35	1	–
A.R.Adams	455.5	101	1508	68	22.17	6-79	4	–
P.J.Franks	386.2	102	1046	41	25.51	3-15	–	–
C.E.Shreck	199	50	577	18	32.05	4-81	–	–
D.J.Pattinson	294.2	49	1128	31	36.38	5-95	1	–
S.R.Patel	311.3	64	954	24	39.75	4-55	–	–
Also bowled:								
S.J.Mullaney	93.4	19	321	9	35.66	4-31	–	–
L.J.Fletcher	144.2	31	508	9	56.44	3-43	–	–

A.D.Brown 7-0-53-0; A.D.Hales 5.5-1-26-0; D.J.Hussey 18-1-82-0; G.P.Swann 26-5-88-2; A.C.Voges 1-0-2-0; G.G.White 23-3-104-1; M.J.Wood 1-0-11-0.

The First-Class Averages (pp 220–237) give the records of Nottinghamshire players in all first-class county matches (Nottinghamshire's other opponents being Durham MCCU), with the exception of S.C.J.Broad and G.P.Swann, whose first-class figures for Nottinghamshire are as above.

NOTTINGHAMSHIRE RECORDS

FIRST-CLASS CRICKET

Highest Total	For 791		v	Essex	Chelmsford	2007
	V 781-7d		by	Northants	Northampton	1995
Lowest Total	For 13		v	Yorkshire	Nottingham	1901
	V 16		by	Derbyshire	Nottingham	1879
	16		by	Surrey	The Oval	1880
Highest Innings	For 312*	W.W.Keeton	v	Middlesex	The Oval	1939
	V 345	C.G.Macartney	for	Australians	Nottingham	1921

Highest Partnership for each Wicket

1st	406*	D.J.Bicknell/G.E.Welton	v	Warwicks	Birmingham	2000
2nd	398	A.Shrewsbury/W.Gunn	v	Sussex	Nottingham	1890
3rd	367	W.Gunn/J.R.Gunn	v	Leics	Nottingham	1903
4th	361	A.O.Jones/J.R.Gunn	v	Essex	Leyton	1905
5th	359	D.J.Hussey/C.M.W.Read	v	Essex	Nottingham	2007
6th	372*	K.P.Pietersen/J.E.Morris	v	Derbyshire	Derby	2001
7th	301	C.C.Lewis/B.N.French	v	Durham	Chester-le-St	1993
8th	220	G.F.H.Heane/R.Winrow	v	Somerset	Nottingham	1935
9th	170	J.C.Adams/K.P.Evans	v	Somerset	Taunton	1994
10th	152	E.B.Alletson/W.Riley	v	Sussex	Hove	1911
	152	U.Afzaal/A.J.Harris	v	Worcs	Nottingham	2000

Best Bowling	For 10-66	K.Smales	v	Glos	Stroud	1956
(Innings)	V 10-10	H.Verity	for	Yorkshire	Leeds	1932
Best Bowling	For 17-89	F.C.L.Matthews	v	Northants	Nottingham	1923
(Match)	V 17-89	W.G.Grace	for	Glos	Cheltenham	1877

Most Runs – Season	2620	W.W.Whysall	(av 53.46)	1929
Most Runs – Career	31592	G.Gunn	(av 35.69)	1902-32
Most 100s – Season	9	W.W.Whysall		1928
	9	M.J.Harris		1971
	9	B.C.Broad		1990
Most 100s – Career	65	J.Hardstaff jr		1930-55
Most Wkts – Season	181	B.Dooland	(av 14.96)	1954
Most Wkts – Career	1653	T.G.Wass	(av 20.34)	1896-1920
Most Career W-K Dismissals	957	T.W.Oates	(733 ct; 224 st)	1897-1925
Most Career Catches in the Field	466	A.O.Jones		1892-1914

LIMITED-OVERS CRICKET

Highest Total	50ov	346-9		v	Ireland	Nottingham	2009
	40ov	329-6		v	Derbyshire	Nottingham	1993
	T20	213-6		v	Northants	Nottingham	2006
Lowest Total	50ov	123		v	Yorkshire	Scarborough	1969
	40ov	57		v	Glos	Nottingham	2009
	T20	91		v	Lancashire	Manchester	2006
Highest Innings	50ov	149*	D.W.Randall	v	Devon	Torquay	1988
	40ov	167*	P.Johnson	v	Kent	Nottingham	1993
	T20	91	M.A.Ealham	v	Yorkshire	Nottingham	2004
Best Bowling	50ov	6-10	K.P.Evans	v	Northumb	Jesmond	1994
	40ov	6-12	R.J.Hadlee	v	Lancashire	Nottingham	1980
	T20	5-26	R.J.Logan	v	Lancashire	Nottingham	2003

SOMERSET

Formation of Present Club: 18 August 1875
Inaugural First-Class Match: 1882
Colours: Black, White and Maroon
Badge: Somerset Dragon
County Champions: (0); best – 2nd (Div 1) 2001, 2010
Gillette/NatWest/C&G/FP Trophy Winners: (3) 1979, 1983, 2001
Benson and Hedges Cup Winners: (2) 1981, 1982
Pro 40/National League (Div 1) Winners: (0); best – 4th 2001
Sunday League Winners: (1) 1979
Clydesdale Bank 40 Winners: (0); best – Finalists 2010
Twenty20 Cup Winners: (1) 2005

Chief Executive: tba, County Ground, Taunton TA1 1JT • Tel: 0845 337 1875 • Fax: 01823 332395 • Email: enquiries@somersetcountycc.co.uk • Web: www.somersetcricketclub.co.uk

Director of Cricket: Brian C.Rose. **Head Coach:** Andy Hurry. **Captain:** M.E.Trescothick. **Vice-Captain:** A.C.Thomas. **Overseas Players:** M.Kartik, B.A.W.Mendis and K.A.Pollard. **2011 Beneficiary:** none. **Scorer:** Gerald A.Stickley. ‡ New registration. ^{NQ} Not qualified for England.

BARROW, Alexander William Rodgerson (King's C, Taunton), b Frome 6 May 1992. 5'7". RHB, RM. Somerset 2nd XI debut 2009. Awaiting 1st XI debut.

BURKE, James Edward, b Plymouth, Devon 25 Jan 1991. RHB, RMF. Somerset 2nd XI debut 2008. Devon 2008-09. Awaiting 1st XI debut.

BUTTLER, Joseph Charles (King's C, Taunton), b Taunton 8 Sep 1990. 6'0". RHB, WK. Debut (Somerset) 2009. Somerset 2nd XI debut 2006. HS 144 v Hants (Southampton) 2010. LO HS 90* v Glamorgan (Taunton) 2010 (CB40). T20 HS 55*.

COMPTON, Nicholas Richard Denis (Harrow S; Durham U), b Durban, South Africa 26 Jun 1983. 6'1". Son of R.Compton (Natal 1978-79 to 1980-81). Grandson of D.C.S.Compton (Middlesex, England, Holkar, Europeans, Commonwealth and Cavaliers 1936-64); great-nephew of L.H.Compton (Middlesex 1938-56). RHB, OB. Middlesex 2004-09; cap 2006. MCC 2007. Somerset debut 2010. ME 2010-11. F-c Tour (Eng A): B 2006-07. 1000 runs (1): 1315 (2006). HS 190 M v Durham (Lord's) 2006. Sm HS 72 v Essex (Taunton) 2010. BB 1-1 v Hants (Southampton) 2010. LO HS 131 M v Kent (Canterbury) 2009 (FPT). LO BB 1-0 M v Scotland (Lord's) 2009 (FPT). T20 HS 74.

DIBBLE, Adam John, b Exeter, Devon 9 Mar 1991. RHB, RMF. Somerset 2nd XI debut 2009. Devon 2009. Awaiting 1st XI debut.

GREGORY, Lewis (Hele's S, Plympton), b Plymouth, Devon 24 May 1992. 6'0". RHB, RMF. Somerset 2nd XI debut 2008, aged 16 years and 87 days. Devon 2008. England U19s 2010 to 2010-11. Awaiting f-c debut. LO HS 0 and LO BB 4-49 v Pakistanis (Taunton) 2010.

HAGGETT, Calum John (Millfield S), b Taunton 30 Oct 1990. LHB, RM. Somerset 2nd XI debut 2009. England U19s 2009-10. Awaiting f-c and l-o debut. T20 HS 2. T20 BB 1-15.

HILDRETH James Charles (Millfield S), b Milton Keynes, Bucks 9 Sep 1984. 5'10". RHB, RMF. Debut (Somerset) 2003; cap 2007. F-c Tour (EL): WI 2010-11. 1000 runs (5); most – 1440 (2010). HS 303* v Warwks (Taunton) 2009. BB 2-39 v Hants (Taunton) 2004. LO HS 151 v Scotland (Taunton) 2009 (FPT). LO BB 2-26 v Worcs (Worcester) 2008 (FPT). T20 HS 77*. T20 BB 3-24.

‡**HUSSAIN, Gemaal** Maqsood (Top Valley CS, Nottingham; High Pavement SFC, Nottingham), b Whipps Cross, London, 10 Oct 1983. 6'5". RHB, RMF. Gloucestershire 2001-02 to; cap 2009. Bradford/Leeds UCCE 2003. HS 28* Gs v Middx (Bristol) 2010. 50 wkts (1): 67 (2010). BB 5-36 (9-98 match) Gs v Northants (Bristol) 2010. LO HS- and BB 2-17 v Notts (Nottingham) 2009 (P40). T20 HS 8. T20 BB 3-22.

JONES, Chris Robert, b Harold Wood, Essex 5 Nov 1990. RHB. Debut (Somerset) 2010, without batting or bowling. Somerset 2nd XI debut 2006. Dorset 2008-09.

NQ**KARTIK, Murali** (educated in New Delhi), b Madras, India 11 Sep 1976. 6'0". LHB, SLA. Railways 1996-97 to date. Central Zone 1997-98 to date. Lancashire 2005-06. Middlesex 2007-09; cap 2007. Somerset debut 2010. **Tests** (I): 8 (1999-00 to 2004-05); HS 43 v B (Dhaka) 2000-01; BB 4-44 v A (Bombay) 2004-05. **LOI** (I): 14 (2001-02 to 2007-08); HS 32* v A (Perth) 2003-04; BB 6-27 v A (Bombay) 2007-08. **IT20** (I): 1 (2007-08); HS and BB- v P (Jaipur) 2007-08. F-c Tours (I A): E 2003; A 2003-04 (I); SA 2001-02; WI 1999-00, 2002-03; P 1997-98; SL 2002; B 2000-01 (I). HS 96 Railways v Rest of India (Delhi) 2005-06. CC HS 62* M v Essex (Chelmsford) 2009. Sm HS 52* v Essex (Colchester) 2010 and v Lancs (Taunton) 2010. 50 wkts (1): 51 (2007). BB 9-70 Rest of India v Bombay (Bombay) 2000-01. CC BB 6-21 M v Glamorgan (Lord's) 2007. Sm BB 6-42 (11-72 match) v Warwks (Birmingham) 2010. LO HS 44 Railways v Rajasthan (Indore) 2008-09. LO BB 6-27 (see LOI). T20 HS 28. T20 BB 5-13 M v Essex (Lord's) 2007 – M record.

KIESWETTER, Craig (Diocesan C; Millfield S), b Johannesburg, South Africa 18 Nov 1987. 6'1". RHB, WK. Debut (Somerset) 2007; cap 2009. Represented South Africa in U19 World Cup 2006. Qualified for England Feb 2010. **LOI**: 12 (2009-10 to 2010); HS 107 v B (Chittagong) 2009-10. **IT20**: 9 (2009-10 to 2010); HS 63 v A (Bridgetown) 2009-10. F-c Tour (EL): WI 2010-11. 1000 runs (1): 1242 (2009). HS 153 v Lancs (Taunton) 2010. LO HS 143 England XI v Bangladesh CB (Fatullah) 2009-10. T20 HS 84.

‡**KIRBY, Steven** Paul (Elton HS; Bury C), b Ainsworth, nr Bolton, Lancs 4 Oct 1977. 6'3½". RHB, RFM. Leicestershire staff 1998 – no f-c appearances. Yorkshire 2001-04, debut as sub for M.J.Hoggard (England duty) taking 7-50; cap 2003. Gloucestershire 2005-10; cap 2005. MCC 2008, 2010. F-c Tour (Eng A): I 2003-04 (part). HS 57 Y v Hants (Leeds) 2002. 50 wkts (2); most – 67 (2003). BB 8-80 (13-154 match) Y v Somerset (Taunton) 2003. LO HS 15 Y v Leics (Leicester) 2003 (NL). LO BB 5-36 Gs v Middx (Lord's) 2007 (FPT). T20 HS 25. T20 BB 3-17.

‡NQ**MENDIS**, Balapuwaduge **Ajantha** Winslo, b Moratuwa, Sri Lanka, 11 March 1985. RHB, LBG. Sri Lanka Army 2006-07 to date. **Tests** (SL): 15 (2008 to 2010-11); HS 78 v I (Colombo, PSS) 2010; BB 6-117 (10-209 match) v I (Galle) 2008. **LOI** (SL): 46 (2007-08 to 2010-11); HS 15* v B (Lahore) 2008 and v UAE (Lahore) 2008; BB 6-13 v I (Karachi) 2008. **IT20** (SL): 19 (2008-09 to 2010); HS 4* v Ireland (Lord's) 2009; BB 4-15 v Z (King City) 2008-09. HS 78 (see Tests). BB 7-37 SL Army v Lankan (Panagoda) 2007-08. LO HS 71* SL Army v Kurunegala Youth (Welisara) 2006-07. LO BB 6-12 SL Army v Seeduwa Raddoluwa (Panagoda) 2010-11. T20 HS 15. T20 BB 4-9.

MESCHEDE, Craig Anthony Joseph, b South Africa 21 Nov 1991. RHB, RMF. Awaiting f-c and l-o debut. Somerset 2nd XI debut 2008. T20 HS 28*.

NQ**POLLARD, Kieron** Adrian, b Tacarigua, Trinidad 12 May 1987. RHB, RMF. Trinidad & Tobago 2006-07 to date, scoring 126 (inc 7 sixes) v Barbados on debut. Somerset (T20 only) 2010. **LOI** (WI): 32 (2006-07 to 2010-11); HS 62 v A (Brisbane) 2009-10; BB 3-27 v SA (Roseau) 2010. **IT20** (WI): 20 (2008 to 2010); HS 38 v NZ (Hamilton) 2008-09; BB 2-22 v SA (North Sound) 2010. HS 174 T&T v Barbados (Pointe-a-Pierre) 2008-09. BB 2-29 T&T v Jamaica (Nain) 2006-07. LO HS 87 T&T v Guyana (Port-of-Spain) 2006-07. LO BB 4-32 T&T v Jamaica (Kingston) 2006-07. T20 HS 89*. T20 BB 4-15 v Kent (Beckenham) 2010 – Sm joint record.

NQSUPPIAH, Arul Vivasvan (Exeter U), b Kuala Lumpur, Malaysia 30 Aug 1983. Son of R.Suppiah (Kuala Lumpur). Brother of R.V.Suppiah (Malaysia 1997-98 to 2006; f-c 2004). 6'0". RHB, SLA. Debut (Somerset) 2002; cap 2009. Malaysia 2000-01 to 2005 (not f-c). Devon 2003-05. 1000 runs (1): 1201 (2009). HS 151 v Notts (Taunton) 2009. BB 3-46 v WI A (Taunton) 2002. CC BB 3-58 v Hants (Taunton) 2009. LO HS 80 v Lancs (Manchester) 2010 (CB40). LO BB 4-39 v Surrey (Oval) 2006 (CGT). T20 HS 32*. T20 BB 3-25.

NQTHOMAS, Alfonso Clive (Ravensmead SS; Parow HS), b Cape Town, South Africa 9 Feb 1977. RHB, RFM. WP 1998-99. North West 2000-01 to 2002-03. Northerns 2003-04 to 2005-06. Titans 2004-05 to 2007-08. Warwickshire 2007. Somerset debut 2008; cap 2008 (Kolpak registration). **IT20** (SA): 1 (2006-07); HS- and BB 3-25 v P (Johannesburg) 2006-07. F-c Tour (SA A): Z 2004. HS 119* North West v Northerns (Pretoria) 2002-03. UK HS 70 v Hants (Taunton) 2009. BB 7-54 Titans v Cape Cobras (Cape Town) 2005-06. UK BB 5-40 v Notts (Taunton) 2010. LO HS 28* v Scotland (Edinburgh) 2009 (FPT). LO BB 4-18 v Glos (Bristol) 2009 (P40). T20 HS 30*. T20 BB 4-27.

TREGO, Peter David (Wyvern CS, W-s-M), b Weston-super-Mare 12 Jun 1981. 6'0". RHB, RMF. Somerset 2000-02, 2006 to date; cap 2007; 2nd XI debut 1997, aged 16 years 20 days. Kent 2003. Middlesex 2005. Herefordshire 2005. HS 140 v WI A (Taunton) 2002. CC HS 135 v Derbys (Taunton) 2006. BB 6-59 M v Notts (Nottingham) 2005. Sm BB 4-26 v Yorks (Leeds) 2010. LO HS 147 v Glamorgan (Taunton) 2010 (CB40) – tournament record. LO BB 5-40 EL v WI A (Worcester) 2010. T20 HS 79. T20 BB 2-17.

TRESCOTHICK, Marcus Edward (Sir Bernard Lovell S), b Keynsham 25 Dec 1975. 6'2". LHB, RM, occ WK. Debut (Somerset) 1993; cap 1999; joint captain 2002; benefit 2008; captain 2010 to date. PCA 2000, 2009. *Wisden* 2004. MBE 2005. **Tests**: 76 (2000 to 2006, 2 as captain); HS 219 v SA (Oval) 2003; BB 1-34 v P (Karachi) 2000-01. **LOI**: 123 (2000 to 2006, 10 as captain); HS 137 v P (Lord's) 2001; BB 2-7 v Z (Manchester) 2000. **IT20**: 3 (2005 to 2006); HS 72 v SL (Southampton) 2006. F-c Tours: A 2002-03; SA 2004-05; WI 2003-04; NZ 1999-00 (Eng A), 2001-02; I 2001-02, 2005-06 (*part*); P 2000-01, 2005-06; SL 2000-01, 2003-04; B 1999-00 (Eng A), 2003-04. 1000 runs (4); most – 1817 (2009). HS 284 v Northants (Northampton) 2007. BB 4-36 (inc hat-trick) v Young A (Taunton) 1995. CC BB 4-82 v Yorks (Leeds) 1998. Hat-trick 1995 (*see above*). LO HS 184 v Glos (Taunton) 2008 (P40) – Sm record. LO BB 4-50 v Northants (Northampton) 2000 (NL). T20 HS 107.

WALLER, Maximilian Thomas Charles (Millfield S; Bournemouth U), b Salisbury, Wiltshire 3 March 1988. 6'0". RHB, LB. Debut (Somerset) 2009. Somerset 2nd XI debut 2006. Dorset 2007-08. HS 28 v Hants (Southampton) 2009. BB 2-27 v Sussex (Hove) 2009. LO HS 5 v Lancs (Manchester) 2010 (CB40). LO BB 2-24 v Unicorns (Exmouth) 2010 (CB40). T20 HS 1*. T20 BB 3-16.

WILLOUGHBY, Charl Myles (Wynberg BHS; Stellenbosch U), b Cape Town, South Africa 3 Dec 1974. 6'2". LHB, LMF. Boland 1994-95 to 1999-00. WP 2000-01 to 2003-04. MCC 2001, 2004. WP-Boland 2004-05. Leicestershire 2005 (Kolpak). Cape Cobras 2005-06 to 2006-07. Somerset debut 2006; cap 2007. Qualifies as UK resident in 2011. Berkshire 2000. **Tests** (SA): 2 (2003); HS – ; BB 1-47 v B (Chittagong) 2002-03. **LOI** (SA): 3 (1999-00 to 2003); HS 0; BB 2-39 v P (Sharjah) 1999-00. F-c Tours (SA): E 2003; WI 2000 (SA A); Z 1998-99 (SA Acad), 2004 (SA A); B 2003. HS 47 v Worcs (Taunton) 2006. 50 wkts (5+2); most – 66 (2006). BB 7-44 v Glos (Taunton) 2006. LO HS 15 v Kent (Canterbury) 2009 (FPT). LO BB 6-16 Le v Somerset (Leicester) 2005 (CGT) – Le record. T20 HS 11. T20 BB 4-9.

RELEASED/RETIRED continued on p 178

SOMERSET 2010

RESULTS SUMMARY

	Place	Won	Lost	Tied	Drew	NR
LV= County Championship (1st Division)	2nd	7	5		4	
All First-Class Matches		7	5		4	
Clydesdale Bank 40 (Group A)	Finalist	11	3			
Friends Provident t20 (South Group)	Finalist	13	5			1

LV= COUNTY CHAMPIONSHIP AVERAGES

BATTING AND FIELDING

Cap		M	I	NO	HS	Runs	Avge	100	50	Ct/St
2007	J.C.Hildreth	16	23	1	151	1440	65.45	7	5	7
1999	M.E.Trescothick	16	28	4	228*	1397	58.20	4	6	26
2008	Z.de Bruyn	14	21	–	95	814	38.76	–	5	10
	D.A.Stiff	2	4	2	40	71	35.50	–	–	–
	D.G.Wright	5	7	–	78	236	33.71	–	2	4
2009	A.V.Suppiah	16	26	3	125	771	33.52	1	4	5
	J.C.Buttler	13	20	3	144	569	33.47	1	2	23
	N.R.D.Compton	11	17	3	72	465	33.21	–	2	5
2007	P.D.Trego	16	23	2	108	693	33.00	1	5	12
	M.Kartik	11	12	5	52*	199	28.42	–	2	9
2009	C.Kieswetter	12	18	1	84	467	27.47	–	4	29
2008	A.C.Thomas	15	20	4	44	328	20.50	–	–	1
	B.J.Phillips	11	15	3	55	179	14.91	–	1	5
2007	C.M.Willoughby	16	18	6	16	85	7.08	–	–	1

Also played: C.R.Jones (1 match) did not bat; M.K.Munday (3) 0, 0, 0* (1 ct).

BOWLING

	O	M	R	W	Avge	Best	5wI	10wM
M.Kartik	383.2	107	882	45	19.60	6- 42	5	2
B.J.Phillips	277.3	79	661	29	22.79	5- 72	1	–
A.C.Thomas	377.5	85	1202	49	24.53	5- 40	2	–
D.G.Wright	154.1	41	377	14	26.92	5- 41	1	–
C.M.Willoughby	512.1	118	1582	58	27.27	6-101	1	–
Z.de Bruyn	94.2	10	386	12	32.16	4- 23	–	–
P.D.Trego	227.1	50	729	22	33.13	4- 26	–	–

Also bowled:
M.K.Munday | 52.1 | 9 | 238 | 6 | 39.66 | 4-105 | – | –

N.R.D.Compton 14.2-0-87-2; J.C.Hildreth 13-0-95-1; D.A.Stiff 40.5-3-207-2; A.V.Suppiah 99-18-300-3.

Somerset played no fixtures outside the County Championship in 2010. The First-Class Averages (pp 220–237) give the records of their players in all first-class county matches.

SOMERSET RECORDS

FIRST-CLASS CRICKET

Highest Total	For 850-7d		v	Middlesex	Taunton	2007
	V 811		by	Surrey	The Oval	1899
Lowest Total	For 25		v	Glos	Bristol	1947
	V 22		by	Glos	Bristol	1920
Highest Innings	For 342	J.L.Langer	v	Surrey	Guildford	2006
	V 424	A.C.MacLaren	for	Lancashire	Taunton	1895

Highest Partnership for each Wicket

1st	346	L.C.H.Palairet/ H.T.Hewett	v	Yorkshire	Taunton	1892
2nd	290	J.C.W.MacBryan/M.D.Lyon	v	Derbyshire	Burton upon T	1924
3rd	319	P.M.Roebuck/M.D.Crowe	v	Leics	Taunton	1984
4th	310	P.W.Denning/I.T.Botham	v	Glos	Taunton	1980
5th	320	J.D.Francis/I.D.Blackwell	v	Durham UCCE	Taunton	2005
6th	265	W.E.Alley/K.E.Palmer	v	Northants	Northampton	1961
7th	279	R.J.Harden/G.D.Rose	v	Sussex	Taunton	1997
8th	172	I.V.A.Richards/I.T.Botham	v	Leics	Leicester	1983
	172	A.R.K.Pierson/P.S.Jones	v	N Zealanders	Taunton	1999
9th	183	C.H.M.Greetham/H.W.Stephenson	v	Leics	Weston-s-Mare	1963
	183	C.J.Tavaré/N.A.Mallender	v	Sussex	Hove	1990
10th	163	I.D.Blackwell/N.A.M.McLean	v	Derbyshire	Taunton	2003

Best Bowling	For 10- 49	E.J.Tyler	v	Surrey	Taunton	1895
(Innings)	V 10- 35	A.Drake	for	Yorkshire	Weston-s-Mare	1914
Best Bowling	For 16- 83	J.C.White	v	Worcs	Bath	1919
(Match)	V 17-137	W.Brearley	for	Lancashire	Manchester	1905

Most Runs – Season	2761	W.E.Alley	(av 58.74)	1961
Most Runs – Career	21142	H.Gimblett	(av 36.96)	1935-54
Most 100s – Season	11	S.J.Cook		1991
Most 100s – Career	49	H.Gimblett		1935-54
Most Wkts – Season	169	A.W.Wellard	(av 19.24)	1938
Most Wkts – Career	2165	J.C.White	(av 18.03)	1909-37
Most Career W-K Dismissals	1007	H.W.Stephenson	(698 ct; 309 st)	1948-64
Most Career Catches in the Field	381	J.C.White		1909-37

LIMITED-OVERS CRICKET

Highest Total	50ov	413-4	v	Devon	Torquay	1990
	40ov	377-9	v	Sussex	Hove	2003
	T20	250-3	v	Glos	Taunton	2006
Lowest Total	50ov	58	v	Middlesex	Southgate	2000
	40ov	58	v	Essex	Chelmsford	1977
	T20	82	v	Kent	Taunton	2010
Highest Innings	50ov	162*	C.J.Tavaré.	v Devon	Torquay	1990
	40ov	184	M.E.Trescothick	v Glos	Taunton	2008
	T20	141*	C.L.White	v Worcs	Worcester	2006
Best Bowling	50ov	8-66	S.R.G.Francis	v Derbyshire	Derby	2004
	40ov	6-24	I.V.A.Richards	v Lancashire	Manchester	1983
	T20	4-15	A.W.Laraman	v Worcs	Taunton	2004
		4-15	K.A.Pollard	v Kent	Beckenham	2010

SURREY

Formation of Present Club: 22 August 1845
Inaugural First-Class Match: 1864
Colours: Chocolate
Badge: Prince of Wales' Feathers

County Champions (since 1890): (18) 1890, 1891, 1892, 1894, 1895, 1899, 1914, 1952, 1953, 1954, 1955, 1956, 1957, 1958, 1971, 1999, 2000, 2002
Joint Champions: (1) 1950
Gillette/NatWest/C&G/FP Trophy Winners: (1) 1982
Benson and Hedges Cup Winners: (3) 1974, 1997, 2001
Pro 40/National League (Div 1) Winners: (1) 2003
Sunday League Winners: (1) 1996
Clydesdale Bank 40 Winners: (0); best – 3rd Group A 2010
Twenty20 Cup Winners: (1) 2003

Chief Executive: Richard A.Gould, The Kia Oval, London, SE11 5SS • Tel: 0871 246 1100 • Fax: 020 7820 5601 • E-mail: enquiries@surreyccc.com • Web: www.kiaoval.com

Cricket Manager: Chris Adams. **Assistant Coach:** Ian D.K.Salisbury. **Captain:** R.J.Hamilton-Brown. **Vice-Captain:** tba. **Overseas Players:** S.W.Tait (T20 only) and Yasir Arafat. **2011 Beneficiary:** none. **Head Groundsman:** Scott Patterson. **Scorer:** Keith R.Booth. ‡ New registration. ᴺᵠ Not qualified for England.

ANSARI, Zafar Shahaan (Hampton S; Cambridge U), b Ascot, Berks 10 Dec 1991. Younger brother of A.S.Ansari (Cambridge U 2008-10). 5'11". LHB, SLA. Surrey 2nd XI debut 2008. Awaiting f-c debut. Summer contract. LO HS 6 and LO BB 1-26 v Sussex (Hove) 2010 (CB40).

BATTY, Gareth Jon (Bingley GS), b Bradford, Yorks 13 Oct 1977. Younger brother of J.D.Batty (Yorkshire and Somerset 1989-96). 5'11". RHB, OB. Yorkshire 1997. Surrey 1999-2001, rejoined in 2010. Worcestershire 2002-09. **Tests:** 7 (2003-04 to 2005); HS 38 v SL (Kandy) 2003-04; BB 3-55 v SL (Galle) 2003-04. Took wicket with his third ball in Test cricket. **LOI:** 10 (2002-03 to 2008-09); HS 17 v WI (Bridgetown) 2008-09; BB 2-40 v WI (Gros Islet, St Lucia) 2003-04. **IT20:** 1 (2008-09); HS 4 v SL (Port-of-Spain) 2008-09. F-c **Tours:** WI 2003-04, 2005-06; NZ 2008-09 (EL); SL 2002-03 (ECB Acad); SL 2003-04; B 2003-04. HS 133 Wo v Surrey (Oval) 2004. Sy HS 67 v Cambridge MCCU (Cambridge) 2010. 50 wkts (2); most – 60 (2003). BB 7-52 (10-113 match) v Northants (Northampton) 2004. Sy BB 5-76 v Northants (Oval) 2010. LO HS 83* v Yorks (Oval) 2001 (NL). LO BB 5-35 Wo v Hants (Southampton) 2009 (FPT). T20 HS 87. T20 BB 4-23.

BROWN, Michael James (Queen Elizabeth GS, Blackburn; Collingwood C, Durham U), b Burnley, Lancs 9 Feb 1980. 6'0" Elder brother of D.O.Brown (*see GLAMORGAN*). RHB, OB. Middlesex 1999-2003. Durham U 2001-02. British U 2001-02. Hampshire 2004-08; cap 2007. Surrey debut 2009. 1000 runs (1): 1078 (2007). HS 133 Ha v Loughborough UCCE (Southampton) 2006. CC HS 126* Ha v Durham (Chester-le-St) 2007. Sy HS 120 v Derbys (Croydon) 2009. LO HS 96* Ha v Worcs (Southampton) 2008 (FPT). T20 HS 77.

BURNS, Rory Joseph (City of London Freemen's S), b Epsom 26 Aug 1990. LHB, WK. Surrey 2nd XI debut 2009. MCC Univs 2010. Hampshire 2nd XI 2010. Awaiting 1st XI debut.

DAVIES, Steven Michael (King Charles I S, Kidderminster), b Bromsgrove, Worcs 17 Jun 1986. 5'10". LHB, WK. Worcestershire 2005-09. Surrey debut 2010. Worcs 2nd XI debut 2001, aged 15 years 8 days. MCC 2006-07. **LOI**: 8 (2009-10 to 2010-11); HS 87 v P (Chester-le-St) 2010. **IT20**: 5 (2008-09 to 2010-11); HS 33 v P (Cardiff) 2010. F-c Tours: A 2010-11; B 2006-07 (Eng A). 1000 runs (3); most – 1090 (2010). HS 192 Wo v Glos (Bristol) 2006. Sy HS 137 v Worcs (Croydon) 2010. LO HS 119 Wo v Glos (Worcester) 2008 (P40). T20 HS 89.

‡**NQDE BRUYN, Zander** (Helpmekaar HS; Randburg HS; Rand Afrikaans U, Jo'burg), b Johannesburg, South Africa 5 Jul 1975. 6'0". RHB, RMF. Transvaal B 1995-96 to 1996-97. Gauteng 1996-97 to 2001-02. Easterns 2002-03 to 2005-06. Titans 2004-05 to 2005-06. Worcestershire 2005. Warriors 2006-07 to 2008-09. Somerset 2008-10 (Kolpak registration); cap 2008. Lions 2009-10 to date. Joins Surrey in 2011 (Kolpak registration). **Tests** (SA): 3 (2004-05); HS 83 v I (Kanpur) 2004-05 – on debut; BB 2-32 v I (Calcutta) 2004-05. F-c Tours (SA): I 2004-05; SL 2005-06 (SA A). 1000 runs (0+1): 1048 (2003-04). HS 266* Easterns v GW (Kimberley) 2003-04. UK HS 161 Wo v Somerset (Worcester) 2005. BB 7-67 Warriors v Titans (Pt Elizabeth) 2007-08. UK BB 4-23 Sm v Essex (Colchester) 2010. LO HS 122* Sm v Pakistanis (Taunton) 2010. LO BB 5-44 Easterns v WP (Cape Town) 2003-04. T20 HS 95*. T20 BB 4-18.

DERNBACH, Jade Winston (St John the Baptist S), b Johannesburg, South Africa 3 Mar 1986. 6'1½". RHB, RMF. Italian passport. UK resident since 1998. Debut (Surrey) 2003, when aged 17. F-c Tour (EL): WI 2010-11. HS 56* v Northants (Northampton) 2010. 50 wkts (1): 51 (2010). BB 6-47 v Leics (Leicester) 2009. LO HS 31 v Somerset (Taunton) 2010 (CB40). LO BB 5-31 v Derbys (Chesterfield) 2008 (P40). T20 HS 12. T20 BB 3-32.

DUNN, Matthew Peter (Bearwood C, Wokingham), b Egham 5 May 1992. 6'2". LHB, RFM. Debut (Surrey) 2010. Surrey 2nd XI debut 2009. England U19s 2010. BB 3-48 v Bangladesh (Oval) 2010.

HAMILTON-BROWN, Rory James (Millfield S), b St John's Wood, London 3 Sep 1987. 6'0". RHB, OB. Surrey 2005; rejoined as captain 2010. No f-c appearances 2006-07. Sussex 2008-09. HS 171* and BB 2-49 Sx v Yorks (Hove) 2009. Sy HS 125 v Worcs (Croydon) 2010. Sy BB 1-17 v Cambridge MCCU (Cambridge) 2010. LO HS 115 v Glamorgan (Oval) 2010 (CB40). LO BB 3-28 v Leics (Leicester) 2007 (P40). T20 HS 87*. T20 BB 4-15.

HARINATH, Arun (Whitgift S; Loughborough U), b Sutton 26 Mar 1987. LHB, OB. Loughborough UCCE 2007-09. MCC 2008. Surrey debut 2009. Surrey 2nd XI debut 2003. Buckinghamshire 2007-08. HS 69 LU v Worcs (Worcester) 2007. Sy HS 63 v Middx (Oval) 2010. BB – . LO HS 21* v Warwks (Oval) 2009 (P40).

JEWELL, Thomas Melvin (Bradfield C), b Reading, Berkshire 13 Jan 1991. RHB, RMF. Debut (Surrey) 2008. Surrey 2nd XI debut 2007. HS 4* v Cambridge MCCU (Cambridge) 2010). CC HS 1 and CC BB 1-56 v Northants (Northampton) 2010. BB 1-16 v Loughborough UCCE (Oval) 2008. LO HS 1 v Northants (Northampton) 2009 (P40). LO BB – .

NQJORDAN, Christopher James (Comber Mere S, Barbados; Dulwich C), b Christ Church, Barbados 4 Oct 1988. 6'0". RHB, RFM. Debut (Surrey) 2007. Missed entire 2010 season with back injury. HS 57 v Notts (Nottingham) 2008. BB 4-84 v Essex (Guildford) 2009. LO HS 38 v Yorks (Guildford) 2008 (P40). LO BB 3-28 v Yorks (Scarborough) 2007 (P40). T20 HS 31. T20 BB 2-34.

KING, Simon James (Warlingham S; John Fisher S), b Warlingham 4 Sep 1987. RHB, OB. Debut (Surrey) 2009. Surrey 2nd XI debut 2005. HS 8 v Derbys (Croydon) 2009. BB 3-61 v Middx (Lord's) 2009 – on debut. LO HS 5* v Kent (Beckenham) 2009.

LANCEFIELD, Thomas John (Whitgift S), b Epsom 8 Oct 1990. 5'9". LHB, LM. Debut (Surrey) 2010. Tamil Union 2010-11. Surrey 2nd XI debut 2009. HS 74 v Worcs (Worcester) 2010. BB 1-12 Tamil Union v Colts (Colombo, CCC) 2010-11. Sy BB – . LO HS 20 v Leics (Leicester) 2009 (P40). T20 HS 27. T20 BB – .

LINLEY, Timothy Edward (St Mary's RC CS, Menston; Notre Dame SFC; Oxford Brookes U), b Leeds, Yorks 23 Mar 1982. 6'2". RHB, RFM. Oxford UCCE 2003-05. British U 2004. Sussex 2006 (1 match). Surrey debut 2009. HS 42 OU v Derbys (Oxford) 2005. Sy HS 36 v Kent (Canterbury) 2009. BB 5-105 v Northants (Northampton) 2010. LO HS 20* v Warwks (Oval) 2009 (P40). LO BB 2-38 v Glamorgan (Oval) 2009 (P40). T20 HS 8. T20 BB 1-17.

‡MAYNARD, Thomas Lloyd (Millfield S; Whitchurch HS, Cardiff), b Cardiff 25 Mar 1989. Son of M.P.Maynard (Glamorgan and England 1985-2005). 6'3". RHB, OB. Glamorgan 2007-10. Wales MC 2006-08. HS 98 Gm v Worcs (Colwyn Bay) 2010. BB – . LO HS 108 Gm v Northants (Colwyn Bay) 2009 (P40). LO BB – . T20 HS 78*.

MEAKER, Stuart Christopher (Cranleigh S), b Durban, South Africa 21 Jan 1989. Moved to UK in 2001. 6'1". RHB, RMF. Debut (Surrey) 2008. England U19s 2007 to 2008. Surrey 2nd XI debut 2007. HS 94 v Bangladeshis (Oval) 2010. CC HS 72 v Essex (Colchester) 2009. BB 5-48 v Glos (Oval) 2010. LO HS 10* and BB 2-21 v Kent (Canterbury) 2009 (P40). T20 HS 10*. T20 BB 2-36.

PIETERSEN, Kevin Peter (Maritzburg C; Natal U), b Pietermaritzburg, South Africa 27 Jun 1980. British passport (English mother) – qualified for England Oct 2004. 6'4". RHB, OB. MBE 2005. *Wisden* 2005. Natal/KwaZulu-Natal 1997-98 to 1999-00. Nottinghamshire 2001-04; cap 2002. MCC 2004. Hampshire 2005-08; cap 2005 (no f-c appearances 2006-07, 2009-10). Dolphins 2009-10. Surrey debut 2010 (on loan). **ECB central contract 2010-11. Tests:** 71 (2005 to 2010-11, 3 as captain); HS 227 v A (Adelaide) 2010-11; BB 1-0 v SA (Lord's) 2008. **LOI:** 110 (2004-05 to 2010-11, 12 as captain); HS 116 v SA (Pretoria) 2004-05; scored 454 runs (av 151.33) in 7-match series, including fastest England 100 off 69 balls (E London), v SA 2004-05; BB 2-22 v SA (Leeds) 2008. **IT20:** 30 (2005 to 2010-11); HS 79 v Z (Cape Town) 2007-08; BB 1-3 v SA (Centurion) 2009-10. F-c Tours: A 2006-07, 2010-11; SA 2004-05; WI 2008-09; NZ 2007-08; I 2003-04 (Eng A), 2005-06, 2008-09 (Captain); P 2005-06; SL 2007-08; B 2009-10. 1000 runs (3); most – 1546 (2003). HS 254* Nt v Middx (Nottingham) 2002. Sy HS 40 v Glos (Bristol) 2010. BB 4-31 Nt v Durham UCCE (Nottingham) 2003. CC BB 3-72 Nt v Hants (Nottingham) 2004. LO HS 147 Nt v Somerset (Taunton) 2002 (NL). LO BB 3-14 Nt v Middx (Lord's) 2004 (NL). T20 HS 79. T20 BB 3-33.

RAMPRAKASH, Mark Ravin (Gayton HS; Harrow Weald SFC), b Bushey, Herts 5 Sep 1969. 5'9". RHB, OB. Middlesex 1987-2000; cap 1990; captain 1997-99. Surrey debut 2001 – scoring 146 v Kent (Oval); cap 2002; joint Testimonial 2008. YC 1991. *Wisden* 2006. PCA 2006. **Tests:** 52 (1991 to 2001-02); HS 154 v WI (Bridgetown) 1997-98; BB 1-2 v WI (Georgetown) 1997-98. **LOI:** 18 (1991 to 2001-02); HS 51 v WI (Port-of-Spain) 1997-98; BB 3-28 v Z (Harare) 2001-02. F-c Tours: A 1994-95 (part), 1998-99; SA 1995-96; WI 1991-92 (Eng A), 1993-94, 1997-98; NZ 1991-92, 2001-02; I 1994-95 (Eng A), 2001-02; P 1990-91 (Eng A); SL 1990-91 (Eng A). 1000 runs (20, inc 2000 (3): 2258 (1995), 2278 (2006), 2026 (2007)). Averaged 103.54 in f-c matches 2006, the second-highest average by any batsman scoring 1000 runs in a season (105.28 in CC), setting world records by scoring 2000 runs in only 20 innings, posting scores of at least 150 in five successive matches and reaching double figures in each of his 24 innings. In 2007 he became the first to score 2000 f-c runs in a season and average over 100 (101.30) twice. Ten hundreds in a season (2): 1995, 2007. HS 301* Nt v Northants (Oval) 2006. BB 3-32 M v Glamorgan (Cardiff) 1998. Sy BB 2-35 v Northants (Northampton) 2004. LO HS 147* M v Worcs (Lord's) 1990 (SL) – M record. LO BB 5-38 M v Leics (Lord's) 1993 (SL). T20 HS 85*.

ROY, Jason Jonathan (Whitgift S), b Durban, South Africa 21 Jul 1990. 6'0". RHB. RM. Debut (Surrey) 2010. Surrey 2nd XI debut 2008. HS 76 v Leics (Leicester) 2010 – on debut. BB – . LO HS 60 v Sussex (Hove) 2010 (CB40). LO BB – . T20 HS 101* v Kent (Beckenham) 2010 – Sy record.

SCHOFIELD, Christopher Paul (Wardle HS), b Birch Hill, Rochdale, Lancs 6 Oct 1978. 6'2". LHB, LBG. Lancashire 1998-2004; cap 2002. Surrey debut 2006. **Tests**: 2 (2000); HS 57 v Z (Nottingham) 2000. BB – . **IT20**: 4 (2007-08); HS 9* and BB 2-15 v Z (Cape Town) 2007-08. F-c Tours (Eng A): WI 2000-01; NZ 1999-00; B 1999-00. HS 144 v Essex (Colchester) 2009. BB 6-120 Eng A v Bangladesh (Chittagong) 1999-00. Sy BB 5-40 v Northants (Northampton) 2009. LO HS 75* v Hants (Southampton) 2007 (FPT). LO BB 5-31 La v Derbys (Manchester) 2001 (NL). T20 HS 27. T20 BB 4-12.

SPRIEGEL, Matthew Neil William (Whitgift S; Loughborough U), b Epsom 4 Mar 1987. 6'3". LHB, OB. Loughborough UCCE 2007-08; captain 2007-08. Surrey debut 2008. Surrey 2nd XI debut 2004. HS 108* v Bangladeshis (Oval) 2010. CC HS 103 v Northants (Oval) 2010. BB 2-28 v Hants (Oval) 2008. LO HS 81* v Leics (Leicester) 2009 (P40). LO BB 2-23 v Kent (Canterbury) 2009 (P40). T20 HS 25*. T20 BB 4-33.

‡NQ**TAIT, Shaun** William (Oakbank Area S, S Aus), b Bedford Park, Adelaide, S Australia 22 Feb 1983. RHB, RF. S Aus 2002-03 to 2008-09. Durham 2004. Glamorgan 2010 (T20 only). Joins Surrey in 2011 for T20 only. **Tests** (A): 3 (2005 to 2007-08); HS 8 v I (Perth) 2007-08; BB 3-97 v E (Nottingham) 2005. **LOI** (A): 28 (2006-07 to 2010-11); HS 11 v E (Sydney) 2006-07; BB 4-39 v SA (Gros Islet) 2006-07. **IT20** (A): 19 (2007-08 to 2010-11); HS 6 v P (Birmingham) 2010; BB 3-13 v P (Melbourne) 2009-10. F-c Tour (A): E 2005. HS 68 S Aus v Vic (Adelaide) 2005-06. CC HS 4. BB 7-29 (10-98 match) S Aus v Q (Brisbane) 2007-08. CC BB – . LO HS 22* Aus A v Z (Perth) 2003-04. LO BB 8-43 inc hat-trick S Aus v Tas (Adelaide) 2003-04, 8th best analysis in all 1-o cricket. T20 HS 14*. T20 BB 4-14.

TREMLETT, Christopher Timothy (Thornden S, Chandler's Ford; Taunton's C, Southampton), b Southampton, Hampshire 2 Sep 1981. Son of T.M.Tremlett (Hampshire 1976-91); grandson of M.F.Tremlett (Somerset, CD and England 1947-60). 6'7". RHB, RMF. Hampshire 2000-09, taking wicket of M.H.Richardson (NZ A) with his first ball; cap 2004. Surrey debut 2010. **Tests**: 6 (2007 to 2010-11); HS 25* v I (Oval) 2007; BB 5-87 v A (Perth) 2010-11. **LOI**: 13 (2005 to 2010-11); HS 19* v I (Birmingham) 2007; BB 4-32 v B (Nottingham) 2005 – on debut (hat-trick ball hit stump without dislodging bails). **IT20**: 1 (2007-08); BB 2-45 v I (Durban) 2007-08. F-c Tours: A 2010-11; SL 2002-03 (ECB Acad). HS 64 H v Glos (Southampton) 2005. Sy HS 53* v Middx (Lord's) 2010. BB 6-44 H v Sussex (Hove) 2005. Sy BB 4-29 v Glos (Bristol) 2010. Hat-trick: H v Notts (Nottingham) 2005. LO HS 38* H v Cheshire (Alderley Edge) 2004 (CGT). LO BB 4-25 H v Essex (Southend) 2002 (NL). T20 HS 13. T20 BB 4-25.

NQ**WILSON, Gary** Craig (Methodist C, Belfast; Manchester Met), b Dundonald, N Ireland 5 Feb 1986. RHB, WK. 5'10". Ireland 2005 to 2010-11. Surrey debut 2010. MCC YC 2005. Surrey 2nd XI debut 2006. **LOI** (Ire): 25 (2007 to 2010-11); HS 113 v Netherlands (Dublin) 2010. **IT20** (Ire): 15 (2008 to 2009-10); HS 29 v Netherlands (Dubai) 2009-10. HS 125 v Leics (Leicester) 2010. BB – . LO HS 113 (see LOI). T20 HS 36*.

‡[NQ]**YASIR ARAFAT** Satti (Gordon C, Rawalpindi), b Rawalpindi, Pakistan 12 Mar 1982. 5'9½". RHB, RMF. Rawalpindi 1997-98 to 2006-07. Pakistan Reserves 1999-00. KRL 2000-01 to date. National Bank 2005-06. Sussex 2006, 2009-10; cap 2006. Kent 2007-08; cap 2007. Federal Areas 2007-08 to 2008-09. Scotland (not f-c) 2004-05. **Tests** (P): 3 (2007-08 to 2008-09); HS 50* v SL (Karachi) 2008-09; BB 5-161 v I (Bangalore) 2007-08 – on debut. **LOI** (P): 11 (1999-00 to 2009); HS 27 v SA (Chandigarh) 2006-07; BB 1-28 v SL (Karachi) 1999-00. **IT20** (P): 7 (2007-08 to 2009-10); HS 17 v Scotland (Durban) 2007-08; BB 3-32 v E (Dubai) 2009-10. F-c Tours (P): WI 2010-11 (Pak A); I 2007-08; SL (Karachi) 1999-00. HS 122 K v Sussex (Canterbury) 2007. 50 wkts (0+4); most – 91 (2001-02). BB 9-35 KRL v SSGC (Rawalpindi) 2008-09. UK BB 6-86 K v Hants (Canterbury) 2008. LO HS 110* v Auckland (Oamaru) 2009-10. LO BB 6-24 Pakistan A v England A (Colombo) 2004-05. T20 HS 49. T20 BB 4-17.

RELEASED/RETIRED
(Having made a County First-Class or List A appearance in 2010)

AFZAAL, Usman (Manvers Pierrepont CS; S Notts C), b Rawalpindi, Pakistan 9 Jun 1977. 6'0". LHB, SLA. Nottinghamshire 1995-2003; cap 2000. MCC 2002. Northamptonshire 2004-07; cap 2005. Surrey debut 2008, scoring 134* v Lancs; cap 2009. **Tests**: 3 (2001); HS 54 and BB 1-49 v A (Oval) 2001. F-c Tours: SA 1996-97 (Nt); WI 2000-01 (Eng A); NZ 2001-02. 1000 runs (7); most – 1365 (2004). HS 204* v Northants (Northampton) 2009. BB 4-101 Nt v Glos (Nottingham) 1998. Sy BB 3-51 v Leics (Leicester) 2009. LO HS 132 Nh v Yorks (Leeds) 2007 (FPT). LO BB 4-49 v Derbys (Chesterfield) 2008 (P40). T20 HS 98*. T20 BB 2-15.

EVANS, L.J. – *see WARWICKSHIRE.*

[NQ]**Rao IFTIKHAR ANJUM**, b 1 Dec 1980 Khanewal, Punjab, Pakistan. RHB, RM. Islamabad 1999-00 to 2006-07. ADBP 2000-01 to 2001-02. ZT Bank 2002-03 to date. Rawalpindi 2003-04 to 2004-05. Federal Areas 2009-00 to date. Surrey 2010. **Tests** (P): 1 (2005-06); HS 9* and BB – v SL (Kandy) 2005-06. **LOI** (P): 62 (2004-05 to 2009-10); HS 32 v Z (Kingston) 2006-07; BB 5-30 v SL (Colombo, RPS) 2009. **IT20** (P): 2 (2007 to 2009); HS – ; BB 1-34 v SL (Colombo, RPS) 2009. F-c Tours (P): E 2006; SL 2005-06; Kenya 2004 (Pak A). HS 78 ZT Bank v Karachi PT (Peshawar) 2003-04. Sy HS 29 and Sy BB 2-53 v Glos (Oval) 2010. BB 7-59 ZT Bank v WAPDA (Hyderabad) 2004-05. LO HS 39 Islamabad v Rawalpindi (Rawalpindi) 1999-00. LO BB 5-30 (*see LOI*). T20 HS 24. T20 BB 2-18.

[NQ]**NEL, Andre** (Dr E.G.Jansen S, Boksburg), b Germiston, Transvaal, South Africa 15 Jul 1977. 6'4". RHB, RFM. Easterns 1996-97 to 2003-04. Northamptonshire 2003; cap 2003. Titans 2004-05. Essex 2005 (one match), 2007-08. Lions 2008-09 to 2009-10. Dolphins 2008-09. Surrey 2009-10 (Kolpak registration). **Tests** (SA): 36 (2001-02 to 2008); HS 34 v WI (Pt Elizabeth) 2007-08; BB 6-32 (10-88 match) v WI (Bridgetown) 2004-05. **LOI** (SA): 79 (2000-01 to 2008); HS 30* v NZ (Pt Elizabeth) 2007-08; BB 5-45 v B (Providence) 2006-07. **IT20** (SA): 2 (2005-06); HS 0* and BB 2-19 v NZ (Johannesburg) 2005-06. F-c Tours (SA): E 2008; A 2005-06; WI 2000-01, 2004-05; NZ 2003-04; P 2003-04, 2007-08; SL 2006; Z 2001-02, 2007 (SA A); Ireland/Scotland 1999 (SA Acad). HS 96 v Northants (Northampton) 2010. BB 6-25 Easterns v Gauteng (Johannesburg) 2001-02. UK BB 6-36 v Northants (Northampton) 2009. LO HS 58 Lions v Cape Cobras (Paarl) 2008-09. LO BB 6-27 Easterns v GW (Benoni) 2000-01. T20 HS 19. T20 BB 2-13.

WALTERS, S.J. – *see GLAMORGAN.*

YOUNUS KHAN – *see WARWICKSHIRE.*

S.R.Waters left the staff, without making a County First-Class or List A appearance in 2010.

SURREY 2010

RESULTS SUMMARY

	Place	Won	Lost	Tied	Drew	NR
LV= County Championship (2nd Division)	7th	4	6		6	
All First-Class Matches		4	6		8	
Clydesdale Bank 40 (Group A)	3rd	6	4	1		1
Friends Provident t20 (South Group)	5th	8	8			

LV= COUNTY CHAMPIONSHIP AVERAGES

BATTING AND FIELDING

Cap		M	I	NO	HS	Runs	Avge	100	50	Ct/St
2002	M.R.Ramprakash	16	28	2	248	1595	61.34	5	5	5
	S.M.Davies	12	20	1	137	887	49.27	1	8	29
	G.C.Wilson	5	7	–	125	339	48.42	1	1	14
	Younus Khan	3	5	1	77*	155	38.75	–	1	2
	J.J.Roy	3	5	–	76	170	34.00	–	2	–
	T.J.Lancefield	7	11	1	74	323	32.30	–	2	3
	R.J.Hamilton-Brown	16	28	1	125	808	29.92	2	3	11
	C.P.Schofield	7	12	–	90	336	28.00	–	2	4
	A.Harinath	12	21	–	63	529	25.19	–	3	3
2009	U.Afzaal	11	19	1	87	451	25.05	–	3	4
	S.J.Walters	6	10	–	53	242	24.20	–	1	8
	G.J.Batty	14	23	2	65	483	23.00	–	1	11
	A.Nel	7	10	–	96	219	21.90	–	1	4
	C.T.Tremlett	12	17	6	53*	230	20.90	–	1	1
	M.N.W.Spriegel	8	12	–	103	248	20.66	1	–	9
	Iftikhar Anjum	3	5	1	29	61	15.25	–	–	1
	J.W.Dernbach	14	20	9	56*	154	14.00	–	1	1
	T.E.Linley	6	10	4	16	55	9.16	–	–	4
	S.C.Meaker	9	12	1	21	63	5.72	–	–	3

Also batted: S.P.Cheetham (1 match) 0*; L.J.Evans (1) 10, 7 (1 ct); T.M.Jewell (1) 1; K.P.Pietersen (2) 0, 1, 40.

BOWLING

	O	M	R	W	Avge	Best	5wI	10wM
C.T.Tremlett	361.5	88	969	48	20.18	4- 29	–	–
J.W.Dernbach	421	89	1344	46	29.21	5- 68	2	–
T.E.Linley	142	34	437	14	31.21	5-105	1	–
A.Nel	227	67	671	21	31.95	4- 68	–	–
S.C.Meaker	241.5	41	896	28	32.00	5- 48	2	–
C.P.Schofield	163	33	541	14	38.64	4- 63	–	–
G.J.Batty	470.3	66	1638	41	39.95	5- 76	1	–
Also bowled:								
U.Afzaal	71.3	9	201	8	25.12	2- 26	–	–
M.N.W.Spriegel	57.3	5	175	5	35.00	1- 5	–	–
Iftikhar Anjum	65	8	240	6	40.00	2- 53	–	–

S.P.Cheetham 16-1-71-2; R.J.Hamilton-Brown 42.3-1-167-0; A.Harinath 2-0-12-0; T.M.Jewell 14-1-74-1; T.J.Lancefield 1-0-9-0; M.R.Ramprakash 1-0-6-0; J.J.Roy 3-0-18-0; S.J.Walters 3-0-15-0; G.C.Wilson 9-0-44-0; Younus Khan 18-0-64-0.

The First-Class Averages (pp 220–237) give the records of Surrey players in all first-class county matches (Surrey's other opponents being Cambridge MCCU and the Bangladeshis), with the exception of K.P.Pietersen, whose first-class figures for Surrey are as above, and:
S.M.Davies 13-21-3-137-1009-50.45-2-8-30ct.
L.J.Evans 2-4-0-98-137-34.25-0-1-1ct. 6-0-30-1.

SURREY RECORDS

FIRST-CLASS CRICKET

Highest Total	For	811		v	Somerset	The Oval	1899
	V	863		by	Lancashire	The Oval	1990
Lowest Total	For	14		v	Essex	Chelmsford	1983
	V	16		by	MCC	Lord's	1872
Highest Innings	For	357*	R.Abel	v	Somerset	The Oval	1899
	V	366	N.H.Fairbrother	for	Lancashire	The Oval	1990

Highest Partnership for each Wicket

1st	428	J.B.Hobbs/A.Sandham	v	Oxford U	The Oval	1926
2nd	371	J.B.Hobbs/E.G.Hayes	v	Hampshire	The Oval	1909
3rd	413	D.J.Bicknell/D.M.Ward	v	Kent	Canterbury	1990
4th	448	R.Abel/T.W.Hayward	v	Yorkshire	The Oval	1899
5th	318	M.R.Ramprakash/Azhar Mahmood	v	Middlesex	The Oval	2005
6th	298	A.Sandham/H.S.Harrison	v	Sussex	The Oval	1913
7th	262	C.J.Richards/K.T.Medlycott	v	Kent	The Oval	1987
8th	205	I.A.Greig/M.P.Bicknell	v	Lancashire	The Oval	1990
9th	168	E.R.T.Holmes/E.W.J.Brooks	v	Hampshire	The Oval	1936
10th	173	A.Ducat/A.Sandham	v	Essex	Leyton	1921

Best Bowling	For	10-43	T.Rushby	v	Somerset	Taunton	1921
(Innings)	V	10-28	W.P.Howell	for	Australians	The Oval	1899
Best Bowling	For	16-83	G.A.R.Lock	v	Kent	Blackheath	1956
(Match)	V	15-57	W.P.Howell	for	Australians	The Oval	1899

Most Runs – Season	3246	T.W.Hayward	(av 72.13)		1906
Most Runs – Career	43554	J.B.Hobbs	(av 49.72)		1905-34
Most 100s – Season	13	T.W.Hayward			1906
	13	J.B.Hobbs			1925
Most 100s – Career	144	J.B.Hobbs			1905-34
Most Wkts – Season	252	T.Richardson	(av 13.94)		1895
Most Wkts – Career	1775	T.Richardson	(av 17.87)		1892-1904
Most Career W-K Dismissals	1221	H.Strudwick	(1035 ct; 186 st)		1902-27
Most Career Catches in the Field	605	M.J.Stewart			1954-72

LIMITED-OVERS CRICKET

Highest Total	50ov	496-4		v	Glos	The Oval	2007
	40ov	386-3		v	Glamorgan	The Oval	2010
	T20	224-5		v	Glos	Bristol	2006
Lowest Total	50ov	74		v	Kent	The Oval	1967
	40ov	64		v	Worcs	Worcester	1978
	T20	94		v	Essex	Chelmsford	2008
Highest Innings	50ov	268	A.D.Brown	v	Glamorgan	The Oval	2002
	40ov	203	A.D.Brown	v	Hampshire	Guildford	1997
	T20	101*	J.J.Roy	v	Kent	Beckenham	2010
Best Bowling	50ov	7-33	R.D.Jackman	v	Yorkshire	Harrogate	1970
	40ov	7-30	M.P.Bicknell	v	Glamorgan	The Oval	1999
	T20	6-24	T.J.Murtagh	v	Middlesex	Lord's	2005

SUSSEX

Formation of Present Club: 1 March 1839
Substantial Reorganisation: August 1857
Inaugural First-Class Match: 1864
Colours: Dark Blue, Light Blue and Gold
Badge: County Arms of Six Martlets
County Champions: (3) 2003, 2006, 2007
Gillette/NatWest/C&G/FP Trophy Winners: (5) 1963, 1964, 1978, 1986, 2006
Benson and Hedges Cup Winners: (0); best –
Semi-Finalist 1982, 1999
Pro 40/National League (Div 1) Winners: (2) 2008, 2009
Sunday League Winners: (1) 1982
Clydesdale Bank Winners: (0) 2nd Group A 2010
Twenty20 Cup Winners: (1) 2009

Chief Executive: David Brooks, County Ground, Eaton Road, Hove BN3 3AN • **Tel:** 0844 264 0202 • **Fax:** 01273 771549 • **Email:** info@sussexcricket.co.uk • **Web:** www.sussexcricket.co.uk

Professional Cricket Manager: Mark A.Robinson. **Club Coach:** Mark J.G.Davis. **Captain:** M.H.Yardy. **Vice-Captain:** none. **Overseas Players:** Naved-ul-Hasan and W.D.Parnell. **2011 Beneficiary:** M.J.G.Davis (testimonial). **Head Groundsman:** Andy Mackay. **Scorer:** M.J. (Mike) Charman. ‡ New registration. [NQ] Not qualified for England.

ADKIN, William Anthony (Sackville S, E Grinstead; Southampton Solent C), b Redhill, Surrey 9 Apr 1990. 6'8½". LHB, RM. Debut (Sussex) 2010. Sussex 2nd XI debut 2006, aged 16 years 88 days. HS 45 and BB 1-38 v Surrey (Guildford) 2010 – only f-c game. LO HS 30 and LO BB 1-16 v Bangladeshis (Hove) 2010 – only l-o game.

ANYON, James Edward (Garstang HS; Preston C; Loughborough U), b Lancaster, Lancs 5 May 1983. 6'1". LHB, RFM. Loughborough UCCE 2003-04. Warwickshire 2005-09. Surrey 2009 (on loan). Sussex debut 2010. Cumberland 2003. HS 37* Wa v Durham (Chester-le-St) 2007. Sx HS 34 v Derbys (Derby) 2010. BB 6-82 Wa v Glamorgan (Cardiff) 2008. Sx BB 3-23 v Northants (Hove) 2010. LO HS 12 Wa v Worcs (Birmingham) 2009 (CGT). LO BB 3-6 Wa v Notts (Nottingham) 2008 (FPT). T20 HS 8*. T20 BB 3-6.

BEER, William Andrew Thomas (Reigate GS; Collyer's C, Horsham), b Crawley 8 Oct 1988. RHB, LB. Debut (Sussex) 2008. No f-c appearances in 2009. Sussex 2nd XI debut 2006. HS 37* and BB 3-31 v Worcs (Worcester) 2010. LO HS 14 v Glos (Bristol) 2009 (FPT). LO BB 2-17 v Durham (Hove) 2010 (P40). T20 HS 22. T20 BB 3-19.

BROWN, Ben Christopher (Ardingly C), b Crawley 23 Nov 1988. RHB, WK. Debut (Sussex) 2007. No f-c appearances in 2008 or 2009. HS 112 v Derbys (Horsham) 2010. LO HS 58 v Bangladeshis (Hove) 2010. T20 HS 7.

GATTING, Joe Stephen, b Brighton (Cardinal Newman C; Brighton C) 25 Nov 1987. 6'0". Son of S.P.Gatting (Middlesex 2nd XI, football for Arsenal, Brighton & Hove Albion, Charlton Athletic), nephew of M.W.Gatting (Middlesex and England 1975-98). RHB, OB. Debut (Sussex) 2009, scoring 152 v Cambridge UCCE (Cambridge). Sussex 2nd XI debut 2005. HS 152 (*see above*). CC HS 70 v Notts (Nottingham) 2009. BB 1-19 v Cambridge MCCU (Cambridge) 2010. LO HS 99* v Yorks (Scarborough) 2009 (P40). T20 HS 30*.

‡[NQ]**GONDAL,** Naveed Arif (Mandi Baha u Din S), b Mandi Baha u Din, Pakistan 2 Nov 1981. 5'10½". EU qualification via Danish wife. LHB, LMF. Gujranwala 2001-02 to 2002-03. Sialkot 2008-09 to 2009-10. F-c Tours (Pak A): A 2009; SL 2009. HS 49 Sialkot v Rawalpindi (Sialkot) 2009-10. BB 7-66 Sialkot v Abbottabad (Abbottabad) 2009-10. LO HS 49 Gujranwala v Sargodha (Sargodha) 2002-03. LO BB 3-19 Sialkot v Peshawar (Sialkot) 2008-09. T20 HS 1*. T20 BB 2-13.

174

NQGOODWIN, Murray William (Newton Moore HS, Bunbury, WA), b Salisbury, Rhodesia 11 Dec 1972. Younger brother of D.G.Goodwin (Zimbabwe 1986-87 to 1989-90). 5'9". Migrated to Australia in Nov 1986 and gained Australian citizenship in Sep 1997. Kolpak registration 2005 to date. RHB, LB. WA 1994-95 to 1996-97, 2000-01 to 2005-06. Mashonaland 1997-98 to 1998-99. Sussex debut/cap 2001. Warriors 2006-07. Netherlands 1997. **Tests** (Z): 19 (1997-98 to 2000); HS 166* v P (Bulawayo) 1997-98. **LOI** (Z): 71 (1997-98 to 2000); HS 112* v WI (Chester-le-St) 2000; BB 1-12 v SL (Sharjah) 1998-99. F-c Tours (Z): E 2000, SA 1999-00; WI 1999-00; NZ 1997-98; P 1998-99; SL 1997-98. 1000 runs (8+1); most – 1654 (2001). HS 344* (Sx record) v Somerset (Taunton) 2009, sharing record Sx 4th wkt partnership of 363 with C.D.Hopkinson. BB 2-23 Z v Lahore City (Lahore) 1998-99. Sx BB – . LO HS 167 WA v NSW (Perth) 2000-01. LO BB 1-9 Mashonaland v Eng A (Harare) 1998-99. T20 HS 102*.

HATCHETT, Lewis James (Steyning GS), b Shoreham-by-Sea 21 Jan 1990. 6'3". LHB, LMF. Debut (Sussex) 2010. Sussex 2nd XI debut 2009. HS 20 v Middx (Uxbridge) 2010. BB 5-47 v Leics (Leicester) 2010.

HODD, Andrew John (Bexhill C), b Chichester 12 Jan 1984. 5'9". RHB, WK. Sussex 2003 (1 match), 2006 to date. Surrey 2005 (1 match). HS 123 v Yorks (Hove) 2007. LO HS 91 v Lancs (Hove) 2010 (CB40). T20 HS 26.

JOYCE, Edmund Christopher (Presentation C, Bray, Co Wicklow; Trinity C, Dublin), b Dublin, Ireland 22 Sep 1978. 5'11". Brother of four Ireland cricketers: Augustine (2000), Dominick (2004-06), Cecilia (2001-07) and Isobel (2007). Twin brother Roy (1999-2007). LHB, RM. Ireland 1997-98. Middlesex 1999-2008; cap 2002. Sussex debut/cap 2009. Qualified for England 2005. MCC 2006, 2008. Named in Ireland's World Cup squad for 2010-11. **LOI:** 17 (2006 to 2006-07); HS 107 v A (Sydney) 2006-07. **IT20:** 2 (2006 to 2006-07); HS 1 v A (Sydney) 2006-07. F-c Tour (Eng A): WI 2005-06. 1000 runs (5); most – 1668 (2005). HS 211 M v Warwks (Birmingham) 2006. Sx HS 183 v Notts (Horsham) 2009. BB M 2-34 v Cambridge UCCE (Cambridge) 2004. CC BB 1-4 M v Glamorgan (Cardiff) 2005. Sx BB 1-9 v Hants (Southampton) 2009. LO HS 146 v Glos (Hove) 2009 (FPT). LO BB 2-10 M v Notts (Nottingham) 2003 (NL). T20 HS 47.

‡KHAN, Amjad (Skolenpa Duevej, Denmark), b Copenhagen, Denmark 14 Oct 1980. 6'0". RHB, RFM. Kent 2001-10. Denmark 1998-2000. Qualified for England Dec 2006. Missed 2007 season following reconstructive knee surgery. **Tests:** 1 (2008-09); HS- and BB 1-111 v WI (Port-of-Spain) 2008-09. **IT20:** 1 (2008-09); HS 2 and BB 2-34 v WI (Port-of-Spain) 2008-09. F-c Tours: WI 2008-09 (*part*); NZ 2008-09 (Eng A – *part*). HS 78 K v Middx (Lord's) 2003. 50 wkts (2); most – 63 (2002). BB 6-52 K v Yorks (Canterbury) 2002. LO HS 65* Denmark v Ireland (Harare) 1999-00. LO BB 4-26 v Leics (Leicester) 2003 (NL). T20 HS 15. T20 BB 3-11.

LIDDLE, Christopher John (Nunthorpe CS), b Middlesbrough, Yorks 1 Feb 1984. 6'5". RHB, LFM. Leicestershire 2005-06. Sussex debut 2007. Missed entire 2009 season with a stress fracture of the right ankle. HS 53 v Worcs (Hove) 2007. BB 3-42 Le v Somerset (Leicester) 2006. Sx BB 2-43 v Sri Lanka A (Hove) 2007. LO HS 11 v Essex (Arundel) 2007 (FPT). LO BB 4-49 v Surrey (Guildford) 2010 (CB40). T20 HS 10*. T20 BB 4-15.

MACHAN, Matthew William (Brighton C), b Brighton 15 Feb 1991. 5'8". LHB, RM/OB. Debut (Sussex) 2010. Sussex 2nd XI debut 2006, aged 15 years 153 days. HS 6 v Cambridge MCCU (Cambridge) 2010 – only f-c game. LO HS 10 v Bangladeshis (Hove) 2010 – only l-o game.

NASH, Christopher David (Collyer's SFC; Loughborough U), b Cuckfield 19 May 1983. 5'11". RHB, OB. Debut (Sussex) 2002 – no f-c appearances 2003-04; cap 2008. Loughborough UCCE 2003-04. British U 2004. 1000 runs (1): 1321 (2009). HS 184 v Leics (Leicester) 2010. BB 4-12 v Glamorgan (Cardiff) 2010. LO HS 85 v Glamorgan (Swansea) 2010 (CB40). LO BB 4-40 v Yorks (Hove) 2009 (FPT). T20 HS 60*. T20 BB 2-17.

^{NQ}NAVED-UL-HASAN, Rana (Government HS, Sheikhpura), b Sheikhpura, Pakistan 28 Feb 1978. 5'11". RHB, RMF. Debut Pakistan A v England A (Multan) 1995-96. Lahore 1999-00. Pakistan Customs 2000-01. Sheikhpura 2000-01 to 2001-02. Allied Bank 2001-02. WAPDA 2002-03 to date. Sialkot 2003-04 to 2005-06. Sussex 2005-07, 2010; cap 2005. Punjab 2006-07. Yorkshire 2008-09. Herefordshire 2002. **Tests** (P): 9 (2004-05 to 2006-07); HS 42* v E (Lahore) 2005-06; BB 3-30 v E (Faisalabad) 2005-06. **LOI** (P): 74 (2002-03 to 2009-10); HS 33 v SL (Colombo, RPS) 2009 and v A (Adelaide) 2009-10. BB 6-27 v I (Jamshedpur) 2004-05. **IT20** (P): 4 (2006 to 2009-10); HS 17* v SA (Johannesburg) 2006-07; BB 3-19 v SL (Colombo, RPS) 2009. F-c Tours (P): A 2004-05; SA 2006-07; WI 2004-05; I 2004-05. HS 139 v Middx (Lord's) 2005. 50 wkts (2+3); most – 91 (2000-01). BB 7-49 Sheikhpura v Sialkot (Muridke) 2001-02. CC BB 7-62 (11-148 match) v Yorks (Leeds) 2006. LO HS 74 Y v Derbys (Derby) 2008. LO BB 6-27 (*see LOI*). T20 HS 95. T20 BB 4-23.

PANESAR, Mudhsuden Singh (*'Monty'*) (Stopsley HS; Bedford Modern S; Loughborough U), b Luton, Beds 25 Apr 1982. 6'0". LHB, SLA. Northamptonshire 2001-09; cap 2006. British U 2002-05. Loughborough UCCE 2004. Lions 2009-10. Sussex debut/cap 2010. MCC 2006. Bedfordshire 1998-99. *Wisden* 2007. **Tests**: 39 (2005-06 to 2009); HS 26 v SL (Nottingham) 2006; BB 6-37 v NZ (Manchester) 2008. **LOI**: 26 (2006-07 to 2007-08); HS 13 v WI (Nottingham) 2007; BB 3-25 v B (Bridgetown) 2006-07. **IT20**: 1 (2006-07); HS 1 and BB 2-40 v A (Sydney) 2006-07. F-c Tours: A 2006-07, 2010-11; WI 2008-09; NZ 2007-08; I 2005-06, 2008-09; SL 2002-03 (ECB Acad), 2007-08. HS 46* v Middx (Hove) 2010. 50 wkts (4); most – 71 (2006). BB 7-181 Nh v Essex (Chelmsford) 2005. Sx BB 5-44 v Glos (Arundel) 2010. LO HS 17* Nh v Leics (Northampton) 2008 (FPT). LO BB 5-20 ECB Acad v SL Acad XI (Colombo) 2002-03. T20 HS 3*. T20 BB 2-22.

‡^{NQ}PARNELL, Wayne Dillon (Grey HS), b Port Elizabeth, South Africa, 30 Jul 1989. 6'1". LHB, LFM. EP 2006-07 to date. Warriors 2008-09 to date. Kent 2009. **Tests** (SA): 3 (2009-10); HS 22 v I (Kolkata) 2009-10; BB 2-17 v E (Johannesburg) 2009-10. **LOI** (SA): 18 (2008-09 to 2010-11); HS 49 v I (Jaipur) 2009-10; BB 5-48 v E (Cape Town) 2009-10. **IT20** (SA): 11 (2008-09 to 2010-11); HS 14 v I (Durban) 2010-11; BB 4-13 v WI (Oval) 2009. F-c Tour (SA): I 2009-10. HS 90 K v Glamorgan (Canterbury) 2009. BB 4-7 EP v KwaZulu Natal (Port Elizabeth) 2006-07. CC BB 4-78 v Essex (Chelmsford) 2009. LO HS 49 (*see LOI*). LO BB 5-48 (*see LOI*). T20 HS 14. T20 BB 4-13.

PRIOR, Matthew James (Brighton C), b Johannesburg, South Africa 26 Feb 1982. 5'11". RHB, WK. Debut (Sussex) 2001; cap 2003. MCC 2005. *Wisden* 2009. **ECB central contract 2010-11. Tests**: 40 (2007 to 2010-11); HS 131* v WI (Port-of-Spain) 2008-09 (scored 126* v WI on debut – first instance while keeping wicket for England). **LOI**: 61 (2004-05 to 2010-11); HS 87 v WI (Birmingham) 2009. **IT20**: 10 (2007 to 2009-10); HS 32 v SA (Cape Town) 2007-08. F-c Tours: A 2010-11; SA 2009-10; WI 2008-09; I 2003-04 (Eng A), 2008-09; SL 2004-05 (Eng A), 2007-08; B 2006-07 (Eng A), 2009-10. 1000 runs (3); most – 1158 (2004). HS 201* v Loughborough UCCE (Hove) 2004. CC HS 153* v Essex (Colchester) 2003. LO HS 144 v Warwks (Hove) 2005 (NL). T20 HS 117 v Glamorgan (Hove) 2010 – Sx record.

RAYNER, Oliver Philip (St Bede's S, Sussex), b Fallingbostel, W Germany, 1 Nov 1985. 6'5". RHB, OB. Debut (Sussex) 2006, scoring 101 v Sri Lankans (Hove) – first hundred on debut for Sussex since 1920. Starts 2011 season on loan at Middlesex. HS 101 (*see above*). CC HS 60 v Hants (Arundel) 2009. BB 5-49 v Hants (Arundel) 2008. LO HS 61 v Lancs (Hove) 2006 (P40). LO BB 2-31 v Durham (Chester-le-St) 2008 (P40). T20 HS 41*. T20 BB 1-16.

‡^{NQ}**VINCENT, Lou** (Westlake BHS; Adelaide S), b Warkworth, Auckland, New Zealand 11 Nov 1978. RHB, RM. Auckland 1997-98 to date. NZ Academy 1998-99. North Is 1999-00. Worcestershire 2006. Lancashire 2008. Suffolk 2005. **Tests** (NZ): 23 (2001-02 to 2007-08); HS 224 v SL (Wellington) 2004-05. **LOI** (NZ): 102 (2000-01 to 2007-08); HS 172 v Z (Bulawayo) 2005-06; BB 1-0 v SA (Cape Town) 2007-08. **IT20** (NZ): 9 (2005-06 to 2007-08); HS 42 v WI (Auckland) 2005-06. F-c Tours (NZ): A 2001-02; SA 2004-05 (NZ A), 2007-08; WI 2002; I 2003-04; P 2002; Z 2005-06. HS 224 (*see Tests*). CC HS 141 Wo v Leics (Worcester) 2006. BB 2-37 Auckland v Wellington (Auckland) 1999-00. UK BB 1-12 Wo v Leics (Leicester) 2006. LO HS 172 (*see LOI*). LO BB 3-7 Auckland v Otago (Auckland) 2010-11. T20 HS 105*. T20 BB 3-28.

WELLS, Luke William Peter (St Bede's S), b Eastbourne 29 Dec 1990. Son of A.P.Wells (Border, Kent, Sussex and England 1981-2000) and nephew of C.M.Wells (Border, Derbyshire, Sussex and WP 1979-96). 6'4". LHB, OB. Debut (Sussex) 2010. Sussex 2nd XI debut 2008. England U19s 2009 to 2010. HS 62 v Worcs (Worcester) 2010 – only f-c match. LO HS 9 v Bangladeshis (Hove) 2010 – only l-o match.

‡^{NQ}**WERNARS, Kirk** Ogilvy, b Constantiaberg, Cape Town, South Africa 14 Jun 1991. 6'3". EU passport. LHB, RMF. WP 2009-10 to date. HS 22* and BB 2-11 WP v Boland (Cape Town) 2009-10 – only f-c match. LO HS 37* WP v Namibia (Windhoek) 2010-11. LO BB 6-27 WP v Gauteng (Johannesburg) 2010-11.

WRIGHT, Luke James (Belvoir HS; Ratcliffe C; Loughborough U), b Grantham, Lincs 7 Mar 1985. 5'11". Younger brother of A.S.Wright (Leicestershire 2001-02). RHB, RMF. Leicestershire 2003 (one f-c match). Sussex debut 2004; cap 2007. **LOI**: 44 (2007 to 2010-11); HS 52 v NZ (Bristol) 2008; BB 2-34 v NZ (Bristol) 2008. **IT20**: 29 (2007-08 to 2010-11); HS 71 v Netherlands (Lord's) 2009; BB 1-5 v A (Bridgetown) 2009-10. F-c Tour (EL): NZ 2008-09. HS 155* v MCC (Lord's) 2008. CC HS 134 v Middx (Uxbridge) 2010. BB 5-65 v Derbys (Derby) 2010. LO HS 125 v Glos (Hove) 2007 (P40). LO BB 4-12 v Middx (Hove) 2004 (NL). T20 HS 103. T20 BB 3-17.

YARDY, Michael Howard (William Parker S, Hastings), b Pembury, Kent 27 Nov 1980. 6'0". LHB, LM/SLA. Debut (Sussex) 2000; cap 2005; captain 2009 to date. **LOI**: 25 (2006 to 2010-11); HS 60* v A (Perth) 2010-11; BB 3-24 v P (Nottingham) 2006 – on debut. **IT20**: 14 (2006 to 2010-11); HS 35* v P (Cardiff) 2010; BB 2-19 v P (Bridgetown) 2009-10. F-c Tours (Eng A, C=Captain): WI 2005-06; I 2007-08C; B 2006-07C. 1000 runs (2); most – 1520 (2005). HS 257 (record Sussex score v touring team) and BB 5-83 v Bangladeshis (Hove) 2005. CC HS 179 v Middx (Lord's) 2005. CC BB 3-15 v Yorks (Leeds) 2009. LO HS 98* v Surrey (Oval) 2006 (CGT). LO BB 6-27 v Warwks (Birmingham) 2005 (NL). T20 HS 76*. T20 BB 3-21.

RELEASED/RETIRED
(Having made a County First-Class or List A appearance in 2010)

AGA, Ragheb Gul (Hillcrest S; Brighton U), b Nairobi, Kenya 10 Jul 1984. RHB, RMF. Kenya 2003-04 to date. Sussex 2008-10. **LOI**: 2 (2004); HS 1 and BB 2-17 v P (Birmingham) 2004. F-c Tours (Kenya): Z 2005-06. HS 66* v Cambridge MCCU (Cambridge) 2010. CC HS 26 v Kent (Hove) 2008. BB 4-63 v Hants (Canterbury) 2008. LO HS 16 Kenya v UAE (Mombasa) 2010-11. LO BB 4-14 Kenya v Zimbabwe A (Harare) 2005-06. T20 HS 28. T20 BB 2-12.

COLLYMORE, C.D. – *see MIDDLESEX.*

KEEGAN, Chad Blake (Durban HS), b Sandton, Johannesburg, South Africa 30 Jul 1979. 6'1". RHB, RFM. Middlesex 2001-06; cap 2003. Sussex l-o only, 2009-10. ME 2010-11. MCC YCs 2000. Qualified for England March 2005. HS 82 ME v SR (Masvingo) 2010-11. CC HS 44 M v Surrey (Oval) 2004. 50 wkts (1): 63 (2003). BB 6-114 M v Leics (Southgate) 2003. LO HS 50 M v Notts (Lord's) 2003 (NL). LO BB 6-33 M v Notts (Nottingham) 2005 (NL). T20 HS 42. T20 BB 3-11.

KIRTLEY, Robert James (Clifton C), b Eastbourne 10 Jan 1975. 6'0". RHB, RFM. Sussex 1995-2009; cap 1998; benefit 2006. TCCB XI 1996. Mashonaland 1996-97. MCC 2002. **Tests**: 4 (2003 to 2003-04); HS 12 v SL (Colombo) 2003-04; BB 6-34 v SA (Nottingham) 2003 – on debut. **LOI**: 11 (2001-02 to 2003-04); HS 1 (*twice*); BB 2-33 v Z (Harare) 2001-02 on debut, and v B (Dhaka) 2003-04. **IT20**: 1 (2007-08); HS 2* and BB- v A (Cape Town) 2007-08. F-c Tours (Eng A): NZ 1999-00; SL 2003-04 (Eng); B 1999-00. HS 59 v Durham (Eastbourne) 1998. 50 wkts (7); most – 75 (2001). BB 7-21 v Hants (Southampton) 1999. LO HS 30* v Middx (Lord's) 2003 (CGT). LO BB 6-50 v Durham (Hove) 2009 (FPT). T20 HS 11*. T20 BB 4-22.

MARTIN-JENKINS, Robin Simon Christopher (Radley C; Durham U), b Guildford, Surrey 28 Oct 1975. Son of C.D.A.Martin-Jenkins (Cricket Broadcaster and Writer). 6'5". RHB, RMF. Sussex 1995-2010; cap 2009. British U 1996. 1000 runs (1): 1008 (2002). HS 205* v Somerset (Taunton) 2002. BB 7-51 v Leics (Horsham) 2002. LO HS 68* v Northants (Hove) 2003 (NL). LO BB 4-22 v Kent (Canterbury) 2002 (BHC). T20 HS 56*. T20 BB 4-20.

THORNELY, Michael Alistair (Brighton C), b Camden, London 19 Oct 1987. 6'1". RHB, RM. Debut (Sussex) 2007. HS 89 v Northants (Hove) 2010. BB 2-14 v Worcs (Hove) 2010. LO HS 67 v Somerset (Taunton) 2010 (CB40).

YASIR ARAFAT – *see SURREY*.

B.B.McCullum and D.R.Smith left the staff, without making a County First-Class or List A appearance in 2010.

SOMERSET RELEASED/RETIRED (continued from p 164)

RELEASED/RETIRED
(Having made a County First-Class or List A appearance in 2010)

De BRUYN, Z. – *see SURREY*.

MUNDAY, Michael Kenneth (Truro S, Cornwall; Corpus Christi C, Oxford), b Nottingham 22 Oct 1984. 5'7½". RHB, LB. Oxford U 2003-06; blue 2003-04-05-06. Somerset 2005-10. Cornwall 2001-09. HS 21 v Lancs (Manchester) 2008. BB 8-55 (10-65 match) v Notts (Taunton) 2007. LO HS – and BB 1-39 Cornwall v Sussex (Truro) 2001 (CGT).

PHILLIPS, B.J. – *see NOTTINGHAMSHIRE*.

STIFF, David Alexander (Batley GS; Wakefield C), b Dewsbury, Yorks 20 Oct 1984. RHB, RFM. Kent 2004-06. Somerset 2009-10. Yorkshire 2nd XI 2001-03. Signed for Leicestershire in 2007 – no 1st XI appearances. HS 49 v Yorks (Taunton) 2009. BB 5-91 v Hants (Taunton) 2009. LO HS- and BB 1-27 Y CB v Glos CB (Bristol) 2001 (CGT).

TURNER, M.L. – *see DERBYSHIRE*.

WRIGHT, D.G. – *see WORCESTERSHIRE*.

R.J.H.Lett left the staff, without making a County First-Class or List A appearance in 2010.

SUSSEX 2010

RESULTS SUMMARY

	Place	Won	Lost	Tied	Drew	NR
LV= County Championship (2nd Division)	**1st**	8	3		5	
All First-Class Matches		9	3		5	
Clydesdale Bank 40 (Group A)	2nd	7	3	1		1
Friends Provident t20 (South Group)	3rd	9	7			

LV= COUNTY CHAMPIONSHIP AVERAGES

BATTING AND FIELDING

Cap		M	I	NO	HS	Runs	Avge	100	50	Ct/St
2000	R.S.C.Martin-Jenkins	9	13	3	130	629	62.90	2	5	4
2001	M.W.Goodwin	16	26	3	142	1201	52.21	4	5	5
2009	E.C.Joyce	9	15	2	164	590	45.38	1	3	15
2007	L.J.Wright	9	12	1	134	465	42.27	1	3	3
2008	C.D.Nash	16	27	2	184	1029	41.16	3	1	10
	B.C.Brown	8	12	1	112	404	36.72	1	2	6/1
	Yasir Arafat	9	9	2	58	255	36.42	–	2	1
	Naved-ul-Hasan	5	8	2	101	208	34.66	1	1	–
2005	M.H.Yardy	9	13	2	100*	345	31.36	1	1	12
2003	M.J.Prior	7	11	1	123*	296	29.60	1	–	19
	A.J.Hodd	10	14	1	109	319	24.53	1	1	29/1
	M.A.Thornely	12	21	1	89	467	23.35	–	4	8
	O.P.Rayner	6	8	1	47	135	19.28	–	–	9
	J.S.Gatting	7	9	–	24	124	13.77	–	–	3
	J.E.Anyon	10	15	–	34	174	11.60	–	–	3
2010	M.S.Panesar	15	19	5	46*	154	11.00	–	–	1
	C.D.Collymore	14	17	8	19*	78	8.66	–	–	3
	L.J.Hatchett	3	4	–	20	30	7.50	–	–	1

Also batted (1 match each): W.A.Adkin 45; R.G.Aga 0; W.A.T.Beer 37* (1 ct);
L.W.P.Wells 62, 8.

BOWLING

	O	M	R	W	Avge	Best	5wI	10wM
R.S.C.Martin-Jenkins	201.1	35	593	30	19.76	5-45	1	–
C.D.Collymore	414	115	1133	57	19.87	6-48	1	–
Yasir Arafat	256	43	896	36	24.88	5-74	2	–
L.J.Wright	154.5	22	573	23	24.91	5-65	1	–
M.S.Panesar	516.2	135	1328	52	25.53	5-44	2	–
Naved-ul-Hasan	162.4	44	532	20	26.60	4-28	–	–
J.E.Anyon	192.2	29	696	26	26.76	3-23	–	–
O.P.Rayner	118.3	32	334	12	27.83	3-24	–	–
Also bowled:								
C.D.Nash	49	8	115	7	16.42	4-12	–	–
L.J.Hatchett	52.2	11	207	8	25.87	5-47	1	–

W.A.Adkin 11-2-38-1; R.G.Aga 7-1-38-0; W.A.T.Beer 14.4-3-61-3; M.A.Thornely
21-2-75-4; L.W.P.Wells 2-0-16-0.

The First-Class Averages (pp 220–237) give the records of Sussex players in all first-class
county matches (Sussex's other opponents being Cambridge MCCU), with the exception of
M.S.Panesar and M.J.Prior, whose full first-class figures for Sussex are as above.

SUSSEX RECORDS

FIRST-CLASS CRICKET

Highest Total	For 742-5d		v	Somerset	Taunton	2009
	V 726		by	Notts	Nottingham	1895
Lowest Total	For 19		v	Surrey	Godalming	1830
	19		v	Notts	Hove	1873
	V 18		by	Kent	Gravesend	1867
Highest Innings	For 344*	M.W.Goodwin	v	Somerset	Taunton	2009
	V 322	E.Paynter	for	Lancashire	Hove	1937

Highest Partnership for each Wicket

1st	490	E.H.Bowley/J.G.Langridge	v	Middlesex	Hove	1933
2nd	385	E.H.Bowley/M.W.Tate	v	Northants	Hove	1921
3rd	385*	M.H.Yardy/M.W.Goodwin	v	Warwicks	Hove	2006
4th	363	M.W.Goodwin/C.D.Hopkinson	v	Somerset	Taunton	2009
5th	297	J.H.Parks/H.W.Parks	v	Hampshire	Portsmouth	1937
6th	255	K.S.Duleepsinhji/M.W.Tate	v	Northants	Hove	1930
7th	344	K.S.Ranjitsinhji/W.Newham	v	Essex	Leyton	1902
8th	291	R.S.C.Martin-Jenkins/M.J.G.Davis	v	Somerset	Taunton	2002
9th	178	H.W.Parks/A.F.Wensley	v	Derbyshire	Horsham	1930
10th	156	G.R.Cox/H.R.Butt	v	Cambridge U	Cambridge	1908

Best Bowling	For 10- 48	C.H.G.Bland	v	Kent	Tonbridge	1899
(Innings)	V 9- 11	A.P.Freeman	for	Kent	Hove	1922
Best Bowling	For 17-106	G.R.Cox	v	Warwicks	Horsham	1926
(Match)	V 17- 67	A.P.Freeman	for	Kent	Hove	1922

Most Runs – Season	2850	J.G.Langridge	(av 64.77)		1949
Most Runs – Career	34150	J.G.Langridge	(av 37.69)		1928-55
Most 100s – Season	12	J.G.Langridge			1949
Most 100s – Career	76	J.G.Langridge			1928-55
Most Wkts – Season	198	M.W.Tate	(av 13.47)		1925
Most Wkts – Career	2211	M.W.Tate	(av 17.41)		1912-37
Most Career W-K Dismissals	1176	H R Butt	(911 ct; 265 st)		1890-1912
Most Career Catches in the Field	779	J.G.Langridge			1928-55

LIMITED-OVERS CRICKET

Highest Total	50ov	384-9	v	Ireland	Belfast	1996
	40ov	325-4	v	Unicorns	Arundel	2010
	T20	239-5	v	Glamorgan	Hove	2010
Lowest Total	50ov	49	v	Derbyshire	Chesterfield	1969
	40ov	59	v	Glamorgan	Hove	1996
	T20	67	v	Hampshire	Hove	2004
Highest Innings	50ov	158* M.W.Goodwin	v	Essex	Chelmsford	2006
	40ov	163 C.J.Adams	v	Middlesex	Arundel	1999
	T20	117 M.J.Prior	v	Glamorgan	Hove	2010
Best Bowling	50ov	6- 9 A.I.C.Dodemaide	v	Ireland	Downpatrick	1990
	40ov	7-41 A.N.Jones	v	Notts	Nottingham	1986
	T20	5-11 Mushtaq Ahmed	v	Essex	Hove	2005

WARWICKSHIRE

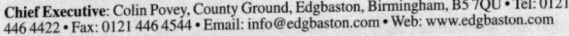

Formation of Present Club: 8 April 1882
Substantial Reorganisation: 19 January 1884
Inaugural First-Class Match: 1894
Colours: Dark Blue, Gold and Silver
Badge: Bear and Ragged Staff
County Champions: (6) 1911, 1951, 1972, 1994, 1995, 2004
Gillette/NatWest/C&G/FP Trophy Winners: (5) 1966, 1968, 1989, 1993, 1995
Benson and Hedges Cup Winners: (2) 1994, 2002
Pro 40/National League (Div 1) Winners: (0); best – 3rd 2001, 2002
Sunday League Winners: (3) 1980, 1994, 1997
Clydesdale Bank 40 Winners: (1) 2010
Twenty20 Cup Winners: (0); best – Finalist 2003

Chief Executive: Colin Povey, County Ground, Edgbaston, Birmingham, B5 7QU • Tel: 0121 446 4422 • Fax: 0121 446 4544 • Email: info@edgbaston.com • Web: www.edgbaston.com

Director of Coaching/First XI Coach: Ashley F.Giles. **Assistant Coach:** Dougie Brown. **Captain:** J.O.Troughton. **Vice-Captain:** tba. **Overseas Player:** Younus Khan. **2011 Beneficiary:** I.R.Bell. **Head Groundsman:** Steve Rouse. **Scorer:** David E.Wainwright. ‡ New registration. NQ Not qualified for England.

ALLIN, Thomas William (Cardiff U), b Devon 27 Nov 1987. Son of A.W.Allin (Glamorgan 1976) and brother of M.L.Allin (Devon 2003). RHB, RMF. Cardiff UCCE (not f-c) 2008-10. Warwickshire 2nd XI debut 2008. Devon 2007. Awaiting 1st XI debut.

AMBROSE, Timothy Raymond (Merewether HS, NSW; TAFE C), b Newcastle, NSW, Australia 1 Dec 1982. ECB qualified – British/EU passport. 5'7". RHB, WK. Sussex 2001-05; cap 2003. Warwickshire debut 2006; cap 2007. **Tests:** 11 (2007-08 to 2008-09); HS 102 v NZ (Wellington) 2007-08. **LOI:** 5 (2008); HS 6 v NZ (Oval) 2008. **IT20:** 1 (2008); HS – . F-c Tours: WI 2008-09; NZ 2007-08. HS 251* v Worcs (Worcester) 2007. LO HS 135 v Durham (Birmingham) 2007 (FPT). T20 HS 77.

BARKER, Keith Hubert Douglas (Moorhead HS; Fulwood C, Preston), b Manchester 21 Oct 1986. 6'3". Son of K.H.Barker (British Guiana 1960-61 to 1963-64). Played football for Blackburn Rovers and Rochdale. LHB, LM. Debut (Warwickshire) 2009. Warwickshire 2nd XI debut 2008. HS 23 v Durham UCCE (Durham) 2009. CC HS 22 v Essex (Southend) 2010. BB 2-22 v Hants (Southampton) 2010. LO HS 40 and LO BB 4-33 v Scotland (Birmingham) 2010 (CB40). T20 HS 46. T20 BB 4-19.

BELL, Ian Ronald (Princethorpe C), b Walsgrave-on-Stowe 11 Apr 1982. 5'9". RHB, RM. Debut (Warwickshire) 1999; cap 2001; benefit 2011. MCC 2004. YC 2004. MBE 2005. **ECB central contract 2010-11. Tests:** 62 (2004 to 2010-11); HS 199 v SA (Lord's) 2008; BB 1-33 v P (Faisalabad) 2005-06. **LOI:** 90 (2004-05 to 2010-11); HS 126* v I (Southampton) 2007; BB 3-9 v Z (Bulawayo) 2004-05 – taking a wicket with his third ball in LOI. **IT20:** 7 (2006 to 2010-11); HS 60* v NZ (Manchester) 2008. F-c Tours: A 2006-07, 2010-11; SA 2009-10; WI 2000-01 (Eng A – part), 2008-09; NZ 2007-08; I 2005-06, 2008-09; P 2005-06; SL 2002-03 (ECB Acad), 2004-05, 2007-08; B 2009-10. 1000 runs (3); most – 1714 (2004). HS 262* v Sussex (Horsham) 2004. BB 4-4 v Middx (Lord's) 2004. LO HS 158 EL v India A (Worcester) 2010. LO BB 5-41 v Essex (Chelmsford) 2003 (NL). T20 HS 85. T20 BB 1-12.

BEST, Paul Merwood, b Nuneaton 8 Mar 1991. LHB, SLA. Warwickshire 2nd XI debut 2009. England U19s 2009-10 to 2010. Awaiting 1st XI debut.

181

BOTHA, Anthony Greyvensteyn (Maritzburg C; Maritzburg Technikon), b Pretoria, South Africa 17 Nov 1976. 6'0". LHB, SLA. Natal/KwaZulu Natal 1995-96 to 1998-99. EP/Easterns 1999-00 to 2002-03. British passport. Derbyshire 2004-07; cap 2004. Moved to Warwickshire in mid-season – debut 2007. HS 156* De v Yorks (Derby) 2005. Wa HS 76 v Kent (Nottingham) 2010. 50 wkts (1): 55 (2007). BB 8-53 Natal B v Northerns B (Pretoria) 1997-98. CC BB 6-101 De v Somerset (Derby) 2007. Wa BB 4-77 v Worcs (Birmingham) 2008. LO HS 60* Easterns v EP (Benoni) 2001-02. LO BB 5-43 v Leics (Leicester) 2008. T20 HS 35*. T20 BB 4-14.

CARTER, Neil Miller (Hottentots Holland HS; Cape Technicon), b Cape Town, South Africa 29 Jan 1975. British passport. 6'2". LHB, LFM. Boland 1999-00 to 2000-01. Warwickshire debut 2001; cap 2005. PCA 2010. HS 103 v Sussex (Hove) 2002 – completed maiden hundred off 67 balls. 50 wkts (1): 51 (2010). BB 6-63 Boland v GW (Kimberley) 2000-01 and 6-63 v Sussex (Birmingham) 2006. LO HS 135 v Scotland (Birmingham) 2006 (CGT). LO BB 5-31 v Durham (Birmingham) 2002 (NL). T20 HS 58. T20 BB 5-19 v Worcs (Birmingham) 2005 – Wa record.

CHOPRA, Varun (Ilford County HS), b Barking, Essex 21 Jun 1987. 6'1". RHB, LB. Essex 2006-09. Warwickshire debut 2010. England U19s 2005 to 2006. HS 155 Ex v Glos (Bristol) 2008. Scored 106 v Glos (Chelmsford) 2006 – on CC debut. Wa HS 54 v Notts (Nottingham) 2010. BB – . LO HS 102 Ex v Middx (Chelmsford) 2007 (FPT). T20 HS 51.

CLARKE, Rikki (Broadwater SS; Godalming C), b Orsett, Essex 29 Sep 1981. 6'4". RHB, RFM. Surrey 2002-07, scoring 107* v Cambridge U (Cambridge) on debut; cap 2005. MCC 2006. Derbyshire cap/captain 2008. Warwickshire debut 2008. YC 2002. **Tests**: 2 (2003-04); HS 55 and BB 2-7 v B (Chittagong) 2003-04. **LOI**: 20 (2003 to 2006); HS 39 v P (Lord's) 2006; BB 2-28 v B (Dhaka) 2003-04. F-c Tours: WI 2003-04, 2005-06; SL 2002-03 (ECB Acad), 2004-05; B 2003-04. 1000 runs (1): 1027 (2006). HS 214 Sy v Somerset (Guildford) 2006. Wa HS 127* v Yorks (Leeds) 2010. BB 6-63 v Kent (Canterbury) 2010. LO HS 98* Sy v Derbys (Derby) 2002 (NL). LO BB 4-49 Sy v Warwks (Birmingham) 2005 (NL). T20 HS 79*. T20 BB 3-11.

EVANS, Laurie John (Whitgift S; The John Fisher S; St Mary's C, Durham), b Lambeth, London 12 Oct 1987. 6'0". RHB, RFM. Durham UCCE 2007. MCC 2007. Surrey 2009-10. Warwickshire debut 2010. HS 133* DU v Lancs (Durham) 2007. CC/Wa HS 15 v Kent (Birmingham) 2010. BB 1-30 Sy v Bangladeshis (Oval) 2010. LO HS 36* v Derbys (Croydon) 2009 (P40). T20 HS 7.

HOLMES, Maurice Gibson (Loughborough U), b Tenterden, Kent 19 May 1990. RHB, OB. Kent 2nd XI 2009. Warwickshire 2nd XI debut 2010. Awaiting 1st XI debut.

JAVID, Ateeq, b Birmingham 15 Oct 1991. RHB, RM. Debut (Warwickshire) 2009. Warwickshire 2nd XI debut 2008. England U19s 2010 to 2010-11. HS 48 v Yorks (Leeds) 2010. BB – .

JOHNSON, Richard Matthew, b Solihull 1 Sep 1988. RHB, WK. Debut (Warwickshire) 2008. Herefordshire 2006. Warwickshire 2nd XI debut 2007. HS 72 v Cambridge UCCE (Cambridge) 2008 – on debut. CC HS 39 v Essex (Birmingham) 2010. LO HS 20 v Northants (Birmingham) 2008 (FPT). T20 HS 6*.

MADDY, Darren Lee (Wreake Valley C), b Leicester 23 May 1974. 5'9". RHB, RM/OB. Leicestershire 1994-2006; cap 1996; benefit 2006. Warwickshire debut/cap 2007; captain 2007-08. **Tests**: 3 (1999 to 1999-00); HS 24 v SA (Durban) 1999-00; BB – . **LOI**: 8 (1998 to 1999-00); HS 53 v Z (Harare) 1999-00. **IT20**: 4 (2007-08); HS 50 and BB 2-6 v NZ (Durban) 2007-08. F-c Tours (Eng A): SA 1996-97 (Le), 1998-99, 1999-00 (Eng); SL 1997-98; Z 1998-99; K 1997-98. 1000 runs (4); most – 1187 (2002). HS 229* Le v Loughborough UCCE (Leicester) 2003. CC HS 162 Le v Durham (Darlington) 1998. Wa HS 148* v Kent (Canterbury) 2007. BB 5-37 Le v Hants (Southampton) 2002. Wa BB 5-63 v Durham (Chester-le-St) 2007. LO HS 167* Le v Scotland (Edinburgh) 2006 (CGT). LO BB 4-16 Le v Somerset (Taunton) 2000 (NL). T20 HS 111 Le v Yorks (Leeds) 2004 – Le record. T20 BB 2-6.

METTERS, Christopher Liam (Coombeshead C; Exeter C), b Torquay, Devon 12 Sep 1990. RHB, SLA. Warwickshire 2nd XI debut 2010. Essex 2nd XI 2010. Devon 2008-10. Awaiting 1st XI debut.

MILLER, Andrew Stephen (St Cecilia's RC HS; Preston C), b Preston, Lancs 27 Sep 1987. 6'4". RHB, RMF. Debut (Warwickshire) 2008. Lancashire 2nd XI 2005. Warwickshire 2nd XI debut 2006. England U19s 2004-05 to 2006. HS 35 v Durham (Birmingham) 2010. BB 5-58 v Lancs (Birmingham) 2010.

MILNES, Thomas Patrick, b Stourbridge, Worcs 6 Oct 1992. RHB, RFM. Warwickshire 2nd XI debut 2009. England U19s 2010-11. Awaiting 1st XI debut.

NEWPORT, Nathan Alexander, b Worcester 10 May 1989. Son of P.J.Newport (Boland, NT, Worcestershire and England 1982-99). RHB, RM. Debut (Warwickshire) 2009; did not bat or bowl. Warwickshire 2nd XI debut 2008.

PIOLET, Steffan Andrew (Warden Park S; Central Sussex C), b Redhill, Surrey 8 Aug 1988. 6'1". RHB, RM. Debut (Warwickshire) 2009. Sussex 2nd XI 2006-08. Warwickshire 2nd XI debut 2008. HS 26* and BB 6-17 (10-43 match) v Durham UCCE (Durham) 2009 – on debut. CC HS 6 and CC BB 1-67 v Yorks (Leeds) 2010. LO HS 4 and LO BB 3-34 v Northants (Northampton) 2009 (P40). T20 HS 7. T20 BB 2-9.

‡**PORTERFIELD, William** Thomas Stuart (Strabane GS; Leeds Met U), b Londonderry, N Ireland 6 Sep 1984. 5'11". LHB, OB. Ireland 2006 to date. MCC 2007. Gloucestershire 2008-10; cap 2008. **LOI** (Ire): 44 (2006 to 2010-11); HS 112* v Bermuda (Nairobi) 2006-07. **IT20** (Ire): 17 (2008 to 2010); HS 46 v Afghanistan (Colombo, PSS) 2009-10. F-c Tour (Ire, C=captain): WI 2009-10C. HS 175 Gs v Worcs (Cheltenham) 2010. BB 1-29 Ire v Jamaica (Spanish Town) 2009-10. UK BB 1-57 Gs v Loughborough UCCE (Bristol) 2008. LO HS 112* (see LOI). T20 HS 65.

RANKIN, William Boyd (Strabane GS; Harper Adams UC), b Londonderry, Co Derry, N Ireland 5 Jul 1984. 6'8". LHB, RMF. Brother of R.J.Rankin (Ireland U19 2003-04). Ireland 2006-07 to 2008. Derbyshire 2007. Warwickshire debut 2008. Middlesex summer contract 2004-05. **LOI** (Ireland): 23 (2006-07 to 2010); HS 7* v SL (St George's) 2006-07; BB 3-32 v P (Kingston) 2006-07. **IT20** (Ire): 6 (2009 to 2009-10); HS 5* v P (Oval) 2009; BB 2-25 v E (Providence) 2009-10. HS 13 v Notts (Nottingham) 2010. BB 5-16 v Essex (Birmingham) 2010. LO HS 9 v Kent (Canterbury) 2009 (FPT). LO BB 4-34 v Kent (Birmingham) 2010 (CB40). T20 HS 5*. T20 BB 2-25.

TAHIR, Naqaash Sarosh (Moseley S; Spring Hill C), b Birmingham 14 Nov 1983. 5'10", RHB, RFM. Debut (Warwickshire) 2004. HS 49 v Worcs (Worcester) 2004. BB 7-107 v Lancs (Blackpool) 2006. LO HS 13* v Leics (Oakham) 2008 (FPT). LO BB 2-47 v Notts (Nottingham) 2010 (FPT).

TROTT, Ian Jonathan Leonard (Rondebosch BHC; Stellenbosch U), b Cape Town, South Africa 22 Apr 1981. 6'0". Stepbrother of K.C.Jackson (WP and Boland 1988-89 to 2001-02). RHB, RM. Boland 2000-01. WP 2001-02. EU/British passport. Warwickshire debut 2003 scoring 134 v Sussex (Birmingham); cap 2005. Otago 2005-06. **ECB central contract 2010-11. Tests**: 18 (2009 to 2010-11); HS 226 and BB 1-16 v B (Lord's) 2010; scored 119 v A (Oval) 2009 on debut. **LOI**: 18 (2009 to 2010-11). HS 137 v A (Sydney) 2010-11. **IT20**: 7 (2007 to 2009-10); HS 51 v SA (Centurion) 2009-10. F-c Tours: A 2010-11; SA 2009-10; NZ 2008-09 (EL); I 2007-08 (EL); B 2009-10. 1000 runs (6); most – 1400 (2009). HS 226 (*see Tests*). CC HS 210 v Sussex (Birmingham) 2005. BB 7-39 v Kent (Canterbury) 2003. LO HS 137 (*see LOI*). LO BB 4-55 v Hants (Lord's) 2005 (CGT). T20 HS 86*. T20 BB 2-19.

TROUGHTON, Jamie Oliver ('**Jim**') (Trinity S; Leamington Spa; Birmingham U), b Camden, London 2 Mar 1979. Great-grandson of H.T.Crichton (Warwicks 1908). 5'11". LHB, SLA. Debut (Warwickshire) 2001; cap 2002; captain 2011. **LOI**: 6 (2003); HS 20 v P (Lord's) 2003. F-c Tour (ECB Acad): SL 2002-03. 1000 runs (1): 1067 (2002). HS 223 v Hants (Birmingham) 2009. BB 3-1 v Cambridge UCCE (Cambridge) 2004. CC BB 2-26 v Lancs (Birmingham) 2006. LO HS 115* and BB 4-23 Wa CB v Cumberland (Millom) 2001 (CGT). T20 HS 66. T20 BB 2-10.

WESTWOOD, Ian James (Wheelers Lane S; Solihull SFC), b Birmingham 13 Jul 1982. 5'7½". LHB, OB. Debut (Warwickshire) 2003; cap 2008; captain 2009-10. HS 178 v WI A (Birmingham) 2006. CC HS 176 v Glamorgan (Cardiff) 2008. BB 2-39 v Hants (Southampton) 2009. LO HS 65 v Northants (Northampton) 2008 (FPT). BB 1-28 Wa CB v Cambs (March) 2001 (CGT). T20 HS 49*. T20 BB 3-29.

WOAKES, Christopher Roger (Barr Beacon Language S, Walsall), b Birmingham 2 March 1989. 6'2". RHB, RMF. Debut (Warwickshire) 2006; cap 2009. MCC 2009. Herefordshire 2006-07. **LOI**: 3 (2010-11); HS 12 v A (Sydney) 2010-11; BB 6-45 v A (Brisbane) 2010-11. **IT20**: 2 (2010-11); HS 19* v A (Adelaide) 2010-11; BB 1-29 v A (Melbourne) 2010-11. F-c Tour (EL): WI 2010-11. HS 136* v Hants (Birmingham) 2010. 50 wkts (1): 58 (2010). BB 6-43 EL v West Indians (Derby) 2009. Wa BB 6-52 (11-197 match) v Kent (Birmingham) 2010. LO HS 49* v Leics (Birmingham) 2010 (CB40). LO BB 6-45 (*see LOI*). T20 HS 28. T20 BB 4-21.

‡^{NO}**YOUNUS KHAN**, Mohammad (Shah Latif SS, Karachi; All Hadeed GHS, Karachi), b Mardan, North-West Frontier Province, Pakistan 29 Nov 1977. 5'11½". RHB, RM/LB. Peshawar 1998-99 to 2004-05. Habib Bank 1999-00 to date. Nottinghamshire 2005. Yorkshire 2007; cap 2007. NW Frontier Province 2007-08 to 2008-09. S Aus 2008-09. Surrey 2010. **Tests** (P): 67 (1999-00 to 2010-11, 9 as captain); HS 313 v SL (Karachi) 2008-09; BB 2-23 v SL (Galle) 2009. **LOI** (P): 213 (1999-00 to 2010-11, 21 as captain); HS 144 v Hong Kong (Colombo, SSC) 2004; BB 1-3 v Hong Kong (Karachi) 2008. **IT20** (P): 25 (2006 to 2010-11, 8 as captain); HS 51 v SL (Johannesburg) 2007. F-c Tours (P) (C=Captain): E 2001, 2006; A 2004-05; SA 2002-03, 2006-07; WI 1999-00, 2004-05; NZ 2000-01, 2010-11; I 2004-05, 2007-08C; SL 2000, 2002-03 (v A), 2005-06, 2009C; Z 2002-03; B 2001-02; UAE 2001-02 (v WI), 2002-03 (v A), 2010-11 (v SA). 1000 runs (0+1): 1315 (1999-00). HS 313 (*see Tests*). UK HS 217* Y v Kent (Scarborough) 2007. BB 4-52 Y v Hants (Southampton) 2007. LO HS 144 (*see LOI*). LO BB 3-5 Nt v Glos (Cheltenham) 2005 (NL). T20 HS 70. T20 BB 3-18.

RELEASED/RETIRED
(Having made a County First-Class or List A appearance in 2010)

IMRAN TAHIR – *see* HAMPSHIRE.

ORD, James Edward (Loughborough U), b Birmingham 9 Nov 1987. RHB, OB. Loughborough UCCE 2009. Warwickshire 2010. Warwickshire 2nd XI debut 2006. HS 9 LU v Hants (Southampton) 2009. Wa HS 6 v Essex (Southend) 2010. LO HS 27 v Northants (Northampton) 2009 (P40).

C.S.MacLeod left the staff, without making a County First-Class or List A appearance in 2010.

WARWICKSHIRE 2010

RESULTS SUMMARY

	Place	Won	Lost	Tied	Drew	NR
LV= County Championship (1st Division)	6th	6	9		1	
All First-Class Matches		6	9		1	
Clydesdale Bank 40 (Group C)	**Winners**	11	3			
Friends Provident t20 (North Group)	QF	11	5			1

LV= COUNTY CHAMPIONSHIP AVERAGES

BATTING AND FIELDING

Cap		M	I	NO	HS	Runs	Avge	100	50	Ct/St
2001	I.R.Bell	6	11	1	104	381	38.10	1	2	10
2005	I.J.L.Trott	6	11	–	150	415	37.72	1	3	10
2005	N.M.Carter	11	20	3	99*	617	36.29	–	4	–
	R.Clarke	15	28	5	127*	673	29.26	1	3	23
2008	I.J.Westwood	16	32	4	86*	726	25.92	–	5	6
	V.Chopra	9	18	1	54	409	24.05	–	1	9
2009	C.R.Woakes	13	21	3	136*	431	23.94	1	1	6
2002	J.O.Troughton	16	30	1	78	585	20.17	–	1	5
2007	D.L.Maddy	14	27	1	61	499	19.19	–	2	16
	A.G.Botha	8	14	–	76	248	17.71	–	1	7
	R.M.Johnson	5	8	1	39	118	16.85	–	–	12/2
2010	Imran Tahir	16	27	4	69*	384	16.69	–	1	4
	K.H.D.Barker	4	5	1	22	57	14.25	–	–	1
2007	T.R.Ambrose	11	20	–	54	267	13.35	–	1	33/3
	A.Javid	4	7	–	48	91	13.00	–	–	3
	N.S.Tahir	3	6	–	34	69	11.50	–	–	2
	A.S.Miller	7	12	5	35	65	9.28	–	–	4
	W.B.Rankin	9	16	7	13	63	7.00	–	–	3

Also played (one match each): L.J.Evans 15, 3 (1 ct); J.E.Ord 1, 6 (1 ct); S.A.Piolet 6, 4 (2 ct).

BOWLING

	O	M	R	W	Avge	Best	5wI	10wM
C.R.Woakes	396.2	100	1165	54	21.57	6- 52	3	1
N.M.Carter	356.2	70	1129	51	22.13	5- 60	4	–
R.Clarke	212.5	31	743	32	23.21	6- 63	1	–
Imran Tahir	430.4	58	1376	56	24.57	8-114	3	–
D.L.Maddy	206.5	62	523	21	24.90	4- 37	–	–
W.B.Rankin	145.3	19	594	22	27.00	5- 16	1	–
A.S.Miller	154.4	42	488	16	30.50	5- 58	2	–

Also bowled:

N.S.Tahir	83	15	238	5	47.60	2- 49		

K.H.D.Barker 36.1-4-135-2; A.G.Botha 50.4-11-175-4; S.A.Piolet 17-3-80-1; I.J.L.Trott 19-4-71-1.

Warwickshire played no first-class fixtures outside the County Championship in 2010. The First-Class Averages (pp 220–237) give the records of Warwickshire players in all first-class county matches, with the exception of I.R.Bell, L.J.Evans, I.J.L.Trott and C.R.Woakes, whose first-class figures for Warwickshire are as above.

WARWICKSHIRE RECORDS

FIRST-CLASS CRICKET

Highest Total	For 810-4d		v	Durham	Birmingham	1994
	V 887		by	Yorkshire	Birmingham	1896
Lowest Total	For 16		v	Kent	Tonbridge	1913
	V 15		by	Hampshire	Birmingham	1922
Highest Innings	For 501*	B.C.Lara	v	Durham	Birmingham	1994
	V 322	I.V.A.Richards	for	Somerset	Taunton	1985

Highest Partnership for each Wicket

1st	377*	N.F.Horner/K.Ibadulla	v	Surrey	The Oval	1960
2nd	465*	J.A.Jameson/R.B.Kanhai	v	Glos	Birmingham	1974
3rd	327	S.P.Kinneir/W.G.Quaife	v	Lancashire	Birmingham	1901
4th	470	A.I.Kallicharran/G.W.Humpage	v	Lancashire	Southport	1982
5th	335	J.O.Troughton/T.R.Ambrose	v	Hampshire	Birmingham	2009
6th	226	T.R.Ambrose/H.H.Streak	v	Worcs	Worcester	2007
7th	289*	I.R.Bell/T.Frost	v	Sussex	Horsham	2004
8th	228	A.J.W.Croom/R.E.S.Wyatt	v	Worcs	Dudley	1925
9th	233	I.J.L.Trott/J.S.Patel	v	Yorkshire	Birmingham	2009
10th	214	N.V.Knight/A.Richardson	v	Hampshire	Birmingham	2002

Best Bowling	For	10-41	J.D.Bannister	v	Comb Servs	Birmingham	1959
(Innings)	V	10-36	H.Verity	for	Yorkshire	Leeds	1931
Best Bowling	For	15-76	S.Hargreave	v	Surrey	The Oval	1903
(Match)	V	17-92	A.P.Freeman	for	Kent	Folkestone	1932

Most Runs – Season	2417	M.J.K.Smith	(av 60.42)	1959
Most Runs – Career	35146	D.L.Amiss	(av 41.64)	1960-87
Most 100s – Season	9	A.I.Kallicharran		1984
	9	B.C.Lara		1994
Most 100s – Career	78	D.L.Amiss		1960-87
Most Wkts – Season	180	W.E.Hollies	(av 15.13)	1946
Most Wkts – Career	2201	W.E.Hollies	(av 20.45)	1932-57
Most Career W-K Dismissals	800	E.J.Smith	(662 ct; 138 st)	1904-30
Most Career Catches in the Field	422	M.J.K.Smith		1956-75

LIMITED-OVERS CRICKET

Highest Total	50ov	392-5		v	Oxfordshire	Birmingham	1984
	40ov	321-7		v	Leics	Birmingham	2010
	T20	205-2		v	Northants	Birmingham	2005
		205-7		v	Glamorgan	Swansea	2005
Lowest Total	50ov	98		v	Leics	Leicester	1998
	40ov	59		v	Yorkshire	Leeds	2001
	T20	114		v	Sussex	Hove	2009
Highest Innings	50ov	206	A.I.Kallicharran	v	Oxfordshire	Birmingham	1984
	40ov	137	I.R.Bell	v	Yorkshire	Birmingham	2005
	T20	89	N.V.Knight	v	Worcs	Worcester	2003
Best Bowling	50ov	6-32	K.Ibadulla	v	Hampshire	Birmingham	1965
		6-32	A.I.Kallicharran	v	Oxfordshire	Birmingham	1984
	40ov	6-15	A.A.Donald	v	Yorkshire	Birmingham	1995
	T20	5-19	N.M.Carter	v	Worcs	Birmingham	2005

WORCESTERSHIRE

Formation of Present Club: 11 March 1865
Inaugural First-Class Match: 1899
Colours: Dark Green and Black
Badge: Shield Argent a Fess between three Pears Sable
County Championships: (5) 1964, 1965, 1974, 1988, 1989
Gillette/NatWest/C&G/FP Trophy Winners: (1) 1994
Benson and Hedges Cup Winners: (1) 1991
Pro 40/National League (Div 1) Winners: (1) 2007
Sunday League Winners: (3) 1971, 1987, 1988
Clydesdale Bank 40 Winners: (0); best 5th Group A
Twenty20 Cup Winners: (0); best – Quarter-Finalist 2004, 2007

Chief Executive: David Leatherdale, County Ground, New Road, Worcester, WR2 4QQ • Tel: 01905 748474 • Fax: 01905 748005 • Email: admin@wccc.co.uk • Web: www.wccc.co.uk

Director of Cricket: Steve J.Rhodes. **Assistant Coaches:** Damian D'Oliveira and Ben Smith. **Captain:** D.K.H.Mitchell. **Vice-Captain:** tba. **Overseas Player:** Saeed Ajmal, Shakib Al Hasan and D.G.Wright. **2011 Beneficiary:** none. **Head Groundsman:** Tim Packwood. **Scorer:** Neil D.Smith. ‡ New registration. NQ Not qualified for England.

Worcestershire revised their capping policy in 2002 and now award players with their County Colours when they make their Championship debut.

ALI, Moeen Munir (Moseley S), b Birmingham, Warwks 18 Jun 1987. Brother of A.K.Ali (*see GLOUCESTERSHIRE*) and cousin of Kabir Ali (*see HAMPSHIRE*). 6'0". LHB, OB. Warwickshire 2005-06, having joined staff when aged 15. Worcestershire debut 2007. HS 153 v Yorks (Leeds) 2009. BB 5-36 v Middx (Lord's) 2010. LO HS 125 v Hants (Southampton) 2009 (FPT). LO BB 3-32 v Yorks (Worcester) 2009 (P40). T20 HS 72. T20 BB 3-19.

ANDREW, Gareth Mark (Ansford Community S; Richard Huish C), b Yeovil, Somerset 27 Dec 1983. 6'0". LHB, RMF. Somerset 2003-05; 2nd XI debut 1999, aged 15 years 247 days. Worcestershire debut 2008. HS 92* v Notts (Worcester) 2009. BB 5-58 v Middx (Kidderminster) 2008. LO HS 104 v Surrey (Oval) 2010 (CB40). LO BB 5-31 v Yorks (Worcester) 2009 (P40). T20 HS 27*. T20 BB 4-22.

BLOFIELD, Alexander David (Shrewsbury S), b Shrewsbury, Shropshire 28 Oct 1991. 6'2". RHB, OB. Worcestershire 2nd XI debut 2009. Shropshire 2009. Awaiting 1st XI debut.

CAMERON, James Gair (St George's C, Harare; U of WA), b Harare, Zimbabwe 31 Jan 1986. LHB, RM. British passport holder. Debut (Worcestershire) 2010. HS 105 v Sussex (Worcester) 2010. BB 2-18 v Northants (Worcester) 2010. LO HS 58 v Unicorns (Kidderminster) 2010 (CB40). LO BB 4-44 v Glamorgan (Cardiff) 2010 (CB40). T20 HS 51*. T20 BB 3-22.

CHOUDHRY, Shaaiq Hussain (Fir Vale S; Bradford U), b Sheffield, Yorkshire 3 Nov 1985. 5'10". RHB, SLA. MCC 2007. Warwickshire 2009. Worcestershire debut 2010. Bradford/Leeds UCCE 2006-08 (not f-c). HS 75 Wa v Durham UCCE (Durham) 2009. CC HS 63 and BB 1-32 v Sussex (Hove) 2010. LO HS 39 v Sussex (Hove) 2010 (CB40). LO BB 4-54 v Surrey (Oval) (CB40). T20 HS 8*. T20 BB 1-24.

COX, Oliver Ben (Bromsgrove S), b Wordsley, Stourbridge 2 Feb 1992. 5'10". RHB, WK. Debut (Worcestershire) 2009, scoring 61 v Somerset (Taunton). Worcestershire 2nd XI debut 2009. HS 61 (*see above*). LO HS 9* v Somerset (Worcester) 2010 (CB40). T20 HS 6*.

D'OLIVEIRA, Brett Louis (Worcester SFC), b Worcester 28 Feb 1992. Son of D.B.D'Oliveira (Worcs 1982-95), grandson of B.L.D'Oliveira (Worcs, EP and England 1964-80). RHB, LB. Worcestershire 2nd XI debut 2010. Awaiting 1st XI debut.

HARRISON, Nicholas Luke (Hardenhuish S, Chippenham), b Bath, Somerset 3 Feb 1992. RHB, RMF. Worcestershire 2nd XI debut 2010. Wiltshire 2009-10. Awaiting 1st XI debut.

JONES, Richard Alan (Grange HS and King Edward VI C, Stourbridge; Loughborough U), b Wordsley, Stourbridge 6 Nov 1986. 6'2". RHB, RFM. Debut (Worcestershire) 2007. HS 53* v Durham (Worcester) 2009. BB 7-115 v Sussex (Hove) 2010. LO HS 11* v Sussex (Worcester) 2010 (CB40). LO BB 1-47 v Glamorgan (Cardiff) 2010 (CB40). T20 HS 9. T20 BB 1-17.

KAPIL, Aneesh (Denstone C), b Wolverhampton 3 Aug 1993. 5'8". RHB, RFM. Worcestershire 2nd XI debut 2008, aged 15 years 10 days. Summer contract. Awaiting 1st XI debut.

[NQ]**KERVEZEE, Alexei** Nicolaas (Duneside HS, Namibia; Grenoobi HS, SA; Segbroek C, Holland), b Walvis Bay, Namibia 11 Sep 1989. 5'8". RHB, OB. Netherlands 2005 to 2009-10. Worcestershire debut 2008. Worcestershire 2nd XI debut 2007. **LOI** (Ne): 30 (2006 to 2010); HS 92 v Kenya (Voorburg) 2010; BB – . **IT20** (Ne): 6 (2009 to 2009-10); HS 39 v Canada (Dubai) 2009-10 and 39 v Afghanistan (Dubai) 2009-10. HS 155 v Derbys (Derby) 2010. BB 1-14 Netherlands v Namibia (Windhoek) 2007-08. LO HS 121* Netherlands v Denmark (Potchefstroom) 2008-09. LO BB – . T20 HS 39.

LEACH, Joseph (Shrewsbury S), b Stafford 30 Oct 1990. 6'1". RHB, RM. Worcestershire 2nd XI debut 2008. Staffordshire 2008-09. Awaiting 1st XI debut.

MANUEL, Jack Kenneth (Wilnecote HS, Tamworth), b Sutton Coldfield, W. Midlands 13 Feb 1991. 6'1". LHB, OB. Worcestershire 2nd XI debut 2008. England U19s 2009 to 2010. Awaiting f-c debut. LO HS 22 v Sussex (Hove) 2010 (CB40). T20 HS 31.

MASON, Matthew Sean (Mazenod C, Lesmurdie, WA), b Claremont, Perth, Australia 20 Mar 1974. British passport. 6'5". RHB, RFM. WA 1996-97 to 1997-98. Worcestershire debut 2002. HS 63 v Warwks (Worcester) 2004. 50 wkts (3); most – 53 (2003, 2005). BB 8-45 (10-117) v Glos (Worcester) 2006. LO HS 25 v Durham (Worcester) 2004 (NL). LO BB 4-34 v Surrey (Guildford) 2003 (NL). T20 HS 8*. T20 BB 3-42.

MITCHELL, Daryl Keith Henry (Prince Henry's HS; University C, Worcester), b Badsey, near Evesham 25 Nov 1983. 5'10". RHB, RM. Debut (Worcestershire) 2005; captain 2011. 1000 runs (2); most – 1180 (2010). HS 298 v Somerset (Taunton) 2009. BB 4-49 v Yorks (Leeds) 2009. LO HS 92 v Somerset (Taunton) 2008 (FPT). LO BB 4-42 v Lancs (Worcester) 2006 (CGT). T20 HS 39. T20 BB 4-11 v Glos (Bristol) 2008 – Wo record.

PARDOE, Matthew Graham (Haybridge HS), b Stourbridge 5 Jan 1991. 6'1". LHB, LM. Worcestershire 2nd XI debut 2007. Awaiting 1st XI debut.

PINNER, Neil Douglas (RGS Worcester), b Wordsley, Stourbridge 29 Sep 1990. 5'11". RHB, OB. Worcestershire 2nd XI debut 2008. Awaiting 1st XI debut.

RICHARDSON, Alan (Alleyne's HS, Stone; Stafford CFE; Durham U), b Newcastle-under-Lyme, Staffs 6 May 1975. 6'2". RHB, RMF. Derbyshire 1995 (one match). Warwickshire 1999-2004; cap 2002. Middlesex 2005-09; cap 2005, taking 7-113 v Notts (Lord's) on debut. Worcestershire debut 2010. Staffordshire 1996-98. Minor Counties 1998. HS 91 Wa v Hants (Birmingham) 2002 - adding Wa record 214 for 10th wicket with N.V.Knight. Wo HS 11 (*twice*) 2010. 50 wkts (2); most – 57 (2005). BB 8-46 Wa v Sussex (Birmingham) 2002. Wo BB 5-44 v Leics (Leicester) 2010. LO HS 21* M v Lancs (Lord's) 2005 (NL). LO BB 5-35 Wa v Staffs (Stone) 2002 (CGT). T20 HS 6*. T20 BB 3-13.

RUSSELL, Christopher James (Medina HS), b Newport, IoW 16 Feb 1989. 6'1". RHB, RMF. Worcestershire 2nd XI debut 2008. Awaiting f-c debut. LO HS- and LO BB 1-23 v Unicorns (Worcester) 2010 (CB40).

‡NQ**SAEED AJMAL**, b Faisalabad, Pakistan 14 Oct 1977. RHB, OB. Faisalabad 1996-97 to 2006-07. KRL 2000-01 to 2008-09. Islamabad 2001-02. Federal Areas 2007-08. ZT Bank 2009-10. **Tests** (P): 9 (2009 to 2010-11); HS 50 and BB 5-82 v E (Birmingham) 2010. **LOI** (P): 35 (2008 to 2010-11); HS 33 and BB 4-33 v NZ (Abu Dhabi) 2009-10. **IT20** (P): 29 (2009 to 2010-11); HS 13* v E (Bridgetown) 2009-10; BB 4-19 v Ireland (Oval) 2009. F-c Tours (P): E 2010; A 2009-10; NZ 2009-10; SL 2009; UAE 2010-11 (v SA). HS 53 Faisalabad v Quetta (Sargodha) 2003-04. 50 wkts (0+1); 62 (2006-07). BB 7-63 KRL v ZT Bank (Rawalpindi) 2008-09. LO HS 33 (*see LOI*). LO BB 5-18 Faisalabad v Karachi (Karachi) 2003-04. T20 HS 13*. T20 BB 4-19.

NQ**SHAKIB AL HASAN**, b Magura, Jessore, Bangladesh 24 Mar 1987. LHB, SLA. Debut Bangladesh CB President's XI 2004-05. Khulna Division 2004-05 to date. Worcestershire debut 2010. **Tests** (B): 21 (2007 to 2010, 8 as captain); HS 100 v NZ (Hamilton) 2009-10; BB 7-36 (9-115 match) v NZ (Chittagong) 2008-09. **LOI** (B): 102 (2006 to 2010-11; 33 as captain); HS 134* v Canada (St John's) 2006-07; BB 4-33 v NZ (Christchurch) 2009-10. **IT20** (B): 14 (2006-07 to 2009-10, 4 as captain); HS 47 v P (Gros Islet) 2009-10; BB 4-34 v WI (Johannesburg) 2007-08. F-c Tours (B) (C=captain): E 2008 (B A), 2010C; SA 2008-09; WI 2009C; NZ 2007-08, 2009-10C; SL 2007; Z 2004-05 (B A), 2006 (B A). HS 129 Khulna v Dhaka (Khulna) 2008-09. Wo HS 90 v Derbys (Derby) 2010. BB 7-32 v Middx (Lord's) 2010. LO HS 134* (*see LOI*). LO BB 4-30 Bangladesh A v Zimbabwe A (Bulawayo) 2006. T20 HS 47. T20 BB 4-34.

SHANTRY, Jack David (Priory SS; Shrewsbury SFC; Liverpool U), b Shrewsbury, Shropshire 29 Jan 1988. Son of B.K.Shantry (Gloucestershire 1978-79) and brother of A.J.Shantry (*see GLAMORGAN*). 6'4". LHB, LM. Debut (Worcestershire) 2009. Shropshire 2007-09. HS 13* v Glos (Worcester) 2010. BB 5-49 v Leics (Leicester) 2010. LO HS 18 v Sussex (Hove) 2010 (CB40). LO BB 3-33 v Unicorns (Worcester) 2010 (CB40). T20 HS 6*. T20 BB 3-23.

SOLANKI, Vikram Singh (Regis S, Wolverhampton), b Udaipur, India 1 Apr 1976. 6'0". RHB, OB, occ WK. Debut (Worcestershire) 1995; cap 1998; captain 2005-10; benefit 2007. Rajasthan 2006-07. **LOI**: 51 (1999-00 to 2006); HS 106 v SA (Oval) 2003; BB 1-17 v SL (Leeds) 2006. **IT20**: 3 (2005 to 2007-08); HS 43 v I (Durban) 2007-08. F-c Tours (Eng A): SA 1998-99, 1999-00 (Eng – *part*); WI 2000-01, 2005-06 (Captain); NZ 1999-00; SL 2004-05; Z 1996-97 (Wo), 1998-99; B 1999-00. 1000 runs (5); most – 1339 (1999). Wo 270 v Glos (Cheltenham) 2008, sharing Wo 2nd wkt record partnership of 316 with S.C.Moore. BB 5-40 v Middx (Lord's) 2004. LO HS 164* v Worcs CB (Worcester) 2003 (CGT). LO BB 4-14 v Somerset (Taunton) 2006 (P40). T20 HS 100. T20 BB 1-6.

WHEELDON, David Anthony (Painsley RC HS; Moorlands SFC), b Stoke-on-Trent, Staffordshire 12 Apr 1989. 5'8". LHB, OB. Debut (Worcestershire) 2009. Worcestershire 2nd XI debut 2006. Staffordshire 2006. HS 87 v Somerset (Taunton) 2009.

WHELAN, Christopher David (St Margaret's HS), b Liverpool, Lancs 8 May 1986. 6'2". RHB, RMF. Middlesex 2005-07. Worcestershire debut 2008. HS 58 v Middx (Kidderminster) 2008. BB 5-95 v Lancs (Worcester) 2009. LO HS 11 v Yorks (Worcester) 2009 (P40). LO BB 4-27 v Hants (Worcester) 2009 (FPT). T20 HS 2*. T20 BB 2-24.

‡^{NO}**WRIGHT, Damien** Geoffrey (Terrigal HS, NSW), b Casino, NSW, Australia 25 Jul 1975. 6'1". RHB, RFM. Tasmania 1997-98 to 2006-07. Scotland 2001 (CGT). Northamptonshire 2003, 2005. Glamorgan 2007. Victoria 2008-09 to date. Sussex 2009. Somerset 2010. Joins Worcestershire for the early part of 2011. HS 111 Tas v Vic (Hobart) 2004-05. UK HS 85 Nh v Worcs (Worcester) 2005. 50 wkts (1): 53 (2005). BB 8-60 Nh v Yorks (Leeds) 2005. LO HS 55 Scotland v Middx CB (Southgate) 2001 (CGT). LO BB 5-37 Nh v Notts (Northampton) 2005. T20 HS 38*. T20 BB 3-17.

RELEASED/RETIRED
(Having made a County First-Class or List A appearance in 2010)

IMRAN ARIF (Govt HS, Saidpur Kotli; Bradford C), b Kotli, Azad Kashmir, Pakistan 15 Jan 1984. UK passport 2009. 5'11". RHB, RFM. Worcestershire 2008-10. Sussex 2nd XI 2007. HS 35 v Sussex (Hove) 2009. BB 5-50 v Glamorgan (Worcester) 2008 – on debut. LO HS 16* v Durham (Worcester) 2008. LO BB 2-43 v Somerset (Bath) 2010 (CB40). T20 HS 6*. T20 BB 1-30.

JAQUES, Philip Anthony (Fig Tree HS, Wollongong; Australian C of PE, Homebush), b Wollongong, NSW, Australia 3 May 1979. 6'1". LHB, SLC. British passport (English parents). NSW 2000-01 to date. Northamptonshire 2003; cap 2003. Yorkshire 2004-05; cap 2005. Worcestershire 2006-07, 2010. **Tests** (A): 11 (2005-06 to 2008); HS 150 v SL (Hobart) 2007-08. **LOI** (A): 6 (2005-06 to 2006-07); HS 94 v SA (Melbourne) 2005-06. F-c Tours (A): WI 2008; P 2005-06 (Aus A), 2007-08 (Aus A); B 2005-06. 1000 runs (4+2); most – 1409 (2003). HS 244 v Essex (Chelmsford) 2006. BB – . LO HS 171* NSW v Q (Sydney) 2009-10. T20 HS 92.

SMITH, Benjamin Francis (Kibworth HS), b Corby, Northants 3 Apr 1972. 5'9". RHB, RM. Leicestershire 1990-2001; cap 1995. MCC 1999-00. CD 2000-01 to 2001-02. Worcestershire 2002-10; captain 2003 to 2004 (*part*). F-c Tours: SA 1996-97 (Le); B 1999-00 (MCC). 1000 runs (8); most – 1546 (2005). HS 204 Le v Surrey (Oval) 1998. Wo HS 203 v Somerset (Taunton) 2006, sharing Wo 4th wkt record partnership of 330 with G.A.Hick. BB 1-5 Le v Essex (Ilford) 1991. Wo BB 1-39 v Surrey (Oval) 2006. LO HS 115 Le v Somerset (Weston-s-M) 1995 (SL). LO BB 1-2 v Worcs CB (Worcester) 2003 (CGT). T20 HS 105.

S.P.D.Smith left the staff, without making a First-Class County or List A appearance in 2010.

WORCESTERSHIRE 2010

RESULTS SUMMARY

	Place	Won	Lost	Tied	Drew	NR
LV= County Championship (2nd Division)	2nd	7	4		5	
All First-Class Matches		7	4		5	
Clydesdale Bank 40 (Group A)	5th	4	8			
Friends Provident t20 (North Group)	9th	5	10			1

LV= COUNTY CHAMPIONSHIP AVERAGES

BATTING AND FIELDING

Cap†		M	I	NO	HS	Runs	Avge	100	50	Ct/St
2008	M.M.Ali	15	28	2	126	1260	48.46	3	9	9
2009	A.N.Kervezee	16	30	3	155	1190	44.07	3	6	14
2005	D.K.H.Mitchell	16	31	3	165*	1180	42.14	4	4	32
2010	J.G.Cameron	10	17	1	105	576	36.00	1	3	7
2008	G.M.Andrew	9	14	1	79	425	32.69	–	4	2
2010	B.J.M.Scott	7	12	2	98	313	31.30	–	3	30/1
2006	P.A.Jaques	8	15	–	94	465	31.00	–	3	9
1998	V.S.Solanki	15	28	1	114	717	26.55	1	4	18
2010	Shakib Al Hasan	8	15	1	90	358	25.57	–	1	3
2002	B.F.Smith	8	14	2	80	282	23.50	–	2	9
2009	D.A.Wheeldon	7	14	1	65	269	20.69	–	2	2
2009	O.B.Cox	9	16	4	59	218	18.16	–	1	18/1
2002	M.S.Mason	8	12	2	51*	137	13.70	–	1	6
2010	A.Richardson	14	18	11	11	71	10.14	–	–	5
2007	R.A.Jones	11	19	2	21*	100	5.88	–	–	7
2009	J.D.Shantry	11	15	5	13*	55	5.50	–	–	3

Also batted: S.H.Choudhry (1 match – cap 2010) 63 (1 ct); Imran Arif (2 – cap 2008) 0, 4, 4* (1 ct); C.D.Whelan (1 – cap 2008) 5, 0 (1 ct).

BOWLING

	O	M	R	W	Avge	Best	5wI	10wM
Shakib Al Hasan	259	48	783	35	22.37	7- 32	3	–
A.Richardson	524	153	1342	55	24.40	5- 44	2	–
M.S.Mason	278	72	849	31	27.38	4- 87	–	–
G.M.Andrew	196.4	32	656	23	28.52	4- 45	–	–
R.A.Jones	298.2	48	1281	38	33.71	7-115	2	–
J.D.Shantry	308	73	945	27	35.00	5- 49	1	–
M.M.Ali	179.4	29	626	17	36.82	5- 36	1	–

Also bowled:
J.G.Cameron 93.5 17 332 8 41.50 2- 18

S.H.Choudhry 10-3-32-1; Imran Arif 33-2-141-4; A.N.Kervezee 4.3-0-63-0; D.K.H.Mitchell 15-3-64-0; V.S.Solanki 29-4-96-1; C.D.Whelan 9-1-34-1.

Worcestershire played no first-class fixtures outside the County Championship in 2010. The First-Class Averages (pp 220–237) give the records of Worcestershire players in all first-class county matches, with the exception of M.M.Ali and Shakib Al Hasan, whose first-class figures for Worcestershire are as above.

† Worcestershire revised their capping policy in 2002 and now award players with their County Colours when they make their Championship debut.

WORCESTERSHIRE RECORDS

FIRST-CLASS CRICKET

Highest Total	For 701-6d		v	Surrey	Worcester	2007
	V 701-4d		by	Leics	Worcester	1906
Lowest Total	For 24		v	Yorkshire	Huddersfield	1903
	V 30		by	Hampshire	Worcester	1903
Highest Innings	For 405*	G.A.Hick	v	Somerset	Taunton	1988
	V 331*	J.D.B.Robertson	for	Middlesex	Worcester	1949

Highest Partnership for each Wicket

1st	309	H.K.Foster/F.L.Bowley	v	Derbyshire	Derby	1901
2nd	316	S.C.Moore/V.S.Solanki	v	Glos	Cheltenham	2008
3rd	438*	G.A.Hick/T.M.Moody	v	Hampshire	Southampton	1997
4th	330	B.F.Smith/G.A.Hick	v	Somerset	Taunton	2006
5th	393	E.G.Arnold/W.B.Burns	v	Warwicks	Birmingham	1909
6th	265	G.A.Hick/S.J.Rhodes	v	Somerset	Taunton	1988
7th	256	D.A.Leatherdale/S.J.Rhodes	v	Notts	Nottingham	2002
8th	184	S.J.Rhodes/S.R.Lampitt	v	Derbyshire	Kidderminster	1991
9th	181	J.A.Cuffe/R.D.Burrows	v	Glos	Worcester	1907
10th	119	W.B.Burns/G.A.Wilson	v	Somerset	Worcester	1906

Best Bowling	For 9- 23	C.F.Root	v	Lancashire	Worcester	1931
(Innings)	V 10- 51	J.Mercer	for	Glamorgan	Worcester	1936
Best Bowling	For 15- 87	A.J.Conway	v	Glos	Moreton-in-M	1914
(Match)	V 17-212	J.C.Clay	for	Glamorgan	Swansea	1937

Most Runs – Season	2654	H.H.I.H.Gibbons	(av 52.03)	1934
Most Runs – Career	34490	D.Kenyon	(av 34.18)	1946-67
Most 100s – Season	10	G.M.Turner		1970
	10	G.A.Hick		1988
Most 100s – Career	106	G.A.Hick		1984-2008
Most Wkts – Season	207	C.F.Root	(av 17.52)	1925
Most Wkts – Career	2143	R.T.D.Perks	(av 23.73)	1930-55
Most Career W-K Dismissals	1095	S.J.Rhodes	(991 ct; 104 st)	1985-2004
Most Career Catches in the Field	528	G.A.Hick		1984-2008

LIMITED-OVERS CRICKET

Highest Total	50ov	404-3	v	Devon	Worcester	1987
	40ov	376-6	v	Surrey	Oval	2010
	T20	227-6	v	Northants	Kidderminster	2007
Lowest Total	50ov	58	v	Ireland	Worcester	2009
	40ov	86	v	Yorkshire	Leeds	1969
	T20	86	v	Northants	Worcester	2006
Highest Innings	50ov	180*	T.M.Moody	v	Surrey	The Oval	1994
	40ov	160	T.M.Moody	v	Kent	Worcester	1991
	T20	116*	G.A.Hick	v	Northants	Luton	2004
Best Bowling	50ov	7-19	N.V.Radford	v	Beds	Bedford	1991
	40ov	6-16	Shoaib Akhtar	v	Glos	Worcester	2005
	T20	4-11	D.K.H.Mitchell	v	Glos	Bristol	2008

YORKSHIRE

Formation of Present Club: 8 January 1863
Substantial Reorganisation: 10 December 1891
Inaugural First-Class Match: 1864
Colours: Dark Blue, Light Blue and Gold
Badge: White Rose
County Championships (since 1890): (30) 1893, 1896, 1898, 1900, 1901, 1902, 1905, 1908, 1912, 1919, 1922, 1923, 1924, 1925, 1931, 1932, 1933, 1935, 1937, 1938, 1939, 1946, 1959, 1960, 1962, 1963, 1966, 1967, 1968, 2001
Joint Champions: (1) 1949
Gillette/NatWest/C&G/FP Trophy Winners: (3) 1965, 1969, 2002
Benson and Hedges Cup Winners: (1) 1987
Pro 40/National League (Div 1) Winners: (0); best – 2nd 2000
Sunday League Winners: (1) 1983
Clydesdale Bank 40 Winners: (0); best – Semi-Finalist 2010
Twenty20 Cup Winners: (0); best – Quarter-Finalist 2007

Chief Executive: Colin Graves, Carnegie Pavilion, Kirkstall Lane, Headingley, Leeds, LS6 3BU • Tel: 0871 971 1222 • Fax: 0113 278 4099 • Email: cricket@yorkshireccc.com • Web: www.yorkshireccc.com

Director of Professional Cricket: Martyn D.Moxon. **Assistant Director:** C.White. **Captain:** A.W.Gale. **Vice-Captain:** tba. **Overseas Players:** none. **2011 Beneficiary:** G.L.Brophy. **Head Groundsman:** Andy Fogarty. **Scorer:** John T.Potter. ‡ New registration. NQ Not qualified for England.

ASHRAF, Moin Aqeeb (Dixons City Academy, Bradford), b Bradford 5 Jan 1992. 6'4". RHB, RMF. Debut (Yorkshire) 2010. Yorkshire 2nd XI debut 2009. HS 10 and BB 5-32 v Kent (Leeds) 2010.

AZEEM Muhammad **RAFIQ** (Holgate S Sports C; Barnsley C), b Karachi, Pakistan 27 Feb 1991. 5'11". RHB, OB. Debut (Yorkshire) 2009. Yorkshire 2nd XI debut 2008. England U19s 2009 to 2010. HS 100 v Worcs (Worcester) 2009. BB 4-92 v Lancs (Manchester) 2010. LO HS – . LO BB 1-36 v Sussex (Scarborough) 2009 (P40). T20 HS 11*. T20 BB 3-23.

BAIRSTOW, Jonathan Marc (St Peter's S, York; Leeds Met U), b Bradford 26 Sep 1989. Son of D.L.Bairstow (Yorkshire, GW, England 1970-90) and brother of A.D.Bairstow (Derbyshire 1995). 6'0". RHB, WK. Debut (Yorkshire) 2009. Inaugural winner of Young Wisden Schools Cricketer of the Year 2008. Yorkshire 2nd XI debut 2007. F-c Tour (EL): WI 2010-11. HS 85 EL v CC&C (Bridgetown) 2010-11. Y HS 84* v Notts (Scarborough) 2009. LO HS 46* v Netherlands (Schiedam) 2010 (CB40). T20 HS 49*.

BALLANCE, Gary Simon (Peterhouse S, Marondera, Zimbabwe; Harrow S; Leeds Met U), b Harare, Zimbabwe 22 Nov 1989. Nephew of G.S.Ballance (Rhodesia B 1978-79) and D.L.Houghton (Rhodesia/Zimbabwe 1978-79 to 1997-98). 6'0". LHB, LB. Debut (Yorkshire) 2008. MWR 2010-11. Derbyshire (List A) 2006-07. HS 132 MWR v ME (Kwekwe) 2010-11. Y HS 43 v Loughborough MCCU (Leeds) 2010. CC HS 31* v Somerset (Taunton) 2010. LO HS 135* MWR v ME (Kwekwe) 2010-11. T20 HS 48*.

BLAIN, John Angus Rae (Penicuik HS; Jewel & Esk Valley C), b Edinburgh, Scotland 4 Jan 1979. 6'1". RHB, RMF. Scotland 1996 to 2008. Northamptonshire 1997-2003. Yorkshire debut 2004. **LOI** (Scot): 33 (1999 to 2008-09); HS 41 v Afghanistan (Benoni) 2008-09; BB 5-22 v Netherlands (Dublin) 2008. **IT20** (Scot): 6 (2007-08 to 2008); HS 3* v Netherlands (Belfast) 2008; BB 2-23 v P (Durban) 2007-08. HS 93 Scotland v Ireland (Belfast) 2007. CC HS 34 Nh v Surrey (Northampton) 2001. Y HS 28* v Notts (Nottingham) 2004. Y HS 28* and Y BB 4-38 v Derbys (Leeds) 2004. BB 6-42 Nh v Kent (Canterbury) 2001. LO HS 41 (*see LOI*). LO BB 5-22 (*see LOI*). T20 HS 3*. T20 BB 2-23.

BRESNAN, Timothy Thomas (Castleford HS and TC; Pontefract New C), b Pontefract 28 Feb 1985. 6'0". RHB, RFM. Debut (Yorkshire) 2003; cap 2006. MCC 2006, 2009. **Tests**: 7 (2009 to 2010-11); HS 91 v B (Dhaka) 2009-10; BB 4-50 v A (Melbourne) 2010-11. **LOI**: 35 (2006 to 2010-11); HS 80 v SA (Centurion) 2009-10; BB 4-28 v SA (Chittagong) 2009-10. **IT20**: 16 (2006 to 2010-11); HS 23* v NZ (Gros Islet) 2009-10; BB 3-10 v P (Cardiff) 2010. F-c Tours: A 2010-11; B 2006-07 (Eng A), 2009-10. HS 126* Eng A v Indians (Chelmsford) 2007. Y HS 116 v Surrey (Oval) 2007, sharing in Y record 9th wicket partnership of 246 with J.N.Gillespie. BB 5-42 v Worcs (Worcester) 2005. LO HS 80 (*see LOI*). BB 4-25 v Somerset (Leeds) 2005 (NL). T20 HS 42. T20 BB 3-10.

BROPHY, Gerard Louis (Christian Brothers C, Boksburg; Witwatersrand TC), b Welkom, OFS, South Africa 26 Nov 1975. 5'11". British/EU passport. Qualified for England 2006. RHB, WK. Transvaal/Gauteng 1996-97 to 1998-99. FS 1999-00 to 2000-01. Northamptonshire 2002-05. Yorkshire debut 2006; cap 2008; benefit 2011. F-c Tour (SA Acad): Z 1998. HS 185 SA Academy v Zim President's XI (Harare) 1998-99. UK HS 181 Nh v Sussex (Hove) 2004. Y HS 103 v Warwks (Leeds) 2010. LO HS 93* v Derbys (Leeds) 2010 (CB40). T20 HS 57*.

GALE, Andrew William (Whitcliffe Mount S; Heckmondwike GS), b Dewsbury 28 Nov 1983. 6'2". LHB, LB. Debut (Yorkshire) 2004; cap 2008; captain 2010 to date. F-c Tour (EL): WI 2010-11. HS 151* v Notts (Nottingham) 2010. BB 1-33 v Loughborough UCCE (Leeds) 2007. LO HS 125* v Essex (Chelmsford) 2010 (CB40). T20 HS 91.

GELDART, Callum John (Huddersfield New C), b Huddersfield 17 Dec 1991. 5'11". LHB, RM. Debut (Yorkshire) 2010. Yorkshire 2nd XI debut 2009. HS 17 v Loughborough MCCU (Leeds) 2010 – only 1st XI appearance.

HANNON-DALBY, Oliver James (Brooksbank S, Leeds Met U), b Halifax 20 Jun 1989. 6'7". LHB, RMF. Debut (Yorkshire) 2008. No 1st XI appearances in 2009. Yorkshire 2nd XI debut 2006. HS 11 v Lancs (Manchester) 2010. BB 5-68 v Warwks (Birmingham) and 5-68 v Somerset (Leeds) 2010 – in consecutive matches.

HODGSON, Lee John (De Brus SS), b Middlesbrough 29 Jun 1986. 5'11". RHB, RFM. Surrey 2008 (1 match). Yorkshire debut 2009. HS 63 Sy v Notts (Oval) 2008 – on debut. Y HS 34 v India A (Leeds) 2010. BB 1-42 v Loughborough MCCU (Leeds) 2010. LO HS 9 v Essex (Leeds) 2009 (P40). LO BB 2-44 v Glos (Leeds) 2009 (P40). T20 HS 39*. T20 BB 2-29.

LEE, James Edward (Immanuel Community C), b Sheffield 23 Dec 1988. 6'1". LHB, RMF. Debut (Yorkshire) 2006. HS 21* v Lancs (Manchester) 2006. BB 2-63 v Somerset (Taunton) 2009. LO HS – . LO BB 3-43 v Glos (Leeds) 2009 (P40).

LEES, Alexander Zak (Holy Trinity SS, Halifax), b Halifax 14 Apr 1993. 6'3". LHB, LB. Debut (Yorkshire) 2010. Yorkshire 2nd XI debut 2010. HS 38 v India A (Leeds) 2010 – only 1st XI appearance.

LYTH, Adam (Caedmon S, Whitby; Whitby Community C), b Whitby 25 Sep 1987. 5'8". LHB, RM. Debut (Yorkshire) 2007; cap 2010. F-c Tour (EL): WI 2010-11. 1000 runs (1): 1509 (2010). HS 142 v Somerset (Taunton) 2010. BB 1-12 v Loughborough UCCE (Leeds) 2007. CC BB 1-20 v Somerset (Scarborough) 2008. LO HS 109* v Sussex (Scarborough) 2009 (P40). T20 HS 59.

McGRATH, Anthony (Yorkshire Martyrs Collegiate S), b Bradford 6 Oct 1975. 6'2". RHB, RM. Debut (Yorkshire) 1995; cap 1999; captain 2003, 2009; benefit 2009. MCC 1999-00. **Tests**: 4 (2003); HS 81 v Z (Chester-le-St) 2003; BB 3-16 v Z (Lord's) 2003. **LOI**: 14 (2003 to 2004); HS 52 v SA (Manchester) 2003; BB 1-13 v WI (Nottingham) 2004. F-c Tours (Eng A): A 1996-97; P 1995-96; Z 1995-96 (Y); B 1999-00 (MCC). 1000 runs (3); most – 1425 (2005). HS 211 v Warwks (Birmingham) 2009. BB 5-39 v Derbys (Derby) 2004. LO HS 148 v Somerset (Taunton) 2006 (P40). LO BB 4-41 v Surrey (Leeds) 2003 (NL). T20 HS 73*. T20 BB 3-27.

PATTERSON, Steven Andrew (Malet Lambert CS; St Mary's SFC, Hull; Leeds U), b Hull 3 Oct 1983.6'4". RHB, RMF. Debut (Yorkshire) 2005. Bradford/Leeds UCCE 2003 (not f-c). HS 46 v Lancs (Manchester) 2006. BB 5-50 v Essex (Scarborough) 2010. LO HS 25* v Worcs (Leeds) 2006 (P40). LO BB 6-32 v Derbys (Leeds) 2010. T20 HS 3*. T20 BB 4-30.

PYRAH, Richard Michael (Ossett S; Wakefield C), b Dewsbury 1 Nov 1982. 6'0". RHB, RM. Debut (Yorkshire) 2004; cap 2010. HS 134* v Loughborough MCCU (Leeds) 2010. CC HS 78 v Worcs (Worcester) 2005. BB 2-8 v Essex (Scarborough) 2010. LO HS 67 v Glos (Bristol) 2009 (FPT). LO BB 5-50 Yorks CB v Somerset (Scarborough) 2002 (CGT). T20 HS 33*. T20 BB 4-20 v Durham (Leeds) 2008 – joint Y record.

RANDHAWA, Gurman Singh, b Huddersfield 25 Jan 1992. LHB, SLA. Yorkshire 2nd XI debut 2009. England U19s 2010-11. Awaiting 1st XI debut.

RASHID, Adil Usman (Belle Vue S, Bradford), b Bradford 17 Feb 1988. 5'8". RHB, LBG. Debut (Yorkshire) 2006; cap 2008. MCC 2007-09. YC 2007. Match double (114, 48, 8-157 and 2-45) for England U19 v India U19 (Taunton) 2006. **LOI**: 5 (2009 to 2009-10); HS 31* v A (Oval) 2009; BB 1-16 v Ireland (Belfast) 2009. **IT20**: 5 (2009 to 2009-10); HS 9* v SA (Nottingham) 2009; BB 1-11 v WI (Oval) 2009. F-c Tours (EL): WI 2010-11; I 2007-08; B 2006-07 (Eng A). HS 157* v Lancs (Leeds) 2009. 50 wkts (2); most – 65 (2008). BB 7-107 v Hants (Southampton) 2008. LO HS 41* v Derbys (Leeds) 2008 (FPT). BB 3-28 v Middx (Scarborough) 2010 (CB40). T20 HS 34. T20 BB 4-20 v Leics (Leeds) 2010 – joint Y record.

ROOT, Joseph Edward (King Ecgbert S, Sheffield; Worksop C), b Sheffield 30 Dec 1990. 6'0". RHB, OB. Debut (Yorkshire) 2010. Yorkshire 2nd XI debut 2007. England U19s 2009-10 to 2010. HS 20* v Loughborough MCCU (Leeds) 2010. LO HS 63 v Essex (Leeds) 2009 (P40).

SANDERSON, Ben William (Ecclesfield CS), b Sheffield 3 Jan 1989. RHB, RMF. Debut (Yorkshire) 2008. Yorkshire 2nd XI debut 2006. HS 6 and CC BB 1-87 v Lancs (Leeds) 2008. BB 5-50 v Loughborough MCCU (Leeds) 2010. LO HS 12* v Essex (Leeds) 2010 (CB40). LO BB 2-17 v Derbys (Leeds) 2010 (CB40). T20 HS – . T20 BB 1-13.

SAYERS, Joseph John (St Mary's RC CS, Menston; Worcester C, Oxford) b Leeds 5 Nov 1983. 6'0". LHB, OB. Oxford U 2002-04; blue 2002-03-04. Yorkshire debut 2004; cap 2007. 1000 runs (1): 1150 (2009). HS 187 v Kent (Tunbridge W) 2007. BB 3-20 v Warwks (Scarborough) 2009. LO HS 62 v Glos (Leeds) 2003 (NL). LO BB 1-31 v Warwks (Birmingham) 2005 (NL). T20 HS 12.

SHAHZAD, Ajmal (Woodhouse Grove S; Bradford U), b Huddersfield 27 Jul 1985. 6'0". RHB, RFM. Debut (Yorkshire) 2006 (first British-born Asian to play for Yorkshire); cap 2010. **Tests**: 1 (2010); HS 5 and BB 3-45 v SA (Manchester) 2010. **LOI**: 9 (2009-10 to 2010-11); HS 9 v A (Brisbane) 2010-11; BB 3-41 v B (Bristol) 2010. **IT20**: 3 (2009-10 to 2010-11); HS 0*; BB 2-38 v P (Dubai) 2009-10. F-c Tours: A 2010-11; B 2009-10. HS 88 v Sussex (Hove) 2009. BB 5-51 v Durham (Chester-le-St) 2010. LO HS 43* v Sussex (Leeds) 2009 (FPT). LO BB 5-51 v Sri Lanka A (Leeds) 2007. T20 HS 17*. T20 BB 2-22.

‡**SIDEBOTTOM, Ryan** Jay (King James's GS, Almondbury), b Huddersfield 15 Jan 1978. Son of A.Sidebottom (Yorks, OFS and England 1973-91). 6'3". LHB, LFM. Yorkshire 1997-2003; cap 2000. Nottinghamshire 2004-10; cap 2004; benefit 2010. **Tests**: 22 (2001 to 2009-10); HS 31 v SL (Kandy) 2007-08; BB 7-47 v NZ (Napier) 2007-08. Hat-trick v NZ (Hamilton) 2007-08. **LOI**: 25 (2001-02 to 2009-10); HS 24 v A (Southampton) 2009; BB 3-19 v SL (Dambulla) 2007-08. **IT20**: 18 (2007 to 2010); HS 5* and BB 3-16 v NZ (Auckland) 2007-08. F-c Tours: SA 2009-10; WI 2000-01 (Eng A), 2008-09; NZ 2007-08; SL 2007-08. HS 54 v Glamorgan (Cardiff) 1998. 50 wkts (2); most – 50 (2005, 2006). BB 7-47 (see Tests). CC BB 7-97 v Derbys (Leeds) 2003. LO HS 32 Nt v Middx (Nottingham) 2005 (NL). LO BB 6-40 v Glamorgan (Cardiff) 1998 (SL). T20 HS 17*. T20 BB 3-16.

WAINWRIGHT, David John (Hemsworth HS and SFC; Loughborough U), b Pontefract 21 Mar 1985. 5'9". LHB, SLA. Debut (Yorkshire) 2004; cap 2010. Loughborough UCCE 2005-06. British U 2006. HS 104* (batting at No 10) v Sussex (Hove) 2008. BB 5-134 v Sussex (Hove) 2009. LO HS 26 v Surrey (Scarborough) 2007 (P40). LO BB 3-26 EL v Pakistan A (Dubai) 2009-10. T20 HS 3*. T20 BB 3-6.

RELEASED/RETIRED
(Having made a County First-Class or List A appearance in 2010)

[NQ]**BEST, Tino** la Bertram, b Richmond Gap, St Michael, Barbados 26 Aug 1981. RHB, RF. Barbados 2001-02 to date. Yorkshire 2010. **Tests** (WI): 14 (2002-03 to 2009); HS 27 v SL (Colombo, SSC) 2005; BB 4-46 v P (Kingston) 2005. **LOI** (WI): 12 (2003-04 to 2009-10); HS 24 v I (Dambulla) 2005; 4-35 v B (Kingstown) 2003-04 – on LOI debut. F-c Tours (WI): E 2002 (WI A), 2004, 2006 (WI A); A 2005-06; SL 2005. HS 51 Barbados v CC&C (Bridgetown) 2008-09; Y HS 40 v India A (Leeds) 2010. BB 7-33 (11-66 match) Barbados v Windward Is (Crab Hill) 2003-04. Y BB 4-86 v Durham (Leeds) 2010. LO HS 24 (see LOI). LO BB 5-24 Barbados v Guyana (Kingston) 2010-11. T20 HS 10*. T20 BB 2-26.

[NQ]**RUDOLPH, Jacobus** Andries ('**Jacques**') (Afrikaanse Hoer Seunskool), b Springs, Transvaal, South Africa 4 May 1981. Elder brother of G.J.Rudolph (Limpopo and Namibia 2006-07 to date). 5'11". LHB, LBG. Northerns 1999-00 to 2003-04. Titans 2004-05, 2008-09 to date. Eagles 2005-06 to 2007-08. Yorkshire 2007-10 (Kolpak registration); scored 122 v Surrey (Oval) on debut; cap 2007. **Tests** (SA): 35 (2003 to 2006); HS 222* v B (Chittagong) 2003 – on debut; BB 1-1 v E (Leeds) 2003. **LOI** (SA): 45 (2003 to 2005-06); HS 81 v B (Dhaka) 2003. **IT20** (SA): 1 (2005-06); HS 6* v A (Brisbane) 2005-06. F-c Tours (SA): E 2003; A 2001-02, 2005-06; WI 2004-05; NZ 2003-04; I 2004-05; SL 2004, 2005-06, 2006; B 2003. 1000 runs (4); most – 1375 (2010). HS 228* v Durham (Leeds) 2010. BB 5-80 Eagles v Cape Cobras (Cape Town) 2007-08. UK BB 1-1 (see Tests). Y BB 1-13 v Somerset (Scarborough) 2008. LO HS 134* South Africa A v Kenya (Laudium) 2001-02. LO BB 4-41 South Africa A v New Zealand A (Colombo) 2005-06. T20 HS 71. T20 BB 3-16.

H.H.Gibbs and C.J.McKay left the staff, without making a County First-Class or List A appearance in 2010.

YORKSHIRE 2010

RESULTS SUMMARY

	Place	Won	Lost	Tied	Drew	NR
LV= County Championship (1st Division)	3rd	6	2		8	
All First-Class Matches		6	2		10	
Clydesdale Bank 40 (Group B)	SF	10	3			
Friends Provident t20 (North Group)	6th	6	9			1

LV= COUNTY CHAMPIONSHIP AVERAGES

BATTING AND FIELDING

Cap		M	I	NO	HS	Runs	Avge	100	50	Ct/St
2010	A.Lyth	16	29	–	142	1509	52.03	3	9	9
2007	J.A.Rudolph	16	29	2	228*	1375	50.92	4	6	20
2008	A.W.Gale	13	23	4	151*	876	46.10	3	3	2
2008	A.U.Rashid	16	24	8	76	732	45.75	–	6	14
2010	D.J.Wainwright	5	5	3	39	89	44.50	–	–	1
1999	A.McGrath	16	29	1	124*	1219	43.53	3	9	9
	J.M.Bairstow	16	29	7	81	918	41.72	–	8	29/5
2010	R.M.Pyrah	6	6	1	61	170	34.00	–	1	4
2007	J.J.Sayers	8	13	–	63	376	28.92	–	5	3
2010	A.Shahzad	9	12	3	45	238	26.44	–	–	1
2008	G.L.Brophy	8	16	1	103	383	25.53	1	–	17
2006	T.T.Bresnan	6	9	1	70	203	25.37	–	2	2
	S.A.Patterson	14	17	4	39*	184	14.15	–	–	3
	T.L.Best	8	8	–	15	46	5.75	–	–	4
	O.J.Hannon-Dalby	16	14	6	11*	21	2.62	–	–	1

Also batted: M.A.Ashraf (2 matches) 0, 10, 0 (1 ct); Azeem Rafiq (2) 4, 13*, 12; G.S.Ballance (1) 4, 31*.

BOWLING

	O	M	R	W	Avge	Best	5wI	10wM
S.A.Patterson	392.5	96	1201	45	26.68	5-50	1	–
A.Shahzad	292.2	47	1013	34	29.79	5-51	1	–
A.U.Rashid	504.4	67	1784	57	31.29	5-87	3	–
T.T.Bresnan	188.2	42	538	17	31.64	5-52	1	–
O.J.Hannon-Dalby	365.4	58	1299	34	38.20	5-68	2	–
T.L.Best	184	19	727	17	42.76	4-86	–	–
D.J.Wainwright	138.2	20	535	12	44.58	3-48	–	–
Also bowled:								
M.A.Ashraf	42	12	106	9	11.77	5-32	1	–
R.M.Pyrah	84.4	16	326	7	46.57	2- 8	–	–

Azeem Rafiq 76-12-222-4; A.Lyth 2-0-16-0; A.McGrath 74-13-226-0; J.A.Rudolph 11-2-43-0; J.J.Sayers 24-3-61-0.

The First-Class Averages (pp 220–237) give the records of Yorkshire players in all first-class county matches (Yorkshire's other opponents being Loughborough MCCU and India A), with the exception of T.T.Bresnan, A.W.Gale and A.Shahzad, whose first-class figures for Yorkshire are as above.

YORKSHIRE RECORDS

FIRST-CLASS CRICKET

Highest Total	For 887		v	Warwicks	Birmingham	1896
	V 681-7d		by	Leics	Bradford	1996
Lowest Total	For 23		v	Hampshire	Middlesbrough	1965
	V 13		by	Notts	Nottingham	1901
Highest Innings	For 341	G.H.Hirst	v	Leics	Leicester	1905
	V 318*	W.G.Grace	for	Glos	Cheltenham	1876

Highest Partnership for each Wicket

1st	555	P.Holmes/H.Sutcliffe	v	Essex	Leyton	1932
2nd	346	W.Barber/M.Leyland	v	Middlesex	Sheffield	1932
3rd	346	J.J.Sayers/A.McGrath	v	Warwicks	Birmingham	2009
4th	358	D.S.Lehmann/M.J.Lumb	v	Durham	Leeds	2006
5th	340	E.Wainwright/G.H.Hirst	v	Surrey	The Oval	1899
6th	276	M.Leyland/E.Robinson	v	Glamorgan	Swansea	1926
7th	254	W.Rhodes/D.C.F.Burton	v	Hampshire	Dewsbury	1919
8th	292	R.Peel/Lord Hawke	v	Warwicks	Birmingham	1896
9th	246	T.T.Bresnan/J.N.Gillespie	v	Surrey	The Oval	2007
10th	149	G.Boycott/G.B.Stevenson	v	Warwicks	Birmingham	1982

Best Bowling	For 10-10	H.Verity	v	Notts	Leeds	1932
(Innings)	V 10-37	C.V.Grimmett	for	Australians	Sheffield	1930
Best Bowling	For 17-91	H.Verity	v	Essex	Leyton	1933
(Match)	V 17-91	H.Dean	for	Lancashire	Liverpool	1913

Most Runs – Season	2883	H.Sutcliffe	(av 80.08)		1932
Most Runs – Career	38558	H.Sutcliffe	(av 50.20)		1919-45
Most 100s – Season	12	H.Sutcliffe			1932
Most 100s – Career	112	H.Sutcliffe			1919-45
Most Wkts – Season	240	W.Rhodes	(av 12.72)		1900
Most Wkts – Career	3597	W.Rhodes	(av 16.02)		1898-1930
Most Career W-K Dismissals	1186	D.Hunter	(863 ct; 323 st)		1888-1909
Most Career Catches in the Field	665	J.Tunnicliffe			1891-1907

LIMITED-OVERS CRICKET

Highest Total	50ov	411-6		v	Devon	Exmouth	2004
	40ov	352-6		v	Notts	Scarborough	2001
	T20	213-7		v	Worcs	Leeds	2010
Lowest Total	50ov	76		v	Surrey	Harrogate	1970
	40ov	54		v	Essex	Leeds	2003
	T20	90-9		v	Durham	Chester-le-St[2]	2009
Highest Innings	50ov	160	M.J.Wood	v	Devon	Exmouth	2004
	40ov	191	D.S.Lehmann	v	Notts	Scarborough	2001
	T20	109	I.J.Harvey	v	Derbyshire	Leeds	2005
Best Bowling	50ov	7-27	D.Gough	v	Ireland	Leeds	1997
	40ov	7-15	R.A.Hutton	v	Worcs	Leeds	1969
	T20	4-20	R.M.Pyrah	v	Durham	Leeds	2008
		4-20	A.U.Rashid	v	Leics	Leeds	2010

FIRST-CLASS UMPIRES 2011

† New appointment. See page 84 for key to abbreviations.

BAILEY, Robert John (Biddulph HS), b Biddulph, Staffs 28 Oct 1963. 6'3". RHB, OB. Northamptonshire 1982-99; cap 1985; benefit 1993; captain 1996-97. Derbyshire 2000-01; cap 2000. Staffordshire 1980. YC 1984. **Tests:** 4 (1988 to 1989-90); HS 43 v WI (Oval) 1988. **LOI:** 4 (1984-85 to 1989-90); HS 43* v SL (Oval) 1988. F-c Tours: SA 1991-92 (Nh); WI 1989-90; Z 1994-95 (Nh). 1000 runs (13); most – 1987 (1990). HS 224* Nh v Glamorgan (Swansea) 1986. BB 5-54 Nh v Notts (Northampton) 1993. F-c career: 374 matches; 21844 runs @ 40.52, 47 hundreds; 121 wickets @ 42.51; 272 ct. Appointed 2006.

BAINTON, Neil Laurence, b Romford, Essex 2 October 1970. No f-c appearances. Appointed 2006.

BENSON, Mark Richard (Sutton Valence S), b Shoreham, Sussex 6 Jul 1958. 5'10". LHB, OB. Kent 1980-95; cap 1981; captain 1991-96 (did not play in 1996); benefit 1991. **Tests:** 1 (1986); HS 30 v I (Birmingham) 1986. **LOI:** 1 (1986); HS 24 v NZ (Leeds) 1986. 1000 runs (11); most – 1725 (1987). HS 257 K v Hants (Southampton) 1991. BB 2-55 K v Surrey (Dartford) 1986. F-c career: 292 matches; 18387 runs @ 40.23, 48 hundreds; 5 wickets @ 98.60; 140 ct. Appointed 2000. Umpired 27 Tests (2004-05 to 2009-10) and 72 LOI (2004 to 2008-09). ICC International Panel 2004-06. **ICC Elite Panel 2006-09**.

BODENHAM, Martin John Dale, b Brighton, Sussex 23 Apr 1950. No f-c appearances. Former football referee who officiated at the 1997 League Cup final and four internationals. Appointed 2009.

COOK, Nicholas Grant Billson (Lutterworth GS), b Leicester 17 Jun 1956. 6'0". RHB, SLA. Leicestershire 1978-85; cap 1982. Northamptonshire 1986-94; cap 1987; benefit 1995. **Tests:** 15 (1983 to 1989); HS 31 v A (Oval) 1989; BB 6-65 (11-83 match) v P (Karachi) 1983-84. **LOI:** 3 (1983-84 to 1989-90); HS – ; BB 2-18 v P (Peshawar) 1987-88. F-c Tours: NZ 1979-80 (DHR), 1983-84; P 1983-84, 1987-88; SL 1985-86 (Eng B); Z 1980-81 (Le), 1984-85 (EC). HS 75 Le v Somerset (Taunton) 1980. 50 wkts (8); most – 90 (1982). BB 7-34 (10-97 match) Nh v Essex (Chelmsford) 1992. F-c career: 356 matches; 3137 runs @ 11.66; 879 wickets @ 29.01; 197 ct. Appointed 2009.

COWLEY, Nigel Geoffrey (Dutchy Manor SS, Mere), b Shaftesbury, Dorset 1 Mar 1953. 5'7". RHB, OB. Dorset 1972. Hampshire 1974-89; cap 1978; benefit 1988. Glamorgan 1990. 1000 runs (1): 1042 (1984). HS 109* H v Somerset (Taunton) 1977. BB 6-48 H v Leics (Southampton) 1982. F-c career: 271 matches; 7309 runs @ 23.35, 2 hundreds; 437 wickets @ 34.04; 105 ct. Appointed 2000.

EVANS, Jeffery Howard, b Llanelli, Carms 7 Aug 1954. No f-c appearances. Appointed 2001. Umpired in Central League 2007-08.

†GALE, Stephen Clifford, b Shrewsbury, Shropshire 3 Jun 1952. No f-c appearances. Shropshire (list A only) 1976-85. Reserve List 2008-10. Appointed 2011.

GARRATT, Steven Arthur, b Nottingham 5 Jul 1953. No f-c appearances. Reserve List 2003-07 standing in 20 f-c matches. Appointed 2008.

GOUGH, Michael Andrew (English Martyrs RCS; Hartlepool SFC), b Hartlepool, Co Durham 18 Dec 1979. Son of M.P.Gough (Durham 1974-77). 6'5". RHB, OB. Durham 1998-2003. F-c Tours (Eng A): NZ 1999-00; B 1999-00. HS 123 Du v CU (Cambridge) 1998. CC HS 103 Du v Essex (Colchester) 2002. BB 5-56 Du v Middx (Chester-le-St) 2001. F-c career: 67 matches; 2952 runs @ 25.44, 2 hundreds; 30 wickets @ 45.00; 57 ct. Reserve List 2006-08. Appointed 2009.

GOULD, Ian James (Westgate SS, Slough), b Taplow, Bucks 19 Aug 1957. 5'8". LHB, WK. Middlesex 1975 to 1980-81, 1996; cap 1977. Auckland 1979-80. Sussex 1981-90; cap 1981; captain 1987; benefit 1990. MCC YC. **LOI:** 18 (1982-83 to 1983); HS 42 v A (Sydney) 1982-83. F-c Tours: A 1982-83; P 1980-81 (Int); Z 1980-81 (M). HS 128 M v Worcs (Worcester) 1978. BB 3-10 Sx v Surrey (Oval) 1989. Middlesex coach 1991-2000.

Reappeared in one match (v OU) 1996. F-c career: 298 matches; 8756 runs @ 26.05, 4 hundreds; 7 wickets @ 52.14; 603 dismissals (536 ct, 67 st). Appointed 2002. Umpired 18 Tests (2008-09 to 2010-11) and 48 LOI (2006 to 2010). **ICC Elite Panel 2009 to date.**

HARTLEY, Peter John (Greenhead GS; Bradford C), b Keighley, Yorks 18 Apr 1960. 6'0". RHB, RMF. Warwickshire 1982. Yorkshire 1985-97; cap 1987; benefit 1996. Hampshire 1998-2000; cap 1998. F-c Tours (Y): SA 1991-92; WI 1986-87; Z 1995-96. HS 127* Y v Lancs (Manchester) 1988. 50 wkts (7); most – 81 (1995). BB 9-41 (inc hat-trick, 4 wkts in 5 balls and 5 in 9; 11-68 match) Y v Derbys (Chesterfield) 1995. Hat-trick 1995. F-c career: 232 matches; 4321 runs @ 19.91, 2 hundreds; 683 wickets @ 30.21; 68 ct. Appointed 2003. Umpired 6 LOI (2007 to 2009). **ICC International Panel 2006-09.**

ILLINGWORTH, Richard Keith (Salts GS), b Bradford, Yorks 23 Aug 1963. 5'11". RHB, SLA. Worcestershire 1982-2000; cap 1986; benefit 1997. Natal 1988-89. Derbyshire 2001. Wiltshire 2005. **Tests:** 9 (1991 to 1995-96); HS 28 v SA (Pt Elizabeth) 1995-96; BB 4-96 v WI (Nottingham) 1995. Took wicket of P.V.Simmons with his first ball in Tests – v WI (Nottingham) 1991. **LOI:** 25 (1991 to 1995-96); HS 14 v P (Melbourne) 1991-92; BB 3-33 v Z (Albury) 1991-92. F-c Tours: SA 1995-96; NZ 1991-92; P 1990-91 (Eng A); SL 1990-91 (Eng A); Z 1989-90 (Eng A), 1990-91 (Wo), 1993-94 (Wo), 1996-97 (Wo). HS 120* Wo v Warwks (Worcester) 1987 – as night-watchman. Scored 106 for England A v Z (Harare) 1989-90 – also as night-watchman. 50 wkts (5); most – 75 (1990). BB 7-50 Wo v OU (Oxford) 1985. F-c career: 376 matches; 7027 runs @ 22.45, 4 hundreds; 831 wickets @ 31.54; 161 ct. Appointed 2006. Umpired 2 LOI (2010). **ICC International Panel (Third Umpire) 2009 to date.**

JESTY, Trevor Edward (Privet County SS, Gosport), b Gosport, Hants 2 Jun 1948. 5'8½". RHB, RM. Hampshire 1966-84; cap 1971; benefit 1982. Surrey 1985-87; cap 1985; captain 1985. Lancashire 1987-88 to 1991; cap 1989. Border 1973-74. GW 1974-75 to 1980-81. Canterbury 1979-80. *Wisden* 1982. **LOI:** 10 (1982-83); HS 52* v NZ (Adelaide) 1982-83; BB 1-23 v A (Sydney) 1982-83. F-c Tours (La): WI 1987-88, 1982-83 (Int); Z 1988-89. 1000 runs (10); most – 1645 (1982). HS 248 H v CU (Cambridge) 1984. Scored 122* La v OU (Oxford) 1991 in his final f-c innings. 50 wkts (2); most – 52 (1981). BB 7-75 H v Worcs (Southampton) 1976. F-c career: 490 matches; 21916 runs @ 32.71, 35 hundreds; 585 wickets @ 27.47; 265 ct, 1 st. Appointed 1994. Umpired in Indian Cricket League 2007-08.

KETTLEBOROUGH, Richard Allan (Worksop C), b Sheffield, Yorks 15 Mar 1973. 6'0". LHB, RM. Yorkshire 1994-97. Middlesex 1998-99. F-c Tour (Y): Z 1995-96. HS 108 Y v Essex (Leeds) 1996. BB 2-26 Y v Notts (Scarborough) 1996. F-c career: 33 matches; 1258 runs @ 25.16, 1 hundred; 3 wickets @ 81.00; 20 ct. Appointed 2006. Umpired 2 Tests (2010-11) and 12 LOI (2009 to 2010-11). **ICC International Panel 2009 to date.**

LLONG, Nigel James (Ashford North S), b Ashford, Kent 11 Feb 1969. 6'0". LHB, OB. Kent 1990-98; cap 1993. F-c Tour (K): Z 1992-93. HS 130 K v Hants (Canterbury) 1996. BB 5-21 K v Middx (Canterbury) 1996. F-c career: 68 matches; 3024 runs @ 31.17, 6 hundreds; 35 wickets @ 35.97; 59 ct. Appointed 2002. Umpired 7 Tests (2007-08 to 2010-11) and 39 LOI (2006 to 2010-11). **ICC International Panel 2004 to date.**

LLOYDS, Jeremy William (Blundell's S), b Penang, Malaya 17 Nov 1954. 6'0". LHB, OB. Somerset 1979-84; cap 1982. Gloucestershire 1985-91; cap 1985. OFS 1983-84 to 1987-88. F-c Tour (Gl): SL 1986-87. 1000 runs (3); most – 1295 (1986). HS 132* Sm v Northants (Northampton) 1982. BB 7-88 Sm v Essex (Chelmsford) 1982. F-c career: 267 matches; 10679 runs @ 31.04, 10 hundreds; 333 wickets @ 38.86; 229 ct. Appointed 1998. Umpired 5 Tests (2003-04 to 2004-05) and 18 LOI (2000 to 2005-06). **ICC International Panel 2003-06.**

MALLENDER, Neil Alan (Beverley GS), b Kirk Sandall, Yorks 13 Aug 1961. 6'0". RHB, RFM. Northamptonshire 1980-86 and 1995-96; cap 1984. Somerset 1987-94; cap 1987; benefit 1994. Otago 1983-84 to 1992-93; captain 1992-93. **Tests:** 2 (1992); HS 4 v P (Oval) 1992; BB 5-50 v P (Leeds) 1992 – on debut. F-c Tour (Nh): Z 1994-95. HS 100* Otago v CD (Palmerston N) 1991-92. UK HS 87* Sm v Sussex (Hove) 1990. 50 wkts (6); most – 56 (1983). BB 7-27 Otago v Auckland (Auckland) 1984-85. UK BB 7-41 Nh v

Derbys (Northampton) 1982. F-c career: 345 matches; 4709 runs @ 17.18, 1 hundred; 937 wickets @ 26.31; 111 ct. Appointed 1999. Umpired 3 Tests (2003-04) and 22 LOI (2001 to 2003-04), including 2002-03 World Cup. **ICC Elite Panel 2004**.

MILLNS, David James (Garibaldi CS; N Notts C; Nottingham Trent U), b Clipstone, Notts 27 Feb 1965. 6'3". LHB, RF. Nottinghamshire 1988-89, 2000-01; cap 2000. Leicestershire 1990-99; cap 1991; benefit 1999. Tasmania 1994-95. Boland 1996-97. F-c Tours: A 1992-93 (Eng A); SA 1996-97 (Le). HS Le v Northants (Northampton) 1997. 50 wkts (4); most – 76 (1994). BB 9-37 (12-91 match) Le v Derbys (Derby) 1991. F-c career: 171 matches; 3082 runs @ 22.01, 3 hundreds; 553 wickets @ 27.35; 76 ct. Reserve List 2007-08. Appointed 2009.

†O'SHAUGHNESSY, Steven Joseph (Harper Green SS, Franworth), b Bury, Lancs 9 Sep 1961. 5'10½". RHB, RM. Lancashire 1980-87; cap 1985. Worcestershire 1988-89. Scored 100 in 35 min to equal world record for La v Leics (Manchester) 1983. 1000 runs (1): 1167 (1984). HS 159* La v Somerset (Bath) 1984. BB 4-66 La v Notts (Nottingham) 1982. F-c career: 112 matches; 3720 runs @ 24.31, 5 hundreds; 114 wickets @ 36.03; 57 ct. Reserve list 2009-10. Appointed 2011.

ROBINSON, Robert Timothy (Dunstable GS; High Pavement SFC; Sheffield U), b Sutton in Ashfield, Notts 21 Nov 1958. 6'0". RHB, RM. Nottinghamshire 1978-99; cap 1983; captain 1988-95; benefit 1992. *Wisden* 1985. **Tests:** 29 (1984-85 to 1989); HS 175 v A (Leeds) 1985. **LOI:** 26 (1984-85 to 1988); HS 83 v P (Sharjah) 1986-87. F-c Tours: A 1987-88; SA 1989-90 (Eng XI), 1996-97 (Nt); NZ 1987-88; WI 1985-86; I/SL 1984-85; P 1987-88. 1000 runs (14) inc 2000 (1): 2032 (1984). HS 220* v Yorks (Nottingham) 1990. BB 1-22. F-c career: 425 matches; 27571 runs @ 42.15, 63 hundreds; 4 wickets @ 72.25; 257 ct. Appointed 2007.

SHARP, George (Elwick Road SS, Hartlepool), b West Hartlepool, Co Durham 12 Mar 1950. 5'11". RHB, WK, occ LM. Northamptonshire 1968-85; cap 1973; benefit 1982. HS 98 Nh v Yorks (Northampton) 1983. BB 1-47. F-c career: 306 matches; 6254 runs @ 19.85; 1 wicket @ 70.00; 655 dismissals (565 ct, 90 st). Appointed 1992. Umpired 15 Tests (1996 to 2001-02) and 31 LOI (1995-96 to 2001-02). **ICC International Panel 1996 to 2001-02.**

STEELE, John Frederick (Endon SS), b Brown Edge, Staffs 23 Jul 1946. 5'10½". RHB, SLA. Brother of D.S. (Northants, Derbys and England 1963-84). Leicestershire 1970-83; cap 1971; benefit 1983. Glamorgan 1984-86; cap 1984. Natal 1973-74 to 1977-78. Staffordshire 1965-69. F-c Tour (DHR): SA 1974-75. 1000 runs (6); most – 1347 (1972). HS 195 Le v Derbys (Leicester) 1971. BB 7-29 Natal B v GW (Umzinto) 1973-74 and 7-29 Le v Glos (Leicester) 1980. F-c career: 379 matches; 15054 runs @ 28.95, 21 hundreds; 584 wickets @ 27.04; 413 ct. Appointed 1997.

WILLEY, Peter (Seaham SS), b Sedgefield, Co Durham 6 Dec 1949. 6'1". RHB, OB. Northamptonshire 1966-83; cap 1971; benefit 1981. Leicestershire 1984-91; cap 1984; captain 1987. EP 1982-83 to 1984-85. Northumberland 1992. **Tests:** 26 (1976 to 1986); HS 102* v WI (St John's) 1980-81; BB 2-73 v WI (Lord's) 1980. **LOI:** 26 (1977 to 1985-86); HS 64 v A (Sydney) 1979-80; BB 3-33 v A (Melbourne) 1979-80. F-c Tours: A 1979-80; SA 1972-73 (DHR), 1981-82 (SAB); WI 1980-81, 1985-86; I 1979-80; SL 1977-78 (DHR). 1000 runs (10); most – 1783 (1982). HS 227 Nh v Somerset (Northampton) 1976. 50 wkts (3); most – 52 (1979). BB 7-37 Nh v OU (Oxford) 1975. F-c career: 559 matches; 24361 runs @ 30.56, 44 hundreds; 756 wickets @ 30.95; 235 ct. Appointed 1993. Umpired 25 Tests (1995-96 to 2003-04) and 34 LOI (1996 to 2003), including 1999 and 2002-03 World Cups. **ICC International Panel 1996 to 2001-02 and 2003-04.**

RESERVE FIRST-CLASS LIST: Paul Baldwin, Ismail Dawood, Mark A.Eggleston, Russell Evans, Andrew Hicks, Graham D.Lloyd, Steven J.Malone, Martin Saggers, Billy Taylor, Alex Wharf.

Test Match statistics to 1 April 2011; LOI statistics to 18 February 2011.

UNIVERSITY FIRST-CLASS REGISTER 2010

CAMBRIDGE († Blue 2010)

Full Names	Birthdate	Birthplace	College	Bat/Bowl	F-C Debut
ACKLAND, Ben James	26.10.89	Nuneaton	(Anglia RU)	RHB/OB	2010
†ANSARI, Akbar Shahzaman	03.07.88	Ascot, Berkshire	Trinity H	RHB/LB	2008
†ASHOK, Anand	28.11.88	Hyderabad, India	Queens'	RHB/RM	2009
BROWN, Francis Andrew	21.03.90	Nottingham	Jesus	RHB/SLA	2009
†GOODWIN, Daniel Michael	26.10.89	London	St John's	RHB/RMF	2010
GRAY, Stephen Kevin	06.07.88	Barking, Essex	(Anglia RU)	RHB/WK	2008
†GREENWOOD, James Murray	20.03.85	Hammersmith, London	Hughes Hall	RHB/RMF	2010
†HESKETH, Richard Lindsay	30.03.88	Cambridge	Christ's	RHB/SLC	2010
†HOPKINS, Charles Edwin Heughan	12.06.87	Peterborough	Jesus	RHB/RMF	2010
†HUGHES, Philip Heywood	17.06.91	Southampton	Downing	RHB/RM	2010
JOSLIN, Andrew James Philip	18.12.89	Leytonstone	(Anglia RU)	RHB/RM	2009
†KENNEDY, Augustus Damian John	10.08.90	London	Corpus Christi	RHB/WK	2010
LEE, Nicholas Trevor	16.10.83	Dartford	(Anglia RU)	RHB/LB	2004
LOTAY, Jivan Daulat Singh	25.07.90	High Wycombe	(Anglia RU)	LHB/OB	2009
†OWEN, Frederick Gerard	25.09.85	Chester	Corpus Christi	RHB	2006
PARK, Craig M.	01.03.86	South Africa	(Anglia RU)	RHB/RMF	2010
†TAYLOR, Michael Hugh	06.12.88	Ballymena	Gonville & Caius	RHB/LB	2010
†TIMMS, Richard Thomas	09.09.84	Bristol	Clare	RHB/RFM	2005
TURNBULL, Peter Thomas	20.07.89	Pontypridd	(Anglia RU)	RHB/RMF	2009
WHEATER, Adam Jack	13.02.90	Whipps Cross	(Anglia RU)	RHB/WK	2008
WOOLLEY, Robert James Joseph	06.08.90	Tameside	(Anglia RU)	RHB/RM	2009

DURHAM

Full Names	Birthdate	Birthplace	College	Bat/Bowl	F-C Debut
ATKINSON, James John	24.08.90	Hong Kong	St Mary's	RHB/WK	2009
BLACKABY, Luke Alexander	01.02.91	Farnborough, Kent		LHB/LM	2010
DURANDT, Luc Etienne	01.09.89	Johannesburg, SA	Collingwood	LHB/RM	2010
GALE, Daniel James	15.06.89	Tadworth, Surrey	St Aidan's	RHB/SLA	2008
GLOVER, John Charles	29.08.89	Cardiff, Wales	St Aidan's	RHB/RMF	2008
HARPER, George Michael	05.12.88	Minnesota, USA	St Hild & St Bede	RHB/LFM	2009
MORGAN, Charles Felix Derrington	09.07.89	Leicester	St Aidan's	RHB/WK	2008
NEWTON, Daniel Charles Alexander	14.12.90	London		RHB/RM	2010
PATEL, Luke Adam	06.10.90	Wakefield, Yorks		LHB/OB	2009
ROPER, Christopher George William	20.05.91	Bristol		RHB/RM	2010
SMITH, Gregory Philip	16.11.88	Leicester	St Hild & St Bede	RHB/LB	2009
WATERS, Seren Robert	11.04.90	Nairobi, Kenya	St Cuthbert's	RHB/LBG	2008-09
WESTLEY, Thomas	13.03.89	Cambridge	St Cuthbert's	RHB/OB	2007

LOUGHBOROUGH

Full Names	Birthdate	Birthplace	Bat/Bowl	F-C Debut
BAKER, Gavin Charles	03.10.88	Edgware, Middlesex	RHB/RMF	2009
COPE, Alan Charles	17.07.88	Guildford, Surrey	RHB/RM	2008
EVANS, Rhodri Francis	06.12.89	Swansea, Glamorgan	LHB/RM	2009
GANDAM, Harvey Singh	21.01.90	Slough, Bucks	RHB/RFM	2010
GROVES, Peter Richard	30.06.88	Bromley, Kent	RHB/RMF	2009
MALAN, Charl Christiaan	23.02.89	London	RHB/OB	2009
MURPHY, David	24.06.89	Welwyn Garden City	RHB/WK	2009
ROSE, Simon Alexander Leslie	06.01.89	Huntingdon, Cambridgeshire	RHB/RMF	2009
TAVARÉ, William Andrew	01.01.90	Bristol, Gloucestershire	RHB/RMF	2009
TAYLOR, Robert Meadows Lombe	21.12.89	Northampton	LHB/LM	2010
WELSH, Alex Stephen	01.09.88	Sheffield, Yorkshire	RHB/LB	2010
WINSLADE, Thomas Simon	28.05.90	Epsom, Surrey	RHB/OB	2010

OXFORD († Blue 2010)

Full Names	Birthdate	Birthplace	College	Bat/Bowl	F-C Debut
ABEL, Edward	30.01.88	Salisbury, Wiltshire	(Brookes U)	LHB/SLA	2008
†AGARWAL, Samridh Sunil	13.07.90	Agra, India	Queens	RHB/OB	2010
BARNARD, Michael Robert	08.02.90	Shrewsbury	(Brookes U)	RHB/RMF	2010
BRADSHAW, Duncan Phillip	19.02.86	Harare, Zimbabwe	(Brookes U)	RHB/RFM	2006
†BRYAN, Thomas Edward	31.10.88	Colchester, Essex	Worcester	RHB/RM	2009
CONWAY, Danny Oliver	01.05.85	Stockton-on-Tees	(Brookes U)	RHB/RMF	2010
COUGHTRIE, Richard George	09.07.88	North Shields	(Brookes U)	RHB/WK	2009
†DINGLE, Lewis Allen	16.09.88	Blackpool	ChristChurch	RHB/RMF	2007
JEAVONS, Aaron Francis	23.04.89	Staffordshire	(Brookes U)	LHB/OB	2010
†KING, Daniel Alexander	26.02.83	Canberra, Australia	Merton	LHB/WK	2009
†KRUGER, Neil	15.08.81	Cape Town, SA	Green Templeton	RHB/RM	2008
†LODWICK, Jonathon Andrew	14.10.89	Reading	Worcester	RHB/RM	2010
MARTIN, Jak	07.09.88	Kingston-upon-Thames	(Brookes U)	LHB/RM	2009
†MEADOWS, Nicholas Axel	26.09.80	Brisbane, Australia	St John's	RHB/OB	2010
MILLIGAN, Marc Jon	01.08.87	Pretoria, SA	(Brookes U)	RHB/RMF	2009
†PASCOE, Daniel Charles	14.05.83	Canberra, Australia	Lincoln	RHB/SLA	2009
†SCOTT, Alex James Dennis	04.05.90	Hong Kong	Keble	RHB/LB	2009
†SHARMA, Avinash Sunil	15.09.81	Whangarei, NZ	Green Templeton	RHB/RM	2009
†SHARMA, Rajiv	10.06.84	Auckland, NZ	Mansfield	RHB/RMF	2009
SMITH, David Thomas	13.09.89	Canterbury	(Brookes U)	RHB/RM	2009
STEBBINGS, Benjamin Robert William	06.10.89	Oxford	(Brookes U)	RHB/RM	2010
WATKINS, Simon Joseph Vernon	20.01.89	London	(Brookes U)	LHB/OB	2010
WATSON, Matthew John Corbett	04.04.87	Barnet	(Brookes U)	RHB/LB	2009
YOUNG, Edward George Christopher	21.05.89	Chertsey	(Brookes U)	RHB/SLA	2009

TOURING TEAMS REGISTER 2010

AUSTRALIA

Full Names	Birthdate	Birthplace	Team	Type	F-C Debut
BOLLINGER, Doug Erwin	24.07.81	Sydney	NSW	LHB/LFM	2002-03
CLARKE, Michael John	02.04.81	Liverpool	NSW	RHB/SLA	1999-00
HILFENHAUS, Benjamin William	15.03.83	Ulverstone	Tasmania	RHB/RFM	2005-06
HUSSEY, Michael Edward Killeen	27.05.75	Morley	W Australia	LHB/RM	1994-95
JOHNSON, Mitchell Guy	02.11.81	Townsville	Queensland	LHB/LF	2001-02
KATICH, Simon Mathew	21.08.75	Middle Swan	NSW	LHB/SLC	1996-97
NORTH, Marcus James	28.07.79	Melbourne	W Australia	LHB/OB	1998-99
PAINE, Timothy David	08.12.84	Hobart	Tasmania	RHB/WK	2005-06
PONTING, Ricky Thomas	19.12.74	Launceston	Tasmania	RHB/RM	1992-93
SMITH, Steven Peter Devereux	02.06.89	Sydney	NSW	RHB/LBG	2007-08
WATSON, Shane Robert	17.06.81	Ipswich	Queensland	RHB/RMF	2000-01

BANGLADESH

Full Names	Birthdate	Birthplace	Team	Type	F-C Debut
ABDUR RAZZAK	15.06.82	Khulna	Khulna	LHB/SLA	2001-02
IMRUL KAYES	02.02.87	Kushtia	Khulna	LHB/WK	2006-07
JAHURUL ISLAM	12.12.86	Rajshahi	Rajshahi	RHB/OB	2002-03
JUNAID SIDDIQUE	30.10.87	Rajshahi	Rajshahi	LHB/OB	2003-04
MAHBUBUL ALAM	01.12.83	Dhaka	Dhaka	RHB/RMF	2003-04
MAHMUDULLAH	04.02.86	Mymensingh	Dhaka	RHB/OB	2004-05
MOHAMMAD ASHRAFUL	07.07.84	Dhaka	Dhaka	RHB/OB	2000-01
MUSHFIQUR RAHIM	01.09.88	Bogra	Sylhet	RHB/WK	2004-05
NAEEM ISLAM	31.12.86	Gaibandha	Rajshahi	RHB/OB	2003-04
ROBIUL ISLAM	20.10.86	Satkhira	Khulna	RHB/RMF	2005-06
RUBEL HOSSAIN	01.01.90	Khulna	Chittagong	RHB/RMF	2007-08
SHAFIUL ISLAM	06.10.89	Bogra	Rajshahi	RHB/RFM	2007-08
SHAHADAT HOSSAIN	07.08.86	Dhaka	Dhaka	RHB/RMF	2003-04
SHAKIB AL HASAN	24.03.87	Magura	Khulna	LHB/SLA	2004-05
TAMIM IQBAL	20.03.89	Chittagong	Chittagong	LHB/SLA	2004-05

INDIA A

Full Names	Birthdate	Birthplace	Team	Type	F-C Debut
DHAWAN, Shikhar	05.12.85	Delhi	Delhi	LHB	2004-05
GANAPATHY, Chandrasekar	10.06.81	Madras	Tamil Nadu	RHB/RM	2003-04
IQBAL ABDULLA	02.12.89	Bombay	Mumbai	LHB/SLA	2007-08
JASKARAN SINGH	04.09.89	Mohali	Punjab	RHB/RM	2010
KULKARNI, Dhawal Sunil	10.12.88	Bombay	Mumbai	RHB/RM	2008-09
MUKUND, Abhinav	06.01.90	Madras	Tamil Nadu	LHB/LBG	2007-08
PANDEY, Manish Krishnanand	10.09.89	Nainital	Karnataka	RHB/OB	2008-09
PUJARA, Cheteshwar Arvind	25.01.89	Rajkot	Saurashtra	RHB/LB	2005-06
RAHANE, Ajinkya Madhukar	05.06.88	Ashwi-Khurd	Mumbai	RHB/RM	2007-08
SAHA, Wriddhiman Prasanta	24.10.84	Shaktigarh	Bengal	RHB/WK	2007-08
TIWARY, Manoj Kumar	14.11.85	Howrah	Bengal	RHB/LBG	2004-05
TYAGI, Sudeep	19.09.87	Ghaziabad	Uttar Pradesh	RHB/RM	2007-08
UNADKAT, Jaidev Dipakbhai	18.10.91	Porbandar	Saurashtra	RHB/LMF	2010

PAKISTAN

Full Names	Birthdate	Birthplace	Team	Type	F-C Debut
ABDUR REHMAN	01.03.80	Sialkot	Habib Bank	LHB/SLA	1997-98
AZHAR ALI	19.02.85	Lahore	KRL	RHB/LB	2001-02
DANISH KANERIA	16.12.80	Karachi	Habib Bank	LHB/LBG	1998-99
FAWAD ALAM	08.10.85	Karachi	National Bank	LHB/SLA	2003-04
IMRAN FARHAT	20.05.82	Lahore	Habib Bank	LHB/LB	1998-99
KAMRAN AKMAL	13.01.82	Lahore	National Bank	RHB/WK	1997-98
MOHAMMAD AAMER	13.04.92	Gujjar Khan	National Bank	LHB/LFM	2008-09
MOHAMMAD ASIF	20.12.82	Sheikhupura	National Bank	LHB/RFM	2000-01
MOHAMMAD YOUSUF	27.08.74	Lahore	WAPDA	RHB/OB	1996-97
SAEED AJMAL	14.10.77	Faisalabad	ZT Bank	RHB/OB	1996-97
SALMAN BUTT	07.10.84	Lahore	National Bank	LHB/OB	2000-01
SHAHID AFRIDI	01.03.80	Khyber Agency	Habib Bank	RHB/LBG	1995-96
SHOAIB MALIK	01.02.82	Sialkot	PIA	RHB/OB	1997
UMAR AKMAL	26.05.90	Lahore	SNGPL	RHB/OB	2007-08
UMAR AMIN	16.10.89	Rawalpindi	National Bank	LHB/RM	2007-08
UMAR GUL	14.04.84	Peshawar	Habib Bank	RHB/RFM	2001-02
WAHAB RIAZ	28.06.85	Lahore	National Bank	LHB/LFM	2001-02
YASIR HAMEED	28.02.78	Peshawar	PIA	RHB/OB	1996-97
ZULQARNAIN HAIDER	23.04.86	Lahore	ZT Bank	RHB/WK	2003-04

WEST INDIES A

Full Names	Birthdate	Birthplace	Team	Type	F-C Debut
BAKER, Lionel Sionne	06.09.84	Montserrat	Leeward Is	LHB/RMF	2002-03
BERNARD, David Eddison	19.07.81	Kingston	Jamaica	RHB/RMF	2000-01
BRATHWAITE, Kraigg Clairmonte	01.12.92	St Michael	Barbados	RHB	2008-09
BROWN, Odean Vernon	08.02.82	Westmoreland	Jamaica	RHB/LB	2003-04
EDWARDS, Kirk Anton	03.11.84	St Peter	Barbados	RHB/OB	2005-06
FLETCHER, Andre David Stephon	28.11.87	La Tante, Grenada	Windward Is	RHB/RMF	2003-04
FUDADIN, Assad Badyr	01.08.85	Berbice	Guyana	RHB/RMF	2003-04
GUILLEN, Justin Christopher	02.01.86	Port-of-Spain	Trinidad & T	LHB/OB	2008-09
KHAN, Imran	06.12.84	Port-of-Spain	Trinidad & T	RHB/SLA	2004-05
PHILLIPS, Omar Jamel	12.10.86	St Peter	Combined C&C	LHB/RM	2007-08
RUSSELL, Andre Dwayne	29.04.88	Jamaica	Jamaica	RHB/RF	2006-07
SMITH, Devon Sheldon	21.10.81	Sauters, Grenada	Windward Is	LHB/OB	1998-99
TONGE, Gavin Courtney	13.02.83	St John's	Leeward Is	RHB/RFM	2002-03
WALTON, Chadwick Antonio Kirkpatrick	03.07.85	Jamaica	Combined C&C	RHB/WK	2007-08

THE 2010 FIRST-CLASS SEASON STATISTICAL HIGHLIGHTS

FIRST TO INDIVIDUAL TARGETS

1000 RUNS	A.Lyth	Yorkshire	5 July
2000 RUNS	–	Most 1595 – M.R.Ramprakash (Surrey)	
50 WICKETS	S.T.Finn	Middlesex and England	24 July
100 WICKETS	–	Most 68 – A.R.Adams (Nottinghamshire)	

TEAM HIGHLIGHTS
HIGHEST INNINGS TOTALS

620-7d	Surrey v Northamptonshire	The Oval
611-5d	Oxford University v Cambridge University	Oxford
610-6d	Yorkshire v Durham	Leeds

HIGHEST FOURTH INNINGS TOTALS

395-4	Northamptonshire (set 394) v Middlesex	Northampton

LOWEST INNINGS TOTALS

44	Derbyshire v Gloucestershire	Bristol
59	Nottinghamshire v Yorkshire	Nottingham
66	Middlesex v Worcestershire	Lord's
70	Gloucestershire v Derbyshire	Bristol
71	Leicestershire v Glamorgan	Leicester
72	Pakistan v England (*2nd Test*)	Birmingham
74	Pakistan v England (*4th Test*)	Lord's
80	Pakistan v England (*1st Test*)	Nottingham
86	Gloucestershire v Northamptonshire	Bristol
88	Australia v Pakistan (*2nd Test*)	Leeds
93	Worcestershire v Northamptonshire	Worcester

MATCH AGGREGATES OF 1400 RUNS

1479-28	Yorkshire (405 & 333-4d) v Somerset (377 & 364-4)	Taunton
1402-25	Middx (442-8d & 258-3d) v Northants (307 & 395-4)	Northampton

LARGE MARGINS OF VICTORY

Inns & 225 runs	England (446) v Pakistan (74 & 147)	Lord's
Inns & 175 runs	Surrey (620-7d) v Northants (240 & 205)	The Oval
354 runs	England (354 & 262-9d) v Pakistan (182 & 80)	Nottingham
329 runs	Leicestershire (295 & 351-4d) v Glos (159 & 158)	Leicester

NARROW MARGINS OF VICTORY

2 wickets	Notts (250 & 250-8) beat Somerset (272 & 227)	Nottingham
2 wickets	Hampshire (305 & 281-8 beat Notts (270 & 315)	Nottingham
10 runs	Surrey (186 & 180-3d) beat Glos (106-5d & 250)	Bristol

FOUR HUNDREDS IN AN INNINGS

Sussex (576-3d) v Derbyshire	Horsham

60 EXTRAS IN AN INNINGS

	B	LB	W	NB		
76	6	19	13	38	Gloucestershire (242) v Derbyshire	Derby
69	20	26	15	8	Middlesex (442-8d) v Northamptonshire	Northampton

BATTING HIGHLIGHTS
DOUBLE HUNDREDS

S.M.Ervine	237*	Hampshire v Somerset	Southampton
D.J.Hussey	251*	Nottinghamshire v Yorkshire	Leeds
R.W.T.Key	261	Kent v Durham	Canterbury
C.A.Pujara	208*	India A v West Indies A	Croydon
M.R.Ramprakash (2)	223	Surrey v Middlesex	The Oval
	248	Surrey v Northamptonshire	The Oval
S.D.Robson	204	Middlesex v Oxford MCCU	Oxford
C.J.L.Rogers	200	Derbyshire v Surrey	The Oval
J.L.Rudolph	228*	Yorkshire v Durham	Leeds
J.W.A.Taylor	206*	Leicestershire v Middlesex	Leicester
M.E.Trescothick	228*	Somerset v Essex	Colchester
I.J.L.Trott	226	England v Bangladesh (*1st Test*)	Lord's

HUNDREDS IN THREE CONSECUTIVE INNINGS

| D.K.H.Mitchell | 104 | 134* | Worcestershire v Gloucestershire | Cheltenham |
| | 165* | | Worcestershire v Glamorgan | Colwyn Bay |

HUNDRED IN EACH INNINGS OF A MATCH

R.S.Bopara	142	102	Essex v Yorkshire	Chelmsford
M.A.Carberry	162	107	Hampshire v Durham	Basingstoke
D.K.H.Mitchell	104	134*	Worcestershire v Gloucestershire	Cheltenham
M.R.Ramprakash	223	103*	Surrey v Middlesex	The Oval
C.J.L.Rogers	200	140*	Derbyshire v Surrey	The Oval

FASTEST HUNDRED AGAINST GENUINE BOWLING

| J.C.Hildreth (102*) | 68 balls | Somerset v Yorkshire | Taunton |

SEVEN SIXES IN AN INNINGS

| 7 | M.E.Trescothick (228*) | Somerset v Essex | Colchester |
| 7 | L.J.Wright (94*) | Sussex v Worcestershire | Worcester |

150 RUNS FROM BOUNDARIES IN AN INNINGS

| *Runs* | *6s* | *4s* | | |
| 170 | 3 | 38 | R.W.T.Key (261) | Kent v Durham | Canterbury |

HUNDRED ON FIRST-CLASS DEBUT

A.S.Sharma   185*   Oxford University v Cambridge University   Oxford
The highest hundred on debut this century.

HUNDRED ON FIRST-CLASS DEBUT IN BRITAIN

S.Dhawan	179	India A v Yorkshire	Leeds
Jahurul Islam	158	Bangladeshis v Surrey	The Oval
A.M.Rahane	118	India A v Yorkshire	Leeds
Umar Akmal	153	Pakistanis v Kent	Canterbury

CARRYING BAT THROUGH COMPLETED INNINGS

| M.J.Di Venuto | 117* | Durham (213) v Yorkshire | Chester-le-Street |
| I.J.Westwood | 82* | Warwickshire (197) v Lancashire | Manchester |

LONG INNINGS (Qualification 600 mins and/or 400 balls)

Mins Balls
635 508   J.H.K.Adams (194)   Hampshire v Lancashire   Liverpool

FIRST-WICKET PARTNERSHIP OF 100 IN EACH INNINGS

163/103   A.J.Strauss/S.A.Newman   Middlesex v Surrey   The Oval

OTHER NOTABLE PARTNERSHIPS († *County record*)

Qualifications: 1st-4th wkts: 250 runs; 5th-6th: 225; 7th: 200; 8th: 175; 9th: 150; 10th: 100.

First Wicket
294   E.C.Joyce/C.D.Nash   Sussex v Derbyshire   Horsham
273   C.J.L.Rogers/W.L.Madsen   Derbyshire v Northants   Northampton
259   D.A.King/S.S.Agarwal   Oxford U v Cambridge U   Oxford

Second Wicket
314   M.A.Carberry/M.J.Lumb   Hampshire v Durham   Basingstoke
272   R.W.T.Key/G.O.Jones   Kent v Loughborough MCCU   Canterbury

Fourth Wicket
360*† J.W.A.Taylor/A.B.McDonald Leicestershire v Middlesex   Leicester
278† J.H.K.Adams/J.M.Vince   Hampshire v Yorkshire   Scarborough
266   O.A.Shah/N.J.Dexter   Middlesex v Leicestershire   Leicester
254   M.A.Carberry/N.D.McKenzie   Hampshire v Kent   Southampton
253   A.V.Suppiah/J.C.Hildreth   Somerset v Kent   Canterbury

Fifth Wicket
339† J.C.Mickleburgh/J.S.Foster   Essex v Durham   Chester-le-Street

Sixth Wicket
270   D.I.Stevens/J.C.Tredwell   Kent v Nottinghamshire   Tunbridge Wells

Seventh Wicket
237   A.D.Brown/C.M.W.Read   Nottinghamshire v Durham   Nottingham
225   M.W.Goodwin/R.S.C.Martin-Jenkins   Sussex v Derbyshire   Derby

Eighth Wicket
332   I.J.L.Trott/S.C.J.Broad   England v Pakistan   Lord's
   This was the highest partnership for the eighth wicket in all Test cricket and in all cricket in England.

Tenth Wicket
123   T.D.Groenewald/P.S.Jones   Derbyshire v Worcestershire   Worcester
118   A.Nel/J.W.Dernbach   Surrey v Northamptonshire   Northampton
118   A.G.Botha/Imran Tahir   Warwickshire v Kent   Birmingham
103   C.R.Woakes/Imran Tahir   Warwickshire v Hampshire   Birmingham

BOWLING HIGHLIGHTS
EIGHT WICKETS IN AN INNINGS

S.C.J.Broad   8- 52   Nottinghamshire v Warwickshire   Birmingham
S.T.Finn   9- 37   Middlesex v Worcestershire   Worcester
Imran Tahir   8-114   Warwickshire v Durham   Birmingham

TEN WICKETS IN A MATCH

J.M.Anderson	11- 71	England v Pakistan (*1st Test*)	Nottingham
S.C.J.Broad	11-131	Nottinghamshire v Warwickshire	Birmingham
M.A.Chambers	10-123	Essex v Nottinghamshire	Chelmsford
S.T.Finn	14-106	Middlesex v Worcestershire	Worcester
M.Kartik (2) #	11- 72	Somerset v Warwickshire	Birmingham
	10-107	Somerset v Kent	Taunton
G.Keedy	10-128	Lancashire v Durham	Manchester
M.Ntini	10-104	Kent v Durham	Chester-le-Street
J.D.Unadkat†	13-103	India A v West Indies A	Leicester
C.R.Woakes	11- 97	Warwickshire v Kent	Birmingham

† *On first-class debut.* # *In successive matches; he took five or more wickets in five consecutive innings.*

FOUR WICKETS IN FIVE BALLS

P.S.Jones	Derbyshire v Gloucestershire	Bristol

HAT-TRICKS

R.D.B.Croft	Glamorgan v Gloucestershire	Cheltenham
A.J.Hall	Northamptonshire v Glamorgan	Northampton
J.C.Tredwell	Kent v Yorkshire	Leeds

MOST RUNS CONCEDED IN AN INNINGS

R.J.Peterson	47-7-170-4	Derbyshire v Worcestershire	Worcester

MOST OVERS BOWLED IN AN INNINGS

G.Keedy	58-13-105-1	Lancashire v Hampshire	Liverpool

WICKET-KEEPING HIGHLIGHTS

SIX WICKET-KEEPING DISMISSALS IN AN INNINGS

S.M.Davies	6ct	England Lions v Bangladeshis	Derby
C.M.W.Read	6ct	Nottinghamshire v Essex	Chelmsford

NINE WICKET-KEEPING DISMISSALS IN A MATCH

D.Murphy	9ct	Northamptonshire v Glamorgan	Northampton

NO BYES CONCEDED IN AN INNINGS OF 600 OR MORE

610-6d	P.Mustard	Durham v Yorkshire	Leeds

FIELDING HIGHLIGHTS

FIVE CATCHES IN THE FIELD IN AN INNINGS

N.J.Edwards	5ct	Nottinghamshire v Kent	Nottingham

SIX CATCHES IN THE FIELD IN A MATCH

C.J.L.Rogers	6ct	Derbyshire v Surrey	Chesterfield

COUNTY CHAMPIONSHIP 2010
LV FINAL TABLES

DIVISION 1

	P	W	L	D	Bat	Bowl	Deduct Points	Total Points
1 **NOTTINGHAMSHIRE** (2)	16	7	5	4	47	43	–	214
2 Somerset (3)	16	6	2	8	53	41	–	214
3 Yorkshire (7)	16	6	2	8	41	42	–	203
4 Lancashire (4)	16	5	3	8	35	43	–	182
5 Durham (1)	16	5	3	8	30	39	–	173
6 Warwickshire (5)	16	6	9	1	20	47	–	166
7 Hampshire (6)	16	3	6	7	47	41	–	157
8 Kent (–)	16	3	7	6	42	44	1	151
9 Essex (–)	16	2	6	8	29	43	2	126

DIVISION 2

	P	W	L	D	Bat	Bowl	Deduct Points	Total Points
1 Sussex (–)	16	8	3	5	45	47	–	235
2 Worcestershire (–)	16	7	4	5	39	42	–	208
3 Glamorgan (5)	16	7	4	5	33	43	–	203
4 Leicestershire (9)	16	7	5	4	31	44	–	199
5 Gloucestershire (4)	16	6	9	1	28	47	2	172
6 Northamptonshire (3)	16	6	7	3	28	34	–	167
7 Surrey (7)	16	4	6	6	43	36	2	159
8 Middlesex (8)	16	4	7	5	37	41	2	155
9 Derbyshire (6)	16	3	7	6	30	42	–	138

SCORING OF CHAMPIONSHIP POINTS 2010

(a) For a win, 16 points, plus any points scored in the first innings.

(b) In a tie, each side to score eight points, plus any points scored in the first innings.

(c) In a drawn match, each side to score three points, plus any points scored in the first innings (see also paragraph (f) below).

(d) If the scores are equal in a drawn match, the side batting in the fourth innings to score eight points plus any points scored in the first innings, and the opposing side to score three points plus any points scored in the first innings.

(e) **First Innings Points** (awarded only for performances **in the first 110 overs** of each first innings and retained whatever the result of the match).

   (i) A maximum of five batting points to be available as under:
      200 to 249 runs – 1 point; 250 to 299 runs – 2 points; 300 to 349 runs – 3 points; 350 to 399 runs – 4 points; 400 runs or over – 5 points.

   (ii) A maximum of three bowling points to be available as under:
      3 to 5 wickets taken – 1 point; 6 to 8 wickets taken – 2 points; 9 to 10 wickets taken – 3 points.

(f) If a match is abandoned without a ball being bowled, each side to score three points.

(g) The side which has the highest aggregate of points gained at the end of the season shall be the Champion County of their respective Division. Should any sides in the Championship table be equal on points, the following tie-breakers will be applied in the order stated: most wins, fewest losses, team achieving most points in contests between teams level on points, most wickets taken, most runs scored. At the end of the season, the top two teams from the Second Division will be promoted and the bottom two teams from the First Division will be relegated.

COUNTY CHAMPIONS

The English County Championship was not officially constituted until December 1889. Prior to that date there was no generally accepted method of awarding the title; although the 'least matches lost' method existed, it was not consistently applied. Rules governing playing qualifications were agreed in 1873 and the first unofficial points system 15 years later.

Research has produced a list of champions dating back to 1826, but at least seven different versions exist for the period from 1864 to 1889 (see *The Wisden Book of Cricket Records*). Only from 1890 can any authorised list of county champions commence.

That first official Championship was contested between eight counties: Gloucestershire, Kent, Lancashire, Middlesex, Nottinghamshire, Surrey, Sussex and Yorkshire. The remaining counties were admitted in the following seasons: 1891 – Somerset, 1895 – Derbyshire, Essex, Hampshire, Leicestershire and Warwickshire, 1899 – Worcestershire, 1905 – Northamptonshire, 1921 – Glamorgan, and 1992 – Durham.

The Championship pennant was introduced by the 1951 champions, Warwickshire, and the Lord's Taverners' Trophy was first presented in 1973. The first sponsors, Schweppes (1977-83), were succeeded by Britannic Assurance (1984-98), PPP Healthcare (1999-2000), CricInfo (2001), Frizzell (2002-2005) and Liverpool Victoria (2006 to 2010). Based on their previous season's positions, the 18 counties were separated into two divisions in 2000. From 2000 to 2005 the bottom three Division 1 teams were relegated and the top three Division 2 sides promoted. This was reduced to two teams from the end of the 2006 season.

1890	Surrey	1932	Yorkshire	1971	Surrey
1891	Surrey	1933	Yorkshire	1972	Warwickshire
1892	Surrey	1934	Lancashire	1973	Hampshire
1893	Yorkshire	1935	Yorkshire	1974	Worcestershire
1894	Surrey	1936	Derbyshire	1975	Leicestershire
1895	Surrey	1937	Yorkshire	1976	Middlesex
1896	Yorkshire	1938	Yorkshire	1977	{ Kent
1897	Lancashire	1939	Yorkshire		Middlesex
1898	Yorkshire	1946	Yorkshire	1978	Kent
1899	Surrey	1947	Middlesex	1979	Essex
1900	Yorkshire	1948	Glamorgan	1980	Middlesex
1901	Yorkshire	1949	{ Middlesex	1981	Nottinghamshire
1902	Yorkshire		Yorkshire	1982	Middlesex
1903	Middlesex	1950	{ Lancashire	1983	Essex
1904	Lancashire		Surrey	1984	Essex
1905	Yorkshire	1951	Warwickshire	1985	Middlesex
1906	Kent	1952	Surrey	1986	Essex
1907	Nottinghamshire	1953	Surrey	1987	Nottinghamshire
1908	Yorkshire	1954	Surrey	1988	Worcestershire
1909	Kent	1955	Surrey	1992	Essex
1910	Kent	1956	Surrey	1993	Middlesex
1911	Warwickshire	1957	Surrey	1994	Warwickshire
1912	Yorkshire	1958	Surrey	1995	Warwickshire
1913	Kent	1959	Yorkshire	1996	Leicestershire
1914	Surrey	1989	Worcestershire	1997	Glamorgan
1919	Yorkshire	1990	Middlesex	1998	Leicestershire
1920	Middlesex	1991	Essex	1999	Surrey
1921	Middlesex	1960	Yorkshire	2000	Surrey
1922	Yorkshire	1961	Hampshire	2001	Yorkshire
1923	Yorkshire	1962	Yorkshire	2002	Surrey
1924	Yorkshire	1963	Yorkshire	2003	Sussex
1925	Yorkshire	1964	Worcestershire	2004	Warwickshire
1926	Lancashire	1965	Worcestershire	2005	Nottinghamshire
1927	Lancashire	1966	Yorkshire	2006	Sussex
1928	Lancashire	1967	Yorkshire	2007	Sussex
1929	Nottinghamshire	1968	Yorkshire	2008	Durham
1930	Lancashire	1969	Glamorgan	2009	Durham
1931	Yorkshire	1970	Kent	2010	Nottinghamshire

COUNTY CHAMPIONSHIP RESULTS 2010

DIVISION 1

	DURHAM	ESSEX	HANTS	KENT	LANCS	NOTTS	SOM'T	WARWKS	YORKS
DURHAM	–	C-le-St Drawn	C-le-St D 5w	C-le-St K I/4	C-le-St Drawn	C-le-St D 210	C-le-St Drawn	C-le-St D 219	C-le-St Y 4w
ESSEX	Chelms Drawn	–	Chelms E 62	Chelms Drawn	Chelms L 8w	Chelms E 143	Colchester S 219	Southend W 7w	Chelms Drawn
HANTS	B'stoke Drawn	So'ton Drawn	–	So'ton H I/111	So'ton Drawn	So'ton N 5w	So'ton Drawn	So'ton W 10w	So'ton Drawn
KENT	Cant D 6w	Cant K 99	Cant H 130	–	Cant L 121	Tun W Drawn	Cant Drawn	Cant W 44	Cant Drawn
LANCS	Man D 6w	Man Drawn	L'pool L 3w	Man Drawn	–	Man Drawn	Man Drawn	Man L 121	Man Drawn
NOTTS	N'ham N I/62	N'ham Drawn	N'ham H 2w	N'ham N I/32	N'ham N 3w	–	N'ham N 2w	N'ham N I/55	N'ham Y 5w
SOM'T	Taunton Drawn	Taunton Drawn	Taunton Drawn	Taunton Drawn	Taunton Drawn	Taunton S 10w	–	Taunton S 9w	Taunton S 6w
WARWKS	B'ham Drawn	B'ham W 7w	B'ham W 8w	B'ham W 95	B'ham L 65	B'ham N 10w	B'ham S 181	–	B'ham Y 4w
YORKS	Leeds Drawn	Scar Y I/96	Scar Drawn	Leeds K 4w	Leeds Drawn	Leeds Drawn	Leeds Y 6w	Leeds Y 6w	–

DIVISION 2

	DERBYS	GLAM	GLOS	LEICS	MIDDX	N'HANTS	SURREY	SUSSEX	WORCS
DERBYS	–	Derby D 8w	Derby Gs 134	Derby L 203	Derby Drawn	C'field Drawn	C'field Sy 42	Derby Drawn	Derby Drawn
GLAM	Cardiff Drawn	–	Cardiff Gm I/4	Swansea Drawn	Cardiff M 6w	Cardiff Gm I/4	Cardiff Drawn	Cardiff Sx 201	Col B Gm 241
GLOS	Bristol D 54	Chelt'm Gm 176	–	Leics Gs 9w	Bristol Gs 10w	Bristol N 94	Bristol Sy 10	Bristol Sx 207	Chelt'm W 6w
LEICS	Leics L 10w	Leics Gm 10w	Leics L 329	–	Leics Drawn	Leics L 6w	Leics Drawn	Leics Sx I/19	Leics W 173
MIDDX	Lord's M I/35	Lord's Gm 78	Lord's Gs 103	Lord's Drawn	–	Lord's N 9w	Lord's M I/44	Uxbridge Drawn	Lord's W 111
N'HANTS	No'ton Drawn	No'ton N 10w	No'ton Gs 7w	No'ton L 10w	No'ton N 6w	–	No'ton Sy 7w	No'ton N 3w	No'ton Drawn
SURREY	Oval D 208	Oval Drawn	Oval Gs 77	Oval L I/60	Oval Drawn	Oval Sy I/175	–	Guildford Drawn	Croydon Drawn
SUSSEX	Horsham Sx I/109	Hove Sx 8w	Arundel Sx 8w	Hove Sx 10w	Hove M 3w	Hove Sx I/19	Hove Sx 10w	–	Hove Drawn
WORCS	Worcs W 8w	Worcs Gm 9w	Worcs Drawn	Worcs L 7w	Worcs W 111	Worcs N 4w	Worcs W 238	Worcs W 4w	–

COUNTY CHAMPIONSHIP RESULTS 2011

KEEP YOUR OWN RECORD (see page 211)

DIVISION 1

	DURHAM	HANTS	LANCS	NOTTS	SOM'T	SUSSEX	WARWKS	WORCS	YORKS
DURHAM	–	C-le-St	C-le-St	C-le-St	C-le-St	C-le-St	C-le-St	C-le-St	C-le-St
HANTS	So'ton	–	So'ton	So'ton	So'ton	So'ton	So'ton	So'ton	So'ton
LANCS	L'pool	Man	–	S'port	L'pool	L'pool	L'pool	B'pool	L'pool
NOTTS	N'ham	N'ham	N'ham	–	N'ham	N'ham	N'ham	N'ham	N'ham
SOM'T	Taunton	Taunton	Taunton	Taunton	–	Taunton	Taunton	Taunton	Taunton
SUSSEX	Hove	Hove	Hove	Hove	Hove	–	Arundel	Horsham	Hove
WARWKS	B'ham	B'ham	B'ham	B'ham	B'ham	B'ham	–	B'ham	B'ham
WORCS	Worcs	Worcs	Worcs	Worcs	Worcs	Worcs	Worcs	–	Worcs
YORKS	Leeds	Leeds	Leeds	Leeds	Leeds	Scar	Leeds	Scar	–

DIVISION 2

	DERBYS	ESSEX	GLAM	GLOS	KENT	LEICS	MIDDX	N'HANTS	SURREY
DERBYS	–	Derby	Derby	Derby	Derby	Derby	Derby	C'field	Derby
ESSEX	C'ford	–	C'ford	Colch'r	C'ford	Southend	C'ford	C'ford	C'ford
GLAM	Cardiff	Cardiff	–	Cardiff	Cardiff	Col B	Cardiff	Swansea	Cardiff
GLOS	Bristol	Bristol	Bristol	–	Chelt'm	Bristol	Bristol	Bristol	Chelt'm
KENT	Cant	Cant	Cant	Cant	–	Tun W	Cant	Cant	Cant
LEICS	Leics	Leics	Leics	Leics	Leics	–	Leics	Leics	Leics
MIDDX	Lord's	Lord's	Lord's	Uxbridge	Lord's	Lord's	–	Lord's	Lord's
N'HANTS	No'ton	No'ton	No'ton	No'ton	No'ton	No'ton	No'ton	–	No'ton
SURREY	Oval	Croydon	Oval	Oval	Oval	Oval	Guildford	Oval	–

CLYDESDALE BANK 40 2010

This latest format of the 40-over competition was launched in 2010, and was the only List-A tournament played in the UK that season. The three Group winners, plus the runner-up with the most points, met in the semi-finals, with the winner decided in the final at Lord's.

GROUP A	P	W	L	T	NR	Pts	Net RR
1 Somerset	12	10	2	–	–	20	+1.49
2 Sussex	12	7	3	1	1	16	+0.90
3 Surrey	12	6	4	1	1	14	–0.01
4 Lancashire	12	6	6	–	–	12	–0.32
5 Worcestershire	12	4	8	–	–	8	–0.20
6 Unicorns	12	3	7	–	2	8	–0.47
7 Glamorgan	12	2	8	–	2	6	–1.59

GROUP B	P	W	L	T	NR	Pts	Net RR
1 Yorkshire	12	10	2	–	–	20	+0.38
2 Essex	12	9	2	–	1	19	+0.31
3 Gloucestershire	12	9	3	–	–	18	0.66
4 Derbyshire	12	4	8	–	–	8	–0.037
5 Northamptonshire	12	4	8	–	–	8	–0.038
6 Middlesex	12	3	7	–	2	8	–0.45
7 Netherlands	12	1	10	–	1	3	–1.00

GROUP C	P	W	L	T	NR	Pts	Net RR
1 Warwickshire	12	9	3	–	–	18	+0.31
2 Kent	12	7	3	–	2	16	+0.77
3 Nottinghamshire	12	7	4	–	1	15	+0.35
4 Hampshire	12	6	6	–	–	12	+0.01
5 Durham	12	5	6	–	1	11	+0.26
6 Leicestershire	12	4	8	–	–	8	–0.22
7 Scotland	12	2	10	–	–	4	–1.23

Win = 2 points. Tie (T)/No Result (NR) = 1 point.

Positions of counties finishing equal on points are decided by most wins or, if equal, the team that achieved the most points in the matches played between them; if still equal, the team with the higher net run rate (ie deducting from the average runs per over scored by that team in matches where a result was achieved, the average runs per over scored against that team).

Statistical Highlights in 2010

Highest total	386-3	Surrey v Glamorgan	The Oval
Biggest victory (runs)	249	Somerset beat Glamorgan	Taunton
Biggest victory (wkts)	10	Yorkshire beat Essex	Chelmsford
Most runs	861 (ave 95.66) J.A.Rudolph (Yorkshire)		
Highest innings	147	P.D.Trego	Somerset v Glamorgan	Taunton
Most sixes	8	R.N.ten Doeschate	Essex v Derbyshire	Leek
Highest partnership	233*	A.W.Gale/J.A.Rudolph	Yorkshire v Essex	Chelmsford
Most wickets	27 (ave 15.92) A.C.Thomas (Somerset)		
Best bowling	7-29	D.A.Payne	Gloucestershire v Essex	Chelmsford
Most economical	8-2-9-0	S.A.Patterson	Yorkshire v Netherlands	Schiedam
Most expensive	8-0-100-0	D.S.Harrison	Glamorgan v Somerset	Taunton

2010 CLYDESDALE BANK 40 FINAL

SOMERSET v WARWICKSHIRE

At Lord's, London, on 18 September (floodlit).
Result: **WARWICKSHIRE** won by three wickets.
Toss: Warwickshire. Award: I.R.Bell.

SOMERSET		Runs	Balls	4/6	Fall
* M.E.Trescothick	c Woakes b Barker	21	17	3	1- 41
† C.Kieswetter	c Barker b Carter	37	43	4	3- 81
P.D.Trego	c Clarke b Barker	11	16	2	2- 62
N.R.D.Compton	lbw b Tahir	60	65	2	7-179
J.C.Hildreth	run out	44	46	3	4-176
J.C.Buttler	lbw b Tahir	0	2	–	5-176
A.V.Suppiah	b Tahir	1	6	–	6-178
B.J.Phillips	c Bell b Tahir	1	11	–	8-180
A.C.Thomas	not out	6	10	–	
M.Kartik	st Johnson b Tahir	3	3	–	9-187
M.L.Turner	c Clarke b Carter	8	16	1	10-199
Extras	(W 5, NB 2)	7			
Total	**(39 overs)**	**199**			

WARWICKSHIRE		Runs	Balls	4/6	Fall
I.J.L.Trott	c Kieswetter b Phillips	17	35	2	3- 39
N.M.Carter	c Trego b Phillips	5	6	1	1- 12
K.H.D.Barker	c Turner b Thomas	3	10	–	2- 20
* I.R.Bell	c Buttler b Thomas	107	95	12	7-199
J.O.Troughton	c Kieswetter b Thomas	30	48	2	4-118
D.L.Maddy	c Kartik b Turner	9	11	–	5-135
R.Clarke	c Hildreth b Trego	19	20	2/1	6-164
A.G.Botha	not out	4	8	–	
C.R.Woakes	not out	1	2	–	
† R.M.Johnson					
Imran Tahir					
Extras	(B 1, LB 2, NB 2)	5			
Total	**(7 wkts; 39 overs)**	**200**			

WARWICKSHIRE	O	M	R	W	SOMERSET	O	M	R	W
Carter	6	0	40	2	Thomas	8	1	33	3
Woakes	8	1	31	0	Phillips	8	0	24	2
Barker	7	0	33	2	Turner	7	0	71	1
Botha	8	0	39	0	Kartik	8	0	27	0
Imran Tahir	8	0	41	5	Trego	7	0	36	1
Maddy	2	0	15	0	Suppiah	1	0	6	0

Umpires: P.J.Hartley and R.A.Kettleborough

SEMI-FINALS

At County Ground, Taunton, on 11 September. Toss: Somerset. SOMERSET won by 95
runs. Somerset 312-6 (40; M.E.Trescothick 79, N.R.D.Compton 55). Essex 217 (29.3;
J.S.Foster 58). Award: M.E.Trescothick.

At North Marine Ground, Scarborough, on 11 September. Toss: Warwickshire.
WARWICKSHIRE won by four wickets (D/L method). Yorkshire 257-5 (37; J.A.Rudolph
106, G.L.Brophy 64). Warwickshire 260-6 (35.5/37; V.Chopra 76, I.R.Bell 57).

CLYDESDALE BANK/PRO40/NATIONAL/SUNDAY LEAGUE CHAMPIONS

1969	Lancashire	1983	Yorkshire	1997	Warwickshire
1970	Lancashire	1984	Essex	1998	Lancashire
1971	Worcestershire	1985	Essex	1999	Lancashire
1972	Kent	1986	Hampshire	2000	Gloucestershire
1973	Kent	1987	Worcestershire	2001	Kent
1974	Leicestershire	1988	Worcestershire	2002	Glamorgan
1975	Hampshire	1989	Lancashire	2003	Surrey
1976	Kent	1990	Derbyshire	2004	Glamorgan
1977	Leicestershire	1991	Nottinghamshire	2005	Essex
1978	Hampshire	1992	Middlesex	2006	Essex
1979	Somerset	1993	Glamorgan	2007	Worcestershire
1980	Warwickshire	1994	Warwickshire	2008	Sussex
1981	Essex	1995	Kent	2009	Sussex
1982	Sussex	1996	Surrey	2010	Warwickshire

PRINCIPAL 40-OVER RECORDS 1969-2010

Highest Total		386-3	Surrey v Glamorgan	The Oval	2010
Highest Total Batting Second		327-4	Unicorns v Sussex	Arundel	2010
Lowest Total		23	Middlesex v Yorks	Leeds	1974
Largest Victory (Runs)		249	Somerset beat Glamorgan	Taunton	2010
Highest Scores	203	A.D.Brown	Surrey v Hampshire	Guildford	1997
	191	D.S.Lehmann	Yorks v Notts	Scarborough	2001
	184	M.E.Trescothick	Somerset v Glos	Taunton	2008
	176	G.A.Gooch	Essex v Glamorgan	Southend	1983
	175*	I.T.Botham	Somerset v Northants	Wellingborough	1986
Fastest Hundred	44 balls	M.A.Ealham	Kent v Derbyshire	Maidstone	1995
Most Sixes (Inns)	13	I.T.Botham	Somerset v Northants	Wellingborough	1986
Highest Partnership for each Wicket					
1st	239	G.A.Gooch/B.R.Hardie	Essex v Notts	Nottingham	1985
2nd	302	M.E.Trescothick/C.Kieswetter	Somerset v Glos	Taunton	2008
3rd	228*	M.W.Goodwin/C.J.Adams	Sussex v Middlesex	Hove	2003
4th	219	C.G.Greenidge/C.L.Smith	Hampshire v Surrey	Southampton	1987
5th	221*	R.R.Sarwan/M.A.Hardinges	Glos v Lancashire	Manchester	2005
6th	167	C.L.Cairns/C.M.W.Read	Notts v Sussex	Nottingham	2003
7th	164	J.N.Snape/M.A.Hardinges	Glos v Notts	Nottingham	2001
8th	116*	N.D.Burns/P.A.J.DeFreitas	Leics v Northants	Leicester	2001
9th	105	D.G.Moir/R.W.Taylor	Derbyshire v Kent	Derby	1984
10th	82	G.Chapple/P.J.Martin	Lancashire v Worcs	Manchester	1996
Best Bowling	8-26	K.D.Boyce	Essex v Lancashire	Manchester	1971
	7-15	R.A.Hutton	Yorkshire v Worcs	Leeds	1969
	7-16	S.D.Thomas	Glamorgan v Surrey	Swansea	1998
	7-29	D.A.Payne	Gloucestershire v Essex	Chelmsford	2010
	7-30	M.P.Bicknell	Surrey v Glamorgan	The Oval	1999
	7-39	A.Hodgson	Northants v Somerset	Northampton	1976
	7-41	A.N.Jones	Sussex v Notts	Nottingham	1986
Four Wkts in Four Balls		A.Ward	Derbyshire v Sussex	Derby	1970
		V.C.Drakes	Notts v Derbys	Nottingham	1999
		D.A.Payne	Gloucestershire v Essex	Chelmsford	2010
Most Economical Analysis					
	8-8-0-0	B.A.Langford	Somerset v Essex	Yeovil	1969
Most Expensive Analysis					
	8-0-100-0	D.S.Harrison	Glamorgan v Somerset	Taunton	2010
Most Wicket-Keeping Dismissals in an Innings					
	7 (6ct, 1st)	R.W.Taylor	Derbyshire v Lancs	Manchester	1975
Most Catches in an Innings by a Fielder					
	5	J.M.Rice	Hampshire v Warwicks	Southampton	1978
	5	D.J.G.Sales	Northants v Essex	Northampton	2007

FRIENDS PROVIDENT t20 2010

In 2010, the Twenty20 competition was sponsored by Friends Provident for the first time. Between 2003 and 2009, three regional leagues competed to qualify for the knockout stages, but this was reduced to two leagues in 2010.

NORTH

	P	W	L	T	NR	Pts	Net RR
Warwickshire	16	11	4	–	1	23	+0.40
Nottinghamshire	16	10	4	–	2	22	+0.64
Lancashire	16	9	6	–	1	19	+0.47
Northamptonshire	16	7	6	3	–	17	–0.16
Derbyshire	16	6	8	–	2	14	–0.15
Yorkshire	16	6	9	1	–	13	–0.12
Leicestershire	16	6	9	–	1	13	–0.23
Durham	16	4	8	–	4	12	–0.29
Worcestershire	16	5	10	–	1	11	–0.65

SOUTH

	P	W	L	T	NR	Pts	Net RR
Somerset	16	11	5	–	–	22	+0.41
Essex	16	10	6	–	–	20	+0.39
Sussex	16	9	7	–	–	18	+0.60
Hampshire	16	8	8	–	–	16	+0.38
Surrey	16	8	8	–	–	16	+0.18
Middlesex	16	8	8	–	–	16	+0.01
Kent	16	7	9	–	–	14	–0.16
Glamorgan	16	6	10	–	–	12	–0.97
Gloucestershire	16	5	11	–	–	10	–0.94

QUARTER-FINALS: HAMPSHIRE beat Warwickshire by five wickets at Birmingham.
NOTTINGHAMSHIRE beat Sussex by 13 runs at Nottingham.
SOMERSET beat Northants by seven wickets at Taunton.
ESSEX beat Lancashire by eight wickets at Chelmsford.

SEMI-FINALS: HAMPSHIRE beat Essex by six wickets at Southampton.
SOMERSET beat Notts by 3 runs (D/L method) at Southampton.

LEADING AGGREGATES AND RECORDS 2010

BATTING (500 runs)

		M	I	NO	HS	Runs	Avge	100	50	R/100b	Sixes
J.H.K.Adams	(Hampshire)	19	19	2	101*	668	39.29	2	2	132.2	17
M.E.Trescothick	(Somerset)	19	19	1	83	572	31.77	–	6	157.1	22
M.J.Cosgrove	(Glamorgan)	16	16	–	89	562	35.12	–	4	132.2	14
T.C.Smith	(Lancashire)	17	17	2	92*	543	36.20	–	3	119.6	10
D.J.Hussey	(Notts)	17	17	5	81*	524	43.66	–	3	142.0	19

BOWLING (25 wkts)

		O	M	R	W	Avge	BB	4w	R/Over
A.C.Thomas	(Somerset)	72.5	3	460	33	13.93	3-11	–	6.31
D.R.Briggs	(Hampshire)	67.0	–	445	31	14.35	3- 5	–	6.64
K.A.Pollard	(Somerset)	58.2	–	438	29	15.10	4-15	1	7.50
S.D.Parry	(Lancashire)	60.0	–	427	26	16.42	4-28	1	7.11
A.U.Rashid	(Yorkshire)	61.0	–	428	26	16.46	4-20	1	7.01

Highest total	239-5		Sussex v Glamorgan	Hove
Highest innings	117	M.J.Prior	Sussex v Glamorgan	Hove
Most sixes	9	L.R.P.L.Taylor	Durham v Leicestershire	Chester-le-St
Best bowling	5-13	A.B.McDonald	Leicestershire v Notts	Nottingham
Most economical	4-2-5-2	A.C.Thomas	Somerset v Hampshire	Southampton
	4-0-5-3	D.R.Briggs	Hampshire v Kent	Canterbury
Most expensive	4-0-64-0	Abdul Razzaq	Hampshire v Somerset	Taunton

2010 FRIENDS PROVIDENT t20 FINAL

HAMPSHIRE v SOMERSET

At The Rose Bowl, Southampton, on 14 August.
Result: **HAMPSHIRE** won by losing fewer wickets.
Toss: Somerset. Award: N.D.McKenzie.

SOMERSET		Runs	Balls	4/6	Fall
* M.E.Trescothick	c Christian b Razzaq	19	8	-/2	1- 41
† C.Kieswetter	c Carberry b Christian	71	59	6/2	4-149
P.D.Trego	c Ervine b Briggs	33	24	3/1	2- 97
J.C.Hildreth	c Christian b Razzaq	12	14	–	3-145
J.C.Buttler	c Vince b Cork	5	7	–	5-173
K.A.Pollard	retired hurt	22	7	1/2	5-173
Z.de Bruyn	not out	0	–	–	–
A.V.Suppiah	c Bates b Cork	0	1	–	6-173
B.J.Phillips	not out	0	1	–	–
A.C.Thomas					
M.Kartik					
Extras	(LB 1, W 8, NB 2)	11			
Total	(6 wkts; 20 overs)	**173**			

HAMPSHIRE		Runs	Balls	4/6	Fall
J.H.K.Adams	b Suppiah	34	24	3/1	3- 84
Abdul Razzaq	c Kieswetter b Trego	33	19	6/1	1- 60
J.M.Vince	run out (Hildreth/Kieswetter)	0	1	–	2- 62
N.D.McKenzie	c Trescothick b Waller	52	39	3/1	4-163
S.M.Ervine	not out	44	31	7	–
M.A.Carberry	c Kieswetter b Phillips	0	2	–	5-164
D.T.Christian	not out	3	4	–	–
* D.G.Cork					
C.P.Wood					
† A.M.Bates					
D.R.Briggs					
Extras	(B 2, LB 4, W 1)	7			
Total	(5 wkts; 20 overs)	**173**			

HAMPSHIRE	O	M	R	W	SOMERSET	O	M	R	W
Cork	4	0	24	2	Thomas	4	0	23	0
Wood	4	0	51	0	Phillips	4	0	44	2
Abdul Razzaq	4	0	37	2	De Bruyn	3	0	29	0
Christian	4	0	30	1	Trego	4	0	38	1
Briggs	4	0	30	1	Kartik	4	0	27	0
					Suppiah	1	0	6	1

Umpires: R.J.Bailey and R.K.Illingworth

TWENTY20 CUP WINNERS

PRINCIPAL TWENTY20 CUP RECORDS 2003-10

Highest Total	250-3		Somerset v Glos	Taunton	2006
Highest Total Batting 2nd	222-3		Northants v Worcs	Kidderminster	2007
Lowest Total	67		Sussex v Hampshire	Hove	2004
Largest Victory (Runs)	128		Essex v Sussex	Chelmsford	2008
Largest Victory (Balls)	75		Hampshire v Glos	Bristol	2010
Highest Scores	152*	G.R.Napier	Essex v Sussex	Chelmsford	2008
	141*	C.L.White	Somerset v Worcs	Worcester	2006
	124*	M.J.Lumb	Hampshire v Essex	Southampton	2009
	117	M.J.Prior	Sussex v Glamorgan	Hove	2010
Fastest Hundred	34 balls	A.Symonds	Kent v Middlesex	Maidstone	2004
Most Sixes (Innings)	16	G.R.Napier	Essex v Sussex	Chelmsford	2008
Most Runs in Career	1870	I.J.L.Trott	Warwickshire		2003-10

Highest Partnership for each Wicket

1st	175	V.S.Solanki/G.A.Hick	Worcs v Northants	Kidderminster	2007
2nd	186	J.L.Langer/C.L.White	Somerset v Glos	Taunton	2006
3rd	144*	J.H.K.Adams/S.M.Ervine	Hampshire v Surrey	Southampton	2010
4th	139	M.R.Ramprakash/R.Clarke	Surrey v Glos	Bristol	2006
5th	117	M.van Jaarsveld/M.J.Walker	Kent v Leicestershire	Leicester	2006
6th	98*	R.W.T.Key/M.J.Walker	Kent v Middlesex	Beckenham	2006
7th	67	O.A.C.Banks/B.J.Phillips	Somerset v Northants	Northampton	2008
8th	68	M.W.Alleyne/J.Lewis	Glos v Glamorgan	Cardiff	2005
9th	59*	G.Chapple/P.J.Martin	Lancashire v Leics	Leicester	2003
10th	59	H.H.Streak/J.E.Anyon	Warwickshire v Worcs	Birmingham	2005

Best Bowling	6-21	A.J.Hall	Northants v Worcs	Northampton	2008
	6-24	T.J.Murtagh	Surrey v Middlesex	Lord's	2005
	5-11	Mushtaq Ahmed	Sussex v Essex	Hove	2005
	5-13	M.Kartik	Middlesex v Essex	Lord's	2007
	5-13	A.B.McDonald	Leicestershire v Notts	Nottingham	2010
Most Wkts in Career	81	S.J.Cook	Kent, Middlesex		2003-10
	81	A.J.Hall	Worcs, Kent, Northants		2003-10
	81	Yasir Arafat	Sussex, Kent		2006-10

Most Economical Innings Analyses (Qualification: 4 overs)

4-2-5-2	A.C.Thomas	Somerset v Hampshire	Southampton	2010
4-0-5-3	D.R.Briggs	Hampshire v Kent	Canterbury	2010
4-1-6-2	J.Louw	Northants v Warwicks	Birmingham	2004
4-0-6-1	M.W.Alleyne	Glos v Worcs	Worcester	2005

Most Maiden Overs in an Innings

4-2-9-1	M.Morkel	Kent v Surrey	Beckenham	2007
4-2-5-2	A.C.Thomas	Somerset v Hampshire	Southampton	2010

Most Expensive Innings Analyses

4-0-67-1	R.J.Kirtley	Sussex v Essex	Chelmsford	2008
4-0-65-2	M.J.Hoggard	Yorkshire v Lancs	Leeds	2005
4-0-64-0	Abdul Razzaq	Hampshire v Somerset	Taunton	2010
4-0-63-1	R.J.Kirtley	Sussex v Surrey	Hove	2004

Most Wicket-Keeping Dismissals in an Innings

5 (5 ct)	M.J.Prior	Sussex v Middlesex	Richmond	2006
5 (4 ct, 1 st)	G.L.Brophy	Yorkshire v Durham	Chester-le-St	2008

Most Catches in an Innings by a Fielder

4	D.Pretorius	Warwickshire v Glamorgan	Swansea	2005
4	W.R.Smith	Nottinghamshire v Surrey	Nottingham	2006
4	D.J.G.Sales	Northamptonshire v Worcs	Northampton	2008
4	G.D.Elliott	Surrey v Kent	The Oval	2009

YOUNG CRICKETER OF THE YEAR

This annual award, made by The Cricket Writers' Club, is currently restricted to players qualified for England, Andrew Symonds meeting that requirement at the time of his award, and under the age of 23 on 1st May. In 1986 their ballot resulted in a dead heat. Up to 1 April 2011 their selections have gained a tally of 2,129 international Test match caps (shown in brackets).

1950	R.Tattersall (16)	1981	M.W.Gatting (79)
1951	P.B.H.May (66)	1982	N.G.Cowans (19)
1952	F.S.Trueman (67)	1983	N.A.Foster (29)
1953	M.C.Cowdrey (114)	1984	R.J.Bailey (4)
1954	P.J.Loader (13)	1985	D.V.Lawrence (5)
1955	K.F.Barrington (82)	1986 {	A.A.Metcalfe
1956	B.Taylor		J.J.Whitaker (1)
1957	M.J.Stewart (8)	1987	R.J.Blakey (2)
1958	A.C.D.Ingleby-Mackenzie	1988	M.P.Maynard (4)
1959	G.Pullar (28)	1989	N.Hussain (96)
1960	D.A.Allen (39)	1990	M.A.Atherton (115)
1961	P.H.Parfitt (37)	1991	M.R.Ramprakash (52)
1962	P.J.Sharpe (12)	1992	I.D.K.Salisbury (15)
1963	G.Boycott (108)	1993	M.N.Lathwell (2)
1964	J.M.Brearley (39)	1994	J.P.Crawley (37)
1965	A.P.E.Knott (95)	1995	A.Symonds (26 – Australia)
1966	D.L.Underwood (86)	1996	C.E.W.Silverwood (6)
1967	A.W.Greig (58)	1997	B.C.Hollioake (2)
1968	R.M.H.Cottam (4)	1998	A.Flintoff (79)
1969	A.Ward (5)	1999	A.J.Tudor (10)
1970	C.M.Old (46)	2000	P.J.Franks
1971	J.Whitehouse	2001	O.A.Shah (6)
1972	D.R.Owen-Thomas	2002	R.Clarke (2)
1973	M.Hendrick (30)	2003	J.M.Anderson (57)
1974	P.H.Edmonds (51)	2004	I.R.Bell (62)
1975	A.Kennedy	2005	A.N.Cook (65)
1976	G.Miller (34)	2006	S.C.J.Broad (34)
1977	I.T.Botham (102)	2007	A.U.Rashid
1978	D.I.Gower (117)	2008	R.S.Bopara (10)
1979	P.W.G.Parker (1)	2009	J.W.A.Taylor
1980	G.R.Dilley (41)	2010	S.T.Finn (11)

THE PROFESSIONAL CRICKETERS' ASSOCIATION
PLAYER OF THE YEAR

Founded in 1967, the Professional Cricketers' Association introduced this award, decided by their membership, in 1970. The NatWest-sponsored award was presented at the PCA's Annual Awards Dinner at the Hurlingham Club in London. Only John Lever and Andrew Flintoff have won the award in successive years.

1970 {	M.J.Procter	1983	K.S.McEwan	1997	S.P.James
	J.D.Bond	1984	R.J.Hadlee	1998	M.B.Loye
1971	L.R.Gibbs	1985	N.V.Radford	1999	S.G.Law
1972	A.M.E.Roberts	1986	C.A.Walsh	2000	M.E.Trescothick
1973	P.G.Lee	1987	R.J.Hadlee	2001	D.P.Fulton
1974	B.Stead	1988	G.A.Hick	2002	M.P.Vaughan
1975	Zaheer Abbas	1989	S.J.Cook	2003	Mushtaq Ahmed
1976	P.G.Lee	1990	G.A.Gooch	2004	A.Flintoff
1977	M.J.Procter	1991	Waqar Younis	2005	A.Flintoff
1978	J.K.Lever	1992	C.A.Walsh	2006	M.R.Ramprakash
1979	J.K.Lever	1993	S.L.Watkin	2007	O.D.Gibson
1980	R.D.Jackman	1994	B.C.Lara	2008	M.van Jaarsveld
1981	R.J.Hadlee	1995	D.G.Cork	2009	M.E.Trescothick
1982	M.D.Marshall	1996	P.V.Simmons	2010	N.M.Carter

2010 FIRST-CLASS AVERAGES

These averages involve the 518 players who appeared in the 171 first-class matches played by 29 teams in England and Wales during the 2010 season.

'Cap' denotes the season in which the player was awarded a 1st XI cap by the county he represented in 2010. If he played for more than one county in 2010, the county(ies) who awarded him his cap is (are) underlined. Durham abolished both their capping and 'awards' system after the 2005 season. Glamorgan's capping system is based on a player's number of appearances. Gloucestershire now cap players on first-class debut. Worcestershire now award county colours when players make their Championship debut.

Team abbreviations: A – Australia(ns); B – Bangladesh(is); CU – Cambridge University/ Cambridge MCCU; De – Derbyshire; Du – Durham; DU – Durham MCCU; E – England; EL – England Lions; Ex – Essex; Gm – Glamorgan; Gs – Gloucestershire; H – Hampshire; IA – India A; K – Kent; La – Lancashire; Le – Leicestershire; LU – Loughborough MCCU; M – Middlesex; Nh – Northamptonshire; Nt – Nottinghamshire; OU – Oxford University/ Oxford MCCU; P – Pakistan(is); Sm – Somerset; Sy – Surrey; Sx – Sussex; Wa – Warwickshire; WI A – West Indies A; Wo – Worcestershire; Y – Yorkshire.

† Left-handed batsman. Cap: a dash (–) denotes a non-county player. A blank denotes uncapped by his current county.

BATTING AND FIELDING

	Cap	M	I	NO	HS	Runs	Avge	100	50	Ct/St
† Abdur Razzak (B)	–	3	6	1	30	99	19.80	–	–	1
† Abdur Rehman (P)	–	1	1	–	30	30	30.00	–	–	–
† E.Abel (OU)	–	1	1	–	60	60	60.00	–	1	–
B.J.Ackland (CU)	–	2	4	1	51*	93	31.00	–	1	1
A.R.Adams (Nt)	2007	14	20	5	37	240	16.00	–	–	13
† J.H.K.Adams (H)	2006	16	29	1	196	1351	48.25	3	8	16
† W.A.Adkin (Sx)		1	1	–	45	45	45.00	–	–	1
S.J.Adshead (Gs)	2004	4	7	2	49	125	25.00	–	–	13
† U.Afzaal (Sy)	2009	13	22	2	159*	682	34.10	1	4	4
R.G.Aga (Sx)		2	2	1	66*	66	66.00	–	1	1
S.S.Agarwal (OU)		3	4	2	117	134	67.00	1	–	1
Kabir Ali (H)		4	8	–	18	64	8.00	–	–	2
Kadeer Ali (Gs)	2005	6	12	1	74	240	21.81	–	2	5
† M.M.Ali (EL/Wo)	2007	16	30	3	126	1270	47.03	3	9	12
J.Allenby (Gm)	2010	16	25	4	105	933	44.42	1	10	16
T.R.Ambrose (Wa)	2007	11	20	–	54	267	13.35	–	1	33/3
H.M.Amla (Nt)	2010	5	7	1	129	463	77.16	1	5	1
† J.M.Anderson (E/La)	2003	10	13	2	25*	69	6.27	–	–	3
† G.M.Andrew (Wo)	2008	9	14	1	79	425	32.69	–	4	2
A.S.Ansari (CU)	–*	4	7	1	26*	66	11.00	–	–	1
† J.E.Anyon (Sx)		11	15	–	34	174	11.60	–	–	3
C.P.Ashling (Gm)		3	5	2	20	37	12.33	–	–	1
A.Ashok (Y)	–	2	4	–	93	157	39.25	–	1	2
M.A.Ashraf (Y)		4	4	–	10	15	3.75	–	–	1
J.J.Atkinson (DU)	–	1	–	–				–	–	–
Azeem Rafiq (Y)		3	3	1	13*	29	14.50	–	–	–
Azhar Ali (P)	–	6	12	1	92*	291	26.45	–	2	3
Azhar Mahmood (K)	2008	8	14	–	64	317	22.64	–	2	1
J.M.Bairstow (Y)		16	29	7	81	918	41.72	–	8	29/5
G.C.Baker (LU/Nh)		3	4	–	35	53	13.25	–	–	1
L.S.Baker (WI A)	–	3	4	2	6	12	6.00	–	–	1
D.J.Balcombe (H)		8	6	1	30	56	11.20	–	–	2

F-C	Cap	M	I	NO	HS	Runs	Avge	100	50	Ct/St
† G.S.Ballance (Y)		3	5	2	43	84	28.00	–	–	1
H.M.C.M.Bandara (K)		6	10	3	29	105	15.00	–	–	5
† V.Banerjee (Gs)	2006	7	14	3	35	108	9.81	–	–	1
† K.H.D.Barker (Wa)		4	5	1	22	57	14.25	–	–	1
M.R.Barnard (OU)	–	1	–	–	0	0	0.00	–	–	–
A.M.Bates (H)		8	11	3	31	92	11.50	–	–	28
G.J.Batty (Sy)		15	24	2	67	550	25.00	–	2	12
J.N.Batty (Gs)	2010	15	30	2	61	450	16.07	–	1	53/3
W.A.T.Beer (Sx)		2	1	1	37*	37	–	–	–	1
I.R.Bell (E/Wa)	2001	8	13	1	128	526	43.83	2	2	11
C.C.Benham (H)		7	13	–	45	278	21.38	–	–	11
D.M.Benkenstein (Du)	2005	16	26	1	114	799	31.96	1	5	13
J.G.E.Benning (Le)		1	2	1	29	55	55.00	–	–	1
G.K.Berg (M)	2010	15	26	5	125	761	36.23	1	3	7
D.E.Bernard (WI A)	–	2	3	–	70	92	30.66	–	1	–
T.L.Best (Y)		9	9	–	40	86	9.55	–	–	4
L.A.Blackaby (DU)		2	1	–	38	38	38.00	–	–	1
† I.D.Blackwell (Du)		15	24	2	86	794	36.09	–	8	2
J.A.R.Blain (Y)		1	–	–	–	–	–	–	–	–
† A.J.Blake (K)		9	17	1	105*	359	22.43	1	–	5
† N.Boje (Nh)	2008	9	15	1	98	471	33.64	–	4	3
D.E.Bollinger (A)	–	2	4	2	21	27	13.50	–	–	–
R.S.Bopara (EL/Ex)	2005	9	17	2	142	590	39.33	2	3	4
P.M.Borrington (De)		7	13	1	79*	246	20.50	–	1	4
S.G.Borthwick (Du)		11	15	3	68	315	26.25	–	2	8
† A.G.Botha (Wa)		8	14	–	76	248	17.71	–	1	7
† M.A.G.Boyce (Le)		15	27	3	90	761	31.70	–	6	19
D.P.Bradshaw (OU)		2	3	–	63	116	38.66	–	1	–
† W.D.Bragg (Gm)		3	6	–	44	56	9.33	–	–	3/1
K.C.Brathwaite (WI A)	–	2	3	–	13	17	5.66	–	–	1
R.M.R.Brathwaite (Du)		1	2	1	2	2	2.00	–	–	–
G.R.Breese (Du)	2005	2	3	–	14	27	9.00	–	–	1
T.T.Bresnan (E/Y)	2006	7	10	1	70	228	25.33	–	2	3
T.Brett (Nh)		1	–	–	–	–	–	–	–	–
D.R.Briggs (H)		13	14	3	28	116	10.54	–	–	2
† S.C.J.Broad (E/Nt)		6	9	–	169	257	28.55	1	–	4
J.A.Brooks (Nh)		14	20	3	53	177	10.41	–	1	2
G.L.Brophy (Y)	2008	9	17	1	103	472	29.50	1	1	20
A.D.Brown (Nt)		17	26	3	134	863	37.52	1	6	12
B.C.Brown (Sx)		9	14	2	112	515	42.91	2	2	9/2
D.O.Brown (Gm)		1	2	–	99	114	57.00	–	1	1
F.A.Brown (CU)	–	2	2	–	30	30	15.00	–	–	–
† K.R.Brown (La)		2	3	–	21	25	8.33	–	–	–
M.J.Brown (Sy)		1	2	–	47	64	32.00	–	–	–
O.V.Brown (WI A)	–	1	1	1	0*	0	–	–	–	–
T.E.Bryan (OU)	–	1	–	–	–	–	–	–	–	1
N.L.Buck (Le)		15	20	5	26	93	6.20	–	–	4
D.A.Burton (Nh)		1	2	1	2*	2	2.00	–	–	1
J.C.Buttler (Sm)		13	20	3	144	569	33.47	1	2	23
J.G.Cameron (Wo)	2010	10	17	1	105	576	36.00	1	3	7
† M.A.Carberry (H)	2006	16	28	1	164	1385	51.29	6	4	9
A.Carter (Ex)		3	5	1	16*	45	11.25	–	–	2

F-C	Cap	M	I	NO	HS	Runs	Avge	100	50	Ct/St
† N.M.Carter (Wa)	2005	11	20	3	99*	617	36.29	–	4	–
M.S.Chadwick (Sx)		1	–	–	–	–	–	–	–	–
M.A.Chambers (Ex)		11	16	5	14	53	4.81	–	–	5
† S.Chanderpaul (La)		8	14	1	120	698	53.69	2	5	2
G.Chapple (La)	1994	14	22	6	54*	403	25.18	–	2	4
S.P.Cheetham (Sy)		1	1	–	0*	0	–	–	–	–
E.Chigumbura (Nh)		6	10	1	44	189	21.00	–	–	–
M.J.Chilton (La)	2002	16	29	4	69	750	30.00	–	4	6
V.Chopra (Wa)		9	18	1	54	409	24.05	–	1	9
S.H.Choudhry (Wo)	2010	1	1	–	63	63	63.00	–	1	1
D.T.Christian (H)		1	2	–	36	64	32.00	–	–	–
J.L.Clare (De)		4	6	–	24	45	7.50	–	–	4
M.J.Clarke (A)		2	4	–	77	139	34.75	–	1	2
R.Clarke (Wa)		15	28	5	127*	673	29.26	1	3	23
† M.E.Claydon (Du)		12	15	4	38*	185	16.81	–	–	2
S.J.Cliff (Le)		1	–	–	–	–	–	–	–	–
J.J.Cobb (Le)		5	10	2	55*	153	19.12	–	1	3
† K.J.Coetzer (Du)		7	13	1	72	302	25.16	–	2	2
M.T.Coles (K)		14	23	6	51	378	22.23	–	1	4
P.D.Collingwood (Du/E)	1998	5	7	–	82	131	18.71	–	1	8
P.T.Collins (M)		10	13	4	13	36	4.00	–	–	–
C.D.Collymore (Sx)		14	17	8	19*	78	8.66	–	–	3
M.A.Comber (Ex)		2	3	–	19	19	6.33	–	–	1
N.R.D.Compton (Sm)		11	17	3	72	465	33.21	–	2	5
D.O.Conway (OU)	–	3	2	1	6	6	6.00	–	–	–
† A.N.Cook (E/EL/Ex)	2005	14	24	1	110	773	33.60	2	3	12
S.J.Cook (K)	2007	15	24	7	26*	205	12.05	–	–	2
A.C.Cope (LU)	–	2	3	–	18	33	11.00	–	–	–
D.G.Cork (H)	2009	13	17	3	55	380	27.14	–	2	8
† M.J.Cosgrove (Gm)	2006	15	24	2	142	1187	49.45	5	4	10
D.A.Cosker (Gm)	2000	16	24	10	49*	268	19.14	–	–	7
R.G.Coughtrie (OU)	–	3	5	1	43	84	21.00	–	–	4
O.B.Cox (Wo)	2009	9	16	4	59	218	18.16	–	1	18/1
R.D.B.Croft (Gm)	1992	9	14	3	63	244	22.18	–	2	–
S.J.Croft (La)	2010	16	26	3	93	883	38.39	–	8	13
G.D.Cross (La)		7	11	1	100*	290	29.00	1	1	12
L.M.Daggett (Nh)		12	17	8	48	167	18.55	–	–	3
J.W.M.Dalrymple (Gm)	2008	15	22	–	105	554	25.18	1	2	19
Danish Kaneria (Ex/P)	2004	9	14	2	16*	82	6.83	–	–	1
J.H.Davey (M)		4	7	–	72	220	31.42	–	3	3
A.M.Davies (Du)	2005	6	5	2	27	32	10.66	–	–	–
† S.M.Davies (EL/Sy)		14	22	3	137	1090	57.36	2	9	38
L.A.Dawson (H)		8	13	1	86	348	29.00	–	3	4
Z.de Bruyn (Sm)	2008	14	21	–	95	814	38.76	–	5	10
J.L.Denly (K)	2008	18	33	–	106	848	25.69	1	5	10
† C.D.J.Dent (Gs)	2010	16	31	3	98	725	25.89	–	4	24
J.W.Dernbach (Sy)		15	20	9	56*	154	14.00	–	1	1
N.J.Dexter (M)	2010	12	21	2	118	907	47.73	2	5	10
† S.Dhawan (IA)	–	3	4	–	179	260	65.00	1	–	1
L.A.Dingle (OU)	–	1	–	–	–	–	–	–	–	–
† M.J.Di Venuto (Du)		16	27	3	129	1092	45.50	3	7	29
P.G.Dixey (K)		1	1	–	22	22	22.00	–	–	–/3

F-C	Cap	M	I	NO	HS	Runs	Avge	100	50	Ct/St
† M.P.Dunn (Sy)		1	–	–	–	–	–	–	–	–
† L.E.Durandt (DU)	–	2	3	2	20*	53	53.00	–	–	1
W.J.Durston (De)		6	11	–	69	240	21.81	–	1	9
J.du Toit (Le)		13	20	1	154	899	47.31	2	6	16
K.A.Edwards (WI A)	–	3	4	–	40	67	16.75	–	–	1
N.J.Edwards (Nt)		7	11	–	85	255	23.18	–	1	17
P.D.Edwards (K)		2	3	1	13	20	10.00	–	–	1
† S.M.Ervine (H)	2005	17	27	4	237*	976	42.43	1	5	7
D.Evans (M)		4	5	2	19*	23	7.66	–	–	1
L.Evans (Du/Nh)		3	4	3	8*	20	20.00	–	–	1
L.J.Evans (Sy/Wa)		3	6	–	98	155	25.83	–	1	2
† R.F.Evans (LU)	–	2	2	–	55	55	27.50	–	1	1
† Fawad Alam (P)	–	1	2	–	68	88	44.00	–	1	–
R.S.Ferley (K)		1	2	–	19	20	10.00	–	–	–
S.T.Finn (E/M)	2009	13	19	9	18	47	4.70	–	–	1
A.D.S.Fletcher (WI A)	–	3	4	–	123	183	45.75	1	–	1
L.J.Fletcher (Nt)		6	9	3	23*	96	16.00	–	–	2
G.W.Flower (Ex)	2005	3	5	2	46	123	41.00	–	–	3
M.H.A.Footitt (Nt)		9	12	3	30	69	7.66	–	–	3
J.S.Foster (Ex)	2001	16	27	1	169	839	32.26	1	4	48/5
J.E.C.Franklin (Gs)	2004	16	29	3	108	862	33.15	1	4	7
† P.J.Franks (Nt)	1999	16	22	1	114	765	36.42	1	6	1
A.B.Fudadin (WI A)	–	1	1	–	3	3	3.00	–	–	–
† A.W.Gale (EL/Y)	2008	14	24	4	151*	950	47.50	3	4	2
D.J.Gale (DU)	–	2	1	–	37	37	37.00	–	–	1
C.Ganapathy (IA)	–	1	1	–	1	1	1.00	–	–	–
H.S.Gandam (LU)	–	2	2	–	33	44	22.00	–	–	1
J.S.Gatting (Sx)		8	11	–	31	155	14.09	–	–	4
† C.J.Geldart (Y)		1	1	–	17	17	17.00	–	–	–
A.P.R.Gidman (Gs)	2004	16	29	–	99	679	23.41	–	3	16
J.C.Glover (DU)	–	2	1	1	4*	4	–	–	–	–
L.J.Goddard (De)		8	11	1	67	165	16.50	–	1	24
† B.A.Godleman (Ex)		12	22	–	106	569	25.86	1	2	12
J.E.Goodman (K)		1	2	1	59	59	59.00	–	1	–
D.M.Goodwin (CU)	–	1	2	–	18	26	13.00	–	–	–
M.W.Goodwin (Sx)	2001	16	26	3	142	1201	52.21	4	5	5
S.K.Gray (CU)	–	3	6	2	35*	131	32.75	–	–	3
J.M.Greenwood (CU)	–	1	2	1	23*	24	24.00	–	–	1
† D.A.Griffiths (H)		5	9	6	9*	34	11.33	–	–	1
T.D.Groenewald (De)		13	19	9	35*	216	21.60	–	–	3
P.R.Groves (LU)	–	2	2	1	43	80	80.00	–	–	–
† J.C.Guillen (WI A)	–	1	2	–	3	3	1.50	–	–	–
H.F.Gurney (Le)		5	4	1	4	6	2.00	–	–	1
A.D.Hales (Nt)		12	20	1	136	677	35.63	1	4	12
A.J.Hall (Nh)	2009	15	27	3	133	696	29.00	1	3	21
R.J.Hamilton-Brown (Sy)		17	29	1	125	844	30.14	2	3	11
T.R.G.Hampton (M)		1	1	1	1*	1	–	–	–	–
† O.J.Hannon-Dalby (Y)		17	15	7	11*	29	3.62	–	–	1
† A.Harinath (Sy)		14	25	1	63	621	25.87	–	4	3
† B.W.Harmison (Du)		6	10	–	96	286	28.60	–	2	1
S.J.Harmison (Du)	1999	9	12	6	11*	36	6.00	–	–	2
G.M.Harper (DU)	–	2	1	–	3	3	3.00	–	–	1

223

F-C	Cap	M	I	NO	HS	Runs	Avge	100	50	Ct/St
A.J.Harris (Le)		4	7	4	20	27	9.00	–	–	2
J.A.R.Harris (EL/Gm)	2010	14	20	2	49	267	14.83	–	–	3
D.S.Harrison (Gm)	2006	12	18	–	35	253	14.05	–	–	2
P.W.Harrison (Nh)		5	8	1	44	137	19.57	–	–	7/2
† L.J.Hatchett (Sx)		4	4	–	20	30	7.50	–	–	1
C.W.Henderson (Le)	2004	16	21	1	33	265	13.25	–	–	6
† H.M.R.K.B.Herath (H)		4	6	3	17*	59	19.66	–	–	1
R.L.Hesketh (CU)	–	2	3	–	20	38	12.66	–	–	1
J.C.Hildreth (Sm)	2007	16	23	1	151	1440	65.45	7	5	7
B.W.Hilfenhaus (A)	–	2	4	1	56*	77	25.66	–	1	–
J.B.Hockley (K)		6	11	1	82	141	14.10	–	1	6
A.J.Hodd (Sx)		10	14	1	109	319	24.53	1	1	29/1
L.J.Hodgson (Y)		2	2	–	34	67	33.50	–	–	1
† K.W.Hogg (La)	2010	9	13	4	88	301	33.44	–	2	3
M.J.Hoggard (Le)	2010	15	17	6	6	31	2.81	–	–	5
C.E.H.Hopkins (CU)	–	3	4	–	14	34	8.50	–	–	–
P.J.Horton (La)	2007	16	30	2	123	634	22.64	1	3	19
D.M.Housego (M)		2	4	1	102*	144	48.00	1	–	1
† B.H.N.Howgego (Nh)		7	13	2	80	292	26.54	–	1	3
† C.F.Hughes (De)		12	21	2	156	784	41.26	2	4	12
P.H.Hughes (CU)		2	4	–	87	198	49.50	–	2	–
† P.J.Hughes (H)		3	6	–	38	85	14.16	–	–	–
G.M.Hussain (Gs)	2009	15	26	10	28*	153	9.56	–	–	1
D.J.Hussey (Nt)	2004	5	7	1	251*	399	66.50	1	3	7
† M.E.K.Hussey (A)	–	2	4	1	56*	69	23.00	–	1	3
Iftikhar Anjum (Sy)		3	5	1	29	61	15.25	–	–	–
Imran Arif (Wo)	2008	2	3	1	4*	8	4.00	–	–	1
† Imran Farhat (P)	–	6	12	–	67	256	21.33	–	1	5
Imran Tahir (Wa)		16	27	4	69*	384	16.69	–	1	4
† Imrul Kayes (B)	–	5	9	–	75	242	26.88	–	1	5
† Iqbal Abdulla (IA)	–	3	2	–	12	12	6.00	–	–	2
A.J.Ireland (Gs)	2007	8	12	2	11	21	2.10	–	–	–
Jahurul Islam (B)	–	5	9	1	158	312	39.00	1	1	6
N.A.James (Gm)		1	2	1	60*	75	75.00	–	1	–
† P.A.Jaques (Wo)	2006	8	15	–	94	465	31.00	–	3	9
Jaskaran Singh (IA)	–	2	1	–	58	58	58.00	–	1	–
A.Javid (Wa)		4	7	–	48	91	13.00	–	–	3
† A.F.Jeavons (OU)	–	1	2	–	62	66	33.00	–	1	1
W.I.Jefferson (Le)		11	20	1	135	722	38.00	2	4	14
T.M.Jewell (Sy)		3	2	1	4*	5	5.00	–	–	1
† M.G.Johnson (A)	–	2	4	–	30	45	11.25	–	–	1
R.M.Johnson (Wa)		5	8	1	39	118	16.85	–	–	12/2
C.R.Jones (Sm)		1	–	–	–	–	–	–	–	–
G.O.Jones (K)	2003	17	31	–	178	1003	32.35	3	2	49/6
P.S.Jones (De)	2010	12	18	4	86	427	30.50	–	1	4
R.A.Jones (Wo)	2007	11	19	2	21*	100	5.88	–	–	7
† S.P.Jones (H)		1	2	2	0*	0	–	–	–	–
R.H.Joseph (K)		2	3	2	18*	30	30.00	–	–	1
A.J.P.Joslin (CU)	–	1	2	–	11	12	6.00	–	–	–
E.C.Joyce (Sx)	2009	10	17	3	164	738	52.71	2	3	17
† Junaid Siddique (B)	–	8	–	74	223	27.87	–	2	3	
Kamran Akmal (P)	–	6	12	–	46	128	10.66	–	–	27/1

224

F-C	Cap	M	I	NO	HS	Runs	Avge	100	50	Ct/St
† M.Kartik (Sm)		11	12	5	52*	199	28.42	–	2	9
† S.M.Katich (A/La)		3	6	–	83	227	37.83	–	2	2
† G.Keedy (La)	2000	7	9	2	34	89	12.71	–	–	–
A.D.J.Kennedy (CU)	–	1	2	1	48*	62	62.00	–	2	–
S.C.Kerrigan (La)		13	15	5	16*	45	4.50	–	–	3
A.N.Kervezee (Wo)	2009	16	30	3	155	1190	44.07	3	6	14
R.W.T.Key (K)	2001	16	28	2	261	814	31.30	2	1	1
A.Khan (K)		12	18	5	24	115	8.84	–	–	5
I.Khan (WI A)	–	3	4	–	62	123	30.75	–	1	3
C.Kieswetter (Sm)	2009	12	18	1	84	467	27.47	–	4	29
† D.A.King (OU)	–	1	1	–	189	189	189.00	1	–	4
S.J.King (Sy)		1	–	–	–	–	–	–	–	–
S.P.Kirby (EL/Gs)	2005	11	18	6	22*	106	8.83	–	–	2
N.Kruger (OU)	–	1	1	–	48	48	48.00	–	–	2
D.S.Kulkarni (IA)	–	3	2	1	13	15	15.00	–	–	–
† T.J.Lancefield (Sy)		8	13	1	74	381	31.75	–	2	3
M.A.K.Lawson (K)		1	1	–	31	31	31.00	–	–	–
N.T.Lee (CU)	–	3	4	–	63	111	27.75	–	1	–
† A.Z.Lees (Y)		1	1	–	38	38	38.00	–	–	–
J.Lewis (Gs)	1998	16	28	2	50	419	16.11	–	1	7
T.E.Linley (Sy)		7	10	4	16	55	9.16	–	–	4
J.A.Lodwick (OU)	–	1	–	–	–	–	–	–	–	1
† A.B.London (M)		4	7	1	77	137	22.83	–	1	3
† J.D.S.Lotay (CU)	–	2	3	1	34*	43	21.50	–	–	1
J.R.Lowe (Y)		1	1	–	5	5	5.00	–	–	–
M.B.Loye (Nh)	1994	10	18	1	164	420	24.70	1	1	–
D.S.Lucas (Nh)	2009	11	17	2	40*	316	21.06	–	–	1
† M.J.Lumb (H)	2008	5	7	–	158	381	54.42	1	1	4
† T.Lungley (De)	2007	7	10	1	21	85	9.44	–	–	6
† A.Lyth (Y)	2010	16	29	–	142	1509	52.03	3	9	9
A.B.McDonald (Le)		6	11	1	176*	442	44.20	2	1	2
B.E.McGain (Ex)		2	4	2	24	46	23.00	–	–	–
A.McGrath (Y)	1999	16	29	1	124*	1219	43.53	3	9	9
† M.W.Machan (Sx)		1	2	–	6	11	5.50	–	–	–
N.D.McKenzie (H)	2010	15	25	5	141*	942	47.10	3	4	21
D.L.Maddy (Wa)	2007	14	27	1	61	499	19.19	–	2	16
W.L.Madsen (De)		16	29	1	179	940	33.57	4	2	11
Mahbubul Alam (B)		1	–	–	–	–	–	–	–	–
S.I.Mahmood (La)	2007	15	20	2	72	564	31.33	–	5	2
Mahmudullah (B)	–	5	9	–	40	200	22.22	–	–	3
C.C.Malan (LU)	–	1	1	–	11	11	11.00	–	–	–
† D.J.Malan (M)	2010	16	29	3	115	1001	38.50	3	5	19
M.N.Malik (Le)		8	9	3	35*	88	14.66	–	–	–
H.J.H.Marshall (Gs)	2006	15	27	2	89*	884	35.36	–	7	15
C.S.Martin (Ex)		1	2	1	11	11	11.00	–	–	–
† J.Martin (OU)		3	5	–	81	195	39.00	–	2	2
R.S.C.Martin-Jenkins (Sx)	2000	9	13	3	130	629	62.90	2	5	6
M.S.Mason (Wo)	2002	8	12	2	51*	137	13.70	–	1	4
D.D.Masters (Ex)	2008	14	22	1	50	356	16.95	–	1	8
† J.K.Maunders (Ex)		7	12	–	126	307	25.58	1	1	6
T.L.Maynard (Gm)		11	18	–	98	495	27.50	–	4	11
N.A.Meadows (OU)	–	1	1	–	38	38	38.00	–	–	4

F-C	Cap	M	I	NO	HS	Runs	Avge	100	50	Ct/St
S.C.Meaker (Sy)		11	14	1	94	175	13.46	–	1	3
J.C.Mickleburgh (Ex)		16	30	–	174	852	28.40	1	3	11
J.D.Middlebrook (Nh)		12	21	3	84	459	25.50	–	3	6
A.S.Miller (Wa)		7	12	5	35	65	9.28	–	–	4
M.J.Milligan (OU)		3	2	–	4	7	3.50	–	–	2
D.K.H.Mitchell (Wo)	2005	16	31	3	165*	1180	42.14	4	4	32
† Mohammad Aamer (P)	–	7	14	3	44*	151	13.72	–	–	–
Mohammad Ashraful (B)	–	5	9	–	89	260	28.88	–	3	–
† Mohammad Asif (P)	–	6	10	3	14	37	5.28	–	–	1
Mohammad Yousuf (P)	–	2	4	–	56	99	24.75	–	1	–
S.C.Moore (La)		9	17	–	61	426	25.05	–	2	6
C.F.D.Morgan (DU)		1	2	1	16	16	16.00	–	–	4/1
† E.J.G.Morgan (E/M)	2008	7	10	1	130	372	41.33	1	2	4
G.J.Muchall (Du)	2005	10	15	1	140*	520	37.14	2	1	3
† A.Mukund (IA)	–	3	4	–	91	201	50.25	–	2	2
S.J.Mullaney (Nt)		11	17	4	100*	512	39.38	1	3	6
M.K.Munday (Sm)		3	3	1	0*	0	0.00	–	–	1
D.Murphy (LU/Nh)		11	18	7	76	421	38.27	–	4	30
† T.J.Murtagh (M)	2008	15	23	10	50*	241	18.53	–	1	4
Mushfiqur Rahim (B)	–	5	9	–	52	117	13.00	–	1	6/1
† P.Mustard (Du)		16	24	5	120	742	39.05	2	4	40/2
Naeem Islam (B)	–	2	3	–	8	13	6.50	–	–	–
J.K.H.Naik (Le)		8	12	3	72	301	33.44	–	1	5
G.R.Napier (Ex)	2003	4	5	–	35	67	13.40	–	–	1
C.D.Nash (Sx)	2008	17	29	2	184	1051	38.92	3	1	12
Naved-ul-Hasan (Sx)		5	8	2	101	208	34.66	1	1	–
A.Nel (Sy)		7	10	–	96	219	21.90	–	1	4
J.D.Nel (K)		3	2	–	4	6	3.00	–	–	2
† T.J.New (Le)	2009	17	27	4	91	746	32.43	–	6	46/1
† S.A.Newman (M)		15	27	–	126	945	35.00	2	6	8
D.C.A.Newton (DU)	–	1	1	–	0	0	0.00	–	–	–
R.I.Newton (Nh)		6	11	–	102	357	32.45	1	2	1
† P.A.Nixon (Le)	1994	16	27	1	106	915	35.19	1	7	4
† M.J.North (A)	–	2	4	–	20	36	9.00	–	–	3
S.A.Northeast (K)		17	30	–	71	719	23.96	–	4	6
M.Ntini (K)		5	8	3	13	25	5.00	–	–	–
I.E.O'Brien (M)		7	9	1	14*	39	4.87	–	–	1
† N.J.O'Brien (Nh)		3	6	–	49	216	36.00	–	–	7/1
J.E.Ord (Wa)		1	2	–	6	7	3.50	–	–	1
M.Osborne (Ex)		2	3	2	5	5	5.00	–	–	–
F.G.Owen (CU)	–	1	2	–	24	33	16.50	–	–	–
W.T.Owen (Gm)		3	4	1	38	38	12.66	–	–	–
T.D.Paine (A)	–	2	4	–	47	104	26.00	–	–	11/1
A.P.Palladino (Ex)		5	9	1	66	130	16.25	–	1	1
M.K.Pandey (IA)	–	3	6	–	36	54	27.00	–	–	2
M.S.Panesar (EL/Sx)	2010	16	20	5	46*	163	10.86	–	–	2
C.M.Park (CU)	–	3	4	–	72	91	22.75	–	1	2
G.T.Park (De)		11	19	2	124*	431	25.35	1	2	6
D.C.Pascoe (OU)	–	2	2	2	33*	64	–	–	–	3
† L.A.Patel (DU)	–	1	1	–	26	26	26.00	–	–	–
R.H.Patel (M)		1	1	1	19*	19	–	–	–	–
S.R.Patel (Nt)	2008	17	28	2	104	750	28.84	1	4	9

F-C	Cap	M	I	NO	HS	Runs	Avge	100	50	Ct/St
S.A.Patterson (Y)		14	17	4	39*	184	14.15	–	–	3
D.J.Pattinson (Nt)	2008	13	14	4	27	101	10.10	–	–	–
S.D.Peters (Nh)	2007	16	30	2	199	1320	47.14	3	7	16
† R.J.Peterson (De)		15	24	3	58	484	23.04	–	2	9
M.L.Pettini (Ex)	2006	15	27	3	96	599	24.95	–	2	7
B.J.Phillips (Sm)		11	15	3	55	179	14.91	–	1	5
† O.J.Phillips (WI A)	–	3	5	1	35	91	22.75	–	–	1
† T.J.Phillips (Ex)	2006	10	16	3	46*	240	18.46	–	–	8
† C.D.Piesley (K)		1	2	–	43	43	21.50	–	–	–
K.P.Pietersen (E/Sy)		8	12	1	80	273	24.81	–	2	6
S.A.Piolet (Wa)		1	2	–	6	10	5.00	–	–	2
L.E.Plunkett (Du/EL)		15	18	–	51	238	13.22	–	1	10
R.T.Ponting (A)	–	2	4	–	66	98	24.50	–	1	2
† W.T.S.Porterfield (Gs)	2008	7	14	–	175	531	37.92	2	1	6
N.Pothas (H)	2003	9	15	–	87	531	35.40	–	4	33
D.B.L.Powell (La)		4	4	1	16*	29	9.66	–	–	–
M.J.Powell (Gm)	2000	7	12	1	55	275	25.00	–	1	1
S.W.Poynter (M)		1	1	–	42	42	42.00	–	–	3
T.Poynton (De)		4	6	–	25	88	14.66	–	–	5
† A.G.Prince (La)		7	13	2	115	450	40.90	1	4	7
M.J.Prior (E/Sx)	2003	13	19	3	123*	639	39.93	2	2	41/1
† L.A.Procter (La)		2	3	–	32	64	31.33	–	–	–
C.A.Pujara (IA)	–	3	4	2	208*	322	161.00	1	1	4
R.M.Pyrah (Y)		7	7	2	134*	304	60.80	1	1	4
A.M.Rahane (IA)	–	3	4	1	118	233	77.66	1	1	–
M.R.Ramprakash (Sy)	2002	16	28	2	248	1595	61.34	5	5	5
† W.B.Rankin (Wa)		9	16	7	13	63	7.00	–	–	3
A.U.Rashid (Y)	2008	16	24	8	76	732	45.75	–	6	14
O.P.Rayner (Sx)		7	10	2	67*	256	32.00	–	2	10
C.M.W.Read (Nt)	1999	17	26	5	124*	945	45.00	2	5	60/4
† D.J.Redfern (De)		9	15	1	85	331	23.64	–	1	3
† G.P.Rees (Gm)	2009	17	30	4	106*	918	35.30	2	5	6
H.Riazuddin (H)		1	1	–				–	–	–
A.Richardson (Wo)	2010	14	18	11	11	71	10.14	–	–	5
M.J.Richardson (Du)		1	1	–	2	2	2.00	–	–	–
Robiul Islam (B)	–	4	6	4	17*	29	14.50	–	–	1
S.D.Robson (M)		8	15	–	204	513	34.20	1	2	8
C.G.Roebuck (Y)		1	1	–	23	23	23.00	–	–	–
C.J.L.Rogers (De)	2008	15	27	3	200	1285	53.54	4	5	19
T.S.Roland-Jones (M)		8	12	1	26	124	11.27	–	–	3
J.E.Root (Y)		2	3	1	20*	38	19.00	–	–	1
C.G.W.Roper (DU)	–	2	1	–	0	0	0.00	–	–	1
S.A.L.Rose (LU)	–	2	2	1	14	14	14.00	–	–	–
A.M.Rossington (M)		1	1	–	1	1	1.00	–	–	1
J.J.Roy (Sy)		3	5	–	76	170	34.00	–	2	–
Rubel Hossain (B)	–	3	4	–	9	23	5.75	–	–	–
† J.A.Rudolph (Y)	2007	16	29	2	228*	1375	50.92	4	6	20
C.Rushworth (Du)		9	14	2	28	127	10.58	–	–	1
A.D.Russell (WI A)	–	2	3	–	19	37	12.33	–	–	–
† J.L.Sadler (De)		3	4	–	16	45	11.25	–	–	3
Saeed Ajmal (P)	–	3	5	2	50	67	22.33	–	1	2
W.P.Saha (IA)	–	2	2	–	62	112	56.00	–	2	2/1

227

F-C	Cap	M	I	NO	HS	Runs	Avge	100	50	Ct/St
D.J.G.Sales (Nh)	1999	15	28	–	127	680	24.28	1	2	20
† Salman Butt (P)	–	7	14	–	92	376	26.85	–	2	1
B.W.Sanderson (Y)		1	–	–	–	–	–	–	–	–
† J.J.Sayers (Y)	2007	9	14	–	63	395	28.21	–	5	3
† C.P.Schofield (Sy)		8	13	–	90	341	26.23	–	2	5
A.J.D.Scott (OU)	–	1	–	–	–	–	–	–	–	–
B.J.M.Scott (Wo)	2010	7	12	2	98	313	31.30	–	3	30/1
B.M.Shafayat (Nt)		7	11	–	159	277	25.18	1	–	7
Shafiul Islam (B)	–	3	6	1	24	56	11.20	–	–	1
O.A.Shah (M)	2000	13	23	1	156	804	36.54	2	3	10
Shahadat Hossain (B)	–	4	6	1	33	80	16.00	–	–	–
Shahid Afridi (P)	–	2	3	–	31	33	11.00	–	–	1
A.Shahzad (E/Y)	2010	10	13	3	45	243	24.30	–	–	3
† Shakib Al Hasan (B/Wo)	2010	11	20	2	90	415	23.05	–	1	4
A.J.Shantry (Gm)		1	1	–	22	22	22.00	–	–	–
† J.D.Shantry (Wo)	2009	11	15	5	13*	55	5.50	–	–	3
A.S.Sharma (OU)	–	1	1	–	185*	185	–	1	–	2
R.Sharma (OU)	–	4	6	–	44	108	18.00	–	–	1
A.Sheikh (De)		1	2	–	6	6	3.00	–	–	1
Shoaib Malik (P)	–	4	8	1	48*	164	23.42	–	–	–
C.E.Shreck (Nt)	2006	5	7	1	7*	10	1.66	–	–	4
† R.J.Sidebottom (Nt)	2004	9	7	7	22*	66	–	–	–	3
J.A.Simpson (M)		16	27	2	101*	657	26.28	1	2	42/2
B.F.Smith (Wo)	2002	8	14	2	80	282	23.50	–	2	9
† D.S.Smith (WI A)	–	3	5	1	170	246	61.50	1	–	6
D.T.Smith (OU)	–	1	2	1	12*	16	16.00	–	–	1
G.M.Smith (De)	2009	16	27	1	165*	721	27.73	1	4	4
G.P.Smith (DU/Le)		7	12	5	158*	652	93.14	3	3	6
S.P.D.Smith (A)	–	2	4	–	77	100	25.00	–	1	1
† T.C.Smith (La)	2010	14	25	3	128	576	26.18	2	2	14
T.M.J.Smith (M)		4	7	1	33	110	18.33	–	–	3
W.R.Smith (Du)		5	8	–	57	171	21.37	–	1	2
S.D.Snell (Gs)	2005	10	19	1	71	322	17.88	–	2	18
V.S.Solanki (Wo)	1998	15	28	1	114	717	26.55	1	4	18
† M.N.W.Spriegel (Sy)		10	14	1	108*	391	30.07	2	–	10
B.R.W.Stebbings (OU)	–	3	3	–	25	44	14.66	–	–	–
D.I.Stevens (K)	2005	15	26	3	197	979	42.56	4	2	6
D.A.Stiff (Sm)		2	4	2	40	71	35.50	–	–	–
B.A.Stokes (Du)		13	19	3	161*	740	46.25	2	2	8
† M.D.Stoneman (Du)		11	17	1	118	525	32.81	1	4	5
† A.J.Strauss (E/M)	2001	14	25	1	92	801	33.37	–	6	25
A.V.Suppiah (Sm)	2009	16	26	3	125	771	33.52	1	4	5
L.D.Sutton (La)	2007	13	21	2	118	530	27.89	2	–	37/5
G.P.Swann (E/Nt)	2005	7	9	–	28	91	10.11	–	–	9
N.S.Tahir (Wa)		3	6	–	34	69	11.50	–	–	2
† Tamim Iqbal (B)	–	3	6	–	108	323	53.83	2	1	4
W.A.Tavaré (LU)	–	2	3	–	49	60	20.00	–	–	–
C.G.Taylor (Gs)	2001	15	27	2	89	803	32.12	–	6	11
J.M.R.Taylor (Gs)	2010	4	6	–	11	11	2.75	–	–	2
J.W.A.Taylor (EL/Le)	2009	17	29	4	206*	1095	43.80	3	4	15
M.H.Taylor (CU)	–	2	4	2	16*	42	21.00	–	–	–
† R.M.L.Taylor (LU)	–	2	2	–	22	39	19.50	–	–	2

F-C	Cap	M	I	NO	HS	Runs	Avge	100	50	Ct/St
R.N.ten Doeschate (Ex)	2006	11	19	2	85	577	33.94	–	5	9
A.C.Thomas (Sm)	2008	15	20	4	44	328	20.50	–	–	1
† M.A.Thornely (Sx)		12	21	1	89	467	23.35	–	4	8
C.D.Thorp (Du)		5	6	1	29	64	12.80	–	–	2
R.T.Timms (CU)	–	1	2	–	36	66	33.00	–	–	1
M.K.Tiwary (IA)	–	3	3	–	36	57	19.00	–	–	3
† J.A.Tomlinson (H)	2008	15	21	5	42	198	12.37	–	–	3
G.C.Tonge (WI A)	–	3	4	1	54	128	42.66	–	1	–
K.S.Toor (M)		1	1	–	15	15	15.00	–	–	–
† J.C.Tredwell (K)	2007	12	20	2	115	489	27.16	1	1	21
P.D.Trego (Sm)	2007	16	23	2	108	693	33.00	1	5	12
C.T.Tremlett (Sy)		12	17	6	53*	230	20.90	–	1	1
† M.E.Trescothick (Sm)	1999	16	28	4	228*	1397	58.20	4	6	26
V.Tripathi (Nh)		4	7	1	71	196	32.66	–	2	3
I.J.L.Trott (E/Wa)	2005	12	21	2	226	1084	57.05	3	5	14
† J.O.Troughton (Wa)	2002	16	30	1	78	585	20.17	–	1	5
P.T.Turnbull (CU)	–	3	4	–	13	25	6.25	–	–	–
S.Tyagi (IA)	–	1	–	–	–	–	–	–	–	–
S.D.Udal (M)	2008	13	19	1	55	216	12.00	–	1	6
Umar Akmal (P)	–	7	13	2	153	393	35.72	1	1	5
† Umar Amin (P)	–	5	10	–	73	174	17.40	–	1	1
Umar Gul (P)	–	5	9	4	65*	126	25.20	–	1	–
J.D.Unadkat (IA)	–	2	1	1	12*	12	–	–	–	–
† W.P.J.U.C.Vaas (Nh)		2	2	–	17	17	8.50	–	–	1
M.van Jaarsveld (K)	2005	17	29	2	110*	1188	44.00	3	6	36
J.M.Vince (H)		16	27	4	180	891	38.73	1	4	11
A.C.Voges (Nt)	2008	3	5	–	126	254	50.80	1	1	1
G.G.Wagg (De)	2007	4	7	–	37	82	11.71	–	–	1
M.A.Wagh (Nt)	2007	16	24	1	139	953	41.43	3	3	8
Wahab Riaz (P)	–	3	4	–	27	35	8.75	–	–	2
† D.J.Wainwright (Y)		7	6	3	39	108	36.00	–	–	1
A.G.Wakely (Nh)		13	22	–	108	627	28.50	1	4	6
† M.J.Walker (Ex)	2010	12	24	2	105	838	38.09	1	4	8
† M.A.Wallace (Gm)	2003	16	24	1	113	626	27.21	1	4	43/4
S.J.Walters (Sy)		6	10	–	53	242	24.20	–	1	8
C.A.K.Walton (WI A)	–	3	4	–	34	51	12.75	–	–	7
H.T.Waters (Gm)		11	13	4	16	67	7.44	–	–	1
S.R.Waters (DU)	–	2	3	1	25*	47	23.50	–	–	2
† S.J.V.Watkins (OU)	–	1	2	1	46*	54	54.00	–	–	–
M.J.C.Watson (OU)	–	3	4	–	22	26	6.50	–	–	1
S.R.Watson (A)	–	2	4	–	31	64	16.00	–	–	2
† L.W.P.Wells (Sx)		1	2	–	62	70	35.00	–	1	–
A.S.Welsh (LU)	–	2	3	1	21	30	15.00	–	–	1
T.Westley (DU/Ex)		10	18	1	132	440	25.88	1	2	4
† I.J.Westwood (Wa)	2008	16	32	4	86*	726	25.92	–	5	6
A.J.Wheater (CU/Ex)		3	5	1	55	167	41.75	–	2	5
† D.A.Wheeldon (Wo)	2009	7	14	1	65	269	20.69	–	2	2
C.D.Whelan (Wo)	2008	1	2	–	5	5	2.50	–	–	1
G.G.White (Nh)		1	1	–	29	29	29.00	–	–	1
R.A.White (Nh)	2008	10	19	1	95	363	20.16	–	2	3
W.A.White (Le)		9	13	2	101*	394	35.81	1	1	4
D.J.Willey (Nh)		3	4	2	18*	41	20.50	–	–	1

F-C	Cap	M	I	NO	HS	Runs	Avge	100	50	Ct/St
† C.M.Willoughby (Sm)	2007	16	18	6	16	85	7.08	–	–	1
G.C.Wilson (Sy)		6	9	1	125	349	43.62	1	1	14
T.S.Winslade (LU)		1	2	–	17	18	9.00	–	–	
C.R.Woakes (EL/Wa)	2009	14	22	3	136*	457	24.05	1	1	7
C.P.Wood (H)		3	4	–	35	68	17.00	–	–	
M.J.Wood (Nt)		4	6	–	72	148	24.66	–	2	1
R.J.J.Woolley (CU)		3	4	1	55*	117	39.00	–	1	
B.J.Wright (Gm)		17	27	1	172	847	32.57	2	4	7
C.J.C.Wright (Ex)		11	17	5	28*	161	13.41	–	–	2
D.G.Wright (Sm)		5	7	–	78	236	33.71	–	2	4
L.J.Wright (Sx)	2007	9	12	1	134	465	42.27	1	3	3
† M.H.Yardy (Sx)	2005	9	13	2	100*	345	31.36	1	1	12
Yasir Arafat (Sx)		9	9	2	58	255	36.42	–	1	4
Yasir Hameed (P)		2	4	–	36	41	10.25	–	–	4
E.G.C.Young (Gs/OU)	2010	4	6	–	79	225	37.50	–	2	5
Younus Khan (Sy)		3	5	1	77*	155	38.75	–	1	2
Zulqarnain Haider (P)		1	2	–	88	88	44.00	–	1	2

BOWLING

See BATTING AND FIELDING section for details of matches and caps

	Cat	O	M	R	W	Avge	Best	5wI	10wM
Abdur Razzak (B)	SLA	73	10	241	6	40.16	2- 67	–	–
Abdur Rehman (P)	SLA	25	4	99	1	99.00	1- 54	–	–
B.J.Ackland (CU)	OB	1	0	3	0				
A.R.Adams (Nt)	RMF	455.5	101	1508	68	22.17	6- 79	4	–
J.H.K.Adams (H)	LM	2	1	5	0				
W.A.Adkin (Sx)	RM	11	2	38	1	38.00	1- 38	–	–
U.Afzaal (Sy)	SLA	75.3	9	217	8	27.12	2- 26	–	–
R.G.Aga (Sx)	RMF	34	10	99	2	49.50	2- 29	–	–
S.S.Agarwal (OU)	OB	80.1	18	249	5	49.80	5- 78	1	–
Kabir Ali (H)	RMF	137.2	27	488	19	25.68	5- 33	2	
M.M.Ali (EL/Wo)	RM	179.4	29	626	17	36.82	5- 36	1	–
J.Allenby (Gm)	RM	330.1	82	885	41	21.58	5- 59	1	
J.M.Anderson (E/La)	RFM	355.2	115	884	48	18.41	6- 17	3	1
G.M.Andrew (Wo)	RMF	196.4	32	656	23	28.52	4- 45	–	
A.S.Ansari (CU)	LB	6	1	32	0				
J.E.Anyon (Sx)	RFM	227.2	41	767	29	26.44	3- 23	–	
C.P.Ashling (Gm)	RFM	55.1	5	200	6	33.33	3- 18	–	–
A.Ashok (CU)	RM	13	2	67	0				
M.A.Ashraf (Y)	RMF	75	20	212	11	19.27	5- 32	1	–
Azeem Rafiq (Y)	OB	88	13	268	5	53.60	4- 92	–	–
Azhar Ali (P)	LB	1	0	9	0				
Azhar Mahmood (K)	RFM	279.3	55	847	30	28.23	5- 62	2	–
G.C.Baker (LU/Nh)	RMF	63.1	11	256	3	85.33	2- 35	–	
L.S.Baker (WI A)	RMF	80.3	18	245	8	30.62	2- 31	–	–
D.J.Balcombe (H)	RFM	246.1	52	812	27	30.07	3- 69	–	–
H.M.C.M.Bandara (K)	LBG	210.4	32	745	18	41.38	4- 42	–	–
V.Banerjee (Gs)	SLA	222	28	793	23	34.47	5- 74	2	–
K.H.D.Barker (Wa)	LM	36.1	4	135	2	67.50	2- 22	–	–
M.R.Barnard (OU)	RFM	22.1	7	64	1	64.00	1- 14	–	–
G.J.Batty (Sy)	OB	488.5	70	1696	42	40.38	5- 76	1	–

F-C	Cat	O	M	R	W	Avge	Best	5wI	10wM
W.A.T.Beer (Sx)	LB	32.4	7	111	5	22.20	3- 31	–	–
D.M.Benkenstein (Du)	RM/OB	81	43	143	4	35.75	2- 17	–	–
J.G.E.Benning (Le)	RM	19	2	59	3	19.66	2- 38	–	–
G.K.Berg (M)	RMF	235	32	877	24	36.54	4- 72	–	–
D.E.Bernard (WI A)	RMF	54	7	160	1	160.00	1-102	–	–
T.L.Best (Y)	RF	198	20	793	18	44.05	4- 86	–	–
L.A.Blackaby (DU)	LM	1	0	11	0			–	–
I.D.Blackwell (Du)	SLA	455.3	129	1205	43	28.02	5- 78	2	–
J.A.R.Blain (Y)	RFM	14	7	20	0			–	–
A.J.Blake (K)	RMF	19	4	69	3	23.00	2- 9	–	–
N.Boje (Nh)	SLA	230.3	42	796	15	53.06	2- 47	–	–
D.E.Bollinger (A)	LFM	53	13	182	5	36.40	3- 51	–	–
R.S.Bopara (EL/Ex)	RM	35.1	5	122	11	11.09	4- 14	–	–
S.G.Borthwick (Du)	LBG	156.5	19	618	15	41.20	2- 22	–	–
A.G.Botha (Wa)	SLA	50.4	11	175	4	43.75	3- 50	–	–
M.A.G.Boyce (Le)	RM	1	0	2	0			–	–
D.P.Bradshaw (OU)	RFM	32	5	103	4	25.75	2- 41	–	–
R.M.R.Brathwaite (Du)	RFM	30.1	2	118	4	29.50	3- 93	–	–
G.R.Breese (Du)	OB	3	1	5	0			–	–
T.T.Bresnan (E/Y)	RFM	238.4	56	707	21	33.66	5- 52	1	–
T.Brett (Nh)	SLA	17	6	38	0			–	–
D.R.Briggs (H)	SLA	377.2	59	1294	34	38.05	4- 93	–	–
S.C.J.Broad (E/Nt)	RFM	179.5	37	626	33	18.96	8- 52	2	1
J.A.Brooks (Nh)	RMF	373.3	86	1260	37	34.05	4- 88	–	–
A.D.Brown (Nt)	LB	9	0	57	0			–	–
F.A.Brown (CU)	SLA	45	0	194	4	48.50	2- 70	–	–
O.V.Brown (WI A)	LB	32.2	4	123	5	24.60	5- 92	1	–
T.E.Bryan (OU)	RMF	5	1	11	0			–	–
N.L.Buck (Le)	RMF	381.5	88	1340	49	27.34	4- 44	–	–
D.A.Burton (M)	RMF	20	4	75	5	15.00	5- 75	1	–
J.G.Cameron (Wo)	RM	93.5	17	332	8	41.50	2- 18	–	–
M.A.Carberry (H)	OB	42	10	110	4	27.50	1- 0	–	–
A.Carter (Ex)	RM	100.5	15	311	13	23.92	5- 40	1	–
N.M.Carter (Wa)	LFM	356.2	70	1129	51	22.13	5- 60	4	–
M.S.Chadwick (Sx)	RMF	19	2	74	1	74.00	1- 41	–	–
M.A.Chambers (Ex)	RFM	269.3	51	909	38	23.92	6- 68	2	1
G.Chapple (La)	RFM	372.4	89	1027	52	19.75	5- 27	2	–
S.P.Cheetham (Sy)	RFM	16	1	71	2	35.50	2- 71	–	–
E.Chigumbura (Nh)	RM	114	17	482	20	24.10	5- 92	1	–
S.H.Choudhry (Wa)	SLA	10	3	32	1	32.00	1- 32	–	–
D.T.Christian (H)	RFM	22.1	1	115	2	57.50	2-115	–	–
J.L.Clare (De)	RMF	69.3	8	324	11	29.45	4- 42	–	–
R.Clarke (Wa)	RFM	212.5	31	743	32	23.21	6- 63	1	–
M.E.Claydon (Du)	RMF	287.1	49	1087	35	31.05	3- 17	–	–
S.J.Cliff (Le)	RM	21	6	54	1	54.00	1- 29	–	–
J.J.Cobb (Le)	LB	8	2	38	0			–	–
K.J.Coetzer (Du)	RM	7	0	33	0			–	–
M.T.Coles (K)	RMF	280	42	1040	27	38.51	4- 55	–	–
P.D.Collingwood (Du/E)	RM	18	4	36	1	36.00	1- 11	–	–
P.T.Collins (M)	LFM	284.4	51	999	36	27.75	4- 46	–	–
C.D.Collymore (Sx)	RFM	414	115	1133	57	19.87	6- 48	2	–
M.A.Comber (Ex)	RMF	22.2	2	94	4	23.50	2- 34	–	–

F-C	Cat	O	M	R	W	Avge	Best	5wI	10wM
N.R.D.Compton (Sm)	OB	14.2	0	87	2	43.50	1- 1	–	–
D.O.Conway (OU)	RM	76	17	249	6	41.50	2- 36	–	–
A.N.Cook (E/EL/Ex)	OB	8	1	36	1	36.00	1- 33	–	–
S.J.Cook (K)	RMF	331.3	68	1132	37	30.59	4- 62	–	–
A.C.Cope (LU)	RM	4	0	24	0			–	–
D.G.Cork (H)	RFM	407.2	102	1042	45	23.15	5- 50	2	–
M.J.Cosgrove (Gm)	RM	35	5	140	3	46.66	1- 12	–	–
D.A.Cosker (Gm)	SLA	432	101	1128	51	22.11	5- 93	1	–
R.D.B.Croft (Gm)	OB	323.3	67	805	26	30.96	4- 20	–	–
S.J.Croft (La)	RMF	14	2	51	1	51.00	1- 17	–	–
L.M.Daggett (Nh)	RFM	321.4	65	1058	30	35.26	4- 25	–	–
J.W.M.Dalrymple (Gm)	OB	127	13	391	11	35.54	4- 71	–	–
Danish Kaneria (Ex/P)	LBG	316.4	56	1130	30	37.66	4- 51	–	–
J.H.Davey (M)	RM	27	2	107	2	53.50	2- 41	–	–
A.M.Davies (Du)	RMF	131	47	282	2	141.00	2- 10	–	–
L.A.Dawson (H)	SLA	33	5	107	1	107.00	1- 61	–	–
Z.de Bruyn (Sm)	RM	94.2	10	386	12	32.16	4- 23	–	–
J.L.Denly (K)	LB	53	2	215	3	71.66	2-100	–	–
C.D.J.Dent (Gs)	SLA	11	0	43	0			–	–
J.W.Dernbach (Sy)	RMF	447	98	1390	51	27.25	5- 68	2	–
N.J.Dexter (M)	RM	120	25	378	13	29.07	3- 50	–	–
S.Dhawan (IA)	RM	9	2	33	1	33.00	1- 18	–	–
L.A.Dingle (OU)	RMF	19	3	73	1	73.00	1- 36	–	–
M.P.Dunn (Sy)	RFM	14.5	7	48	3	16.00	3- 48	–	–
W.J.Durston (De)	OB	16	0	76	1	76.00	1- 9	–	–
J.du Toit (Le)	RM	2	0	20	0			–	–
P.D.Edwards (K)	RMF	34	10	145	3	48.33	2- 60	–	–
S.M.Ervine (H)	RM	362.5	77	1073	20	53.65	4- 31	–	–
D.Evans (M)	RFM	102.3	19	397	11	36.09	5- 87	1	–
L.Evans (Du/Nh)	RMF	59	10	212	5	42.40	3- 53	–	–
L.J.Evans (Sy/Wa)	RFM	6	0	30	1	30.00	1- 30	–	–
R.F.Evans (LU)	RM	24	0	100	1	100.00	1- 57	–	–
Fawad Alam (P)	SLA	4	1	8	0			–	–
R.S.Ferley (K)	SLA	26	2	142	2	71.00	1- 54	–	–
S.T.Finn (E/M)	RFM	407.1	92	1410	64	22.03	9- 37	4	1
A.D.S.Fletcher (WI A)	RMF	5	0	19	0			–	–
L.J.Fletcher (Nt)	RMF	169.2	40	563	12	46.91	3- 39	–	–
G.W.Flower (Ex)	SLA	9	0	32	1	32.00	1- 19	–	–
M.H.A.Footitt (De)	LFM	239.2	48	786	23	34.17	4- 78	–	–
J.E.C.Franklin (IA)	LFM	334.2	69	1083	46	23.54	7- 14	1	–
P.J.Franks (Nt)	RMF	410.2	106	1129	42	26.88	3- 15	–	–
A.B.Fudadin (WI A)	RMF	14	1	42	0			–	–
D.J.Gale (DU)	SLA	78	8	287	8	35.87	4- 94	–	–
C.Ganapathy (IA)	RM	19	5	77	1	77.00	1- 53	–	–
J.S.Gatting (Sx)	OB	5	2	19	1	19.00	1- 19	–	–
A.P.R.Gidman (Gs)	RM	53	7	203	9	22.55	2- 10	–	–
J.C.Glover (DU)	RMF	45	8	180	2	90.00	2- 82	–	–
J.E.Goodman (K)	RM	6	0	16	1	16.00	1- 16	–	–
D.M.Goodwin (CU)	RMF	35	6	142	1	142.00	1-142	–	–
J.M.Greenwood (CU)	RMF	19	1	97	0			–	–
D.A.Griffiths (H)	RFM	152	18	646	19	34.00	5- 85	1	–
T.D.Groenewald (De)	RFM	413.5	105	1295	38	34.07	5- 86	1	–

F-C	Cat	O	M	R	W	Avge	Best	5wI	10wM
P.R.Groves (LU)	RMF	29	2	142	3	47.33	2- 55	–	–
H.F.Gurney (Le)	LFM	96	22	332	10	33.20	3- 82	–	–
A.D.Hales (Nt)	RM	5.5	1	26	0			–	–
A.J.Hall (Nh)	RFM	318	57	1047	33	31.72	4- 44	–	–
R.J.Hamilton-Brown (Sy)	OB	47.3	1	184	1	184.00	1- 17	–	–
T.R.G.Hampton (M)	RM	14	3	42	1	42.00	1- 15	–	–
O.J.Hannon-Dalby (Y)	RMF	382.4	61	1372	34	40.35	5- 68	2	–
A.Harinath (Sy)	OB	2	0	12	0			–	–
B.W.Harmison (Du)	RMF	86.4	10	402	14	28.71	4- 70	–	–
S.J.Harmison (Du)	RF	245.4	51	819	30	27.30	7- 29	1	–
G.M.Harper (DU)	LFM	49	1	248	2	124.00	2- 89	–	–
A.J.Harris (Le)	RM	96.4	23	385	9	42.77	3- 43	–	–
J.A.R.Harris (EL/Gm)	RFM	463.4	117	1356	63	21.52	5- 56	2	–
D.S.Harrison (Gm)	RMF	323.3	44	1156	37	31.24	7- 45	2	–
L.J.Hatchett (Sx)	LMF	66.4	15	256	12	21.33	5- 47	1	–
C.W.Henderson (Le)	SLA	489.3	136	1179	56	21.05	6- 21	3	–
H.M.R.K.B.Herath (H)	SLA	175.3	42	463	10	46.30	4- 98	–	–
R.L.Hesketh (CU)	SLC	3	0	21	0			–	–
J.C.Hildreth (Sm)	RMF	13	0	95	1	95.00	1- 95	–	–
B.W.Hilfenhaus (A)	RFM	61.5	15	190	8	23.75	3- 39	–	–
J.B.Hockley (K)	OB	43	5	175	2	87.50	1- 8	–	–
L.J.Hodgson (Y)	RFM	30.5	6	128	2	64.00	1- 42	–	–
K.W.Hogg (La)	RFM	202.2	48	650	20	32.50	4- 53	–	–
M.J.Hoggard (Le)	RMF	416.4	105	1222	50	24.44	6- 63	3	–
C.E.H.Hopkins (CU)	RMF	61	9	305	2	152.50	1- 66	–	–
B.H.N.Howgego (Nh)	RM	2	0	16	0			–	–
C.F.Hughes (De)	SLA	11	0	81	1	81.00	1- 9	–	–
G.M.Hussain (Gs)	RMF	417.4	86	1497	67	22.34	5- 36	2	–
D.J.Hussey (Nt)	OB	18	1	82	0			–	–
Iftikhar Anjum (Sy)	RM	65	8	240	6	40.00	2- 53	–	–
Imran Arif (Wo)	RFM	33	2	141	4	35.25	2- 63	–	–
Imran Farhat (P)	LBG	14	1	40	0			–	–
Imran Tahir (Wa)	LBG	430.4	58	1376	56	24.57	8-114	3	–
Iqbal Abdulla (IA)	SLA	97.2	26	232	10	23.20	4- 42	–	–
A.J.Ireland (Gs)	RMF	222.5	33	784	36	21.77	5- 25	2	–
N.A.James (Gm)	SLA	1	0	1	0			–	–
Jaskaran Singh (RM)	RM	45	6	174	1	174.00	1- 97	–	–
T.M.Jewell (Sy)	RFM	40	10	127	3	42.33	1- 22	–	–
M.G.Johnson (A)	LF	53.4	8	217	3	72.33	1- 31	–	–
G.O.Jones (K)	WK	1	0	8	0			–	–
P.S.Jones (De)	RMF	313.5	68	959	31	30.93	4- 26	–	–
R.A.Jones (Wo)	RMF	298.2	48	1281	38	33.71	7-115	2	–
S.P.Jones (H)	RFM	22	5	60	4	15.00	4- 60	–	–
R.H.Joseph (K)	RFM	52	9	185	2	92.50	2-112	–	–
M.Kartik (Sm)	SLA	383.2	107	882	45	19.60	6- 42	5	2
G.Keedy (La)	SLA	246.5	43	688	31	22.19	7- 68	2	1
S.C.Kerrigan (La)	SLA	319	66	967	30	32.23	6- 74	3	–
A.N.Kervezee (Wo)	OB	4.3	0	63	0			–	–
R.W.T.Key (K)	RM/OB	15.2	3	45	2	22.50	2- 31	–	–
A.Khan (K)	RFM	372.2	82	1258	38	33.10	5- 43	1	–
I.Khan (WI A)	LB	52	5	217	2	108.50	1- 18	–	–
S.J.King (Sy)	OB	28	1	134	1	134.00	1-134	–	–

F-C	Cat	O	M	R	W	Avge	Best	5wI	10wM
S.P.Kirby (EL/Gs)	RFM	280.4	63	912	33	27.63	4- 50	–	–
D.S.Kulkarni (IA)	RM	87.3	24	253	7	36.14	5- 31	1	–
T.J.Lancefield (Sy)	LM	1	0	9	0				
M.A.K.Lawson (K)	LB	34	2	164	6	27.33	4- 93	–	–
J.Lewis (Gs)	RMF	419.3	103	1222	54	22.62	4- 25	–	–
T.E.Linley (Sy)	RFM	170	46	483	16	30.18	5-105	1	–
J.A.Lodwick (OU)	RM	18	4	60	0				
A.B.London (M)	OB	8	3	15	1	15.00	1- 15	–	–
J.D.S.Lotay (CU)	OB	37	3	146	2	73.00	1- 43	–	–
D.S.Lucas (Nh)	LMF	300.4	59	1038	32	32.43	5- 64	1	–
T.Lungley (De)	RM	165	25	630	19	33.15	3- 39	–	–
A.Lyth (Y)	RM	2	0	16	0				
A.B.McDonald (Le)	RFM	103	21	320	12	26.66	5- 40	1	–
B.E.McGain (Ex)	LBG	64.3	4	260	10	26.00	5-151	1	–
A.McGrath (Y)	RM	74	13	226	0				
N.D.McKenzie (H)	RM	32	3	95	2	47.50	2- 30	–	–
D.L.Maddy (Wa)	RM/OB	206.5	62	523	21	24.90	4- 37	–	–
W.L.Madsen (De)	OB	8.2	0	68	1	68.00	1- 68	–	–
Mahbubul Alam (B)	RMF	24	2	88	2	44.00	1- 38	–	–
S.I.Mahmood (La)	RF	348	54	1263	33	38.27	5- 55	1	–
Mahmudullah (B)	OB	93.4	7	329	5	65.80	2- 70	–	–
C.C.Malan (LU)	OB	10	1	28	1	28.00	1- 28	–	–
D.J.Malan (M)	LB	74.1	2	339	6	56.50	2- 51	–	–
M.M.Malik (Le)	RFM	193.2	45	599	21	28.52	4- 32	–	–
H.J.H.Marshall (Gs)	RM	61	19	153	0				
C.S.Martin (Ex)	RFM	25	10	84	1	84.00	1- 84	–	–
R.S.C.Martin-Jenkins (Sx)	RFM	201.1	35	593	30	19.76	5- 45	1	–
M.S.Mason (Wo)	RFM	278	72	849	31	27.38	4- 87	–	–
D.D.Masters (Ex)	RMF	487	138	1223	53	23.07	5- 43	1	–
T.L.Maynard (Gm)	OB	3	0	20	0				
S.C.Meaker (Sy)	RMF	269.4	48	998	29	34.41	5- 48	2	–
J.C.Mickleburgh (Ex)	RMF	1.1	0	11	0				
J.D.Middlebrook (Nh)	OB	251.2	40	863	18	47.94	3- 23	–	–
A.S.Miller (Wa)	RFM	154.4	42	488	16	30.50	5- 58	2	–
M.J.Milligan (OU)	RFM	52	8	205	1	205.00	1- 49	–	–
D.K.H.Mitchell (Wo)	RM	15	3	64	0				
Mohammad Aamer (P)	LFM	224.5	47	656	35	18.74	6- 84	3	–
Mohammad Ashraful (B)	OB	16	0	81	0				
Mohammad Asif (P)	RFM	211.1	46	657	23	28.56	5- 77	1	–
G.J.Muchall (Du)	RM	1	0	2	0				
A.Mukund (IA)	LBG	3	1	3	0				
S.J.Mullaney (Nt)	RM	93.4	19	321	9	35.66	4- 31	–	–
M.K.Munday (Sm)	LB	52.1	9	238	6	39.66	4-105	–	–
T.J.Murtagh (M)	RFM	459.2	127	1405	38	36.97	5- 52	2	–
Naeem Islam (B)	OB	31	3	133	0				
J.K.H.Naik (Le)	OB	205	40	619	35	17.48	7- 96	1	–
G.R.Napier (Ex)	RM	95	18	280	3	93.33	1- 47	–	–
C.D.Nash (Sx)	OB	56	10	126	8	15.75	4- 12	–	–
Naved-ul-Hasan (Y)	RMF	162.4	44	532	20	26.60	4- 28	–	–
A.Nel (Sy)	RFM	227	67	671	21	31.95	4- 68	–	–
J.D.Nel (K)	RMF	54	12	190	10	19.00	6- 62	1	–
R.I.Newton (Nh)	LB	2.1	0	19	0				

F-C	Cat	O	M	R	W	Avge	Best	5wI	10wM
P.A.Nixon (Le)	RM	2.1	1	7	1	7.00	1- 7	–	–
M.J.North (A)	OB	18.1	1	55	6	9.16	6- 55	1	–
S.A.Northeast (K)	OB	6	3	8	0				
M.Ntini (K)	RFM	164	44	474	24	19.75	6- 51	2	1
I.E.O'Brien (M)	RMF	205.1	36	628	23	27.30	7- 48	1	–
M.Osborne (Ex)	RMF	36	5	151	6	25.16	3- 35	–	–
W.T.Owen (Gm)	RMF	54	8	232	3	77.33	3- 65	–	–
A.P.Palladino (Ex)	RMF	142	30	499	18	27.72	4- 57	–	–
M.K.Pandey (IA)	OB	2	0	12	0				
M.S.Panesar (EL/Sx)	SLA	518.2	135	1336	52	25.69	5- 44	2	–
C.M.Park (CU)	RMF	49	3	219	2	109.50	1- 34	–	–
G.T.Park (De)	RM	83.3	9	327	9	36.33	2- 20	–	–
D.C.Pascoe (OU)	SLA	107	37	245	12	20.41	6- 68	2	–
R.H.Patel (M)	SLA	47	8	134	5	26.80	3- 52	–	–
S.R.Patel (Nt)	SLA	345.3	73	1044	26	40.15	4- 55	–	–
S.A.Patterson (Y)	RMF	392.5	96	1201	45	26.68	5- 50	1	–
D.J.Pattinson (Nt)	RFM	310.2	54	1180	33	35.75	5- 95	1	–
R.J.Peterson (De)	SLA	553.3	129	1566	51	30.70	4- 10	–	–
B.J.Phillips (Sm)	RFM	277.3	79	661	29	22.79	5- 72	1	–
T.J.Phillips (Ex)	SLA	246.2	45	752	20	37.60	4- 94	–	–
K.P.Pietersen (E/Sy)	OB	1	0	2	0				
S.A.Piolet (Wa)	RM	17	3	80	1	80.00	1- 67	–	–
L.E.Plunkett (Du/EL)	RFM	415.4	64	1499	40	37.47	4-107	–	–
W.T.S.Porterfield (Gs)	OB	5	0	49	0				
D.B.L.Powell (La)	RMF	99	16	343	7	49.00	2- 45	–	–
T.Poynton (De)	(WK)	8	0	96	2	48.00	2- 96	–	–
L.A.Procter (La)	RM	7.3	0	47	1	47.00	1- 26	–	–
R.M.Pyrah (Y)	RM	84.4	16	326	7	46.57	2- 8	–	–
A.M.Rahane (IA)	RM	3	1	5	0				
M.R.Ramprakash (Sy)	OB	1	0	6	0				
W.B.Rankin (Wa)	RFM	145.3	19	594	22	27.00	5- 16	1	–
A.U.Rashid (Y)	LB	504.4	67	1784	57	31.29	5- 87	3	–
O.P.Rayner (Sx)	OB	148.2	38	412	18	22.88	4- 62	–	–
D.J.Redfern (De)	OB	3	0	14	0				
G.P.Rees (Gm)	LM	1	0	3	0				
H.Riazuddin (H)	RFM	13	6	29	2	14.50	1- 0	–	–
A.Richardson (Wo)	RMF	524	153	1342	55	24.40	5- 44	2	–
Robiul Islam (B)	RMF	104	10	432	12	36.00	4- 77	–	–
S.D.Robson (M)	LBG	2	0	17	0				
C.J.L.Rogers (De)	LBG	1	0	5	0				
T.S.Roland-Jones (M)	RMF	230.2	34	745	38	19.60	5- 41	2	–
J.E.Root (Y)	OB	7	0	27	0				
C.G.W.Roper (DU)	RM	42	3	249	2	124.50	1- 61	–	–
S.A.L.Rose (LU)	RMF	53	8	216	1	216.00	1- 72	–	–
J.J.Roy (Sy)	RM	3	0	18	0				
Rubel Hossain (B)	RMF	58.1	5	250	5	50.00	2- 30	–	–
J.A.Rudolph (Y)	LBG	11	2	43	0				
C.Rushworth (Du)	RMF	214.4	43	821	21	39.09	4- 90	–	–
A.D.Russell (WI A)	RF	68	18	207	11	18.81	5- 68	1	–
Saeed Ajmal (P)	OB	125.1	19	353	12	29.41	5- 82	1	–
D.J.G.Sales (Nh)	RM	1	0	10	0				
B.W.Sanderson (Y)	RMF	18	3	50	5	10.00	5- 50	1	–

235

F–C	Cat	O	M	R	W	Avge	Best	5wI	10wM
J.J.Sayers (Y)	OB	24	3	61	0			–	–
C.P.Schofield (Sy)	LBG	184	34	606	14	43.28	4- 63	–	–
A.J.D.Scott (OU)	LB	47.5	8	147	8	18.37	4- 52	–	–
Shafiul Islam (B)	RFM	66.2	14	187	5	37.40	2- 44	–	–
O.A.Shah (M)	OB	43.5	5	133	4	33.25	1- 16	–	–
Shahadat Hossain (B)	RMF	108.3	12	416	13	32.00	5- 98	1	–
Shahid Afridi (P)	LBG	17	0	69	1	69.00	1- 44	–	–
A.Shahzad (E/Y)	RFM	309.2	51	1076	38	28.31	5- 51	1	–
A.J.Shantry (Gm)	LFM	14	4	41	1	41.00	1- 21	–	–
J.D.Shantry (Wo)	LM	308	73	945	27	35.00	5- 49	1	–
Shakib Al Hasan (B/Wo)	SLA	345.3	56	1088	43	25.30	7- 32	4	–
R.Sharma (OU)	RMF	67.5	14	188	2	94.00	1- 14	–	–
A.Sheikh (De)	LMF	25	1	152	5	30.40	3- 78	–	–
Shoaib Malik (P)	OB	44.3	6	134	6	22.33	2- 17	–	–
C.E.Shreck (Nt)	RFM	199	50	577	18	32.05	4- 81	–	–
R.J.Sidebottom (Nt)	LFM	236	62	630	30	21.00	5- 35	1	–
D.S.Smith (WI A)	OB	1	0	5	0				
D.T.Smith (OU)	RM	0.3	0	5	0				
G.M.Smith (De)	OB/RM	414.3	77	1368	42	32.57	5- 54	1	–
S.P.D.Smith (A)	LBG	31	7	82	3	27.33	3- 51	–	–
T.C.Smith (La)	RMF	279.5	58	913	32	28.53	6- 94	1	–
T.M.J.Smith (M)	SLA	72	12	262	2	131.00	1- 30	–	–
W.R.Smith (Du)	OB	4	0	27	0				
V.S.Solanki (Wo)	OB	29	4	96	1	96.00	1- 22	–	–
M.N.W.Spriegel (Sy)	OB	65.3	3	207	5	41.40	1- 5	–	–
D.I.Stevens (K)	RM	280.1	74	768	28	27.42	4- 38	–	–
D.A.Stiff (Sm)	RFM	40.5	3	207	2	103.50	1- 42	–	–
B.A.Stokes (Du)	RMF	66.3	6	328	5	65.60	2- 32	–	–
A.V.Suppiah (Sm)	SLA	99	18	300	3	100.00	1- 21	–	–
G.P.Swann (E/Nt)	OB	200.1	58	567	30	18.90	6- 65	3	–
N.S.Tahir (Wa)	RFM	83	15	238	5	47.60	2- 49	–	–
C.G.Taylor (Gs)	OB	52.5	5	172	3	57.33	1- 19	–	–
J.M.R.Taylor (Gs)	OB	5	2	13	1	13.00	1- 8	–	–
J.W.A.Taylor (EL/Le)	LB	4	0	15	0				
M.H.Taylor (CU)	LB	50.5	4	235	4	58.75	4-161	–	–
R.M.L.Taylor (LU)	LM	46	6	202	5	40.40	2- 60	–	–
R.N.ten Doeschate (Ex)	RMF	191.3	16	716	27	26.51	5- 13	1	–
A.C.Thomas (Sm)	RFM	377.5	85	1202	49	24.53	5- 40	2	–
M.A.Thornely (Sx)	RM	21	2	75	4	18.75	2- 14	–	–
C.D.Thorp (Du)	RMF	148.3	39	427	13	32.84	4- 54	–	–
R.T.Timms (CU)	RFM	11	0	51	0				
M.K.Tiwary (IA)	LBG	32	3	93	2	46.50	2- 72	–	–
J.A.Tomlinson (H)	LFM	559.1	149	1624	46	35.30	7- 85	2	–
G.C.Tonge (WI A)	RFM	95	20	321	9	35.66	3- 53	–	–
K.S.Toor (M)	LB	25	2	84	1	84.00	1- 36	–	–
J.C.Tredwell (K)	OB	377	71	1151	38	30.28	7- 22	2	–
P.D.Trego (Sm)	RMF	227.1	50	729	22	33.13	4- 26	–	–
C.T.Tremlett (Sy)	RFM	361.5	88	969	48	20.18	4- 29	–	–
V.Tripathi (Nh)	LB	6	0	28	0				
I.J.L.Trott (E/Wa)	RM	25	4	94	5	18.80	2- 20	–	–
P.T.Turnbull (CU)	RMF	108.2	22	366	10	36.60	5- 92	1	–
S.Tyagi (IA)	RM	5	2	4	0				

F-C	Cat	O	M	R	W	Avge	Best	5wI	10wM
S.D.Udal (M)	OB	284.3	38	917	27	33.96	5-128	1	–
Umar Akmal (P)	OB	1	0	10	0				
Umar Amin (P)	RM	22	4	63	3	21.00	1- 7	–	–
Umar Gul (P)	RFM	119.4	21	391	14	27.92	4- 61	–	–
J.D.Unadkat (IA)	LMF	83.3	24	203	16	12.68	7- 41	2	1
W.P.J.U.C.Vaas (Nh)	LMF	73.2	20	161	6	26.83	4- 49	–	–
M.van Jaarsveld (K)	OB	123	17	332	5	66.40	2- 50	–	–
J.M.Vince (H)	RM	5.2	1	24	0				
A.C.Voges (Nt)	SLA	1	0	2	0				
G.G.Wagg (De)	LM	77	13	246	10	24.60	3- 31	–	–
Wahab Riaz (P)	LFM	71.2	11	283	8	35.37	5- 63	1	–
D.J.Wainwright (Y)	SLA	184.2	27	716	14	51.14	3- 48	–	–
A.G.Wakely (Nh)	OB	9.1	0	57	1	57.00	1- 4	–	–
M.J.Walker (Ex)	RM	18	2	71	3	23.66	3- 35	–	–
M.A.Wallace (Gm)	(WK)	1	0	3	0				
S.J.Walters (Sy)	RM	3	0	15	0				
H.T.Waters (Gm)	RMF	297.4	79	898	26	34.53	4- 39	–	–
S.R.Waters (DU)	LBG	16	3	65	2	32.50	1- 18	–	–
S.J.V.Watkins (OU)	OB	17	1	73	0				
M.J.C.Watson (OU)	LB	31	2	128	0				
S.R.Watson (A)	RMF	29.5	5	117	11	10.63	6- 33	2	–
L.W.P.Wells (Sx)	OB	2	0	16	0				
A.S.Welsh (LU)	LB	42.4	2	152	4	38.00	3- 32	–	–
T.Westley (DU/Ex)	OB	88.3	15	229	10	22.90	4- 55	–	–
C.D.Whelan (Wo)	RMF	9	1	34	1	34.00	1- 21	–	–
G.G.White (Nh)	SLA	23	3	104	1	104.00	1-104	–	–
R.A.White (Nh)	LB	1	0	7	0				
W.A.White (Le)	RMF	134.2	20	531	8	66.37	4- 58	–	–
D.J.Willey (Nh)	LFM	56.5	8	218	6	36.33	2- 47	–	–
C.M.Willoughby (Sm)	LMF	512.1	118	1582	58	27.27	6-101	1	–
G.C.Wilson (Sy)	(WK)	9	0	44	0				
C.R.Woakes (EL/Wa)	RMF	424.2	107	1246	58	21.48	6- 52	3	1
C.P.Wood (H)	LM	71.1	17	240	13	18.46	5- 54	1	–
M.J.Wood (Nt)	OB	1	0	11	0				
R.J.J.Woolley (CU)	RM	89	8	394	6	65.66	3- 73	–	–
B.J.Wright (Gm)	RM	2	0	7	0				
C.J.C.Wright (Ex)	RFM	301.5	55	1156	31	37.29	5- 70	1	–
D.G.Wright (Sm)	RFM	154.1	41	377	14	26.92	5- 41	1	–
L.J.Wright (Sx)	RM	154.5	22	573	23	24.91	5- 65	1	–
Yasir Arafat (Sx)	RMF	256	43	896	36	24.88	5- 74	1	–
Yasir Hameed (P)	OB	1	1	0	0				
E.G.C.Young (Gs/OU)	SLA	54	3	228	1	228.00	1- 75	–	–
Younus Khan (Sy)	RM/LB	18	0	64	0				

FIRST-CLASS CAREER RECORDS

Compiled by Philip Bailey

The following career records are for all players who appeared in first-class cricket during the 2010 season, and are complete to the end of that season. Some players who did not appear in 2010 but may do so in 2011 are included.

BATTING AND FIELDING

'1000' denotes instances of scoring 1000 runs in a season. Where these have been achieved outside the British Isles they are shown after a plus sign.

	M	I	NO	HS	Runs	Avge	100	50	1000	Ct/St
Abdul Razzaq	116	182	27	203*	5195	33.51	8	27	–	32
Abdur Razzak	49	81	14	83	1387	20.70	–	7	–	17
Abdur Rehman	104	142	16	96	2288	18.15	–	11	–	47
Abel, E.	5	6	1	60	154	30.80	–	1	–	4
Ackland, B.J.	2	4	1	51*	93	31.00	–	1	–	1
Adams, A.R.	115	153	16	124	3158	23.05	3	12	–	81
Adams, J.H.K.	104	186	16	262*	6423	37.78	10	36	3	91
Adkin, W.A.	1	1	–	45	45	45.00	–	–	–	–
Adshead, S.J.	77	125	20	156*	3304	31.46	3	17	–	205/15
Afzaal, U.	235	406	47	204*	14055	39.15	32	74	7	104
Aga, R.G.	19	29	5	66*	340	14.16	–	1	–	7
Agarwal, S.S.	3	4	2	117	134	67.00	1	–	–	1
Ali, Kabir	117	164	23	84*	2383	16.90	–	7	–	32
Ali, Kadeer	99	180	10	161	4906	28.85	6	26	–	54
Ali, M.M.	49	84	7	153	2697	35.02	5	18	1	21
Allenby, J.	63	96	15	138*	3175	39.19	4	25	–	60
Ambrose, T.R.	120	185	15	251*	5533	32.54	9	31	–	279/19
Amla, H.M.	132	219	20	253*	9688	48.68	29	48	0+2	100
Anderson, J.M.	111	132	54	37*	792	10.15	–	–	–	44
Andrew, G.M.	42	59	10	92*	1178	24.04	–	7	–	12
Ansari, A.S.	11	17	4	193	514	39.53	2	1	–	3
Anyon, J.E.	58	74	25	37*	538	10.97	–	–	–	18
Ashling, C.P.	4	6	2	20	49	12.25	–	–	–	–
Ashok, A.	3	6	1	112	288	57.60	1	1	–	2
Ashraf, M.A.	4	4	–	10	15	3.75	–	–	–	1
Atkinson, J.J. –	3	4	–	16	21	5.25	–	–	–	3
Azeem Rafiq	7	8	1	100	146	20.85	1	–	–	1
Azhar Ali	56	92	12	153*	3080	38.50	11	11	–	52
Azhar Mahmood	163	254	29	204*	6952	30.89	9	35	–	127
Bairstow, J.M.	28	48	13	84*	1510	43.14	–	14	–	50/5
Baker, G.C.	5	7	1	66	196	32.66	–	2	–	1
Baker, L.S.	29	41	14	32	268	9.92	–	–	–	11
Balcombe, D.J.	29	36	7	73	422	14.55	–	1	–	8
Ballance, G.S.	4	7	2	43	90	18.00	–	–	–	1
Bandara, H.M.C.M.	150	214	45	108	3415	20.20	1	14	–	95
Banerjee, V.	40	62	20	35	386	9.19	–	–	–	9
Barker, K.H.D.	7	9	1	23	85	10.62	–	–	–	1
Barnard, M.R.	1	1	–	0	0	0.00	–	–	–	–
Bates, A.M.	8	11	3	31	92	11.50	–	–	–	28
Batty, G.J.	150	228	38	133	4852	25.53	2	24	–	103
Batty, J.N.	206	324	36	168*	9238	32.07	20	39	1	553/67
Beer, W.A.T.	4	3	2	37*	43	43.00	–	–	–	1
Bell, I.R.	171	290	27	262*	11575	44.01	31	60	3	126

F-C	M	I	NO	HS	Runs	Avge	100	50	1000	Ct/St
Benham, C.C.	48	80	3	111	2103	27.31	2	10	–	51
Benkenstein, D.M.	226	343	38	259	13741	45.05	34	72	4	153
Benning, J.G.E.	42	67	7	128	1938	32.30	4	8	–	17
Berg, G.K.	31	54	7	125	1547	32.91	1	10	–	17
Bernard, D.E.	82	137	10	120	3616	28.47	4	19	–	67
Best, T.L.	81	107	19	51	1102	12.52	–	1	–	23
Blackaby, L.A.	2	1	–	38	38	38.00	–	–	–	–
Blackwell, I.D.	181	271	21	247*	9936	39.74	23	55	3	61
Blain, J.A.R.	43	47	16	93	495	15.96	–	2	–	12
Blake, A.J.	14	22	1	105*	484	23.04	1	–	–	6
Boje, N.	212	318	55	226*	8975	34.12	8	55	–	123
Bollinger, D.E.	64	69	30	31*	301	7.71	–	–	–	23
Bopara, R.S.	103	172	22	229	6332	42.21	17	25	1	67
Borrington, P.M.	26	42	5	105	1109	29.97	2	5	–	16
Borthwick, S.G.	13	18	4	68	341	24.35	–	2	–	9
Bosman, L.E.	94	169	12	140	4568	29.09	5	23	–	51
Botha, A.G.	135	209	27	156*	4311	23.68	4	20	–	102
Botha, J.	63	105	16	109	3087	34.68	1	22	–	46
Boyce, M.A.G.	49	85	6	106	2188	27.69	1	15	–	26
Bradshaw, D.P.	12	17	3	127*	529	37.78	1	2	–	2
Bragg, W.D.	14	22	–	92	474	21.54	–	2	–	7/1
Brathwaite, K.C.	7	13	1	73	353	29.41	–	2	–	4
Brathwaite, R.M.R.	13	14	4	76*	144	14.40	–	.1	–	–
Bravo, D.J.	94	173	7	197	5193	31.28	8	29	–	81
Breese, G.R.	116	185	20	165*	4359	26.41	4	27	–	96
Bresnan, T.T.	96	127	22	126*	2882	27.44	3	14	–	41
Brett, T.	1	–	–	–	–	–	–	–	–	–
Briggs, D.R.	16	17	3	36	153	10.92	–	–	–	3
Broad, S.C.J.	73	94	18	169	1905	25.06	1	11	–	21
Brooks, J.A.	17	23	6	53	197	11.58	–	1	–	3
Brophy, G.L.	115	184	22	185	5118	31.59	7	26	–	286/21
Brown, A.D.	280	438	49	295*	16669	42.85	46	74	8	276/1
Brown, B.C.	10	15	2	112	561	43.15	2	2	–	9/2
Brown, D.O.	24	41	4	99	1089	29.43	–	8	–	13
Brown, F.A.	4	4	–	30	61	15.25	–	–	–	1
Brown, K.R.	9	15	1	40	181	12.92	–	–	–	7
Brown, M.J.	93	166	16	133	5195	34.63	9	28	1	71
Brown, O.V.	38	51	15	33	361	10.02	–	–	–	23
Bryan, T.E.	2	2	–	16	17	8.50	–	–	–	1
Buck, N.L.	19	25	7	26	122	6.77	–	–	–	5
Burton, D.A.	5	8	4	52*	58	14.50	–	1	–	1
Butler, I.G.	43	56	18	68	648	17.05	–	2	–	11
Buttler, J.C.	14	21	3	144	599	33.27	1	2	–	23
Cameron, J.G.	10	17	1	105	576	36.00	1	3	–	7
Carberry, M.A.	112	198	18	204	7832	43.51	23	36	3	50
Carter, A.	5	6	1	16*	49	9.80	–	–	–	2
Carter, N.M.	107	148	24	103	2872	23.16	1	13	–	24
Chadwick, M.S.	1	–	–	–	–	–	–	–	–	–
Chambers, M.A.	22	30	16	14	83	5.92	–	–	–	7
Chanderpaul, S.	261	424	75	303*	19007	54.46	55	97	1+1	146
Chapple, G.	252	346	65	155	7104	25.28	6	33	–	83
Cheetham, S.P.	2	1	1	0*	0	–	–	–	–	1
Chigumbura, E.	70	122	9	186	4014	34.90	3	28	–	29
Chilton, M.J.	182	297	27	131	8909	32.99	20	36	1	132
Chopra, V.	57	99	6	155	2661	28.61	2	17	–	49
Choudhry, S.H.	3	4	2	75	199	99.50	–	3	–	1

239

F-C	M	I	NO	HS	Runs	Avge	100	50	1000	Ct/St
Christian, D.T.	19	30	3	72	664	24.59	–	4	–	18
Clare, J.L.	24	32	5	129*	655	24.25	1	5	–	10
Clarke, M.J.	120	204	20	201*	8475	46.05	28	34	–	118
Clarke, R.	118	188	19	214	6023	35.63	12	28	1	161
Claydon, M.E.	31	33	6	40	391	14.48	–	–	–	5
Cliff, S.J.	7	7	2	26	71	14.20	–	–	–	1
Cobb, J.J.	28	48	5	148*	1105	25.69	1	7	–	12
Coetzer, K.J.	42	74	9	172	2248	34.58	5	7	–	26
Coles, M.T.	16	25	6	51	408	21.47	–	1	–	4
Collingwood, P.D.	188	325	26	206	10977	36.71	24	56	2	214
Collins, P.T.	141	178	51	25	837	6.59	–	–	–	30
Collymore, C.D.	134	187	85	23	819	8.02	–	–	–	45
Comber, M.A.	2	3	–	19	19	6.33	–	–	–	1
Compton, N.R.D.	65	114	12	190	3453	33.85	8	14	1	33
Conway, D.O.	3	2	1	6	6	6.00	–	–	–	–
Cook, A.N.	133	237	18	195	9700	44.29	26	52	4	127
Cook, S.J.	132	170	29	93*	2312	16.39	–	6	–	33
Cope, A.C.	3	5	–	51	84	16.80	–	1	–	–
Cork, D.G.	312	450	60	200*	9797	25.12	8	53	–	231
Cosgrove, M.J.	90	160	11	233	6449	43.28	19	37	1	61
Cosker, D.A.	178	232	71	52	2174	13.50	–	1	–	110
Coughtrie, R.G.	5	7	1	43	115	19.16	–	–	–	6
Cox, O.B.	10	17	4	61	279	21.46	–	2	–	22/2
Croft, R.D.B.	391	576	103	143	12609	26.65	8	54	–	175
Croft, S.J.	59	90	9	122	2509	30.97	1	17	–	48
Crook, S.P.	35	47	7	97	1261	31.52	–	9	–	12
Cross, G.D.	15	24	2	100*	599	27.22	1	4	–	39/8
Daggett, L.M.	39	50	21	48	302	10.41	–	–	–	5
Dalrymple, J.W.M.	123	192	16	244	6013	34.16	10	32	1	82
Danish Kaneria	180	229	81	65	1508	10.18	–	1	–	61
Davey, J.H.	4	7	–	72	220	31.42	–	3	–	3
Davies, A.M.	83	107	41	62	733	11.10	–	1	–	17
Davies, S.M.	91	152	18	192	5371	40.08	8	28	3	275/14
Dawson, L.A.	29	44	6	100*	1112	29.26	1	7	–	17
Dawson, R.K.J.	103	153	17	87	2927	21.52	–	12	–	63
de Bruyn, Z.	167	279	27	266*	10008	39.71	21	54	0+1	103
Denly, J.L.	70	121	5	149	3906	33.67	10	19	1	33
Dent, C.D.J.	16	31	3	98	725	25.89	–	4	–	24
Dernbach, J.W.	49	62	23	56*	404	10.35	–	1	–	4
de Wet, F.	47	65	13	56	812	15.61	–	1	–	19
Dexter, N.J.	51	81	12	146	2955	42.82	7	15	–	44
Dhawan, S.	50	79	5	224	3408	46.05	9	15	–	45
Dingle, L.A.	3	3	1	6*	7	3.50	–	–	–	–
Di Venuto, M.J.	315	556	41	254*	23974	46.55	57	141	10	379
Dixey, P.G.	13	22	1	103	334	15.90	1	–	–	27/6
Dunn, M.P.	1	–	–	–	–	–	–	–	–	–
Durandt, L.E.	2	3	2	20*	53	53.00	–	–	–	1
Durston, W.J.	40	68	12	146*	1966	35.10	1	14	–	43
du Toit, J.	28	43	3	154	1599	39.97	4	9	–	24
Edwards, K.A.	22	41	3	107	1361	35.81	1	11	–	13
Edwards, N.J.	56	93	–	212	3153	33.90	3	16	1	52
Edwards, P.D.	12	15	8	43	121	17.28	–	–	–	2
Ervine, S.M.	117	185	19	237*	5863	35.31	11	30	–	96
Evans, D.	19	23	6	19*	75	4.41	–	–	–	4
Evans, L.	4	6	4	8*	21	10.50	–	–	–	1
Evans, L.J.	9	18	1	133*	543	31.94	1	3	–	6

240

F-C	M	I	NO	HS	Runs	Avge	100	50	1000	Ct/St
Evans, R.F.	4	4	–	44	67	16.75	–	–	–	2
Fawad Alam	57	98	19	296*	4423	55.98	8	28	0+1	32
Ferley, R.S.	34	41	10	78*	650	20.96	–	2	–	10
Finn, S.T.	46	62	21	26*	245	5.97	–	–	–	11
Fletcher, A.D.S.	30	55	4	123	1595	31.27	2	10	–	30/1
Fletcher, L.J.	15	17	6	92	217	19.72	–	1	–	2
Flower, G.W.	188	318	25	243*	10898	37.19	23	58	–	174
Footitt, M.H.A.	18	19	8	30	118	10.72	–	–	–	4
Foster, J.S.	174	263	30	212	8213	35.24	14	41	1	484/44
Franklin, J.E.C.	132	201	28	219	5949	34.38	11	26	–	50
Franks, P.J.	175	249	44	123*	5643	27.52	4	30	–	56
Fudadin, A.B.	33	54	4	93	1500	30.00	–	7	–	24
Fuller, J.K.	2	3	–	24	31	10.33	–	–	–	1
Gale, A.W.	61	97	5	151*	3290	35.76	9	14	–	26
Gale, D.J.	7	9	7	37	59	29.50	–	–	–	4
Ganapathy, C.	31	43	17	126	1101	42.34	2	3	–	13
Gandam, H.S.	2	2	–	33	44	22.00	–	–	–	1
Gatting, J.S.	12	17	–	152	465	27.35	1	1	–	6
Geldart, C.J.	1	1	–	17	17	17.00	–	–	–	–
Gibbs, H.H.	193	331	13	228	13425	42.21	31	60	–	176
Gidman, A.P.R.	130	227	20	176	7348	35.49	15	40	4	80
Gidman, W.R.S.	1	2	–	8	8	4.00	–	–	–	–
Glover, J.C.	8	10	2	14	41	5.12	–	–	–	1
Goddard, L.J.	18	25	5	91	489	24.45	–	3	–	46
Godleman, B.A.	48	81	3	113*	2376	30.46	3	12	–	42
Goodman, J.E.	1	2	1	59	59	59.00	–	1	–	–
Goodwin, D.M.	1	2	–	18	26	13.00	–	–	–	1
Goodwin, M.W.	266	461	38	344*	20381	48.18	63	84	8+1	144
Gray, S.K.	8	13	4	35*	190	21.11	–	–	–	12/1
Greenwood, J.M.	1	2	1	23*	24	24.00	–	–	–	1
Griffiths, D.A.	22	32	14	31*	141	7.83	–	–	–	2
Groenewald, T.D.	39	51	14	78	778	21.02	–	3	–	16
Groves, P.R.	5	4	2	52	139	69.50	–	1	–	–
Guillen, J.C.	14	27	–	134	667	24.70	1	1	–	17
Guptill, M.J.	33	57	2	189	1694	30.80	2	9	–	20
Gurney, H.F.	16	17	8	24*	61	6.77	–	–	–	2
Hales, A.D.	20	32	2	136	1124	37.46	1	8	–	15
Hall, A.J.	173	254	32	163	7606	34.26	8	47	1	156
Hamilton-Brown, R.J.	25	42	3	171*	1277	32.74	4	4	–	17
Hampton, T.R.G.	1	1	1	1*	1	–	–	–	–	–
Hannon-Dalby, O.J.	18	16	7	11*	30	3.33	–	–	–	1
Harinath, A.	24	40	1	69	1001	25.66	–	7	–	7
Harmison, B.W.	37	62	5	110	1488	26.10	3	7	–	23
Harmison, S.J.	199	258	74	49*	1812	9.84	–	–	–	29
Harper, G.M.	3	3	–	3	3	1.00	–	–	–	1
Harris, A.J.	147	197	50	41*	1253	8.52	–	–	–	38
Harris, J.A.R.	42	59	9	87*	886	17.72	–	2	–	8
Harrison, D.S.	102	141	18	88	2017	16.39	–	7	–	30
Harrison, P.W.	18	28	5	54	488	21.21	–	1	–	23/2
Hatchett, L.J.	4	4	–	20	30	7.50	–	–	–	1
Henderson, C.W.	239	326	70	81	4775	18.65	–	15	–	82
Henderson, T.	86	137	17	81	1897	15.80	–	6	–	31
Herath, H.M.R.K.B.	184	262	60	80*	3304	16.35	–	12	–	84
Hesketh, R.L.	2	3	–	20	38	12.66	–	–	–	1
Hildreth, J.C.	110	179	14	303*	7110	43.09	19	35	2	78
Hilfenhaus, B.W.	50	66	22	56*	544	12.36	–	2	–	17

241

	M	I	NO	HS	Runs	Avge	100	50	1000	Ct/St
Hockley, J.B.	30	49	5	82	804	18.27	–	4	–	21
Hodd, A.J.	48	68	11	123	1686	29.57	4	8	–	93/11
Hodgson, L.J.	4	5	–	63	165	33.00	–	1	–	3
Hogg, K.W.	64	78	11	88	1649	24.61	–	11	–	16
Hoggard, M.J.	210	263	77	89*	1684	9.05	–	4	–	60
Hopkins, C.E.H.	3	4	–	14	34	8.50	–	–	–	–
Horton, P.J.	75	129	12	173	4319	36.91	9	23	2	68/1
Housego, D.M.	7	14	1	102*	296	22.76	1	–	–	3
Howego, B.H.N.	14	26	4	80	527	23.95	–	1	–	6
Hughes, C.F.	12	21	2	156	784	41.26	2	4	–	12
Hughes, P.H.	2	4	–	87	198	49.50	–	2	–	–
Hughes, P.J.	43	77	6	198	3967	55.87	13	21	–	30
Hunter, I.D.	63	81	21	65	1064	17.73	–	2	–	18
Hussain, G.M.	16	28	10	28*	169	9.38	–	–	–	12
Hussey, D.J.	147	227	22	275	11417	55.69	39	50	4+1	180
Hussey, M.E.K.	235	419	43	331*	19906	52.94	52	92	4	255
Iftikhar Anjum	99	149	33	78	1963	16.92	–	5	–	56
Imran Arif	17	19	9	35	102	10.20	–	–	–	6
Imran Farhat	135	234	13	242	9029	40.85	20	39	0+1	129
Imran Tahir	123	155	32	77*	1794	14.58	–	3	–	56
Imrul Kayes	35	66	1	138	1667	25.64	2	6	–	22
Iqbal Abdulla	19	20	5	69	437	29.13	–	4	–	10
Ireland, A.J.	36	53	16	16*	135	3.64	–	–	–	9
Jahurul Islam	66	121	12	158	3953	36.26	8	25	0+1	69/2
James, N.A.	2	3	1	60*	109	54.50	–	1	–	1
Jaques, P.A.	147	261	10	244	12808	51.02	36	61	4+2	109
Jaskaran Singh	2	1	–	58	58	58.00	–	1	–	–
Javid, A.	7	13	–	48	146	11.23	–	–	–	6
Jeavons, A.F.	1	2	–	62	66	33.00	–	1	–	1
Jefferson, W.I.	102	179	13	222	6014	36.22	14	24	1	102
Jewell, T.M.	4	2	1	4*	5	5.00	–	–	–	–
Johnson, M.G.	64	87	19	123*	1649	24.25	1	8	–	16
Johnson, R.M.	7	11	1	72	223	22.30	–	1	–	20/2
Jones, C.R.	1	–	–	–	–	–	–	–	–	–
Jones, G.O.	143	218	20	178	6699	33.83	15	32	2	431/31
Jones, P.S.	146	175	43	114	2655	20.11	2	8	–	33
Jones, R.A.	23	36	5	53*	349	11.25	–	1	–	11
Jones, S.P.	89	110	37	46	899	12.31	–	–	–	17
Joseph, R.H.	46	59	22	36*	414	11.18	–	–	–	9
Joslin, A.J.P.	2	4	–	33	74	18.50	–	–	–	1
Joyce, E.C.	152	251	21	211	10344	44.97	24	56	5	126
Junaid Siddique	42	78	1	114*	1943	25.23	2	11	–	28
Kamran Akmal	152	240	27	174	6623	31.09	12	30	–	518/45
Kartik, M.	160	199	33	96	3249	19.57	–	16	–	117
Katich, S.M.	223	382	47	306	18134	54.13	50	97	3+4	204
Keedy, G.	194	219	106	64	1290	11.41	–	2	–	46
Keegan, C.B.	47	57	6	44	607	11.90	–	–	–	14
Kennedy, A.D.J.	1	2	1	48*	62	62.00	–	–	–	2
Kerrigan, S.C.	13	15	5	16*	45	4.50	–	–	–	3
Kervezee, A.N.	36	62	5	155	2126	37.29	3	11	1	21
Key, R.W.T.	226	390	28	270*	15039	41.54	43	56	6	127
Khan, A.	87	102	32	78	1138	16.25	–	4	–	16
Khan, I.	25	42	3	125	959	24.58	1	5	–	21
Khawaja, U.T.	20	32	2	172*	1457	48.56	5	6	–	13
Kieswetter, C.	59	84	11	153	2721	37.27	4	16	1	171/2
Killeen, N.	102	145	31	48	1302	11.42	–	–	–	26

242

F-C	M	I	NO	HS	Runs	Avge	100	50	1000	Ct/St
King, D.A.	2	3	–	189	191	63.66	1	–	–	4
King, S.J.	3	2	–	8	8	4.00	–	–	–	–
Kirby, S.P.	130	181	58	57	1067	8.67	–	1	–	24
Kirtley, R.J.	170	231	76	59	2040	13.16	–	4	–	60
Kruger, N.	3	5	–	172	381	76.20	1	1	–	4
Kulkarni, D.S.	29	27	14	87	411	31.61	–	2	–	10
Lancefield, T.J.	8	13	1	74	381	31.75	–	2	–	3
Langeveldt, C.K.	93	116	39	56	1106	14.36	–	1	–	25
Lawson, M.A.K.	24	29	8	44	311	14.80	–	–	–	10
Lee, N.T.	13	20	4	79*	490	30.62	–	3	–	2
Lees, A.Z.	1	1	–	38	38	38.00	–	–	–	–
Lewis, J.	212	302	61	62	3666	15.21	–	9	–	53
Liddle, C.J.	14	14	5	53	113	12.55	–	1	–	5
Linley, T.E.	20	24	5	42	228	12.00	–	–	–	6
Lodwick, J.A.	1	–	–	–	–	–	–	–	–	1
London, A.B.	8	15	2	77	327	25.15	–	3	–	4
Lotay, J.D.S.	5	6	1	34*	87	17.40	–	–	–	2
Lowe, J.R.	1	1	–	5	5	5.00	–	–	–	–
Loye, M.B.	256	410	38	322*	14936	40.15	42	61	6	119
Lucas, D.S.	75	98	25	55*	1391	19.05	–	1	–	14
Lumb, M.J.	134	224	15	219	7266	34.76	12	45	2	92
Lungley, T.	55	77	16	50	885	14.50	–	1	–	25
Lyth, A.	36	59	–	142	2425	41.10	4	16	1	21
McCullum, N.L.	48	73	6	106*	1804	26.92	1	11	–	51
McDonald, A.B.	69	112	25	176*	3230	37.12	6	18	–	51
McGain, B.E.	32	35	13	25	242	11.00	–	–	–	11
McGrath, A.	231	389	27	211	13565	37.47	32	66	3	164
Machan, M.W.	1	2	–	6	11	5.50	–	–	–	–
McKay, C.J.	22	28	2	55	489	18.80	–	2	–	5
McKenzie, N.D.	209	353	42	226	13563	43.61	35	66	–	184
McLaren, R.	80	115	19	140	2711	28.23	2	14	–	40
Maddy, D.L.	258	422	28	229*	12807	32.50	26	60	4	269
Madsen, W.L.	49	86	7	179	3057	38.69	8	14	–	51
Mahbubul Alam	32	40	11	20	178	6.13	–	–	–	12
Mahmood, S.I.	96	122	18	94	1698	16.32	–	8	–	22
Mahmudullah	51	92	11	152	2859	35.29	5	13	–	48
Malan, C.C.	4	4	–	24	43	10.75	–	–	–	–
Malan, D.J.	46	82	8	132*	2699	36.47	4	18	1	45
Malik, M.N.	74	96	33	41	646	10.25	–	–	–	10
Marshall, H.J.H.	153	260	17	170	8709	35.83	18	43	1	88
Martin, C.S.	155	192	95	25	389	4.01	–	–	–	30
Martin, J.	6	9	–	81	290	32.22	–	2	–	3
Martin-Jenkins, R.S.C.	184	276	41	205*	7448	31.69	5	41	1	55
Mascarenhas, A.D.	181	271	30	131	6185	25.66	8	22	–	72
Mason, M.S.	98	127	31	63	1320	13.75	–	4	–	27
Masters, D.D.	132	165	27	119	2039	14.77	1	5	–	45
Maunders, J.K.	90	159	3	180	4689	30.05	8	23	–	56
Maynard, T.L.	24	35	1	98	727	21.38	–	5	–	22
Meadows, N.A.	1	1	–	38	38	38.00	–	–	–	4
Meaker, S.C.	18	25	2	94	411	17.86	–	3	–	3
Mendis, B.A.W.	35	47	4	78	572	13.30	–	1	–	11
Mickleburgh, J.C.	25	46	–	174	1287	27.97	1	7	–	17
Middlebrook, J.D.	156	225	32	127	4884	25.30	4	19	–	78
Miller, A.S.	11	16	7	35	70	7.77	–	–	–	4
Milligan, M.J.	5	3	–	4	9	3.00	–	–	–	2
Mitchell, D.K.H.	64	117	16	298	4002	39.62	9	18	2	75

F-C	M	I	NO	HS	Runs	Avge	100	50	1000	Ct/St
Mohammad Aamer	28	45	9	44*	508	14.11	–	–	–	5
Mohammad Ashraful	104	196	5	263	5320	27.85	13	22	–	54
Mohammad Asif	87	120	44	42	598	7.86	–	–	–	30
Mohammad Yousuf	134	226	20	223	10152	49.28	29	49	–	84
Moore, S.C.	112	204	16	246	7288	38.76	15	35	3	55
Morgan, C.F.D.	5	6	–	38	61	10.16	–	–	–	5/1
Morgan, E.J.G.	55	91	12	209*	2930	37.08	7	13	1	47/1
Morkel, J.A.	65	93	15	204*	3296	42.25	5	20	–	27
Muchall, G.J.	115	200	10	219	5576	29.34	10	26	–	77
Mukund, A.	28	43	1	300*	2235	53.21	8	6	–	19
Mullaney, S.J.	15	22	5	165*	769	45.23	2	3	–	9
Munday, M.K.	31	28	11	21	107	6.29	–	–	–	12
Muralitharan, M.	232	276	83	67	2192	11.35	–	1	–	123
Murphy, D.	16	24	8	76	522	32.62	–	5	–	41/1
Murtagh, T.J.	98	139	43	74*	2168	22.58	–	9	–	29
Mushfiqur Rahim	47	85	10	115*	2190	29.20	3	13	–	78/11
Mustard, P.	118	182	20	130	4771	29.45	4	27	–	389/15
Myburgh, J.G.	73	132	18	203	5180	45.43	13	30	–	50
Naeem Islam	52	88	10	126	2790	35.76	5	18	–	35/1
Naik, J.K.H.	21	29	9	109*	561	28.05	1	1	–	11
Nannes, D.P.	23	24	8	31*	108	6.75	–	–	–	7
Napier, G.R.	103	142	30	125	3350	29.91	3	20	–	39
Nash, C.D.	79	134	11	184	4734	38.48	9	24	3	32
Naved Arif	30	38	12	49	410	15.76	–	–	–	11
Naved-ul-Hasan	122	174	20	139	3560	23.11	5	10	–	56
Needham, J.	19	31	12	48	384	20.21	–	–	–	10
Nel, A.	132	153	43	96	1692	15.38	–	4	–	53
Nel, J.D.	18	23	10	36	154	11.84	–	–	–	6
New, T.J.	85	141	18	125	3926	31.91	2	29	–	141/7
Newby, O.J.	43	37	8	38*	238	8.20	–	–	–	8
Newman, S.A.	116	199	3	219	7721	39.39	16	46	4	85
Newton, D.C.A.	1	1	–	0	0	0.00	–	–	–	–
Newton, R.I.	6	11	–	102	357	32.45	1	2	–	1
Nixon, P.A.	351	526	111	173*	14401	34.70	21	72	1	889/67
North, M.J.	153	267	25	239*	10400	42.97	28	55	0+1	119
Northeast, S.A.	29	51	2	128*	1391	28.38	1	7	–	16
Ntini, M.	186	217	82	34*	1274	9.43	–	–	–	40
O'Brien, I.E.	91	113	26	44	756	8.68	–	–	–	17
O'Brien, N.J.	83	126	14	176	3971	35.45	9	16	–	240/26
Onions, G.	71	93	32	41	758	12.42	–	–	–	17
Ord, J.E.	2	4	–	9	17	4.25	–	–	–	1
Osborne, M.	2	3	2	5	5	5.00	–	–	–	–
Owen, F.G.	5	9	–	50	174	19.33	–	1	–	–
Owen, W.T.	4	4	1	38	38	12.66	–	–	–	–
Paine, T.D.	39	71	5	215	2024	30.66	1	14	–	110/4
Palladino, A.P.	52	66	18	66	620	12.91	–	2	–	24
Pandey, M.K.	18	28	3	194	1203	48.12	4	7	–	22
Panesar, M.S.	131	168	53	46*	1021	8.87	–	–	–	29
Park, C.M.	3	4	–	72	91	22.75	–	1	–	2
Park, G.T.	45	76	10	178*	2335	35.37	4	14	1	41
Parnell, W.D.	23	28	3	90	542	21.68	–	3	–	6
Parry, S.D.	3	2	–	2	3	1.50	–	–	–	1
Pascoe, D.C.	3	4	2	37	131	65.50	–	–	–	1
Patel, A.	3	6	2	69*	153	38.25	–	1	–	2
Patel, L.A.	1	1	–	26	26	26.00	–	–	–	–
Patel, R.H.	1	1	1	19*	19	–	–	–	–	–

244

F-C	M	I	NO	HS	Runs	Avge	100	50	1000	Ct/St
Patel, S.R.	77	118	8	176	4430	40.27	10	24	–	41
Patterson, S.A.	29	33	9	46	350	14.58	–	–	–	6
Pattinson, D.J.	51	58	10	59	561	11.68	–	1	–	5
Peters, S.D.	194	334	27	199	10685	34.80	24	53	4	153
Petersen, A.N.	97	176	10	152	6352	38.26	19	27	0+1	81
Peterson, R.J.	114	177	22	130	3964	25.57	6	14	–	49
Pettini, M.L.	93	158	20	208*	4663	33.78	5	26	1	67
Phillips, B.J.	108	150	26	100*	2581	20.81	1	14	–	31
Phillips, O.J.	22	43	3	204	1236	30.90	1	5	–	23
Phillips, T.J.	61	85	11	89	1436	19.40	–	4	–	40
Piesley, C.D.	1	2	–	43	43	21.50	–	–	–	–
Pietersen, K.P.	154	256	18	254*	11726	49.26	38	49	3	119
Piolet, S.A.	2	4	1	26*	41	13.66	–	–	–	2
Plunkett, L.E.	100	136	24	94*	2305	20.58	–	10	–	60
Pollard, K.A.	20	33	1	174	1199	37.46	3	5	–	32
Ponting, R.T.	246	418	54	257	20873	57.34	73	90	–	261
Porterfield, W.T.S.	43	75	2	175	2431	33.30	4	13	–	45
Pothas, N.	210	325	59	165	11135	41.86	24	58	–	592/45
Powell, D.B.L.	102	144	23	69	1525	12.60	–	4	–	31
Powell, M.J.	200	335	31	299	11786	38.76	25	59	5	122
Poynter, S.W.	1	1	–	42	42	42.00	–	–	–	3
Poynton, T.	7	11	–	25	105	9.54	–	–	–	12/2
Prince, A.G.	189	304	41	254	11418	43.41	28	55	0+1	127
Prior, M.J.	173	272	29	201*	9651	39.71	22	55	3	416/26
Procter, L.A.	2	3	–	32	64	21.33	–	–	–	–
Pujara, C.A.	49	78	13	302*	3925	60.38	14	13	0+1	24/1
Pyrah, R.M.	22	28	4	134*	801	33.37	2	4	–	13
Rahane, A.M.	39	64	7	265*	3670	64.38	12	16	0+2	27
Ramprakash, M.R.	442	729	91	301*	34839	54.60	113	144	20	249
Rankin, W.B.	34	42	17	13	128	5.12	–	–	–	12
Rashid, A.U.	69	97	21	157*	2937	38.64	4	19	–	37
Rayner, O.P.	38	45	9	101	782	21.72	1	3	–	42
Read, C.M.W.	239	354	61	240	10700	36.51	18	57	2	707/40
Redfern, D.J.	32	51	4	95	1338	28.46	–	8	–	17
Redmond, A.J.	86	147	10	146	4529	33.05	8	27	–	66
Rees, G.P.	63	106	8	154	3580	36.53	10	18	2	50
Riazuddin, H.	3	2	–	4	7	3.50	–	–	–	–
Richardson, A.	122	127	53	91	832	11.24	–	1	–	38
Richardson, M.J.	1	1	–	2	2	2.00	–	–	–	–
Robiul Islam	34	54	21	21	214	6.48	–	–	–	16
Robson, S.D.	15	28	–	204	954	34.07	2	4	–	20
Roebuck, C.G.	1	1	–	23	23	23.00	–	–	–	–
Rogers, C.J.L.	173	305	22	319	14791	52.26	45	68	4+2	173
Roland-Jones, T.S.	8	12	1	26	124	11.27	–	–	–	3
Root, J.E.	2	3	1	20*	38	19.00	–	–	–	1
Roper, C.G.W.	2	1	–	0	0	0.00	–	–	–	1
Rose, S.A.L.	2	2	1	14	14	14.00	–	–	–	1
Rossington, A.M.	1	1	–	1	1	1.00	–	–	–	–
Roy, J.J.	3	5	–	76	170	34.00	–	2	–	–
Rubel Hossain	20	31	9	17	83	3.77	–	–	–	8
Rudolph, J.A.	186	317	21	228*	13337	45.05	38	61	4	174
Rushworth, C.	9	14	2	28	127	10.58	–	–	–	1
Russell, A.D.	10	14	1	108*	294	22.61	1	–	–	4
Sadler, J.L.	66	111	15	145	3047	31.73	3	16	1	46
Saeed Ajmal	91	122	42	53	963	12.03	–	3	–	30
Saha, W.P.	28	44	5	159	1404	36.00	3	7	–	67/4

F-C	M	I	NO	HS	Runs	Avge	100	50	1000	Ct/St
Sales, D.J.G.	204	329	28	303*	12145	40.34	24	59	6	189
Salman Butt	90	159	7	290	6232	41.00	17	24	–	33
Sanderson, B.W.	3	2	1	6	6	6.00	–	–	–	–
Sayers, J.J.	85	139	10	187	4360	33.79	10	22	1	51
Schofield, C.P.	100	143	18	144	3644	29.15	1	26	–	57
Scott, A.J.D.	1	–	–	–	–	–	–	–	–	–
Scott, B.J.M.	77	119	22	164*	2710	27.93	3	16	–	211/22
Shafayat, B.M.	119	201	7	161	5828	30.04	9	31	1	107/9
Shafiul Islam	18	28	7	53	298	14.19	–	1	–	5
Shah, O.A.	222	379	34	203	14521	42.08	39	72	8	170
Shahadat Hossain	52	89	28	40	731	11.98	–	–	–	11
Shahid Afridi	111	183	4	164	5631	31.45	12	30	–	75
Shahzad, A.J.	32	40	12	88	796	28.42	–	2	–	7
Shakib Al Hasan	54	100	9	129	2991	32.86	4	14	–	28
Shantry, A.J.	29	37	12	100	444	17.76	1	–	–	6
Shantry, J.D.	15	20	6	13*	67	4.78	–	–	–	5
Sharma, A.S.	1	1	1	185*	185	–	1	–	–	2
Sharma, R.	8	12	2	58*	287	28.70	–	1	–	2
Sheikh, A.	1	2	–	6	6	3.00	–	–	–	1
Shoaib Malik	95	147	17	148*	3856	29.66	8	17	–	44
Shreck, C.E.	85	97	54	19	154	3.58	–	–	–	31
Sidebottom, R.J.	147	184	59	54	1592	12.73	–	1	–	49
Simpson, J.A.	19	33	2	101*	827	26.67	1	3	–	47/2
Smith, B.F.	334	529	58	204	18777	39.86	40	100	8	214
Smith, D.R.	81	134	9	155	3679	29.43	7	14	–	78
Smith, D.S.	129	229	9	212	8138	36.99	18	36	0+1	122
Smith, D.T.	2	3	1	12*	22	11.00	–	–	–	2
Smith, G.M.	71	122	10	165*	3308	29.53	3	22	–	19
Smith, G.P.	20	36	6	158*	1098	36.60	3	5	–	11
Smith, S.P.D.	15	26	4	177	1112	50.54	4	3	–	22
Smith, T.C.	56	78	16	128	1626	26.22	3	5	–	50
Smith, T.M.J.	6	10	1	33	123	13.66	–	–	–	3
Smith, W.R.	76	122	8	201*	3628	31.82	8	12	–	36
Snell, S.D.	41	69	7	127	1679	27.08	1	13	–	96/3
Solanki, V.S.	267	446	26	270	15039	35.80	27	79	5	276
Spriegel, M.N.W.	31	50	3	108*	1203	25.59	3	3	–	23
Stebbings, B.R.W.	3	3	–	25	44	14.66	–	–	–	–
Stevens, D.I.	170	276	20	208	8836	34.51	21	42	2	128
Stiff, D.A.	20	24	10	49	321	22.92	–	–	–	1
Stirling, P.R.	8	12	–	100	338	28.16	1	1	–	6
Stokes, B.A.	14	21	3	161*	798	44.33	2	3	–	8
Stoneman, M.D.	45	75	3	118	1789	24.84	2	9	–	28
Strauss, A.J.	199	353	17	177	14061	41.84	35	63	4	175
Styris, S.B.	126	210	19	212*	5964	31.22	10	29	–	100
Suppiah, A.V.	60	99	5	151	3296	35.06	5	18	1	34
Sutton, L.D.	160	254	39	151*	6780	31.53	11	19	–	408/22
Swann, G.P.	200	276	22	183	6740	26.53	4	35	–	146
Tahir, N.S.	52	59	16	49	658	15.30	–	–	–	7
Tait, S.W.	50	70	29	68	509	12.41	–	2	–	15
Tamim Iqbal	40	73	1	151	2928	40.66	6	20	–	20
Tavaré, W.A.	2	3	–	49	60	20.00	–	–	–	–
Taylor, C.G.	144	250	18	196	7944	34.24	17	37	2	96
Taylor, J.M.R.	2	4	–	6	11	2.75	–	–	–	2
Taylor, J.W.A.	40	64	11	207*	2405	45.37	6	11	2	29
Taylor, L.R.P.L.	71	120	3	217	4774	40.80	10	26	–	89
Taylor, M.H.	2	4	2	16*	42	21.00	–	–	–	–

F-C	M	I	NO	HS	Runs	Avge	100	50	1000	Ct/St
Taylor, R.M.L.	2	2	–	22	39	19.50	–	–	–	2
ten Doeschate, R.N.	81	118	15	259*	4950	48.05	16	17	–	44
Thomas, A.C.	112	158	33	119*	3158	25.26	2	11	–	31
Thompson, J.G.	1	2	–	21	32	16.00	–	–	–	–
Thornely, M.A.	17	30	2	89	522	18.64	–	4	–	15
Thorp, C.D.	56	74	9	79*	976	15.01	–	3	–	33
Timms, R.T.	8	15	–	57	308	20.53	–	2	–	6
Tiwary, M.K.	42	62	7	210*	2903	52.78	11	7	–	46
Tomlinson, J.A.	65	85	35	42	530	10.60	–	–	–	16
Tonge, G.C.	34	54	9	57	541	12.02	–	2	–	17
Toor, K.S.	1	1	–	15	15	15.00	–	–	–	–
Tredwell, J.C.	101	145	19	123*	3004	23.84	3	13	–	106
Trego, P.D.	99	143	20	140	4352	35.38	8	27	–	37
Tremlett, C.T.	104	139	37	64	1868	18.31	–	7	–	28
Trescothick, M.E.	271	466	27	284	18042	41.09	43	91	4	340
Tripathi, V.	4	7	1	71	196	32.66	–	2	–	3
Trott, I.J.L.	153	257	31	226	10183	45.05	23	51	6	148
Troughton, J.O.	126	196	15	223	6498	35.90	16	31	1	58
Turnbull, P.T.	4	5	1	13	25	6.25	–	–	–	1
Turner, M.L.	9	8	2	57	89	14.83	–	1	–	3
Tyagi, S.	19	22	7	12	32	2.13	–	–	–	1
Udal, S.D.	301	430	79	117*	7931	22.59	1	34	–	127
Umar Akmal	42	72	7	248	3061	47.09	7	18	–	34
Umar Amin	34	60	4	153	2113	37.73	4	13	–	17
Umar Gul	61	78	12	65*	864	13.09	–	1	–	15
Unadkat, J.D.	2	1	1	12*	12	–	–	–	–	1
Vaas, W.P.J.U.C.	202	272	57	134	5525	25.69	4	24	–	57
van Jaarsveld, M.	239	402	36	262*	16775	45.83	51	81	6+1	364
Vince, J.M.	25	40	5	180	1192	34.05	1	5	–	14
Vincent, L.	92	151	11	224	4922	35.15	10	29	–	109
Voges, A.C.	82	138	18	180	4867	40.55	10	27	–	100
Wagg, G.G.	68	94	11	108	2024	24.38	1	10	–	23
Wagh, M.A.	203	332	27	315	12187	39.95	31	58	6	88
Wahab Riaz	67	92	15	68	1156	15.01	–	3	–	22
Wainwright, D.J.	31	37	11	104*	925	35.57	2	2	–	10
Wakely, A.G.	34	58	2	113*	1371	24.48	2	9	–	21
Walker, M.J.	212	356	37	275*	11610	36.39	28	47	4	142
Wallace, M.A.	167	265	17	139	6848	27.61	9	32	–	418/37
Waller, M.T.C.	4	6	1	28	67	13.40	–	–	–	1
Walters, S.J.	34	54	1	188	1336	25.20	2	4	–	38
Walton, C.A.K.	30	52	3	87	1160	23.67	–	6	–	83/6
Warner, D.A.	4	6	1	48*	131	26.20	–	–	–	3
Waters, H.T.	34	50	22	34	212	7.57	–	–	–	7
Waters, S.R.	6	11	2	157*	354	39.33	1	–	–	5
Watkins, S.J.V.	1	2	1	46*	54	54.00	–	–	–	–
Watson, M.J.C.	6	6	1	22	69	13.80	–	–	–	1
Watson, S.R.	84	146	16	203*	5940	45.69	14	32	–	69
Wells, L.W.P.	1	2	–	62	70	35.00	–	1	–	–
Welsh, A.S.	2	3	1	21	30	15.00	–	–	–	1
Wernars, K.O.	1	2	1	22*	30	30.00	–	–	–	1
Westley, T.	35	61	9	132	1517	29.17	2	7	–	15
Westwood, I.J.	82	144	16	178	4149	32.41	7	23	–	40
Wheater, A.J.	7	8	1	55	225	32.14	–	2	–	17
Wheeldon, D.A.	12	20	1	87	429	22.57	–	3	–	5
Whelan, C.D.	22	27	6	58	302	14.38	–	1	–	4
White, G.G.	9	11	2	65	169	18.77	–	1	–	2

F-C	M	I	NO	HS	Runs	Avge	100	50	1000	Ct/St
White, R.A.	97	169	16	277	5045	32.97	7	26	1	58
White, W.A.	32	48	7	101*	880	21.46	1	2	–	14
Wigley, D.H.	50	62	22	70	532	13.30	–	2	–	22
Willey, D.J.	13	21	3	60	372	20.66	–	1	–	4
Williams, R.E.M.	9	15	5	31	119	11.90	–	–	–	4
Willoughby, C.M.	209	233	102	47	801	6.11	–	–	–	42
Wilson, G.C.	16	23	2	125	583	27.76	1	2	–	31/1
Winslade, T.S.	1	2	–	17	18	9.00	–	–	–	–
Woakes, C.R.	46	60	15	136*	1226	27.24	2	3	–	23
Wood, C.P.	3	4	–	35	68	17.00	–	–	–	–
Wood, M.J.	101	170	8	297	5332	32.91	9	34	1	31
Woolley, R.J.J.	6	6	1	55*	135	27.00	–	1	–	4
Wright, B.J.	38	60	3	172	1527	26.78	3	7	–	25
Wright, C.J.C.	54	70	18	76	916	17.61	–	3	–	13
Wright, D.G.	108	163	22	111	3500	24.82	1	19	–	53
Wright, L.J.	66	93	15	155*	2867	36.75	8	15	–	29
Wyatt, A.C.F.	3	3	1	3	4	2.00	–	–	–	1
Yardy, M.H.	129	217	21	257	7606	38.80	15	38	2	99
Yasir Arafat	168	250	37	122	5788	27.17	4	31	–	45
Yasir Hameed	137	227	14	300	7733	36.30	16	35	–	108
Young, E.G.C.	7	9	1	79	265	33.12	–	2	–	6
Younus Khan	150	244	28	313	10873	50.33	34	44	0+1	158
Zulqarnain Haider	71	109	18	161	3172	34.85	3	18	–	211/13

BOWLING

'50wS' denotes instances of taking 50 or more wickets in a season. Where these have been achieved outside the British Isles they are shown after a plus sign.

	Runs	Wkts	Avge	Best	5wI	10wM	50wS
Abdul Razzaq	10778	340	31.70	7- 51	11	2	–
Abdur Razzak	4987	157	31.76	7- 11	5	1	–
Abdur Rehman	9529	363	26.25	8- 53	18	4	0+1
Ackland, B.J.	3	0					
Adams, A.R.	11090	463	23.95	6- 25	17	2	1
Adams, J.H.K.	662	11	60.18	2- 16	–	–	–
Adkin, W.A.	38	1	38.00	1- 38	–	–	–
Afzaal, U.	5078	98	51.81	4-101	–	–	–
Aga, R.G.	1024	29	35.31	4- 63	–	–	–
Agarwal, S.S.	249	5	49.80	5- 78	1	–	–
Ali, Kabir	12008	448	26.80	8- 50	23	4	5
Ali, Kadeer	304	3	101.33	1- 4	–	–	–
Ali, M.M.	1659	27	61.44	5- 36	1	–	–
Allenby, J.	2777	99	28.05	5- 59	2	–	–
Ambrose, T.R.	1	0					
Amla, H.M.	224	1	224.00	1- 10	–	–	–
Anderson, J.M.	11342	409	27.73	7- 43	22	3	2
Andrew, G.M.	3654	101	36.17	5- 58	2	–	–
Ansari, A.S.	461	12	38.41	4- 50	–	–	–
Anyon, J.E.	5276	141	37.41	6- 82	2	–	–
Ashling, C.P.	316	9	35.11	3- 18	–	–	–
Ashok, A.	82	1	82.00	1- 15	–	–	–
Ashraf, M.A.	212	11	19.27	5- 32	1	–	–
Azeem Rafiq	755	15	50.33	4- 92	–	–	–
Azhar Ali	639	17	37.58	4- 34	–	–	–
Azhar Mahmood	14277	566	25.22	8- 61	24	3	0+1
Baker, G.C.	390	5	78.00	2- 35	–	–	–

F-C	Runs	Wkts	Avge	Best	5wI	10wM	50wS
Baker, L.S.	2344	78	30.05	8- 31	3	1	–
Balcombe, D.J.	2832	72	39.33	5-112	1	–	–
Bandara, H.M.C.M.	10943	432	25.33	8- 49	14	2	0+1
Banerjee, V.	4184	93	44.98	5- 74	2	–	–
Barker, K.H.D.	310	3	103.33	2- 22	–	–	–
Barnard, M.R.	64	1	64.00	1- 14	–	–	–
Batty, G.J.	14076	410	34.33	7- 52	16	1	2
Batty, J.N.	61	1	61.00	1- 21	–	–	–
Beer, W.A.T.	192	6	32.00	3- 31	–	–	–
Bell, I.R.	1564	47	33.27	4- 4	–	–	–
Benham, C.C.	37	0					
Benkenstein, D.M.	3375	97	34.79	4- 16	–	–	–
Benning, J.G.E.	1433	24	59.70	3- 43	–	–	–
Berg, G.K.	1934	52	37.19	5- 55	2	–	–
Bernard, D.E.	4343	144	30.15	6- 40	3	–	–
Best, T.L.	6756	239	28.26	7- 33	10	2	–
Blackaby, L.A.	11	0					
Blackwell, I.D.	12431	333	37.33	7- 85	12	–	–
Blain, J.A.R.	4286	120	35.71	6- 42	4	–	–
Blake, A.J.	101	3	33.66	2- 9	–	–	–
Boje, N.	18756	577	32.50	8- 93	22	2	–
Bollinger, D.E.	6324	222	28.48	6- 47	12	2	–
Bopara, R.S.	4585	107	42.85	5- 75	1	–	–
Borrington, P.M.	5	0					
Borthwick, S.G.	797	26	30.65	4- 27	–	–	–
Bosman, L.E.	343	8	42.87	3- 25	–	–	–
Botha, A.G.	10496	302	34.75	8- 53	9	1	1
Botha, J.	4503	147	30.63	6- 42	4	1	–
Boyce, M.A.G.	63	0					
Bradshaw, D.P.	407	6	67.83	2- 41	–	–	–
Bragg, W.D.	23	0					
Brathwaite, K.C.	3	1	3.00	1- 3	–	–	–
Brathwaite, R.M.R.	1294	30	43.13	5- 54	1	–	–
Bravo, D.J.	5621	168	33.45	6- 11	7	–	–
Breese, G.R.	8369	280	29.88	7- 60	12	3	–
Bresnan, T.T.	8109	250	32.43	5- 42	4	–	–
Brett, T.	38	0					
Briggs, D.R.	1589	42	37.83	4- 93	–	–	–
Broad, S.C.J.	7342	253	29.01	8- 52	12	1	–
Brooks, J.A.	1585	46	34.45	4- 76	–	–	–
Brophy, G.L.	1	0					
Brown, A.D.	775	6	129.16	3- 25	–	–	–
Brown, D.O.	1251	28	44.67	5- 38	1	–	–
Brown, F.A.	330	8	41.25	3- 26	–	–	–
Brown, K.R.	44	2	22.00	2- 30	–	–	–
Brown, M.J.	20	0					
Brown, O.V.	3335	148	22.53	8- 54	10	3	0+1
Bryan, T.E.	17	0					
Buck, N.L.	1616	52	31.07	4- 44	–	–	–
Burton, D.A.	550	14	39.28	5- 68	2	–	–
Butler, I.G.	3989	126	31.65	6- 46	2	–	–
Cameron, J.G.	332	8	41.50	2- 18	–	–	–
Carberry, M.A.	873	13	67.15	2- 85	–	–	–
Carter, A.	475	16	29.68	5- 40	1	–	–
Carter, N.M.	10258	297	34.53	6- 63	13	–	1
Chadwick, M.S.	74	1	74.00	1- 41	–	–	–

F-C	Runs	Wkts	Avge	Best	5wI	10wM	50wS
Chambers, M.A.	1770	62	28.54	6-68	2	1	–
Chanderpaul, S.	2453	56	43.80	4-48	–	–	–
Chapple, G.	21124	780	27.08	7-53	31	2	5
Cheetham, S.P.	198	3	66.00	2-71	–	–	–
Chigumbura, E.	4709	167	28.19	5-33	4	–	–
Chilton, M.J.	667	12	55.58	2- 3	–	–	–
Chopra, V.	78	0					
Choudhry, S.H.	86	1	86.00	1-32	–	–	–
Christian, D.T.	1786	56	31.89	5-24	2	–	–
Clare, J.L.	1805	62	29.11	7-74	2	–	–
Clarke, M.J.	1470	31	47.41	6- 9	1	–	–
Clarke, R.	6598	168	39.27	6-63	1	–	–
Claydon, M.E.	2493	70	35.61	4-90	–	–	–
Cliff, S.J.	513	14	36.64	4-42	–	–	–
Cobb, J.J.	243	5	48.60	2-11	–	–	–
Coetzer, K.J.	71	2	35.50	2-16	–	–	–
Coles, M.T.	1170	29	40.34	4-55	–	–	–
Collingwood, P.D.	4928	121	40.72	5-52	1	–	–
Collins, P.T.	12523	478	26.19	6-24	13	–	0+1
Collymore, C.D.	10717	406	26.39	7-57	12	2	1
Comber, M.A.	94	4	23.50	2-34	–	–	–
Compton, N.R.D.	215	3	71.66	1- 1	–	–	–
Conway, D.O.	249	6	41.50	2-36	–	–	–
Cook, A.N.	205	6	34.16	3-13	–	–	–
Cook, S.J.	10526	330	31.89	8-63	12	–	–
Cope, A.C.	24	0					
Cork, D.G.	25637	967	26.51	9-43	35	5	7
Cosgrove, M.J.	1437	35	41.05	3- 3	–	–	–
Cosker, D.A.	15890	445	35.70	6-91	7	1	1
Croft, R.D.B.	39995	1133	35.30	8-66	49	9	10
Croft, S.J.	1375	31	44.35	4-51	–	–	–
Crook, S.P.	2842	59	48.16	5-71	1	–	–
Daggett, L.M.	3328	91	36.57	8-94	2	–	–
Dalrymple, J.W.M.	6893	160	43.08	5-49	1	–	–
Danish Kaneria	23489	884	26.57	8-59	61	10	3+1
Davey, J.H.	107	2	53.50	2-41	–	–	–
Davies, A.M.	5726	253	22.63	8-24	12	2	1
Dawson, L.A.	741	17	43.58	2- 3	–	–	–
Dawson, R.K.J.	8770	199	44.07	6-82	5	–	–
de Bruyn, Z.	7573	191	39.64	7-67	3	–	–
Denly, J.L.	662	13	50.92	2-13	–	–	–
Dent, C.D.J.	43	0					
Dernbach, J.W.	4505	129	34.92	6-47	5	–	1
de Wet, F.	4576	194	23.58	7-61	10	2	0+1
Dexter, N.J.	1167	28	41.67	3-50	–	–	–
Dhawan, S.	62	1	62.00	1-18	–	–	–
Dingle, L.A.	171	1	171.00	1-36	–	–	–
Di Venuto, M.J.	484	5	96.80	1- 0	–	–	–
Dunn, M.P.	48	3	16.00	3-48	–	–	–
Durston, W.J.	1496	25	59.84	3-23	–	–	–
du Toit, J.	355	5	71.00	3-31	–	–	–
Edwards, N.J.	194	2	97.00	1-16	–	–	–
Edwards, P.D.	965	15	64.33	3-72	–	–	–
Ervine, S.M.	7838	181	43.30	6-82	5	–	–
Evans, D.	1710	49	34.89	6-35	3	–	–
Evans, L.	327	9	36.33	3-53	–	–	–

F-C	Runs	Wkts	Avge	Best	5wI	10wM	50wS
Evans, L.J.	30	1	30.00	1- 30	–	–	–
Evans, R.F.	217	2	108.50	1- 57	–	–	–
Fawad Alam	745	22	33.86	4- 27	–	–	–
Ferley, R.S.	3018	66	45.72	6-136	1	–	–
Finn, S.T.	4589	162	28.32	9- 37	5	1	2
Fletcher, A.D.S.	68	0					
Fletcher, L.J.	1433	42	34.11	4- 38	–	–	–
Flower, G.W.	5605	166	33.76	7- 31	3	–	–
Footitt, M.H.A.	1515	46	32.93	5- 45	2	–	–
Foster, J.S.	128	1	128.00	1-122	–	–	–
Franklin, J.E.C.	10871	411	26.45	7- 14	13	1	–
Franks, P.J.	14685	460	31.92	7- 56	11	–	2
Fudadin, A.B.	248	5	49.60	2- 34	–	–	–
Fuller, J.K.	231	2	115.50	1- 33	–	–	–
Gale, A.W.	47	1	47.00	1- 33	–	–	–
Gale, D.J.	435	9	48.33	4- 94	–	–	–
Ganapathy, C.	2118	72	29.41	5- 59	3	–	–
Gatting, J.S.	19	1	19.00	1- 19	–	–	–
Gibbs, H.H.	78	3	26.00	2- 14	–	–	–
Gidman, A.P.R.	4251	97	43.82	4- 47	–	–	–
Gidman, W.R.S.	86	4	21.50	3- 37	–	–	–
Glover, J.C.	601	15	40.06	5- 38	1	–	–
Godleman, B.A.	35	0					
Goodman, J.E.	16	1	16.00	1- 16	–	–	–
Goodwin, D.M.	142	1	142.00	1-142	–	–	–
Goodwin, M.W.	376	7	53.71	2- 23	–	–	–
Greenwood, J.M.	97	0					
Griffiths, D.A.	2303	65	35.43	5- 85	1	–	–
Groenewald, T.D.	3345	98	34.13	6- 50	4	–	–
Groves, P.R.	349	11	31.72	5- 72	1	–	–
Guillen, J.C.	1	0					
Guptill, M.J.	127	4	31.75	3- 37	–	–	–
Gurney, H.F.	1334	28	47.64	5- 82	1	–	–
Hales, A.D.	166	3	55.33	2- 63	–	–	–
Hall, A.J.	12863	490	26.25	6- 77	15	1	–
Hamilton-Brown, R.J.	378	7	54.00	2- 49	–	–	–
Hampton, T.R.G.	42	1	42.00	1- 15	–	–	–
Hannon-Dalby, O.J.	1486	35	42.45	5- 68	2	–	–
Harinath, A.	30	0					
Harmison, B.W.	1144	33	34.66	4- 27	–	–	–
Harmison, S.J.	19927	713	27.94	7- 12	27	1	6
Harper, G.M.	297	6	49.50	4- 49	–	–	–
Harris, A.J.	14733	451	32.66	7- 54	17	3	2
Harris, J.A.R.	4027	150	26.84	7- 66	4	1	1
Harrison, D.S.	9276	257	36.09	7- 45	8	–	1
Hatchett, L.J.	256	12	21.33	5- 47	1	–	–
Henderson, C.W.	24413	791	30.86	7- 57	30	1	1
Henderson, T.	7024	262	26.80	7- 67	10	1	–
Herath, H.M.R.K.B.	16602	668	24.85	8- 43	38	5	0+2
Hesketh, R.L.	21	0					
Hildreth, J.C.	411	5	82.20	2- 39	–	–	–
Hilfenhaus, B.W.	5870	204	28.77	7- 58	7	1	0+1
Hockley, J.B.	408	5	81.60	1- 8	–	–	–
Hodd, A.J.	7	0					
Hodgson, L.J.	216	2	108.00	1- 42	–	–	–
Hogg, K.W.	4406	124	35.53	5- 48	1	–	–

F-C	Runs	Wkts	Avge	Best	5wI	10wM	50wS
Hoggard, M.J.	19510	718	27.17	7- 49	25	1	3
Hopkins, C.E.H.	305	2	152.50	1- 66	–	–	–
Horton, P.J.	10	0					
Housego, D.M.	17	0					
Howgego, B.H.N.	16	0					
Hughes, C.F.	81	1	81.00	1- 9	–	–	–
Hughes, P.J.	9	0					
Hunter, I.D.	5835	150	38.90	5- 46	3	–	–
Hussain, G.M.	1604	69	23.24	5- 36	2	–	1
Hussey, D.J.	1486	21	70.76	4-105	–	–	–
Hussey, M.E.K.	875	22	39.77	3- 34	–	–	–
Iftikhar Anjum	9504	394	24.12	7- 59	22	3	0+4
Imran Arif	1615	43	37.55	5- 50	2	–	–
Imran Farhat	2900	97	29.89	7- 31	2	–	–
Imran Tahir	12765	505	25.27	8- 76	35	7	2+2
Imrul Kayes	11	0					
Iqbal Abdulla	1806	61	29.60	4- 42	–	–	–
Ireland, A.J.	3271	113	28.94	7- 36	4	1	–
Jahurul Islam	7	1	7.00	1- 0	–	–	–
James, N.A.	7	1	7.00	1- 6	–	–	–
Jaques, P.A.	87	0					
Jaskaran Singh	174	1	174.00	1- 97	–	–	–
Javid, A.	78	0					
Jefferson, W.I.	60	1	60.00	1- 16	–	–	–
Jewell, T.M.	143	4	35.75	1- 16	–	–	–
Johnson, M.G.	7373	244	30.21	8- 61	7	3	–
Jones, G.O.	26	0					
Jones, P.S.	14122	384	36.77	6- 25	10	1	2
Jones, R.A.	2461	68	36.19	7-115	3	–	–
Jones, S.P.	8007	264	30.32	6- 45	15	1	–
Joseph, R.H.	4258	130	32.75	6- 32	5	–	1
Joyce, E.C.	1025	11	93.18	2- 34	–	–	–
Junaid Siddique	119	1	119.00	1- 30	–	–	–
Kartik, M.	13738	537	25.58	9- 70	31	5	1
Katich, S.M.	3462	95	36.44	7-130	3	–	–
Keedy, G.	18498	585	31.62	7- 68	29	6	3
Keegan, C.B.	4887	140	34.90	6-114	6	–	1
Kerrigan, S.C.	967	30	32.23	6- 74	3	–	–
Kervezee, A.N.	145	2	72.50	1- 14	–	–	–
Key, R.W.T.	198	3	66.00	2- 31	–	–	–
Khan, A.	9151	286	31.99	6- 52	8	–	2
Khan, I.	1847	85	21.72	7- 71	5	1	–
Khawaja, U.T.	17	0					
Killeen, N.	8215	262	31.35	7- 70	9	–	1
King, S.J.	290	5	58.00	3- 61	–	–	–
Kirby, S.P.	13008	464	28.03	8- 80	15	4	2
Kirtley, R.J.	16607	614	27.04	7- 21	29	4	7
Kulkarni, D.S.	2396	92	26.04	7- 50	6	–	–
Lancefield, T.J.	9	0					
Langeveldt, C.K.	8670	310	27.96	6- 48	9	1	1
Lawson, M.A.K.	2279	52	43.82	6- 88	4	–	–
Lee, N.T.	24	1	24.00	1- 24	–	–	–
Lewis, J.	19102	733	26.06	8- 95	33	5	8
Liddle, C.J.	962	17	56.58	3- 42	–	–	–
Linley, T.E.	1461	38	38.44	5-105	1	–	–
Lodwick, J.A.	60	0					

252

F-C	Runs	Wkts	Avge	Best	5wI	10wM	50wS
London, A.B.	54	1	54.00	1- 15	–	–	–
Lotay, J.D.S.	333	7	47.57	3-147	–	–	–
Loye, M.B.	61	1	61.00	1- 8	–	–	–
Lucas, D.S.	6614	207	31.95	7- 24	8	1	1
Lumb, M.J.	242	6	40.33	2- 10	–	–	–
Lungley, T.	4784	149	32.10	5- 20	3	–	1
Lyth, A.	171	3	57.00	1- 12	–	–	–
McCullum, N.L.	4176	100	41.76	6- 90	2	–	–
McDonald, A.B.	4602	159	28.94	6- 34	4	–	–
McGain, B.E.	3467	100	34.67	6-112	5	–	–
McGrath, A.	4234	114	37.14	5- 39	1	–	–
McKay, C.J.	2015	81	24.87	6- 75	2	–	–
McKenzie, N.D.	464	9	51.55	2- 13	–	–	–
McLaren, R.	6361	255	24.94	8- 38	10	1	1+1
Maddy, D.L.	7208	227	31.75	5- 37	5	–	–
Madsen, W.L.	372	7	53.14	3- 45	–	–	–
Mahbubul Alam	2552	91	28.04	5- 47	1	–	–
Mahmood, S.I.	8754	264	33.15	6- 30	7	1	–
Mahmudullah	2430	69	35.21	5- 51	1	–	–
Malan, C.C.	178	4	44.50	1- 28	–	–	–
Malan, D.J.	1141	24	47.54	4- 20	–	–	–
Malik, M.N.	7066	200	35.33	6- 46	7	–	–
Marshall, H.J.H.	1483	30	49.43	4- 24	–	–	–
Martin, C.S.	15434	477	32.35	6- 54	18	1	0+1
Martin-Jenkins, R.S.C.	12253	384	31.90	7- 51	8	–	–
Mascarenhas, A.D.	11818	418	28.27	6- 25	16	–	1
Mason, M.S.	8410	311	27.04	8- 45	10	1	3
Masters, D.D.	10892	376	28.96	6- 24	12	–	1
Maunders, J.K.	928	24	38.66	4- 15	–	–	–
Maynard, T.L.	38	0					
Meaker, S.C.	1635	43	38.02	5- 48	2	–	–
Mendis, B.A.W.	3597	185	19.44	7- 37	11	2	0+1
Mickleburgh, J.C.	50	0					
Middlebrook, J.D.	13313	341	39.04	6- 82	8	1	1
Miller, A.S.	782	27	28.96	5- 58	2	–	–
Milligan, M.J.	280	2	140.00	1- 17	–	–	–
Mitchell, D.K.H.	596	16	37.25	4- 49	–	–	–
Mohammad Aamer	2578	120	21.48	7- 61	7	1	.0+1
Mohammad Ashraful	3940	113	34.86	7- 99	5	–	–
Mohammad Asif	8848	360	24.57	7- 35	22	5	0+1
Mohammad Yousuf	24	0					
Moore, S.C.	321	5	64.20	1- 13	–	–	–
Morgan, E.J.G.	46	2	23.00	2- 24	–	–	–
Morkel, J.A.	5049	169	29.87	6- 36	4	–	–
Muchall, G.J.	617	15	41.13	3- 26	–	–	–
Mukund, A.	183	7	26.14	3- 5	–	–	–
Mullaney, S.J.	405	10	40.50	4- 31	–	–	–
Munday, M.K.	2534	86	29.46	8- 55	4	2	–
Muralitharan, M.	26997	1374	19.64	9- 51	119	34	3+3
Murtagh, T.J.	8641	280	30.86	7- 82	12	1	2
Myburgh, J.G.	1326	30	44.20	4- 56	–	–	–
Naeem Islam	1085	21	51.66	3- 7	–	–	–
Naik, J.K.H.	1500	51	29.41	7- 96	1	–	–
Nannes, D.P.	2327	93	25.02	7- 50	2	1	–
Napier, G.R.	8134	210	38.73	6-103	3	–	–
Nash, C.D.	1167	27	43.22	4- 12	–	–	–

F-C	Runs	Wkts	Avge	Best	5wI	10wM	50wS
Naved Arif	3375	145	23.27	7- 66	10	1	0+1
Naved-ul-Hasan	12761	523	24.39	7- 49	27	4	2+3
Needham, J.	1268	35	36.22	6- 49	1	–	–
Nel, A.	12212	446	27.38	6- 25	14	1	–
Nel, J.D.	1374	51	26.94	6- 62	2	–	–
New, T.J.	211	5	42.20	2- 18	–	–	–
Newby, O.J.	3505	105	33.38	5- 69	1	–	–
Newman, S.A.	57	0					
Newton, R.I.	19	0					
Nixon, P.A.	157	1	157.00	1- 7	–	–	–
North, M.J.	4953	121	40.93	6- 55	2	–	–
Northeast, S.A.	10	0					
Ntini, M.	18586	648	28.68	7- 37	27	5	–
O'Brien, I.E.	8392	322	26.06	8- 55	14	1	–
O'Brien, N.J.	16	2	8.00	1- 4	–	–	–
Onions, G.	6923	230	30.10	8-101	9	–	2
Osborne, M.	151	6	25.16	3- 35	–	–	–
Owen, W.T.	269	3	89.66	3- 65	–	–	–
Paine, T.D.	3	0					
Palladino, A.P.	3994	117	34.13	6- 41	2	–	–
Pandey, M.K.	21	0					
Panesar, M.S.	13562	419	32.36	7-181	21	3	4
Park, C.M.	219	2	109.50	1- 34	–	–	–
Park, G.T.	958	18	53.22	3- 25	–	–	–
Parnell, W.D.	1992	56	35.57	4- 7	–	–	–
Parry, S.D.	256	9	28.44	5- 23	1	–	–
Pascoe, D.C.	324	14	23.14	6- 68	2	–	–
Patel, A.	76	1	76.00	1- 34	–	–	–
Patel, R.H.	134	5	26.80	3- 52	–	–	–
Patel, S.R.	3805	93	40.91	6- 84	2	–	–
Patterson, S.A.	2184	67	32.59	5- 50	1	–	–
Pattinson, D.J.	4709	133	35.40	6- 30	6	–	–
Peters, S.D.	31	1	31.00	1- 19	–	–	–
Petersen, A.N.	125	4	31.25	2- 7	–	–	–
Peterson, R.J.	10547	321	32.85	6- 67	14	1	1
Pettini, M.L.	191	0					
Phillips, B.J.	7121	238	29.92	6- 29	5	–	–
Phillips, T.J.	5046	110	45.87	5- 41	1	–	–
Pietersen, K.P.	3279	61	53.75	4- 31	–	–	–
Piolet, S.A.	123	11	11.18	6- 17	1	1	–
Plunkett, L.E.	9520	306	31.11	6- 63	8	1	3
Pollard, K.A.	313	6	52.16	2- 29	–	–	–
Ponting, R.T.	768	14	54.85	2- 10	–	–	–
Porterfield, W.T.S.	135	2	67.50	1- 29	–	–	–
Pothas, N.	63	1	63.00	1- 16	–	–	–
Powell, D.B.L.	9318	276	33.76	6- 49	6	–	–
Powell, M.J.	132	2	66.00	2- 39	–	–	–
Poynton, T.	96	2	48.00	2- 96	–	–	–
Prince, A.G.	166	4	41.50	2- 11	–	–	–
Procter, L.A.	47	1	47.00	1- 26	–	–	–
Pujara, C.A.	83	5	16.60	2- 4	–	–	–
Pyrah, R.M.	817	16	51.06	2- 8	–	–	–
Rahane, A.M.	63	0					
Ramprakash, M.R.	2202	34	64.76	3- 32	–	–	–
Rankin, W.B.	2867	101	28.38	5- 16	3	–	–
Rashid, A.U.	7593	228	33.30	7-107	13	–	2

254

F-C	Runs	Wkts	Avge	Best	5wI	10wM	50wS
Rayner, O.P.	3086	89	34.67	5- 49	3	–	–
Read, C.M.W.	90	0					
Redfern, D.J.	255	5	51.00	1- 7	–	–	–
Redmond, A.J.	4314	100	43.14	4- 30	–	–	–
Rees, G.P.	3	0					
Riazuddin, H.	200	5	40.00	1- 0	–	–	–
Richardson, A.	10699	369	28.99	8- 46	11	1	2
Robiul Islam	3400	114	29.82	5- 30	6	1	–
Robson, S.D.	22	0					
Rogers, C.J.L.	131	1	131.00	1- 16	–	–	–
Roland-Jones, T.S.	745	38	19.60	5- 41	2	–	–
Root, J.E.	27	0					
Roper, C.G.W.	249	2	124.50	1- 61	–	–	–
Rose, S.A.L.	216	1	216.00	1- 72	–	–	–
Roy, J.J.	18	0					
Rubel Hossain	2106	36	58.50	5- 60	2	–	–
Rudolph, J.A.	2521	58	43.46	5- 80	3	–	–
Rushworth, C.	821	21	39.09	4- 90	–	–	–
Russell, A.D.	607	23	26.39	5- 68	2	–	–
Sadler, J.L.	250	3	83.33	1- 5	–	–	–
Saeed Ajmal	8354	299	27.93	7- 63	18	1	0+1
Sales, D.J.G.	184	9	20.44	4- 25	–	–	–
Salman Butt	653	11	59.36	4- 82	–	–	–
Sanderson, B.W.	190	6	31.66	5- 50	1	–	–
Sayers, J.J.	147	3	49.00	3- 20	–	–	–
Schofield, C.P.	8399	232	36.20	6-120	6	–	–
Scott, A.J.D.	147	8	18.37	4- 52	–	–	–
Scott, B.J.M.	1	0					
Shafayat, B.M.	642	8	80.25	2- 25	–	–	–
Shafiul Islam	1361	39	34.89	4- 38	–	–	–
Shah, O.A.	1489	26	57.26	3- 33	–	–	–
Shahadat Hossain	5162	134	38.52	6- 27	7	–	–
Shahid Afridi	7023	258	27.22	6-101	8	–	–
Shahzad, A.	2933	91	32.23	5- 51	1	–	–
Shakib Al Hasan	4898	164	29.86	7- 32	12	–	–
Shantry, A.J.	1923	81	23.74	5- 49	4	1	–
Shantry, J.D.	1327	35	37.91	5- 49	1	–	–
Sharma, R.	398	9	44.22	5- 81	1	–	–
Sheikh, A.	152	5	30.40	3- 78	–	–	–
Shoaib Malik	5559	179	31.05	7- 81	5	1	–
Shreck, C.E.	9390	307	30.58	8- 31	18	2	2
Sidebottom, R.J.	12106	475	25.48	7- 47	20	2	2
Smith, B.F.	488	4	122.00	1- 5	–	–	–
Smith, D.R.	4054	124	32.69	4- 22	–	–	–
Smith, D.S.	218	2	109.00	1- 2	–	–	–
Smith, D.T.	5	0					
Smith, G.M.	4090	113	36.19	5- 54	2	–	–
Smith, G.P.	64	1	64.00	1- 64	–	–	–
Smith, S.P.D.	1352	29	46.62	7- 64	1	–	–
Smith, T.C.	3792	116	32.68	6- 46	2	–	–
Smith, T.M.J.	411	3	137.00	1- 30	–	–	–
Smith, W.R.	552	8	69.00	3- 34	–	–	–
Snell, S.D.	15	0					
Solanki, V.S.	4120	86	47.90	5- 40	4	1	–
Spriegel, M.N.W.	767	17	45.11	2- 28	–	–	–
Stevens, D.I.	3407	94	36.24	4- 36	–	–	–

F-C	Runs	Wkts	Avge	Best	5wI	10wM	50wS
Stiff, D.A.	1906	43	44.32	5- 91	1	–	–
Stirling, P.R.	113	3	37.66	2- 45	–	–	–
Stokes, B.A.	365	6	60.83	2- 32	–	–	–
Strauss, A.J.	89	2	44.50	1- 16	–	–	–
Styris, S.B.	6353	203	31.29	6- 32	9	1	–
Suppiah, A.V.	1932	32	60.37	3- 46	–	–	–
Swann, G.P.	17608	553	31.84	7- 33	24	4	1
Tahir, N.S.	3815	128	29.80	7-107	2	–	–
Tait, S.W.	5661	198	28.59	7- 29	7	1	0+1
Tamim Iqbal	77	0					
Taylor, C.G.	1452	27	53.77	4- 52	–	–	–
Taylor, J.M.R.	13	1	13.00	1- 8	–	–	–
Taylor, J.W.A.	160	0					
Taylor, L.R.P.L.	330	4	82.50	2- 34	–	–	–
Taylor, M.H.	235	4	58.75	4-161	–	–	–
Taylor, R.M.L.	202	5	40.40	2- 60	–	–	–
ten Doeschate, R.N.	5258	158	33.27	6- 20	7	–	–
Thomas, A.C.	9655	353	27.35	7- 54	16	1	–
Thornely, M.A.	100	4	25.00	2- 14	–	–	–
Thorp, C.D.	4168	159	26.21	7- 88	7	1	1
Timms, R.T.	126	0					
Tiwary, M.K.	760	14	54.28	2- 42	–	–	–
Tomlinson, J.A.	6735	190	35.44	8- 46	8	1	1
Tonge, G.C.	2794	95	29.41	7- 58	4	–	–
Toor, K.S.	84	1	84.00	1- 36	–	–	–
Tredwell, J.C.	9534	267	35.70	8- 66	9	3	1
Trego, P.D.	6256	166	37.68	6- 59	1	–	–
Tremlett, C.T.	9252	337	27.45	6- 44	7	–	–
Trescothick, M.E.	1551	36	43.08	4- 36	–	–	–
Tripathi, V.	28	0					
Trott, I.J.L.	2471	56	44.12	7- 39	1	–	–
Troughton, J.O.	1416	22	64.36	3- 1	–	–	–
Turnbull, P.T.	469	11	42.63	5- 92	1	–	–
Turner, M.L.	853	17	50.17	4- 30	–	–	–
Tyagi, S.	1690	60	28.16	6- 46	2	1	–
Udal, S.D.	26695	822	32.47	8- 50	37	5	7
Umar Akmal	10	0					
Umar Amin	261	9	29.00	1- 0	–	–	–
Umar Gul	6844	249	27.48	8- 78	14	1	0+1
Unadkat, J.D.	203	16	12.68	7- 41	2	1	–
Vaas, W.P.J.U.C.	17068	683	24.98	7- 54	27	3	0+2
van Jaarsveld, M.	1848	47	39.31	5- 33	1	–	–
Vince, J.M.	61	0					
Vincent, L.	527	10	52.70	2- 37	–	–	–
Voges, A.C.	1370	40	34.25	4- 92	–	–	–
Wagg, G.G.	7024	216	32.51	6- 35	8	1	2
Wagh, M.A.	4611	100	46.11	7-222	2	–	–
Wahab Riaz	6579	228	28.85	6- 64	10	2	0+1
Wainwright, D.J.	2552	70	36.45	5-134	1	–	–
Wakely, A.G.	252	4	63.00	2- 62	–	–	–
Walker, M.J.	1214	25	48.56	3- 35	–	–	–
Wallace, M.A.	3	0					
Waller, M.T.C.	320	5	64.00	2- 27	–	–	–
Walters, S.J.	239	3	79.66	1- 4	–	–	–
Walton, C.A.K.	23	0					
Warner, D.A.	19	1	19.00	1- 0	–	–	–

F-C	Runs	Wkts	Avge	Best	5wI	10wM	50wS
Waters, H.T.	2377	65	36.56	5-86	1	–	–
Waters, S.R.	68	2	34.00	1-18	–	–	–
Watkins, S.J.V.	73	0					
Watson, M.J.C.	271	4	67.75	4-78	–	–	–
Watson, S.R.	4478	159	28.16	7-69	5	1	–
Wells, L.W.P.	16	0					
Welsh, A.S.	152	4	38.00	3-32	–	–	–
Wernars, K.O.	30	3	10.00	2-11	–	–	–
Westley, T.	415	14	29.64	4-55	–	–	–
Westwood, I.J.	222	6	37.00	2-39	–	–	–
Whelan, C.D.	1715	44	38.97	5-95	1	–	–
White, G.G.	498	6	83.00	2-35	–	–	–
White, R.A.	807	14	57.64	2-30	–	–	–
White, W.A.	2583	58	44.53	5-87	1	–	–
Wigley, D.H.	4932	136	36.26	6-72	4	–	–
Willey, D.J.	513	12	42.75	2-21	–	–	–
Williams, R.E.M.	755	23	32.82	5-70	2	–	–
Willoughby, C.M.	19646	774	25.38	7-44	31	3	5+2
Wilson, G.C.	46	0					
Woakes, C.R.	3936	154	25.55	6-43	8	2	1
Wood, C.P.	240	13	18.46	5-54	1	–	–
Wood, M.J.	79	0					
Woolley, R.J.J.	689	11	62.63	3-71	–	–	–
Wright, B.J.	137	2	68.50	1-14	–	–	–
Wright, C.J.C.	5110	123	41.54	6-22	2	–	–
Wright, D.G.	9999	349	28.65	8-60	12	–	1
Wright, L.J.	3924	101	38.85	5-65	3	–	–
Wyatt, A.C.F.	159	7	22.71	3-42	–	–	–
Yardy, M.H.	2003	26	77.03	5-83	1	–	–
Yasir Arafat	16236	674	24.08	9-35	39	5	0+4
Yasir Hameed	735	7	105.00	2-46	–	–	–
Young, E.G.C.	379	3	126.33	2-74	–	–	–
Younus Khan	1560	35	44.57	4-52	–	–	–
Zulqarnain Haider	26	0					

LEADING CURRENT FIRST-CLASS PLAYERS

These are the leading career batting/bowling averages and wicket-keeping/fielding aggregates among players currently registered for first-class county cricket at the time of going to press. All figures are to the end of the 2010 English season.

BATTING (Qualification: 100 innings)

	Runs	Avge		Runs	Avge
D.J.Hussey	11417	55.69	J.C.Hildreth	7110	43.09
M.R.Ramprakash	34839	54.60	A.D.Brown	16669	42.85
C.J.L.Rogers	14791	52.26	R.S.Bopara	6332	42.21
Younus Khan	10873	50.33	O.A.Shah	14521	42.08
K.P.Pietersen	11726	49.26	N.Pothas	11135	41.86
M.W.Goodwin	20381	48.18	A.J.Strauss	14061	41.84
R.N.ten Doeschate	4950	48.05	R.W.T.Key	15039	41.54
M.J.Di Venuto	23974	46.55	M.E.Trescothick	18042	41.09
M.van Jaarsveld	16775	45.83	A.C.Voges	4867	40.55
J.G.Myburgh	5180	45.43	D.J.G.Sales	12145	40.34
D.M.Benkenstein	13741	45.05	S.R.Patel	4430	40.27
I.J.L.Trott	10183	45.05	M.B.Loye	14936	40.15
E.C.Joyce	10344	44.97	S.M.Davies	5371	40.08
A.N.Cook	9700	44.29	M.A.Wagh	12187	39.95
I.R.Bell	11575	44.01	I.D.Blackwell	9936	39.74
N.D.McKenzie	13563	43.61	Z.de Bruyn	10008	39.71
M.A.Carberry	7832	43.51	M.J.Prior	9651	39.71
M.J.Cosgrove	6449	43.28	D.K.H.Mitchell	4002	39.62

BOWLING (Qualification: 100 wickets)

	Wkts	Avge		Wkts	Avge
B.A.W.Mendis	185	19.44	M.Kartik	537	25.58
M.Muralitharan	1374	19.64	J.Lewis	733	26.06
A.M.Davies	253	22.63	A.J.Hall	490	26.25
N.A.Gondal	145	23.27	C.D.Collymore	406	26.39
F.de Wet	194	23.58	J.E.C.Franklin	411	26.45
A.R.Adams	463	23.95	D.G.Cork	967	26.51
Yasir Arafat	674	24.08	Kabir Ali	448	26.80
Naved-ul-Hasan	523	24.39	J.A.R.Harris	150	26.84
R.McLaren	255	24.94	M.S.Mason	311	27.04
W.P.J.U.C.Vaas	683	24.98	G.Chapple	780	27.08
Azhar Mahmood	566	25.22	M.J.Hoggard	718	27.17
Imran Tahir	505	25.27	Shahid Afridi	258	27.22
C.M.Willoughby	774	25.38	A.C.Thomas	353	27.35
R.J.Sidebottom	475	25.48	C.T.Tremlett	337	27.45
C.R.Woakes	154	25.55			

WICKET-KEEPING (Qualification: 400 dismissals, exc catches taken in the field)

	Total	Ct	St		Total	Ct	St
P.A.Nixon	950	883	67	G.O.Jones	459	428	31
C.M.W.Read	746	706	40	M.A.Wallace	452	415	37
N.Pothas	627	582	45	L.D.Sutton	418	396	22
J.N.Batty	620	553	67	M.J.Prior	411	385	26
J.S.Foster	527	483	44	P.Mustard	404	389	15

FIELDING (Qualification: 250 catches)

M.J.Di Venuto	379	V.S.Solanki	276
M.van Jaarsveld	364	A.D.Brown	273
M.E.Trescothick	340	D.L.Maddy	269

LIMITED-OVERS CAREER RECORDS

Compiled by Philip Bailey

The following career records, to the end of the 2010 season, include all players currently registered with first-class counties. These records are restricted to performances in limited-overs matches of 'List A' status as defined by the Association of Cricket Statisticians and Historians now incorporated by ICC into their Classification of Cricket. The following matches qualify for List A status and are included in the figures that follow: Limited-Overs Internationals; Other International matches (e.g. Commonwealth Games, 'A' team internationals); Premier domestic limited-overs tournaments in Test status countries; Official tourist matches against the main first-class teams.

The following matches do NOT qualify for inclusion: World Cup warm-up games; Tourist matches against first-class teams outside the major domestic competitions (e.g. Universities, Minor Counties etc.); Festival, pre-season friendly games and Twenty20 Cup matches.

	M	Runs	Avge	HS	100	50	Wkts	Avge	Best	Econ
Adams, A.R.	149	1437	17.74	90*	–	1	180	29.89	5- 7	4.76
Adams, J.H.K.	47	1554	37.90	131	1	12	1	105.00	1-34	7.97
Adkin, W.A.	1	30	30.00	30	–	–	1	16.00	1-16	2.66
Adshead, S.J.	104	1580	22.89	87	–	8	–	–	–	109/31
Ali, Kabir	157	1092	15.16	92	–	3	227	25.33	5-36	5.16
Ali, M.M.	63	1507	26.43	125	3	8	19	42.36	3-32	5.62
Allenby, J.	59	1189	25.29	91*	–	6	49	31.10	5-43	5.17
Ambrose, T.R.	111	2258	28.22	135	3	8	–	–	–	115/20
Anderson, J.M.	184	252	8.12	15	–	–	251	28.43	5-23	4.81
Andrew, G.M.	83	640	16.41	104	1	1	83	34.03	5-31	6.27
Ansari, Z.S.	1	6	6.00	6	–	–	1	26.00	1-26	5.20
Anyon, J.E.	38	34	5.66	12	–	–	41	30.58	3- 6	5.47
Ashling, C.P.	8	11	5.50	6*	–	–	5	60.80	2-33	6.65
Azeem Rafiq	2	–	–	–	–	–	1	36.00	1-36	7.20
Azhar Mahmood	291	3946	21.21	101*	2	15	310	31.99	6-18	4.63
Bairstow, J.M.	17	179	17.90	46*	–	–	–	–	–	11/–
Baker, G.C.	1	0	0.00	0	–	–	1	63.00	1-63	9.00
Balbirnie, A.	4	29	7.25	17	–	–	–	–	–	1/–
Balcombe, D.J.	9	4	1.33	2	–	–	10	37.80	2-39	5.90
Ball, A.J.	1	5	5.00	5	–	–	1	16.00	1-16	3.20
Ball, J.T.	2	6	3.00	6	–	–	4	16.25	3-32	4.64
Ballance, G.S.	5	162	32.40	73	–	1	–	–	–	–
Banerjee, V.	12	12	4.00	6	–	–	18	24.27	3-47	4.60
Barker, K.H.D.	23	221	22.10	40	–	–	26	27.88	4-33	5.67
Bates, A.M.	6	3	1.50	2*	–	–	–	–	–	5/2
Batty, G.J.	194	2050	16.80	83*	–	5	172	33.66	5-35	4.56
Batty, J.N.	185	2808	22.28	158*	1	14	–	–	–	195/34
Beer, W.A.T.	14	34	8.50	14	–	–	8	52.50	2-17	4.66
Bell, I.R.	205	6811	38.92	158	7	49	33	34.48	5-41	5.29
Benkenstein, D.M.	279	6826	35.18	107*	1	42	86	29.90	4-16	5.02
Berg, G.K.	33	550	23.91	65	–	2	24	29.33	4-50	5.45
Blackwell, I.D.	241	5533	27.12	134*	3	33	194	34.52	5-26	4.78
Blain, J.A.R.	102	635	15.48	41	–	–	143	25.72	5-22	5.03
Blake, A.J.	18	285	40.71	81*	–	2	1	61.00	1-25	5.08
Bopara, R.S.	164	4607	37.45	201*	6	24	109	27.00	4-38	5.34
Borrington, P.M.	1	25	25.00	25	–	–	–	–	–	–
Borthwick, S.G.	10	21	21.00	10*	–	–	5	48.80	2-11	7.62
Botha, A.G.	145	1660	23.05	60*	–	4	142	29.57	5-43	4.86
Botha, J.	134	1381	20.92	55*	–	3	121	37.62	4-19	4.53
Boyce, M.A.G.	32	720	28.80	80	–	4	–	–	–	–

259

L-O	M	Runs	Avge	HS	100	50	Wkts	Avge	Best	Econ
Bragg, W.D.	13	283	25.72	78	–	1	0	–	–	2/–
Brathwaite, R.M.R.	1	–	–	–	–	–	1	19.00	1-19	6.33
Breese, G.R.	149	1740	20.23	68*	–	3	155	28.47	5-41	4.64
Bresnan, T.T.	169	1583	19.54	80	–	4	178	34.21	4-25	5.05
Brett, T.	5	2	–	2*	–	–	3	59.66	1-24	4.97
Briggs, D.R.	11	17	8.50	9*	–	–	6	69.66	2-36	4.80
Broad, S.C.J.	90	418	12.29	45*	–	–	149	26.00	5-23	5.17
Brooks, J.A.	9	14	4.66	10	–	–	6	50.33	3-41	5.11
Brophy, G.L.	112	1992	27.28	93*	–	13	–	–	–	110/22
Brown, A.D.	399	11168	30.85	268	19	50	14	40.07	3-39	6.47
Brown, B.C.	11	112	28.00	58	–	1	–	–	–	8/1
Brown, D.O.	38	500	20.83	63*	–	1	14	57.42	3-29	6.59
Brown, K.R.	12	358	32.54	65*	–	3	–	–	–	–
Brown, M.J.	30	922	34.14	96*	–	7	–	–	–	–
Buck, N.L.	9	26	26.00	21	–	–	11	32.27	2-16	5.75
Burton, D.A.	3	2	2.00	2	–	–	2	47.00	1-26	6.26
Buttler, J.C.	16	443	49.22	90*	–	4	–	–	–	11/1
Cameron, J.G.	12	236	29.50	58	–	1	7	41.71	4-44	6.61
Carberry, M.A.	118	2901	29.01	121*	2	21	4	42.50	2-11	5.86
Carter, A.	10	25	5.00	12	–	–	12	23.25	3-32	5.69
Carter, N.M.	167	2853	22.46	135	3	12	220	26.38	5-31	4.84
Chambers, M.A.	3	1	–	1*	–	–	3	31.00	1-26	6.20
Chapple, G.	270	2000	17.69	81*	–	9	299	29.15	6-18	4.51
Cheetham, S.P.	10	20	10.00	13*	–	–	14	28.50	4-32	6.33
Chilton, M.J.	184	4480	30.47	115	5	21	42	24.07	5-26	5.48
Chopra, V.	38	1335	38.14	102	2	12	0	–	–	6.00
Choudhry, S.H.	7	115	57.50	39	–	–	6	35.50	4-54	6.45
Clare, J.L.	24	193	11.35	34	–	–	15	49.06	3-39	5.61
Clark, J.	1	32	32.00	32	–	–	–	–	–	-/–
Clarke, R.	150	2694	25.41	98*	–	12	80	41.21	4-49	5.71
Claydon, M.E.	28	86	7.16	19	–	–	28	34.75	3-31	4.83
Cobb, J.J.	17	222	17.07	43*	–	–	3	39.66	1-12	5.40
Coetzer, K.J.	58	1479	30.18	127	1	9	0	–	–	6.00
Coles, M.T.	10	11	3.66	5	–	–	18	15.27	4-45	6.70
Collingwood, P.D.	359	9469	34.06	120*	8	54	221	34.61	6-31	4.86
Collymore, C.D.	131	151	6.04	13*	–	–	139	31.46	5-27	4.27
Comber, M.A.	1	52	–	52*	–	1	–	–	–	–
Compton, N.R.D.	71	1957	36.92	131	4	12	1	53.00	1- 0	5.21
Cook, A.N.	75	2486	36.55	125	5	14	0	–	–	3.33
Cook, S.J.	179	1244	16.81	67*	–	2	224	27.65	6-37	4.72
Cork, D.G.	308	4157	21.31	93	–	19	380	27.38	6-21	4.31
Cosgrove, M.J.	96	3178	35.70	121	3	25	17	56.70	2-21	6.39
Cosker, D.A.	201	646	10.94	50*	–	1	205	33.27	5-54	4.79
Cox, O.B.	7	9	9.00	9*	–	–	–	–	–	7/2
Croft, R.D.B.	402	6474	23.45	143	4	32	409	32.44	6-20	4.33
Croft, S.J.	76	1663	31.98	93*	–	11	39	31.82	4-24	5.34
Crook, S.P.	30	281	15.61	72	–	1	21	50.42	4-20	6.05
Cross, G.D.	42	599	19.32	76	–	1	2	13.00	2-26	24/11
Daggett, L.M.	41	78	26.00	14*	–	–	54	26.27	4-17	4.93
Davey, J.H.	7	74	12.33	24	–	–	6	19.66	5- 9	5.05
Davies, A.M.	73	166	7.54	31*	–	–	68	30.69	4-13	4.19
Davies, S.M.	107	3183	34.22	119	5	19	–	–	–	96/27
Davis, C.A.L.	1	–	–	–	–	–	0	–	–	5.86
Dawson, L.A.	38	632	25.28	69*	–	2	27	34.37	4-45	5.34
Dawson, R.K.J.	127	626	10.43	41	–	–	128	30.60	4-13	4.93
de Bruyn, Z.	181	4829	36.58	122*	5	30	128	31.60	5-44	5.42

L-O	M	Runs	Avge	HS	100	50	Wkts	Avge	Best	Econ
Denly, J.L.	77	2296	33.76	115	4	11	1	35.00	1-20	7.00
Dent, C.D.J.	6	13	4.33	8	–	–	1	17.00	1-17	8.50
Dernbach, J.W.	60	147	8.64	31	–	–	95	27.28	5-31	6.33
de Wet, F.	52	258	28.66	56*	–	1	61	30.72	5-59	4.78
Dexter, N.J.	52	1250	33.78	135*	2	5	19	50.94	3-17	5.18
Di Venuto, M.J.	299	9082	33.02	173*	15	46	5	36.20	1-10	5.43
Durston, W.J.	68	1342	32.73	117	1	8	24	42.79	3-44	6.02
du Toit, S.J.	36	888	27.75	144	2	3	2	33.00	2-30	6.00
Edwards, N.J.	8	141	20.14	65	–	1	–	–	–	–
Elstone, S.L.	4	66	22.00	30	–	–	1	22.00	1-22	6.00
Ervine, S.M.	169	4035	31.77	167*	6	17	166	33.60	5-50	5.58
Evans, L.	5	1	1.00	1*	–	–	5	31.20	2-53	6.50
Evans, L.J.	2	39	39.00	36*	–	–	–	–	–	–
Finn, S.T.	32	35	5.00	13	–	–	37	30.05	3-23	5.17
Fletcher, L.J.	21	79	11.28	40*	–	–	20	37.15	2-35	5.19
Footitt, M.H.A.	9	1	1.00	1*	–	–	10	29.10	3-20	5.59
Foster, J.S.	163	2411	27.08	83*	–	11	–	–	–	193/53
Franklin, J.E.C.	180	3065	30.95	133*	2	14	169	34.43	5-42	4.81
Franks, P.J.	167	1802	20.95	84*	–	5	176	29.26	6-27	5.00
Gale, A.W.	92	2285	30.87	125*	1	12	–	–	–	–
Gatting, J.S.	23	555	29.21	99*	–	4	0	–	–	3.75
Gidman, A.P.R.	154	3420	26.30	116	4	17	61	42.50	5-42	5.19
Gidman, W.R.S.	18	105	13.12	21	–	–	19	22.26	4-36	4.51
Godleman, B.A.	17	342	21.37	82	–	1	–	–	–	–
Goodman, J.E.	3	38	38.00	26*	–	–	–	–	–	–
Goodwin, M.W.	340	10384	36.05	167	13	66	7	43.71	1- 9	5.23
Gregory, L.	1	0	0.00	0	–	–	4	12.25	4-49	4.90
Griffiths, D.A.	5	3	–	3*	–	–	6	37.83	4-29	6.13
Groenewald, T.D.	46	330	13.20	36	–	–	41	36.17	3-25	5.59
Guptill, M.J.	67	2115	35.84	156	5	11	2	26.50	2- 7	4.89
Gurney, H.F.	16	7	2.33	7	–	–	12	42.50	5-24	5.17
Hales, A.D.	26	797	36.22	150*	2	3	–	–	–	–
Hall, A.J.	286	5451	29.14	129*	6	29	329	27.50	5-18	4.70
Hamilton-Brown, R.J.	48	1020	26.15	115	1	4	28	33.96	3-28	5.72
Harinath, A.	1	21	–	21*	–	–	–	–	–	–
Harmison, B.W.	47	950	24.35	67	–	3	24	35.00	3-43	5.86
Harmison, S.J.	143	267	8.09	25*	–	–	184	30.75	5-33	4.96
Harris, J.A.R.	21	98	7.53	21	–	–	27	28.51	4-48	5.20
Harrison, D.S.	85	454	12.61	37*	–	–	98	30.76	5-26	5.04
Henderson, C.W.	241	1110	15.41	45	–	–	304	25.24	6-29	4.30
Henderson, T.	114	1608	21.72	126*	1	9	130	27.43	5- 5	4.35
Hildreth, J.C.	124	3332	32.99	151	4	14	6	30.83	2-26	7.40
Hodd, A.J.	37	552	25.09	91	–	1	–	–	–	29/8
Hodgson, L.J.	6	9	9.00	9	–	–	2	80.00	2-44	6.15
Hogg, K.W.	126	935	16.40	66*	–	1	127	29.80	4-20	4.74
Hoggard, M.J.	140	88	4.63	17*	–	–	190	25.78	5-28	4.50
Horton, P.J.	55	1376	29.27	111*	2	7	–	–	–	–
Howell, B.A.C.	2	17	8.50	12	–	–	2	27.50	1-23	5.00
Howgego, B.H.N.	1	7	7.00	7	–	–	–	–	–	–
Hughes, C.F.	20	492	27.33	72	–	5	2	81.00	1-17	5.22
Hussain, G.M.	1	–	–	–	–	–	2	8.50	2-17	3.40
Hussey, D.J.	174	5636	40.25	130	8	37	30	43.40	3-26	5.27
Imran Tahir	87	304	14.47	41*	–	–	125	23.36	5-27	4.56
Ireland, A.J.	65	90	5.62	17	–	–	88	28.63	4-16	5.39
James, N.A.	13	127	18.14	30	–	–	9	21.66	2-19	4.43
Jefferson, W.I.	96	3092	35.13	132	4	18	2	4.50	2- 9	2.25

L-O	M	Runs	Avge	HS	100	50	Wkts	Avge	Best	Econ
Jewell, T.M.	2	1	1.00	1	–	–	0	–	–	9.33
Johnson, R.M.	8	30	15.00	20	–	–	–	–	–	7/2
Jones, A.J.	1	5	5.00	5	–	–	0	–	–	9.25
Jones, G.O.	160	2702	24.12	86	–	11	–	–	–	174/35
Jones, P.S.	184	676	12.75	42	–	–	245	29.61	6-56	5.26
Jones, R.A.	7	19	9.50	11*	–	–	1	269.00	1-47	7.07
Jones, S.P.	35	76	15.20	26	–	–	32	40.00	5-32	5.11
Joseph, R.H.	33	43	21.50	15	–	–	39	28.56	5-13	5.11
Joyce, E.C.	191	5997	37.01	146	8	37	6	51.50	2-10	7.02
Kartik, M.	180	669	11.53	44	–	–	233	28.54	6-27	4.36
Keedy, G.	75	141	9.40	33	–	–	90	26.47	5-30	4.63
Keogh, R.I.	1	11	11.00	11	–	–	–	–	–	–
Kervezee, A.N.	52	1436	31.21	121*	2	6	0	–	–	9.12
Key, R.W.T.	194	5467	31.41	120*	5	34	–	–	–	–
Khan, A.	62	281	12.21	65*	–	1	65	32.69	4-26	5.20
Khawaja, U.T.	4	136	34.00	56	–	1	–	–	–	–
Kieswetter, C.	69	2359	38.67	143	6	9	–	–	–	67/15
Kirby, S.P.	77	88	4.19	15	–	–	97	30.62	5-36	5.56
Lancefield, T.J.	1	20	20.00	20	–	–	–	–	–	–
Lewis, J.	209	873	11.19	54	–	1	277	26.30	5-19	4.54
Liddle, C.J.	17	16	4.00	11	–	–	15	43.86	4-49	6.45
Linley, T.E.	12	37	37.00	20*	–	–	5	80.80	2-38	5.77
London, A.B.	2						0	–	–	5.00
Loye, M.B.	299	8884	34.16	127	10	58	–	–	–	–
Lucas, D.S.	65	205	10.78	32*	–	–	77	30.41	4-27	5.63
Lumb, M.J.	164	4752	32.32	110	3	37	0	–	–	14.00
Lyth, A.	42	883	26.75	109*	1	3	0	–	–	4.66
McCullum, B.B.	215	4617	29.40	170	5	21	–	–	–	232/15
McCullum, N.L.	95	1204	19.11	71	–	6	79	39.31	3-21	5.28
McDonald, A.B.	77	1475	32.06	67	–	8	68	38.82	4-50	5.08
McGrath, A.	288	7472	33.06	148	7	44	80	32.62	4-41	5.05
Machan, M.W.	1	10	10.00	10	–	–	–	–	–	–
McKenzie, N.D.	228	6365	36.37	131*	8	43	4	62.00	2-19	5.83
McLaren, R.	105	1561	32.52	82*	–	8	105	31.63	5-46	5.08
Maddy, D.L.	337	8546	30.85	167*	11	51	198	29.55	4-16	5.12
Madsen, W.L.	24	627	34.83	71*	–	5	5	14.80	2-18	4.35
Mahmood, S.I.	137	435	8.52	29	–	–	192	27.04	5-16	5.17
Malan, D.J.	42	742	19.52	60	–	2	10	40.50	2- 4	5.88
Malik, M.N.	73	105	10.50	11	–	–	73	34.58	4-40	5.27
Manuel, J.K.	2	26	13.00	22	–	–	–	–	–	–
Marshall, H.J.H.	239	5770	28.42	122	6	38	4	64.50	2-21	6.24
Mascarenhas, A.D.	244	4107	25.35	79	–	27	281	26.24	5-27	4.25
Mason, M.S.	81	171	7.43	25	–	–	94	28.14	4-34	4.30
Masters, D.D.	131	467	12.28	39	–	–	126	32.23	5-17	4.46
Maynard, T.L.	41	1109	30.80	108	2	7	0	–	–	16.00
Meaker, S.C.	15	16	8.00	10*	–	–	11	47.63	2-21	6.39
Mendis, B.A.W.	69	450	16.66	71*	–	2	123	17.43	6-13	4.08
Mickleburgh, J.C.	4	84	21.00	46	–	–	–	–	–	–
Middlebrook, J.D.	157	1406	19.52	57*	–	1	122	34.95	4-27	4.65
Mitchell, D.K.H.	54	1030	31.21	92	–	7	28	39.35	4-42	5.36
Moore, S.C.	103	2536	28.49	118	4	13	1	53.00	1- 1	7.75
Morgan, E.J.G.	135	4049	37.84	161	7	23	0	–	–	7.00
Muchall, G.J.	97	2153	29.09	101*	1	10	1	144.00	1-15	5.14
Muchall, P.B.	1	22	22.00	22	–	–	1	34.00	1-34	8.50
Mullaney, S.J.	19	206	17.16	41	–	–	23	19.04	3-13	5.25
Muralitharan, M.	434	924	7.27	33*	–	–	654	22.38	7-30	3.83

L-O	M	Runs	Avge	HS	100	50	Wkts	Avge	Best	Econ
Murphy, D.	8	69	69.00	31*	–	–	–	–	–	7/3
Murtagh, T.J.	115	595	12.14	35*	–	–	165	26.77	4-14	5.18
Mustard, P.	128	3135	29.02	108	2	22	–	–	–	129/31
Myburgh, J.G.	90	2239	29.46	112	1	13	23	60.04	2-22	5.02
Naik, J.K.H.	21	85	9.44	18	–	–	19	36.52	3-21	5.14
Napier, G.R.	196	2370	17.95	79	–	12	225	24.85	6-29	5.08
Nash, C.D.	50	1292	27.48	85	–	8	16	26.18	4-40	5.63
Naved Arif	10	77	19.25	49	–	–	9	40.11	3-19	6.56
Naved-ul-Hasan	170	2094	21.81	74	–	10	261	26.91	6-27	5.24
Needham, J.	41	223	13.11	42	–	–	26	45.23	3-36	5.16
Nel, J.D.	84	202	9.61	36*	–	–	83	35.77	4-25	5.24
New, T.J.	54	1114	26.52	68	–	4	–	–	–	26/7
Newby, O.J.	18	36	6.00	12*	–	–	16	42.31	4-41	5.86
Newman, S.A.	94	2692	30.59	177	4	16	–	–	–	–
Newton, R.I.	8	203	25.37	66	–	1	–	–	–	–
Nixon, P.A.	406	7300	26.35	101	1	33	0	–	–	419/99
Northeast, S.A.	11	159	19.87	69	–	1	–	–	–	–
Onions, G.	53	107	6.68	19	–	–	60	31.96	3-39	5.22
O'Shea, M.P.	17	504	33.60	90	–	3	5	66.80	2-37	6.38
Owen, W.T.	8	35	7.00	12	–	–	13	24.61	5-49	6.53
Palladino, A.P.	35	125	7.81	31	–	–	83	36.15	3-32	5.47
Panesar, M.S.	66	135	10.38	17*	–	–	65	34.24	5-20	4.52
Park, G.T.	38	648	24.92	64	–	1	9	77.42	2-40	5.84
Parnell, W.D.	41	305	19.06	49	–	–	65	28.04	5-48	5.73
Parry, S.D.	22	102	11.33	31	–	–	27	28.55	3-48	4.70
Patel, A.	7	173	24.71	41	–	–	2	17.00	2-34	6.80
Patel, R.H.	1	–	–	–	–	–	0	–	–	7.60
Patel, S.R.	114	2559	31.59	114	2	13	97	27.28	6-13	5.14
Patterson, S.A.	39	83	41.50	25*	–	–	44	32.11	6-32	5.05
Pattinson, D.J.	43	69	6.90	13*	–	–	56	27.05	4-29	5.26
Payne, D.A.	9	25	25.00	13	–	–	22	11.50	7-29	5.07
Peters, S.D.	161	3063	22.19	107	2	18	–	–	–	–
Petersen, A.N.	116	3316	31.88	124	5	22	3	46.66	1-13	5.21
Pettini, M.L.	112	2529	26.07	144	4	17	–	–	–	–
Phillips, B.J.	125	946	18.54	51*	–	1	147	28.34	4-25	4.86
Phillips, T.J.	48	263	15.47	41	–	–	52	23.36	5-34	5.06
Pietersen, K.P.	217	6931	41.75	147	13	41	40	49.95	3-14	5.29
Piolet, S.A.	12	6	3.00	4	–	–	13	24.38	3-34	5.38
Plunkett, L.E.	110	907	18.89	72	–	2	130	31.99	4-15	5.38
Pollard, K.A.	48	1109	27.72	87	–	7	57	21.29	4-32	5.16
Porterfield, W.T.S.	96	3135	34.45	112*	5	17	–	–	–	–
Pothas, N.	235	4552	35.56	114*	3	24	–	–	–	211/53
Powell, M.J.	204	4665	26.96	114*	1	25	1	26.00	1-26	6.50
Poynton, T.	6	52	26.00	24	–	–	–	–	–	5/1
Prior, M.J.	203	4719	27.75	144	4	26	–	–	–	174/27
Procter, L.A.	7	167	41.75	97	–	2	9	22.55	3-29	5.34
Pyrah, R.M.	82	775	19.37	67	–	1	100	24.59	5-50	5.69
Ramprakash, M.R.	407	13273	40.22	147*	17	85	46	29.43	5-38	4.68
Rankin, W.B.	52	50	8.33	9	–	–	70	24.54	4-34	5.02
Rashid, A.U.	55	343	14.29	41*	–	–	43	39.16	3-28	5.04
Rayner, O.P.	20	213	26.62	61	–	1	14	47.85	2-31	5.98
Read, C.M.W.	262	4334	27.60	135	2	15	–	–	–	256/60
Redfern, D.J.	27	496	21.56	57*	–	2	5	37.60	2-10	4.99
Rees, G.P.	21	556	30.88	123*	1	4	–	–	–	–
Riazuddin, H.	17	42	14.00	23*	–	–	11	53.81	2-47	4.81
Richardson, A.	64	105	10.50	21*	–	–	62	35.46	5-35	4.70

L-O	M	Runs	Avge	HS	100	50	Wkts	Avge	Best	Econ
Robson, S.D.	4	69	34.50	48	–	–	–	–	–	–
Rogers, C.J.L.	128	4173	35.66	140	4	28	2	13.00	2-22	6.50
Roland-Jones, T.S.	8	56	14.00	23*	–	–	11	32.90	3-55	5.93
Root, J.E.	1	63	63.00	63	–	1	–	–	–	–
Roy, J.J.	9	104	13.00	60	–	1	0	–	–	12.00
Rushworth, C.	10	16	8.00	7*	–	–	15	17.46	3- 6	4.44
Russell, C.J.	2	–	–	–	–	–	1	68.00	1-23	7.55
Saeed Ajmal	130	296	8.22	33	–	–	184	27.57	5-18	4.49
Sales, D.J.G.	241	6761	34.14	161	4	48	0	–	–	4.78
Sanderson, B.W.	7	12	–	12*	–	–	7	23.85	2-17	5.75
Sayers, J.J.	21	444	23.36	62	–	4	1	71.00	1-31	7.88
Schofield, C.P.	137	1794	23.92	75*	–	8	141	27.35	5-31	5.22
Scollay, T.E.	6	78	13.00	32	–	–	1	21.00	1-21	5.25
Shah, O.A.	325	9406	34.83	134	13	60	27	33.18	4-11	5.89
Shahid Afridi	392	8971	25.63	124	8	49	386	23.39	6-38	4.63
Shahzad, A.	30	149	14.90	43*	–	–	39	29.20	5-51	4.82
Shakib Al Hasan	117	3057	31.51	134*	4	19	132	30.37	4-30	4.20
Shantry, A.J.	12	48	16.00	19*	–	–	13	25.00	5-37	4.77
Shantry, J.D.	17	42	14.00	18	–	–	23	30.39	3-33	6.04
Shreck, C.E.	52	45	6.42	9*	–	–	63	31.90	5-19	5.22
Sidebottom, R.J.	173	500	11.36	32	–	–	178	31.30	6-40	4.36
Simpson, J.A.	18	327	25.15	82	–	1	–	–	–	11/4
Smith, D.R.	133	2274	21.86	96	–	14	94	33.22	6-29	4.84
Smith, G.M.	62	1346	23.61	88	–	5	49	33.73	4-53	5.75
Smith, G.P.	10	139	15.44	58	–	1	–	–	–	–
Smith, T.C.	45	742	26.50	87*	–	6	57	25.73	3- 8	4.96
Smith, T.M.J.	18	118	19.66	65	–	1	15	41.13	3-26	5.66
Smith, W.R.	70	1527	25.45	103	1	11	2	25.50	1- 6	5.77
Solanki, V.S.	362	9775	31.94	164*	14	55	28	34.75	4-14	5.23
Spriegel, M.N.W.	36	794	37.80	81*	–	6	20	47.10	2-23	5.38
Stevens, D.I.	218	5454	30.30	133	4	36	51	35.41	5-32	4.96
Stirling, P.R.	37	1130	31.38	177	1	8	10	29.90	4-11	4.54
Stokes, B.A.	13	204	18.54	39	–	–	5	15.80	2-22	5.64
Stoneman, M.D.	5	94	18.80	25	–	–	–	–	–	–
Strauss, A.J.	240	7118	32.50	163	9	46	0	–	–	3.00
Styris, S.B.	312	7667	33.33	141	5	52	287	30.36	6-25	4.60
Suppiah, A.V.	68	1347	28.06	80	–	7	35	34.00	4-39	5.78
Sutton, L.D.	159	2055	19.75	83	–	6	–	–	–	176/24
Swann, G.P.	230	2945	19.00	83	–	14	259	25.94	5-17	4.41
Tahir, N.S.	15	19	9.50	13*	–	–	5	87.80	2-47	5.03
Tait, S.W.	88	108	6.75	22*	–	–	162	23.27	8-43	5.08
Taylor, C.G.	169	3383	26.02	105	1	20	16	38.31	2- 5	5.25
Taylor, J.W.A.	81	1150	46.00	103*	2	7	5	34.00	4-61	7.39
ten Doeschate, R.N.	126	3328	46.87	134*	5	19	125	26.55	5-50	5.48
Thomas, A.C.	134	504	14.82	28*	–	–	178	27.62	4-18	5.08
Thorp, C.D.	38	286	16.82	52	–	1	47	27.36	6-17	4.37
Thorpe, J.A.	1	3	–	3*	–	–	1	26.00	1-26	8.66
Tomlinson, J.A.	27	34	3.77	14	–	–	29	31.37	4-47	5.01
Tredwell, J.C.	152	1253	18.15	88	–	4	144	33.39	6-27	4.71
Trego, P.D.	108	1581	22.26	147	1	6	111	31.81	5-40	5.57
Tremlett, C.T.	119	509	10.38	38*	–	–	164	27.02	4-25	4.85
Trescothick, M.E.	334	11136	37.62	184	27	55	57	28.84	4-50	4.90
Trott, I.J.L.	173	5952	45.78	125*	12	40	52	25.59	4-55	5.61
Troughton, J.O.	137	3130	29.25	115*	2	18	25	25.76	4-23	5.25
Turner, M.L.	22	49	12.25	15*	–	–	31	26.45	4-36	6.13
Vaas, W.P.J.U.C.	392	2903	16.12	76*	–	6	480	26.97	8-19	4.14

L-O	M	Runs	Avge	HS	100	50	Wkts	Avge	Best	Econ
van Jaarsveld, M.	261	8361	41.39	132*	15	52	35	36.94	3-13	5.27
Vince, J.M.	17	520	32.50	93	–	3	–	–	–	–
Vincent, L.	199	5119	28.43	172	7	27	4	61.25	2-25	6.04
Voges, A.C.	103	3219	41.26	104*	2	25	22	49.63	3-25	5.26
Wagg, G.G.	76	901	17.32	48*	–	–	86	30.60	4-35	5.47
Wagh, M.A.	113	2720	27.20	102*	1	21	25	34.48	4-35	4.71
Wainwright, D.J.	41	136	17.00	26	–	–	33	35.87	3-26	4.75
Wakely, A.G.	21	256	14.22	35	–	–	2	10.00	2-14	5.00
Walker, M.J.	280	6153	28.61	117	3	36	30	25.30	4-24	5.03
Wallace, M.A.	153	1829	19.45	85	–	3	–	–	–	142/38
Waller, M.T.C.	16	12	12.00	5	–	–	11	42.27	2-24	5.53
Walters, S.J.	45	1000	28.57	91	–	6	3	59.66	1-12	6.50
Waters, H.T.	20	24	4.80	8	–	–	14	57.78	3-47	6.22
Wells, L.W.P.	1	9	9.00	9	–	–	–	–	–	–
Wernars, K.O.	2	41	41.00	28*	–	–	0	–	–	9.16
Westley, T.	6	41	10.25	36	–	–	1	59.00	1-34	5.36
Westwood, I.J.	59	929	23.22	65	–	3	3	71.66	1-28	5.11
Wheater, A.J.	7	96	48.00	55*	–	1	–	–	–	1/–
Whelan, C.D.	24	41	4.10	11	–	–	27	28.07	4-27	6.06
White, G.G.	20	52	7.42	14	–	–	21	26.28	5-35	5.24
White, R.A.	83	1782	23.44	111	2	10	2	27.50	2-18	6.11
White, W.A.	36	345	20.29	46*	–	–	31	38.48	6-29	6.25
Whiteley, R.A.	4	41	13.66	24	–	–	0	–	–	7.00
Willey, D.J.	18	149	12.41	25	–	–	6	56.33	2-40	5.84
Williams, R.E.M.	6	2	–	2*	–	–	2	124.00	2-60	8.04
Willoughby, C.M.	209	147	5.06	15	–	–	255	27.81	6-16	4.18
Wilson, G.C.	70	1287	22.57	113	1	9	–	–	–	51/15
Woakes, C.R.	40	191	13.64	49*	–	–	37	36.05	4-38	5.22
Wood, C.P.	10	5	1.25	3	–	–	18	20.44	4-35	5.17
Wright, B.J.	49	966	24.15	79	–	5	1	126.00	1-19	5.72
Wright, C.J.C.	59	121	8.06	23	–	–	51	41.52	3- 3	5.59
Wright, D.G.	104	929	16.89	55	–	4	128	28.98	5-37	4.19
Wright, L.J.	140	2069	22.98	125	1	5	100	38.26	4-12	5.28
Wyatt, A.C.F.	4	1	1.00	1	–	–	3	41.00	1-24	6.36
Yardy, M.H.	165	2893	23.90	98*	–	19	102	38.53	6-27	4.92
Yasir Arafat	207	2333	21.20	110*	1	7	330	24.88	6-24	4.93
Young, E.G.C.	8	47	9.40	25	–	–	3	68.66	2-42	5.61
Younus Khan	264	7684	34.45	144	10	48	27	38.33	3- 5	5.72

FIRST-CLASS CRICKET RECORDS

To the end of the 2010 season

TEAM RECORDS

HIGHEST INNINGS TOTALS

1107	Victoria v New South Wales	Melbourne	1926-27
1059	Victoria v Tasmania	Melbourne	1922-23
952-6d	Sri Lanka v India	Colombo	1997-98
951-7d	Sind v Baluchistan	Karachi	1973-74
944-6d	Hyderabad v Andhra	Secunderabad	1993-94
918	New South Wales v South Australia	Sydney	1900-01
912-8d	Holkar v Mysore	Indore	1945-46
910-6d	Railways v Dera Ismail Khan	Lahore	1964-65
903-7d	England v Australia	The Oval	1938
900-6d	Queensland v Victoria	Brisbane	2005-06
887	Yorkshire v Warwickshire	Birmingham	1896
863	Lancashire v Surrey	The Oval	1990
860-6d	Tamil Nadu v Goa	Panjim	1988-89
850-7d	Somerset v Middlesex	Taunton	2007

Excluding penalty runs in India, there have been 34 innings totals of 800 runs or more in first-class cricket. Tamil Nadu's total of 860-6d was boosted to 912 by 52 penalty runs.

HIGHEST SECOND INNINGS TOTAL

770	New South Wales v South Australia	Adelaide	1920-21

HIGHEST FOURTH INNINGS TOTAL

654-5	England (set 696 to win) v South Africa	Durban	1938-39

HIGHEST MATCH AGGREGATE

2376-37	Maharashtra v Bombay	Poona	1948-49

RECORD MARGIN OF VICTORY

Innings and 851 runs: Railways v Dera Ismail Khan	Lahore	1964-65

MOST RUNS IN A DAY

721	Australians v Essex	Southend	1948

MOST HUNDREDS IN AN INNINGS

6	Holkar v Mysore	Indore	1945-46

LOWEST INNINGS TOTALS

12	†Oxford University v MCC and Ground	Oxford	1877
12	Northamptonshire v Gloucestershire	Gloucester	1907
13	Auckland v Canterbury	Auckland	1877-78
13	Nottinghamshire v Yorkshire	Nottingham	1901
14	Surrey v Essex	Chelmsford	1983
15	MCC v Surrey	Lord's	1839
15	†Victoria v MCC	Melbourne	1903-04
15	†Northamptonshire v Yorkshire	Northampton	1908
15	Hampshire v Warwickshire	Birmingham	1922

† Batted one man short

There have been 27 instances of a team being dismissed for under 20.

LOWEST MATCH AGGREGATE BY ONE TEAM

34 (16 and 18) Border v Natal   East London   1959-60

LOWEST COMPLETED MATCH AGGREGATE BY BOTH TEAMS

105   MCC v Australians   Lord's   1878

FEWEST RUNS IN AN UNINTERRUPTED DAY'S PLAY

95   Australia (80) v Pakistan (15-2)   Karachi   1956-57

TIED MATCHES

Before 1949 a match was considered to be tied if the scores were level after the fourth innings, even if the side batting last had wickets in hand when play ended. Law 22 was amended in 1948 and since then a match has been tied only when the scores are level after the fourth innings has been completed. There have been 56 tied first-class matches, five of which would not have qualified under the current law. The most recent are:

Warwickshire (446-7d & forfeit) v Essex (66-0d & 380)   Birmingham   2003
Worcestershire (262 & 247) v Zimbabweans (334 & 175)   Worcester   2003

BATTING RECORDS
HIGHEST INDIVIDUAL INNINGS

501*	B.C.Lara	Warwickshire v Durham	Birmingham	1994
499	Hanif Mohammed	Karachi v Bahawalpur	Karachi	1958-59
452*	D.G.Bradman	New South Wales v Queensland	Sydney	1929-30
443*	B.B.Nimbalkar	Maharashtra v Kathiawar	Poona	1948-49
437	W.H.Ponsford	Victoria v Queensland	Melbourne	1927-28
429	W.H.Ponsford	Victoria v Tasmania	Melbourne	1922-23
428	Aftab Baloch	Sind v Baluchistan	Karachi	1973-74
424	A.C.MacLaren	Lancashire v Somerset	Taunton	1895
405*	G.A.Hick	Worcestershire v Somerset	Taunton	1988
400*	B.C.Lara	West Indies v England	St John's	2003-04
394	Naved Latif	Sargodha v Gujranwala	Gujranwala	2000-01
390	S.C.Cook	Lions v Warriors	East London	2009-10
385	B.Sutcliffe	Otago v Canterbury	Christchurch	1952-53
383	C.W.Gregory	New South Wales v Queensland	Brisbane	1906-07
380	M.L.Hayden	Australia v Zimbabwe	Perth	2003-04
377	S.V.Manjrekar	Bombay v Hyderabad	Bombay	1990-91
375	B.C.Lara	West Indies v England	St John's	1993-94
374	D.P.M.D.Jayawardena	Sri Lanka v South Africa	Colombo	2006
369	D.G.Bradman	South Australia v Tasmania	Adelaide	1935-36
366	N.H.Fairbrother	Lancashire v Surrey	The Oval	1990
366	M.V.Sridhar	Hyderabad v Andhra	Secunderabad	1993-94
365*	C.Hill	South Australia v NSW	Adelaide	1900-01
365*	G.St A.Sobers	West Indies v Pakistan	Kingston	1957-58
364	L.Hutton	England v Australia	The Oval	1938
359*	V.M.Merchant	Bombay v Maharashtra	Bombay	1943-44
359	R.B.Simpson	New South Wales v Queensland	Brisbane	1963-64
357*	R.Abel	Surrey v Somerset	The Oval	1899
357	D.G.Bradman	South Australia v Victoria	Melbourne	1935-36
356	B.A.Richards	South Australia v W Australia	Perth	1970-71
355*	G.R.Marsh	W Australia v S Australia	Perth	1989-90
355	B.Sutcliffe	Otago v Auckland	Dunedin	1949-50
353	V.V.S.Laxman	Hyderabad v Karnataka	Bangalore	1999-00
352	W.H.Ponsford	Victoria v New South Wales	Melbourne	1926-27
350	Rashid Israr	Habib Bank v National Bank	Lahore	1976-77

There have been 177 triple hundreds in first-class cricket, W.V.Raman (313) and Arjan Kripal Singh (302*) for Tamil Nadu v Goa at Panjim in 1988-89 providing the only instance of two batsmen scoring 300 in the same innings.

MOST HUNDREDS IN SUCCESSIVE INNINGS

6	C.B.Fry	Sussex and Rest of England		1901
6	D.G.Bradman	South Australia and D.G.Bradman's XI		1938-39
6	M.J.Procter	Rhodesia		1970-71

TWO DOUBLE HUNDREDS IN A MATCH

244	202*	A.E.Fagg	Kent v Essex	Colchester	1938

TRIPLE HUNDRED AND HUNDRED IN A MATCH

333	123	G.A.Gooch	England v India	Lord's	1990

DOUBLE HUNDRED AND HUNDRED IN A MATCH MOST TIMES

4	Zaheer Abbas	Gloucestershire	1976-81

TWO HUNDREDS IN A MATCH MOST TIMES

8	Zaheer Abbas	Gloucestershire and PIA	1976-82
8	R.T.Ponting	Tasmania, Australia and Australians	1992-2006
7	W.R.Hammond	Gloucestershire, England and MCC	1927-45

MOST HUNDREDS IN A SEASON

18	D.C.S.Compton	1947	16	J.B.Hobbs	1925

100 HUNDREDS IN A CAREER

	Total		100th Hundred	
	Hundreds	Inns	Season	Inns
J.B.Hobbs	197	1315	1923	821
E.H.Hendren	170	1300	1928-29	740
W.R.Hammond	167	1005	1935	679
C.P.Mead	153	1340	1927	892
G.Boycott	151	1014	1977	645
H.Sutcliffe	149	1088	1932	700
F.E.Woolley	145	1532	1929	1031
G.A.Hick	136	871	1998	574
L.Hutton	129	814	1951	619
G.A.Gooch	128	990	1992-93	820
W.G.Grace	126	1493	1895	1113
D.C.S.Compton	123	839	1952	552
T.W.Graveney	122	1223	1964	940
D.G.Bradman	117	338	1947-48	295
I.V.A.Richards	114	796	1988-89	658
M.R.Ramprakash	113	729	2008	676
Zaheer Abbas	108	768	1982-83	658
A.Sandham	107	1000	1935	871
M.C.Cowdrey	107	1130	1973	1035
T.W.Hayward	104	1138	1913	1076
G.M.Turner	103	792	1982	779
J.H.Edrich	103	979	1977	945
L.E.G.Ames	102	951	1950	915
G.E.Tyldesley	102	961	1934	919
D.L.Amiss	102	1139	1986	1081

MOST 400s: 2 – B.C.Lara, W.H.Ponsford
MOST 300s or more: 6 – D.G.Bradman; 4 – W.R.Hammond, W.H.Ponsford
MOST 200s or more: 37 – D.G.Bradman; 36 – W.R.Hammond; 22 – E.H.Hendren

MOST RUNS IN A MONTH

1294 (avge 92.42)   L.Hutton   Yorkshire   June 1949

MOST RUNS IN A SEASON

Runs			I	NO	HS	Avge	100	Season
3816	D.C.S.Compton	Middlesex	50	8	246	90.85	18	1947
3539	W.J.Edrich	Middlesex	52	8	267*	80.43	12	1947
3518	T.W.Hayward	Surrey	61	8	219	66.37	13	1906

The feat of scoring 3000 runs in a season has been achieved 28 times, the most recent instance being by W.E.Alley (3019) in 1961. The highest aggregate in a season since 1969 is 2755 by S.J.Cook in 1991.

1000 RUNS IN A SEASON MOST TIMES

28   W.G.Grace (Gloucestershire), F.E.Woolley (Kent)

HIGHEST BATTING AVERAGE IN A SEASON

(Qualification: 12 innings)

Avge			I	NO	HS	Runs	100	Season
115.66	D.G.Bradman	Australians	26	5	278	2429	13	1938
104.66	D.R.Martyn	Australians	14	5	176*	942	5	2001
103.54	M.R.Ramprakash	Surrey	24	2	301*	2278	8	2006
102.53	G.Boycott	Yorkshire	20	5	175*	1538	6	1979
102.00	W.A.Johnston	Australians	17	16	28*	102	–	1953
101.70	G.A.Gooch	Essex	30	3	333	2746	12	1990
101.30	M.R.Ramprakash	Surrey	25	5	266*	2026	10	2007
100.12	G.Boycott	Yorkshire	30	5	233	2503	13	1971

FASTEST HUNDRED AGAINST AUTHENTIC BOWLING

35 min   P.G.H.Fender   Surrey v Northamptonshire   Northampton   1920

FASTEST DOUBLE HUNDRED

113 min   R.J.Shastri   Bombay v Baroda   Bombay   1984-85

FASTEST TRIPLE HUNDRED

181 min   D.C.S.Compton   MCC v NE Transvaal   Benoni   1948-49

MOST SIXES IN AN INNINGS

16   A.Symonds   Gloucestershire v Glamorgan   Abergavenny   1995

MOST SIXES IN A MATCH

20   A.Symonds   Gloucestershire v Glamorgan   Abergavenny   1995

MOST SIXES IN A SEASON

80   I.T.Botham   Somerset and England   1985

MOST FOURS IN AN INNINGS

72   B.C.Lara   Warwickshire v Durham   Birmingham   1994

MOST RUNS OFF ONE OVER

| 36 | G.St A.Sobers | Nottinghamshire v Glamorgan | Swansea | 1968 |
| 36 | R.J.Shastri | Bombay v Baroda | Bombay | 1984-85 |

Both batsmen hit for six all six balls of overs bowled by M.A.Nash and Tilak Raj respectively.

MOST RUNS IN A DAY

390*   B.C.Lara   Warwickshire v Durham   Birmingham   1994

There have been 19 instances of a batsman scoring 300 or more runs in a day.

1015 min R.Nayyar (271) Himachal Pradesh v Jammu & Kashmir Chamba 1999-00

HIGHEST PARTNERSHIPS FOR EACH WICKET

First Wicket

561	Waheed Mirza/Mansoor Akhtar	Karachi W v Quetta	Karachi	1976-77
555	P.Holmes/H.Sutcliffe	Yorkshire v Essex	Leyton	1932
554	J.T.Brown/J.Tunnicliffe	Yorkshire v Derbys	Chesterfield	1898

Second Wicket

580	Rafatullah Mohmand/Aamer Sajjad	WAPDA v SSGC	Sheikhupura	2009-10
576	S.T.Jayasuriya/R.S.Mahanama	Sri Lanka v India	Colombo	1997-98
480	E.Elgar/R.R.Rossouw	Eagles v Titans	Centurion	2009-10
475	Zahir Alam/L.S.Rajput	Assam v Tripura	Gauhati	1991-92
465*	J.A.Jameson/R.B.Kanhai	Warwickshire v Glos	Birmingham	1974

Third Wicket

624	K.C.Sangakkara/D.P.M.D.Jayawardena	Sri Lanka v South Africa	Colombo	2006
467	A.H.Jones/M.D.Crowe	N Zealand v Sri Lanka	Wellington	1990-91
459	C.J.L.Rogers/M.J.North	W Australia v Victoria	Perth	2006-07
456	Khalid Irtiza/Aslam Ali	United Bank v Multan	Karachi	1975-76
451	Mudassar Nazar/Javed Miandad	Pakistan v India	Hyderabad	1982-83
445	P.E.Whitelaw/W.N.Carson	Auckland v Otago	Dunedin	1936-37
438*	G.A.Hick/T.M.Moody	Worcestershire v Hants	Southampton	1997

Fourth Wicket

577	V.S.Hazare/Gul Mahomed	Baroda v Holkar	Baroda	1946-47
574*	C.L.Walcott/F.M.M.Worrell	Barbados v Trinidad	Port-of-Spain	1945-46
502*	F.M.M.Worrell/J.D.C.Goddard	Barbados v Trinidad	Bridgetown	1943-44
470	A.I.Kallicharran/G.W.Humpage	Warwickshire v Lancs	Southport	1982

Fifth Wicket

520*	C.A.Pujara/R.A.Jadeja	Saurashtra v Orissa	Rajkot	2008-09
464*	M.E.Waugh/S.R.Waugh	NSW v W Australia	Perth	1990-91
420	Mohd. Ashraful/Marshall Ayub	Dhaka v Chittagong	Chittagong	2006-07
410*	A.S.Chopra/S.Badrinath	India A v South Africa A	Delhi	2007-08
405	S.G.Barnes/D.G.Bradman	Australia v England	Sydney	1946-47
401	M.B.Loye/D.Ripley	Northants v Glamorgan	Northampton	1998

Sixth Wicket

487*	G.A.Headley/C.C.Passailaigue	Jamaica v Tennyson's	Kingston	1931-32
428	W.W.Armstrong/M.A.Noble	Australians v Sussex	Hove	1902
411	R.M.Poore/E.G.Wynyard	Hampshire v Somerset	Taunton	1899

Seventh Wicket

460	Bhupinder Singh jr/P.Dharmani	Punjab v Delhi	Delhi	1994-95
347	D.St E.Atkinson/C.C.Depeiza	W Indies v Australia	Bridgetown	1954-55
344	K.S.Ranjitsinhji/W.Newham	Sussex v Essex	Leyton	1902

Eighth Wicket

433	V.T.Trumper/A.Sims	Australians v C'bury	Christchurch	1913-14
332	I.J.L.Trott/S.C.J.Broad	England v Pakistan	Lord's	2010
313	Wasim Akram/Saqlain Mushtaq	Pakistan v Zimbabwe	Sheikhupura	1996-97

Ninth Wicket

283	J.Chapman/A.Warren	Derbys v Warwicks	Blackwell	1910
268	J.B.Commins/N.Boje	SA 'A' v Mashonaland	Harare	1994-95
251	J.W.H.T.Douglas/S.N.Hare	Essex v Derbyshire	Leyton	1921

Tenth Wicket

307	A.F.Kippax/J.E.H.Hooker	NSW v Victoria	Melbourne	1928-29
249	C.T.Sarwate/S.N.Banerjee	Indians v Surrey	The Oval	1946
239	Aqil Arshad/Ali Raza	Lahore Whites v Hyderabad	Lahore	2004-05
235	F.E.Woolley/A.Fielder	Kent v Worcs	Stourbridge	1909

35,000 RUNS IN A CAREER

	Career	I	NO	HS	Runs	Avge	100
J.B.Hobbs	1905-34	1315	106	316*	**61237**	50.65	197
F.E.Woolley	1906-38	1532	85	305*	**58969**	40.75	145
E.H.Hendren	1907-38	1300	166	301*	**57611**	50.80	170
C.P.Mead	1905-36	1340	185	280*	**55061**	47.67	153
W.G.Grace	1865-1908	1493	105	344	**54896**	39.55	126
W.R.Hammond	1920-51	1005	104	336*	**50551**	56.10	167
H.Sutcliffe	1919-45	1088	123	313	**50138**	51.95	149
G.Boycott	1962-86	1014	162	261*	**48426**	56.83	151
T.W.Graveney	1948-71/72	1223	159	258	**47793**	44.91	122
G.A.Gooch	1973-2000	990	75	333	**44846**	49.01	128
T.W.Hayward	1893-1914	1138	96	315*	**43551**	41.79	104
D.L.Amiss	1960-87	1139	126	262*	**43423**	42.86	102
M.C.Cowdrey	1950-76	1130	134	307	**42719**	42.89	107
A.Sandham	1911-37/38	1000	79	325	**41284**	44.82	107
G.A.Hick	1983/84-2008	871	84	405*	**41112**	52.23	136
L.Hutton	1934-60	814	91	364	**40140**	55.51	129
M.J.K.Smith	1951-75	1091	139	204	**39832**	41.84	69
W.Rhodes	1898-1930	1528	237	267*	**39802**	30.83	58
J.H.Edrich	1956-78	979	104	310*	**39790**	45.47	103
R.E.S.Wyatt	1923-57	1141	157	232	**39405**	40.04	85
D.C.S.Compton	1936-64	839	88	300	**38942**	51.85	123
G.E.Tyldesley	1909-36	961	106	256*	**38874**	45.46	102
J.T.Tyldesley	1895-1923	994	62	295*	**37897**	40.60	86
K.W.R.Fletcher	1962-88	1167	170	228*	**37665**	37.77	63
C.G.Greenidge	1970-92	889	75	273*	**37354**	45.88	92
J.W.Hearne	1909-36	1025	116	285*	**37252**	40.98	96
L.E.G.Ames	1926-51	951	95	295	**37248**	43.51	102
D.Kenyon	1946-67	1159	59	259	**37002**	33.63	74
W.J.Edrich	1934-58	964	92	267*	**36965**	42.39	86
J.M.Parks	1949-76	1227	172	205*	**36673**	34.76	51
M.W.Gatting	1975-98	861	123	258	**36549**	49.52	94
D.Denton	1894-1920	1163	70	221	**36479**	33.37	69
G.H.Hirst	1891-1929	1215	151	341	**36323**	34.13	60
I.V.A.Richards	1971/72-93	796	63	322	**36212**	49.40	114
A.Jones	1957-83	1168	72	204*	**36049**	32.89	56
W.G.Quaife	1894-1928	1203	185	255*	**36012**	35.37	72
R.E.Marshall	1945/46-72	1053	59	228*	**35725**	35.94	68
G.Gunn	1902-32	1061	82	220	**35208**	35.96	62

BOWLING RECORDS
ALL TEN WICKETS IN AN INNINGS

This feat has been achieved 81 times in first-class matches (excluding 12-a-side fixtures).

Three Times: A.P.Freeman (1929, 1930, 1931)
Twice: V.E.Walker (1859, 1865); H.Verity (1931, 1932); J.C.Laker (1956)

Instances since 1945:

W.E.Hollies	Warwickshire v Notts	Birmingham	1946
J.M.Sims	East v West	Kingston on Thames	1948
J.K.R.Graveney	Gloucestershire v Derbyshire	Chesterfield	1949
T.E.Bailey	Essex v Lancashire	Clacton	1949
R.Berry	Lancashire v Worcestershire	Blackpool	1953
S.P.Gupte	President's XI v Combined XI	Bombay	1954-55
J.C.Laker	Surrey v Australians	The Oval	1956
K.Smales	Nottinghamshire v Glos	Stroud	1956
G.A.R.Lock	Surrey v Kent	Blackheath	1956

J.C.Laker	England v Australia	Manchester	1956
P.M.Chatterjee	Bengal v Assam	Jorhat	1956-57
J.D.Bannister	Warwicks v Combined Services	Birmingham (M & B)	1959
A.J.G.Pearson	Cambridge U v Leicestershire	Loughborough	1961
N.I.Thomson	Sussex v Warwickshire	Worthing	1964
P.J.Allan	Queensland v Victoria	Melbourne	1965-66
I.J.Brayshaw	Western Australia v Victoria	Perth	1967-68
Shahid Mahmood	Karachi Whites v Khairpur	Karachi	1969-70
E.E.Hemmings	International XI v W Indians	Kingston	1982-83
P.Sunderam	Rajasthan v Vidarbha	Jodhpur	1985-86
S.T.Jefferies	Western Province v OFS	Cape Town	1987-88
Imran Adil	Bahawalpur v Faisalabad	Faisalabad	1989-90
G.P.Wickremasinghe	Sinhalese v Kalutara	Colombo	1991-92
R.L.Johnson	Middlesex v Derbyshire	Derby	1994
Naeem Akhtar	Rawalpindi B v Peshawar	Peshawar	1995-96
A.Kumble	India v Pakistan	Delhi	1998-99
D.S.Mohanty	East Zone v South Zone	Agartala	2000-01
O.D.Gibson	Durham v Hampshire	Chester-le-Street	2007
M.W.Olivier	Warriors v Eagles	Bloemfontein	2007-08
Zulfiqar Babar	Multan v Islamabad	Multan	2009-10

MOST WICKETS IN A MATCH

19	J.C.Laker	England v Australia	Manchester	1956

MOST WICKETS IN A SEASON

Wkts		Season	Matches	Overs	Mdns	Runs	Avge
304	A.P.Freeman	1928	37	1976.1	423	5489	18.05
298	A.P.Freeman	1933	33	2039	651	4549	15.26

The feat of taking 250 wickets in a season has been achieved on 12 occasions, the last instance been by A.P.Freeman in 1933. 200 or more wickets in a season have been taken on 59 occasions, the last being by G.A.R.Lock (212 wickets, average 12.02) in 1957.

The highest aggregates of wickets taken in a season since the reduction of County Championship matches in 1969 are as follows:

Wkts		Season	Matches	Overs	Mdns	Runs	Avge
134	M.D.Marshall	1982	22	822	225	2108	15.73
131	L.R.Gibbs	1971	23	1024.1	295	2475	18.89
125	F.D.Stephenson	1988	22	819.1	196	2289	18.31
121	R.D.Jackman	1980	23	746.2	220	1864	15.40

Since 1969 there have been 50 instances of bowlers taking 100 wickets in a season.

MOST HAT-TRICKS IN A CAREER

7	D.V.P.Wright
6	T.W.J.Goddard, C.W.L.Parker
5	S.Haigh, V.W.C.Jupp, A.E.G.Rhodes, F.A.Tarrant

2000 WICKETS IN A CAREER

	Career	Runs	Wkts	Avge	100w
W.Rhodes	1898-1930	69993	4187	16.71	23
A.P.Freeman	1914-36	69577	3776	18.42	17
C.W.L.Parker	1903-35	63817	3278	19.46	16
J.T.Hearne	1888-1923	54352	3061	17.75	15
T.W.J.Goddard	1922-52	59116	2979	19.84	16
W.G.Grace	1865-1908	51545	2876	17.92	10
A.S.Kennedy	1907-36	61034	2874	21.23	15
D.Shackleton	1948-69	53303	2857	18.65	20
G.A.R.Lock	1946-70/71	54709	2844	19.23	14
F.J.Titmus	1949-82	63313	2830	22.37	16

	Career	Runs	Wkts	Avge	100w
M.W.Tate	1912-37	50571	2784	18.16	13+1
G.H.Hirst	1891-1929	51282	2739	18.72	15
C.Blythe	1899-1914	42136	2506	16.81	14
D.L.Underwood	1963-87	49993	2465	20.28	10
W.E.Astill	1906-39	57783	2431	23.76	9
J.C.White	1909-37	43759	2356	18.57	14
W.E.Hollies	1932-57	48656	2323	20.94	14
F.S.Trueman	1949-69	42154	2304	18.29	12
J.B.Statham	1950-68	36999	2260	16.37	13
R.T.D.Perks	1930-55	53771	2233	24.07	16
J.Briggs	1879-1900	35431	2221	15.95	12
D.J.Shepherd	1950-72	47302	2218	21.32	12
E.G.Dennett	1903-26	42571	2147	19.82	12
T.Richardson	1892-1905	38794	2104	18.43	10
T.E.Bailey	1945-67	48170	2082	23.13	9
R.Illingworth	1951-83	42023	2072	20.28	10
F.E.Woolley	1906-38	41066	2068	19.85	8
N.Gifford	1960-88	48731	2068	23.56	4
G.Geary	1912-38	41339	2063	20.03	11
D.V.P.Wright	1932-57	49307	2056	23.98	10
J.A.Newman	1906-30	51111	2032	25.15	9
A.Shaw	1864-97	24580	2026+1	12.12	9
S.Haigh	1895-1913	32091	2012	15.94	11

ALL-ROUND RECORDS
THE 'DOUBLE'

3000 runs and 100 wickets: J.H.Parks (1937)

2000 runs and 200 wickets: G.H.Hirst (1906)

2000 runs and 100 wickets: F.E.Woolley (4), J.W.Hearne (3), W.G.Grace (2), G.H.Hirst (2), W.Rhodes (2), T.E.Bailey, D.E.Davies, G.L.Jessop, V.W.C.Jupp, J.Langridge, F.A.Tarrant, C.L.Townsend, L.F.Townsend

1000 runs and 200 wickets: M.W.Tate (3), A.E.Trott (2), A.S.Kennedy

Most Doubles: 16 – W.Rhodes; 14 – G.H.Hirst; 10 – V.W.C.Jupp

Double in Debut Season: D.B.Close (1949) – aged 18, the youngest to achieve this feat.

The feat of scoring 1000 runs and taking 100 wickets in a season has been achieved on 305 occasions, R.J.Hadlee (1984) and F.D.Stephenson (1988) being the only players to complete the 'double' since the reduction of County Championship matches in 1969.

WICKET-KEEPING RECORDS
EIGHT DISMISSALS IN AN INNINGS

9	(8ct, 1st)	Tahir Rashid	Habib Bank v PACO	Gujranwala	1992-93
9	(7ct, 2st)	W.R.James	Matabeleland v Mashonaland CD	Bulawayo	1995-96
8	(8ct)	A.T.W.Grout	Queensland v W Australia	Brisbane	1959-60
8	(8ct)	D.E.East	Essex v Somerset	Taunton	1985
8	(8ct)	S.A.Marsh	Kent v Middlesex	Lord's	1991
8	(6ct, 2st)	T.J.Zoehrer	Australians v Surrey	The Oval	1993
8	(7ct, 1st)	D.S.Berry	Victoria v South Australia	Melbourne	1996-97
8	(7ct, 1st)	Y.S.S.Mendis	Bloomfield v Kurunegala Youth	Colombo	2000-01
8	(7ct, 1st)	S.Nath	Assam v Tripura (on debut)	Gauhati	2001-02
8	(8ct)	J.N.Batty	Surrey v Kent	The Oval	2004
8	(8ct)	Golam Mabud	Sylhet v Dhaka	Dhaka	2005-06
8	(8ct)	D.C.de Boorder	Otago v Wellington	Wellington	2009-10

TWELVE DISMISSALS IN A MATCH

13	(11ct, 2st)	W.R.James	Matabeleland v Mashonaland CD	Bulawayo	1995-96
12	(8ct, 4st)	E.Pooley	Surrey v Sussex	The Oval	1868
12	(9ct, 3st)	D.Tallon	Queensland v NSW	Sydney	1938-39
12	(9ct, 3st)	H.B.Taber	NSW v South Australia	Adelaide	1968-69
12	(12ct)	P.D.McGlashan	Northern Districts v Central Districts	Whangarei	2009-10

MOST DISMISSALS IN A SEASON

128 (79ct, 49st) L.E.G.Ames   1929

1000 DISMISSALS IN A CAREER

	Career	Dismissals	Ct	St
R.W.Taylor	1960-88	**1649**	1473	176
J.T.Murray	1952-75	**1527**	1270	257
H.Strudwick	1902-27	**1497**	1242	255
A.P.E.Knott	1964-85	**1344**	1211	133
R.C.Russell	1981-2004	**1320**	1192	128
F.H.Huish	1895-1914	**1310**	933	377
B.Taylor	1949-73	**1294**	1083	211
S.J.Rhodes	1981-2004	**1263**	1139	124
D.Hunter	1889-1909	**1253**	906	347
H.R.Butt	1890-1912	**1228**	953	275
J.H.Board	1891-1914/15	**1207**	852	355
H.Elliott	1920-47	**1206**	904	302
J.M.Parks	1949-76	**1181**	948	178
R.Booth	1951-70	**1126**	1088	93
L.E.G.Ames	1926-51	**1121**	703	418
D.L.Bairstow	1970-90	**1099**	961	138
G.Duckworth	1923-47	**1096**	753	343
H.W.Stephenson	1948-64	**1082**	748	334
J.G.Binks	1955-75	**1071**	895	176
T.G.Evans	1939-69	**1066**	816	250
A.Long	1960-80	**1046**	922	124
G.O.Dawkes	1937-61	**1043**	895	148
R.W.Tolchard	1965-83	**1037**	912	125
W.L.Cornford	1921-47	**1017**	675	342

FIELDING RECORDS
MOST CATCHES IN AN INNINGS

7	M.J.Stewart	Surrey v Northamptonshire	Northampton	1957
7	A.S.Brown	Gloucestershire v Nottinghamshire	Nottingham	1966

MOST CATCHES IN A MATCH

10	W.R.Hammond	Gloucestershire v Surrey	Cheltenham	1928

MOST CATCHES IN A SEASON

78	W.R.Hammond	1928	77	M.J.Stewart	1957

750 CATCHES IN A CAREER

1018	F.E.Woolley	1906-38	784	J.G.Langridge	1928-55
887	W.G.Grace	1865-1908	764	W.Rhodes	1898-1930
830	G.A.R.Lock	1946-70/71	758	C.A.Milton	1948-74
819	W.R.Hammond	1920-51	754	E.H.Hendren	1907-38
813	D.B.Close	1949-86			

ENGLAND LIMITED-OVERS INTERNATIONALS 2010

PAKISTAN v ENGLAND

TWENTY20 INTERNATIONALS
Dubai International Cricket Stadium, 19 February. Toss: Pakistan. **ENGLAND** won by seven wickets. Pakistan 129-8 (20). England 130-3 (18.3; E.J.G.Morgan 67*). Award: E.J.G.Morgan.

Dubai International Cricket Stadium, 20 February. Toss: Pakistan. **PAKISTAN** won by four wickets. England 148-6 (20; K.P.Pietersen 62, Yasir Arafat 3-32). Pakistan 149-6 (19; G.P.Swann 3-16). Award: Abdul Razzaq (46* in 18 balls). England debut: A.Shahzad.

BANGLADESH v ENGLAND

LIMITED-OVERS INTERNATIONALS
Shere Bangla National Stadium, Mirpur, 28 February. Toss: England. **ENGLAND** won by six wickets. Bangladesh 228 (45.4; Tamim Iqbal 125, G.P.Swann 3-32). England 229-4 (46; P.D.Collingwood 75*, A.N.Cook 64, Naeem Islam 3-49). Award: Tamim Iqbal. England debut: C.Kieswetter.
In this match, P.D.Collingwood became the first England player to take 100 catches in the field.

Shere Bangla National Stadium, Mirpur, 2 March. Toss: England. **ENGLAND** won by two wickets. Bangladesh 260-6 (50; Mushfiqur Rahim 76, Imrul Kayes 63, T.T.Bresnan 3-51). England 261-8 (48.5; E.J.G.Morgan 110*, A.N.Cook 60, Shakib Al Hasan 3-32, Abdur Razzak 3-52). Award: E.J.G.Morgan. England debut: J.C.Tredwell.
E.J.G.Morgan became the first man to score an LOI century for two different countries, having previously done so for Ireland.

Chittagong Divisional Stadium, 5 March. Toss: Bangladesh. **ENGLAND** won by 45 runs. England 284-5 (50; C.Kieswetter 107). Bangladesh 239-9 (50; T.T.Bresnan 4-28). Award: C.Kieswetter. Series Award: E.J.G.Morgan. England debut: A.Shahzad.

ICC WORLD TWENTY20 2010

See pages 277-278 for details of these matches.

ENGLAND v SCOTLAND

LIMITED-OVERS INTERNATIONAL
Grange CC, Raeburn Place, Edinburgh, 19 June. Toss: Scotland. **ENGLAND** won by seven wickets. Scotland 211 (49.5; K.J.Coetzer 51, M.H.Yardy 3-41). England 213-3 (33.4; C.Kieswetter 69, A.J.Strauss 61).

ENGLAND v AUSTRALIA

NATWEST LIMITED-OVERS INTERNATIONAL SERIES
Rose Bowl, Southampton, 22 June. Toss: Australia. **ENGLAND** won by four wickets. Australia 267-7 (50; M.J.Clarke 87*). England 268-6 (46; E.J.G.Morgan 103*, R.J.Harris 3-42). Award: E.J.G.Morgan.

Sophia Gardens, Cardiff, 24 June. Toss: Australia. **ENGLAND** won by four wickets. Australia 239-7 (50; C.L.White 86*, S.R.Watson 57, S.C.J.Broad 4-44). England 243-6 (45.2; E.J.G.Morgan 52, A.J.Strauss 51, D.E.Bollinger 3-46). Award: S.C.J.Broad.
In this match P.D.Collingwood became England's leading runscorer in LOIs, overhauling A.J.Stewart's record of 4677.

Old Trafford, Manchester, 27 June. Toss: England. **ENGLAND** won by one wicket. Australia 212 (46; S.R.Watson 61, G.P.Swann 4-37, J.M.Anderson 3-22). England 214-9 (49.1; A.J.Strauss 87, D.E.Bollinger 3-20, S.W.Tait 3-28). Award: G.P.Swann.

The Oval, London, 30 June. Toss: England. **AUSTRALIA** won by 78 runs. Australia 290-5 (50; M.J.Clarke 99*, R.T.Ponting 92). England 212 (42.4; M.H.Yardy 57, R.J.Harris 5-32). Award: R.J.Harris.

Lord's, London, 3 July. Toss: Australia. **AUSTRALIA** won by 42 runs. Australia 277-7 (50; M.E.K.Hussey 79, S.E.Marsh 59, T.D.Paine 54, S.C.J.Broad 4-64, G.P.Swann 3-32). England 235 (46.3; P.D.Collingwood 95, S.W.Tait 4-48). Award: S.W.Tait. Series Award: E.J.G.Morgan.

ENGLAND v BANGLADESH
NATWEST LIMITED-OVERS INTERNATIONAL SERIES
Trent Bridge, Nottingham, 8 July. Toss: Bangladesh. **ENGLAND** won by six wickets. Bangladesh 250-9 (50; Raqibul Hasan 76, Junaid Siddique 51, J.M.Anderson 3-74). England 251-4 (45.1; I.R.Bell 84*, A.J.Strauss 50). Award: I.R.Bell.

County Ground, Bristol, 10 July. Toss: England. **BANGLADESH** won by 5 runs. Bangladesh 236-7 (50; Imrul Kayes 76, A.Shahzad 3-41). England 231 (49.3; I.J.L.Trott 94). Award: Mashrafe Mortaza (Bangladesh, 22 and 2-42).

Edgbaston, Birmingham, 12 July. Toss: Bangladesh. **ENGLAND** won by 144 runs. England 347-5 (50; A.J.Strauss 154, I.J.L.Trott 110, Mashrafe Mortaza 3-31). Bangladesh 203 (45; R.S.Bopara 4-38). Award: A.J.Strauss. Series Award: A.J.Strauss.
England's 2nd wicket partnership of 250 between A.J.Strauss and I.J.L.Trott was the biggest for England in all LOIs, beating the previous record of 226 between A.J.Strauss and A.Flintoff v West Indies at Lord's in 2004.

ENGLAND v PAKISTAN
NATWEST TWENTY20 SERIES
Sophia Gardens, Cardiff, 5 September. Toss: England. **ENGLAND** won by five wickets. Pakistan 126-4 (20). England 129-5 (17.1). Award: M.H.Yardy (1-21 and 35*).

Sophia Gardens, Cardiff, 7 September. Toss: Pakistan. **ENGLAND** won by six wickets. Pakistan 89 (18.4; T.T.Bresnan 3-10). England 90-4 (14). Award: T.T.Bresnan.
NATWEST LIMITED-OVERS INTERNATIONAL SERIES
Riverside Ground, Chester-le-Street, 10 September. Toss: Pakistan. **ENGLAND** won by 24 runs. England 274-6 (41; S.M.Davies 87, I.J.L.Trott 69, Saeed Ajmal 4-58). Pakistan 250-9 (41; Kamran Akmal 53). Award: S.M.Davies.

Headingley, Leeds, 12 September. Toss: Pakistan. **ENGLAND** won by four wickets. Pakistan 294-8 (50; Kamran Akmal 74, Asad Shafiq 50, S.C.J.Broad 4-81). England 295-6 (49.3; A.J.Strauss 126, I.J.L.Trott 53). Award: A.J.Strauss.

The Oval, London, 17 September. Toss: Pakistan. **PAKISTAN** won by 23 runs. Pakistan 241 (49.4; Fawad Alam 64, J.M.Anderson 3-26, T.T.Bresnan 3-51). England 218 (45.4; E.J.G.Morgan 61, A.J.Strauss 57, Umar Gul 6-42). Award: Umar Gul.

Lord's, London, 20 September. Toss: Pakistan. **PAKISTAN** won by 38 runs. Pakistan 265-7 (50; Mohammad Hafeez 64, G.P.Swann 4-37). England 227 (46.1; A.J.Strauss 68, Umar Gul 4-32, Shoaib Akhtar 3-59). Award: Abdul Razzaq (44* in 20 balls).

Rose Bowl, Southampton, 22 September. Toss: Pakistan. **ENGLAND** won by 121 runs. England 256-6 (50; E.J.G.Morgan 107*, Shoaib Akhtar 3-40). Pakistan 135 (37; S.C.J.Broad 3-25, G.P.Swann 3-26). Award: E.J.G.Morgan. Series Award: A.J.Strauss.

ICC WORLD TWENTY20 2010

The third ICC World Twenty20 took place in the West Indies between 30 April and 16 May.

GROUP A	P	W	L	T	A	Pts	Net RR
Australia	2	2	–	–	–	4	+1.52
Pakistan	2	1	1	–	–	2	–0.32
Bangladesh	2	–	2	–	–	0	–1.20

GROUP B	P	W	L	T	A	Pts	Net RR
New Zealand	2	2	–	–	–	4	+0.42
Sri Lanka	2	1	1	–	–	2	+0.35
Zimbabwe	2	–	2	–	–	0	–1.59

GROUP C	P	W	L	T	A	Pts	Net RR
India	2	2	–	–	–	4	+1.49
South Africa	2	1	1	–	–	2	+1.12
Afghanistan	2	–	2	–	–	0	–2.44

GROUP D	P	W	L	T	A	Pts	Net RR
West Indies	2	2	–	–	–	4	+2.78
England	2	–	1	1	1	1	–0.45
Ireland	2	–	1	1	1	1	–3.50

Providence Stadium, Guyana, 3 May. Toss: West Indies. **WEST INDIES** won by eight wickets (D/L method). England 191-5 (20; E.J.G.Morgan 55). West Indies 60-2 (5.5/6). Award: D.J.G.Sammy (West Indies, 2-22). England debuts: C.Kieswetter and M.J.Lumb.

Providence Stadium, Guyana, 4 May. Toss: Ireland. **NO RESULT**. England 120-8 (20). Ireland 14-1 (3.3).

SUPER EIGHTS

GROUP E	P	W	L	T	A	Pts	Net RR
England	3	3	–	–	–	6	+0.96
Pakistan	3	1	2	–	–	2	+0.04
New Zealand	3	1	2	–	–	2	–0.37
South Africa	3	1	2	–	–	2	–0.61

Kensington Oval, Bridgetown, Barbados, 6 May. Toss: England. **ENGLAND** won by six wickets. Pakistan 147-9 (20). England 151-4 (19.3; K.P.Pietersen 73*). Award: K.P.Pietersen.

Kensington Oval, Bridgetown, Barbados, 6 May. Toss: South Africa. **SOUTH AFRICA** won by 13 runs. South Africa 170-4 (20). New Zealand 157-7 (20). Award: J.A.Morkel (South Africa, 40).

Kensington Oval, Bridgetown, Barbados, 8 May. Toss: Pakistan. **NEW ZEALAND** won by 1 run. New Zealand 133-7 (20). Pakistan 132-7 (20; Salman Butt 67*, I.G.Butler 3-19). Award: I.G.Butler.

Kensington Oval, Bridgetown, Barbados, 8 May. Toss: England. **ENGLAND** won by 39 runs. England 168-7 (20; K.P.Pietersen 53). South Africa 129 (19; R.J.Sidebottom 3-23, G.P.Swann 3-24). Award: K.P.Pietersen.

Beausejour Stadium, Gros Islet, St Lucia, 10 May. Toss: Pakistan. **PAKISTAN** won by 11 runs. Pakistan 148-7 (20; Umar Akmal 51, C.K.Langeveldt 4-19). South Africa 137-7 (20; A.B.de Villiers 53, Saeed Ajmal 4-26). Award: Umar Akmal.

Beausejour Stadium, Gros Islet, St Lucia, 10 May. Toss: New Zealand. **ENGLAND** won by three wickets. New Zealand 149-6 (20). England 153-7 (19.1). Award: T.T.Bresnan (England, 1-20 and 23*).

GROUP F	P	W	L	T	A	Pts	Net RR
Australia	3	3	–	–	–	6	+2.73
Sri Lanka	3	2	1	–	–	4	–0.33
West Indies	3	1	2	–	–	2	–1.28
India	3	–	3	–	–	0	–1.11

Kensington Oval, Bridgetown, Barbados, 7 May. Toss: India. **AUSTRALIA** won by 49 runs. Australia 184-5 (20; D.A.Warner 72, S.R.Watson 54). India 135 (17.4; R.G.Sharma 79*, S.W.Tait 3-21, D.P.Nannes 3-25). Award: D.A.Warner.

Kensington Oval, Bridgetown, Barbados, 7 May. Toss: Sri Lanka. **SRI LANKA** won by 57 runs. Sri Lanka 195-3 (20; D.P.M.D.Jayawardena 98*, K.C.Sangakkara 68). West Indies 138-8 (20; B.A.W.Mendis 3-24, S.L.Malinga 3-28). Award: D.P.M.D.Jayawardena.

Kensington Oval, Bridgetown, Barbados, 9 May. Toss: India. **WEST INDIES** won by 14 runs. West Indies 169-6 (20; C.H.Gayle 98, A.Nehra 3-35). India 155-9 (20). Award: C.H.Gayle.

Kensington Oval, Bridgetown, Barbados, 9 May. Toss: Australia. **AUSTRALIA** won by 81 runs. Australia 168-5 (20; C.L.White 85*, H.K.S.R.Kaluhalamulla 3-20). Sri Lanka 87 (16.2; M.G.Johnson 3-15). Award: C.L.White.

Beausejour Stadium, Gros Islet, St Lucia, 11 May. Toss: India. **SRI LANKA** won by five wickets. India 163-5 (20; S.K.Raina 63). Sri Lanka 167-5 (20). Award: A.D.Mathews (Sri Lanka, 46).

Beausejour Stadium, Gros Islet, St Lucia, 11 May. Toss: West Indies. **AUSTRALIA** won by six wickets. West Indies 105 (19; S.P.D.Smith 3-20). Australia 109-4 (16.2). Award: S.P.D.Smith.

SEMI-FINALS

Beausejour Stadium, Gros Islet, St Lucia, 13 May. Toss: Sri Lanka. **ENGLAND** won by seven wickets. Sri Lanka 128-6 (20; A.D.Mathews 58). England 132-3 (16). Award: S.C.J.Broad (England, 2-21).

Beausejour Stadium, Gros Islet, St Lucia, 14 May. Toss: Australia. **AUSTRALIA** won by three wickets. Pakistan 191-6 (20; Umar Akmal 56*, Kamran Akmal 50). Australia 197-7 (19.5; M.E.K.Hussey 60*, Mohammad Aamer 3-35). Award: M.E.K.Hussey.

FINAL

Kensington Oval, Bridgetown, Barbados, 16 May. Toss: England. **ENGLAND** won by seven wickets. Australia 147-6 (20; D.J.Hussey 59). England 148-3 (17; C.Kieswetter 63). Award: C.Kieswetter.

RECORDS
Match

Highest score	197-7 (19.5)	Australia v Pakistan	Semi-final	Gros Islet
Lowest score	68 (16.4)	Ireland v West Indies	Group D	Providence
Highest innings	101	S.K.Raina	India v South Africa	Group C	Gros Islet
Fastest fifty	22 balls	M.E.K.Hussey	Australia v Pakistan	Semi-final	Gros Islet
Highest partnership	166	D.P.M.D.Jayawardena K.C.Sangakkara	Sri Lanka v West Indies	Group F	Bridgetown
Best analysis	4-18	D.P.Nannes	Australia v Bangladesh	Group A	Bridgetown
Most dismissals	4 (4ct)	M.S.Dhoni	India v Afghanistan	Group C	Gros Islet

Tournament

Man of the Series	K.P.Pietersen	England (248 runs @ 62.00, strike rate 137.7)
Most runs	302	D.P.M.D.Jayawardena	Sri Lanka (302 runs @ 60.40, strike rate 159.7)
Highest strike rate	175.7	M.E.K.Hussey	Australia (188 runs in 107 balls) Qual: 100 runs
Most sixes	12	C.L.White	Australia (100 runs)
Most wickets	14	D.P.Nannes	Australia (ave 13.07, economy 7.03)
Most economical	5.53	S.W.Tait	Australia (131 runs in 23.4 overs) Qual: 15 overs
Most dismissals	9 (3ct, 6st)	Kamran Akmal	Pakistan
Most catches	8	M.E.K.Hussey, D.A.Warner	Australia

LIMITED-OVERS INTERNATIONALS CAREER RECORDS

These records, complete to 18 February 2011 (before the start of the ICC World Cup), include all players registered for county cricket for the 2011 season at the time of going to press, plus those who have appeared in LOI matches for ICC full member countries since 6 October 2009.

ENGLAND – BATTING AND FIELDING

	M	I	NO	HS	Runs	Avge	100	50	Ct/St
K.Ali	14	9	3	39*	93	15.50	–	–	1
T.R.Ambrose	5	5	1	6	10	2.50	–	–	3
J.M.Anderson	137	58	30	20*	183	6.53	–	–	37
G.J.Batty	10	8	2	17	30	5.00	–	–	4
I.R.Bell	90	87	8	126*	2776	35.13	1	16	28
I.D.Blackwell	34	29	2	82	403	14.92	–	1	8
R.S.Bopara	54	50	10	60	1140	28.50	–	4	18
T.T.Bresnan	35	29	11	80	455	25.27	–	1	8
S.C.J.Broad	73	43	14	45*	372	12.82	–	–	17
A.D.Brown	16	16	–	118	354	22.12	1	1	6
G.Chapple	1	1	–	14	14	14.00	–	–	–
R.Clarke	20	13	–	39	144	11.07	–	–	11
P.D.Collingwood	193	177	36	120*	5031	35.68	5	26	107
A.N.Cook	26	26	–	102	858	33.00	1	5	10
D.G.Cork	32	21	3	31*	180	10.00	–	–	6
R.D.B.Croft	50	36	12	32	345	14.37	–	–	11
S.M.Davies	8	8	–	87	244	30.50	–	1	8
J.L.Denly	9	9	–	67	268	29.77	–	2	5
S.T.Finn	3	2	–	34	35	17.50	–	–	1
J.S.Foster	11	6	3	13	41	13.66	–	–	13/7
P.J.Franks	1	1	–	4	4	4.00	–	–	–
S.J.Harmison	58	25	14	18*	91	8.27	–	–	10
M.J.Hoggard	26	6	2	7	17	4.25	–	–	5
G.O.Jones	49	41	8	80	815	24.69	–	4	68/4
S.P.Jones	8	1	1	1	1	1.00	–	–	–
E.C.Joyce	17	17	–	107	471	27.70	1	3	6
R.W.T.Key	5	5	–	19	54	10.80	–	–	–
C.Kieswetter	12	12	–	107	320	26.66	1	1	11/2
M.B.Loye	7	7	–	45	142	20.28	–	–	–
A.McGrath	14	12	2	52	166	16.60	–	1	4
D.L.Maddy	8	6	–	53	113	18.83	–	1	1
S.I.Mahmood	26	15	4	22*	85	7.72	–	–	1
A.D.Mascarenhas	20	13	2	52	245	22.27	–	1	4
E.J.G.Morgan †	38	38	9	110*	1160	40.00	3	5	13
P.Mustard	10	10	–	83	233	23.30	–	1	9/2
P.A.Nixon	19	18	4	49	297	21.21	–	–	20/3
G.Onions	4	1	–	1	1	1.00	–	–	–
M.S.Panesar	26	8	3	13	26	5.20	–	–	4
S.R.Patel	11	5	–	31	116	23.20	–	–	4
K.P.Pietersen	110	100	15	116	3517	41.37	7	21	32
L.E.Plunkett	29	25	10	56	315	21.00	–	1	7
M.J.Prior	61	56	8	87	1204	25.08	–	3	64/5
A.U.Rashid	5	4	1	31*	60	20.00	–	–	1
C.M.W.Read	36	24	7	30*	300	17.64	–	–	41/2
O.A.Shah	71	66	6	107*	1834	30.56	1	12	21
A.Shahzad	9	6	1	9	32	6.40	–	–	4
R.J.Sidebottom	25	18	8	24	133	13.30	–	–	6
V.S.Solanki	51	46	5	106	1097	26.75	2	5	16

	M	I	NO	HS	Runs	Avge	100	50	Ct/St
A.J.Strauss	120	119	8	154	3871	34.87	5	26	56
G.P.Swann	44	28	4	34	299	12.45	–	–	19
J.C.Tredwell	3	2	1	16	18	18.00	–	–	–
C.T.Tremlett	13	10	4	19*	47	7.83	–	–	3
M.E.Trescothick	123	122	6	137	4335	37.37	12	21	49
I.J.L.Trott	18	18	2	137	858	53.62	3	6	5
J.O.Troughton	6	5	1	20	36	9.00	–	–	1
C.R.Woakes	3	3	1	12	20	10.00	–	–	1
L.J.Wright	44	33	3	52	656	21.86	–	2	17
M.H.Yardy	25	21	8	60*	307	23.61	–	2	9

ENGLAND – BOWLING

	O	M	R	W	Avge	Best	4wI	R/Over
K.Ali	112.1	4	682	20	34.10	4-45	1	6.08
J.M.Anderson	1134	92	5667	186	30.46	5-23	9	4.99
G.J.Batty	73.2	1	366	5	73.20	2-40	–	4.99
I.R.Bell	14.4	0	88	6	14.66	3- 9	–	6.00
I.D.Blackwell	205	8	877	24	36.54	3-26	–	4.27
R.S.Bopara	65.1	3	331	10	33.10	4-38	1	5.07
T.T.Bresnan	285.3	13	1523	40	38.07	4-28	1	5.33
S.C.J.Broad	618.2	38	3187	124	25.70	5-23	5	5.15
A.D.Brown	1	0	5	0	–	–	–	5.00
G.Chapple	4	0	14	0	–	–	–	3.50
R.Clarke	78.1	3	415	11	37.72	2-28	–	5.30
P.D.Collingwood	841.2	14	4178	110	37.98	6-31	4	4.96
D.G.Cork	295.2	18	1368	41	33.36	3-27	–	4.63
R.D.B.Croft	411	25	1743	45	38.73	3-51	–	4.24
S.T.Finn	30	1	169	3	56.33	2-51	–	5.63
P.J.Franks	9	0	48	0	–	–	–	5.33
S.J.Harmison	483.1	29	2481	76	32.64	5-33	3	5.13
M.J.Hoggard	217.4	13	1152	32	36.00	5-49	1	5.29
S.P.Jones	58	9	275	7	39.28	2-43	–	4.74
A.McGrath	38	2	175	4	43.75	1-13	–	4.60
S.I.Mahmood	199.3	7	1169	30	38.96	4-50	1	5.85
A.D.Mascarenhas	137	6	634	13	48.76	3-23	–	4.62
G.Onions	34	1	185	4	46.25	2-58	–	5.44
M.S.Panesar	218	10	980	24	40.83	3-25	–	4.49
S.R.Patel	56.4	2	319	11	29.00	5-41	1	5.62
K.P.Pietersen	51.4	0	289	7	41.28	2-22	–	5.59
L.E.Plunkett	227.1	7	1321	39	33.87	3-24	–	5.81
A.U.Rashid	34	0	191	3	63.66	1-16	–	5.61
O.A.Shah	32.1	1	184	7	26.28	3-15	–	5.72
A.Shahzad	80	5	394	14	28.14	3-41	–	4.92
R.J.Sidebottom	212.5	12	1039	29	35.82	3-19	–	4.88
V.S.Solanki	18.3	0	105	1	105.00	1-17	–	5.67
A.J.Strauss	1	0	3	0	–	–	–	3.00
G.P.Swann	327	10	1478	60	24.63	5-28	4	4.51
J.C.Tredwell	21	0	114	0	–	–	–	5.42
C.T.Tremlett	118.1	7	620	15	41.33	4-32	1	5.24
M.E.Trescothick	38.4	0	219	4	54.75	2- 7	–	5.66
I.J.L.Trott	28.3	0	152	2	76.00	2-31	–	5.33
C.R.Woakes	26.2	0	149	7	21.28	6-45	1	5.65
L.J.Wright	162	5	828	15	55.20	2-34	–	5.11
M.H.Yardy	196	6	916	19	48.21	3-24	–	4.67

† *E.J.G.Morgan made 23 appearances for Ireland (see below).*

AUSTRALIA – BATTING AND FIELDING

	M	I	NO	HS	Runs	Avge	100	50	Ct/St
D.E.Bollinger	32	6	2	30	40	10.00	–	–	2
M.J.Clarke	188	172	36	130	5928	43.58	5	45	73
M.J.Cosgrove	3	3	–	74	112	37.33	–	1	–
M.J.Di Venuto	9	9	–	89	241	26.77	–	2	1
X.J.Doherty	5	1	1	3*	3	–	–	–	4
C.J.Ferguson	28	24	9	71*	660	44.00	–	5	7
B.J.Haddin	76	71	6	110	2079	31.98	2	11	103/7
R.J.Harris	17	11	6	21	43	8.60	–	–	4
J.W.Hastings	7	6	2	18*	61	15.25	–	–	1
N.M.Hauritz	58	32	17	53*	336	22.40	–	1	24
M.C.Henriques	2	2	–	12	18	9.00	–	–	–
B.W.Hilfenhaus	15	7	4	16	29	9.66	–	–	7
J.R.Hopes	84	61	8	63*	1326	25.01	–	3	25
D.J.Hussey	30	27	1	111	834	32.07	1	6	16
M.E.K.Hussey	151	126	40	109*	4469	51.96	2	33	85
P.A.Jaques	6	6	–	94	125	20.83	–	1	3
M.G.Johnson	89	50	16	73*	599	17.61	–	2	22
J.J.Krejza	1	1	1	6*	6	–	–	–	1
B.Lee	192	96	39	57	938	16.45	–	2	46
C.J.McKay	15	4	2	6	12	6.00	–	–	1
G.A.Manou	4	1	–	7	7	7.00	–	–	5
S.E.Marsh	33	33	1	112	1172	36.62	2	7	7
D.P.Nannes	1	1	–	1	1	1.00	–	–	–
T.D.Paine	25	25	1	111	730	30.41	1	5	34/4
R.T.Ponting	352	343	37	164	13082	42.75	29	79	152
P.M.Siddle	17	4	2	9*	21	10.50	–	–	1
S.P.D.Smith	15	12	3	46*	240	26.66	–	–	6
M.A.Starc	2	–	–	–	–	–	–	–	–
S.W.Tait	28	6	4	11	25	12.50	–	–	7
A.C.Voges	15	14	5	80*	392	43.55	–	2	2
S.R.Watson	123	105	23	161*	3353	40.89	5	19	38
C.L.White	79	66	13	105	1947	36.73	2	11	36

AUSTRALIA – BOWLING

	O	M	R	W	Avge	Best	4wI	R/Over
D.E.Bollinger	265.4	24	1208	50	24.16	5-35	4	4.54
M.J.Clarke	374.3	7	1895	52	36.44	5-35	2	5.06
M.J.Cosgrove	5	0	13	1	13.00	1- 1	–	2.60
X.J.Doherty	41	1	184	6	30.66	4-46	1	4.48
R.J.Harris	140.5	13	661	41	16.12	5-19	3	4.69
J.W.Hastings	58	1	289	6	48.16	2-35	–	4.98
N.M.Hauritz	454	12	2152	63	34.15	4-29	2	4.74
M.C.Henriques	15	0	84	1	84.00	1-51	–	5.60
B.W.Hilfenhaus	126.2	11	717	18	39.83	2-42	–	5.67
J.R.Hopes	526.1	32	2384	67	35.58	5-14	1	4.53
D.J.Hussey	65.5	0	366	10	36.60	4-21	1	5.55
M.E.K.Hussey	39	1	227	2	113.50	1-22	–	5.82
M.G.Johnson	716.5	42	3563	135	26.39	5-26	6	4.97
J.J.Krejza	9	0	53	2	26.50	2-53	–	5.88
B.Lee	1629.4	121	7720	335	23.04	5-22	20	4.73
C.J.McKay	130	12	632	30	21.06	5-33	2	4.86
D.P.Nannes	7	1	20	1	20.00	1-20	–	2.85
R.T.Ponting	25	0	104	3	34.66	1-12	–	4.16
P.M.Siddle	125.1	9	581	15	38.73	3-55	–	4.64
S.P.D.Smith	83.5	0	439	17	25.82	3-33	–	5.23
M.A.Starc	17.5	0	78	4	19.50	4-27	1	4.37

	O	M	R	W	Avge	Best	4wI	R/Over
S.W.Tait	229.2	8	1197	51	23.47	4-39	2	5.21
A.C.Voges	25	0	159	1	159.00	1-22	–	6.36
S.R.Watson	733	23	3567	127	28.08	4-36	3	4.86
C.L.White	54.1	2	345	12	28.75	3- 5	–	6.36

SOUTH AFRICA – BATTING AND FIELDING

	M	I	NO	HS	Runs	Avge	100	50	Ct/St
H.M.Amla	42	41	5	140	2156	59.88	7	12	16
D.M.Benkenstein	23	20	3	69	305	17.94	–	1	3
L.L.Bosman	14	12	–	88	301	25.08	–	2	3
J.Botha	69	42	14	46	517	18.46	–	–	31
M.V.Boucher	292	218	56	147*	4664	28.79	1	26	400/22
A.B.de Villiers	114	110	15	146	4170	43.89	9	25	85/2
J.P.Duminy	71	64	17	129	1970	41.91	2	12	27
F.du Plessis	3	3	–	60	69	23.00	–	1	3
H.H.Gibbs	248	240	16	175	8094	36.13	21	37	108
A.J.Hall	88	56	13	81	905	21.04	–	3	29
C.W.Henderson	4	–	–	–	–	–	–	–	–
C.A.Ingram	11	10	2	124	328	41.00	2	–	3
J.H.Kallis	307	293	53	139	11002	45.84	17	80	116
C.K.Langeveldt	72	21	10	12	73	6.63	–	–	11
N.D.McKenzie	64	55	10	131*	1688	37.51	2	10	21
R.McLaren	10	8	2	12	37	6.16	–	–	5
D.A.Miller	13	10	3	51	186	26.57	–	1	4
J.A.Morkel	51	38	8	97	679	22.63	–	2	14
M.Morkel	38	16	5	25	111	10.09	–	–	13
A.Nel	79	22	12	30*	127	12.70	–	–	21
W.D.Parnell	18	7	2	49	116	22.20	–	–	2
A.N.Petersen	14	12	1	80	377	34.27	–	4	2
R.J.Peterson	40	18	4	36	188	13.42	–	–	9
G.C.Smith	165	163	10	141	6097	39.84	8	43	89
D.W.Steyn	48	19	6	35	108	8.30	–	–	10
J.Theron	4	1	–	5	5	5.00	–	–	4
L.L.Tsotsobe	19	5	4	4*	6	6.00	–	–	5
R.E.van der Merwe	13	7	3	12	39	9.75	–	–	3
M.van Jaarsveld	11	7	1	45	124	20.66	–	–	4
M.N.van Wyk	8	8	–	82	266	33.25	–	3	1
C.M.Willoughby	3	2	–	0	0	0.00	–	–	–

SOUTH AFRICA – BOWLING

	O	M	R	W	Avge	Best	4wI	R/Over
D.M.Benkenstein	10.5	1	44	4	11.00	3- 5	–	4.06
J.Botha	563.1	11	2619	65	40.29	4-19	1	4.65
A.B.de Villiers	2	0	22	0	–	–	–	11.00
J.P.Duminy	140.1	2	704	18	39.11	3-31	–	5.02
F.du Plessis	3	0	26	0	–	–	–	8.66
A.J.Hall	556.5	30	2515	95	26.47	5-18	4	4.51
C.W.Henderson	36.1	2	132	7	18.85	4-17	1	3.64
J.H.Kallis	1711.4	75	8264	259	31.90	5-30	4	4.82
C.K.Langeveldt	581.3	29	2962	100	29.62	5-39	3	5.09
N.D.McKenzie	7.4	0	27	0	–	–	–	3.52
R.McLaren	72	6	366	8	45.75	3-51	–	5.08
J.A.Morkel	322.3	13	1763	50	35.26	4-29	2	5.46
M.Morkel	321.5	14	1564	65	24.06	4-21	4	4.85
A.Nel	633.3	58	2935	106	27.68	5-45	4	4.63

SOUTH AFRICA – BOWLING (continued)

	O	M	R	W	Avge	Best	4wI	R/Over
W.D.Parnell	154.2	8	941	31	30.35	5-48	3	6.09
A.N.Petersen	1	0	7	0	–	–	–	7.00
R.J.Peterson	249.3	4	1208	24	50.33	3-42	–	4.84
G.C.Smith	171	0	951	18	52.83	3-30	–	5.56
D.W.Steyn	391.4	26	2046	69	29.65	4-16	3	5.22
J.Theron	32.2	0	173	12	14.41	5-44	1	5.35
L.L.Tsotsobe	157.4	13	717	36	19.91	4-22	4	4.54
R.E.van der Merwe	117.3	2	561	17	33.00	3-27	–	4.77
M.van Jaarsveld	5.1	1	18	2	9.00	1- 0	–	3.48
C.M.Willoughby	28	2	148	2	74.00	2-39	–	5.28

WEST INDIES – BATTING AND FIELDING

	M	I	NO	HS	Runs	Avge	100	50	Ct/St
A.B.Barath	8	8	–	113	256	32.00	1	1	2
C.S.Baugh	33	24	8	49	300	18.75	–	–	22/5
S.J.Benn	19	11	1	31	93	9.30	–	–	1
D.E.Bernard	20	12	2	38	141	14.10	–	–	7
D.J.Bravo	109	89	16	112*	1786	24.46	1	5	44
D.M.Bravo	13	11	2	79	345	38.33	–	2	3
S.Chanderpaul	263	247	39	150	8664	41.65	11	59	73
C.D.Collymore	84	35	17	13*	104	5.77	–	–	12
N.Deonarine	20	19	3	65*	510	31.87	–	4	6
T.M.Dowlin	11	11	2	100*	228	25.33	1	1	2
A.D.S.Fletcher	15	15	–	54	256	17.06	–	2	5/3
C.H.Gayle	223	218	15	153*	7917	39.00	19	42	96
W.W.Hinds	119	111	10	127*	2880	28.51	5	14	29
N.O.Miller	36	22	9	51	236	18.15	–	1	13
R.S.Morton	56	51	6	110*	1519	33.75	2	10	20
K.A.Pollard	32	29	–	62	546	18.82	–	1	10
D.Ramdin	81	62	16	74*	899	19.54	–	2	109/5
R.Rampaul	53	21	3	26*	166	9.22	–	–	6
D.M.Richards	8	7	–	59	179	25.57	–	2	5
K.A.J.Roach	15	9	4	10	29	5.80	–	–	1
D.J.G.Sammy	46	35	12	58*	536	23.30	–	2	23
R.R.Sarwan	159	149	30	115*	5245	44.07	4	35	43
L.M.P.Simmons	19	18	2	70	308	19.25	–	2	4
D.R.Smith	77	61	4	68	925	16.22	–	3	26
J.E.Taylor	66	30	7	43*	204	8.86	–	–	17

WEST INDIES – BOWLING

	O	M	R	W	Avge	Best	4wI	R/Over
S.J.Benn	160	10	686	17	40.35	4-38	1	4.28
D.E.Bernard	104	5	526	14	37.57	3-32	–	5.05
D.J.Bravo	725	28	3808	132	28.84	4-19	4	5.25
S.Chanderpaul	123.2	0	636	14	45.42	3-18	–	5.15
S.Chattergoon	13.2	0	48	1	48.00	1- 1	–	3.60
C.D.Collymore	679	45	2924	83	35.22	5-51	2	4.30
N.Deonarine	53.3	0	312	6	52.00	2-18	–	5.83
C.H.Gayle	1150	37	5447	156	34.91	5-46	4	4.73
W.W.Hinds	157.3	1	837	28	29.89	3-24	–	5.31
N.O.Miller	250.4	14	1156	30	38.53	4-43	1	4.61
R.S.Morton	1	0	2	0	–	–	–	2.00
K.A.Pollard	159	4	851	30	28.36	3-27	–	5.35
R.Rampaul	343.4	21	1744	51	34.19	4-37	3	5.07
K.A.J.Roach	120.5	5	583	26	22.42	5-44	2	4.82

WEST INDIES – BOWLING (continued)

	O	M	R	W	Avge	Best	4wI	R/Over
D.J.G.Sammy	317.2	17	1438	31	46.38	4-26	1	4.53
R.R.Sarwan	96.5	3	586	16	36.62	3-31	–	6.05
L.M.P.Simmons	1	0	9	0	–	–	–	9.00
D.R.Smith	418.2	18	2060	56	36.78	5-45	4	4.92
J.E.Taylor	546.4	31	2629	98	26.82	5-48	4	4.80

NEW ZEALAND – BATTING AND FIELDING

	M	I	NO	HS	Runs	Avge	100	50	Ct/St
H.K.Bennett	8	4	3	4*	7	7.00	–	–	–
S.E.Bond	82	40	22	31*	292	16.22	–	–	15
N.T.Broom	22	22	3	71	333	17.52	–	1	2
I.G.Butler	26	13	5	25	84	10.50	–	–	8
G.D.Elliott	37	28	6	115	716	32.54	1	4	6
J.E.C.Franklin	83	59	22	98*	909	24.56	–	3	22
M.J.Guptill	44	42	4	122*	1310	34.47	1	9	18
G.J.Hopkins	25	17	1	45	236	14.75	–	–	27/1
J.M.How	39	35	1	139	1020	30.00	1	7	19
P.J.Ingram	8	7	–	69	193	27.57	–	1	3
B.B.McCullum	184	156	22	166	3781	28.21	2	18	206/13
N.L.McCullum	19	17	2	65	349	23.26	–	2	6
A.J.McKay	13	7	5	4*	10	5.00	–	–	3
H.J.H.Marshall	66	62	9	101*	1454	27.43	1	12	18
M.J.Mason	26	7	4	13*	24	8.00	–	–	4
K.D.Mills	126	77	26	54	836	16.39	–	2	34
J.D.P.Oram	145	104	13	101*	2230	24.50	1	12	43
A.J.Redmond	6	6	–	52	152	25.33	–	1	3
J.D.Ryder	28	25	1	107	857	35.70	2	4	9
T.G.Southee	43	24	8	32	148	9.25	–	–	7
S.L.Stewart	4	4	–	14	26	6.50	–	–	–
S.B.Styris	180	155	23	141	4341	32.88	4	27	70
L.R.P.L.Taylor	99	91	13	128*	2731	35.01	3	19	73
D.R.Tuffey	94	52	21	36	295	9.51	–	–	20
D.L.Vettori	266	169	50	83	2052	17.24	–	4	76
L.Vincent	102	99	10	172	2413	27.11	3	11	41
B.J.Watling	7	7	–	55	84	14.00	–	1	3
K.S.Williamson	11	10	–	108	253	25.30	1	–	3
L.J.Woodcock	2	1	–	11	11	11.00	–	–	–

NEW ZEALAND – BOWLING

	O	M	R	W	Avge	Best	4wI	R/Over
H.K.Bennett	57.1	1	303	14	21.64	4-46	1	5.30
S.E.Bond	715.5	88	3070	147	20.88	6-19	11	4.28
I.G.Butler	184.5	6	1038	28	37.07	4-44	1	5.61
G.D.Elliott	95.3	7	464	19	24.42	4-31	1	4.85
J.E.C.Franklin	551.5	33	2840	72	39.44	5-42	1	5.14
M.J.Guptill	10.5	0	53	2	26.50	2- 7	–	4.89
N.L.McCullum	133.3	2	612	12	51.00	3-35	–	4.58
A.J.McKay	98.3	5	512	19	26.94	4-62	1	5.19
M.J.Mason	196.3	15	1024	31	33.03	4-24	1	5.21
K.D.Mills	1035.4	93	4924	186	26.47	5-25	8	4.75
J.D.P.Oram	1029.1	83	4476	147	30.44	5-26	4	4.34
J.D.Ryder	49.4	0	318	10	31.80	3-29	–	6.40
T.G.Southee	338.4	13	1840	52	35.38	5-33	4	5.43
S.B.Styris	990.2	39	4712	133	35.42	6-25	5	4.75
L.R.P.L.Taylor	7	0	35	0	–	–	–	5.00

NEW ZEALAND – BOWLING (continued)

	O	M	R	W	Avge	Best	4wI	R/Over
D.R.Tuffey	722.1	70	3534	110	32.12	4-24	2	4.89
D.L.Vettori	2107.3	86	8725	279	31.27	5- 7	9	4.13
L.Vincent	3.2	1	25	1	25.00	1- 0	–	7.50
K.S.Williamson	21	1	103	1	103.00	1- 2	–	4.90
L.J.Woodcock	13	0	73	0	–	–	–	5.61

INDIA – BATTING AND FIELDING

	M	I	NO	HS	Runs	Avge	100	50	Ct/St
R.Ashwin	7	2	–	38	38	19.00	–	–	2
P.P.Chawla	22	11	5	13*	36	6.00	–	–	9
S.Dhawan	1	1	–	0	0	0.00	–	–	–
M.S.Dhoni	177	158	39	183*	5808	48.80	7	37	174/57
A.B.Dinda	5	3	–	16	18	6.00	–	–	–
G.Gambhir	105	101	10	150*	3680	40.43	9	21	32
Harbhajan Singh	217	117	32	49	1125	13.23	–	–	63
R.A.Jadeja	35	22	5	61*	535	31.47	–	4	11
K.D.Karthik	52	44	7	79	1008	27.24	–	5	31/5
M.Kartik	37	14	5	32*	126	14.00	–	–	10
Z.Khan	182	95	35	34*	763	12.71	–	–	38
V.Kohli	45	42	6	118	1672	46.44	4	12	20
P.Kumar	48	24	7	54*	225	13.23	–	1	11
A.Mithun	2	2	–	24	28	14.00	–	–	–
A.Nehra	117	44	21	24	140	6.08	–	–	17
N.V.Ojha	1	1	–	1	1	1.00	–	–	1
P.P.Ojha	16	9	8	16*	41	41.00	–	–	7
M.M.Patel	54	23	14	15	73	8.11	–	–	9
P.A.Patel	18	14	2	56*	290	24.16	–	2	14/3
Y.K.Pathan	45	31	10	123*	694	33.04	2	3	14
S.K.Raina	111	93	18	116*	2639	35.18	3	16	47
W.P.Saha	3	1	–	4	4	4.00	–	–	6
V.Sehwag	228	222	9	146	7380	34.64	13	36	84
I.Sharma	45	14	6	13	47	5.87	–	–	11
R.G.Sharma	42	39	10	70*	743	25.62	–	4	18
S.Sreesanth	51	21	10	10*	44	4.00	–	–	7
S.R.Tendulkar	444	433	41	200*	17629	44.97	46	93	134
S.S.Tiwary	3	2	2	37*	49	–	–	–	1
S.Tyagi	4	1	1	1*	1	–	–	–	–
M.Vijay	11	11	–	33	196	17.81	–	–	6
R.Vinay Kumar	2	–	–	–	–	–	–	–	1
Yuvraj Singh	265	244	34	139	7689	36.61	12	45	81

INDIA – BOWLING

	O	M	R	W	Avge	Best	4wI	R/Over
R.Ashwin	66	3	325	14	23.21	3-24	–	4.92
P.P.Chawla	190.4	6	943	28	33.67	4-23	2	4.94
M.S.Dhoni	2	0	14	1	14.00	1-14	–	7.00
A.B.Dinda	37.5	1	228	3	76.00	2-44	–	6.02
G.Gambhir	1	0	13	0	–	–	–	13.00
Harbhajan Singh	1892.5	78	8154	246	33.14	5-31	5	4.30
R.A.Jadeja	255.4	11	1245	29	42.93	4-32	1	4.86
M.Kartik	317.5	19	1612	37	43.56	6-27	1	5.07
Z.Khan	1521.2	111	7480	252	29.68	5-42	8	4.91
V.Kohli	9.4	0	60	0	–	–	–	6.20
P.Kumar	377.2	35	1914	57	33.57	4-31	3	5.07
A.Mithun	12	0	87	0	–	–	–	7.25
A.Nehra	934.5	54	4861	154	31.56	6-23	7	5.19

	O	M	R	W	Avge	Best	4wI	R/Over
P.P.Ojha	139.1	5	601	20	30.05	4-38	1	4.31
M.M.Patel	403.1	33	1930	65	29.69	4-29	2	4.78
Y.K.Pathan	186.2	1	1043	30	34.76	3-49	–	5.59
S.K.Raina	78.2	0	418	7	59.71	1-13	–	5.33
V.Sehwag	705	12	3716	92	40.39	4- 6	1	5.27
I.Sharma	339.1	13	1947	63	30.90	4-38	3	5.74
R.G.Sharma	33.5	2	160	2	80.00	2-27	–	4.72
S.Sreesanth	399.4	16	2403	75	32.04	6-55	3	6.01
S.R.Tendulkar	1336.4	24	6817	154	44.26	5-32	6	5.10
S.Tyagi	27.3	4	144	3	48.00	1-15	–	5.23
R.Vinay Kumar	17	1	122	2	61.00	2-51	–	7.17
Yuvraj Singh	730.2	16	3683	94	39.18	4- 6	2	5.04

PAKISTAN – BATTING AND FIELDING

	M	I	NO	HS	Runs	Avge	100	50	Ct/St
Abdul Razzaq	254	220	55	112	4959	30.05	3	22	33
Abdur Rehman	15	12	3	31	69	7.66	–	–	2
Ahmed Shehzad	9	9	1	115	294	36.75	1	–	2
Asad Shafiq	12	12	–	50*	266	22.16	–	1	2
Azhar Mahmood	143	110	26	67	1521	18.10	–	3	37
Danish Kaneria	18	10	8	6*	12	6.00	–	–	2
Fawad Alam	27	25	9	64	603	37.68	–	4	9
Iftikhar Anjum	62	34	19	32	234	15.60	–	–	10
Imran Farhat	37	37	1	107	1114	30.94	1	7	13
Kamran Akmal	129	113	13	124	2717	27.17	5	8	128/21
Khalid Latif	5	5	–	64	147	29.40	–	1	1
Misbah-ul-Haq	63	56	12	93*	1757	39.93	–	11	32
Mohammad Aamer	15	12	4	73*	167	20.87	–	1	6
Mohammad Asif	38	16	7	6	34	3.77	–	–	5
Mohammad Hafeez	64	64	2	115	1410	22.74	1	7	26
Mohammad Irfan	2	1	1	3*	3	–	–	–	–
Mohammad Yousuf	288	273	40	141*	9720	41.71	15	64	58
Naved-ul-Hasan	74	51	18	33	524	15.87	–	–	16
Saeed Ajmal	35	24	10	33	115	8.21	–	–	6
Salman Butt	78	78	4	136	2725	36.82	8	14	20
Sarfraz Ahmed	9	3	–	19	32	10.66	–	–	7/3
Shahid Afridi	312	293	18	124	6583	23.93	6	31	101
Shahzaib Hasan	3	3	–	50	100	33.33	–	1	–
Shoaib Akhtar	160	83	40	43	394	9.16	–	–	20
Shoaib Malik	192	172	21	143	5188	34.35	7	31	68
Sohail Tanvir	36	21	6	59	232	15.46	–	1	9
Umar Akmal	30	29	3	102*	878	33.76	1	6	13
Umar Amin	3	3	–	22	34	11.33	–	–	1
Umar Gul	80	39	10	33	246	8.48	–	–	10
Wahab Riaz	13	11	3	21	55	6.87	–	–	4
Yasir Arafat	11	8	3	27	74	14.80	–	–	2
Younus Khan	213	206	19	144	6028	32.23	6	39	112
Zulqarnain Haider	4	4	2	19*	48	24.00	–	–	1/1

PAKISTAN – BOWLING

	O	M	R	W	Avge	Best	4wI	R/Over
Abdul Razzaq	1770.3	100	8342	262	31.83	6-35	11	4.71
Abdur Rehman	130	6	556	12	46.33	2-20	–	4.27
Ahmed Shehzad	2	0	16	0	–	–	–	8.00
Azhar Mahmood	1040.2	58	4813	123	39.13	6-18	5	4.62
Danish Kaneria	142.2	11	683	15	45.53	3-31	–	4.79

	O	M	R	W	Avge	Best	4wI	R/Over
Fawad Alam	60.2	0	332	4	83.00	1- 8	–	5.50
Iftikhar Anjum	493.2	41	2430	77	31.55	5-30	3	4.92
Imran Farhat	19.2	2	110	6	18.33	3-10	–	5.68
Misbah-ul-Haq	4	0	30	0	–	–	–	7.50
Mohammad Aamer	131.3	9	600	25	24.00	4-28	1	4.56
Mohammad Asif	323.3	29	1524	46	33.13	3-28	–	4.71
Mohammad Hafeez	380.5	10	1728	49	35.26	3-17	–	4.53
Mohammad Irfan	12.3	0	77	0	–	–	–	6.16
Mohammad Yousuf	0.2	0	1	1	1.00	1- 0	–	3.00
Naved-ul-Hasan	577.4	25	3221	110	29.28	6-27	7	5.57
Saeed Ajmal	303	6	1343	44	39.52	4-33	–	4.43
Salman Butt	11.3	0	90	0	–	–	–	7.82
Shahid Afridi	2226.2	54	10343	292	35.42	6-38	5	4.64
Shoaib Akhtar	1270	98	6047	244	24.78	6-16	10	4.76
Shoaib Malik	1064	31	4864	134	36.29	4-19	1	4.57
Sohail Tanvir	291	15	1512	48	31.50	5-48	3	5.19
Umar Gul	635.5	42	3259	119	27.38	6-42	5	5.12
Wahab Riaz	104	7	561	23	24.39	3-22	–	5.39
Yasir Arafat	99	2	373	4	93.25	1-28	–	5.40
Younus Khan	39.2	1	239	2	119.50	1- 3	–	6.07

SRI LANKA – BATTING AND FIELDING

	M	I	NO	HS	Runs	Avge	100	50	Ct/St
H.M.C.M.Bandara	31	17	4	31	160	12.30	–	–	9
L.D.Chandimal	4	4	2	111	143	71.50	1	–	4/1
T.M.Dilshan	194	170	29	160	4956	35.14	8	20	81/1
C.R.D.Fernando	141	57	33	20	239	9.95	–	–	27
H.M.R.K.B.Herath	11	3	1	2	4	2.00	–	–	4
S.T.Jayasuriya	444	432	18	189	13428	32.43	28	68	123
D.P.M.D.Jayawardena	332	312	33	128	9119	32.68	12	55	170
H.K.S.R.Kaluhalamulla	21	11	1	56	156	15.60	–	1	5
S.H.T.Kandamby	33	31	6	93*	814	32.56	–	5	5
C.K.Kapugedera	85	70	7	95	1440	22.85	–	7	28
K.M.D.N.Kulasekara	83	51	23	57*	475	16.96	–	1	20
R.A.S.Lakmal	6	1	1	0*	0	–	–	–	2
M.F.Maharoof	94	64	15	69*	984	20.08	–	2	20
S.L.Malinga	77	36	12	56	210	8.75	–	1	12
A.D.Mathews	35	27	7	77*	702	35.10	–	6	12
B.A.W.Mendis	46	22	9	15*	99	7.61	–	–	6
B.M.A.J.Mendis	5	3	1	35*	47	23.50	–	–	2
M.T.T.Mirando	38	27	6	54*	392	18.66	–	1	4
M.Muralitharan	341	160	62	33*	667	6.80	–	–	129
N.L.T.C.Perera	16	10	2	36*	139	17.37	–	–	7
M.Pushpakumara	3	1	1	7*	7	–	–	–	–
T.T.Samaraweera	44	35	7	105*	752	26.85	2	–	14
K.C.Sangakkara	282	264	28	138*	8699	36.86	10	59	276/70
L.P.C.Silva	64	54	7	107*	1437	30.57	1	11	20
W.U.Tharanga	112	107	5	120	3503	34.34	9	18	19
H.D.R.L.Thirimanne	3	2	–	22	37	18.50	–	–	1
W.P.J.U.C.Vaas	322	220	72	50*	2025	13.68	–	1	60
U.W.M.B.C.A.Welegedera	10	3	2	2*	4	4.00	–	–	6

SRI LANKA – BOWLING

	O	M	R	W	Avge	Best	4wI	R/Over
H.M.C.M.Bandara	245	6	1232	36	34.22	4-31	2	5.02
T.M.Dilshan	496.1	13	2369	54	43.87	4-29	2	4.77

	O	M	R	W	Avge	Best	4wI	R/Over
C.R.D.Fernando	1031.2	49	5362	180	29.78	6-27	4	5.19
H.M.R.K.B.Herath	75	3	302	11	27.45	3-28	–	4.02
S.T.Jayasuriya	2473	45	11825	322	36.72	6-29	12	4.78
D.P.M.D.Jayawardena	97	1	558	7	79.71	2-56	–	5.75
H.K.S.R.Kaluhalamulla	158.2	5	737	22	33.50	3-23	–	4.65
S.H.T.Kandamby	28	1	164	2	82.00	2-37	–	5.85
C.K.Kapugedera	43	0	218	2	109.00	1-24	–	5.06
K.M.D.N.Kulasekara	638.5	61	2904	100	29.04	4-40	2	4.54
R.A.S.Lakmal	45	2	298	4	74.50	2-55	–	6.62
M.F.Maharoof	655.2	46	3133	121	25.89	6-14	6	4.78
S.L.Malinga	626	36	3081	114	27.02	5-34	6	4.92
A.D.Mathews	184	13	853	27	31.59	6-20	1	4.63
B.A.W.Mendis	364.3	18	1607	82	19.59	6-13	7	4.40
B.M.A.J.Mendis	28	0	129	4	32.25	2-12	–	4.60
M.T.T.Mirando	279.2	17	1393	50	27.86	5-47	1	4.98
M.Muralitharan	3064.1	197	12035	519	23.18	7-30	24	3.92
N.L.T.C.Perera	98.4	7	518	25	20.72	5-28	2	5.25
M.Pushpakumara	5	0	21	0	–	–	–	4.20
T.T.Samaraweera	115	2	538	10	53.80	3-34	–	4.67
L.P.C.Silva	4	1	21	1	21.00	1-21	–	5.25
W.P.J.U.C.Vaas	2629.1	279	11014	400	27.53	8-19	13	4.18
U.W.M.B.C.A.Welegedara	76.1	5	433	15	28.86	5-66	1	5.68

ZIMBABWE – BATTING AND FIELDING

	M	I	NO	HS	Runs	Avge	100	50	Ct/St
A.M.Blignaut	54	41	8	63*	626	18.96	–	5	11
R.W.Chakabva	5	5	1	45	126	31.50	–	–	3
C.J.Chibhabha	56	56	–	73	1169	20.87	–	8	23
E.Chigumbura	122	114	12	79	2461	24.12	–	13	39
C.K.Coventry	34	31	1	194*	803	26.76	1	3	18/1
A.G.Cremer	37	23	7	31*	217	13.56	–	–	12
K.M.Dabengwa	37	34	7	45	514	19.03	–	–	12
C.R.Ervine	14	12	2	67*	324	32.40	–	1	1
S.M.Ervine	42	34	7	100	698	25.85	1	2	5
G.W.Flower	221	214	18	142*	6571	33.52	6	40	86
T.N.Garwe	1	–	–	–	–	–	–	–	–
M.W.Goodwin	71	70	3	112*	1818	27.13	2	8	20
A.J.Ireland	26	13	5	8*	30	3.75	–	–	2
K.M.Jarvis	9	5	2	13	19	6.33	–	–	1
G.A.Lamb	9	8	1	37	134	19.14	–	–	–
T.Maruma	8	7	–	32	53	7.57	–	–	3
H.Masakadza	102	102	4	178*	2653	27.07	3	16	43
S.W.Masakadza	6	4	2	45*	75	37.50	–	–	2
S.Matsikenyeri	109	106	9	90	2196	22.63	–	13	36
K.O.Meth	7	5	–	53	76	15.20	–	1	1
C.B.Mpofu	49	28	14	6	31	2.21	–	–	7
F.Mutizwa	9	8	1	79	263	37.57	–	3	5/2
I.A.Nicholson	2	2	–	14	14	7.00	–	–	–
R.W.Price	83	47	12	46	312	8.91	–	–	14
E.C.Rainsford	39	23	13	9*	55	5.50	–	–	8
V.Sibanda	85	84	2	116	1796	21.90	1	12	27
T.Taibu	130	117	20	107*	2812	28.98	2	16	107/28
B.R.M.Taylor	112	111	11	145*	3242	32.42	3	20	60/18
P.Utseya	121	96	34	68*	984	15.87	–	3	38
M.A.Vermeulen	43	43	4	92	868	22.25	–	6	18

	M	I	NO	HS	Runs	Avge	100	50	Ct/St
M.N.Waller	14	13	1	63	189	15.75	–	1	4
S.C.Williams	45	44	7	75	1088	29.40	–	11	16

ZIMBABWE – BOWLING

	O	M	R	W	Avge	Best	4wI	R/Over
A.M.Blignaut	391.2	12	2063	50	41.26	4-43	2	5.27
C.J.Chibhabha	145	2	1035	20	51.75	2-28	–	7.13
E.Chigumbura	513.1	22	3100	81	38.27	4-28	1	6.04
A.G.Cremer	294.3	13	1390	47	29.57	6-46	3	4.71
K.M.Dabengwa	184.5	2	936	23	40.69	3-15	–	5.06
S.M.Ervine	274.5	10	1561	41	38.07	3-29	–	5.67
G.W.Flower	910.2	11	4225	104	40.62	4-32	2	4.64
T.N.Garwwe	6	0	50	1	50.00	1-50	–	8.33
M.W.Goodwin	41.2	1	210	4	52.50	1-12	–	5.08
A.J.Ireland	221	13	1115	38	29.34	3-41	–	5.04
K.M.Jarvis	68.5	1	422	10	42.20	3-36	–	6.13
G.A.Lamb	67	3	267	8	33.37	3-45	–	3.98
T.Maruma	34.3	1	204	4	51.00	2-50	–	5.91
H.Masakadza	161.4	4	887	26	34.11	3-39	–	5.48
S.W.Masakadza	45.4	0	366	11	33.27	4-86	1	8.01
S.Matsikenyeri	153.2	2	778	16	48.62	2-25	–	5.08
K.O.Meth	30.4	1	178	1	178.00	1- 6	–	5.80
I.A.Nicholson	12	0	118	2	59.00	1-44	–	9.83
C.B.Mpofu	383.1	28	2000	54	37.03	6-52	2	5.21
R.W.Price	719.4	61	2794	80	34.92	4-22	1	3.88
E.C.Rainsford	317.5	33	1401	45	31.13	5-36	2	4.40
V.Sibanda	23	1	148	2	74.00	1-12	–	6.43
T.Taibu	14	1	61	2	30.50	2-42	–	4.35
B.R.M.Taylor	63	0	383	9	42.55	3-54	–	6.07
P.Utseya	1027.3	51	4289	93	46.11	4-38	2	4.17
M.A.Vermeulen	0.5	0	5	1	5.00	1- 5	–	6.00
M.N.Waller	16	0	109	0	–	–	–	6.81
S.C.Williams	127.3	2	645	10	64.50	3-23	–	5.05

BANGLADESH – BATTING AND FIELDING

	M	I	NO	HS	Runs	Avge	100	50	Ct/St
Abdur Razzak	111	70	29	33	563	13.73	–	–	25
Aftab Ahmed	85	85	6	92	1954	24.73	–	14	29
Dolar Mahmud	7	4	–	41	61	15.25	–	–	–
Enamul Haque[2]	10	5	1	5	12	3.00	–	–	\ 8
Faisal Hossain	6	5	1	17	43	10.75	–	–	2
Imrul Kayes	30	30	–	101	894	29.80	1	6	5
Jahurul Islam	6	6	1	41	156	31.20	–	–	6
Junaid Siddique	46	45	1	100	1056	24.00	1	6	19
Mahmudullah	61	51	14	64*	1070	28.91	–	4	13
Mashrafe Mortaza	118	92	16	51*	1177	15.48	–	1	37
Mohammad Ashraful	164	157	13	109	3360	23.33	3	20	34
Mushfiqur Rahim	84	75	13	98	1460	23.54	–	7	56/22
Naeem Islam	40	33	14	73*	544	28.63	–	1	14
Nazmul Hossain	34	20	12	6*	35	4.37	–	–	5
Raqibul Hasan	49	48	6	89	1231	29.30	–	8	17
Rubel Hossain	21	10	6	4	10	2.50	–	–	4
Shafiul Islam	23	11	4	16	52	7.42	–	–	5
Shahadat Hossain	46	25	15	16*	79	7.90	–	–	5
Shahriar Nafees	64	64	5	123*	1976	33.49	4	11	11

	M	I	NO	HS	Runs	Avge	100	50	Ct/St
Shakib Al Hasan	102	98	17	134*	2834	34.98	5	17	28
Suhrawadi Shuvo	11	7	1	14*	59	9.83	–	–	6
Syed Rasel	52	27	11	15	81	5.06	–	–	8
Tamim Iqbal	89	89	–	154	2640	29.66	3	16	25

BANGLADESH – BOWLING

	O	M	R	W	Avge	Best	4wI	R/Over
Abdur Razzak	980.5	48	4358	162	26.90	5-29	8	4.44
Aftab Ahmed	123.1	0	656	12	54.66	5-31	1	5.32
Dolar Mahmud	35	1	258	8	32.25	4-28	1	7.37
Enamul Haque[2]	96	3	422	14	30.14	3-16	–	4.39
Faisal Hossain	12.1	0	53	1	53.00	1-27	–	4.35
Junaid Siddique	2	0	13	0	–	–	–	6.50
Mahmudullah	307	6	1598	31	51.54	3-52	–	5.20
Mashrafe Mortaza	979.4	87	4515	146	30.92	6-26	6	4.60
Mohammad Ashraful	95	4	554	15	36.93	3-26	–	5.83
Naeem Islam	233	5	1121	29	38.65	3-32	–	4.81
Nazmul Hossain	244.5	20	1268	38	33.36	4-40	1	5.17
Rubel Hossain	158.3	6	918	25	36.72	4-25	2	5.79
Shafiul Islam	160.5	6	1010	32	31.56	4-43	1	6.27
Shahadat Hossain	321.2	18	1824	42	43.42	3-34	–	5.67
Shakib Al Hasan	873.2	53	3716	129	28.80	4-33	3	4.25
Suhrawadi Shuvo	90	5	381	8	47.62	3-14	–	4.23
Syed Rasel	442.5	41	2051	61	33.62	4-22	1	4.63
Tamim Iqbal	1	0	13	0	–	–	–	13.00

ASSOCIATES – BATTING AND FIELDING

	M	I	NO	HS	Runs	Avge	100	50	Ct/St
K.J.Coetzer (Scotland)	5	5	–	51	132	26.40	–	1	3
J.H.Davey (Scotland)	4	4	–	24	46	11.50	–	–	2
A.N.Kervezee (Netherlands)	30	27	2	92	664	26.56	–	3	12
E.J.G.Morgan (Ireland)	23	23	6	115	744	35.42	1	5	9
D.P.Nannes (Netherlands)	1	1	–	1	1	1.00	–	–	–
J.D.Nel (Scotland)	19	10	8	11*	31	15.50	–	–	3
K.J.O'Brien (Ireland)	52	47	8	142	1336	34.25	1	7	22
N.J.O'Brien (Ireland)	40	40	3	72	924	24.97	–	7	30/6
W.T.S.Porterfield (Ireland)	44	44	3	112*	1371	33.43	5	4	22
W.B.Rankin (Ireland)	23	8	6	7*	25	12.50	–	–	4
P.R.Stirling (Ireland)	23	23	1	177	899	40.86	1	6	12
R.N.ten Doeschate (Netherlands)	27	26	8	109*	1234	68.55	3	8	11
G.C.Wilson (Ireland)	25	24	2	113	607	27.59	1	4	16/6

ASSOCIATES – BOWLING

	O	M	R	W	Avge	Best	4wI	R/Over
K.J.Coetzer	2	0	23	0	–	–	–	11.50
J.H.Davey	20.2	3	94	6	15.66	5- 9	1	4.62
A.N.Kervezee	4	0	34	0	–	–	–	8.50
D.P.Nannes	7	1	20	1	20.00	1-20	–	2.85
J.D.Nel	121.4	10	649	14	46.35	4-25	1	5.33
K.J.O'Brien	269.4	18	1299	43	30.20	3-18	–	4.81
A.N.Kervezee	1	0	8	0	–	–	–	8.00
W.B.Rankin	168.2	14	815	33	24.69	3-32	–	4.84
P.R.Stirling	67.5	0	306	10	30.60	4-11	1	4.51
R.N.ten Doeschate	211.2	16	1005	48	20.93	4-31	3	4.75

LIMITED-OVERS INTERNATIONALS RESULTS

1970-71 to 18 February 2011

This chart excludes all matches involving multinational teams.

	Opponents	Matches	Won											Tied	NR
			E	A	SA	WI	NZ	I	P	SL	Z	B	Ass		
England	Australia	113	42	67	–	–	–	–	–	–	–	–	–	2	2
	South Africa	44	18	–	23	–	–	–	–	–	–	–	–	1	2
	West Indies	82	37	–	–	41	–	–	–	–	–	–	–	–	4
	New Zealand	70	29	–	–	–	35	–	–	–	–	–	–	2	4
	India	70	30	–	–	–	–	38	–	–	–	–	–	–	2
	Pakistan	68	38	–	–	–	–	–	28	–	–	–	–	–	2
	Sri Lanka	44	23	–	–	–	–	–	–	21	–	–	–	–	–
	Zimbabwe	30	21	–	–	–	–	–	–	–	8	–	–	–	1
	Bangladesh	14	13	–	–	–	–	–	–	–	–	1	–	–	–
	Associates	14	13	–	–	–	–	–	–	–	–	–	0	–	1
Australia	South Africa	77	–	39	35	–	–	–	–	–	–	–	–	3	–
	West Indies	125	–	63	–	57	–	–	–	–	–	–	–	2	3
	New Zealand	123	–	84	–	–	34	–	–	–	–	–	–	–	5
	India	104	–	61	–	–	–	35	–	–	–	–	–	–	8
	Pakistan	85	–	52	–	–	–	–	29	–	–	–	–	1	3
	Sri Lanka	71	–	47	–	–	–	–	–	22	–	–	–	–	2
	Zimbabwe	27	–	25	–	–	–	–	–	–	1	–	–	–	1
	Bangladesh	16	–	15	–	–	–	–	–	–	–	1	–	–	–
	Associates	14	–	14	–	–	–	–	–	–	–	–	0	–	–
S Africa	West Indies	50	–	–	37	12	–	–	–	–	–	–	–	–	1
	New Zealand	51	–	–	30	–	17	–	–	–	–	–	–	–	4
	India	65	–	–	39	–	–	24	–	–	–	–	–	–	2
	Pakistan	57	–	–	38	–	–	–	18	–	–	–	–	–	1
	Sri Lanka	46	–	–	22	–	–	–	–	22	–	–	–	1	1
	Zimbabwe	32	–	–	29	–	–	–	–	–	2	–	–	–	1
	Bangladesh	13	–	–	12	–	–	–	–	–	–	1	–	–	–
	Associates	17	–	–	17	–	–	–	–	–	–	–	0	–	–
W Indies	New Zealand	51	–	–	–	24	20	–	–	–	–	–	–	–	7
	India	95	–	–	–	54	–	38	–	–	–	–	–	1	2
	Pakistan	114	–	–	–	64	–	–	48	–	–	–	–	2	–
	Sri Lanka	49	–	–	–	26	–	–	–	20	–	–	–	–	3
	Zimbabwe	41	–	–	–	31	–	–	–	–	9	–	–	–	1
	Bangladesh	16	–	–	–	11	–	–	–	–	–	3	–	–	2
	Associates	17	–	–	–	15	–	–	–	–	–	–	1	–	1
N Zealand	India	88	–	–	–	–	37	46	–	–	–	–	–	–	5
	Pakistan	88	–	–	–	–	34	–	51	–	–	–	–	1	2
	Sri Lanka	72	–	–	–	–	35	–	–	32	–	–	–	1	4
	Zimbabwe	28	–	–	–	–	19	–	–	–	7	–	–	1	1
	Bangladesh	21	–	–	–	–	16	–	–	–	–	5	–	–	–
	Associates	11	–	–	–	–	11	–	–	–	–	–	0	–	–
India	Pakistan	119	–	–	–	–	–	46	69	–	–	–	–	–	4
	Sri Lanka	128	–	–	–	–	–	67	–	50	–	–	–	–	11
	Zimbabwe	51	–	–	–	–	–	39	–	–	10	–	–	2	–
	Bangladesh	22	–	–	–	–	–	20	–	–	–	2	–	–	–
	Associates	22	–	–	–	–	–	20	–	–	–	–	2	–	–
Pakistan	Sri Lanka	120	–	–	–	–	–	–	70	46	–	–	–	1	3
	Zimbabwe	40	–	–	–	–	–	–	36	–	2	–	–	1	1
	Bangladesh	26	–	–	–	–	–	–	25	–	–	1	–	–	–
	Associates	17	–	–	–	–	–	–	16	–	–	–	1	–	–
Sri Lanka	Zimbabwe	46	–	–	–	–	–	–	–	38	7	–	–	–	1
	Bangladesh	29	–	–	–	–	–	–	–	27	–	2	–	–	–
	Associates	13	–	–	–	–	–	–	–	12	–	–	1	–	–
Zimbabwe	Bangladesh	51	–	–	–	–	–	–	–	–	23	28	–	–	–
	Associates	41	–	–	–	–	–	–	–	–	32	–	6	1	2
Bangladesh	Associates	30	–	–	–	–	–	–	–	–	–	20	10	–	–
Associates	Associates	121	–	–	–	–	–	–	–	–	–	–	116	–	5
		3089	264	467	282	335	258	373	390	290	101	64	137	23	105

MERIT TABLE OF ALL L-O INTERNATIONALS
1970-71 to 18 February 2011

	Matches	Won	Lost	Tied	No Result	% Won (exc NR)
South Africa	452	282	153	5	12	64.09
Australia	755	467	256	8	24	63.89
West Indies	640	335	276	5	24	54.38
Pakistan	734	390	322	6	16	54.32
India	764	373	354	3	34	51.10
England	549	264	262	5	18	49.72
Sri Lanka	618	290	300	3	25	48.90
New Zealand	603	258	308	5	32	45.18
Bangladesh	238	64	172	–	2	27.12
Zimbabwe	387	101	272	5	9	26.72
Associate Members (v Full*)	196	21	170	1	4	10.94

* Results of games between two Associate Members are excluded from this list; Associate Members have participated in 317 LOIs, 121 LOIs being between Associate Members.

TEAM RECORDS
HIGHEST TOTALS

443-9	(50 overs)	Sri Lanka v Holland	Amstelveen	2006
438-9	(49.5 overs)	South Africa v Australia	Johannesburg	2005-06
434-4	(50 overs)	Australia v South Africa	Johannesburg	2005-06
418-5	(50 overs)	South Africa v Zimbabwe	Potchefstroom	2006-07
414-7	(50 overs)	India v Sri Lanka	Rajkot	2009-10
413-5	(50 overs)	India v Bermuda	Port-of-Spain	2006-07
411-8	(50 overs)	Sri Lanka v India	Rajkot	2009-10
402-2	(50 overs)	New Zealand v Ireland	Aberdeen	2008
401-3	(50 overs)	India v South Africa	Gwalior	2009-10
399-6	(50 overs)	South Africa v Zimbabwe	Benoni	2010-11
398-5	(50 overs)	Sri Lanka v Kenya	Kandy	1995-96
397-5	(44 overs)	New Zealand v Zimbabwe	Bulawayo	2005
392-4	(50 overs)	India v New Zealand	Christchurch	2008-09
392-6	(50 overs)	South Africa v Pakistan	Pretoria	2006-07
391-4	(50 overs)	England v Bangladesh	Nottingham	2005
387-5	(50 overs)	India v England	Rajkot	2008-09
385-7	(50 overs)	Pakistan v Bangladesh	Dambulla	2010
377-6	(50 overs)	Australia v South Africa	Basseterre	2006-07
376-2	(50 overs)	India v New Zealand	Hyderabad, India	1999-00
374-4	(50 overs)	India v Hong Kong	Karachi	2008
373-6	(50 overs)	India v Sri Lanka	Taunton	1999
371-9	(50 overs)	Pakistan v Sri Lanka	Nairobi	1996-97
368-5	(50 overs)	Australia v Sri Lanka	Sydney	2005-06
365-2	(50 overs)	South Africa v India	Ahmedabad	2009-10
363-3	(50 overs)	South Africa v Zimbabwe	Bulawayo	2001-02
363-5	(50 overs)	New Zealand v Canada	Gros Islet	2006-07
363-5	(50 overs)	India v Sri Lanka	Colombo (RPS)	2008-09
363-7	(55 overs)	England v Pakistan	Nottingham	1992
360-4	(50 overs)	West Indies v Sri Lanka	Karachi	1987-88
359-2	(50 overs)	Australia v India	Johannesburg	2002-03
359-5	(50 overs)	Australia v India	Sydney	2003-04
358-4	(50 overs)	South Africa v Bangladesh	Benoni	2008-09
358-5	(50 overs)	Australia v Netherlands	Basseterre	2006-07
357-9	(50 overs)	Sri Lanka v Bangladesh	Lahore	2008
356-4	(50 overs)	South Africa v West Indies	St George's	2006-07
356-9	(50 overs)	India v Pakistan	Vishakhapatnam	2004-05
354-3	(50 overs)	South Africa v Kenya	Cape Town	2001-02
354-6	(50 overs)	South Africa v England	Cape Town	2009-10
354-7	(50 overs)	India v Australia	Nagpur	2009-10
353-3	(40 overs)	South Africa v Holland	Basseterre	2006-07
353-5	(50 overs)	India v New Zealand	Hyderabad, India	2003-04

353-6	(50 overs)	Pakistan v England	Karachi	2005-06
351-3	(50 overs)	India v Kenya	Paarl	2001-02
351-4	(50 overs)	Pakistan v South Africa	Durban	2006-07
351-6	(50 overs)	South Africa v Zimbabwe	Bloemfontein	2010-11
351-7	(50 overs)	Zimbabwe v Kenya	Mombasa	2008-09
350-4	(50 overs)	Australia v India	Hyderabad, India	2009-10
350-6	(50 overs)	India v Sri Lanka	Nagpur	2005-06
350-9	(49.3 overs)	New Zealand v Australia	Hamilton	2006-07

The highest for Bangladesh is 320-8 (v Zimbabwe, Bulawayo, 2009).

HIGHEST TOTALS BATTING SECOND

| **WINNING:** | 438-9 | (49.5 overs) | South Africa v Australia | Johannesburg | 2005-06 |
| **LOSING:** | 411-8 | (50.0 overs) | Sri Lanka v India | Rajkot | 2009-10 |

HIGHEST MATCH AGGREGATES

| 872-13 | (99.5 overs) | South Africa v Australia | Johannesburg | 2005-06 |
| 825-15 | (100 overs) | India v Sri Lanka | Rajkot | 2009-10 |

LARGEST RUNS MARGINS OF VICTORY

290 runs	New Zealand beat Ireland	Aberdeen	2008
272 runs	South Africa beat Zimbabwe	Benoni	2010-11
257 runs	India beat Bermuda	Port-of-Spain	2006-07
256 runs	Australia beat Namibia	Potschefstroom	2002-03
256 runs	India beat Hong Kong	Karachi	2008
245 runs	Sri Lanka beat India	Sharjah	2000-01
243 runs	Sri Lanka beat Bermuda	Port-of-Spain	2006-07
234 runs	Sri Lanka beat Pakistan	Lahore	2008-09
233 runs	Pakistan beat Bangladesh	Dhaka	1999-00
232 runs	Australia beat Sri Lanka	Adelaide	1984-85
229 runs	Australia beat Holland	Basseterre	2006-07
224 runs	Australia beat Pakistan	Nairobi	2002
221 runs	South Africa beat Holland	Basseterre	2006-07
217 runs	Pakistan beat Sri Lanka	Sharjah	2001-02
215 runs	Australia beat New Zealand	St George's	2006-07
212 runs	South Africa beat Zimbabwe	Centurion	2009-10
210 runs	New Zealand beat USA	The Oval	2004
209 runs	South Africa beat West Indies	Cape Town	2003-04
208 runs	South Africa beat Kenya	Cape Town	2001-02
208 runs	Australia beat India	Sydney	2003-04
208 runs	West Indies beat Canada	Kingston	2009-10
206 runs	New Zealand beat Australia	Adelaide	1985-86
206 runs	Sri Lanka beat Holland	Colombo (RPS)	2002-03
203 runs	Australia beat Scotland	Basseterre	2006-07
202 runs	England beat India	Lord's	1975
202 runs	South Africa beat Kenya	Nairobi	1996-97
202 runs	Zimbabwe beat Kenya	Dhaka	1998-99
200 runs	India beat Bangladesh	Dhaka	2002-03
200 runs	New Zealand beat India	Dambulla	2010

LOWEST TOTALS (Excluding reduced innings)

35	(18.0 overs)	Zimbabwe v Sri Lanka	Harare	2003-04
36	(18.4 overs)	Canada v Sri Lanka	Paarl	2002-03
38	(15.4 overs)	Zimbabwe v Sri Lanka	Colombo (SSC)	2001-02
43	(19.5 overs)	Pakistan v West Indies	Cape Town	1992-93
44	(24.5 overs)	Zimbabwe v Bangladesh	Chittagong	2009-10
45	(40.3 overs)	Canada v England	Manchester	1979
45	(14.0 overs)	Namibia v Australia	Potschefstroom	2002-03
54	(26.3 overs)	India v Sri Lanka	Sharjah	2000-01
54	(23.2 overs)	West Indies v South Africa	Cape Town	2003-04
55	(28.3 overs)	Sri Lanka v West Indies	Sharjah	1986-87

63	(25.5 overs)	India v Australia	Sydney	1980-81
64	(35.5 overs)	New Zealand v Pakistan	Sharjah	1985-86
65	(24.0 overs)	USA v Australia	Southampton	2004
65	(24.3 overs)	Zimbabwe v India	Harare	2005
67	(31.0 overs)	Zimbabwe v Sri Lanka	Harare	2008-09
68	(31.3 overs)	Scotland v West Indies	Leicester	1999
69	(28.0 overs)	South Africa v Australia	Sydney	1993-94
69	(22.5 overs)	Zimbabwe v Kenya	Harare	2005-06
70	(25.2 overs)	Australia v England	Birmingham	1977
70	(26.3 overs)	Australia v New Zealand	Adelaide	1985-86

The lowest for England is 86 (v A, Manchester, 2001), and for Bangladesh 74 (v A, Darwin, 2008).

LOWEST MATCH AGGREGATES

73-11	(23.2 overs)	Canada (36) v Sri Lanka (37-1)	Paarl	2002-03
75-11	(27.2 overs)	Zimbabwe (35) v Sri Lanka (40-1)	Harare	2003-04
78-11	(20.0 overs)	Zimbabwe (38) v Sri Lanka (40-1)	Colombo (SSC)	2001-02

BATTING RECORDS

HIGHEST INDIVIDUAL INNINGS

200*	S.R.Tendulkar	India v South Africa	Gwalior	2009-10
194*	C.K.Coventry	Zimbabwe v Bangladesh	Bulawayo	2009
194	Saeed Anwar	Pakistan v India	Madras	1996-97
189*	I.V.A.Richards	West Indies v England	Manchester	1984
189	S.T.Jayasuriya	Sri Lanka v India	Sharjah	2000-01
188*	G.Kirsten	South Africa v UAE	Rawalpindi	1995-96
186*	S.R.Tendulkar	India v New Zealand	Hyderabad	1999-00
183*	M.S.Dhoni	India v Sri Lanka	Jaipur	2005-06
183	S.C.Ganguly	India v Sri Lanka	Taunton	1999
181*	M.L.Hayden	Australia v New Zealand	Hamilton	2006-07
181	I.V.A.Richards	West Indies v Sri Lanka	Karachi	1987-88
178*	H.Masakadza	Zimbabwe v Kenya	Harare	2009-10
177	P.R.Stirling	Ireland v Canada	Toronto	2010
175*	Kapil Dev	India v Zimbabwe	Tunbridge Wells	1983
175	H.H.Gibbs	South Africa v Australia	Johannesburg	2005-06
175	S.R.Tendulkar	India v Australia	Hyderabad, India	2009-10
173	M.E.Waugh	Australia v West Indies	Melbourne	2000-01
172*	C.B.Wishart	Zimbabwe v Namibia	Harare	2002-03
172	A.C.Gilchrist	Australia v Zimbabwe	Hobart	2003-04
172	L.Vincent	New Zealand v Zimbabwe	Bulawayo	2005
171*	G.M.Turner	New Zealand v East Africa	Birmingham	1975
169*	D.J.Callaghan	South Africa v New Zealand	Pretoria	1994-95
169	B.C.Lara	West Indies v Sri Lanka	Sharjah	1995-96
167*	R.A.Smith	England v Australia	Birmingham	1993
166	B.B.McCullum	New Zealand v Ireland	Aberdeen	2008
164	R.T.Ponting	Australia v South Africa	Johannesburg	2005-06
163*	S.R.Tendulkar	India v New Zealand	Christchurch	2008-09
161*	S.R.Watson	Australia v England	Melbourne	2010-11
161	A.C.Hudson	South Africa v Holland	Rawalpindi	1995-96
161	J.A.H.Marshall	New Zealand v Ireland	Aberdeen	2008
160	Imran Nazir	Pakistan v Zimbabwe	Kingston	2006-07
160	T.M.Dilshan	Sri Lanka v India	Rajkot	2009-10
159*	D.Mongia	India v Zimbabwe	Gauhati	2001-02
158	D.I.Gower	England v New Zealand	Brisbane	1982-83
158	M.L.Hayden	Australia v West Indies	North Sound	2006-07
157*	X.M.Marshall	West Indies v Canada	King City (NW)	2008
157	S.T.Jayasuriya	Sri Lanka v Holland	Amstelveen	2006
156	B.C.Lara	West Indies v Pakistan	Adelaide	2004-05
156	A.Symonds	Australia v New Zealand	Wellington	2005-06
156	H.Masakadza	Zimbabwe v Kenya	Harare	2009-10

294

154	A.C.Gilchrist	Australia v Sri Lanka	Melbourne	1998-99
154	Tamim Iqbal	Bangladesh v Zimbabwe	Bulawayo	2009
154	A.J.Strauss	England v Bangladesh	Birmingham	2010
153*	I.V.A.Richards	West Indies v Australia	Melbourne	1979-80
153*	M.Azharuddin	India v Zimbabwe	Cuttack	1997-98
153*	S.C.Ganguly	India v New Zealand	Gwalior	1999-00
153*	C.H.Gayle	West Indies v Zimbabwe	Bulawayo	2003-04
153	B.C.Lara	West Indies v Pakistan	Sharjah	1993-94
153	R.S.Dravid	India v New Zealand	Hyderabad	1999-00
153	H.H.Gibbs	South Africa v Bangladesh	Potchefstroom	2002-03
152*	D.L.Haynes	West Indies v India	Georgetown	1988-89
152*	C.H.Gayle	West Indies v South Africa	Johannesburg	2003-04
152	C.H.Gayle	West Indies v Kenya	Nairobi	2001-02
152	S.R.Tendulkar	India v Namibia	Pietermaritzburg	2002-03
152	A.J.Strauss	England v Bangladesh	Nottingham	2005
152	S.T.Jayasuriya	Sri Lanka v England	Leeds	2006
151*	S.T.Jayasuriya	Sri Lanka v India	Bombay	1996-97
151	A.Symonds	Australia v Sri Lanka	Sydney	2005-06
150*	G.Gambhir	India v Sri Lanka	Kolkata	2009-10
150	S.Chanderpaul	West Indies v South Africa	East London	1998-99
150	G.Gambhir	India v Sri Lanka	Colombo (RPS)	2008-09

HUNDRED ON DEBUT

D.L.Amiss	103	England v Australia	Manchester	1972
D.L.Haynes	148	West Indies v Australia	St John's	1977-78
A.Flower	115*	Zimbabwe v Sri Lanka	New Plymouth	1991-92
Salim Elahi	102*	Pakistan v Sri Lanka	Gujranwala	1995-96
M.J.Guptill	122*	New Zealand v West Indies	Auckland	2008-09
C.A.Ingram	124	South Africa v Zimbabwe	Bloemfontein	2010-11

Shahid Afridi scored 102 for P v SL, Nairobi, 1996-97, in his second match having not batted in his first.

Fastest 100	37 balls	Shahid Afridi (102)	P v SL	Nairobi	1996-97
Fastest 50	17 balls	S.T.Jayasuriya (76)	SL v P	Singapore	1995-96

CARRYING BAT THROUGH INNINGS (SIDE ALL OUT)

G.W.Flower	84*	Zimbabwe (205) v England	Sydney	1994-95
Saeed Anwar	103*	Pakistan (219) v Zimbabwe	Harare	1994-95
N.V.Knight	125*	England (246) v Pakistan	Nottingham	1996
R.D.Jacobs	49*	West Indies (110) v Australia	Manchester	1999
D.R.Martyn	116*	Australia (191) v New Zealand	Auckland	1999-00
H.H.Gibbs	59*	South Africa (101†) v Pakistan	Sharjah	1999-00
A.J.Stewart	100*	England (192) v West Indies	Nottingham	2000
Javed Omar	33*	Bangladesh (103) v Zimbabwe	Harare	2000-01

† One batsman retired hurt.

5000 RUNS IN A CAREER

		LOI	I	NO	HS	Runs	Avge	100	50
S.R.Tendulkar	I	444	433	41	200*	**17629**	44.97	46	93
S.T.Jayasuriya	SL/Asia	444	432	18	189	**13428**	32.43	28	68
R.T.Ponting	A/ICC	352	343	37	164	**13082**	42.75	29	79
Inzamam-ul-Haq¯	P/Asia	378	350	53	137*	**11739**	39.52	10	83
S.C.Ganguly	I/Asia	311	300	23	183	**11363**	41.02	22	72
J.H.Kallis	SA/Afr/ICC	307	293	53	139	**11002**	45.84	17	80
R.S.Dravid	I/Asia/ICC	339	313	40	153	**10765**	39.43	12	82
B.C.Lara	WI/ICC	299	289	32	169	**10405**	40.48	19	63
Mohammad Yousuf	P/Asia	288	272	40	141*	**9720**	41.71	15	64
A.C.Gilchrist	A/ICC	287	279	11	172	**9619**	35.89	16	55
M.Azharuddin	I	334	308	54	153*	**9378**	36.92	7	58
P.A.de Silva	SL	308	296	30	145	**9284**	34.90	11	64
D.P.M.D.Jayawardena	SL/Asia	332	312	33	128	**9119**	32.68	12	55

		LOI	I	NO	HS	Runs	Avge	100	50
Saeed Anwar	P	247	244	19	194	8824	39.21	20	43
K.C.Sangakkara	SL/Asia/ICC	282	264	28	138*	8699	36.86	10	59
S.Chanderpaul	WI	263	247	39	150	8664	41.65	11	59
D.L.Haynes	WI	238	237	28	152*	8648	41.37	17	57
M.S.Atapattu	SL	268	259	32	132*	8529	37.57	11	59
M.E.Waugh	A	244	236	20	173	8500	39.35	18	50
H.H.Gibbs	SA	248	240	16	175	8094	36.13	21	37
S.P.Fleming	NZ/ICC	280	269	21	134*	8037	32.40	8	49
C.H.Gayle	WI/ICC	223	218	15	153*	7917	39.00	19	42
Yuvraj Singh	I/Asia	265	244	34	139	7689	36.61	12	45
S.R.Waugh	A	325	288	58	120*	7569	32.90	3	45
A.Ranatunga	SL	269	255	47	131*	7456	35.84	4	49
Javed Miandad	P	233	218	41	119*	7381	41.70	8	50
V.Sehwag	I/Asia/ICC	228	222	9	146	7380	34.64	13	36
Salim Malik	P	283	256	38	102	7170	32.88	5	47
N.J.Astle	NZ	223	217	14	145*	7090	34.92	16	41
M.G.Bevan	A	232	196	67	108*	6912	53.58	6	46
G.Kirsten	SA	185	185	19	188*	6798	40.95	13	45
A.Flower	Z	213	208	16	145	6786	35.34	4	55
I.V.A.Richards	WI	187	167	24	189*	6721	47.00	11	45
Shahid Afridi	P/Asia/ICC	312	293	18	124	6583	23.93	6	31
G.W.Flower	Z	221	214	18	142*	6571	33.52	6	40
Ijaz Ahmed	P	250	232	29	139*	6564	32.33	10	37
A.R.Border	A	273	252	39	127*	6524	30.62	3	39
R.B.Richardson	WI	224	217	30	122	6248	33.41	5	44
M.L.Hayden	A/ICC	161	155	15	181*	6133	43.80	10	36
G.C.Smith	SA/Afr	165	163	10	141	6097	39.84	8	43
D.M.Jones	A	164	161	25	145	6068	44.61	7	46
Younus Khan	P	213	206	19	144	6028	32.23	6	39
D.C.Boon	A	181	177	16	122	5964	37.04	5	37
J.N.Rhodes	SA	245	220	51	121	5935	35.11	2	33
M.J.Clarke	A	188	172	36	130	5928	43.58	5	45
Ramiz Raja	P	198	197	15	119*	5841	32.09	9	31
M.S.Dhoni	I/Asia	177	158	39	183*	5808	48.80	7	37
C.L.Hooper	WI	227	206	43	113*	5761	35.34	7	29
W.J.Cronje	SA	188	175	31	112	5565	38.64	2	39
A.Jadeja	I	196	179	36	119	5359	37.47	6	30
D.R.Martyn	A	208	182	51	144*	5346	40.80	5	37
R.R.Sarwan	WI	159	149	30	115*	5245	44.07	4	35
Shoaib Malik	P	192	172	21	143	5188	34.35	7	31
A.D.R.Campbell	Z	188	184	14	131*	5185	30.50	7	30
R.S.Mahanama	SL	213	198	23	119*	5162	29.49	4	35
C.G.Greenidge	WI	128	127	13	133*	5134	45.03	11	31
A.Symonds	A	198	161	33	156	5088	39.75	6	30
P.D.Collingwood	E	193	177	36	120*	5031	35.68	5	26

The most for Bangladesh is 3360 in 156 innings by Mohammad Ashraful.

15 HUNDREDS

		Inns	100	E	A	SA	WI	NZ	I	P	SL	Z	B	Ass
S.R.Tendulkar	I	433	46	1	9	4	4	5	–	5	8	5	–	5
R.T.Ponting	A	343*	29	5	–	2	2	6	5	1	4	1	1	1
S.T.Jayasuriya	SL	432	28	2	2	–	1	5	7	3	–	1	4	1
S.C.Ganguly	I	300	22	1	1	3	–	3	–	2	4	3	1	4
H.H.Gibbs	SA	240	21	2	5	2	2	2	2	1	2	1	–	3
Saeed Anwar	P	244	20	1	–	2	4	4	–	7	2	–	–	
C.H.Gayle	WI	218	19	2	3	–	1	4	3	–	2	1	3	
B.C.Lara	WI	289	19	1	3	3	–	2	–	5	2	1	1	1
M.E.Waugh	A	236	18	1	–	2	3	3	3	1	1	3	1	–
D.L.Haynes	WI	237	17	2	4	–	–	4	2	1	–	–		
J.H.Kallis	SA	307	17	1	1	–	4	3	2	1	3	1	–	1
N.J.Astle	NZ	217	16	2	1	1	1	–	5	2	–	3	–	1

	Inns	100	E	A	SA	WI	NZ	I	P	SL	Z	B	Ass
A.C.Gilchrist	A	279*	**16**	2	–	2	–	2	1	1	6	1	–
Mohammad Yousuf	P	273	**15**	–	1	2	2	1	–	2	3	3	–

* = Includes hundred scored against multi-national side. The most for England is 12 by M.E.Trescothick (in 122 innings), for Zimbabwe 7 by A.D.R.Campbell (184), and for Bangladesh 5 by Shakib Al Hasan (98).

HIGHEST PARTNERSHIP FOR EACH WICKET

1st	286	W.U.Tharanga/S.T.Jayasuriya	Sri Lanka v England	Leeds	2006
2nd	331	S.R.Tendulkar/R.Dravid	India v New Zealand	Hyderabad (Ind)	1999-00
3rd	237*	R.Dravid/S.R.Tendulkar	India v Kenya	Bristol	1999
4th	275*	M.Azharuddin/A.Jadeja	India v Zimbabwe	Cuttack	1997-98
5th	223	M.Azharuddin/A.Jadeja	India v Sri Lanka	Colombo (RPS)	1997-98
6th	218	D.P.M.D.Jayawardena/M.S.Dhoni	Asia XI v Africa XI	Chennai	2007
7th	130	A.Flower/H.H.Streak	Zimbabwe v England	Harare	2001-02
8th	138*	J.M.Kemp/A.J.Hall	South Africa v India	Cape Town	2006-07
9th	132	A.D.Mathews/S.L.Malinga	Sri Lanka v Australia	Melbourne	2010-11
10th	106*	I.V.A.Richards/M.A.Holding	West Indies v England	Manchester	1984

BOWLING RECORDS
SIX WICKETS IN AN INNINGS

8-19	W.P.J.U.C.Vaas	Sri Lanka v Zimbabwe	Colombo (SSC)	2001-02
7-15	G.D.McGrath	Australia v Namibia	Potschefstroom	2002-03
7-20	A.J.Bichel	Australia v England	Port Elizabeth	2002-03
7-30	M.Muralitharan	Sri Lanka v India	Sharjah	2000-01
7-36	Waqar Younis	Pakistan v England	Leeds	2001
7-37	Aqib Javed	Pakistan v India	Sharjah	1991-92
7-51	W.W.Davis	West Indies v Australia	Leeds	1983
6-12	A.Kumble	India v West Indies	Calcutta	1993-94
6-13	B.A.W.Mendis	Sri Lanka v India	Karachi	2008
6-14	G.J.Gilmour	Australia v England	Leeds	1975
6-14	Imran Khan	Pakistan v India	Sharjah	1984-85
6-14	M.F.Maharoof	Sri Lanka v West Indies	Bombay	2006-07
6-15	C.E.H.Croft	West Indies v England	Kingstown	1980-81
6-16	Shoaib Akhtar	Pakistan v New Zealand	Karachi	2001-02
6-18	Azhar Mahmood	Pakistan v West Indies	Sharjah	1999-00
6-19	H.K.Olonga	Zimbabwe v England	Cape Town	1999-00
6-19	S.E.Bond	New Zealand v Zimbabwe	Harare	2005
6-20	B.C.Strang	Zimbabwe v Bangladesh	Nairobi	1997-98
6-20	A.D.Mathews	Sri Lanka v India	Colombo ((RPS)	2009-10
6-22	F.H.Edwards	West Indies v Zimbabwe	Harare	2003-04
6-22	M.Ntini	South Africa v Australia	Cape Town	2005-06
6-23	A.A.Donald	South Africa v Kenya	Nairobi	1996-97
6-23	A.Nehra	India v England	Durban	2002-03
6-23	S.E.Bond	New Zealand v Australia	Port Elizabeth	2002-03
6-25	S.B.Styris	New Zealand v West Indies	Port-of-Spain	2002
6-25	W.P.J.U.C.Vaas	Sri Lanka v Bangladesh	Pietermaritzburg	2002-03
6-26	Waqar Younis	Pakistan v Sri Lanka	Sharjah	1989-90
6-26	Mashrafe Mortaza	Bangladesh v Kenya	Nairobi	2006
6-27	Naved-ul-Hasan	Pakistan v India	Jamshedpur	2004-05
6-27	M.Kartik	India v Australia	Bombay	2007-08
6-27	C.R.D.Fernando	Sri Lanka v England	Colombo (RPS)	2007-08
6-28	H.K.Olonga	Zimbabwe v Kenya	Bulawayo	2002-03
6-29	B.P.Patterson	West Indies v India	Nagpur	1987-88
6-29	S.T.Jayasuriya	Sri Lanka v England	Moratuwa	1992-93
6-29	B.A.W.Mendis	Sri Lanka v Zimbabwe	Harare	2008-09
6-30	Waqar Younis	Pakistan v New Zealand	Auckland	1993-94
6-31	P.D.Collingwood	England v Bangladesh	Nottingham	2005
6-35	S.M.Pollock	South Africa v West Indies	East London	1998-99
6-35	Abdul Razzaq	Pakistan v Bangladesh	Dhaka	2001-02
6-38	Shahid Afridi	Pakistan v Australia	Dubai	2009
6-39	K.H.MacLeay	Australia v India	Nottingham	1983
6-41	I.V.A.Richards	West Indies v India	Delhi	1989-90
6-42	A.B.Agarkar	India v Australia	Melbourne	2003-04

6-42	Umar Gul	Pakistan v England	The Oval	2010
6-44	Waqar Younis	Pakistan v New Zealand	Sharjah	1996-97
6-45	C.R.Woakes	England v Australia	Brisbane	2010-11
6-46	A.G.Cremer	Zimbabwe v Kenya	Harare	2009-10
6-49	L.Klusener	South Africa v Sri Lanka	Lahore	1997-98
6-50	A.H.Gray	West Indies v Australia	Port-of-Spain	1990-91
6-52	C.B.Mpofu	Zimbabwe v Kenya	Nairobi (Gym)	2008-09
6-55	S.Sreesanth	India v England	Indore	2005-06
6-59	Waqar Younis	Pakistan v Australia	Nottingham	2001
6-59	A.Nehra	India v Sri Lanka	Colombo (RPS)	2005

150 WICKETS IN A CAREER

		LOI	Balls	R	W	Avge	Best	5w	R/Over
M.Muralitharan	SL/Asia/ICC	341	18385	12035	519	23.18	7-30	10	3.92
Wasim Akram	P	356	18186	11812	502	23.52	5-15	6	3.89
Waqar Younis	P	262	12698	9919	416	23.84	7-36	13	4.68
W.P.J.U.C.Vaas	SL/Asia	322	15775	11014	400	27.53	8-19	4	4.18
S.M.Pollock	SA/Afr/ICC	303	15712	9631	393	24.50	6-35	5	3.67
G.D.McGrath	A/ICC	250	12970	8391	381	22.02	7-15	7	3.88
A.Kumble	I/Asia	271	14496	10412	337	30.89	6-12	2	4.30
B.Lee	A	192	9778	7720	335	23.04	5-22	9	4.73
S.T.Jayasuriya	SL	444	14838	11825	323	36.72	6-29	4	4.78
J.Srinath	I	229	11935	8847	315	28.08	5-23	3	4.44
S.K.Warne	A/ICC	194	10642	7541	293	25.73	5-33	1	4.25
Shahid Afridi	P/Asia/ICC	312	13358	10343	292	35.42	6-38	3	4.64
Saqlain Mushtaq	P	169	8770	6275	288	21.78	5-20	6	4.29
A.B.Agarkar	I	191	9484	8021	288	27.85	6-42	2	5.07
D.L.Vettori	NZ/ICC	266	12645	8725	279	31.27	5- 7	2	4.13
A.A.Donald	SA	164	8561	5926	272	21.78	6-23	2	4.15
M.Ntini	SA/ICC	173	8687	6559	266	24.65	6-22	4	4.53
Abdul Razzaq	P/Asia	254	10623	8342	262	31.83	6-35	3	4.71
J.H.Kallis	SA/Afr/ICC	307	10270	8264	259	31.90	5-30	2	4.82
Kapil Dev	I	225	11202	6945	253	27.45	5-43	1	3.72
Z.Khan	I/Asia	182	9128	7480	252	29.68	5-42	1	4.91
Harbhajan Singh	I/Asia	217	11357	8154	246	33.14	5-31	3	4.30
Shoaib Akhtar	P/Asia/ICC	160	7620	6047	244	24.78	6-16	4	4.76
H.H.Streak	Z/Afr	189	9468	7129	239	29.82	5-32	1	4.51
D.Gough	E/ICC	159	8470	6209	235	26.42	5-44	2	4.39
C.A.Walsh	WI	205	10822	6918	227	30.47	5- 1	1	3.83
C.E.L.Ambrose	WI	176	9353	5429	225	24.12	5-17	4	3.48
C.J.McDermott	A	138	7460	5018	203	24.71	5-44	1	4.03
C.Z.Harris	NZ	250	10667	7613	203	37.50	5-42	1	4.28
C.L.Cairns	NZ/ICC	215	8168	6594	201	32.80	5-42	1	4.84
B.K.V.Prasad	I	161	8129	6332	196	32.30	5-27	1	4.67
S.R.Waugh	A	325	8883	6761	195	34.67	4-33	–	4.56
C.L.Hooper	WI	227	9573	6958	193	36.05	4-34	–	4.36
L.Klusener	SA	171	7336	5751	192	29.95	6-49	6	4.70
K.D.Mills	NZ	126	6214	4924	186	26.47	5-25	1	4.75
J.M.Anderson	E	137	6804	5681	186	30.46	5-23	1	4.99
Aqib Javed	P	163	8012	5721	182	31.43	7-37	4	4.28
Imran Khan	P	175	7461	4844	182	26.61	6-14	1	3.89
C.R.D.Fernando	SL/Asia	141	6188	5362	180	29.78	6-27	1	5.19
N.W.Bracken	A	116	5759	4240	174	24.36	5-47	2	4.41
A.Flintoff	E/ICC	141	5624	4121	169	24.38	5-19	2	4.39
Abdur Razzak	B	111	5885	4358	162	26.90	5-29	3	4.44
Mushtaq Ahmed	P	144	7543	5361	161	33.29	5-36	1	4.26
R.J.Hadlee	NZ	115	6182	3407	158	21.56	5-25	5	3.31
M.Prabhakar	I	130	6360	4534	157	28.87	5-33	2	4.27
M.D.Marshall	WI	136	7175	4233	157	26.96	4-18	–	3.54
G.B.Hogg	A	123	5564	4188	156	26.84	5-32	2	4.51
C.H.Gayle	WI/ICC	223	6900	5447	156	34.91	5-46	1	4.73
A.Nehra	I	117	5609	4861	154	31.56	6-23	2	5.19
S.R.Tendulkar	I	444	8020	6817	154	44.26	5-32	2	5.10
I.K.Pathan	I	107	5194	4547	152	29.91	5-27	1	5.25
U.D.U.Chandana	SL	147	6142	4818	151	31.90	5-61	1	4.70

HAT-TRICKS

Jalaluddin	Pakistan v Australia	Hyderabad	1982-83
B.A.Reid	Australia v New Zealand	Sydney	1985-86
C.Sharma	India v New Zealand	Nagpur	1987-88
Wasim Akram	Pakistan v West Indies	Sharjah	1989-90
Wasim Akram	Pakistan v Australia	Sharjah	1989-90
Kapil Dev	India v Sri Lanka	Calcutta	1990-91
Aqib Javed	Pakistan v India	Sharjah	1991-92
D.K.Morrison	New Zealand v India	Napier	1993-94
Waqar Younis	Pakistan v New Zealand	East London	1994-95
Saqlain Mushtaq	Pakistan v Zimbabwe	Peshawar	1996-97
E.A.Brandes	Zimbabwe v England	Harare	1996-97
A.M.Stuart	Australia v Pakistan	Melbourne	1996-97
Saqlain Mushtaq	Pakistan v Zimbabwe	The Oval	1999
W.P.J.U.C.Vaas	Sri Lanka v Zimbabwe	Colombo (SSC)	2001-02
Mohammad Sami	Pakistan v West Indies	Sharjah	2001-02
W.P.J.U.C.Vaas[1]	Sri Lanka v Bangladesh	Pietermaritzburg	2002-03
B.Lee	Australia v Kenya	Durban	2002-03
J.M.Anderson	England v Pakistan	The Oval	2003
S.J.Harmison	England v India	Nottingham	2004
C.K.Langeveldt	South Africa v West Indies	Bridgetown	2004-05
Shahadat Hossain	Bangladesh v Zimbabwe	Harare	2006
J.E.Taylor	West Indies v Australia	Bombay	2006-07
S.E.Bond	New Zealand v Australia	Hobart	2006-07
S.L.Malinga[2]	Sri Lanka v South Africa	Providence	2006-07
A.Flintoff	England v West Indies	St Lucia	2008-09
M.F.Maharoof	Sri Lanka v India	Dambulla	2010
Abdur Razzak	Bangladesh v Zimbabwe	Dhaka	2010-11

[1] The first three balls of the match. Took four wickets in opening over (W W W 4 wide W 0).
[2] Four wickets in four balls.

WICKET-KEEPING RECORDS
SIX DISMISSALS IN AN INNINGS

6	(6ct)	A.C.Gilchrist	Australia v South Africa	Cape Town	1999-00
6	(6ct)	A.J.Stewart	England v Zimbabwe	Manchester	2000
6	(5ct/1st)	R.D.Jacobs	West Indies v Sri Lanka	Colombo (RPS)	2001-02
6	(6ct)	A.C.Gilchrist	Australia v England	Sydney	2002-03
6	(6ct)	A.C.Gilchrist	Australia v Namibia	Potchefstroom	2002-03
6	(6ct)	A.C.Gilchrist	Australia v Sri Lanka	Colombo (RPS)	2003-04
6	(6ct)	M.V.Boucher	South Africa v Pakistan	Cape Town	2006-07
6	(5ct/1st)	M.S.Dhoni	India v England	Leeds	2007
6	(6ct)	A.C.Gilchrist	Australia v India	Baroda	2007-08
6	(5ct/1st)	A.C.Gilchrist	Australia v India	Sydney	2007-08
6	(6ct)	M.J.Prior	England v South Africa	Nottingham	2008

100 DISMISSALS IN A CAREER

Total			LOI	Ct	St
472‡	A.C.Gilchrist	Australia/ICC	287	417	55
421	M.V.Boucher	South Africa/Africa	292	399	22
327†‡	K.C.Sangakkara	Sri Lanka/Asia/ICC	282	257	70
287‡	Moin Khan	Pakistan	219	214	73
233	I.A.Healy	Australia	168	194	39
231	M.S.Dhoni	India/Asia	177	174	57
220‡	Rashid Latif	Pakistan	166	182	38
212†‡	B.B.McCullum	New Zealand	184	199	13
206‡	R.S.Kaluwitharana	Sri Lanka	187	131	75
204‡	P.J.L.Dujon	West Indies	169	183	21
189	R.D.Jacobs	West Indies	147	160	29
165	D.J.Richardson	South Africa	122	148	17
165†‡	A.Flower	Zimbabwe	213	133	32
163†‡	A.J.Stewart	England	170	148	15
154‡	N.R.Mongia	India	140	110	44

Total			LOI	Ct	St
149	Kamran Akmal	Pakistan	129	128	21
136†‡	A.C.Parore	New Zealand	179	111	25
133	T.Taibu	Zimbabwe/Africa	130	105	28
126	Khaled Masud	Bangladesh	126	91	35
124	R.W.Marsh	Australia	92	120	4
114	D.Ramdin	West Indies	81	109	5
110	B.J.Haddin	Australia	76	103	7
103	Salim Yousuf	Pakistan	86	81	22

† *Excluding catches taken in the field.* ‡ *Excluding matches when not wicket-keeper.*

FIELDING RECORDS
FIVE CATCHES IN AN INNINGS

5	J.N.Rhodes	South Africa v West Indies	Bombay (BS)	1993-94

100 CATCHES IN A CAREER

Total			LOI
170	D.P.M.D.Jayawardena	Sri Lanka/Asia	332
156	M.Azharuddin	India	334
152	R.T.Ponting	Australia/ICC	352
134	S.R.Tendulkar	India	444
133	S.P.Fleming	New Zealand/ICC	280
129	M.Muralitharan	Sri Lanka/Asia/ICC	341
127	A.R.Border	Australia	273
124	R.S.Dravid	India/Asia/ICC	339
123	S.T.Jayasuriya	Sri Lanka/Asia	444
120	C.L.Hooper	West Indies	227
120	B.C.Lara	West Indies/ICC	299
116	J.H.Kallis	South Africa/Africa/ICC	307
113	Inzamam-ul-Haq	Pakistan/Asia	378
111	S.R.Waugh	Australia	325
109	R.S.Mahanama	Sri Lanka	213
108	H.H.Gibbs	South Africa	248
108	S.M.Pollock	South Africa/Africa/ICC	303
108	M.E.Waugh	Australia	244
107	P.D.Collingwood	England	193
107	Younus Khan	Pakistan	213
105	J.N.Rhodes	South Africa	245
101	Shahid Afridi	Pakistan/Asia/ICC	312
100	S.C.Ganguly	India/Asia	311
100	I.V.A.Richards	West Indies	187

The most for Zimbabwe is 86 by G.W.Flower (221), and for Bangladesh 36 by Mashrafe Mortaza (116).

ALL-ROUND RECORDS
50 RUNS AND 5 WICKETS IN A MATCH

I.V.A.Richards	119	5-41	West Indies v New Zealand	Dunedin	1986-87
K.Srikkanth	70	5-27	India v New Zealand	Vishakhapatnam	1988-89
M.E.Waugh	57	5-24	Australia v West Indies	Melbourne	1992-93
L.Klusener	54	6-49	South Africa v Sri Lanka	Lahore	1997-98
Abdul Razzaq	70*	5-48	Pakistan v India	Hobart	1999-00
G.A.Hick	80	5-33	England v Zimbabwe	Harare	1999-00
Shahid Afridi	61	5-40	Pakistan v England	Lahore	2000-01
S.C.Ganguly	71*	5-34	India v Zimbabwe	Kanpur	2000-01
S.B.Styris	63*	6-25	New Zealand v West Indies	Port-of-Spain	2002
R.C.Irani	53	5-26	England v India	The Oval	2002
C.H.Gayle	60	5-46	West Indies v Australia	St George's	2002-03
P.D.Collingwood	112*	6-31	England v Bangladesh	Nottingham	2005
S.Dhaniram	79	5-32	Canada v Bermuda	King City (NW)	2008

APPEARANCE RECORDS

250 MATCHES

444	S.T.Jayasuriya	Sri Lanka/Asia		288	Mohammad Yousuf	Pakistan/Asia
444	S.R.Tendulkar	India		287	A.C.Gilchrist	Australia/ICC
378	Inzamam-ul-Haq	Pakistan/Asia		283	Salim Malik	Pakistan
356	Wasim Akram	Pakistan		282	K.C.Sangakkara	Sri Lanka/Asia/ICC
352	R.T.Ponting	Australia/ICC		280	S.P.Fleming	New Zealand/ICC
341	M.Muralitharan	Sri Lanka/Asia/ICC		273	A.R.Border	Australia
339	R.S.Dravid	India/Asia/ICC		271	A.Kumble	India/Asia
334	M.Azharuddin	India		269	A.Ranatunga	Sri Lanka
332	D.P.M.D.Jayawardena	Sri Lanka/Asia		268	M.S.Atapattu	Sri Lanka
325	S.R.Waugh	Australia		266	D.L.Vettori	New Zealand/ICC
322	W.P.J.U.C.Vaas	Sri Lanka/Asia		265	Yuvraj Singh	India/Asia
312	Shahid Afridi	Pakistan/Asia/ICC		263	S.Chanderpaul	West Indies
311	S.C.Ganguly	India/Asia		262	Waqar Younis	Pakistan
308	P.A.de Silva	Sri Lanka		254	Abdul Razzaq	Pakistan/Asia
307	J.H.Kallis	South Africa/Africa/ICC		250	Ijaz Ahmed	Pakistan
303	S.M.Pollock	South Africa/Africa/ICC		250	C.Z.Harris	New Zealand
299	B.C.Lara	West Indies/ICC		250	G.D.McGrath	Australia/ICC
292	M.V.Boucher	South Africa/Africa				

The most for England is 193 by P.D.Collingwood, for Zimbabwe 221 by G.W.Flower, and for Bangladesh 162 by Mohammad Ashraful.

The most consecutive appearances is 185 by S.R.Tendulkar for India (Apr 1990-Apr 1998).

100 MATCHES AS CAPTAIN

LOI			W	L	T	NR	% Won (exc NR)
221	R.T.Ponting	Australia/ICC	160	48	2	11	76.19
218	S.P.Fleming	New Zealand	98	106	1	13	47.80
193	A.Ranatunga	Sri Lanka	89	95	1	8	48.10
178	A.R.Border	Australia	107	67	1	3	61.14
174	M.Azharuddin	India	90	76	2	6	53.57
147	S.C.Ganguly	India/Asia	76	66	–	5	53.52
143	G.C.Smith	South Africa/Africa	87	49	1	6	63.50
139	Imran Khan	Pakistan	75	59	1	4	55.55
138	W.J.Cronje	South Africa	99	35	1	3	73.33
125	B.C.Lara	West Indies	59	59	–	7	50.42
118	S.T.Jayasuriya	Sri Lanka	66	47	2	3	57.39
109	Wasim Akram	Pakistan	66	41	2	–	60.55
106	S.R.Waugh	Australia	67	35	3	1	63.80
105	I.V.A.Richards	West Indies	67	36	–	2	65.04

The most for England is 60 by M.P.Vaughan, for Zimbabwe 86 by A.D.R.Campbell, and for Bangladesh 69 by Habibul Bashar.

100 LOI UMPIRING APPEARANCES

209	R.E.Koertzen	South Africa	09.12.1992	to	09.06.2010
181	S.A.Bucknor	West Indies	18.03.1989	to	29.03.2009
172	D.R.Shepherd	England	09.06.1983	to	12.07.2005
169	D.J.Harper	Australia	14.01.1994	to	02.02.2011
159	S.J.A.Taufel	Australia	13.01.1999	to	23.01.2011
150	B.F.Bowden	New Zealand	23.03.1995	to	16.01.2011
139	D.B.Hair	Australia	14.12.1991	to	24.08.2008
138	Alim Dar	Pakistan	16.02.2000	to	02.11.2010
118	R.B.Tiffin	Zimbabwe	25.10.1992	to	30.09.2010
110	E.A.R.de Silva	Sri Lanka	22.08.1999	to	06.02.2011
107	D.L.Orchard	South Africa	02.12.1994	to	07.12.2003
101	B.R.Doctrove	West Indies	04.04.1998	to	22.09.2010
100	R.S.Dunne	New Zealand	06.02.1989	to	26.02.2002

INTERNATIONAL TWENTY20 RECORDS

MATCH RESULTS

2004-05 to 1 April 2011

Team	Opponents	Matches	E	A	SA	WI	NZ	I	P	SL	Z	B	Ass	Tied	NR
England	Australia	7	3	3	–	–	–	–	–	–	–	–	–	–	1
	South Africa	5	2	–	3	–	–	–	–	–	–	–	–	–	–
	West Indies	5	1	–	–	4	–	–	–	–	–	–	–	–	–
	New Zealand	5	4	–	–	–	1	–	–	–	–	–	–	–	–
	India	2	1	–	–	–	–	1	–	–	–	–	–	–	–
	Pakistan	7	5	–	–	–	–	–	2	–	–	–	–	–	–
	Sri Lanka	2	1	–	–	–	–	–	–	1	–	–	–	–	–
	Zimbabwe	1	1	–	–	–	–	–	–	–	0	–	–	–	–
	Bangladesh	0	0	–	–	–	–	–	–	–	–	–	–	–	–
	Associates	2	0	–	–	–	–	–	–	–	–	–	–	1	1
Australia	South Africa	6	–	3	3	–	–	–	–	–	–	–	–	–	–
	West Indies	5	–	3	–	2	–	–	–	–	–	–	–	–	–
	New Zealand	5	–	4	–	–	0	–	–	–	–	–	–	1	–
	India	4	–	2	–	–	–	2	–	–	–	–	–	–	–
	Pakistan	7	–	3	–	–	–	–	4	–	–	–	–	–	–
	Sri Lanka	4	–	2	–	–	–	–	–	2	–	–	–	–	–
	Zimbabwe	1	–	0	–	–	–	–	–	–	1	–	–	–	–
	Bangladesh	2	–	2	–	–	–	–	–	–	–	0	–	–	–
	Associates	0	–	0	–	–	–	–	–	–	–	–	0	–	–
S Africa	West Indies	6	–	–	5	1	–	–	–	–	–	–	–	–	–
	New Zealand	5	–	–	4	–	1	–	–	–	–	–	–	–	–
	India	5	–	–	1	–	–	4	–	–	–	–	–	–	–
	Pakistan	5	–	*	3	–	–	–	2	–	–	–	–	–	–
	Sri Lanka	0	–	–	–	–	–	–	–	0	–	–	–	–	–
	Zimbabwe	2	–	–	2	–	–	–	–	–	0	–	–	–	–
	Bangladesh	2	–	–	2	–	–	–	–	–	–	0	–	–	–
	Associates	2	–	–	2	–	–	–	–	–	–	–	0	–	–
W Indies	New Zealand	3	–	–	–	0	1	–	–	–	–	–	–	2	–
	India	2	–	–	–	2	–	0	–	–	–	–	–	–	–
	Pakistan	0	–	–	–	–	–	–	0	–	–	–	–	–	–
	Sri Lanka	3	–	–	–	0	–	–	–	3	–	–	–	–	–
	Zimbabwe	1	–	–	–	0	–	–	–	–	1	–	–	–	–
	Bangladesh	2	–	–	–	1	–	–	–	–	–	1	–	–	–
	Associates	1	–	–	–	1	–	–	–	–	–	–	0	–	–
N Zealand	India	3	–	–	–	–	3	0	–	–	–	–	–	–	–
	Pakistan	8	–	–	–	–	3	–	5	–	–	–	–	–	–
	Sri Lanka	9	–	–	–	–	5	–	–	4	–	–	–	–	–
	Zimbabwe	1	–	–	–	–	1	–	–	–	0	–	–	–	–
	Bangladesh	1	–	–	–	–	1	–	–	–	–	0	–	–	–
	Associates	3	–	–	–	–	3	–	–	–	–	–	0	–	–
India	Pakistan	2	–	–	–	–	–	1	0	–	–	–	–	1	–
	Sri Lanka	4	–	–	–	–	–	2	–	2	–	–	–	–	–
	Zimbabwe	2	–	–	–	–	–	2	–	–	0	–	–	–	–
	Bangladesh	1	–	–	–	–	–	1	–	–	–	0	–	–	–
	Associates	3	–	–	–	–	–	2	–	–	–	–	0	–	1
Pakistan	Sri Lanka	6	–	–	–	–	–	–	4	2	–	–	–	–	–
	Zimbabwe	1	–	–	–	–	–	–	1	–	0	–	–	–	–
	Bangladesh	4	–	–	–	–	–	–	4	–	–	0	–	–	–
	Associates	5	–	–	–	–	–	–	5	–	–	–	0	–	–
Sri Lanka	Zimbabwe	2	–	–	–	–	–	–	–	2	0	–	–	–	–
	Bangladesh	1	–	–	–	–	–	–	–	1	–	0	–	–	–
	Associates	3	–	–	–	–	–	–	–	3	–	–	0	–	–
Zimbabwe	Bangladesh	1	–	–	–	–	–	–	–	–	0	1	–	–	–
	Associates	2	–	–	–	–	–	–	–	–	1	0	1	–	–
Bangladesh	Associates	2	–	–	–	–	–	–	–	–	–	1	1	–	–
Associates	Associates	25	–	–	–	–	–	–	–	–	–	–	24	–	1
		198	18	22	25	11	19	15	27	20	3	3	26	5	4

MATCH RESULTS SUMMARY

	Matches	Won	Lost	Tied	NR	Win %
Netherlands	10	6	3	0	1	66.66
South Africa	38	25	13	0	0	65.78
Pakistan	45	27	17	1	0	60.00
Sri Lanka	34	20	14	0	0	58.82
India	28	15	11	1	1	55.55
Australia	41	22	17	1	1	55.00
England	36	18	16	0	2	52.94
Afghanistan	8	4	4	0	0	50.00
Ireland	17	7	8	0	2	46.66
New Zealand	43	19	21	3	0	44.18
West Indies	28	11	15	2	0	39.28
Kenya	12	4	8	0	0	33.33
Canada	11	3	7	1	0	27.27
Zimbabwe	14	3	10	1	0	21.42
Bangladesh	16	3	13	0	0	18.75
Scotland	12	2	9	0	1	18.18
Bermuda	3	0	3	0	0	0.00

INTERNATIONAL TWENTY20 RECORDS

(To 1 April 2011)

TEAM RECORDS

HIGHEST INNINGS TOTALS

† Batting Second

260-6	Sri Lanka v Kenya	Johannesburg	2007-08
241-6	South Africa v England	Centurion	2009-10
221-5	Australia v England	Sydney	2006-07
218-4	India v England	Durban	2007-08
215-5	Sri Lanka v India	Nagpur	2009-10
214-5	Australia v New Zealand	Auckland	2004-05
214-6	New Zealand v Australia	Christchurch	2009-10
214-4†	Australia v New Zealand	Christchurch	2009-10
211-5	South Africa v Scotland	The Oval	2009
211-4†	India v Sri Lanka	Mohali	2009-10
209-3	Australia v South Africa	Brisbane	2005-06
208-2†	South Africa v West Indies	Johannesburg	2007-08
208-8	West Indies v England	The Oval	2007
206-7	Sri Lanka v India	Mohali	2009-10
205-6	West Indies v South Africa	Johannesburg	2007-08
203-5	Pakistan v Bangladesh	Karachi	2007-08
202-6	England v South Africa	Johannesburg	2009-10
201-4	South Africa v Australia	Johannesburg	2005-06
200-6†	England v India	Durban	2007-08

The highest total for Zimbabwe is 186-7 (v South Africa, Kimberley, 2010-11) and for Bangladesh 166 (v Zimbabwe, Khulna, 2006-07).

LOWEST COMPLETED INNINGS TOTALS

† Batting Second

67	(17.2)	Kenya v Ireland	Belfast	2008
68	(16.4)	Ireland v West Indies	Providence	2009-10
70		Bermuda v Canada	Belfast	2008
73	(16.5)	Kenya v New Zealand	Durban	2007-08
74	(17.3)	India v Australia	Melbourne	2007-08

75† (19.2)	Canada v Zimbabwe	King City (NW)	2008-09
78 (17.3)	Bangladesh v New Zealand	Hamilton	2009-10
79† (14.3)	Australia v England	Southampton	2005
79-7†	West Indies v Zimbabwe	Port-of-Spain	2009-10
80† (16.0)	Afghanistan v South Africa	Bridgetown	2009-10
80† (15.5)	New Zealand v Pakistan	Christchurch	2010-11
81† (15.4)	Scotland v South Africa	The Oval	2009
81 (17.3)	New Zealand v Sri Lanka	Lauderhill	2010
83† (15.5)	Bangladesh v Sri Lanka	Johannesburg	2007-08
84 (15.1)	Zimbabwe v New Zealand	Providence	2009-10
86† (15.3)	Netherlands v Ireland	Dubai	2009-10
87† (16.2)	Sri Lanka v Australia	Bridgetown	2009-10
88† (19.3)	Kenya v Sri Lanka	Johannesburg	2007-08
89 (18.4)	Pakistan v England	Cardiff	2010

The lowest total for England is 111 (v South Africa, Nottingham, 2009) and for South Africa 114 (v Australia, Brisbane, 2005-06).

BATTING RECORDS
600 RUNS IN A CAREER

Runs			M	I	NO	HS	Avge	50	R/100B
1100	B.B.McCullum	NZ	40	40	7	116*	33.33	7	128.3
958	G.C.Smith	SA	31	31	2	89*	33.03	5	129.1
937	K.P.Pietersen	E	30	30	4	79	36.03	5	142.8
784	D.P.M.D.Jayawardena	SL	32	32	4	100	28.00	5	141.7
777	K.C.Sangakkara	SL	29	28	3	78	31.08	6	119.1
758	T.M.Dilshan	SL	32	31	5	96*	29.15	5	120.7
706	D.A.Warner	A	25	25	–	89	28.24	4	144.6
704	Kamran Akmal	P	38	33	3	73	23.46	5	124.6
671	Shahid Afridi	P	42	40	3	54*	18.13	3	144.6
659	L.R.P.L.Taylor	NZ	37	34	4	63	21.96	3	116.8
648	J.P.Duminy	SA	30	29	8	96*	30.85	3	126.3
637	Misbah-ul-Haq	P	31	27	10	87*	37.47	3	113.5
636	Shoaib Malik	P	32	31	6	57	25.44	2	113.7
622	D.J.Hussey	P	28	26	3	88*	27.04	3	127.1
621	G.Gambhir	I	23	22	–	75	28.22	6	124.2
621	S.T.Jayasuriya	SL	30	29	3	88	23.88	4	129.6
617	C.H.Gayle	WI	20	20	1	117	32.47	6	144.4
604	A.B.de Villiers	SA	33	32	6	79*	23.23	4	123.0

HIGHEST INDIVIDUAL INNINGS

Score	Balls				
117	57	C.H.Gayle	WI v SA	Johannesburg	2007-08
116*	56	B.B.McCullum	NZ v A	Christchurch	2009-10
101	60	S.K.Raina	I v SA	Gros Islet	2009-10
100	64	D.P.M.D.Jayawardena	SL v Z	Providence	2009-10
98*	55	R.T.Ponting	A v NZ	Auckland	2004-05
98*	56	D.P.M.D.Jayawardena	SL v WI	Bridgetown	2009-10
98	66	C.H.Gayle	WI v I	Bridgetown	2009-10
96*	57	T.M.Dilshan	SL v WI	The Oval	2009
96*	54	J.P.Duminy	SA v Z	Kimberley	2010-11
96	56	D.R.Martyn	A v SA	Brisbane	2005-06
94	45	L.L.Bosman	SA v E	Centurion	2009-10
90*	55	H.H.Gibbs	SA v WI	Johannesburg	2007-08
89*	58	G.C.Smith	SA v A	Johannesburg	2005-06
89*	56	J.M.Kemp	SA v NZ	Durban	2007-08

89*	43	D.A.Warner	A v SA	Melbourne	2008-09
88*	44	D.J.Hussey	A v SA	Johannesburg	2008-09
88*	61	H.Patel	C v Ire	Colombo (SSC)	2009-10
88	44	S.T.Jayasuriya	SL v K	Johannesburg	2007-08
88	50	C.H.Gayle	WI v A	The Oval	2009
88	44	G.C.Smith	SA v E	Centurion	2009-10
87*	53	Misbah-ul-Haq	P v B	Karachi	2007-08
85*	46	A.Symonds	A v NZ	Perth	2007-08
85*	45	E.J.G.Morgan	E v SA	Johannesburg	2009-10
85*	49	C.L.White	A v SL	Bridgetown	2009-10

HIGHEST PARTNERSHIP FOR EACH WICKET

1st	170	G.C.Smith/L.L.Bosman	SA v E	Centurion	2009-10
2nd	166	D.P.M.D.Jayawardena/K.C.Sangakkara	SL v WI	Bridgetown	2009-10
3rd	120*	H.H.Gibbs/J.M.Kemp	SA v WI	Johannesburg	2007-08
4th	112*	K.P.Pietersen/E.J.G.Morgan	E v P	Dubai	2009-10
5th	119*	Shoaib Malik/Misbah-ul-Haq	P v A	Johannesburg	2009-10
6th	101*	C.L.White/M.E.K.Hussey	A v SL	Bridgetown	2009-10
7th	91	P.D.Collingwood/M.H.Yardy	E v WI	The Oval	2007
8th	61	S.K.Raina/Harbhajan Singh	I v NZ	Christchurch	2008-09
9th	44	S.L.Malinga/C.R.D.Fernando	SL v NZ	Auckland	2006-07
10th	31*	Wahab Riaz/Shoaib Akhtar	P v NZ	Auckland	2010-11

BOWLING RECORDS

25 WICKETS IN A CAREER

Wkts			Matches	Overs	Mdns	Runs	Avge	Best	R/Over
53	Shahid Afridi	P	42	158.5	3	975	18.39	4-11	6.13
47	Umar Gul	P	34	116.1	1	752	16.00	5- 6	6.47
41	Saeed Ajmal	P	29	104.0	–	661	16.12	4-19	6.35
35	D.L.Vettori	NZ	28	108.1	1	580	16.57	4-20	5.36
35	S.L.Malinga	SL	29	98.0	–	728	20.80	3-12	7.42
35	S.C.J.Broad	E	29	101.5	–	755	21.57	3-17	7.41
34	M.G.Johnson	A	26	93.2	1	642	18.88	3-15	6.87
33	B.A.W.Mendis	SL	19	72.0	1	409	12.39	4-15	5.68
32	G.P.Swann	E	22	75.0	1	494	15.43	3-14	6.58
29	D.W.Steyn	SA	21	78.0	–	531	18.31	4- 9	6.80
28	D.P.Nannes	A/Ne	17	61.0	2	459	16.39	4-18	7.52
28	S.W.Tait	A	19	71.4	2	498	17.78	3-13	6.94
27	J.Botha	SA	26	88.0	–	555	20.55	3-16	6.30
26	N.L.McCullum	NZ	25	67.2	–	426	16.38	4-16	6.32
25	M.Morkel	SA	17	62.5	2	395	15.80	4-17	6.28
25	S.E.Bond	NZ	20	77.3	2	543	21.72	3-18	7.00
25	K.D.Mills	NZ	22	81.4	–	701	28.04	3-37	8.58

BEST FIGURES IN AN INNINGS

5- 6	Umar Gul	P v NZ	The Oval	2009
5-18	T.G.Southee	NZ v P	Auckland	2010-11
5-19	R.McLaren	SA v WI	North Sound	2009-10
5-20	N.Odhiambo	K v Sc	Nairobi (Gym)	2009-10
5-26	D.J.G.Sammy	WI v Z	Port-of-Spain	2009-10
4- 6	S.J.Benn	WI v Z	Port-of-Spain	2009-10
4- 7	M.R.Gillespie	NZ v K	Durban	2007-08
4- 8	Umar Gul	P v A	Dubai	2009
4- 9	D.W.Steyn	SA v WI	Port Elizabeth	2007-08

4-11	Shahid Afridi	P v Ne	Lord's	2009
4-13	R.P.Singh	I v SA	Durban	2007-08
4-13	Umar Gul	P v SL	King City (NW)	2008-09
4-13	W.D.Parnell	SA v WI	The Oval	2009
4-14	Shahid Afridi	P v NZ	Christchurch	2010-11
4-15	B.A.W.Mendis	SL v Z	King City (NW)	2008-09
4-15	S.R.Watson	A v E	Adelaide	2010-11

HAT-TRICKS

B.Lee	Australia v Bangladesh	Melbourne	2007-08
J.D.P.Oram	New Zealand v Sri Lanka	Colombo (RPS)	2009
T.G.Southee	New Zealand v Pakistan	Auckland	2010-11

WICKET-KEEPING RECORDS

15 DISMISSALS IN A CAREER

Dis			Matches	Ct	St
45	Kamran Akmal	Pakistan	38	17	28
23	K.C.Sangakkara	Sri Lanka	29	14	9
21	D.Ramdin	West Indies	22	19	2
20	B.B.McCullum	New Zealand	40	16	4
19	M.V.Boucher	South Africa	25	18	1
18	N.E.O'Brien	Ireland	16	10	8
17	A.C.Gilchrist	Australia	13	17	–
16	B.J.Haddin	Australia	23	12	4

MOST DISMISSALS IN AN INNINGS

4 (4 ct)	A.C.Gilchrist	Australia v Zimbabwe	Cape Town	2007-08
4 (4 ct)	M.J.Prior	England v South Africa	Cape Town	2007-08
4 (4 ct)	A.C.Gilchrist	Australia v New Zealand	Perth	2007-08
4 (4 st)	Kamran Akmal	Pakistan v Netherlands	Lord's	2009
4 (3 ct, 1 st)	N.J.O'Brien	Ireland v Sri Lanka	Lord's	2009
4 (4 ct)	M.S.Dhoni	India v Afghanistan	Gros Islet	2009-10
4 (2 ct, 2 st)	A.B.de Villiers	South Africa v West Indies	North Sound	2009-10

MOST STUMPINGS IN AN INNINGS

4	Kamran Akmal	Pakistan v Netherlands	Lord's	2009

FIELDING RECORDS

15 CATCHES IN A CAREER

Total			Matches	Total			Matches
23	L.R.P.L.Taylor	New Zealand	37	16	D.J.Hussey	Australia	28
22	A.B.de Villiers	South Africa	33	15	D.A.Warner	Australia	25
18	M.E.K.Hussey	Australia	27	15	J.Botha	South Africa	26
18	G.C.Smith	South Africa	31	15	J.P.Duminy	South Africa	30

MOST CATCHES IN AN INNINGS

4	D.J.G.Sammy	West Indies v Ireland	Providence	2009-10

APPEARANCE RECORDS
30 APPEARANCES

42	Shahid Afridi	Pakistan		32	D.M.P.D.Jayawardena	Sri Lanka
40	B.B.McCullum	New Zealand		32	Shoaib Malik	Pakistan
38	Kamran Akmal	Pakistan		31	Misbah-ul-Haq	Pakistan
37	L.R.P.L.Taylor	New Zealand		31	J.A.Morkel	South Africa
35	P.D.Collingwood	England		31	G.C.Smith	South Africa
34	M.J.Clarke	Australia		31	S.B.Styris	New Zealand
34	Umar Gul	Pakistan		30	J.P.Duminy	South Africa
33	A.B.de Villiers	South Africa		30	S.T.Jayasuriya	Sri Lanka
32	T.M.Dilshan	Sri Lanka		30	K.P.Pietersen	England

20 MATCHES AS CAPTAIN

IT20			W	L	T	NR	%age wins
30	P.D.Collingwood	England	17	11	–	2	60.71
28	D.L.Vettori	New Zealand	13	13	2	–	46.42
27	G.C.Smith	South Africa	18	9	–	–	66.66
25	M.S.Dhoni	India	12	11	1	1	50.00
21	K.S.Sangakkara	Sri Lanka	12	9	–	–	57.14

UNIVERSITY MATCH RESULTS

Played: 165. Wins: Cambridge 57; Oxford 54. Drawn: 54. Abandoned: 1

In 2001, for the very-first time, Cambridge hosted the University Match, cricket's oldest surviving first-class fixture, after the ECB's re-organisation of university cricket around six centres of excellence had removed it from Lord's. Dating from 1827 it has, wartime interruptions apart, been played annually since 1838. With the exception of five matches played in the area of Oxford (1829, 1843, 1846, 1848 and 1850), all the previous fixtures had been staged at Lord's. Since 2001 it has been played over four days rather than three.

In 2003, Oxford (with Brookes), Cambridge (with Anglia) and Durham were joined by Loughborough in playing three first-class matches against counties. The other two centres – Cardiff (with UWIC and Glamorgan), and Leeds (with Bradford and Leeds Metropolitan) – also play three counties apiece, but without first-class status.

1827	Drawn	1878	Cambridge	1925	Drawn	1974	Drawn
1829	Oxford	1879	Cambridge	1926	Cambridge	1975	Drawn
1836	Oxford	1880	Cambridge	1927	Cambridge	1976	Oxford
1838	Oxford	1881	Oxford	1928	Drawn	1977	Drawn
1839	Cambridge	1882	Cambridge	1929	Drawn	1978	Drawn
1840	Cambridge	1883	Cambridge	1930	Cambridge	1979	Cambridge
1841	Cambridge	1884	Oxford	1931	Oxford	1980	Drawn
1842	Cambridge	1885	Cambridge	1932	Drawn	1981	Drawn
1843	Cambridge	1886	Oxford	1933	Drawn	1982	Cambridge
1844	Drawn	1887	Oxford	1934	Drawn	1983	Drawn
1845	Cambridge	1888	Drawn	1935	Cambridge	1984	Oxford
1846	Oxford	1889	Cambridge	1936	Cambridge	1985	Drawn
1847	Cambridge	1890	Cambridge	1937	Oxford	1986	Cambridge
1848	Oxford	1891	Cambridge	1938	Drawn	1987	Drawn
1849	Cambridge	1892	Oxford	1939	Oxford	1988	Abandoned
1850	Oxford	1893	Cambridge	1946	Oxford	1989	Drawn
1851	Cambridge	1894	Oxford	1947	Drawn	1990	Drawn
1852	Oxford	1895	Cambridge	1948	Oxford	1991	Drawn
1853	Oxford	1896	Oxford	1949	Cambridge	1992	Cambridge
1854	Oxford	1897	Cambridge	1950	Drawn	1993	Oxford
1855	Oxford	1898	Oxford	1951	Oxford	1994	Drawn
1856	Cambridge	1899	Drawn	1952	Drawn	1995	Oxford
1857	Oxford	1900	Drawn	1953	Cambridge	1996	Drawn
1858	Oxford	1901	Drawn	1954	Drawn	1997	Drawn
1859	Cambridge	1902	Cambridge	1955	Drawn	1998	Cambridge
1860	Cambridge	1903	Oxford	1956	Drawn	1999	Drawn
1861	Cambridge	1904	Drawn	1957	Drawn	2000	Drawn
1862	Cambridge	1905	Cambridge	1958	Cambridge	2001	Oxford
1863	Oxford	1906	Cambridge	1959	Oxford	2002	Drawn
1864	Oxford	1907	Cambridge	1960	Drawn	2003	Oxford
1865	Oxford	1908	Oxford	1961	Drawn	2004	Oxford
1866	Oxford	1909	Drawn	1962	Drawn	2005	Oxford
1867	Cambridge	1910	Oxford	1963	Drawn	2006	Oxford
1868	Cambridge	1911	Oxford	1964	Drawn	2007	Drawn
1869	Cambridge	1912	Cambridge	1965	Drawn	2008	Drawn
1870	Cambridge	1913	Cambridge	1966	Oxford	2009	Cambridge
1871	Oxford	1914	Oxford	1967	Drawn	2010	Oxford
1872	Cambridge	1919	Oxford	1968	Drawn		
1873	Oxford	1920	Drawn	1969	Drawn		
1874	Oxford	1921	Cambridge	1970	Drawn		
1875	Oxford	1922	Cambridge	1971	Drawn		
1876	Cambridge	1923	Oxford	1972	Cambridge		
1877	Oxford	1924	Cambridge	1973	Drawn		

CAMBRIDGE UNIVERSITY RECORDS

ALL FIRST-CLASS MATCHES

Highest Total	For 703-9d		v	Sussex	Hove	1890
	V 730-3		by	W Indians	Cambridge	1950
Lowest Total	For 30		v	Yorkshire	Cambridge	1928
	V 32		by	Oxford U	Lord's	1878
Highest Innings	For 254*	K.S.Duleepsinhji	v	Middlesex	Cambridge	1927
	V 304*	E.de C.Weekes	for	W Indians	Cambridge	1950
Highest Partnership						
(2nd wicket)	429*	J.G.Dewes/G.H.G.Doggart	v	Essex	Cambridge	1949
Best Innings Bowling	10-69	S.M.J.Woods	v	Thornton's XI	Cambridge	1890
Best Match Bowling	15-88	S.M.J.Woods	v	Thornton's XI	Cambridge	1890
Most Runs – Season	1581	D.S.Sheppard		(av 79.05)		1952
Most Runs – Career	4310	J.M.Brearley		(av 38.48)		1961-68
Most 100s – Season	7	D.S.Sheppard				1952
Most 100s – Career	14	D.S.Sheppard				1950-52
Most Wkts – Season	80	O.S.Wheatley		(av 17.63)		1958
Most Wkts – Career	208	G.Goonesena		(av 21.82)		1954-57

UNIVERSITY MATCH RECORDS

Highest Total	604		Oxford	2002
Lowest Total	39		Lord's	1858
Highest Innings	211	G.Goonesena	Lord's	1957
Best Innings Bowling	8-44	G.E.Jeffery	Lord's	1873
Best Match Bowling	13-73	A.G.Steel	Lord's	1878

Hat Tricks: F.C.Cobden (1870), A.G.Steel (1879), P.H.Morton (1880), J.F.Ireland (1911), R.G.H.Lowe (1926)

OXFORD UNIVERSITY RECORDS

ALL FIRST-CLASS MATCHES

Highest Total	For 651		v	Sussex	Hove	1895
	V 679-7d		by	Australians	Oxford	1938
Lowest Total	For 12		v	MCC	Oxford	1877
	V 24		by	MCC	Oxford	1846
Highest Innings	For 281	K.J.Key	v	Middlesex	Chiswick Park	1887
	V 338	W.W.Read	for	Surrey	The Oval	1888
Highest Partnership						
(3rd wicket)	408	S.Oberoi/D.R.Fox	v	Cambridge U	Cambridge	2005
Best Innings Bowling	10-38	S.E.Butler	v	Cambridge U	Lord's	1871
Best Match Bowling	15-65	B.J.T.Bosanquet	v	Sussex	Oxford	1900
Most Runs – Season	1307	Nawab of Pataudi sr		(av 93.35)		1931
Most Runs – Career	3319	N.S.Mitchell-Innes		(av 47.41)		1934-37
Most 100s – Season	6	Nawab of Pataudi sr				1931
	6	M.P.Donnelly				1946
Most 100s – Career	9	A.M.Crawley				1927-30
	9	Nawab of Pataudi sr				1928-31
	9	N.S.Mitchell-Innes				1934-37
	9	M.P.Donnelly				1946-47
Most Wkts – Season	70	I.A.R.Peebles		(av 18.15)		1930
Most Wkts – Career	182	R.H.B.Bettington		(av 19.38)		1920-23

UNIVERSITY MATCH RECORDS

Highest Total	611-5d		Oxford	2010
Lowest Total	32		Lord's	1878
Highest Innings	247	S.Oberoi	Cambridge	2005
Best Innings Bowling	10-38	S.E.Butler	Lord's	1871
Best Match Bowling	15-95	S.E.Butler	Lord's	1871

Match Doubles: P.R.le Couteur (160 and 11-66 in 1910); G.J.Toogood (149 and 10-93 in 1985)

INDIAN PREMIER LEAGUE 2010

The third IPL tournament was held in India between 12 March and 25 April. Following bomb explosions outside the ground in Bangalore on 17 April, the semi-finals were moved from that city to Mumbai.

	Team	P	W	L	T	NR	Pts	Net RR
1	Mumbai Indians (7)	14	10	4	–	–	20	+1.08
2	Deccan Chargers (4)	14	8	6	–	–	16	–0.29
3	Chennai Super Kings (2)	14	7	7	–	–	14	+0.27
4	Royal Challengers Bangalore (3)	14	7	7	–	–	14	+0.21
5	Delhi Daredevils (1)	14	7	7	–	–	14	+0.02
6	Kolkata Knight Riders (8)	14	7	7	–	–	14	–0.34
7	Rajasthan Royals (6)	14	6	8	–	–	12	–0.51
8	Kings XI Punjab (5)	14	4	10	–	–	8	–0.47

1st Semi-Final: At Dr D.Y.Patil Sports Academy, Mumbai, 21 April (floodlit). Toss: Mumbai Indians. **MUMBAI INDIANS** won by 35 runs. Mumbai Indians 184-5 (20; S.S.Tiwary 52*). Royal Challengers Bangalore 149-9 (20; K.A.Pollard 3-17). Award: K.A.Pollard 33* and 3-17.

2nd Semi-Final: At Dr D.Y.Patil Sports Academy, Mumbai, 22 April (floodlit). Toss: Chennai Super Kings. **CHENNAI SUPER KINGS** won by 38 runs. Chennai Super Kings 142-7 (20; R.J.Harris 3-29). Deccan Chargers 104 (19.2; D.E.Bollinger 4-13). Award: D.E.Bollinger.

3rd Place Play-off: At Dr D.Y.Patil Sports Academy, Mumbai, 24 April (floodlit). Toss: Deccan Chargers. **ROYAL CHALLENGERS BANGALORE** won by nine wickets. Deccan Chargers 82 (18.3; A.Kumble 4-16). Royal Challengers Bangalore 86-1 (13.5). Award: A.Kumble.

FINAL: At Dr D.Y.Patil Sports Academy, Mumbai, 25 April (floodlit). Toss: Chennai Super Kings. **CHENNAI SUPER KINGS** won by 22 runs. Chennai Super Kings 168-5 (20; S.K.Raina 57*). Mumbai Indians 146-9 (20). Award: S.K.Raina. Series award: S.R.Tendulkar (Mumbai Indians).

IPL winners: 2008 Rajasthan Royals   2009 Deccan Chargers

TEAM RECORDS
HIGHEST TOTALS

246-5 (20)	Chennai v Rajasthan	Chennai	2010
240-5 (20)	Chennai v Punjab	Mohali	2008

LOWEST TOTALS

58	(15.1)	Rajasthan v Bangalore	Cape Town	2009
67	(15.2)	Kolkata v Mumbai	Mumbai	2008

LARGEST MARGINS OF VICTORY

140 runs	Kolkata (222-3) v Bangalore (82)	Bangalore	2008
10 wickets	Mumbai (154-7) v Deccan (155-0)	Mumbai	2008
10 wickets	Rajasthan (92) v Bangalore (93-0)	Bangalore	2010

Delhi beat Punjab by ten wickets in a reduced game in 2009.

BATTING RECORDS
600 RUNS IN A SEASON

Runs			Year	M	I	NO	HS	Ave	100	50	6s	4s	R/100B
618	S.R.Tendulkar	Mumbai	2010	15	15	2	89*	47.53	–	5	3	86	132.6
616	S.E.Marsh	Punjab	2008	11	11	2	115	68.44	1	5	26	59	139.7

HIGHEST SCORES

Score	Balls				
158*	73	B.B.McCullum	Kolkata v Bangalore	Bangalore	2008
127	56	M.Vijay	Chennai v Rajasthan	Chennai	2010
117*	53	A.Symonds	Deccan v Rajasthan	Hyderabad	2008
116*	54	M.E.K.Hussey	Chennai v Punjab	Mohali	2008
115	69	S.E.Marsh	Punjab v Rajasthan	Mohali	2008

FASTEST HUNDRED

37 balls	Y.K.Pathan (100)	Rajasthan v Mumbai	Mumbai (BS)	2010

MOST SIXES IN AN INNINGS

13	B.B.McCullum	Kolkata v Bangalore	Bangalore	2008
11	S.T.Jayasuriya	Mumbai v Chennai	Mumbai	2008
11	M.Vijay	Chennai v Rajasthan	Chennai	2010

HIGHEST STRIKE RATE IN A SEASON (Qualification: 100 runs or more)

R/100B	Score	Balls			
204.34	188	92	B.B.McCullum	Kolkata	2008

HIGHEST STRIKE RATE IN AN INNINGS (Qualification: 25 runs, 300+ strike rate)

R/100B	Score	Balls				
385.7	27*	7	B.Akhil	Bangalore v Deccan	Hyderabad	2008
346.1	45*	13	K.A.Pollard	Mumbai v Delhi	Mumbai (BS)	2010
306.2	49	16	Yuvraj Singh	Punjab v Rajasthan	Mohali	2008

BOWLING RECORDS
20 WICKETS IN A SEASON

Wkts			Year	P	O	M	Runs	Avge	Best 4w	R/Over
23	R.P.Singh	Deccan	2009	16	59.4	1	417	18.13	4-22 1	6.98
22	Sohail Tanvir	Rajasthan	2008	11	41.1	—	266	12.09	6-14 2	6.46
21	A.Kumble	Bangalore	2009	16	59.1	1	347	16.52	5- 5 2	5.86
21	P.P.Ojha	Deccan	2010	16	58.5	—	429	20.42	3-26 —	7.29

MOST WICKETS IN AN INNINGS

6-14	Sohail Tanvir	Rajasthan v Chennai	Jaipur	2008
5- 5	A.Kumble	Bangalore v Rajasthan	Cape Town	2009
5-17	A.Mishra	Delhi v Deccan	Delhi	2008
5-24	L.Balaji	Chennai v Punjab	Chennai	2008

HAT-TRICKS

L.Balaji	Chennai v Punjab	Chennai	2008
A.Mishra	Delhi v Deccan	Delhi	2008
M.Ntini	Chennai v Kolkata	Kolkata	2008
R.G.Sharma	Deccan v Mumbai	Centurion	2009
Yuvraj Singh	Punjab v Deccan	Johannesburg	2009
P.Kumar	Bangalore v Rajasthan	Bangalore	2010

MOST ECONOMICAL BOWLING ANALYSIS

O	M	R	W				
4	1	6	0	F.H.Edwards	Deccan v Kolkata	Cape Town	2009
4	1	6	1	A.Nehra	Delhi v Punjab	Bloemfontein	2009

MOST EXPENSIVE BOWLING ANALYSIS

O	M	R	W				
4	0	59	1	R.P.Singh	Deccan v Kolkata	Hyderabad	2008
4	0	58	0	Mashrafe Mortaza	Kolkata v Deccan	Johannesburg	2009

CHAMPIONS LEAGUE TWENTY20 2010

The second Champions League Twenty20 tournament took place in South Africa between 10 and 26 September. Ten teams took part, having qualified from their domestic Twenty20 competitions: three from India's IPL, two each from Australia and South Africa, and one each from New Zealand, Sri Lanka and West Indies. No teams from England participated, because the competition coincided with the English season. The winners of the first Champions League tournament, held in India, were New South Wales.

GROUP A

Team	P	W	L	T	NR	Pts	Net RR
1 Chennai Super Kings	4	3	1	–	–	6	+2.05
2 Warriors	4	3	1	–	–	6	+0.58
3 Victoria	4	3	1	–	–	6	+0.36
4 Wayamba	4	1	3	–	–	2	–1.12
5 Central Districts	4	–	4	–	–	0	–1.84

GROUP B

Team	P	W	L	T	NR	Pts	Net RR
1 South Australia	4	4	–	–	–	8	+0.58
2 Royal Challengers Bangalore	4	2	2	–	–	4	+0.75
3 Lions	4	2	2	–	–	4	+0.40
4 Mumbai Indians	4	2	2	–	–	4	+0.22
5 Guyana	4	–	4	–	–	0	–2.08

1st Semi-Final: At Kingsmead, Durban, 24 September (floodlit). Toss: Chennai Super Kings. **CHENNAI SUPER KINGS** won by 52 runs (D/L method). Chennai Super Kings 174-4 (17; S.K.Raina 94*). Royal Challengers Bangalore 123 (16.2; M.K.Pandey 52, D.E.Bollinger 3-27). Award: S.K.Raina.

2nd Semi-Final: At Centurion Park, Pretoria, 25 September (floodlit). Toss: Warriors. **WARRIORS** won by 30 runs. Warriors 175-6 (20; D.J.Jacobs 61, D.J.Harris 3-18). South Australia 145-7 (20; C.J.Ferguson 71). Award: D.J.Jacobs.

FINAL: At New Wanderers Stadium, Johannesburg, 26 September (floodlit). Toss: Warriors. **CHENNAI SUPER KINGS** won by eight wickets. Warriors 128-7 (20; M.Muralitharan 3-16). Chennai Super Kings 132-2 (19; M.Vijay 58, M.E.K.Hussey 51*). Award: M.Vijay. Series award: R.Ashwin (Chennai Super Kings).

TOURNAMENT RECORDS 2009-10

Highest total	213-4		Trinidad & Tobago v Eagles	Hyderabad	2009
Lowest total	70		Central Districts v Wayamba	Port Elizabeth	2010
Largest victory	97 runs		Chennai (200-3) v Wayamba (103)	Centurion	2010
Highest score	104*	A.G.Puttick	Cape Cobras v Otago	Hyderabad	2009
Most runs overall	294	M.Vijay (ave 49.00)	Chennai Super Kings		2010
Most runs in season	294	M.Vijay (ave 49.00)	Chennai Super Kings		2010
Highest partnership	147	D.J.Jacobs/A.G.Prince	Warriors v CD	Port Elizabeth	2010
Best bowling	4-17	C.J.D.de Villiers	Eagles v Somerset	Hyderabad	2009
Hat-trick		I.Udana	Wayamba v Central Districts	Port Elizabeth	2010
Most wickets overall	16	D.J.Bravo (ave 17.31)	Trinidad & Tobago, Mumbai		2009-10
Most wickets in season	13	R.Ashwin (ave 11.69)	Chennai Super Kings		2010
Most economical	4-0-7-2	H.M.R.K.B.Herath	Wayamba v CD	Port Elizabeth	2010
Most expensive	4-0-59-0	A.Mishra	Delhi v Bangalore	Bangalore	2009

1934-35 to 1 April 2011

RESULTS SUMMARY

	Opponents	Tests	E	A	NZ	SA	WI	I	P	SL	Ire	H	Drawn
						Won by							Drawn
England	Australia	45	8	11	–	–	–	–	–	–	–	–	26
	New Zealand	23	6	–	0	–	–	–	–	–	–	–	17
	South Africa	6	2	–	–	0	–	–	–	–	–	–	4
	West Indies	3	2	–	–	–	0	–	–	–	–	–	1
	India	12	1	–	–	–	–	1	–	–	–	–	10
Australia	New Zealand	13	–	4	1	–	–	–	–	–	–	–	8
	West Indies	2	–	0	–	–	0	–	–	–	–	–	2
	India	9	–	4	–	–	–	0	–	–	–	–	5
New Zealand	South Africa	3	–	–	1	0	–	–	–	–	–	–	2
	India	6	–	–	0	–	–	0	–	–	–	–	6
South Africa	India	1	–	–	–	0	–	1	–	–	–	–	–
	Holland	1	–	–	–	1	–	–	–	–	0	–	–
West Indies	India	6	–	–	–	–	1	1	–	–	–	–	4
	Pakistan	1	–	–	–	–	0	–	0	–	–	–	1
Pakistan	Sri Lanka	1	–	–	–	–	–	–	0	1	–	–	–
	Ireland	1	–	–	–	–	–	–	0	–	1	–	–
		133	19	19	2	1	1	3	0	1	1	0	86

	Tests	Won	Lost	Drawn	Toss Won
England	89	19	12	58	53
Australia	69	19	9	41	23
New Zealand	45	2	10	33	21
South Africa	11	1	4	6	6
West Indies	12	1	3	8	6†
India	34	3	6	25	16†
Pakistan	3	–	2	1	1
Sri Lanka	1	1	–	–	1
Ireland	1	1	–	–	–
Holland	1	–	1	–	1

† *Results of tosses in five of the six India v West Indies Tests in 1976-77 are not known*

TEAM RECORDS
HIGHEST INNINGS TOTALS

569-6d	Australia v England	Guildford	1998
525	Australia v India	Ahmedabad	1983-84
517-8	New Zealand v England	Scarborough	1996
503-5d	England v New Zealand	Christchurch	1934-35
497	England v South Africa	Shenley	2003
467	India v England	Taunton	2002
455	England v South Africa	Taunton	2003
440	West Indies v Pakistan	Karachi	2003-04
427-4d	Australia v England	Worcester	1998
426-7d	Pakistan v West Indies	Karachi	2003-04
426-9d	India v England	Blackpool	1986
414	England v New Zealand	Scarborough	1996
414	England v Australia	Guildford	1998

| 404-9d | India v South Africa | Paarl | 2001-02 |
| 403-8d | New Zealand v India | Nelson | 1994-95 |

The highest totals for countries not included above are:

316	South Africa v England	Shenley	2003
193-3d	Ireland v Pakistan	Dublin	2000
108	Holland v South Africa	Rotterdam	2007

LOWEST INNINGS TOTALS

35	England v Australia	Melbourne	1957-58
38	Australia v England	Melbourne	1957-58
44	New Zealand v England	Christchurch	1934-35
47	Australia v England	Brisbane	1934-35
50	Holland v South Africa	Rotterdam	2007
53	Pakistan v Ireland	Dublin	2000

The lowest innings totals for countries not included above are:

65	India v West Indies	Jammu	1976-77
67	West Indies v England	Canterbury	1979
89	South Africa v New Zealand	Durban	1971-72

BATTING RECORDS
1000 RUNS IN TESTS

		Career	M	I	NO	HS	Avge	100	50
1935	J.A.Brittin (E)	1979-98	27	44	5	167	49.61	5	11
1594	R.Heyhoe-Flint (E)	1960-79	22	38	3	179	45.54	3	10
1522	C.M.Edwards (E)	1996-2011	19	35	3	117	49.09	4	8
1301	D.A.Hockley (NZ)	1979-96	19	29	4	126*	52.04	4	7
1164	C.A.Hodges (E)	1984-92	18	31	2	158*	40.13	2	6
1110	S.Agarwal (I)	1984-95	13	23	1	190	50.45	4	4
1078	E.Bakewell (E)	1968-79	12	22	4	124	59.88	4	7
1030	S.C.Taylor (E)	1999-2009	15	27	2	177	41.20	4	2
1007	M.E.Maclagan (E)	1934-51	14	25	1	119	41.95	2	6
1002	K.L.Rolton (A)	1995-2009	14	22	4	209*	55.66	2	5

HIGHEST INDIVIDUAL INNINGS

242	Kiran Baluch	P v WI	Karachi	2003-04
214	M.Raj	I v E	Taunton	2002
209*	K.L.Rolton	A v E	Leeds	2001
204	K.E.Flavell	NZ v E	Scarborough	1996
204‡	M.A.J.Goszko	A v E	Shenley	2001
200	J.Broadbent	A v E	Guildford	1998
193	D.A.Annetts	A v E	Collingham	1987
190	S.Agarwal	I v E	Worcester	1986
189	E.A.Snowball	E v NZ	Christchurch	1934-35
179	R.Heyhoe-Flint	E v A	The Oval	1976
177	S.C.Taylor	E v SA	Shenley	2003
176*	K.L.Rolton	A v E	Worcester	1998
167	J.A.Brittin	E v A	Harrogate	1998
161*	E.C.Drumm	E v A	Christchurch	1994-95
160	B.A.Daniels	E v NZ	Scarborough	1996
158*	C.A.Hodges	E v NZ	Canterbury	1984
155*	P.F.McKelvey	NZ v E	Wellington	1968-69

‡ *On debut*

314

FIVE HUNDREDS

		M	I	E	A	NZ	SA	WI	IND	P	SL	IRE
						Opponents						
5	J.A.Brittin (E)	27	44	–	3	1	–	–	1	–	–	–

HIGHEST PARTNERSHIP FOR EACH WICKET

1st	241	Kiran Baluch/Sajjida Shah	P v WI	Karachi	2003-04
2nd	235	E.A.Snowball/M.E.Hide	E v NZ	Christchurch	1934-35
3rd	309	L.A.Reeler/D.A.Annetts	A v E	Collingham	1987
4th	253	K.L.Rolton/L.C.Broadfoot	A v E	Leeds	2001
5th	138	J.Logtenberg/C.van der Westhuizen	SA v E	Shenley	2003
6th	229	J.M.Fields/R.L.Haynes	A v E	Worcester	2009
7th	157	M.Raj/J.Goswami	I v E	Taunton	2002
8th	181	S.J.Griffiths/D.L.Wilson	A v NZ	Auckland	1989-90
9th	107	B.Botha/M.Payne	SA v NZ	Cape Town	1971-72
10th	119	S.Nitschke/C.R.Smith	A v E	Hove	2005

BOWLING RECORDS

50 WICKETS IN TESTS

Wkts		*Career*	*M*	*Balls*	*Runs*	*Avge*	*Best*	*5wI*	*10wM*
77	M.B.Duggan (E)	1949-63	17	3734	1039	13.49	7- 6	5	–
68	E.R.Wilson (A)	1948-58	11	2885	803	11.80	7- 7	4	2
63	D.F.Edulji (I)	1976-91	20	5098†	1624	25.77	6- 64	1	–
60	M.E.Maclagan (E)	1934-51	14	3432	935	15.58	7- 10	3	–
60	C.L.Fitzpatrick (A)	1991-2006	13	3603	1147	19.11	5-292	–	–
60	S.Kulkarni (I)	1976-91	19	3320†	1647	27.45	6- 99	5	–
57	R.H.Thompson (A)	1972-85	16	4304	1040	18.24	5- 33	1	–
55	J.Lord (NZ)	1966-79	15	3108	1049	19.07	6-119	4	1
50	E.Bakewell (E)	1968-79	12	2697	831	16.62	7- 61	3	1

† Excludes balls bowled in Sixth Test v West Indies 1976-77

TEN WICKETS IN A TEST

13-226	Shaiza Khan	P v WI	Karachi	2003-04
11- 16	E.R.Wilson	A v E	Melbourne	1957-58
11- 63	J.M.Greenwood	E v WI	Canterbury	1979
11-107	L.C.Pearson	E v A	Sydney	2002-03
10- 65	E.R.Wilson	A v NZ	Wellington	1947-48
10- 75	E.Bakewell	E v WI	Birmingham	1979
10- 78	J.Goswami	I v E	Taunton	2006
10-107	K.Price	A v I	Lucknow	1983-84
10-118	D.A.Gordon	A v E	Melbourne	1968-69
10-137	J.Lord	NZ v A	Melbourne	1978-79

SEVEN WICKETS IN AN INNINGS

8-53	N.David	I v E	Jamshedpur	1995-96
7- 6	M.B.Duggan	E v A	Melbourne	1957-58
7- 7	E.R.Wilson	A v E	Melbourne	1957-58
7-10	M.E.Maclagan	E v A	Brisbane	1934-35
7-18	A.Palmer	A v E	Brisbane	1934-35
7-24	L.Johnston	A v NZ	Melbourne	1971-72
7-34	G.E.McConway	E v I	Worcester	1986
7-41	J.A.Burley	NZ v E	The Oval	1966
7-51	L.C.Pearson	E v A	Sydney	2002-03
7-59	Shaiza Khan	P v WI	Karachi	2003-04
7-61	E.Bakewell	E v WI	Birmingham	1979

HAT-TRICKS

E.R.Wilson	Australia v England	Melbourne	1957-58
Shaiza Khan	Pakistan v West Indies	Karachi	2003-04
R.M.Farrell	Australia v England	Sydney	2010-11

WICKET-KEEPING AND FIELDING RECORDS
25 DISMISSALS IN TESTS

Total			Tests	Ct	St	
58	C.Matthews	Australia	20	46	12	1984-95
43	J.Smit	England	21	39	4	1992-2006
36	S.A.Hodges	England	11	19	17	1969-79
28	B.A.Brentnall	New Zealand	10	16	12	1966-72

EIGHT DISMISSALS IN A TEST

9 (8ct, 1st)	C.Matthews	A v I	Adelaide	1990-91
8 (6ct, 2st)	L.Nye	E v NZ	New Plymouth	1991-92

SIX DISMISSALS IN AN INNINGS

8 (6ct, 2st)	L.Nye	E v NZ	New Plymouth	1991-92
6 (2ct, 4st)	B.A.Brentnall	NZ v SA	Johannesburg	1971-72

20 CATCHES IN THE FIELD IN TESTS

Total			Tests	
25	C.A.Hodges	England	18	1984-92
21	S.Shah	India	20	1976-91
20	L.A.Fullston	Australia	12	1984-87

APPEARANCE RECORDS
25 TEST MATCH APPEARANCES

27	J.A.Brittin	England	1979-98

12 MATCHES AS CAPTAIN

			Won	Lost	Drawn	
14	P.F.McKelvey	New Zealand	2	3	9	1966-79
12	R.Heyhoe-Flint	England	2	–	10	1966-76
12	S.Rangaswamy	India	1	2	9	1976-84

ENGLAND WOMEN'S TEST MATCH RESULT IN 2010-11

At Bankstown Oval, Sydney, 22, 23, 24, 25 January. Toss: England. Result: **AUSTRALIA** won by seven wickets. England 207 (C.M.Edwards 114, E.A.Perry 4-56) and 149 (R.M.Farrell 5-23). Australia 159-9d and 198-3 (S.J.Elliott 81*, A.J.Blackwell 74). England debuts: L.P.Griffiths, D.Hazell, H.C.Knight.

WOMEN'S LIMITED-OVERS RECORDS

1973 to 1 March 2011
RESULTS SUMMARY

	LOI	Won	Lost	Tied	No Result
Australia	243	187	50	1	5
Denmark	33	6	27	–	–
England	254	139	104	2	9
India	183	96	82	1	4
International XI	18	3	14	–	1
Ireland	112	35	74	–	3
Jamaica	5	1	4	–	–
Japan	5	–	5	–	–
Netherlands	93	18	75	–	–
New Zealand	246	127	112	2	5
Pakistan	76	15	60	–	1
Scotland	8	1	7	–	–
South Africa	83	38	40	1	4
Sri Lanka	83	41	40	–	2
Trinidad & Tobago	6	2	4	–	–
West Indies	84	37	44	1	2
Young England	6	1	5	–	–

TEAM RECORDS
HIGHEST INNINGS TOTALS

455-5 (50)	New Zealand v Pakistan	Christchurch	1996-97
412-3 (50)	Australia v Denmark	Bombay	1997-98

HIGHEST MATCH AGGREGATES

570-14	New Zealand (263) v Australia (307-4)	Hamilton	2008-09
563-16	England (272) v New Zealand (291-6)	Chennai	2006-07

LARGEST RUNS MARGIN OF VICTORY

408 runs	New Zealand beat Pakistan	Christchurch	1996-97
374 runs	Australia beat Pakistan	Melbourne	1996-97
363 runs	Australia beat Denmark	Bombay	1997-98

LOWEST INNINGS TOTALS

22 (23.4)	Netherlands v West Indies	Deventer	2008
23 (24.1)	Pakistan v Australia	Melbourne	1996-97
24 (21.3)	Scotland v England	Reading	2001

BATTING RECORDS
HIGHEST INDIVIDUAL INNINGS

229*	B.J.Clark	Australia v Denmark	Bombay	1997-98
173*	C.M.Edwards	England v Ireland	Poona	1997-98
168	S.W.Bates	New Zealand v Pakistan	Sydney	2008-09
156*	L.M.Keightley	Australia v Pakistan	Melbourne	1996-97
156*	S.C.Taylor	England v India	Lord's	2006
154*	K.L.Rolton	Australia v Sri Lanka	Christchurch	2000-01
153*	J.Logtenberg	South Africa v Netherlands	Deventer	2007
151	K.L.Rolton	Australia v Ireland	Dublin	2005

2000 RUNS IN A CAREER

Runs		Career	M	I	NO	HS	Avge	100	50
4844	B.J.Clark (A)	1991-2005	118	114	12	229*	47.49	5	30
4814	K.L.Rolton (A)	1995-2009	141	132	32	154*	48.14	8	33
4300	C.M.Edwards (E)	1997-2011	145	135	18	173*	36.75	4	35
4064	D.A.Hockley (NZ)	1982-2000	118	115	18	117	41.89	4	34
4007	M.Raj (I)	1999-2011	125	112	31	114*	49.46	3	32
3963	S.C.Taylor (E)	1998-2010	122	116	18	156*	40.43	8	22
2919	H.M.Tiffen (NZ)	1999-2009	117	111	16	100	30.72	1	18
2844	E.C.Drumm (NZ)	1992-2006	101	94	13	116	35.11	2	19
2777	A.Chopra (I)	1999-2010	121	106	21	100	32.67	1	18
2630	L.M.Keightley (A)	1995-2005	82	78	12	156*	39.84	4	21
2463	L.C.Sthalekar (A)	2001-2011	103	94	20	104*	33.28	2	16
2201	R.J.Rolls (E)	1997-2007	104	91	3	114	25.01	2	12
2121	J.A.Brittin (E)	1979-1998	63	59	9	138*	42.42	5	8
2091	J.Sharma (I)	2002-2008	77	75	7	138*	30.75	2	14

HIGHEST PARTNERSHIP FOR EACH WICKET

1st	268	S.J.Taylor/C.M.G.Atkins	E v SA	Lord's	2008
2nd	262	H.M.Tiffen/S.W.Bates	NZ v P	Sydney	2008-09
3rd	244	K.L.Rolton/L.C.Sthalekar	A v Ire	Dublin	2005
4th	224*	J.Logtenberg//M.du Preez	SA v Ne	Deventer	2007
5th	188*	S.C.Taylor/J.Cassar	E v SL	Lincoln, NZ	2001-02
6th	139*	S.J.McGlashan/N.J.Browne	NZ v SA	Bowral	2008-09
7th	104*	S.J.Tsukigawa/N.J.Browne	NZ v E	Madras	2006-07
8th	85*	S.L.Clarke/N.J.Shaw	E v Sc	Reading	2001
9th	73	L.R.F.Askew/I.T.Guha	E v NZ	Madras	2006-07
10th	43	A.Sharma/G.Sultana	I v E	Sydney	2008-09

BOWLING RECORDS
SIX WICKETS IN AN INNINGS

7- 4	Sajjida Shah	Pakistan v Japan	Amsterdam	2003
7- 8	J.M.Chamberlain	England v Denmark	Haarlem	1991
7-24	S.Nitschke	Australia v England	Kidderminster	2005
6-10	J.Lord	New Zealand v India	Auckland	1981-82
6-10	M.Maben	India v Sri Lanka	Kandy	2003-04
6-20	G.L.Page	New Zealand v Trinidad & T	St Albans	1973
6-32	B.H.McNeill	New Zealand v England	Lincoln, NZ	2007-08

100 WICKETS IN A CAREER

Wkts		Career	M	Overs	Runs	Avge	Best	4wI
180	C.L.Fitzpatrick (A)	1993-2007	109	1002.5	3023	16.79	5-14	11
141	N.David (I)	1995-2008	97	815.2	2305	16.34	5-20	6
124	J.Goswami (I)	2002-2011	110	864.3	2715	21.89	5-16	4
117	L.C.Sthalekar (A)	2001-2011	103	788.5	2934	25.07	5-35	2
102	C.E.Taylor (E)	1988-2005	105	856.4	2443	23.95	4-13	2

WICKET-KEEPING AND FIELDING RECORDS
SIX DISMISSALS IN AN INNINGS

6 (4ct, 2st)	S.L.Illingworth	New Zealand v Australia	Beckenham	1993
6 (1ct, 5st)	V.Kalpana	India v Denmark	Slough	1993
6 (2ct, 4st)	Batool Fatima	Pakistan v West Indies	Karachi	2003-04

100 DISMISSALS IN A CAREER

Total			Career	LOI	Ct	St
133	R.J.Rolls	New Zealand	1997-2007	104	89	44
114	J.Smit	England	1993-2007	109	69	45

FOUR CATCHES IN AN INNINGS IN THE FIELD

4	Z.J.Goss	Australia v New Zealand	Adelaide		1995-96

40 CATCHES IN THE FIELD IN A CAREER

Total			LOI	Career
45	B.J.Clark	Australia	118	1991-2005
41	D.A.Hockley	New Zealand	118	1982-2000
41	J.Goswani	India	110	2002-2011

APPEARANCE RECORDS

120 APPEARANCES

145	C.M.Edwards	England	1997-2011
141	K.L.Rolton	Australia	1995-2009
125	M.Raj	India	1999-2011
122	S.C.Taylor	England	1998-2010
121	A.Chopra	India	1995-2010

100 MATCHES AS CAPTAIN

			Won	Lost	No Result	
101	B.J.Clark	Australia	83	17	1	1994-2005

DUCKWORTH/LEWIS – A BRIEF EXPLANATION

The Duckworth/Lewis (D/L) method has been around now for 12 years and it is generally accepted as being a very fair method for resetting targets in interrupted one-day matches. However, ask a typical cricket fan as to how the calculations are done and the fallback excuse of not being good at maths at school is frequently trotted out. But if you can work out how much tax you have to pay on your net income then D/L calculations are well within your grasp.

You may well have heard that the D/L method is based on the idea of resources – these are the combination of wickets and overs that a team has for its innings. However, it's not just the numbers of these that matter; it is also their relative value – wickets and overs have different relative importance as an innings progresses. For example, having lots of wickets in hand without overs left in which to use them is of little value, just as if lots of overs remain they have little value if there are no wickets left with which to use them. In conducting their innings, teams need to manage these twin resources in order to maximise the total they set or maximise their chances of winning the match. Through some neat behind-the-scenes mathematics and statistical analysis of hundreds of matches, Duckworth and Lewis have produced a table that represents the average percentages remaining of their twin resources of a 50-over innings. In the extract of the table supplied you will see that teams start with all 50 overs and 10 wickets – and therefore 100% of their resources. As an innings progresses a team receives its overs, loses its wickets and thereby consumes its resources. The table works always in overs left – in that way it can be used for matches that are shorter than 50 overs – and tells us what percentage of their combined resources remains.

Wickets lost:	0	2	4	6	9
Overs remaining:-					
50	100.0	85.1	62.7	34.9	4.7
40	89.3	77.8	59.5	34.6	4.7
30	75.1	67.3	54.1	33.6	4.7
25	66.5	60.5	50.0	32.6	4.7
20	56.6	52.4	44.6	30.8	4.7
10	32.1	30.8	28.3	22.8	4.7
5	17.2	16.8	16.1	14.3	4.6

Suppose that a team has batted for 45 overs and has lost 6 wickets. With 5 overs left, for 6 wickets lost the table shows it has 14.3% of its resources remaining. If its innings is now terminated, these resources are lost and it has had available for its innings 100 – 14.3 = 85.7% resources compared with the 100% for a complete 50-over innings.

These figures came into play in a crucial Group match of the 2003 World Cup in South Africa. Against the host nation, Sri Lanka scored 268 in their 100% resources of 50 overs. Rain began to fall and abandonment looked likely at the end of the 45th over of South Africa's innings. Charts of the D/L method were consulted and the relevant figure was obtained through the comparative resources of the two teams. The calculation was 268 × 85.7/100 = 229.676. This meant that in order to win SA needed to reach 230 by the end of the 45th over if the match were abandoned. A score of 229 would be the score to tie.

How would South Africa know this? You will have seen the D/L par-score displayed on scoreboards. These numbers come from the par-score sheet that is distributed during the interval to team camps, match officials and the media. The par-score is given for the end of every one of the combinations of overs left and wickets lost (and even on a ball-by-ball basis). This sheet is clearly labelled as the score needed to tie. In the World Cup match the SA camp told the batsmen, Boucher and Klusener, that they needed to get to 229 by the end of the over. Thanks to a six from Boucher off the penultimate ball of the over, they achieved this – and to avoid losing his wicket, which would have raised the par-score, Boucher blocked the last ball. Play was duly abandoned at the end of the over but the dismay in the SA camp was palpable when it was finally realised that the 229 the batsmen had been told to score was in fact the

320

score to tie and not to win the match. So a tie it was and the misreading of the clear information available led to the elimination of the host nation from the tournament.

Whenever a stoppage occurs within an innings, the table provides the information by which to calculate the resources lost. Suppose that there are 20 overs left with only 4 wickets down and a stoppage reduces the innings by 10 overs so there are now only 10 overs left on the resumption. You will see from the table that the team went off with 44.6% resources left and came back with 28.3% left. The stoppage would have cost it 44.6 – 28.3 = 16.3% of its resources so that it would have available 100 – 16.3 = 83.7% resources for its innings if there are no more stoppages (but if there are, the resources available are further reduced in the same way) and, in most cases, the target comes from reducing the first innings score in proportion to the resources available as in the World Cup example.

Sometimes teams start with fewer than 50 overs either due to a shorter match competition, such as the Pro40 or Twenty20, or due to a delayed start. For a 25-over innings, for instance, teams start with 66.5% resources compared with a 50-over innings. Although they have half the overs they still have all 10 wickets and therefore more than half their resources – the table says about two-thirds compared with a 50-over innings. Any loss of overs would reduce this further in the same way and using the same figures as in the table.

So you see that it really is simple to calculate targets following interruptions during the second innings. The method is simply to adjust the first innings score in proportion to the resources available to the two teams – rounding up to win and one fewer to tie.

A distinctive feature of the D/L method compared with previous methods of adjusting targets is that it compensates the team batting first for stoppages within its innings – its batting strategy has been based on the full 50 overs and so to have it curtailed is usually a disadvantage. The D/L method usually sets an enhanced target, that is, a target which is quite a few runs more than the team batting first scored. This has the effect of compensating it for the unexpected shortening of the first innings and the advantage that the team batting second has from knowing in advance of its shorter innings.

How this is achieved, together with further detailed descriptions of the Duckworth/Lewis method and some frequently asked questions, can be found at the Cricinfo website: www.cricinfo.com/db/ABOUT_CRICKET/RAIN_RULES/ and a booklet is available from Acumen Books at www.acumenbooks.co.uk/ducklew.htm.

One of these FAQs concerns the effect that powerplays have on D/L calculations. Data on powerplays are not yet sufficient to do a thorough analysis, but the logic is similar to the old 15-over rule on which there are plenty of data. These show that the greater runs scored in these overs are consistent with what is expected from the D/L method for the overs and the *wickets* used up in those periods of more attacking fields. Consequently it is unlikely that the powerplays have any significant effect on D/L target calculations. But the situation will be kept under review.

Although rain is usually the cause of stoppages and D/L adjusted targets, interruptions have occurred for several other causes including sandstorms, snow, floodlight failures, crowd disturbances and, on a few occasions, due to the sun!

Cases at the higher levels of the game usually run to 80-100 per year and the total usage is approaching 1000 since the method's first use on 1st January 1997 in which England lost to Zimbabwe when they would have won by the old, unfair average run-rate method.

There have been some advances in the methodology since January 1997. With higher totals being more prevalent, and the introduction of Twenty20 matches which fit well into the D/L system, teams need to score a bigger percentage of their runs in the earlier stages of their innings than those suggested by the standard tables. Consequently, higher scores lead to the need for the table to be adjusted and this needs the computer to do the calculations. Whereas what is now known as the Standard Edition, using a single table of resources as described here, is used at lower levels of the game where computers aren't necessary or available, the higher levels of the game now use the more advanced computerised version called the Professional Edition. In this edition, the computer in effect produces a different table of resources for every match, but thereafter the calculations are the same as described here.

MCCA FIXTURES 2011

Sun 1 May
Neston
Oswestry
Abergavenny
Corsham
Welwyn Garden City
Challow
Henley
March

KNOCK-OUT TROPHY
Cheshire v Cumberland (1)
Shropshire v Staffordshire (1)
Wales MC v Cornwall (2)
Wiltshire v Buckinghamshire (2)
Hertfordshire v Herefordshire (3)
Oxfordshire v Dorset (3)
Berkshire v Suffolk (4)
Cambridgeshire v Lincolnshire (4)

Sun 8 May
Jesmond
Knypersley
Marlow
Instow
Ampthill
Colwall
Woodhall Spa (tbc)
Manor Park

KNOCK-OUT TROPHY
Northumberland v Shropshire (1)
Staffordshire v Cheshire (1)
Buckinghamshire v Wales MC (2)
Devon v Wiltshire (2)
Bedfordshire v Hertfordshire (3)
Herefordshire v Oxfordshire (3)
Lincolnshire v Berkshire (4)
Norfolk v Cambridgeshire (4)

Sun 15 May
Marple
Penrith
Truro
Ebbw Vale
Weymouth
Banbury
Falkland
Ipswich S

KNOCK-OUT TROPHY
Cheshire v Northumberland (1)
Cumberland v Staffordshire (1)
Cornwall v Buckinghamshire (2)
Wales MC v Devon (2)
Dorset v Herefordshire (3)
Oxfordshire v Bedfordshire (3)
Berkshire v Norfolk (4)
Suffolk v Lincolnshire (4)

Sun 29 May
Jesmond
Shifnal
Bovey Tracey
Trowbridge
Dunstable
North Mymms
Clare C, Cambridge
Manor Park

KNOCK-OUT TROPHY
Northumberland v Cumberland (1)
Shropshire v Cheshire (1)
Devon v Cornwall (2)
Wiltshire v Wales MC (2)
Bedfordshire v Dorset (3)
Hertfordshire v Oxfordshire (3)
Cambridgeshire v Berkshire (4)
Norfolk v Suffolk (4)

Sun 5 June
Netherfield
Leek
Tring Park
Redruth
Dorchester
Eastnor
Bracebridge Heath
Bury St Edmunds

KNOCK-OUT TROPHY
Cumberland v Shropshire (1)
Staffordshire v Northumberland (1)
Buckinghamshire v Devon (2)
Cornwall v Wiltshire (2)
Dorset v Hertfordshire (3)
Herefordshire v Bedfordshire (3)
Lincolnshire v Norfolk (4)
Suffolk v Cambridgeshire (4)

Sun 12-Tue 14 June
Luton
Henley

MCCA CHAMPIONSHIP
Bedfordshire v Suffolk
Berkshire v Cornwall

Furness	Cumberland v Buckinghamshire
Dean Park	Dorset v Devon
Colwall	Herefordshire v Cheshire
Bishop's Stortford	Hertfordshire v Cambridgeshire
Sleaford	Lincolnshire v Staffordshire
Jesmond	Northumberland v Norfolk
Challow	Oxfordshire v Wiltshire
Pontarddulais	Wales MC v Shropshire

Sun 19 June   **K-O TROPHY Quarter-finals**

Match 1	Winner 2 v Runner-up 3
Match 2	Winner 3 v Runner-up 1
Match 3	Winner 1 v Runner-up 4
Match 4	Winner 4 v Runner-up 2

Sun 26-Tue 28 June   **MCCA CHAMPIONSHIP**

Gerrards Cross	Buckinghamshire v Cambridgeshire
Chester, B'ton Hall	Cheshire v Cornwall
Swalwell	Northumberland v Lincolnshire
Gt & Little Tew	Oxfordshire v Devon
Bridgnorth	Shropshire v Herefordshire
Hem Heath	Staffordshire v Hertfordshire
Mildenhall	Suffolk v Cumberland
Usk	Wales MC v Berkshire
Devizes	Wiltshire v Dorset

Sun 3 July   **K-O TROPHY Semi-finals**
(Res day 4 July)

	Winner Match 4 v Winner Match 2
	Winner Match 1 v Winner Match 3

Sun 10-Tue 12 July   **MCCA CHAMPIONSHIP**

Falkland	Berkshire v Wiltshire
March	Cambridgeshire v Lincolnshire
Falmouth	Cornwall v Wales MC
Sedburgh S	Cumberland v Bedfordshire
Torquay	Devon v Cheshire
Brockhampton	Herefordshire v Dorset
Hertford	Hertfordshire v Norfolk
Whitchurch	Shropshire v Oxfordshire
Knypersley	Staffordshire v Northumberland
Ipswich S	Suffolk v Buckinghamshire

Sun 24-Tue 26 July   **MCCA CHAMPIONSHIP**

Bedford Modern S	Bedfordshire v Cambridgeshire
Finchampstead	Berkshire v Herefordshire
High Wycombe	Buckinghamshire v Staffordshire
Nantwich	Cheshire v Wales MC
St Austell	Cornwall v Shropshire
Dean Park	Dorset v Oxfordshire
Cleethorpes	Lincolnshire v Hertfordshire
Manor Park	Norfolk v Cumberland
Jesmond	Northumberland v Suffolk
Corsham	Wiltshire v Devon

Sun 31 July-Tue 2 August   **MCCA CHAMPIONSHIP**

Manor Park	Norfolk v Bedfordshire

Sun 7-Tue 9 August	MCCA CHAMPIONSHIP
March	Cambridgeshire v Northumberland
Truro	Cornwall v Herefordshire
Exmouth	Devon v Shropshire
Long Marston	Hertfordshire v Cumberland
Grantham	Lincolnshire v Buckinghamshire
Manor Park	Norfolk v Suffolk
Banbury	Oxfordshire v Berkshire
Old Hill	Staffordshire v Bedfordshire
Abergavenny	Wales MC v Dorset
Trowbridge	Wiltshire v Cheshire

Sun 21-Tue 23 August	MCCA CHAMPIONSHIP
Luton	Bedfordshire v Lincolnshire
Slough	Buckinghamshire v Norfolk
Wisbech	Cambridgeshire v Staffordshire
Alderley Edge	Cheshire v Oxfordshire
Barrow	Cumberland v Northumberland
Sidmouth	Devon v Berkshire
Dean Park	Dorset v Cornwall
Eastnor	Herefordshire v Wales MC
Shrewsbury	Shropshire v Wiltshire
Bury St Edmunds	Suffolk v Hertfordshire

Thu 25 August	K-O TROPHY Final
Lord's	(Reserve day 11 September)

Sun 4-Wed 7 Sept	MCCA CHAMPIONSHIP
East Div winner	FINAL

MCCA KNOCK-OUT TROPHY GROUPS

Group 1	*Group 2*	*Group 3*	*Group 4*
Cheshire	Buckinghamshire	Bedfordshire	Berkshire
Cumberland	Cornwall	Dorset	Cambridgeshire
Northumberland	Devon	Herefordshire	Lincolnshire
Shropshire	Wales MC	Hertfordshire	Norfolk
Staffordshire	Wiltshire	Oxfordshire	Suffolk

MCC UNIVERSITIES CHALLENGE 2011

Sun 10, Mon 11 April		**Tue 10, Wed 11 May**	
Weetwood, Leeds	Leeds/Bradford v Loughborough	Durham	Durham v Cardiff
Sat 16, Sun 17 April		**Mon 16, Tue 17 May**	
Cambridge	Cambridge v Oxford	Cambridge	Cambridge v Cardiff
Loughborough	Loughborough v Cardiff	**Tue 31 May, Wed 1 June**	
Durham	Durham v Leeds/Bradford	Oxford	Oxford v Loughborough
Thu 21, Fri 22 April		**Mon 6, Tue 7 June**	
Oxford	Oxford v Durham	Usk	Cardiff v Leeds/Bradford
Mon 25, Tue 26 April		**Tue 14, Wed 15 June**	
Loughborough	Loughborough v Cambridge	Panteg	Cardiff v Oxford
Sat 30 April, Sun 1 May		Durham	Durham v Loughborough
Weetwood, Leeds	Leeds/Bradford v Oxford	Weetwood, Leeds	Leeds/Bradford v Cambridge
Thu 5, Fri 6 May		**Mon 27 June**	
Cambridge	Cambridge v Durham	Lord's	tbc

SECOND XI CHAMPIONSHIP FIXTURES 2011

THREE-DAY MATCHES (* FOUR DAYS)

APRIL

Tue 12	High Wycombe	MCC YC v Glos
Mon 18	The Oval	MCC YC v Surrey
Wed 20	Lady Bay	Notts v Durham
	Taunton Vale	Somerset v Sussex
Wed 27	Cardiff	Glam v Glos
	Radlett	Middx v Sussex
	North Perrott	Somerset v MCC YC
	Moseley	Warwicks v Leics

MAY

Wed 4	Longhirst	Durham v Warwicks
	Chelmsford	Essex v Middx
	Nantwich	Lancs v Worcs
	Ashby Hastings	Leics v Derbys
	Taunton Vale	Somerset v Glam
	Reigate Priory	Surrey v Glos
	Barnsley	Yorks v Notts
Mon 9	Southampton	Hants v Glam
Tue 10	Richmond	Middx v Somerset
Wed 11	Leicester Ivanhoe	Leics v Lancs
	Radlett	MCC YC v Essex
	Kidderminster	Worcs v Derbys
Tue 17	Pontarddulais	Glam v MCC YC
	Bristol	Glos v Sussex
	Southampton	Hants v Middx
	Taunton	Somerset v Surrey
Wed 18	Chester-le-St	Durham v Leics
	Lady Bay	Notts v Worcs
	Coventry/N Warwk	Warwicks v Yorks

JUNE

Wed 1	Bishop's Stortford	Essex v Glos
	Radlett	Middx v Kent
	Stowe S	Northants v Warwicks
	Lady Bay	Notts v Leics
Tue 14	Coggleshall	Essex v Surrey
	Campbell P, Milton K	Northants v Durham
	Lady Bay	Notts v Warwicks
	Kidderminster	Worcs v Leics
	Stamford Bridge	Yorks v Derbys
Wed 15	Radlett	Middx v MCC YC
Mon 20	Derby	Derbys v Lancs
Tue 21	Darlington	Durham v Yorks
	Finedon	Northants v Notts
	Horsham	Sussex v Essex
Wed 22	Beckenham	Kent v MCC YC
Tue 28	Marton	Durham v Derbys
	Desborough	Leics v Northants
Wed 29	Southend	Essex v Hants
	Durham	MCC Univs v Lancs

JULY

Mon 4	Horsham	Sussex v Surrey
Tue 5	York	Yorks v MCC Univs
Wed 6	Southampton	Hants v Kent
Tue 12	Alderley Edge	Lancs v Northants
	Weetwood, Leeds	MCC Univs v Notts
	Newclose, IoW	MCC YC v Hants
Wed 13	Kings S, Canterbury	Kent v Essex
	Radlett	Middx v Glam
	Coventry/N Warwk	Warwicks v Derbys
	Worcester	Worcs v Durham
Tue 19	Canterbury	Kent v Sussex
Wed 20	Denby	Derbys v Northants
	Hartlepool	Durham v MCC Univs
	Cardiff	Glam v Essex
	Bristol	Glos v Somerset
	Todmorden	Lancs v Notts
	Worcester RGS	Worcs v Warwicks
Tue 26	Maidstone	Kent v Somerset
	Wimbledon	Surrey v Hants
	Stamford Bridge	Yorks v Lancs
Wed 27	Bristol	Glos v Middx
	Northampton	Northants v Worcs
	Birmingham	Warwicks v MCC Univs

AUGUST

Tue 2	Guildford	Surrey v Middx
	Hove	Sussex v MCC YC
Wed 3	Belper Meadows	Derbys v MCC Univs
	Cheltenham C	Glos v Hants
	Maidstone	Kent v Glam
	Taunton Vale	Somerset v Essex
	Rugby S	Warwicks v Lancs
Wed 10	Southampton	Hants v Sussex
	Kibworth	Leics v MCC Univs
	Cheam	Surrey v Kent
	Leeds	Yorks v Northants
Tue 16	Bristol	Glos v Kent
	Hove	Sussex v Glam
Wed 17	Denby	Derbys v Notts
	Southampton	Hants v Somerset
	St Annes	Lancs v Durham
	Hinckley Town	Leics v Yorks
	Cambridge	MCC Univs v Worcs
Tue 23	Cardiff	Glam v Surrey
	Cambridge	MCC Univs v Northants
	Worcester	Worcs v Yorks

SEPTEMBER

Tue 6	tbc	FINAL*

SECOND XI TROPHY FIXTURES 2011

(ONE DAY)

APRIL

Mon 11	High Wycombe	MCC YC v Glos
Wed 13	Chelmsford	Essex v Surrey
Tue 19	Lady Bay	Notts v Durham
	Taunton Vale	Somerset v Sussex
Tue 26	Cardiff	Glam v Glos
	Radlett	Middx v Sussex
	North Perrott	Somerset v MCC YC
	Kings Heath	Warwicks v Leics

MAY

Tue 3	Longhirst	Durham v Warwicks
	Chelmsford	Essex v Middx
	Northop Hall	Lancs v Worcs
	Leicester	Leics v Derbys
	Taunton Vale	Somerset v Glam
	Reigate Priory	Surrey v Glos
	Leeds	Yorks v Notts
Mon 9	Richmond	Middx v Somerset
Tue 10	Leicester	Leics v Lancs
	Radlett	MCC YC v Essex
	Kidderminster	Worcs v Derbys
Thu 12	Southampton	Hants v Glam
Mon 16	Pontarddulais	Glam v MCC YC
	Bristol	Glos v Sussex
	Taunton Vale	Somerset v Surrey
Tue 17	Chester-le-St	Durham v Leics
	Lady Bay	Notts v Worcs
	Knowle & D	Warwicks v Yorks
Wed 18	Boughton Hall	Unicorns A v Northants
Thu 19	Boughton Hall	Unicorns A v Lancs
Tue 31	Bishop's Stortford	Essex v Glos
	Radlett	Middx v Kent
	Stowe S	Northants v Warwicks
	Notts HS	Notts v Leics

JUNE

Thu 2	Brandon	Durham v Unicorns A
Fri 3	Todmorden	Yorks v Unicorns A
Mon 13	tbc	Northants v Durham
	Lady Bay	Notts v Warwicks
	Horsham	Sussex v Surrey
	Kidderminster	Worcs v Leics
	Marske	Yorks v Derbys
Tue 14	Radlett	Middx v MCC YC
Wed 15	Tonbridge S	Kent v Sussex
Mon 20	Darlington	Durham v Yorks
	Wellingborough S	Northants v Notts
	Imber Court	Surrey v Hants
	Horsham	Sussex v Essex
Tue 21	Beckenham	Kent v MCC YC

Fri 24	Glossop	Derbys v Lancs
Mon 27	Stokesley	Durham v Derbys
	Oundle S	Leics v Northants
Tue 28	Southend	Essex v Hants
	Imber Court	Surrey v Middx
Wed 29	Tring	Unicorns A v Notts
Thu 30	Radlett	MCC YC v Surrey
	Tring	Unicorns A v Worcs

JULY

Mon 4	Derby	Derbys v Unicorns A
Tue 5	Southampton	Hants v Kent
	Leicester	Leics v Unicorns A
Mon 11	Heywood	Lancs v Northants
	Newclose, IoW	MCC YC v Hants
Tue 12	Radlett	Middx v Glam
	Walmley	Warwicks v Derbys
	Worcester	Worcs v Durham
Tue 19	Leek	Derbys v Northants
	Cardiff	Glam v Essex
	Bristol	Glos v Somerset
	Todmorden	Lancs v Notts
	Worcester RGS	Worcs v Warwicks
Mon 25	Maidstone	Kent v Somerset
	Bingley	Yorks v Lancs
Tue 26	Bristol	Glos v Middx
	Northampton	Northants v Worcs

AUGUST

Mon 1	Hove	Sussex v MCC YC
Tue 2	Cheltenham C	Glos v Hants
	Maidstone	Kent v Glam
	Taunton Vale	Somerset v Essex
	Knowle & Dorridge	Warwicks v Lancs
Tue 9	Southampton	Hants v Sussex
	Cheam	Surrey v Kent
	Pudsey Congs	Yorks v Northants
Mon 15	Bristol	Glos v Kent
	Hove	Sussex v Glam
Tue 16	Denby	Derbys v Notts
	Southampton	Hants v Somerset
	Lytham	Lancs v Durham
	Leicester	Leics v Yorks
Thu 18	King Edward's S	Warwicks v Unicorns A
Mon 22	St Fagans	Glam v Surrey
	Worcester	Worcs v Yorks
Mon 29	tbc	Semi-finals

SEPTEMBER

| Mon 12 | tbc | FINAL |

326

SECOND XI T20 FIXTURES 2011

MAY		
Mon 16	Chelmsford	Essex v Northants
Mon 23	Alvaston & B	Derbys v Durham
	Southampton	Hants v MCC YC
	Dunstable	Northants v Middx
	Kidderminster	Worcs v Glos
Tue 24	Blackpool	Lancs v Durham
	Leicester	Leics v Essex
	Radlett	MCC YC v Kent
	Preston Nomads	Sussex v Surrey
	Ombersley	Worcs v Warwicks
Wed 25	Wellingborough S	Northants v Unicorns A
	Leeds	Yorks v Derbys
Thu 26	Bristol	Glos v Glam
	Folkestone	Kent v Surrey
	Ealing	Middx v Unicorns A
	Olton & W Warks	Warwicks v Somerset
	Leeds	Yorks v Notts
Fri 27	Brandon	Durham v Notts
	Taunton Vale	Somerset v Glam
	Purley	Surrey v MCC YC
Mon 30	Neston	Lancs v Yorks

	Hastings	Sussex v Kent
Tue 31	Purley	Surrey v Hants
JUNE		
Mon 6	Derby	Derbys v Lancs
	Chester-le-St	Durham v Yorks
	Chelmsford	Essex v Middx
	Cardiff	Glam v Warwicks
	Southampton	Hants v Sussex
	Leicester	Leics v Northants
	Taunton Vale	Somerset v Worcs
Tue 7	Bristol	Glos v Somerset
	Trent College	Notts v Lancs
	Shrewsbury S	Unicorns A v Leics
Wed 8	Cardiff	Glam v Worcs
	Canterbury	Kent v Hants
	Radlett	MCC YC v Sussex
	Uxbridge	Middx v Leics
	Trent College	Notts v Derbys
	Shrewsbury S	Unicorns A v Essex
	Coventry/N Warwk	Warwicks v Glos
Fri 10	Cambridge (tbc)	Semi-finals and FINAL

TEST MATCH CHAMPIONSHIP SCHEDULE

Months indicate the start of a series. Number of Tests in brackets. All series involving Pakistan and Zimbabwe are subject to confirmation.

2011	Apr	Bangladesh hosts Australia (2)			Australia hosts India (4)
		West Indies hosts Pakistan (2)			South Africa hosts Sri Lanka (3)
	May	**England hosts Sri Lanka (3)**			New Zealand hosts Zimbabwe (2)
	Jun	West Indies hosts India (4)	2012	Jan	**Pakistan hosts England (3)**
	Jul	**England hosts India (4)**		Mar	**Sri Lanka hosts England (3)**
	Aug	Sri Lanka hosts Australia (3)			New Zealand hosts South Africa (3)
	Oct	South Africa hosts Australia (3)			India hosts Pakistan (3)
		Bangladesh hosts West Indies (2)			West Indies hosts Australia (3)
		Pakistan hosts Sri Lanka (3)		Apr	Pakistan hosts Bangladesh (2)
	Nov	India hosts West Indies (3)			West Indies hosts New Zealand (3)
		Australia hosts New Zealand (2)		May	**England hosts West Indies (3)**
	Dec	Bangladesh hosts Pakistan (2)		July	**England hosts South Africa (3)**

WOMEN'S INTERNATIONAL FIXTURES 2011

Thu 23 June

T20	Billericay	Australia v India
T20	Chelmsford	England v New Zealand

Sat 25 June

T20	Bristol	England v Australia
T20	Clifton C	New Zealand v India

Sun 26 June

T20	Taunton	England v India
T20	Taunton Vale	New Zealand v Australia

Mon 27 June

T20	tbc	3rd/4th place play-off
T20	Southampton	Final

Thu 30 June

LOI	Chesterfield	Australia v India
LOI^F	Derby	England v New Zealand

Sat 2 July

LOI	Derby	England v India
LOI	Chesterfield	New Zealand v Australia

Tue 5 July

LOI	Lord's	England v Australia
LOI	Southgate	New Zealand v India

Thu 7 July

LOI	Wormsley	3rd/4th place play-off or Final
LOI	Aston Rowant	3rd/4th place play-off or Final

INTERNATIONAL UNDER-19 CRICKET 2011

LIMITED-OVERS INTERNATIONALS

England v South Africa

LOI	Edgbaston	Saturday 16 July		LOI	Taunton	Tuesday 26 July
LOI	Northampton	Monday 18 July		LOI	Canterbury	Thursday 28 July
LOI	Arundel	Thursday 21 July		LOI	Canterbury	Saturday 30 July
LOI	Arundel	Saturday 23 July				

PRINCIPAL FIXTURES 2011

CC1	LV= County Championship (1st Div)
CC2	LV= County Championship (2nd Div)
F	Floodlit
FCF	First-Class Friendly
LOI	NatWest Limited-Overs International
40L	Clydesdale Bank 40

T20	Friends Provident t20
IT20	Twenty20 International
[T20]	Other Twenty20 Match
TM	npower Test Match
MCCU	MCC University

Sun 27 – Wed 30 March

FCF	Abu Dhabi	MCC v Notts

Sat 2 – Mon 4 April

FCF	Cambridge	Cambridge MCCU v Essex
	Cardiff	Glamorgan v Cardiff MCCU
FCF	Loughborough	Loughborough MCCU v Northants
FCF	Oxford	Oxford MCCU v Lancashire
	Worcester	Worcs v Leeds/Bradford MCCU

Sun 3 – Tue 5 April

FCF	Durham	Durham MCCU v Durham

Fri 8 – Mon 11 April

CC1	Southampton	Hampshire v Durham
CC1	Liverpool	Lancashire v Sussex
CC1	Worcester	Worcs v Yorkshire
CC2	Chelmsford	Essex v Kent
CC2	Bristol	Glos v Derbyshire
CC2	Leicester	Leics v Glamorgan
CC2	The Oval	Surrey v Northants

Sat 9 – Mon 11 April

FCF	Cambridge	Cambridge MCCU v Middlesex
FCF	Durham	Durham MCCU v Warwicks
FCF	Oxford	Oxford MCCU v Notts
	Taunton Vale	Somerset v Cardiff MCCU

Thu 14 – Sun 17 April

CC1	Nottingham	Notts v Hampshire
CC1	Taunton	Somerset v Warwicks
CC1	Leeds	Yorkshire v Durham
CC2	Derby	Derbyshire v Leics
CC2	Cardiff	Glamorgan v Glos
CC2	Lord's	Middlesex v Essex
CC2	Northampton	Northants v Kent

Wed 20 – Sat 23 April

CC1	Chester-le-St	Durham v Sussex
CC1	Liverpool	Lancashire v Somerset
CC1	Worcester	Worcs v Warwicks
CC1	Leeds	Yorkshire v Notts
CC2	Derby	Derbyshire v Middlesex
CC2	Cardiff	Glamorgan v Surrey
CC2	Northampton	Northants v Essex

Wed 20 – Fri 22 April

	Bristol	Glos v Cardiff MCCU
FCF	Leicester	Leics v Loughborough MCCU
	Southampton	Hampshire v Leeds/Bradford MCCU

Sun 24 April

40L	Chester-le-St	Durham v Scotland

40L	Bristol	Glos v Glamorgan
40L	Southampton	Hampshire v Warwicks
40L	Manchester	Lancashire v Unicorns
40L	Northampton	Northants v Leics
40L	Nottingham	Notts v Somerset
40L	Worcester	Worcs v Middlesex
40L	Leeds	Yorkshire v Netherlands

Mon 25 April

40L	Derby	Derbyshire v Netherlands
40L	Leicester	Leics v Scotland

Tue 26 – Fri 29 April

CC1	Chester-le-St	Durham v Warwicks
CC1	Nottingham	Notts v Worcs
CC1	Hove	Sussex v Lancashire
CC2	Chelmsford	Essex v Glamorgan
CC2	Canterbury	Kent v Glos

Wed 27 – Sat 30 April

CC1	Southampton	Hampshire v Somerset
CC2	Leicester	Leics v Derbyshire
CC2	Lord's	Middlesex v Surrey

Sun 1 May

40L	Derby	Derbyshire v Sussex
40L	Chester-le-St	Durham v Northants
40L	Chelmsford	Essex v Notts
40L	Canterbury	Kent v Worcs
40L	Lord's	Middlesex v Netherlands
40L	The Oval	Surrey v Scotland
40L	Wormsley	Unicorns v Somerset
40L	Birmingham	Warwicks v Leics

Mon 2 May

40L	Chelmsford	Essex v Lancashire
40L	Bristol	Glos v Unicorns
40L	Southampton	Hampshire v Surrey
40L	Leicester	Leics v Durham
40L	Lord's	Middlesex v Kent
40L	Taunton	Somerset v Glamorgan
40L	Hove	Sussex v Netherlands
40L	Birmingham	Warwicks v Scotland
40L	Leeds	Yorkshire v Derbyshire

Wed 4 – Sat 7 May

CC1	Southampton	Hampshire v Sussex
CC1	Nottingham	Notts v Yorkshire
CC1	Taunton	Somerset v Worcs
CC1	Birmingham	Warwicks v Lancashire
CC2	Bristol	Glos v Middlesex

CC2	Canterbury	Kent v Northants
CC2	The Oval	Surrey v Leics

Wed 4 – Fri 6 May

	Derby	Derbyshire v Leeds/Bradford MCCU

Fri 6 May

40L^F	Cardiff	Glamorgan v Essex

Sun 8 May

40L	Canterbury	Kent v Yorkshire
40L	Manchester	Lancashire v Glamorgan
40L	Northampton	Northants v Warwicks
40L	Taunton	Somerset v Glos
40L	The Oval	Surrey v Leics
40L	Hove	Sussex v Middlesex
40L	Bury St Edmunds	Unicorns v Essex
40L	Worcester	Worcs v Derbyshire

Tue 10 – Fri 13 May

CC1	Chester-le-St	Durham v Somerset
CC1	Hove	Sussex v Notts
CC2	Derby	Derbyshire v Essex
CC2	Cardiff	Glamorgan v Kent

Wed 11 – Sat 14 May

CC1	Birmingham	Warwicks v Worcs
CC1	Leeds	Yorkshire v Hampshire
CC2	Bristol	Glos v Northants

Wed 11 – Fri 13 May

FCF	Cambridge	Cambridge MCCU v Surrey

Thu 12 May

40L	Deventer	Netherlands v Middlesex

Sat 14 – Mon 16 May

FCF	Uxbridge	Middlesex v Sri Lankans

Sun 15 May

40L	Chester-le-St	Durham v Hampshire
40L	Cardiff	Glamorgan v Glos
40L	Leicester	Leics v Warwicks
40L	Edinburgh	Scotland v Surrey
40L	Taunton	Somerset v Lancashire
40L	Hove	Sussex v Derbyshire
40L	Wormsley	Unicorns v Nottinghamshire
40L	Leeds	Yorkshire v Kent

Mon 16 May

40L	Edinburgh	Scotland v Durham

Tue 17 May

40L^F	Lord's	Middlesex v Worcs
40L	Deventer	Netherlands v Derbyshire

Wed 18 – Sat 21 May

CC1	Liverpool	Lancashire v Yorkshire
CC1	Nottingham	Notts v Warwicks
CC1	Hove	Sussex v Somerset
CC1	Worcester	Worcs v Durham
CC2	Leicester	Leics v Glos
CC2	Croydon	Surrey v Essex

Wed 18 – Fri 20 May

FCF	Canterbury	Kent v Loughborough MCCU

Thu 19 – Sun 22 May

CC2	Lord's	Middlesex v Glamorgan
FCF	Derby	England Lions v Sri Lankans

Fri 20 May

40L^F	Southampton	Hampshire v Northants

Sun 22 May

40L	Chelmsford	Essex v Unicorns
40L	Canterbury	Kent v Sussex
40L	Manchester	Lancashire v Notts
40L	Northampton	Northants v Scotland
40L	Croydon	Surrey v Hampshire
40L	Birmingham	Warwicks v Durham
40L	Worcester	Worcs v Yorkshire

Tue 24 – Fri 27 May

CC1	Southampton	Hampshire v Lancashire
CC1	Taunton	Somerset v Yorkshire
CC1	Birmingham	Warwicks v Durham
CC2	Chelmsford	Essex v Middlesex
CC2	Canterbury	Kent v Derbyshire
CC2	Northampton	Northants v Leics
CC2	The Oval	Surrey v Glamorgan

Wed 25 – Fri 27 May

FCF	Oxford	Oxford MCCU v Sussex

Wed 25 May

40L^F	Nottingham	Notts v Glos

Thu 26 – Mon 30 May

TM1	Cardiff	ENGLAND v SRI LANKA

Sun 29 May – Wed 1 June

CC1	Chester-le-St	Durham v Lancashire
CC1	Hove	Sussex v Yorkshire
CC1	Worcester	Worcs v Notts
CC2	Derby	Derbyshire v Surrey
CC2	Bristol	Glos v Essex
CC2	Tunbridge Wells	Kent v Leics
CC2	Northampton	Northants v Glamorgan

Wed 1 June

T20	Southampton	Hampshire v Somerset

Thu 2 June

T20	Derby	Derbyshire v Lancashire
T20	Chester-le-St	Durham v Warwicks
T20^F	The Oval	Surrey v Glos
T20	Hove	Sussex v Essex

Fri 3 – Tue 7 June

TM2	Lord's	ENGLAND v SRI LANKA

Fri 3 June

T20^F	Chelmsford	Essex v Glos
T20^F	Cardiff	Glamorgan v Middlesex
T20^F	Southampton	Hampshire v Surrey
T20	Tunbridge Wells	Kent v Somerset
T20	Manchester	Lancashire v Worcs
T20^F	Northampton	Northants v Leics
T20	Nottingham	Notts v Derbyshire
T20	Leeds	Yorkshire v Warwicks

Sun 5 June
T20	Bristol	Glos v Sussex
T20	Tunbridge Wells	Kent v Hampshire
T20	Leicester	Leics v Lancashire
T20	Nottingham	Notts v Middlesex
T20	Taunton	Somerset v Middlesex
T20	Birmingham	Warwicks v Northants
T20	Worcester	Worcs v Durham

Wed 8 June
T20 F	Chelmsford	Essex v Sussex
T20	Southampton	Hampshire v Glamorgan
T20	Manchester	Lancashire v Leics
T20	Birmingham	Warwicks v Notts

Thu 9 June
T20 F	Lord's	Middlesex v Essex
T20	Northampton	Northants v Durham
T20	Leeds	Yorkshire v Worcs

Fri 10 – Sun 12 June
| FCF | Chelmsford | Essex v Sri Lankans |

Fri 10 June
T20	Derby	Derbyshire v Durham
T20	Gloucester	Glos v Hampshire
T20	Manchester	Lancashire v Yorkshire
T20	Leicester	Leics v Notts
T20	Taunton	Somerset v Kent
T20	The Oval	Surrey v Glamorgan
T20 F	Hove	Sussex v Middlesex
T20	Worcester	Worcs v Northants

Sat 11 June
T20 F	Cardiff	Glamorgan v Kent
T20	Gloucester	Glos v Surrey
T20	Nottingham	Notts v Warwicks

Sun 12 June
T20	Chester-le-St	Durham v Derbyshire
T20	Leicester	Leics v Warwicks
T20	Taunton	Somerset v Hampshire
T20	Worcester	Worcs v Lancashire
T20	Leeds	Yorkshire v Northants

Mon 13 June
| T20 F | The Oval | Surrey v Essex |

Tue 14 June
T20	Chester-le-St	Durham v Notts
T20	Richmond	Middlesex v Glamorgan
T20 F	Hove	Sussex v Somerset

Wed 15 June
T20 F	Derby	Derbyshire v Worcs
T20 F	Chelmsford	Essex v Somerset
T20	Beckenham	Kent v Glos
T20	Northampton	Northants v Warwicks

Thu 16 – Mon 20 June
| TM3 | Southampton | ENGLAND v SRI LANKA |

Thu 16 June
| T20 F | Lord's | Middlesex v Sussex |
| T20 F | Nottingham | Notts v Durham |

Fri 17 June
T20	Cardiff	Glamorgan v Hampshire
T20	Bristol	Glos v Essex
T20	Leicester	Leics v Durham
T20 F	Northampton	Northants v Derbyshire
T20	Taunton	Somerset v Surrey
T20 F	Hove	Sussex v Kent
T20	Birmingham	Warwicks v Worcs
T20	Leeds	Yorkshire v Lancashire

Sat 18 – Tue 21 June
| CC1 | Chester-le-St | Durham v Yorkshire |
| CC1 | Worcester | Worcs v Hampshire |

Sat 18 June
T20	Derby	Derbyshire v Leics
T20 F	Canterbury	Kent v Middlesex
T20	Nottingham	Notts v Northants

Sun 19 – Wed 22 June
CC2	Leicester	Leics v Northants
CC2	Lord's	Middlesex v Kent
CC2	The Oval	Surrey v Glos

Sun 19 June
| T20 | Birmingham | Warwicks v Lancashire |

Mon 20 – Thu 23 June
| CC1 | Nottingham | Notts v Lancashire |
| CC1 | Birmingham | Warwicks v Somerset |

Tue 21 June
| T20 F | Cardiff | Glamorgan v Essex |

Wed 22 June
| | Worcester | Worcs v Sri Lankans |
| T20 | Leeds | Yorkshire v Derbyshire |

Thu 23 June
T20 F	Chelmsford	Essex v Hampshire
T20 F	Cardiff	Glamorgan v Sussex
T20 F	The Oval	Surrey v Middlesex

Fri 24 June
T20	Chester-le-St	Durham v Lancashire
T20 F	Chelmsford	Essex v Surrey
T20 F	Southampton	Hampshire v Glos
T20	Uxbridge	Middlesex v Kent
T20	Nottingham	Notts v Leics
T20	Taunton	Somerset v Sussex
T20	Birmingham	Warwicks v Yorkshire
T20	Worcester	Worcs v Derbyshire

Sat 25 – Tue 28 June
| CC2 | Chelmsford | Essex v Northants |

Sat 25 June
| IT20 | Bristol | England v Sri Lanka |
| T20 | Leicester | Leics v Worcs |

Sun 26 June
T20	Leek	Derbyshire v Warwicks
T20	Chester-le-St	Durham v Leics
T20	Beckenham	Kent v Surrey
T20	Uxbridge	Middlesex v Glos
T20	Nottingham	Notts v Lancashire

T20	Taunton	Somerset v Glamorgan
T20	Worcester	Worcs v Yorkshire
	Lord's	Oxford U v Cambridge U

Mon 27 – Thu 30 June

CC1	Liverpool	Lancashire v Durham
CC2	Cardiff	Glamorgan v Derbyshire
CC2	Uxbridge	Middlesex v Glos

Mon 27 June

| T20 F | Southampton | Hampshire v Sussex |

Tue 28 June

| LOI F | The Oval | England v Sri Lanka |

Wed 29 June – Sat 2 July

| CC1 | Arundel | Sussex v Warwicks |

Wed 29 June

| T20 | Milton Keynes | Northants v Worcs |
| T20 | Leicester | Leics v Yorkshire |

Thu 30 June

| T20 F | Southampton | Hampshire v Kent |
| T20 F | The Oval | Surrey v Somerset |

Fri 1 July

LOI	Leeds	England v Sri Lanka
T20 F	Derby	Derbyshire v Notts
T20 F	Cardiff	Glamorgan v Surrey
T20 F	Bristol	Glos v Somerset
T20 F	Canterbury	Kent v Essex
T20	Manchester	Lancashire v Durham
T20	Uxbridge	Middlesex v Hampshire
T20 F	Northampton	Northants v Yorkshire
T20	Worcester	Worcs v Leics

Sat 2 July

| T20 | Chelmsford | Essex v Middlesex |

Sun 3 July

LOI	Lord's	England v Sri Lanka
T20	Chester-le-St	Durham v Worcs
T20	Canterbury	Kent v Glamorgan
T20	Manchester	Lancashire v Derbyshire
T20	Leicester	Leics v Northants
T20	Arundel	Sussex v Glos
T20	Leeds	Yorkshire v Notts

Mon 4 July

| T20 | Bath | Somerset v Essex |
| T20 | Croydon | Surrey v Sussex |

Tue 5 – Fri 8 July

| FCF | Cambridge | Cambridge U v Oxford U |

Tue 5 July

| T20 F | Cardiff | Glamorgan v Somerset |
| T20 | Worcester | Worcs v Notts |

Wed 6 July

LOI F	Nottingham	England v Sri Lanka
T20	Bristol	Glos v Kent
T20 F	Southampton	Hampshire v Essex
T20	Birmingham	Warwicks v Derbyshire
T20	Leeds	Yorkshire v Leics

Thu 7 July

| T20 F | Lord's | Middlesex v Surrey |
| T20 F | Hove | Sussex v Glamorgan |

Fri 8 July

T20	Chester-le-St	Durham v Yorkshire
T20 F	Chelmsford	Essex v Glamorgan
T20 F	Canterbury	Kent v Sussex
T20	Leicester	Leics v Derbyshire
T20 F	Northampton	Northants v Notts
T20	Taunton	Somerset v Glos
T20 F	The Oval	Surrey v Hampshire
T20	Worcester	Worcs v Warwicks

Sat 9 July

| LOI | Manchester | England v Sri Lanka |
| T20 | Derby | Derbyshire v Northants |

Sun 10 – Wed 13 July

| CC2 | Leicester | Leics v Essex |
| CC2 | The Oval | Surrey v Kent |

Sun 10 July

T20	Bristol	Glos v Glamorgan
T20	Manchester	Lancashire v Notts
T20	Southgate	Middlesex v Somerset
T20	Hove	Sussex v Hampshire
T20	Scarborough	Yorkshire v Durham

Mon 11 – Thu 14 July

CC1	Nottingham	Notts v Somerset
CC1	Hove	Sussex v Hampshire
CC1	Scarborough	Yorkshire v Worcs
CC2	Derby	Derbyshire v Glamorgan

Mon 11 July

| T20 | Birmingham | Warwicks v Durham |

Tue 12 July

| T20 | Northampton | Northants v Lancashire |

Wed 13 July

| T20 | Bristol | Glos v Middlesex |
| T20 F | Manchester | Lancashire v Warwicks |

Thu 14 July

| T20 | Chester-le-St | Durham v Northants |
| T20 F | The Oval | Surrey v Kent |

Fri 15 – Sun 17 July

| FCF | Taunton | Somerset v Indians |

Fri 15 July

T20 F	Derby	Derbyshire v Yorkshire
T20 F	Chelmsford	Essex v Kent
T20 F	Cardiff	Glamorgan v Glos
T20 F	Southampton	Hampshire v Middlesex
T20 F	Manchester	Lancashire v Northants
T20 F	Nottingham	Notts v Worcs
T20 F	Hove	Sussex v Surrey
T20 F	Birmingham	Warwicks v Leics

Sun 17 July

40L	Chester-le-St	Durham v Surrey
40L	Cardiff	Glamorgan v Unicorns
40L	Leicester	Leics v Hampshire

40L	Rotterdam	Netherlands v Kent
40L	Nottingham	Notts v Essex
40L	Edinburgh	Scotland v Northants
40L	Leeds	Yorkshire v Middlesex

Mon 18 July

40L	Manchester	Lancashire v Somerset
40L	Rotterdam	Netherlands v Worcs
40L	Nottingham	Notts v Unicorns
40L	Edinburgh	Scotland v Warwicks

Tue 19 July

40L F	Southampton	Hampshire v Durham

Wed 20 – Sat 23 July

CC1	Southampton	Hampshire v Notts
CC1	Birmingham	Warwicks v Sussex
CC1	Leeds	Yorkshire v Lancashire
CC2	Cheltenham	Glos v Kent
CC2	Northampton	Northants v Derbyshire
CC2	Guildford	Surrey v Middlesex
FCF	Leicester	Leics v Sri Lanka A

Wed 20 July

40L	Chelmsford	Essex v Glamorgan

Thu 21 – Mon 25 July

TM1	Lord's	ENGLAND v INDIA

Thu 21 – Sun 24 July

CC1	Taunton	Somerset v Durham

Sun 24 July

40L	Derby	Derbyshire v Kent
40L	Cheltenham	Glos v Notts
40L	Leicester	Leics v Northants
40L	Guildford	Surrey v Warwicks
40L	Colwyn Bay	Unicorns v Lancashire
40L	Worcester	Worcs v Sussex

Mon 25 July

40L F	Northampton	Northants v Hampshire

Tue 26 – Fri 29 July

CC1	Southport	Lancashire v Notts
CC1	Worcester	Worcs v Somerset

Tue 26 July

40L	Cheltenham	Glos v Essex
40L F	Birmingham	Warwicks v Hampshire

Wed 27 – Sat 30 July

CC2	Southend	Essex v Leics
CC2	Swansea	Glamorgan v Northants
CC2	Cheltenham	Glos v Surrey
FCF	Chester-le-St	Durham v Sri Lanka A

Wed 27 July

40L F	Hove	Sussex v Yorkshire

Thu 28 July

40L F	Lord's	Middlesex v Derbyshire

Fri 29 July – Tue 2 August

TM2	Nottingham	ENGLAND v INDIA

Fri 29 July – Mon 1 August

CC2	Lord's	Middlesex v Derbyshire

Sat 30 July

40L	Amstelveen	Netherlands v Sussex

Sun 31 July

40L	Chester-le-St	Durham v Warwicks
40L	Southend	Essex v Somerset
40L	Swansea	Glamorgan v Notts
40L	Cheltenham	Glos v Lancashire
40L	Southampton	Hampshire v Leics
40L	Amstelveen	Netherlands v Yorkshire
40L	Worcester	Worcs v Kent

Mon 1 – Thu 4 August

CC1	Liverpool	Lancashire v Warwicks

Tue 2 – Fri 5 August

CC1	Chester-le-St	Durham v Notts
CC1	Southampton	Hampshire v Yorkshire
CC1	Taunton	Somerset v Sussex
CC2	Cardiff	Glamorgan v Essex
CC2	Leicester	Leics v Kent
FCF	Scarborough	England Lions v Sri Lanka A

Wed 3 August

40L F	The Oval	Surrey v Northants

Thu 4 August

40L F	Derby	Derbyshire v Worcs

Fri 5 – Sat 6 August

	Northampton	Northants v Indians

Fri 5 August

40L F	Manchester	Lancashire v Glos

Sat 6 August

T20		Quarter-finals 1 & 2

Sun 7 August

T20		Quarter-final 3

Mon 8 August

	Manchester	Lancashire v Sri Lanka A
T20		Quarter-final 4

Wed 10 – Sun 14 August

TM3	Birmingham	ENGLAND v INDIA

Wed 10 – Sat 13 August

CC1	Chester-le-St	Durham v Hampshire
CC1	Horsham	Sussex v Worcs
CC2	Derby	Derbyshire v Glos
CC2	Canterbury	Kent v Surrey

Wed 10 August

40L	Lord's	Middlesex v Yorkshire
	Nottingham	Notts v Sri Lanka A

Thu 11 – Sun 14 August

CC2	Lord's	Middlesex v Northants

Fri 12 August

40L F	Nottingham	Notts v Glamorgan
	Worcester	England Lions v Sri Lanka A

Sat 13 August

40L	Edinburgh	Scotland v Leics

Sun 14 August

40L	Chesterfield	Derbyshire v Yorkshire

40L	Chester-le-St	Durham v Leics
40L	Cardiff	Glamorgan v Somerset
40L	Canterbury	Kent v Netherlands
40L	Manchester	Lancashire v Essex
40L	Edinburgh	Scotland v Hampshire
40L	Horsham	Sussex v Worcs
40L	Exmouth	Unicorns v Glos
	Worcester	England Lions v Sri Lanka A

Mon 15 August

| 40L [F] | Northampton | Northants v Surrey |
| 40L [F] | Taunton | Somerset v Notts |

Tue 16 August

| 40L [F] | Canterbury | Kent v Middlesex |
| | Northampton | England Lions v Sri Lanka A |

Wed 17 – Sat 20 August

CC1	Blackpool	Lancashire v Worcs
CC1	Taunton	Somerset v Notts
CC1	Scarborough	Yorkshire v Sussex
CC2	Chesterfield	Derbyshire v Northants
CC2	Colchester	Essex v Glos
CC2	Colwyn Bay	Glamorgan v Leics
CC2	Canterbury	Kent v Middlesex

Wed 17 August

| 40L [F] | Birmingham | Warwicks v Surrey |

Thu 18 – Mon 22 August

| TM4 | The Oval | ENGLAND v INDIA |

Thu 18 – Sun 21 August

| CC1 | Birmingham | Warwicks v Hampshire |

Sun 21 August

40L	Chesterfield	Derbyshire v Middlesex
40L	Colchester	Essex v Glos
40L	Colwyn Bay	Glamorgan v Lancashire
40L	Leicester	Leics v Surrey
40L	Northampton	Northants v Durham
40L	Taunton	Somerset v Unicorns
40L	Worcester	Worcs v Netherlands
40L	Scarborough	Yorkshire v Sussex

Mon 22 – Thu 25 August

| CC1 | Nottingham | Notts v Durham |

Tue 23 – Fri 26 August

CC1	Southampton	Hampshire v Worcs
CC1	Leeds	Yorkshire v Warwicks
CC2	Chelmsford	Essex v Derbyshire
CC2	Leicester	Leics v Surrey
CC2	Northampton	Northants v Middlesex

Tue 23 August

| 40L [F] | Hove | Sussex v Kent |

Wed 24 August

| 40L [F] | Bristol | Glos v Somerset |

Thu 25 August

| LOI | Dublin | Ireland v England |
| | Hove | Sussex v Indians |

Fri 26 August

| [F] | Canterbury | Kent v Indians |

Sat 27 August

| T20 [F] | Birmingham | Semi-finals and FINAL |

Mon 29 August

40L	Southampton	Hampshire v Scotland
40L	Canterbury	Kent v Derbyshire
40L	Lord's	Middlesex v Sussex
40L	Nottingham	Notts v Lancashire
40L	Taunton	Somerset v Essex
40L	The Oval	Surrey v Durham
40L	Wormsley	Unicorns v Glamorgan
40L	Birmingham	Warwicks v Northants
40L	Leeds	Yorkshire v Worcs
[T20]	Leicester	Leics v Indians

Tue 30 August – Fri 2 September

| CC2 | Lord's | Middlesex v Leics |

Wed 31 August – Sat 3 September

CC1	Taunton	Somerset v Hampshire
CC1	Hove	Sussex v Durham
CC1	Birmingham	Warwicks v Yorkshire
CC1	Worcester	Worcs v Lancashire
CC2	Bristol	Glos v Glamorgan
CC2	Canterbury	Kent v Essex
CC2	Northampton	Northants v Surrey

Wed 31 August

| IT20 [F] | Manchester | England v India |

Sat 3 September

| LOI | Chester-le-St | England v India |

Sun 4 September

| 40L | tbc | Semi-finals |

Tue 6 September

| LOI | Southampton | England v India |

Wed 7 – Sat 10 September

CC1	Manchester	Lancashire v Hampshire
CC1	Birmingham	Warwicks v Notts
CC1	Worcester	Worcs v Sussex
CC1	Leeds	Yorkshire v Somerset
CC2	Derby	Derbyshire v Kent
CC2	Chelmsford	Essex v Surrey
CC2	Cardiff	Glamorgan v Middlesex
CC2	Bristol	Glos v Leics

Fri 9 September

| LOI [F] | The Oval | England v India |

Sun 11 September

| LOI | Lord's | England v India |

Mon 12 – Thu 15 September

CC1	Chester-le-St	Durham v Worcs
CC1	Southampton	Hampshire v Warwicks
CC1	Nottingham	Notts v Sussex
CC1	Taunton	Somerset v Lancashire
CC2	Canterbury	Kent v Glamorgan
CC2	Leicester	Leics v Middlesex
CC2	Northampton	Northants v Glos
CC2	The Oval	Surrey v Derbyshire

FIELDING CHART

(For a right-handed batsman)

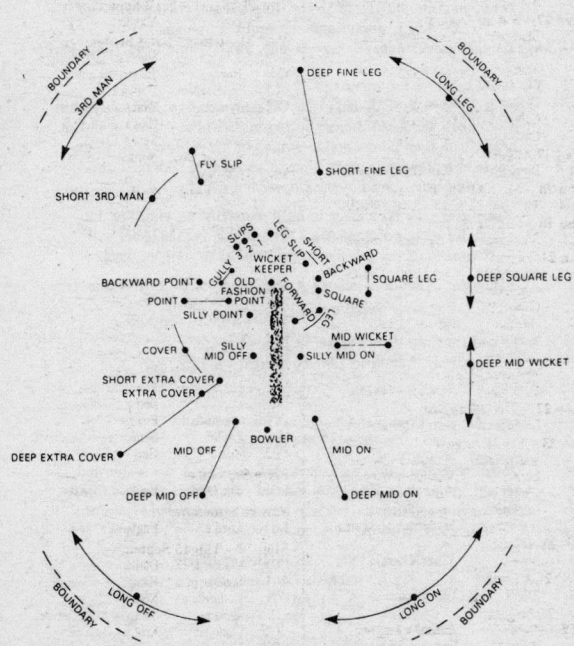

Sun 14th:
Tues 16th:

First published in 2011 by
HEADLINE PUBLISHING GROUP

Cover photographs:
(*Front and spine*) Graeme Swann, England and Nottinghamshire
© Mike Egerton/Empics Sport/Press Association
(*Back*) England team's Ashes victory January 2011 © Tom Shaw/Getty Images

1

Cataloguing in Publication Data is available from the British Library

ISBN 978 0 7553 6067 3

Typeset in Times by
Letterpart Limited, Reigate, Surrey

Preface by Graham Gooch

Printed and bound in Great Britain by
Clays Ltd St Ives plc

Headline's policy is to use papers that are natural, renewable and
recyclable products and made from wood grown in sustainable forests.
The logging and manufacturing processes are expected to conform
to the environmental regulations of the country of origin.

HEADLINE PUBLISHING GROUP
An Hachette UK Company
338 Euston Road
London NW1 3BH
www.headline.co.uk
www.hachette.co.uk